Industrial Efficiency in Six Nations

Industrial Efficiency in Six Nations

Richard E. Caves

in association with
Sheryl D. Bailey, John Baldwin, Fabienne Fecher, Alison Green,
Chris M. Harris, David G. Mayes, Sergio Perelman, Akio Torii,
and Seong Min Yoo

The MIT Press
Cambridge, Massachusetts
London, England

This book was set in Times Roman by Asco Trade Typesetting Ltd., Hong Kong and was printed and bound in the United States of America.

Library of Congress Cataloging-in-Publication Data

Industrial efficiency in six nations / Richard E. Caves in
 association with Sheryl D. Bailey ... [et al.].
    p. cm.
 Includes bibliographical references and index.
 ISBN 0-262-03193-0
 1. Industrial productivity—Case studies. 2. Efficiency,
Industrial—Case studies. I. Caves, Richard E. II. Bailey, Sheryl D.
HC79.I52I53 1992
338'.06—dc20   92-3851
                                                      CIP

Contents

Contributors

Sheryl D. Bailey
City of Norfolk
Norfolk, Virginia

John Baldwin
Statistics Canada
Ottawa, Canada

Richard E. Caves
Harvard University
Cambridge, Massachusetts

Fabienne Fecher
University of Liège
Liège, Belgium

Alison Green
Polytechnic South-West
Plymouth, U.K.

Chris M. Harris
Bureau of Industry Economics
Department of Industry, Technology, and Commerce
Canberra, Australia

David G. Mayes
National Institute of Economic and Social Research
London, U.K.

Sergio Perelman
University of Liège
Liège, Belgium

Akio Torii
Yokohama National University
Yokohama, Japan

Seong Min Yoo
Korea Development Institute
Seoul, Korea

Acknowledgments

We are grateful to the Alfred P. Sloan Foundation for a grant that supported a conference and concluding editorial work on this volume. The conference provided a valuable opportunity for the contributors to compare their findings and obtain reactions from other scholars who attended the conference. In the capacity of discussants and commentators on the project Finn R. Førsund, Zvi Griliches, Lennart Hjalmarsson, Richard R. Nelson, F. M. Scherer, Peter Schmidt, and Hideki Yamawaki offered many useful suggestions and points of perspective.

Several persons made contributions to the organization and development of this project that are not fully reflected in the papers. The project had its genesis a decade ago in discussions with Derek Morris at the U.K. National Economic Development Office, and his successor David G. Mayes aided in bringing the work to completion. Masu Uekusa took part in an earlier version of the Japanese study and helped with the organization of the project, as did John Baldwin and David R. Barton, the coauthor of the preceding U.S. study. Ann Flack looked after the organization of the conference and helped coordinate the subsequent assembly of this volume.

Industrial Efficiency in Six Nations

1 Introduction and Summary

Central to the concerns of microeconomics is allocative efficiency, the study of processes and policies that distribute resources among activities and sectors so they are put to their best uses. Much less attended—indeed often dismissed as uninteresting or unresearchable—is efficiency in the popular sense of whether we accomplish a given task with the minimum effort or use of scarce resources. This issue of technical or productive efficiency of course arises in macroeconomics and the economics of development, where economists have long sought to explain why labor and other resources may be left idle and what policies may restore them to productive use. In microeconomics, however, the hypothesis of profit maximization has mutated into an axiom ever ready to deny any allegation of productive inefficiency: If it paid to do something more efficiently, someone would already have seized the opportunity.

Two developments have combined to checkmate this dismissal and make productive efficiency a subject for serious empirical inquiry. The first is theoretical research into market failures involving information costs and asymmetries, agency problems, contract and bargaining costs that cogently limit the ability of utility-maximizing economic decision makers to achieve first-best efficiency (Arrow 1977). The second is an attractive research methodology for measuring productive inefficiency and thereby assessing its extent and testing hypotheses about its determinants. That is the stochastic frontier production function (SFPF), readily estimated from the data on establishments or enterprises that are collected in every country's industrial census.

The concept of technical or productive inefficiency was defined formally by Farrell (1957). It saw little empirical use until the late 1970s, when the SFPF was proposed by Aigner, Lovell, and Schmidt (1977) and by Meeusen and van den Broeck (1977) as a tool for estimating technical efficiency on the basis of assumptions that are both parsimonious and responsive to the typical limitations of actual data. Various applications to particular industries followed, showing that the SFPF gives plausible estimates and can be used to test hypotheses about differences in the efficiency levels of an industry's members.

The SFPF was applied more broadly in the study that precedes this volume, in which Caves and Barton (1990) measured the efficiency of about 350 U.S. manufacturing industries for 1977 and set forth and tested a number of hypotheses about the factors explaining industries' efficiency levels—both factors with direct normative significance and those representing forms of heterogeneity and disequilibrium that have mainly behavioral interest.

In this book appear studies that replicate the U.S. investigation on the manufacturing sectors of five other countries, in the process developing the theory and research methodology in numerous ways. Other papers extend the approach in time and space, observing and explaining how technical efficiency changes over time and comparing its extent and determinants between countries. We feel that we have learned a great deal: procedurally about how this methodology works in practice and what are its strengths and limitations, and substantively about the factors determining efficiency in manufacturing industries and their consistency from country to country.

This chapter summarizes those conclusions. The first section deals with the research methodology, the second and third review the substantive findings, and the last reflects on lines of future research.

1.1 Research Methodology

Farrell (1957) established that any given production process can be inefficient in either or both of two ways.[1] It could be technically inefficient, employing a larger bundle of inputs than the minimum required to obtain the actual output, or it could be allocatively inefficient, selecting the wrong combination of inputs given their relative prices and marginal productivities. Farrell's work led directly to the measurement of efficiency by means of linear programming techniques that simultaneously estimate the frontier and identify the fully efficient units. That approach asks a great deal of the accuracy of the data, however, because in general the number of an industry's units that it deems fully efficient is related to the number of parameters in the production function being fitted. Should a spurious observation (due to a data error or some other sort of unsuitability) land in the efficient set, the consequent measurement of inefficiency could be substantially in error.

The SFPF escaped this difficulty by formulating the production function for statistical estimation as

$$y = f(x) \exp(v - u),$$

where y is output, x is a vector of inputs, and the error term is composed of two elements. The usual normally distributed v represents random disturbances, measurement errors, and minor omitted variables affecting the deterministic kernel. The other component $u \geq 0$ represents some one-sided distribution of technical efficiency beneath the frontier. Thus a particular data point might lie above the estimated regression plane because of a "lucky" random component; it might lie beneath the plane either due to an unlucky draw or because it is technically inefficient.[2] The simple intuition about the procedure is that if the model correctly identifies an industry's inefficiency, the residuals from its fitted production function will be negatively skewed. The second and third moments of the residuals that are used to calculate skewness are also the source of the measures of (in)efficiency that are obtained from the SFPFs. Specifically the moments yield the estimated standard deviations of the v and u components of the composed residuals (σ_v and σ_u), from which measures of technical (in)efficiency are calculated. In our analyses these measures then become dependent variables in cross-sectional (interindustry) regression models to test hypotheses about technical efficiency.

Before we identify the efficiency measures, it is important to recognize that the procedure does not always work because σ_v and σ_u cannot always be calculated. The following chapters refer to failures of two types. A type I failure occurs when the skewness of the residuals is positive, implying that $\sigma_u < 0$. A type II failure occurs when the third moment of the residuals is so large relative to the second that it implies $\sigma_v < 0$. The logic of the composed-error approach suggests the conjecture that industries subject to type I failures are likely to harbor little inefficiency, with the positive skewness reflecting an oddity of the random residuals v in the particular sample. This conjecture tempts the researcher to retain such industries in the interindustry analysis of efficiency's determinants and to score them as "fully efficient." Caution argues against this choice, however, because on another interpretation an industry with positively skewed residuals could be highly inefficient.[3] Industries with type II failures might be regarded as extremely inefficient because the one-sided component swamps the prevalent random noise, but again this interpretation is not necessary.

In the absence of these failures several measures of efficiency can be calculated and in fact are defined and used in the following chapters. The most popular has been expected technical efficiency (based on Lee and Tyler 1978), an absolute measure that depends only on σ_u and lies in the (0, 1) interval. Closely related to it is average technical inefficiency, a measure based on σ_u normalized by the mean of the dependent variable (or the estimated mean on the efficient frontier). A term used in deriving the SFPF that has been taken over as an efficiency measure is λ, which normalizes σ_u by the standard deviation of the normally distributed component of the error σ_v. Finally, since these three measures are all lost when a type I or II failure occurs in estimation, skewness has been used directly as an efficiency measure by making the assumption that the likelihood of no substantial technical inefficiency increases with the value of positive skewness.[4] That assumption is related to the assumption that industries with type I failures are fully efficient and just as much open to challenge. Nonetheless, some studies in this volume make apparently successful use of skewness as an efficiency measure.

Although the focus of this project is empirical rather than theoretical or methodological, the papers do make some noteworthy extensions of the methodology. Some of these concern the statistical distribution chosen to represent the inefficiency component of the residuals. Previous research employed the half-normal and the exponential distributions only for their simplicity and tractability. Akio Torii, however, shows (subsection 2.3.1) that such distributions of inefficiency can be derived from models of specific processes that generate inefficiency. One model turns on capital-vintage effects and fixed costs of replacement and relates the distribution of inefficiency to the distribution among production units of the slippage of capital productivity below the frontier. The other model turns on organizational inefficiency: if inefficiency tends to creep upward in the absence of specific managerial effort (a fixed cost) to combat it, the specific form of a distribution of inefficiency can again be derived.

An objection made to the use of the half-normal (or exponential) distribution to depict inefficiency is the implicit assumption that the modal level of inefficiency is zero. There is no reason, however, why the number of units that are fully efficient should exceed the number that exhibit any given positive amount of inefficiency. Chris Harris (subsection 5.2.4) makes operational the use of a truncated normal distribution rather than a half-normal, allowing the modal level of inefficiency to be strictly positive and identifying it in the estimation. (The empirical results are mentioned below.)

An econometric problem considered by Akio Torii is the possibility of bias in the estimator of σ_u obtained by the convenient (and consistent) corrected ordinary least squares (COLS) method. One problem arises from the bounded value of the third moment of the residuals from which σ_u is estimated, which can cause asymmetrical biases near the boundaries of the region in which efficiency can be estimated (that is, where the results edge toward a type I or II failure). Because the biases depend on the estimated values of σ_u and σ_v, he is able to develop (subsection 2.2.6) a way to relate the true value of σ_u to these estimates, yielding an adjusted measure of expected technical efficiency that is used throughout his empirical work. The other problem arises from the effect on the estimator of σ_u of nonlinear terms in the production function, inherent in use of the popular translogarithmic function to estimate technical efficiency. Although these indeed bias the COLS estimator, his Monte Carlo analysis (subsection 2.2.5) shows the magnitudes of the biases to be trivial.

Another methodological consideration is developed by John Baldwin (chapter 7). Unable to compute proper SFPFs for Canadian industries because data on plant-level capital stocks are lacking, he employs a simpler research strategy that harks back to Timmer (1971). Working with output per person employed, he assumes that some fraction (10 to 40 percent) of each industry's total output emanates from efficient plants. He can then calculate average efficiency as the ratio of the weighted average of output–employment ratios for the remaining plants that are deemed inefficient to the corresponding weighted average for plants on the assumed frontier. Should this technique perform well compared to the SFPF, it can claim two virtues. First, it does not remove (as the SFPF does) the influence of any scale inefficiency (e.g., suboptimal-scale plants) and diverse input combinations (possibly due to factor-market imperfections) from the raw variance of units' productivity levels before estimating technical inefficiency. These kinds of inefficiencies remain included in the measure of technical efficiency, and thus hypotheses about their interindustry determinants can be tested. Second, his method is much simpler than estimating SFPFs. In general, in this project we showed respect for the hazard of undue complexity; chapters 4 and 9 address the possibility that the simple dispersion of plant-productivity levels within an industry (the second moment of production-function residuals) is a more productive object of analysis than their skewness (the third moment).

1.2 Evaluating Estimated Levels of Efficiency

Now we turn to the empirical results of estimating SFPFs for manufacturing industries in six industrial countries, phase 1 in the project's jargon. A general strategy for the tactical choices in estimating frontier production functions was first worked out in the U.S. study (largely by experimentation on a small panel of industries). The results of this experience were made available to researchers in the other countries, but they did not necessarily seek to replicate the U.S. procedures in all respects. Certain features of the research design are common to all:

1.   A preference for the translogarithmic production function was shared among the researchers. With each national team fitting production functions to many industries, practicality dictated selecting a specific form a priori. Because of its flexibility and the importance of enveloping the data for each industry well, the translog seemed clearly the weapon of choice.

2.   Each team implemented a generally similar set of rules for editing data. Our impression is that the national census organizations vary considerably in the resources they devote to checking the correctness and consistency of data they receive from individual establishments, at least prior to their aggregation. The data editing rules sought to exclude establishments that might be reporting accurate data but be unsuitable for analysis (e.g., start-ups) as well as establishments reporting data that are internally inconsistent or simply wildly implausible. For Australia the data-editing rules were found clearly to improve the quality of the results (chapter 5). For the United States the proportion of reporting establishments excluded from the analysis proved unrelated to how well we could explain an industry's efficiency in cross section, suggesting that varying the rates of deletion did not bias the measures of efficiency (Caves and Barton 1990, 54–58, 106–107).[5]

3.   The measure of plants' outputs used to estimate SFPFs could be either value of output or value added. An argument can be made for and against each. The research teams therefore carried out their computations using both of them, getting dissimilar yields of successful estimates and mean efficiency levels.[6]

4.   The year chosen for the analysis was 1977 or 1978. This choice was purely fortuitous. When the U.S. project began, 1977 was the most recent year in which the full Census of Manufactures had been completed. That or an adjacent year was then chosen by the other investigators. Although macroeconomic conditions in the 1970s were undesirably disturbed in all countries, no obviously superior year was available at the time the projects were started.

Although these common decisions were expected to make the results of the studies basically comparable, many differences remain that stem from irreparable differences in the countries' methods of gathering and reporting their data. A principal difference is in the inclusion of small establishments. In the U.S. data establishments smaller than 250 employees are sampled, while the other primary data sets truncate the small establishments at some (lower) threshold. This truncation was not thought undesirable because, for small units, the proportional amount of random noise in the data was expected to decline sharply with establishment size, and SFPFs were in most cases estimated from unweighted (not size-weighted) establishment data. For Korea efficiency measures were calculated both including and excluding establishments with fewer than 20 employees. Estimated mean efficiency levels rise when they are excluded; more important and dismaying, the interindustry correlations between efficiency measures with and without the small establishments are low, at most 0.555 for expected technical efficiency (table 3.11).

Other differences among the studies arise in the measurement of the inputs of factors of production. Establishment-level capital-stock data are available for Japan and Korea as well as the United States, although their values were surely distorted by the inflation of the 1970s. Elsewhere these stocks were approximated by allocating company-level stocks (Australia) or substituting data on flows of capital expenditures (Britain). With regard to labor inputs, numerous small differences in reporting procedure clearly exist but were not investigated because we expected that they could neither be controlled nor their effects predicted.

An important comparative feature of the country studies is the incidence of type I and II estimation failures. Table 1.1 summarizes the numbers of industries available for analysis in each country and the incidence of estimation failures. The success rate varies markedly between a high of 80 percent (United States) and a low of 41 percent (Japan). The percentage of type I failures (that arguably might represent highly efficient industries) ranges more narrowly, while the prevalence of type II failures varies wildly from none to one-third. The pattern is related in no obvious way to the characteristics of the countries or their data. A simulation analysis by Akio Torii (summarized in subsection 4.1.5) suggests that the incidence of type II failures should be quite low. Despite this diversity we feel that the minority status of type I failures is important in one regard. Consider the following insidious null hypothesis: The composed-error model fundamen-

Table 1.1
Numbers of industries and rates of success in estimating stochastic frontier production functions

Country	Industries analyzed	Estimation failures		Successes
		Type I	Type II	
Australia	140	49	0	91
	100%	35%	0%	65%
Japan	351	86	121	144
	100%	25%	34%	41%
Korea[a]	242	85	29	128
	100%	35%	12%	53%
United Kingdom	151	48	31	72
	100%	32%	20%	48%
United States[b]	434	87	0	347
	100%	20%	0%	80%

Note: Some studies report alternative estimations; the one chosen here involves the deletion of outlying observations, inclusion of control variables, and use of ordinary least squares estimation.
a. Based on gross output per employee. Other countries based on value added per unit of labor input (denominator varies).
b. Taken from Caves and Barton (1990), table 4.1. Other data are from chapters 2–5.

tally fails to capture technical inefficiency, and the third moments of the SFPFs represent nothing more than sample-based skewness in residuals that are normal in the population (but not necessarily in the particular sample). If that hypothesis were correct, half the industries should incur type I failures, and the putative measures of technical efficiency would be meaningless. Ultimately it is our ability to explain cogently the inter-industry differences in measured technical efficiency that lets us proclaim this fearsome dragon to be slain. Meanwhile the fact that type I estimation failures are overall in the minority is a substantial comfort.

An international study of efficiency naturally seeks to learn which country is the most (least) efficient. We came reluctantly to the conclusion that SFPFs do not yield a reliable answer to this question. First, for any given country the mean value of efficiency was found to vary greatly with the efficiency measure chosen and the tactical choices made in estimating the SFPFs. Second, we do not know what to make of industries with estimation failures. Third, neither the data nor the estimation procedures were fully standardized between countries, and we have no way to know whether the differences substantially affected mean estimated efficiency. The question of comparative efficiency is pursued in detail (but to agnostic conclusions) for Japan and the United States in subsection 11.3.2.

What we have learned at this stage from estimating efficiency from SFPFs seems rather unpromising. The yields of estimates are somewhat puny, and the patterns differ considerably among the countries although without yielding any compensating conclusions about international differences in efficiency. Fortunately the situation changes for the better as we turn to the project's second phase, investigating the determinants of interindustry differences in efficiency.

1.2 Determinants of Interindustry Differences in Efficiency

Several families of hypotheses about the determinants of an industry's efficiency level were set forth in Caves and Barton (1990, ch. 5).[7] Although the international project sheds new light on some individual hypotheses and the variables that embody them, that taxonomy still stands. The major families of hypotheses are:

1. *Competitive conditions.* Many hypotheses connect competitive conditions to efficiency. High concentration permits inefficiency to persist, should individual firms' managers not be optimally motivated to eliminate it. Incomplete collusive bargains among firms in a concentrated industry can induce rent-seeking enlargements of those outlays that affect a competitor's position in nonprice rivalry. Finally, when the number of market participants is small, there are fewer agents to experiment and try for improved ways of doing things, and fewer peers from whom to learn.

2. *Organizational factors.* Modern theory of corporate governance provides explanations why firms may not be fully motivated to minimize costs. The slippage can arise from second-best principal-agent relations that distort the use of resources (e.g., collective-bargaining agreements) or from bargaining costs that preclude rectification. Although this project is not designed to test hypotheses about differences in efficiency between firms, it can address any firm-based differences that vary from industry to industry due to observable factors (e.g., the prevalence of trade-union organization).

3. *Structural heterogeneity.* Technical efficiency estimated from the SFPF can pick up many sorts of heterogeneity in the revenue-productivity levels of an industry's plants or firms. These include product differentiation and

its counterpart spatial differentiation in markets with high transportation costs. One might expect these forms of heterogeneity primarily to expand the second rather than the third moment of the SFPF's residuals, but we thought it important to control for the possibility of effects on the third moment (and thus on the efficiency measures) as well.

4. *Dynamic disturbances.* The distribution of units efficiency levels may reflect not only units' diverse long-run equilibrium situations but also the effects of incompletely absorbed disturbances or discrepancies between short- and long-run equilibrium. Falling under this heading might be capital-vintage effects (units with old vintages appear inefficient), market growth (strongly related to the entry of new firms that suffer transient inefficiencies in the shakedown or shakeout process), and innovation (successful innovators appear efficient, but late adapters appear inefficient). Although these factors clearly can affect estimated efficiency, their sign predictions are ambiguous: Innovation can alleviate or offset inefficiency, or it can lift the frontier and make noninnovators appear less efficient.

5. *Regulation.* Government regulation can constrain firms to inefficient choices or protect those that have become inefficient on their own. Such regulation can affect technical efficiency insofar as it generates or sustains efficiency differences among units. No effect would be evident if it makes all of an industry's units inefficient. Although most manufacturing industries are not subject to such intrusive regulation (or regulation of measurable intensity), tests of some hypotheses about regulation proved feasible.

Each research team developed its own variants on these hypotheses and the exogenous variables to test them. As in the estimation of the SFPFs, the collection of exogenous variables was limited by peculiarities of national data sources, but it was also enriched by the development of new hypotheses or methods of testing them. It is difficult to summarize the results obtained due to differences in the quality of data (exogenous variables), problems of robustness in the results, and the like. We present in table 1.2 a bald summary of the results. For each variable and country we report a clearly significant effect of a variable on efficiency ($+ +$ or $- -$), an effect that is marginally significant or not fully robust ($+$ or $-$), a result of insignificance (0), or an indication that no test was made ($\cdot\cdot$).[8] Footnotes to the table cover the more important qualifications (but only those). In

Table 1.2
Summary of results of interindustry analysis of determinants of technical efficiency, by country and family of hypotheses

Exogenous variable	United States	Japan	Korea	Britain	Canada	Australia
A. Competition						
1. Concentration: internal maximum efficiency	Yes	Yes	Yes	No	Yes	Yes
2. Concentration: linear effect	0	0	0	− −	− −	0
3. Import competition	+	−	0	+ +	−[a]	0
4. Exports–shipments ratio	− −	0	0	− −	+[b]	..
B. Organization						
1. Scale of typical plant	+ +[c]	−	+ +[c]	..	+[c]	+
2. Inbound diversification	− −[d]	+ +	0	..	− −[d]	0
3. Outbound diversification	− −[e]	−	− −	+	..	−
4. Multiplant operation	−	− −	−	0	− −	..
5. Extent of subcontracting	..	+	−	..	..	..
6. Prevalence of foreign investment	0	..	..	..	−	−
7. Union members % employees	−	0	..	..	−	..
8. Use of part-time employees	+ +	+	..	..	+	..
C. Structural heterogeneity						
1. Interplant dispersion of capital intensity	− −	..	− −	..	..	..
2. Capital intensity (vintage)	− −[f]	− −[g]	0[h]	−	..	..
3. Interplant dispersion of materials–labor ratio	..	..	..	..	− −	..
4. Intraplant diversity of industry's products	0	− −	..	0	− −	..
5. Intraindustry diversity of plant scale	..	− −	..	..	0	..
6. Product differentiation (advertising–sales ratio)	− −	−	0	0	− −	..
7. Product differentiation (attribute complexity)	0	..	..	..	..	..
8. Nonproduction workers proportion	− −[i]	− −	..	+	− −	0
9. Regional dispersion	−	..	..	− −	0	− −
10. Fuel intensity	0	+ +	0	..	..	..
D. Dynamic disturbances						
1. Research and development expenditures/sales	− −	+ +	0	0	0	..
2. Technology imports payments	..	+ +	..	..	+	..
3. Technology exports receipts	..	+ +	..	..	..	..
4. Rate of productivity growth	0	−	..	..	..	+
5. Rate of output growth	0	− −	..	− −	0	0

Table 1.2 (continued)

Exogenous variable	United States	Japan	Korea	Britain	Canada	Australia
6. Variability of output growth rate	..	— —	..	..	0	..
E. Public policy						
1. Tariff protection	0	— —ʲ	0	..	..	— —ᵏ
2. Regulation of entry	..	— —	..	..	..	..

Note: The symbol $+ +$ ($- -$) indicates a significant and robust positive (negative) influence on efficiency; $+$ ($-$) indicates a positive (negative) influence that is marginally significant or imperfectly robust; 0 indicates no significant effect; $\cdot\cdot$ indicates that no test was made.
a. In homogeneous-product industries that undertake heavy advertising.
b. Associated with resource-intensive production of undifferentiated products.
c. Relative to market size (otherwise, absolute size measure).
d. Based on enterprise data (otherwise, based on establishment data).
e. Based on enterprise data; 0 when based on establishment data (like other observations in this line).
f. Dispersion of vintages of industry's capital.
g. Measure of indivisibility of plant's capital.
h. Measure of newness of capital.
i. The coefficient of variation of plants' ratios of nonproduction workers to employees.
j. Includes rate of direct subsidy to industry.
k. Includes natural protection from transport costs.

the following paragraphs we provide a qualitative assessment of this tabulation, starting with competitive conditions.

One dramatic regularity of the results is the effect of the concentration of domestic producers (lines A1, A2). In every country high concentration is found hostile to technical efficiency. In four of them a quadratic relationship indicates that maximum efficiency comes at an intermediate level of concentration (a fairly low one for United States and Australia, higher for Japan and Korea). In the other two a linear negative effect dominates, although for Canada a quadratic relation is also significant (not reported in chapter 7).[9] The prevalence of the quadratic relation of course raises the question why highly unconcentrated industries should appear inefficient. Torii provides a theoretical model (subsection 2.3.1), and we return to the empirical question below. A curious finding about competition comes from Australia (subsection 6.3.2), for which SFPFs were estimated with the truncation of the distribution of inefficiency endogenized. The extra inefficiency thus exposed is positively and significantly related to concentration and to the prevalence of foreign direct investment.[10]

International competition raises efficiency less robustly than does domestic competition, increasing it significantly for only two countries (A3).

Its effect is negative for Japan (where we might expect none given manu-facturing's heavy orientation toward exports) and Canada (where a specific structural interpretation for the seemingly perverse result is offered). On the other hand, tariff protection as a restraint on import competition significantly reduces efficiency in Japan (E1). Exporting activity may serve as a form of competitive exposure for a national industry (A4), but the implied positive effect turns up only for Canada. The significant negative effects found for the United States and Britain may arise because exporting is a source of structural heterogeneity among establishments: some do much, others little or none.

The organization of an industry and its member firms can affect effi-ciency in many ways. One salient feature is the sizes of plants (absolute, or relative to the market): Various hypotheses based on the effect of fixed costs of replacing equipment or rooting out inefficiency hold that efficiency should increase with plant size. Each country yielded some definite results (B1), although neither model specifications nor findings are entirely con-gruent. For the United States, Canada, and Korea efficiency increases with the sizes of plants relative to the market, which the authors justify on the basis of fixed costs per plant of achieving or sustaining efficiency. However, absolute plant sizes may provide a more cogent test of that hypothesis than of sizes relative to the market, and in that form Australia also yielded positive results. There could, however, be scale diseconomies rather than economies in plant coordination, predicting the negative effect found for Japan. However, the contrary finding for Japan, robust in the analysis presented in chapter 2, is called into question by some findings about Japanese industries disaggregated into their small-plant and large-plant halves (section 10.4). Some more evidence on the unresolved effect of plant size appears below.

Other influences on efficiency stem from the organization of enterprises. Caves and Barton (1990, chs. 6, 7) found strong evidence that diversifica-tion by large enterprises is a significant source of inefficiency. This result was attributed to the diversifying mergers and conglomerate development of large U.S. enterprises, probably near its peak in 1977 and fated for substantial reversal in the 1980s. Because the diversification wave did not wash over other industrial nations, we did not expect to replicate the result elsewhere. We can distinguish between diversification "inbound" to and "outbound" from an industry. Inbound diversification by an enter-prise based elsewhere depresses efficiency in Canada as in the United

States, but Australia and Korea yielded no result (consistent with their smaller and less diversified enterprises), and Japanese efficiency responds positively to a rather different measure of diversification (B2). For outbound diversification the U.S. study also found a negative effect at the enterprise level, although no effect turned up of diversification within individual plants. Three other countries exhibit negative effects of plant-level diversification, although for Britain the effect is positive (B3). Multiplant operation by enterprises within an industry perhaps surprisingly diminishes efficiency in four of five countries (B4). The efficiency of subcontracting in Japan was weakly confirmed (stronger evidence appears in chapter 11), but the Korean data are in disagreement (B5). No effect was found of foreign direct investment flowing from the United States, but flows into Canada and Australia may depress efficiency there (B6).

Labor organization affects efficiency in the United States through two channels: The use of part-time employees increases it, while trade-union organization reduces it (weak significance) (B7, B8).[11] The two variables themselves are negatively correlated, leaving the strengths of their respective effects in some doubt. National labor-relations systems differ greatly, raising doubts about replicating these results in other countries. They are indeed replicated in Canada, the nation most similar to the United States. Japan's results diverge, although they come somewhat more into line in the Japan–U.S. comparison (chapter 11). The relation was not tested directly for Britain, but indirect confirmation comes in chapter 9.

The next class of efficiency determinants covers structural forces that cause competing units to exhibit heterogeneous levels of productivity in long-run equilibrium. Numerous sources of heterogeneity were tested. Although their significance or insignificance generally has no clear normative implications, their inclusion both cuts the chances of biased estimates for normatively significant regressors and provides useful information about their behavioral importance. The process of estimating SFPFs generated direct measures of the heterogeneity of some activities among plants classified to an industry; tests of hypotheses can employ either these direct variance-type measures or indirect indicators based on industry structure (e.g., regional dispersion of plants).

The heterogeneity of plants' capital–labor ratios is found negatively related to efficiency in both the United States and Korea (C1). For Japan Torii argues that the positive influence of fuel intensity indicates the presence of a rigid, fixed-coefficient technology that discourages diversity in plants' factor proportions (C10), and certain results for the United States indirectly support his inference (Caves and Barton 1990, 102–105). For the United States the dispersion of the vintages of an industry's capital could be measured directly and its negative effect confirmed; indirect tests support the same conclusion for Japan and Britain, though not for Korea (C2).

Of other forms of heterogeneity among plants, diverse ratios of materials to labor inputs decrease efficiency in Canada (C3). The diversity of products classified to an industry and produced in its plants also reduces measured efficiency in two countries but not in two others (C4). For Japan (though not for Canada) the dispersion of plant sizes also exerts a negative influence (C5).

Other forms of heterogeneity were inferred from broad traits of market structures. In exploring product differentiation, Caves and Barton (1990) distinguished two of its aspects: The U.S. industry's level of sales-promotion outlays depresses efficiency (C6), while the product's intrinsic complexity or diversity of attributes has no effect (C7). Sales promotion's negative effect is confirmed in Canada, though not in Britain or Korea (intrinsic complexity was not tested elsewhere). One mechanism by which sales promotion and other nonproduction activities affect efficiency is through the diverse proportions of nonproduction workers classified to manufacturing establishments (some such activities are contracted out, others performed in separate establishments). The proportion of workers in nonproduction activities appears to depress efficiency in the United States, Japan, and Canada (C8). The geographic fragmentation of markets reduces estimated efficiency in three countries (C9).[12] Fuel intensity was initially expected to decrease estimated efficiency, because in 1977 producers had not completed their adjustments to the 1973 energy price shock. That hypothesis was not confirmed for the United States or Korea, and the contrary result for Japan was given a different interpretation (C10). Overall the strength and regularity of these relationships is high, surprisingly so given the lack of a clear theoretical link between interplant heterogeneity and the third moment of the SFPF residuals (and thus measured inefficiency).

Dynamic disturbances can both shift the efficient frontier and churn the positions of individual plants relative to it, and so the directions of their effects are neither predictable nor necessarily identical among countries. The intensity of research and development (R&D) activities reduces estimated efficiency in the United States but increases it in Japan while exerting no systematic effect elsewhere (D1). The creation and diffusion of technology is of course an international process, and international flows (which could well let technological laggards catch up) increase efficiency in both Japan and Canada (D2, D3). With R&D controlled, productivity growth reduces estimated efficiency in Japan but has no effect in the United States (where the negative effect of R&D probably captures the same dynamic process) (D4). In Canada productivity growth is associated with declining efficiency over time. The growth rate of real output depresses efficiency in both Japan and Britain (though not in the United States, Canada, or Australia), and for Japan the variability of industry growth exerts a negative effect independent of its pace (D5, D6). In summary, the type of dynamic disturbance that depresses estimated efficiency differs from country to country but four of the six countries exhibit some such centrifugal effect. The seemingly inconsistent results on innovation are arguably consistent with the countries' respective positions in the international creation and dissemination of technology.

This project was not designed to test the effect of government intervention and regulation on efficiency, but it yielded a few results. Tariff protection reduces efficiency in Japan and Australia (E1), as does direct regulation of entry and business operations in Japan (E2).

We hoped that parallel analyses of the interindustry determinants of technical efficiency in several countries would confirm that estimated technical efficiency captures a lot of true variations in efficiency and that the mechanisms determining it are broadly similar from country to country. The results summarized in table 1.2 vary among families of hypotheses, but overall we feel that they confirm the second hope directly, and the first one by implication. In highlighting the evidence of similarity, however, this summary loses the elements of national distinctiveness. For the United States the analysis confirms the hubris of corporate diversification in the decade preceding 1977. For Japan we affirm the country's efficiency as an absorber of frontier technologies and (relative to the United States) the effectiveness of its subcontracting system. In Britain, where competition has long been suspected to lack ferocity, efficiency declines uniformly with an industry's difference from atomistic rivalry, and competition reduces technical inefficiency even as it increases the overall dispersion of competitors' productivity levels. Australia's economic geography (widely dispersed and inefficiently diversified state-level markets) imprints itself strongly on industrial efficiency. Canada's results are aptly similarly to those for its close neighbor and industrial twin, the United States, while the most striking feature of Korea's results is their similarity to those of the substantially more developed nations.

1.3 Extensions in Space and Time

The remainder of the volume proceeds beyond these core static tests to address a variety of related questions—the stability of technical efficiency over time, its variation with size of establishment within industries, and its direct comparability between countries.

1.3.1 Technical Efficiency over Time

The analysis of efficiency's static determinants raises many questions about how efficiency changes over time. Some forms of inefficiency are tied to intertemporally stable structural features of competition and the organization of industries. We hence expect the inefficiencies associated with them to be stable over time, although the eternal incentive to profit by eliminating inefficiency should have its way. Apparent inefficiency associated with structural heterogeneity should be quite stable, as it provides no opportunities to profit by making repairs. On the other hand, the dynamic disturbances that affect efficiency wax and wane over time. Furthermore, apart from economic causation, the statistical inference of technical efficiency based on third moments is itself potentially sensitive to changes in the pattern of random disturbances (see chapter 8). We have some bases for expecting intertemporal stability of estimated efficiency, some for expecting instability, and a lengthy agenda of interesting substantive questions about the dynamic processes involved.

We address that agenda in analyses of three countries. Only for Korea could technical efficiency be estimated for each industry over time (annually 1978–88) in order to expose its stability directly (chapter 8). For Canada efficiency was measured for two years a decade apart (1970 and 1979) and the changes between them analyzed (chapter 7). For Britain data on the dispersion of plants' productivity levels were available for eight years during 1963–79 (with irregular gaps), so the variability and trends over time in industries' productivity dispersions could be measured and explained (chapter 9).

The findings of Seong Min Yoo about technical efficiency over time in Korea are at first sight dismaying. Many industries bounce back and forth over time between estimation successes and failures. Between pairs of adjacent years the rank correlations of industries' estimated efficiency levels are very low, although improved when the average technical inefficiency measure is employed. The only bright spot is that the typical industry's annual values of estimated efficiency are strongly correlated with its period-long mean, suggesting that estimated efficiency may exhibit a lot of random vibration around a stable mean.

Yoo's findings lead directly to the work of John Baldwin on Canada and Sheryl D. Bailey on Britain. Baldwin can observe individual plants that survived over the decade 1970–79, as well as those that entered and departed. With data in hand on their labor-productivity levels, changes in industry efficiency can be related to the turnover of plants (replacement of less by more efficient ones) and to changes in their shares (gains for the efficient, losses for the inefficient) (section 7.4). The turnover of plants is considerable and contributes importantly to industry productivity: The normalized efficiency in 1979 of new plants is about 25 percent higher than that in 1970 of plants destined to close, and 5 percent higher than plants that stayed alive over 1970–79 but lost share. Ongoing plants' gains and losses of share were associated with their gains or losses in normalized productivity. Overall industry efficiency in 1979 would have been 6.5 percent lower without turnover, half the benefit coming from the changing shares of continuing plants and one-third from newly constructed plants.

Baldwin shows that turnover and efficiency share a complex relationship because, while turnover increases efficiency, disturbances to efficiency also affect turnover. For example, parallel to the negative effect of R&D on efficiency in U.S. industries, productivity growth and the *change* in industry efficiency are inversely related in Canada. Turnover also varies with other efficiency-relevant factors such as market growth, trade-union activity, inbound diversification, and the prevalence of plants smaller than optimal scale (section 7.5).

Taken in conjunction with the findings about static efficiency and dynamic disturbances summarized previously, these conclusions show that an industry's efficiency can vibrate extensively and unsystematically from year to year as such disturbances wax and wane.[13] However, they also suggest that such vibrations (consistent with Yoo's findings on Korea) might take place around a stable and structurally determined mean value.[14]

Although this project's resources did not permit pursuing those questions by estimating technical efficiency on a panel of establishment data, Sheryl D. Bailey reports a parallel analysis of variations over time in the industrywide dispersions of British plants' labor-productivity levels. Her results should apply fairly well to intertemporal variations in technical efficiency because of the close relation we repeatedly found between the behavior of the second and third moments of production-function residuals (especially the findings about Britain in chapter 4). She finds little evidence that industries' dispersions display either systematic trends or autocorrelation. However, industries' rates of random vibration[15] over time can be explained rather well by a series of hypotheses adduced from the general proposition that the stability of an industry's plant-productivity dispersion should decrease with the incidence of disturbances and increase with the adjustment speed and flexibility of resource use in the industry.

Bailey's conclusions align nicely with the static findings summarized in table 1.2. Oligopolistic rivalry appears to destabilize the productivity dispersion over time, confirming one mechanism by which concentration can (as it does) depress static efficiency. International competition (especially from the import side) is a source of destabilizing disturbances, which may explain why it does not appear a more robust competitive inducer of efficiency. The multiplant operation of leading firms is stabilizing, a finding that contrasts with (and thus qualifies) its negative effect on static efficiency. Divisive labor relations destabilize the productivity dispersion over time, consistent with the static effects found for Canada and the United States. Instability tends to increase with the sunkenness of capital (inferred inversely from the importance of rented and hence fungible capital).[16] A supplemental analysis shows that most of the vibration of industries' distributions of net output per head is due to the output rather than the labor-input term.

One happy feature of these findings about efficiency over time is that they reinforce the cross-sectional structural analyses summarized in section 1.2. A standard criticism of cross-sectional analyses of industrial performance holds that it neglects the feedback to the supposedly exogenous structural determinants that occurs as firms react to any prevailing abnormalities in their industry's performance. The finding that efficiency tends to exhibit random vibration over time but not autocorrelation or trends suggests that these feedback loops are not strong. So does the consistency between the determinants of the level and intertemporal stability of efficiency.

1.3.2 Efficiency and Plant Size within Industries

The study of U.S. technical efficiency divided industries with sufficient numbers of plants into their large-plant and small-plant halves and estimated their efficiency levels separately. This inquiry was spurred by a number of questions about units' sizes and efficiency levels. The empirical findings summarized in section 1.2 yield for each of the six countries some evidence that highly atomistic industries may tend to be inefficient.[17] Subdividing industries in order to focus on their smaller participants is one way to probe this finding. Small units tend to be price-takers whose market situations resemble those of all members of an atomistic industry. They are also likely to include many new entrants who may suffer from factor-market imperfections and/or be subject to shakedown and shakeout. Caves and Barton (1990, ch. 7) accordingly were not surprised to find smaller half units on average to be about 6 percent less efficient than their larger competitors (the difference is statistically significant). In accord with this result is the finding that mean estimated efficiency in Korea is slightly (2 percent) higher when establishments with fewer than 20 employees are omitted in estimation of the SFPFs (subsection 3.3.4), but with the margin of difference varying widely among industries.

In a comparison of small-plant and large-plant efficiency in Japan (chapter 10) we expect to observe at least as large a difference as in the United States. Discussions of the "small and medium enterprise problem" have long identified factor-market and other distortions that create (at the least) factor-allocation distortions between small and large firms. Although market forces have been eliminating these distortions, few would judge that they had vanished by 1977. Akio Torii developed a Bayesian procedure in order to estimate efficiency for both the smaller and larger halves of the plant populations of 74 Japanese industries. Surprisingly he finds no difference in estimated efficiency, although the mean labor-productivity differential is very large, 27 percent greater in large establishments. Furthermore for both Japan and the United States the symmetrical component of variance around the SFPF (σ_v) is greater in small plants.

The difference between expected efficiency in large and small plants is analyzed among Japanese industries, parallel to the U.S. study. Several explanatory factors are common to both countries, although institutional differences do weigh heavily. The common factors are these:

1. In both countries a higher total capital cost for an efficient-scale plant increases the relative efficiency of the small-plant sector. (For Japan the result in this reduced sample diverges from that of the larger sample [of whole industries] analyzed in chapter 2.)

2. Excess diversification in larger units impairs their relative efficiency in both countries. (In the United States this loss is associated with large firms' ownership of plants classified to alien industries; in Japan it is associated with plant-level diversification.)

3. The flexibility gained by part-time employment benefits the relative efficiency of small units in each country.

Other conclusions reflect institutional differences. In the United States an industry's research intensity (which reduces estimated efficiency overall) raises the relative efficiency of large units, while in Japan technology imports favor the efficiency of large units. In Japan public policy strongly affects relative efficiency: Tariffs and subsidies impair the efficiency of smaller units, entry regulation the efficiency of larger units. The efficiency benefits of subcontracting favor the smaller units. In the United States advertising-related product differentiation reduces the relative efficiency of small units while export intensity lowers the apparent relative efficiency of large units.

The Japanese study goes farther to show that although efficiency on average does not differ between small and large units, their relative-efficiency differences among industries are a significant (positive) influence on the difference in labor productivity between large and small units (section 10.5). That is, where the small-plant sector is relatively more efficient, aggregate small-plant productivity is higher. Furthermore Torii shows that this link between relative efficiency and relative productivity runs through the relative price-cost margins of the large and small units. That is, differential efficiency translates itself into differential rents to the more efficient units (section 10.6).

1.3.3   International Comparisons

Through its parallel national research designs this study as a whole constitutes an international comparison. Nonetheless, several gains might come from a closer comparative analysis effected by matching individual industries between countries. Matching provides assurance that any differences (or similarities) in efficiency patterns or determinants between countries noted in section 1.2 are not artifacts of different samples of industries. With matched industries we can test hypotheses about the relative positions of two countries' production frontiers because the positions of the (unobserved) frontiers can be inferred from relative average productivity adjusted for relative technical efficiency.

Between Japan and the United States 205 industries could be matched and their relative efficiency compared. The data suggest that, if anything, Japanese industries are more efficient, but the main conclusion is that the methodology does not yield confident comparisons of countries' average levels of efficiency. Fortunately international levels in the several measures of efficiency of matched industries are highly correlated, sustaining the conclusion that the SFPF method is as good for exposing interindustry differences as it is bad for determining unconditional averages (subsection 11.3.3).

Although problems of robustness do arise, the analysis of relative efficiency yields a number of interesting conclusions (section 11.4.1). Relative efficiency decreases with the extent of each matched industry's departure from its own country's optimal concentration level. The relative prevalence of trade-union membership reduces relative efficiency, although in Japanese industries alone (chapter 2) no influence of labor organization was found. Relative use of part-time employment exerts the expected positive influence. The strong negative effect of enterprise diversification on U.S. national efficiency does not translate into a significant effect on relative efficiency, raising questions about Japanese institutions (*keiretsu* groupings) that play somewhat related roles. However, the adverse effects of tariffs and subsidies on Japanese efficiency do extend to affect relative efficiency as well.

These results confirm and extend the Japanese and U.S. national studies, but new territory is entered in the analysis of relative frontier efficiency. A method is developed for integrating technical efficiency formally into the analysis of relative average productivity in matched industries (section

11.5). Although not many hypotheses could be tested, it does appear that the efficient frontier in Japan advances with the prevalence of subcontracting. Japan's frontier is relatively advanced in industries whose U.S. branches use substantial amounts of old-vintage capital. The Japanese frontier may be superior in industries whose production activities entail the coordination of large quantities of skilled labor. No effect was found, however, of either relative R&D activities or of international technology imports to Japan.[18]

To analyze relative frontier productivity is essentially to test the bases of international comparative advantage. In chapter 12 Fabienne Fecher and Sergio Perelman pursue the same goal through a very different extension of the SFPF methodology. Adapting a framework of Nishimizu and Page (1982), they regard each national branch of an industry as a more or less efficient unit in the world industry represented by the OECD countries. Observing these country-industry cells over 16 years, they undertake a pooled estimation of a production function for each sector that yields estimated rates of total factor productivity growth and a conditional estimate of efficiency for each industry-year cell. Their estimate of lambda, 0.36, places the bulk of the variance in the symmetrical error term but indicates considerable scope for technical inefficiency. In cross section, U.S. industries continued to dominate the efficiency frontier in the 1970s, but leading countries (notably the United States and Germany) showed weaker gains in productivity than did small countries such as Belgium and Denmark. Most countries and industries experienced gains in technical efficiency,[19] but these were small relative to productivity gains except in sectors whose productivity grew slowly.

Fecher and Perelman report simple tests of hypotheses about interindustry and intercountry differences analogous to the interindustry analyses reported in other studies. The most substantial positive conclusions concern research and development: The R&D spending of the main innovating countries improves the efficiency standings of their industries, while the association is negative for the technology absorbers. Capital expenditure is found to raise a sector's efficiency through (presumably) its embodiment of new technology. Surprisingly the study's results are negative on the correlation between estimated efficiency and international trade. That import competition has a mixed relation to efficiency is not too surprising (given results mentioned above for Canada and Australia), but the prevailing negative relation between efficiency and exporting activity is perverse and unexplained. It should be kept in mind that data limitations constrain the authors to working with excessively aggregated industries.

1.4 Concluding Reflections

Because this study represents a major research expedition on previously untrod ground, we close with a few candid reflections on what has and has not been achieved and what implications emerge for future research.

1. Technical efficiency is a fit topic for serious economic research and deserves much more attention than it has received. Contrary to a widely held view, cogent hypotheses about it can be formulated and successfully tested. Measured technical efficiency picks up much variance that does not represent inefficiency in any normative sense, but even those components are behaviorally interesting for what they can tell us about the heterogeneity of industrial activities and their dynamic adjustment.

2. The methodology of stochastic frontier production functions has its strengths and weaknesses. Its substantial strength is to expose interindustry differences in efficiency that seem "real" in the sense that they are broadly related to hypothesized causes of (in)efficiency. However, in retrospect by our heavy reliance on the SFPF we may have imposed too much structure on the analysis (despite the theoretically attractive properties of that structure noted in section 1.1). Although our hypotheses were formulated specifically to address inefficiency revealed by the third moment of production-function residuals, they seem in several instances to apply about as well to the second moment—the incidence of seemingly random noise.[20] Furthermore theoretically well-founded measures of efficiency obtained from the SFPF do not always outperform not-so-proper ones such as skewness, which seems to gain more in explanatory value from preserving degrees of freedom than it loses in the ambiguous meaning of the variance in its positive range.

3. Although this study only begins to analyze the dynamics of technical efficiency, it does show that the static measurement of efficiency can be integrated with the dynamic microanalysis of productivity growth and efficiency changes. The availability for research of longitudinal data bases on individual establishments in the United States and other countries will no doubt stimulate much work of the sort introduced by John Baldwin in

this volume, research that relates the traits of an establishment at a point in time to its transit through the establishment distribution over time.

4. We close with a qualified view of the value of the stochastic frontier production function. We have established that it can be usefully applied in a mechanical way to large numbers of industries (most previous applications were tailored to data for a single sector). It seems from our tests of hypotheses to capture a great deal of valuable information about differences in efficiency among industries. On the other hand, it does not clearly outperform simpler and cheaper measures. Its emphasis on the asymmetrical component of production-function residuals does not clearly beat approaches focused on the simple variance of those residuals. And in intertemporal analyses it probably can reveal less than approaches that track the productivities of individual establishments over time. The SFPF clearly belongs in the research arsenal, but in some battles it will yield to other weapons.

Notes

1. The exposition here is nontechnical. More sophisticated treatments can be found in chapters 2, 3, and 5 of this volume. For useful surveys see Førsund, Lovell, and Schmidt (1980), Schmidt (1985–86), and Caves and Barton (1990, ch. 2). A recent symposium of papers can be found in *Journal of Econometrics* 46 (October–November 1990).

2. In this form the estimation procedure does not pick up Farrell's allocative inefficiency—the use of the wrong input combination given factor prices. Techniques are available to identify that inefficiency component as well by estimating factor-demand equations jointly with the SFPF. That extension entails the use of maximum-likelihood techniques and (more to the point) requires comprehensive data on input prices that are not available for the broadly based studies reported in this volume.

3. Chris M. Harris pointed out in an earlier version of chapter 5 that positive skewness could arise because most units are in fact similarly inefficient, with the efficient minority elongating the upper tail.

4. In its negative range skewness is closely related to λ, and so the case for using λ applies equally to skewness. Akio Torii shows (subsection 2.2.3) that the association of negative skewness with inefficiency does not depend on the half-normal distribution of inefficiency and also follows if inefficiency is assumed to follow an exponential distribution.

5. Only after the publication of Caves and Barton was it discovered that a programming error made in the early stages at the Bureau of the Census pervasively affects the details of the quantitative results. Fortunately very few qualitative conclusions changed when it was corrected, but a few findings mentioned in this chapter will consequently be at variance with the published text. A memorandum of corrections is available from the authors.

6. In the event value added as the dependent variable produced better results in the SFPFs (fewer estimation failures, more satisfactory tests of hypotheses about interindustry differences). Only in Korea was this difference not evident, and expected efficiency based on gross output was relied upon to test hypotheses about the interindustry determinants of efficiency.

It appears that the high correlation in annual data between plants' gross outputs and materials input levels injects noise into the estimation of efficiency.

7. A form of slippage between hypotheses and interindustry tests is that most of the hypotheses apply to firms as decision units while establishments provide the data used in estimating SFPFs. We generally ignore the distinction except for letting the term "unit" refer interchangeably to firm and establishment.

8. Robustness here refers to the insensitivity of a partial relationship to changes in the exogenous variables included in a model, and to the consistency of statistical significance when alternative efficiency measures (dependent variables) are employed. Principal weight was placed on whatever efficiency measures(s) the author found yielded the more satisfying results. A few results for Canada noted in table 1.2 were not reported in chapter 7.

9. The fact that efficiency was estimated from data on establishments rather than enterprises qualifies findings about competitive conditions. We can get some feeling for the force of the qualifications by determining whether the prevalence of multiplant firms affects efficiency measured from establishment data. We note below that multiplant operation generally bears a negative relation to efficiency. Because an industry's largest firms typically operate more plants, and multiplant operation increases with concentration, the finding that concentration depresses efficiency seems unimpugned.

10. The inefficiency measures based on truncated distributions are, however, quite unrelated to any other determinants that performed robustly in Australia and elsewhere, casting doubt on the conclusion.

11. Most hypotheses discussed in this section have reasonably well established theoretical and/or empirical bases that were set forth by Caves and Barton (1990, ch. 5). Part-time employment was tested an the basis of only a casual conjecture, but Abraham (1988) subsequently developed both theory and evidence on its value to employers as a source of flexibility.

12. The negative effect of regional dispersion for Canada appears in industries whose minimum efficient plant sizes are large.

13. This observation is consistent with the failure to find any relation between technical efficiency in Britain and the gross turnover of firms in the preceding four years (section 4.7).

14. It is unfortunate that data on the gross turnover of firms and/or establishments are not available for the cross-sectional analyses of static efficiency. Mayes and Green addressed the relation using less-than-ideal data and obtained negative results.

15. Measured by calculating for each industry and year a coefficient of variation in net output per head from primary (but grouped) data, then calculating a coefficient of variation over eight years for the annual observations on each industry.

16. Industries that hold large finished-good inventories also exhibit large vibrations of the productivity distribution. Because inventories themselves are a buffer, the conclusion presumably means that producers increase their inventory levels with the incidence of shocks that are not controlled in this analysis.

17. For four countries a significant quadratic relation indicates maximum efficiency at a moderate concentration level. In Canada there is some evidence of inefficiency in atomistic import-competing industries. Only in Britain does no substantial basis arise for concern about efficiency in highly unconcentrated industries.

18. Despite the value of these results, the authors voice some pessimism about the method of international comparisons of matched industries. The limitation lies not in one major defect but a series of small tactical difficulties: the imperfections of matching industries between countries, the loss of observations to type I and II errors, the problems of incompletely comparable data, and the like.

19. Variance decomposition nonetheless shows that most of the variance in technical efficiency is among countries and sectors and not over time (the opposite holds for the variance of total factor productivity).

20. Striking examples are Baldwin's method of measuring efficiency for Canadian manufacturing industries and Bailey's conclusions about the intertemporal behavior of the dispersion of plant-productivity levels of British manufacturing industries.

References

Abraham, K. G. 1988. Flexible staffing arrangements and employers' short-term adjustment strategies. National Bureau of Economic Research, Working Paper No. 2617.

Aigner, D. J., C. A. K. Lovell, and P. Schmidt. 1977. Formulation and estimation of stochastic frontier production function models. *Journal of Econometrics* 6: 21–38.

Arrow, K. J. 1977. The organization of economic activity: Issues pertinent to the choice of market versus nonmarket allocations. In R. H. Haveman and J. Margolis, eds., *Public Expenditure and Policy Analysis*. Chicago: Rand McNally, pp. 67–81.

Caves, R. E., and D. R. Barton. 1990. *Efficiency in U.S. Manufacturing Industries*. Cambridge: MIT Press.

Førund, F. R., C. A. Knox Lovell, and P. Schmidt. 1980. A survey of frontier production functions and of their relationship to efficiency measurement. *Journal of Econometrics* 13: 5–25.

Lee, L.-F., and W. G. Tyler. 1978. The stochastic frontier production function and average efficiency: An empirical analysis. *Journal of Econometrics* 7: 385–389.

Meeusen, W. and J. van den Broeck. 1977. Efficiency estimation of Cobb-Douglas production functions with composed error. *International Economic Review* 18: 435–444.

Nishimizu, M., and J. M. Page, Jr. 1982. Total factor productivity growth, technological progress, and technical efficiency change: Dimensions of productivity change in Yugoslavia, 1965–78. *Economic Journal* 92: 920–938.

Schmidt, P. 1985–86. Frontier production functions. *Econometric Reviews* 4: 289–328.

Timmer, C. P. 1971. Using a probabilistic frontier production function to measure technical inefficiency. *Journal of Political Economy* 79: 775–795.

I EFFICIENCY IN NATIONAL MANUFACTURING SECTORS

2 Technical Efficiency in Japanese Industries

Akio Torii

2.1 Introduction

As a concept of measurement technical inefficiency has been chiefly developed and applied by specialists in econometrics. Since the work of Farrell (1957) technical inefficiency has been estimated as an adjunct to the estimation of the production frontier. Generally, the production frontier is defined as the maximum output technically possible for specified amounts of all inputs. If some production takes place beneath this frontier, the situation is considered to be technically inefficient. Since, by definition, technical inefficiency is the discrepancy of the actual output level from the production frontier, its estimation cannot proceed without the estimation of the production frontier itself. Both deterministic and stochastic functions are employed in the estimation of technical inefficiency. Aigner, Lovell, and Schmidt (1977) and Meeusen and van den Broeck (1977) established the methods for estimating stochastic production frontiers, and succeeding contributions have developed more sophisticated methodologies.

The normative context of technical inefficiency comes from industrial organization theory. In industrial organization theory it is often argued that attaining technical efficiency has a stronger effect on social gain than repairing allocative inefficiency (see Caves and Uekusa 1976). Technical efficiency in this view is, as noted in Caves and Barton (1990), "efficiency in the popular sense of the word." In this respect the efficiency of Japanese industry has been believed to be high, at least for recent decades. One reason for high Japanese efficiency is considered to be the relative newness of its productive assets, thanks to high capital investment in periods of rapid economic growth. That is why one newspaper report claiming the assets of Japanese industry to be of older average vintage than those of the United States proved controversial several years ago (see Suzuki and Miyagawa 1986, ch. 2).

Is the efficiency of Japanese industries really higher than that of other industrialized nations? If it is, what is the difference in Japan's efficiency level, and what accounts for that difference? Indeed technical efficiency measures only one aspect of general efficiency. It is a more trouble-free measure than other measures of productivity because it is less sensitive to the method of measurement. But it is the *level* of technical efficiency that is a topic of great interest.

Exploratory studies of specific industries in various countries suggest that the observed average level of efficiency is distributed in the 50 to 80 percent range (see Schmidt 1985–86; and Caves and Barton 1990). These studies confirm the importance of technical efficiency relative to other aspects of efficiency. Although in ordinary use the concept of inefficiency seems to have the meaning of "remediable defect," estimates of technical inefficiency do not imply that if we improve some aspect of the industrial environment, we can increase output by tens of percent immediately. There are two ways of looking at the difference between observed technical inefficiency and so-called remediable inefficiency. These views correspond to the difference between technical efficiency measured in connection with production frontier and its normative context in industrial organization.

The first view recognizes the normative concept of technical efficiency. For example, when there is technological progress, the optimal conduct of an agent is to replace equipment at a finite rate if the embodiment of new technology is not costless. The agent would choose the optimal point in the trade-off between the cost reduction effects of new technology and the costs of replacement investment. The frontier production function used as the benchmark in measurement is the "current best-practice technology."[1] So the existence of any older plants causes some apparent inefficiency,[2] and some positive level of technical inefficiency will be observed. This example is technically inefficient in an econometric sense but not in the normative sense. Thus the economically efficient, rational agent can behave in a way that econometrically appears to be technically inefficient. This suggests that the observed level of technical inefficiency reflects a wider range of influences than does the normative concept.

The second view is closely related to the first view. As a purely econometric measure, technical inefficiency corresponds nicely to the intuitive meaning of inefficiency: Something is not being done as effectively as possible. The concept's inclusion of all sorts of asymmetrical distortions helps it to embrace this intuitive meaning. The cost of that transparency becomes evident, however, when we try to explain inefficiency as a condition flowing from the rational conduct of economic agents. The standard neoclassical postulate is that every agent acts to maximize his or her welfare. Does this postulate imply that technical inefficiency cannot exist? Does purely irrational conduct exist? Clearly the normative concept of technical efficiency has the same problem as that flagged in the debate over "X-efficiency" (see Frantz 1988).

If an agent's circumstances are not fully known, rational conduct may appear irrational. Although this suggests a similarity between normative and measured technical efficiency, a distinction can be made. An economic agent's conduct may be efficient in the normative context even if it can be measured as being inefficient. The agent's conduct may be efficient because it is cost minimizing and thus increases social welfare. On the other hand, even if seemingly inefficient conduct can be explained by such a model, it may not be socially optimal. We may say that an action of an agent is rational, but the rationality depends on the utility function of the agent, which is something we cannot directly observe. There might in addition be various environmental factors that affect social welfare in the way described by Caves and Barton (1990).[3] If such factors can be characterized as frictions of the economic system, the relationship between the frictions and the level of technical efficiency is worth investigating.

In this chapter we estimate the levels of technical efficiency of Japanese industries and analyze some explanatory factors for their technical inefficiency. We will not depend on a strict theoretical interpretation of technical inefficiency, however.

In section 2.2 we explain the methodology for estimating the level of technical efficiency and the production frontier, and then we examine the properties of various measures of technical efficiency. In section 2.3 we present some hypotheses about determinants of technical inefficiency and test them in an ordinal structure-performance, cross-sectional analysis. In the final section we use a simultaneous equations analysis to investigate the relationship between technical efficiency and dynamic efficiency involving R&D outlays.

2.2   Estimating Technical Efficiency

2.2.1   Stochastic Production Frontier

In estimating the level of technical efficiency in Japanese manufacturing, we employ the composed-error stochastic production function. This methodology was introduced by Aigner, Lovell, and Schmidt (1977) and Meeusen and van den Broeck (1977), who assumed that technical inefficiency is described by the half-normal distribution. The stochastic production frontier model is an expansion of the deterministic production frontier model, which was designed to relieve excessive sensitivity to outliers. It deals with this sensitivity by regarding outlying observations, such as statistical errors or changing environmental factors, as uncontrollable noise. The stochastic production frontier model is expressed as

$$y_i = f(x_i) + v_i - u_i, \qquad u_i \geqq 0, \tag{1}$$

where y is output, x is input, v is some symmetric error term, and u is an asymmetric error term caused by technical inefficiency. The production frontier is $f(x) + v$, and by definition, it can vary.

There are two components of v. The first is pure statistical noise, such as measurement and aggregation errors. The performance of the real object has no relation to these errors. The other component of v consists of factors absorbed into this term because they are uncontrollable or unobservable. Included in v might be the physical conditions of an individual plant or even weather conditions, both of which are uncontrollable, and factors such as the condition of equipment which is unobservable. The error u would result from technical inefficiency.

The difference between the second component of v and technical inefficiency is that noise gives rise to symmetrical deviations whereas technical inefficiency generates asymmetrical deviations. If the ability of the operator of a machine has a symmetrical distribution, it will affect output symmetrically. It will hence be treated as noise that displaces the production frontier. The production frontier is the maximum output possible from a certain amount of input. With the deterministic production frontier, this output is unique. But on the stochastic production frontier the maximum output is subjected to disturbances caused by the kinds of conditions mentioned above. This intuitive definition of the difference between noise and technical inefficiency is sufficient in most cases; nevertheless, we will also examine the theoretical relationship between the concept of technical inefficiency and the shape of its distribution.

2.2.2 Corrected Ordinary Least Squares Method

Once we have assigned some distribution functions to v and u, we look at several methods of estimating the parameters. The method of corrected ordinary least squares (COLS) is a very convenient and easy method to use for the calculations. COLS, which was proposed by Aigner, Lovell, and Schmidt (1977), offers a consistent estimator. The efficiency of COLS was tested by Olson, Schmidt, and Waldman (1980) (henceforth OSW), who compared the Monte Carlo results of COLS estimators with maximum-likelihood (ML) estimators. They found the COLS estimators to be as efficient as ML estimators for a wide range of sample sizes and values of $\lambda = \sigma_u/\sigma_v$. OSW set forth the model as $y = X\beta + \varepsilon$ and $\varepsilon = v - u$. Then they generated X and β nonstochastically, and v and u stochastically using $N(0, \sigma_v^2)$ and the absolute value of $N(0, \sigma_u^2)$, respectively. After summing up y, they applied COLS and ML, as well as one other method.

COLS estimators are computed from the second and third moments of the OLS residuals. The estimated moments are

$$\mu_2 = \sigma_v^2 + \frac{\pi - 2}{\pi}\sigma_u^2, \qquad \mu_3 = \sqrt{\frac{2}{\pi}}\left(1 - \frac{4}{\pi}\right)\sigma_u^3. \tag{2}$$

The symmetric v has no effect on the third moment, and the σ_u estimator is reckoned only from the third moment of the residuals. This fact grants the estimator some robustness in the OSW-type Monte Carlo study because any misspecification that affects the residuals symmetrically has no effect on the σ_u estimator. For example, if the estimating method fails to obtain an unbiased estimator of β and gets $\tilde{\beta} \neq \beta$, the residuals are $\tilde{\varepsilon} = y - X\tilde{\beta}$. It is obvious that if X is distributed symmetrically, then $\varepsilon = y - X\beta$ and $\tilde{\varepsilon}$ have the same third moments. In OSW the set of X was generated by i.i.d. $N(0, 1)$ symmetrically. Therefore the σ_u estimator was not affected by the biases of the estimator of β.

On the other hand, where the distribution of X is not symmetrical, the bias of the estimator of β may influence the σ_u estimator. These asymmetrically distributed X are caused not only by the existence of outliers but also by nonlinearity of estimated functions. For example, when the estimated production frontier is the translog type, as in this chapter, some columns of X are quadratics of other columns. One of these columns should have a skewed distribution. Such asymmetrically distributed X add asymmetrically distributed errors to the OLS residuals when the estimator of β is not precise. Thus the consistency and efficiency of the coefficient estimator could be crucial to the σ_u estimator, and the analysis by OSW does not go far enough. Therefore we undertake another Monte Carlo study that examines the robustness of COLS estimator with a translog production function.

The fact that only the third moment of the OLS residuals determines the σ_u estimator creates another problem. OLS residuals are errors composed of a normal distribution v and a half-normal distribution u, so the moments of the residuals are weighted averages of the normal and the half-normal distributions. The third moment of the residual has to lie between 0 (the expected value of the third moment of the normal distribution) and $\sqrt{(2/\pi)}[1 - (4/\pi)]\sigma_u^3$ (the expected value of the third moment of the half-normal distribution with $\sigma = \sigma_u$). Here the value that σ_u can take is bounded by the observed second moment. That is, $\mu_2 \geq (\pi - 2/\pi)\sigma_u^2$. Therefore the third moment has a lower bound.[4]

We lack efficient estimators for the moments of higher orders, so there is a strong possibility that the estimated third moment is not in the limited region. OSW called such a failure a *type I failure* when the third moment is positive and a *type II failure* when the moment is lower than the lower bound. When we encounter these failures, we cannot obtain a reasonable σ_u estimator, and this seriously complicates any empirical study.

Table 2.1, gives the failure results for the Monte Carlo study that we conducted. We obtained our results by generating v and u from $N(0, \sigma_v^2)$ and the absolute value of $N(0, \sigma_u^2)$, that is, $\sigma_v^2 = 1$ and $\sigma_u^2 = 1$. Then we estimated σ_u from series of $v_i - u_i$, which are the residuals from OLS. As we argued earlier, the σ_u estimator is not affected by how a linear model is calibrated when explanatory variables are arranged nonstochastically and symmetrically. Therefore the likelihood of type I failure was not affected by this simplified method. However, the likelihood of type II failure could be affected because the σ_v estimator is exposed to the estimation error of regression coefficient β even when X are distributed symmetrically.

As shown in the table, type I failure proves to be a more serious problem than type II failure, especially when the value of σ_v is large compared to the value of σ_u. Increasing the sample size does not significantly improve the situation. Of course the problem lies not in these failures but in the biases in the estimator. Because we cannot obtain an estimator of σ_u or σ_v, there is discontinuity as we encounter these failures of the estimator. The treatable region of the third moment of residuals is bounded from both sides. The estimators might be biased asymmetrically near these borders, since in this fringe area estimator bias can be ruled out only on one side. We refer to such a bias as the "boundary effect."

One way to avoid the problem of an asymmetric bias is to extend mathematically the formula for converting the OLS residuals to the estimators. That conversion does not allow both a positive third moment of the residuals and a negative σ_v^2 estimator. It is rather easy to extend the formula to admit these embarrassing values of accepting negative u and σ_u^2, but, besides the theoretical problem of admitting negative u and σ_u^2, there

Table 2.1
Numbers of failures in 2,000 simulation experiments

Value of σ_v	N	Value of σ_u: type I failure						Value of σ_u: type II failure					
		0.1	0.2	0.5	1.0	2.0	5.0	0.1	0.2	0.5	1.0	2.0	5.0
0.1	20	840	498	156	87	89	60	72	182	420	522	528	547
	50	741	244	11	8	2	4	13	89	446	586	639	669
	100	602	74	0	0	0	0	0	28	380	614	693	699
	200	450	14	0	0	0	0	0	6	322	554	727	733
	500	239	0	0	0	0	0	0	0	157	536	674	721
0.2	20	1019	867	386	139	87	78	39	63	241	405	508	606
	50	941	718	124	10	1	2	4	15	179	443	594	632
	100	965	599	15	0	0	0	0	1	81	367	618	708
	200	897	450	1	0	0	0	0	0	19	293	602	748
	500	855	224	0	0	0	0	0	0	0	150	498	714
0.5	20	1003	981	863	487	206	86	49	27	76	163	376	496
	50	1031	1024	707	240	29	4	2	4	11	99	374	632
	100	982	965	610	104	1	0	0	0	1	36	259	644
	200	1011	978	485	16	0	0	0	0	0	2	176	575
	500	1003	925	239	0	0	0	0	0	0	0	51	542
1.0	20	997	979	954	821	503	136	37	33	56	72	158	414
	50	1036	1004	939	704	250	11	2	7	3	12	101	439
	100	968	1030	921	586	78	0	0	0	0	2	39	372
	200	1028	1006	919	461	12	0	0	0	0	0	4	297
	500	1023	1036	834	265	0	0	0	0	0	0	0	147
2.0	20	982	1066	976	995	846	393	30	34	38	49	57	236
	50	993	1097	1033	908	739	119	2	4	3	4	16	142
	100	995	1010	1065	910	635	20	0	0	0	0	1	78
	200	998	1021	965	902	441	0	0	0	0	0	0	30
	500	1028	1015	987	880	244	0	0	0	0	0	0	0
5.0	20	1003	1018	1022	1012	995	844	34	45	50	37	35	60
	50	1002	1036	1027	1030	981	734	3	1	1	3	5	17
	100	984	987	995	980	963	617	0	0	0	0	0	1
	200	1001	1021	1005	1038	916	509	0	0	0	0	0	0
	500	1028	1054	997	986	950	252	0	0	0	0	0	0

is a technical problem in using the extended results for comparison between industries. This problem is mentioned in section 2.3. Still, even when we do not employ an extended σ_u estimator, there can be a bias in the estimators. This situation will be analyzed later when we examine the results of our empirical estimation.

2.2.3 Measures of Technical (In)Efficiency

To investigate the factors that determine industries' levels of technical inefficiency, we need efficiency measures that are comparable among industries. Several possible indexes can be used. One type consists of only functions of σ_u. It includes the σ_u estimator itself, the average efficiency measure proposed by Lee and Tyler (1978), and average technical inefficiency measure used by Caves and Barton (1990). Another type of index involves σ_u to σ_v ratios or functions of this ratio, that is, $\lambda = \sigma_u/\sigma_v$ and the skewness of COLS or OLS residuals.

σ_u and Functions of σ_u

The basic frontier model used here is

$$\ln(y) = \ln(f(X;\beta)) + v - u, \tag{3}$$

or

$$y = f(X;\beta) \cdot \exp(v) \cdot \exp(-u).$$

The frontier term is $f(X;\beta) \cdot \exp(v)$, so the ratio of the real output to the frontier is $\exp(-u)$. The σ_u estimator indexes the level of inefficiency. The measure of average efficiency proposed by Lee and Tyler (1978) is the expected value of $\exp(-u)$:

$$2 \cdot \exp(\sigma_u^2) \cdot [1 - F(\sigma_u)],$$

where the half-normal distribution with standard deviation σ_u is assumed. Here F is the cumulative distribution function of the standard normal distribution. The other index was proposed by Caves and Barton (1990). It is the ratio of the intercept shift of the production frontier. COLS uses the fact that when the half-normal distribution of σ_u is assumed, the production frontier shifts downward by $-\sqrt{(2/\pi)}\sigma_u$. This estimator is the ratio of this intercept shift of the frontier to the average position of the production frontier:

$$\frac{\sqrt{(2/\pi)}\sigma_u}{\bar{y} + \sqrt{(2/\pi)}\sigma_u}.$$

To avoid dependence on measurement scales, the data should be normalized beforehand.

Both indexes are monotonically increasing functions of σ_u, so they have a one-to-one correspondence if the $\bar{y}$'s are the same. The average efficiency measure of Lee-Tyler is more intuitive and is consistent with the ordinary meaning of "efficiency."

As mentioned in subsection 2.2.2, the σ_u estimator can be extended analytically to cover cases of type I and type II failure. One problem with this extension concerns the distribution of the estimated value of this index. By equation (2) the σ_u estimator is calculated from the third moment. The slope of this transformation from the third moment to σ_u is infinite when $\mu_3 = 0$ or $\sigma_u = 0$. The variance in the σ_u estimator is so large compared to the treatable range that we find numerous estimates near or beyond the boundaries. Therefore around the boundaries even a very small deviation of μ_3 displaces the σ_u estimator far from the true value. This distortion in practice causes the distribution of estimated σ_u to split into two peaks at $\sigma_u = 0$, whereas the distribution of μ_3 is symmetrical. The split distribution of σ_u makes it difficult to compare levels of technical inefficiency among industries. In using regression analysis to compare performance indexes among industries, we have to assume normally distributed deviations from estimated relations. Of course the real difficulty in handling these results is in the consistency of underlying theory with the estimators. Several alternative measures of technical efficiency are possible, as mentioned earlier in this section. We do not know a priori which index is the best for comparing technical efficiency levels. Some theories imply that mistakes in managing corporations give rise to symmetrical deviations in one measure of technical inefficiency, and so that measure would be distributed symmetrically. Nevertheless, even though we can assume that some theoretically grounded function describes the distribution of σ_u or other measures of technical inefficiency, statistical deviations in μ_3 can cause distortions in the σ_u estimator that are difficult to treat.

λ and Skewness

The measures λ and skewness are calculated from both σ_u and the symmetric component of OLS residuals σ_v. That is, the magnitude of asymmetry is normalized by the symmetric standard deviation. λ is a simple ratio of σ_u to σ_v:

$$\lambda = \frac{\sigma_u}{\sigma_v}. \tag{4}$$

Skewness is the skewness of OLS residuals:

$$\text{skewness} = \frac{\mu_3}{\mu_2^{3/2}}. \tag{5}$$

Using equation (2), we restate λ as

$$\lambda = \frac{[\sqrt{(\pi/2)}(\pi/\pi - 4)s]^{1/3}}{\{1 - (\pi - 2/\pi)[\sqrt{(\pi/2)}(\pi/\pi - 4)s]^{2/3}\}^{1/2}}, \tag{6}$$

where s is skewness. Then λ is expessed as a monotonically decreasing function of the skewness in the range:

$$\left(\frac{\pi}{\pi - 2}\right)^{3/2} \sqrt{\left(\frac{2}{\pi}\right)} \left(\frac{\pi - 4}{\pi}\right) < s \leqq 0. \tag{7}$$

Therefore we see that skewness is also a function of the ratio of σ_u to σ_v. λ has mainly been used in an econometric context as the relative magnitude of technical inefficiency. For OLS residuals it is used to normalize deviations due to technical inefficiency by deviations due to the random production frontier.

Skewness has a similar function. The deviations from the production frontier are asymmetrical in character and thus differ from the variations of the frontier. The greater the technical inefficiency, the more negatively skewed is the composed error term $\varepsilon = v - u$. This quality, which is an indicator of technical inefficiency, does not depend on any specific assumptions about the distribution function. For example, when an exponential distribution rather than a half-normal distribution is assumed of u, such that

$$u \sim \frac{\exp(-u/\phi)}{\phi} \qquad \text{for } u \geqq 0, E(u) = \phi, V(u) = \phi^2,$$

the second and the expected value of the third moment of residuals are

$$\mu_2 = \sigma_v^2 + \phi^2, \qquad \mu_3 = -2\phi^3.$$

Then consistent estimators of σ_v and ϕ are

$$\hat{\phi} = \left(\frac{-\mu_3}{2}\right)^{1/3}, \qquad \hat{\sigma}_v = \left[\mu_2 - \left(\frac{-\mu_3}{2}\right)^{2/3}\right]^{1/2}.$$

And the estimator of λ is

$$\hat{\lambda} = \frac{\hat{\phi}}{\hat{\sigma}_v} = \frac{(-s/2)^{1/3}}{[1 - (-s/2)^{2/3}]^{1/2}},$$

which is also a monotonically decreasing function of the skewness in the range of $-2 < s \leqq 0$.

Skewness is often used in tests of the normality of regression residuals, and hence its distribution has been the subject of much research.[5] The combined use of skewness and kurtosis has also received much attention.[6] In addition Schmidt and Lin (1984) have discussed the effectiveness of employing skewness to test the hypothesis that deviations from the production frontier are composed of symmetrical and asymmetrical distributions. Ordinarily Lagrangean multiplier tests are used to test this hypothesis, but they present many difficulties.

One advantage of using skewness as an index of technical inefficiency is that it circumvents the difficulty of devising an extended estimator. Strictly speaking, skewness is valid only when the estimator is in the range given by equation (7), where both type I and type II failures can be avoided. That is because only when skewness is in that range can the estimator be explained by an error composed of normal and half-normal distributions. Nevertheless, extending the estimator where $\mu_3 > 0$ or $\sigma_v^2 < 0$ becomes easy because the discontinuity in the mapping from μ_3 to the index has disappeared in equation (5). Were the estimator not extended, the truncation of the distribution at the boundary would become a problem. Hence it is natural to use skewness in this extended sense, as we will in the rest of this chapter.

Properties of Technical Inefficiency Indexes

Since a consistent estimator of σ_u and σ_v can be derived by COLS, all the aforementioned indexes will be consistent. Before using them for inter-industry comparisons, we will examine the unbiasedness and efficiency of these indexes. We do not want an index to be affected by our choice of distribution for technical efficiency because then there would be insufficient theoretical basis for deriving its shape.

To investigate the distribution of estimators, the distribution of the third moment of the OLS residuals is needed, but that distribution is difficult to obtain. We conducted a Monte Carlo study to find the distribution of the estimators of the indexes. We investigated the case of $\sigma_u = 1$ and $\sigma_v = 1$ so that $\lambda = 1$. The method we employed is the same as that which we used to examine type I and type II failures. That is, we directly calculated σ_u, skewness, and λ from the composite random number of $N(0, \sigma_v^2 = 1) - |N(0, \sigma_u^2 = 1)|$. The distributions of other indexes that are functions of σ_u can be easily obtained from the distribution of σ_u. The number of iterations is 5,000 for each case.

The distribution of skewness is expected to be biased upward, as shown by D'Agostino and Person (1973). When $\lambda = 1$, the corresponding value of skewness expected from equation (6) is about -0.137. The standard deviation of skewness inferred from the asymptotic variance is about 0.113 when the sample size is 500.[7] This standard deviation is much larger than on average, so a considerable number of the experiments encounter type I failure. With a sample size as large as this,[8] there is a greater probability of type I failure; therefore the boundary effect discussed in subsection 2.2.2 cannot be neglected. The boundary effect for type I failure will bias the estimator of σ_u upward because the negative part of the distribution of σ_u^2 is cut off.

Table 2.2 presents a summary of the statistics of the Monte Carlo investigation we undertook. As expected, skewness and σ_u are both biased upward when the sample size is small. These biases diminish as sample size increases because the estimators are consistent. In the skewed shape of the distribution of σ_u, which is not given here, the boundary effect of the

Table 2.2
Monte Carlo study of biases in distribution of skewness

Sample size	Maximum	Minimum	Mean	Standard deviation
Distribution of skewness				
10	1.939	−2.070	−0.085	0.613
20	1.868	−1.833	−0.108	0.491
50	0.922	−1.224	−0.128	0.330
100	0.920	−1.072	−0.129	0.240
200	0.496	−0.766	−0.126	0.175
500	0.252	−0.508	−0.124	0.112
Distribution of σ_u				
10	2.852	0.083	1.276	0.497
20	2.560	0.081	1.283	0.431
50	2.312	0.066	1.223	0.370
100	2.181	0.201	1.142	0.330
200	1.866	0.124	1.061	0.295
500	1.598	0.114	0.982	0.248
Distribution of λ				
10	26.516	0.150	2.333	2.343
20	20.560	0.077	2.064	1.899
50	28.420	0.054	1.644	1.273
100	33.292	0.163	1.366	1.124
200	3.795	0.102	1.154	0.453
500	2.204	0.100	1.013	0.331

truncation at $\sigma_u = 0$ would be evident.[9] The estimator for λ would also be biased upward.

As discussed in subsection 2.2.2, the robustness of estimators can be affected by biases in the estimated coefficients of the production function when the factor-input variables have skewed distributions, as in the case of translog production functions. Hence, to analyze the robustness of the estimators, we conducted a Monte Carlo investigation of the regression residuals; the results are reported in subsection 2.2.5. It became apparent that the likelihood of encountering type I and type II failures depends on the values of σ_u and σ_v and therefore that the biases in estimators depend on their absolute values. As a result, we had to repeat the Monte Carlo investigation for various estimators. These experiments are discussed in subsection 2.2.6.

2.2.4 The Production Function

Translog Production Function

We used the translog production function to specify the production frontier. In using a translog function, we do not need to impose any strong a priori assumptions about the Allen partial elasticity of substitution or separability.[10] More important, we do not need to assume homotheticity. The optimal capital–labor ratio can differ, as it does between the large and small plants of manufacturing industries in Japan. This dual structure in Japanese industries is well known and underlies the prevalent differences between the large and small firms in labor productivity, average wages, and value added per capita, for example. Many theorists have tried to identify the cause of the dual structure and have explained it as due to the insufficient capital–labor ratio of the smaller firms. As far as possible we will avoid such assumptions about the homotheticity of the production function. Rather, we will look at the relation of the dual structure to technical efficiency.[11]

Certain problems arise in the estimation of the translog production function. The efficiency of the estimator may be impaired somewhat because of the COLS method employed in this study. The simple OLS estimator of coefficients might not be efficient because collinearity among the explaining variables cannot be avoided. Hence many studies have used the maximum-likelihood method rather than OLS, but with restrictions on cost-share functions. The data necessary for the estimation of the share functions are not available here. Moreover estimation of the translog production function consumes many degrees of freedom which can cause another inefficiency of the estimators when the number of observations is small.

Nevertheless, since the purpose of this study is to obtain appropriate indexes of technical efficiency, not precise parameters of production functions, the COLS method of estimating the level of the technical efficiency suffices. As we reported earlier, Olson, Schmidt, and Waldman (1980) have demonstrated the efficiency of COLS estimators relative to the ML estimator in the case of the Cobb-Douglas production function. We turn next to specifying the production function; then we will investigate the case of the translog production function.

Estimated Production Functions There are two alternative translog production functions that we can use.[12] They differ only in that Z_i in version I is an independent variable.

Version I:

$$\log\left(\frac{VA}{L}\right) = a_0 + a_1 \cdot \log\left(\frac{K}{L}\right) + a_2 \cdot \log(L) + a_3 \cdot \log\left(\frac{K}{L}\right)^2$$

$$+ a_4 \cdot \log(L)^2 + a_5 \cdot \log\left(\frac{K}{L}\right) \cdot \log(L) + V - U, \tag{8}$$

Version II:

$$\log\left(\frac{VA}{L}\right) = a_0 + a_1 \cdot \log\left(\frac{K}{L}\right) + a_2 \cdot \log(L) + a_3 \cdot \log\left(\frac{K}{L}\right)^2$$

$$+ a_4 \cdot \log(L)^2 + a_5 \cdot \log\left(\frac{K}{L}\right) \cdot \log(L) + a_6 \cdot Z_1 + a_7 \cdot Z_2$$

$$+ a_8 \cdot Z_3 + a_9 \cdot Z_4 + a_{10} \cdot Z5 + V - U,$$

where

VA = value added,

K = capital,

L = labor (measured by compensation),

Z_1 = ratio of the number of production workers to the total number of workers,

Z_2 = ratio of energy cost to total material costs,

Z_3 = ratio of value of inventories to capital stock,

Z_4 = an index of specialization,

Z_5 = ratio of payment for subcontracting work to total material costs (see appendix A for more precise definitions of these variables),

U = deviation from production frontier caused by technical inefficiency,

V = regression residuals caused by random factors or any statistical errors.

In a preliminary study we tried an alternate set of production functions in which we used gross output as the dependent variable and added materials input as an explanatory variable. However, high correlations between the variables prevented us from getting reasonable coefficients, so we dropped gross output as a dependent variable of the production function. Z_i are included in version II to correct for the heterogeneity of inputs (see Caves and Barton 1990, 32). Some of the variables serve more effectively to explain differences in technical inefficiency than to explain differences in productivity, since technical inefficiency may be caused by heterogeneity of the technologies employed in an industry. However, heterogeneity can also affect measured productivity asymmetrically, that is, cause technical inefficiency.

2.2.5   Monte Carlo Study of Sensitivity of COLS to Biases in Coefficients

In this subsection we examine the robustness of COLS estimators of technical inefficiency for the case of the translog frontier production function. A problem arises from inefficiency of estimators of coefficients of translog production functions. Asymmetry in input factors, which is caused by the function's quadratic form, can generate asymmetric deviations from production functions. Asymmetric deviations can introduce estimator biases in the technical inefficiency indexes. Therefore we will evaluate the correlation of the deviation in product function coefficients with the estimator biases of technical inefficiency indexes.

We use the basic method of OSW; that is, we generate a series of factor inputs X with uniform distribution $U(0, 1)$, symmetrical deviation v from the frontier by the normal distribution $N(0, \sigma_v^2)$, and asymmetrical deviation u by the absolute value of the normal distribution $|N(0, \sigma_u^2)|$. Then we calculate $y = X\beta + v - u$, and obtain from the OLS estimator of β, $\bar{\beta}$,

Table 2.3a
Monte Carlo analysis of biases in estimation using translog production function: biases in estimated coefficients

Number of observations	Case	Coefficient					
		a_0	a_1	a_2	a_3	a_4	a_5
50	A	0.5997	0.5086	0.0024	0.5052	0.0005	0.0040
		(0.1563)	(0.1928	(0.3099)	(0.0529)	(0.1292)	(0.1535)
	B	0.5971	0.4975	−0.0005	0.9014	0.0125	−0.1631
		(0.1135)	(1.3050)	(0.2842)	(2.0410)	(0.1997)	(1.2680)
100	A	0.5951	0.4981	0.0034	0.4988	0.0015	−0.0025
		(0.1019)	(0.1103)	(0.1802)	(0.0267)	(0.0705)	(0.0763)
	B	0.5991	0.4567	0.0115	0.4671	0.0022	−0.0040
		(0.0683)	(0.7574)	(0.1798)	(0.5357)	(0.0923)	(0.5045)
200	A	0.5947	0.4901	0.0004	0.4992	−0.0011	−0.0039
		(0.0691)	(0.0760)	(0.1143)	(0.0181)	(0.0408	(0.0489)
	B	0.5979	0.5306	−0.0078	0.4825	−0.0060	0.0296
		(0.0507)	(0.4903)	(0.1067)	(0.3228)	(0.0500)	(0.3383)
400	A	0.5960	0.5024	0.0005	0.5008	0.0006	0.0019
		(0.0487)	(0.0461)	(0.0752)	(0.0100)	(0.0256)	(0.0297)
	B	0.5922	0.5156	−0.0067	0.4998	−0.0012	0.0045
		(0.0339)	(0.2986)	(0.0784)	(0.0916)	(0.0371)	(0.1659)

Note: Standard deviations appear below average values of estimated coefficients. σ_u and σ_v are each set at 0.50 and 0.17.

residuals $\varepsilon = y - \bar{y} = y - X\bar{\beta}$. We use the moments of ε to find the estimators of σ_u and σ_v and other technical inefficiency indexes.

We are able to obtain efficient estimators of the coefficients because the series of input factors generated are independent. To create distortions in the estimated coefficients, we make the series of factor inputs X collinear. Then we compare the two sets of estimators of the technical inefficiency indexes. We will denote the first procedure as case A and the second as case B.

For each case A or B, σ_u and σ_v represent the mean values of Japanese industries.[14] They are 0.50 and 0.17, respectively. We repeated the computations for sample sizes $N = 50, 100, 200,$ and 400. For every set of σ_u, σ_v, and N, the computations were repeated 200 times. The shape of the production function estimated was made as simple as possible; that is, $a_0 = 1$, $a_1 = 1/2, a_2 = 0, a_3 = 1/2, a_4 = 0, a_5 = 0$, so that

$$\log\left(\frac{VA}{L}\right) = 1 + \frac{1}{2}\log\left(\frac{K}{L}\right) + \frac{1}{2}\log\left(\frac{K}{L}\right)^2.$$

Table 2.3b
Monte Carlo analysis of biases in estimation using translog production: biases in estimated parameters of technical efficiency

| Number of observations | Case | Index of efficiency | | | | Number of successful trials[a] |
		Skewness	σ_u	σ_v	λ	
50	A	−0.5227	0.4037	0.1975	2.359	168
		(0.3407)	(0.1053)	(0.0533)	(1.348)	
	B	−0.5386	0.4114	0.1936	2.670	165
		(0.3696)	(0.1073)	(0.0596)	(2.119)	
100	A	−0.5816	0.4475	0.1900	2.687	188
		(0.2639)	(0.0829)	(0.0495)	(1.432)	
	B	−0.5679	0.4400	0.1904	2.797	184
		(0.2588)	(0.0883)	(0.0545)	(2.247)	
200	A	−0.6032	0.4674	0.1812	2.982	193
		(0.2049)	(0.0650)	(0.0477)	(1.730)	
	B	−0.6158	0.4718	0.1756	3.382	195
		(0.1926)	(0.0630)	(0.0456)	(4.589)	
400	A	−0.6110	0.4791	0.1778	2.872	199
		(0.1370)	(0.0471)	(0.0344)	(0.977)	
	B	−0.6348	0.4895	0.1733	3.158	198
		(0.1371)	(0.0451)	(0.0364)	(2.193)	

Note: Standard deviations appear below average values of estimated coefficients. σ_u and σ_v are each set at 0.50 and 0.17.
a. There were 200 trials in which all parameters except skewness could be estimated.

This function is homothetic and has constant elasticity of substitution. The results are shown in table 2.3. Table 2.3a reports the estimated coefficients of the production function for each case. The table shows larger standard deviations for case B, in which distortions have been introduced by the independent variables being made collinear, than in case A. In particular the deviations for a_1 and a_3 are very large relative to the value of the estimated coefficient. The biases in the a_0 estimator are manifestations of the asymmetric term u, technical inefficiency.

Table 2.3b gives the estimated parameters of technical inefficiency. The expected values of λ and skewness are 2.941 and −0.658. Type II failures are more apt to occur because expected skewness −0.658 is nearer to the lower bound $[(\pi/\pi - 2)]^{3/2}\sqrt{(2/\pi)}(\pi - 4/\pi)$, which is about −0.995, than to the upper bound 0. Because type II failure cuts off the larger part of σ_u, the σ_u estimator is biased downward. Likewise the estimators of λ have a tendency to downward bias. However, the nonlinearity of the transformation from skewness to λ makes the λ estimator biased upward when the estimation of the production function is distorted by collinearity. When the estimator of the skewness falls near the lower bound, the λ estimator becomes extraordinarily high. This effect pulls up both the average value and the standard deviation of the λ estimator.

Nevertheless, this effect is trivial. Because λ becomes infinite at the lower bound corresponding to type II failure and because the minimum estimated value of skewness is always smaller than the lower bound for each case, λ takes a high value only when skewness happens to be slightly larger than the lower bound. It is these extraordinarily high values of λ that pull up the standard deviation of estimated λ. Excepting the λ estimator, the table shows that the estimators have adequate robustness in relation to the estimation error of the production functions.

2.2.6 Monte Carlo Study of Biases of COLS Estimators and Absolute Values of Estimators

As discussed in the preceding subsection, the biases of the COLS estimators of technical inefficiency are contingent on the absolute values of σ_i. These biases are related to type I and type II failures. Of course when the estimated parameters are nonlinear, there can be other biases. And when the sample size is small, there is a strong possibility of type I and type II failures occurring. Such biases are not apparent in asymptotic properties of the distributions of estimators.

One way around these biases is to build a consistent estimator that allows for type I and II failures another way is to invent an estimator using the ex ante information that σ_u cannot be outside the range given by equation (7), but this has proved to be difficult to accomplish. Still another approach is to estimate the degrees of biases and try to correct them. We conducted a Monte Carlo study for this purpose; it was similar in design to our preceding study. We produced data sets for various values of σ_u, σ_v, and sample size N. The alternative values of σ_u were 0.1, 0.5, 1.0, 2.0, and 4.0; of σ_v 0.1, 0.5, 1.0, 2.0, 3.0, and 4.0; and for N, 50, 100, and 200. For each of 90 (5 × 6 × 3) combinations, 200 experiments were conducted. The settings for β and $v - u$ were the same as previously, but there was no collinearity imposed on the factor-input variables.

Table 2.4 shows the results of these procedures for the estimators of skewness, σ_u, σ_v, and λ. Strong biases in σ_u are caused by the boundary effect. When the true value of λ is low, type I failures pull up the value of the estimated σ_u. When λ is high, type II failures depress it. Biases in σ_v are opposite in direction to the biases of σ_u. The magnitudes of differences are in the order of the estimated values. For every sample size and every value of σ_u, the higher the value of σ_v, the higher is the average value of the estimate. For the σ_u estimate, however, the relationship breaks down when the value of σ_v is high.

If the relationship between the true value and the estimator is systematic, we can estimate the unbiased value using the information of the estimator. If the source of the biases is in the boundary effect, the expected bias is stronger, the nearer to either bound is the true value of skewness, so we must choose an appropriate method to help us correct the estimator. However, the boundary effects are not always the only source of biases. We can calculate the asymptotic variances of the estimators from the results reported in the appendix of OSW. The asymptotic variance of the estimator of σ_u^2 is

$$V(\hat{\sigma}_u^2) = \frac{4\sigma_u^4}{9N(4-\pi)^2}\left[(\pi-3)(3\pi^2+8\pi+48)\right.$$

$$\left. + \frac{9\pi(\pi^2-8)}{\lambda^2} + \frac{9\pi^2(\pi-2)}{\lambda^4} + \frac{3\pi^3}{\lambda^6}\right]. \tag{9}$$

Hence the ratio of asymptotic variance to asymptotic mean skyrockets when the value of the λ approaches 0. Table 2.5 shows this ratio $V(\hat{\sigma}_u^2)/(\hat{\sigma}_u^2)^2$ for sample sizes of 20, 50, 100, 200, and 500. When the value of σ_v becomes high relative to the value of σ_u, the skew generated by the dispersed v overwhelms the skew generated by technical inefficiency factor u. Thus when λ is small, it becomes hard to retain the true value of σ_u from observed moments.

The relation between the true value and the observed value of σ_u and σ_v makes it almost impossible to identify the original value of σ_u from observed moments when λ is less than 1. On the other hand, when λ is high, it is possible to estimate the unbiased value of σ_u. To determine whether the relation between the true value and the COLS estimator can be approximated by a linear relation, the following regression analysis was conducted over all cells of the Monte Carlo study above various lower thresholds of λ (skewness). The dependent variable is the true value of σ_u used in the Monte Carlo study. The explanatory variables are the mean values of estimated $\hat{\sigma}_u$, $\hat{\sigma}_v$ in each cell, and the inverse of the square root of sample size, $1/\sqrt{N}$.[15] The threshold levels of skewness s are 0.1, 0.0, -0.1, -0.2,

Table 2.4
Monte Carlo analysis of relation between biases of COLS estimators and absolute values of estimators

Number of iterations	Values of σ_v	Values of σ_u				
		0.1	0.5	1.0	2.0	4.0
Estimators of skewness						
50	0.1	−0.1628	−0.6802	−0.7231	−0.7944	−0.7650
	0.5	0.0392	−0.0535	−0.3603	−0.6488	−0.7393
	1.0	−0.0149	−0.0241	−0.1129	−0.3384	−0.6308
	2.0	−0.0212	0.0165	−0.0035	−0.1160	−0.3392
	3.0	−0.0120	0.0182	−0.0187	−0.0192	−0.1778
	4.0	0.0412	0.0420	−0.0380	0.0368	−0.1121
100	0.1	−0.1303	−0.7718	−0.8261	−0.8643	−0.8572
	0.5	−0.0221	−0.1247	−0.3899	−0.6830	−0.8386
	1.0	0.0200	−0.0387	−0.1125	−0.3853	−0.7227
	2.0	−0.0019	−0.0038	−0.0268	−0.1346	−0.3948
	3.0	−0.0050	0.0004	−0.0071	−0.0513	−0.2157
	4.0	−0.0012	0.0141	−0.0192	−0.0098	−0.1293
200	0.1	−0.1193	−0.7950	−0.8849	−0.9020	−0.9165
	0.5	0.0056	−0.1271	−0.4270	−0.7366	−0.8723
	1.0	−0.0131	−0.0016	−0.1225	−0.3965	−0.7212
	2.0	−0.0087	−0.0064	−0.0222	−0.1433	−0.3997
	3.0	−0.0071	0.0080	0.0113	−0.0241	−0.2149
	4.0	0.0149	0.0103	−0.0026	−0.0198	−0.1143
Estimators of σ_u						
50	0.1	0.1206	0.4104	0.7640	1.570	3.021
	0.5	0.4505	0.5510	0.8612	1.687	3.045
	1.0	0.8888	0.9378	1.142	1.763	3.162
	2.0	1.750	1.820	1.951	2.414	3.373
	3.0	2.921	2.646	2.730	2.895	3.992
	4.0	3.490	3.574	3.768	3.818	4.575
100	0.1	0.1038	0.4482	0.8599	1.707	3.408
	0.5	0.4349	0.5395	0.9177	1.758	3.440
	1.0	0.8123	0.8653	1.106	1.808	3.575
	2.0	1.673	1.750	1.826	2.307	3.634
	3.0	2.492	2.562	2.547	2.906	3.847
	4.0	3.348	3.502	3.422	3.485	4.527
200	0.1	0.1044	0.4634	0.9220	1.801	3.634
	0.5	0.3868	0.5185	0.9512	1.868	3.651
	1.0	0.7788	0.7872	1.029	1.835	3.730
	2.0	1.562	1.473	1.676	2.119	3.688
	3.0	2.360	2.250	2.397	2.614	3.815
	4.0	3.019	3.029	3.224	3.319	3.996

Table 2.4 (continued)

Number of iterations	Values of σ_v	Values of σ_u				
		0.1	0.5	1.0	2.0	4.0
Estimators of σ_v						
50	0.1	0.0805	0.1473	0.2776	0.5239	1.133
	0.5	0.3614	0.4260	0.4846	0.6300	1.169
	1.0	0.7445	0.7455	0.8213	0.9751	1.307
	2.0	1.499	1.421	1.476	1.564	2.002
	3.0	2.033	2.183	2.255	2.384	2.592
	4.0	3.002	2.911	2.901	3.038	3.302
100	0.1	0.0907	0.1356	0.2470	0.4692	0.9357
	0.5	0.3983	0.4520	0.5029	0.6141	0.9639
	1.0	0.8147	0.8326	0.8992	1.002	1.225
	2.0	1.581	1.623	1.668	1.767	2.025
	3.0	2.425	2.436	2.461	2.519	2.803
	4.0	3.218	3.152	3.219	3.437	3.650
200	0.1	0.0938	0.1261	0.2060	0.4157	0.7783
	0.5	0.4296	0.4767	0.5010	0.5644	0.8668
	1.0	0.8577	0.8942	0.9509	1.046	1.163
	2.0	1.693	1.752	1.749	1.894	2.051
	3.0	2.555	2.596	2.581	2.712	2.941
	4.0	3.393	3.433	3.422	3.549	3.837
Estimators of λ						
50	0.1	1.672	3.331	3.393	6.532	3.475
	0.5	1.380	1.437	2.202	3.619	3.253
	1.0	1.324	1.413	1.543	2.155	3.517
	2.0	1.281	1.526	1.524	1.700	2.036
	3.0	1.642	1.372	1.368	1.328	1.766
	4.0	1.275	1.334	1.457	1.365	1.552
100	0.1	1.216	4.161	4.208	4.736	4.389
	0.5	1.177	1.265	2.041	3.811	4.554
	1.0	1.052	1.126	1.324	2.323	3.419
	2.0	1.123	1.167	1.154	1.426	1.949
	3.0	1.090	1.100	1.097	1.320	1.614
	4.0	1.083	1.191	1.144	1.074	1.338
200	0.1	1.191	4.936	5.941	6.225	6.185
	0.5	0.9327	1.134	2.138	4.106	5.067
	1.0	0.9381	0.9167	1.129	1.880	4.019
	2.0	0.9538	0.8736	1.004	1.170	1.897
	3.0	0.9539	0.8964	0.9569	0.9963	1.364
	4.0	0.9317	0.9114	0.9736	0.9753	1.096

Table 2.5
Ratio of asymptotic variance to the square of the asymptotic mean

λ	$N = 20$	$N = 50$	$N = 100$	$N = 200$	$N = 500$
0.1	30,831.4993	12,332.5997	6,166.2999	3,083.1499	1,233.2599
0.2	1,962.9259	785.1703	392.5851	196.2926	78.5170
0.3	399.0482	159.6193	79.8096	39.9048	15.9619
0.4	131.2738	52.5095	26.2548	13.1274	5.2510
0.5	56.4692	22.5877	11.2938	5.6469	2.2588
0.6	28.8825	11.5530	5.7765	2.8883	1.1553
0.7	16.6928	6.6771	3.3386	1.6693	0.6677
0.8	10.5725	4.2290	2.1144	1.0573	0.4229
0.9	7.1920	2.8768	1.4384	0.7192	0.2877
1.0	5.1815	2.0726	1.0363	0.5182	0.2073
1.2	3.0729	1.2292	0.6146	0.3073	0.1229
1.4	2.0811	0.8324	0.4162	0.2081	0.0832
1.6	1.5502	0.6201	0.3100	0.1550	0.0620
1.8	1.2376	0.4950	0.2475	0.1238	0.0495
2.0	1.0397	0.4159	0.2079	0.1040	0.0416
2.5	0.7779	0.3111	0.1556	0.0778	0.0311
3.0	0.6570	0.2628	0.1314	0.0657	0.0263
3.5	0.5913	0.2365	0.1182	0.0591	0.0237
4.0	0.5517	0.2207	0.1103	0.0552	0.0221
5.0	0.5081	0.2032	0.1016	0.0508	0.0202

-0.3, and -0.4, and t-statistics are in parentheses. When the threshold is 0.1, no cells are excluded.

When $s < 0.1$,

$$\sigma_u = 0.4729 - 5.1427\frac{1}{\sqrt{N}} + 1.6044\hat{\sigma}_u - 1.2013\hat{\sigma}_v,$$
$$\quad\quad (2.00) \quad\quad (16.08) \quad\quad (10.68)$$

$\bar{R}^2 = 0.7499, \quad N = 90.$

When $s < 0.0$,

$$\sigma_u = 0.1322 - 2.5466\frac{1}{\sqrt{N}} + 1.5400\hat{\sigma}_u - 0.9684\hat{\sigma}_v,$$
$$\quad\quad (1.01) \quad\quad (16.57) \quad\quad (8.67)$$

$\bar{R}^2 = 0.8096, \quad N = 75.$

When $s < -0.1$,

$$\sigma_u = -0.1719 + 1.9013 \frac{1}{\sqrt{N}} + 1.2583\hat{\sigma}_u - 0.3642\hat{\sigma}_v,$$
$$\quad\;\; (1.56) \quad\;\; (28.37) \quad\; (5.84)$$

$$\bar{R}^2 = 0.9731, \quad N = 47.$$

When $s < -0.2$,

$$\sigma_u = -0.5453 + 5.2224 \frac{1}{\sqrt{N}} + 1.2193\hat{\sigma}_u - 0.1760\hat{\sigma}_v,$$
$$\quad\;\; (6.24) \quad\;\; (37.69) \quad\; (3.27)$$

$$\bar{R}^2 = 0.9906, \quad N = 32.$$

When $s < -0.3$,

$$\sigma_u = -0.5404 + 5.0925 \frac{1}{\sqrt{N}} + 1.2011\hat{\sigma}_u - 0.1129\hat{\sigma}_v,$$
$$\quad\;\; (5.85) \quad\;\; (32.37) \quad\; (1.39)$$

$$\bar{R}^2 = 0.9907, \quad N = 30.$$

When $s < -0.4$,

$$\sigma_u = -0.4794 + 4.5577 \frac{1}{\sqrt{N}} + 1.0673\hat{\sigma}_u + 0.3335\hat{\sigma}_v,$$
$$\quad\;\; (3.99) \quad\;\; (15.44) \quad\; (1.52)$$

$$\bar{R}^2 = 0.9921, \quad N = 22.$$

The adjusted R^2 increases as the conditions become more stringent, and in each case seems high enough to accept the linearity of these relations, although the number of synthetic observations retained in the regression analysis decreases with the tightened constraint. It should be noted that as we choose a stricter threshold, the number of industries decreases for which efficiency can be estimated. There is a trade-off between the size of the feasible data set and the accuracy of the analysis.[16] Therefore, because of the small gain in accuracy from including observations falling above that threshold, the condition that skewness < -0.2 is employed in the empirical interindustry analysis. Under this condition an estimator is calculated by the regression equation. We call this estimator "an *adjusted* σ_u estimator." That is, when skewness < -0.2, the adjusted σ_u estimator is

$$\sigma_u = -0.5453 + 5.2224 \frac{1}{\sqrt{N}} + 1.2193\hat{\sigma}_u - 0.1760\hat{\sigma}_v.$$

2.2.7 Estimation of Technical Inefficiency Levels

Variations in the Method of Estimation

The basic method we used to estimate the levels of technical efficiency in Japanese industries was introduced in subsection 2.2.4, but we explored several alternatives. First, as we argued previously, we considered whether to include or exclude Z_i variables that control for heterogeneity in factor inputs. Second, we considered whether OLS or weighted least squares (WLS) should be used to estimate the coefficients of the production funtions. Third, to limit the effect of outliers, we considered a procedure that would omit from the industry data sets observations with extraordinarily large or small gross ouput, material inputs, value added, or tangible assets not in the range $(m - 4.5s, m + 4.5s)$, where m is the industry mean and s is the standard deviation. Because the stochastic production frontier model is designed to avoid the effect of outliers, the value of the second and third procedures was unclear, and so these two procedures were employed as alternatives.

Combinations of the three alternatives yielded eight different ways to estimate indexes of technical inefficiency. Henceforth we will denote these eight ways as follows:

	Z_i	Estimation procedure	Outliers
IWD	Include	WLS	Delete
IWR	Include	WLS	Retain
IOD	Include	OLS	Delete
IOR	Include	OLS	Retain
EWD	Exclude	WLS	Delete
EWR	Exclude	WLS	Retain
EOD	Exclude	OLS	Delete
EOR	Exclude	OLS	Retain

Plants and Industries Excluded from the Analysis

Purged from our observations were establishment data with zero values of tangible or fixed assets (at the beginning or end of the year), total number of employees or regular production workers, total compensation of employees or production workers, materials costs, shipments, or non-positive value added. To obtain enough degrees of freedom in the regressions, we applied the analysis only to industries exhibiting at least 20 plant observations after these exclusions. As a result the total number of industries investigated is 351 when production functions include Z_i and 352 when the Z_i are omitted.[17]

The estimator of technical inefficiency is obtained only if the value of skewness falls in the range defined in equation (7). The number of industries that met type I and type II failures are

Case	Number of industries analyzed	Type I failure	Type II failure
IWD	351	81	102
IWR	351	95	82
IOD	351	86	121
IOR	351	99	100
EWD	352	85	108
EWR	352	103	88
EOD	352	83	119
EOR	352	102	103

In each case more than half of the industries experienced type I or type II failure, and the rates of failure differ little among the alternative methods.

To develop cross-industry or cross-country comparisons effectively, we want to include as many industries as possible. When λ, σ_u, or functions of σ_u are used, the small number of industries may restrict the analysis, making the use of skewness attractive for these purposes.

Correlations between Measures of Technical Inefficiency

Table 2.6 gives the basic statistics and simple correlation coefficients among the indexes estimated by different procedures. The indexes calculated are skewness, $\hat{\sigma}_u$,

Table 2.6
Simple correlation coefficients between indexes (case IWD)

	Index						
	σ_u	σ_v	λ	Skewness	LTE	LTF	N
σ_u	1.0000	−0.1131	0.2845	−0.7255	−0.9907	−0.8464	−0.0111
σ_v		1.0000	−0.4049	0.7052	0.0722	−0.0264	0.1520
λ			1.0000	−0.4156	−0.4745	−0.2285	−0.0447
Skewness				1.0000	0.7397	0.5645	0.0638
LTE					1.0000	0.8484	0.0146
LTF						1.0000	0.3921
Maximum	1.1120	0.6676	89.76	1.599	0.9467	1.0000	3356
Minimum	0.0697	0.0086	0.14	−5.124	0.4938	0.4295	21
Mean	0.5318	0.2627	3.48	−0.723	0.6990	0.6407	148.3
Standard deviation	0.2197	0.1093	8.28	1.107	0.0950	0.0988	261.6
Number	148	148	148	338	144	113	351

$\hat{\sigma}_v$, λ, the Lee-Tyler estimator of average efficiency (LTE), and the Lee-Tyler estimator using the adjusted estimator of σ_u discussed in subsection 2.2.6 (LTF). The last rows of the table report the numbers of industries for which the indexes can be obtained. The estimation method is IWD.

The mean of observed skewness in the table indicates that negatively skewed distributions of the deviations from the production frontiers prevail, as predicted by the theory. The dispersion of skewness is so large that the standard deviation exceeds the width of the feasible range defined in equation (7), which is less than 1.

The mean of estimated λ is 3.48, which shows that the magnitude of deviations caused by technical inefficiency generally exceeds those caused by symmetrical deviations. The mean of LTE is 0.7 and that of LTF is 0.64, so the adjustment discussed in subsection 2.2.6 reduced the value of estimators of average efficiency by one-tenth. One possible explanation is that type II failures caused the downward bias in the σ_u estimator, as suggested by the fact that the average value of skewness is nearer to the lower bound than to the upper bound. This adjustment fortunately reduced the number of industries by only 22 percent. The adjustment causes industries likely to face type I failure to be purged from calculation of LTF, strengthening the downward tendency just mentioned.

As mentioned earlier, when the sample size is small the estimators are prone to certain biases. The table shows that sample size has no significant correlations except with LTF in this case, IWD. In other cases the same tendencies are seen when the production functions are estimated including Z_i as explanatory variables, while no correlation between sample size and LTF appears when Z_i are excluded from explanatory variables. Considering the low correlations between sample size and σ_u, the adjustment process employing the sample size could strengthen the correlation.

The high correlation between LTE and the σ_u estimator is due to the functional correspondence between them. The same correspondence should but failed to make λ and skewness highly correlated, probably due to the discontinuous relation when skewness lies near the lower bound corresponding to type II failure.

The correlation between LTE and LTF, about 0.85, expresses indirectly the relationship between σ_u and LTF. Because σ_u and σ_v have no significant correlation with each other, skewness and λ have opposite-sign correlations with σ_u and σ_v independently. The relationship between LTF and skewness or λ is weaker than the relationship between LTE and them. The adjustment from LTE to LTF reduces these correlations and tends to discourage substituting LTE for LTF in order to enlarge the number of industries available for interindustry comparison. However, skewness is not a mere substitute index but has its own meaning as an index normalized by σ_v and independent of assumptions about the distribution of technical inefficiency. Moreover skewness still has correlations with LTE and LTF that exceed 0.5, which make it seem a worthwhile substitute.

Correlations among Indexes Estimated by Alternative Methods

These tendencies of the estimated indexes reappear for each method alternative to IWD. The smallest mean value of observed skewness is -0.7231 (IWD), and the maximum is -0.5748 (IOR), which implies that technical inefficiency is observed robustly. The means of estimated λ are distributed around 3. The means of LTE are slightly less than 0.7 (maximum: 0.7047 [IOD], minimum: 0.6678 [EOR]) and those of LTF are distributed around 62 to 63 percent, as shown in table 2.7. The table also shows correlations between LTF indexes estimated by the various procedures; the high correlations confirm its robustness.

The same high correlations are seen for other (in)efficiency indexes, σ_u, skewness, and LTE. However, correlations between λ estimators derived by various methods are lower: The minimum is 0.1239 (between EWD and

Table 2.7
Simple correlation coefficients between various measures: adjusted Lee-Tyler average efficiency

	Method of estimation							
	IWD	IWR	IOD	IOR	EWD	EWR	EOD	EOR
IWD	1.0000	0.9278	0.9717	0.9151	0.9289	0.8612	0.8953	0.8278
IWR		1.0000	0.8906	0.9733	0.8672	0.9272	0.8382	0.8985
IOD			1.0000	0.9154	0.9232	0.8243	0.9091	0.8355
IOR				1.0000	0.8709	0.9238	0.8763	0.9169
EWD					1.0000	0.9237	0.9885	0.9041
EWR						1.0000	0.9064	0.9899
EOD							1.0000	0.9154
Maximum	1.0000	0.8795	0.8657	0.9279	0.8667	0.8385	0.8608	0.8474
Minimum	0.4295	0.4327	0.4357	0.3918	0.4090	0.3865	0.3531	0.3576
Mean	0.6407	0.6336	0.6413	0.6280	0.6289	0.6226	0.6299	0.6244
Standard deviation	0.0988	0.0958	0.0936	0.0980	0.1012	0.0940	0.0995	0.1026
Number[a]	113	125	125	134	116	116	125	131

a. Refers to the cases in which the index could be estimated.

IWD), and the maximum is 0.9346 (between EOR and EWD). Outliers with extraordinarily high values and the large variance of the estimator may cause these relatively low correlation coefficients for λ.

2.3   Determinants of Technical Efficiency Level

Table 2.8 presents the distributions of LTF estimated by IWD. The table shows that efficiency is distributed around an average of two-thirds, indicating about one-third shortfall from the production frontier. Many insist that modern Japanese industries are very efficient, which suggests that these values could be underestimated.[18] How should we evaluate this estimated level?

The mean value does not cover all industries, since those with type I or type II failure are omitted. They can be interpreted, respectively, as perfectly efficient or so inefficient that the level cannot be inferred on the assumption of a half-normal distribution of technical inefficiency. If they were, respectively, assigned efficiency levels of 100 percent and some low number, a different level of average efficiency would be obtained, but the industries with 100 percent efficiency would make the distribution of this index discontinuous at 100 percent. Table 2.8 also shows the histogram of

Table 2.8
Distribution of estimated values of technical efficiency (LTF) and skewness

LTF		Skewness	
Range	Frequency	Range	Frequency
0.35–0.40	0	−5.5– −5.0	1
0.40–0.45	3	−5.0– −4.5	6
0.45–0.50	4	−4.5– −4.0	0
0.50–0.55	12	−4.0– −3.5	3
0.55–0.60	26	−3.5– −3.0	6
0.60–0.65	16	−3.0– −2.5	4
0.65–0.70	22	−2.5– −2.0	19
0.70–0.75	17	−2.0– −1.5	19
0.75–0.80	6	−1.5– −1.0	50
0.80–0.85	5	−1.0– −0.5	66
0.85–0.90	1	−0.5–0.0	83
0.90–0.95	0	0.0–0.5	52
0.95–1.00	1	0.5–1.0	24
		1.0–1.5	4

observed values of skewness. The distribution of observed skewness has a long negative tail. These large negative values of skewness cannot be explained by technical inefficiency if it is assumed to be half-normally distributed.

Because of the difficulties with the estimation procedure adduced in section 2.2, it may be best not to emphasize mean absolute values of the indexes. The information contained in the indexes could prove to be more valuable for interindustry comparisons. If some relations predicted theoretically are identified as explaining differences in levels of technical efficiency among industries, that in itself affirms the validity of these estimations.[19] However, to explain the differences statistically, we must be able to explain inefficiency theoretically. As was argued in section 2.1, the purely econometric concept of technical inefficiency is so generous that it embraces two types of technical inefficiency. One results from purposive choices by economic agents, explained by their rational behavior. The other is from "irrational" aspects of resource allocation. Since observed inefficiencies are probably a mixture of these two types of inefficiency, they could be explained in part by factors deduced from economic models of rational agents and in part by structural factors that affect measures of inefficiency.

In this section we first introduce two models that examine the effects of optimal conduct on technical efficiency. Then we add some structural variables to represent determinants of efficiency. To identify these effects more precisely, we embed the interindustry test of these hypotheses about technical inefficiency in a broader regression analysis of the dependence of performance on structure. Technical inefficiency does not only have static dimensions; dynamic aspects such as technological progress can lead to technical inefficiency as well. And there is yet another static concept— allocative efficiency exhibited in differences among industries' price-cost margins—that can be related to technical inefficiency. At the end of this section we investigate the simultaneous effects of these efficiencies.

2.3.1 Two Models Explaining Technical Efficiency Level

Economists have proposed many hypotheses about the origins of technical inefficiency, but none has explicitly derived the half-normal or exponential distribution of technical inefficiency. These special forms of the distribution are assumed only because they are convenient for statistical control.

In this subsection we set up some hypotheses for specific types of distributions of technical inefficiency. We developed these hypotheses by looking at possible sources of technical inefficiency. One hypothesis deals with technical inefficiency associated with technological improvement. As new, more efficient technology develops, existing plants can become obsolete and inefficient. To restore frontier efficiency, firms must replace their outmoded plants or machines; this process should be continual rather than instantaneous. The other hypothesis is similar to Leibenstein's X-inefficiency, and it considers technical inefficiency to result from incomplete managerial control.

After setting forth these hypotheses, relations between structural variables and the level of technical efficiency will be investigated. We assume that economic agents are rational in their conduct. For the second model, where managers' control over the performance of the production line is incomplete, we assume that the managers are rational in determining the extent of effort devoted to preserving performance level. The assumption of rationality thus indicates the applicability limit of such models.

Model Analysis A: A Vintage Model of Technical Inefficiency

We look first at the case where the half-normal distribution of technical inefficiency can be derived. We take a putty-clay-type vintage model to explain a distribution of vintage on the basis of the growth rate of technology and a firm's scrapping decisions. The model we use to analyze this problem relates the conditions of technological growth and scrappage to the level of the technical inefficiency when the vintage distribution is appoximated by a half-normal distribution.

Each firm is assumed to have many plants; we could think of each as a machine. Each plant produces one unit of product in a unit time interval, and plants are so small that they can be indexed continuously. Each plant's production cost reflects the newest technology at the time when the plant was constructed. The speed of construction of new plants is v. That is, the number of plants constructed in a unit time interval is v. When the firm's output is constant, the same number of plants is scrapped in each unit time interval. In general, the oldest plants exceeding the firm's optimal production level are scrapped. Due to technological growth the production cost of the newest plants decreases at the common rate α. α is the rate of technological progress.

Consider at time t a firm with plants that were constructed z periods ago. We denote the production cost of a plant at time t constructed z periods ago as $C(z, t)$. Then

$$C(z, t) = C(0, t - z). \tag{10}$$

By assumption

$$C(0, t) = C_0 \exp(-\alpha t). \tag{11}$$

Here C_0 is defined as $C(0, 0)$. By (10) and (11),

$$C(z, t) = C_0 \exp[-\alpha(t - z)]. \tag{12}$$

The newer a plant, the lower is its production cost. Hence, if we sort plants by their construction times, we get the marginal cost function at a given time. If the firm produces q units at time t, it chooses to operate its newest q plants. Then the oldest plant operated is $z = q/v$ periods old. Therefore the oldest plant's cost (marginal cost) is

$$C_0 \exp[-\alpha(t - z)] = C_0 \exp(-\alpha t) \cdot \left(\frac{\alpha q}{v}\right).$$

The distribution function of the vintage is rectangular. If we denote the production level as q^*, this density is v/q^* because the oldest plant is q^*/v periods old. From this we get the distribution function of efficiency. The production cost of plants z periods old is $\exp(\alpha z)$ times as high as the newest plants. That is, the output of the same input is $\exp(-\alpha z)$ times as large as the newest. Here we define an efficiency index ε as $\varepsilon = \exp(-\alpha z)$, $\varepsilon \leqq 1$. The newest plant's ε is 1. We get the density function of ε by the distribution of z.

$$\frac{v}{q^*} dz = \frac{v}{q^*} \left| \frac{dz}{d\varepsilon} \right| d\varepsilon = \frac{v}{q^*} \left| -\frac{1}{\alpha\varepsilon} \right| d\varepsilon = \frac{v}{q^*\alpha\varepsilon} d\varepsilon. \tag{13}$$

Therefore the density function of ε is $v/(q^*\alpha\varepsilon)$ for $\exp(-\alpha q^*/v) \leqq \varepsilon \leqq 1$, from the oldest operated ($\exp[-\alpha q^*/v]$) to the newest (1).

Incidentally, in the stochastic production frontier models, this efficiency ε is $\exp(-u) = y/f(x) \exp(v)$. When u's distribution function is half-normal,

$$u \sim \left(\sqrt{\frac{2}{\pi}} \right) \left(\frac{1}{\sigma_u} \right) e^{-(u/\sigma_u)^2/2} \qquad \text{for } u \geqq 0.$$

Then the distribution of ε is

$$\varepsilon \sim \left(\sqrt{\frac{2}{\pi}} \right) \left(\frac{1}{\sigma_u} \right) e^{-(\ln(\varepsilon)/\sigma_u)^2/2} \frac{1}{\varepsilon}.$$

This function is approximated by Taylor series expanded at $\varepsilon = 1$ as

$$\left(\sqrt{\frac{2}{\pi}} \right) \left(\frac{1}{\sigma_u \varepsilon} \right) + O[(\varepsilon - 1)^2].$$

Here $O(\cdot)$ is Landau's symbol, and $a_t = O(b_t)$ indicates that a_t is at most of order b_t. The first term is the same functional form of distribution as that of equation (13). By comparing coefficients of these terms, we get

$$\sigma_u = \left(\sqrt{\frac{2}{\pi}} \right) \left(\frac{\alpha q^*}{v} \right). \tag{14}$$

The standard deviation of technical inefficiency σ_u is proportional to the speed of technology growth α and inversely proportional to the relative speed of embodiment of the new technology (v/q^*), which is the ratio of the number of newly constructed plants to total plants.

Model Analysis B. Optimal Distribution of Vintage and Level of Technical Inefficiency

We now turn to an analysis of the distribution of the level of inefficiency. In model analysis A we saw that inefficiency is a function of the growth rate of technology and the speed of its embodiment. By fixing the rate of technology growth at some level, we can find the determinants of the speed of embodiment of new technology by an optimizing firm. If the speed is dependent on the market structure, the level of inefficiency is also dependent on the market structure.

Notation used in model analysis B is

p = price,

p_0, p_1, a = parameters of demand function,

q = level of production of a firm,

r = discount ratio,

π_t = profit of a firm at time t,

V = discounted cash flow,

Q = total supply in the market,

W_t = consumer surplus and the sum of firms' profits at time t,

N = number of firms.

The market's inverse demand curve is $p = p_1 - aQ$, and the subjective demand curve for firm i is $p = p_0 - aq_i$.

Some more assumptions are needed besides those in model analysis A. The construction cost of new plants for a firm is proportional to its speed. It costs cv to construct v plants in a unit time interval. Here c is a constant, the cost to construct one plant in a time interval. Firms maximize the discounted cash flow $\pi_t \exp(-rt)$. The growth rate of technology α is small enough that we can neglect α^2. There are N firms in the market. The total supply by these firms is Q. Each firm selects its supply strategy, assuming that its level of supply does not affect other firms' strategies. They select their optimal strategy at time 0.

A firm's marginal cost function at time t is $c_0 \exp(-\alpha t) \cdot \exp(\alpha q_i/v_i)$, and its marginal revenue is $p_0 - 2aq_i$. Then the optimal production level q_i^* is the solution of

$$p_0 - 2aq_i^* = c_0 \exp(-\alpha t) \cdot \exp\left(\frac{\alpha q_i^*}{v_i}\right).$$

With α^2 neglected, the right side is approximated as $c_0(1 - \alpha t + \alpha q_i^*/v_i)$. Therefore

$$q_i^* \simeq \frac{p_0 - c_0 + c_0\alpha t}{2a} - \frac{(p_0 - c_0)c_0\alpha}{4a^2 v_i}. \tag{15}$$

The profit of the firm at time t is[20]

$$\pi_{ti} = (p_0 - aq_i^*)q_i^* - c_0 \exp(-\alpha t) \int_0^{q_i^*} \exp\left(\frac{\alpha q}{v}\right) dq - cv_i$$

$$\simeq q_i^* \frac{p_0 - c_0 + c_0\alpha t}{2} - v_i c$$

$$\simeq \frac{(p_0 - c_0)^2 [1 - (c_0\alpha/2av_i)] + 2(p_0 - c_0)c_0\alpha t}{4a} - v_i c.$$

From this

$$V_i \simeq \frac{(p_0 - c_0)^2 [1 - (c_0\alpha/2av)]r + 2(p_0 - c_0)c_0\alpha}{4ar^2} - \frac{v_i c}{r}.$$

Maximizing V_i by v_i, we get

$$\frac{\alpha}{v_i} = \left(\frac{2a}{p_0 - c_0}\right)\left(\sqrt{\frac{2c\alpha}{c_0}}\right). \tag{16}$$

When there is only one firm in the market, $p_0 = p_1$, the quantity supplied is expressed by equation (15), and the replacement speed is

$$v^M = \left(\frac{p_1 - c_0}{2a}\right)\left(\sqrt{\frac{c_0\alpha}{2c}}\right), \tag{17}$$

where v^M is replacement speed with monopoly. σ_u calculated from equation (14) is

$$\left(\frac{1}{p_1 - c_0}\right)\left(\sqrt{\frac{2}{\pi}}\right)\left\{[p_1 - c_0(1 - \alpha t)]\sqrt{\frac{2c\alpha}{c_0}} - 2c\alpha\right\}.$$

The level of technical efficiency depends on time. At $t = 0$ this value takes

$$\sigma_u^M = \sqrt{\frac{2}{\pi}}\left(\sqrt{\frac{2c\alpha}{c_0}} - \frac{2c\alpha}{p_1 - c_0}\right). \tag{18}$$

Here σ_u^M is denoted as the value of σ_u for a monopoly at $t = 0$.

Next consider the first-best case which maximizes the discounted flow of sum of consumer surplus and firms' profit. First, we define W_t, the sum of consumer surplus and firms' profit at time t, as

$$W_t = \int_0^Q \left[p_1 - aq - c_0 \exp\left(-\alpha t + \frac{\alpha q}{v} \right) \right] dq - cv$$

$$\simeq Q\left[p_1 - c_0(1 - \alpha t) - \frac{aQ}{2} - \frac{c_0 \alpha Q}{2v} \right) \right] - cv,$$

which is maximized when

$$Q = \frac{p_1 - c_0(1 - \alpha t)}{a + c_0(\alpha/v)} \simeq \frac{p_1 - c_0(1 - \alpha t)}{a} - \frac{(p_1 - c_0)c_0\alpha}{a^2 v}. \tag{19}$$

We denote this value of Q as $\overline{Q}_t$ and the maximized value of W_t as $\overline{W}_t$ when $Q = \overline{Q}_t \cdot \overline{W}_t$ is

$$\overline{W}_t = \frac{\overline{Q}_t}{2} [p_1 - c_0(1 - \alpha t)] - vc.$$

The discounted sum of $\overline{W}_t$ is

$$\int_0^\infty \overline{W}_t e^{-rt} \, dt = \frac{(p_1 - c_0)^2 [1 - (c_0\alpha/av)]r + 2(p_1 - c_0)c_0\alpha}{2ar^2} - \frac{vc}{r},$$

which is maximized when the speed of replacement investment is chosen as

$$\frac{\alpha}{v^F} = \left(\frac{a}{p_1 - c_0} \right)\left(\sqrt{\frac{2c\alpha}{c_0}} \right),$$

or

$$v^F = \left(\frac{p_1 - c_0}{a} \right)\left(\sqrt{\frac{c_0\alpha}{2c}} \right), \tag{20}$$

where v^F is the first-best replacement speed. Then the value of σ_u, when $Q = \overline{Q}_t$ and $v = v^F$, is

$$\frac{1}{p_1 - c_0} \left(\sqrt{\frac{2}{\pi}} \right)\left\{ [p_1 - c_0(1 - \alpha t)] \sqrt{\frac{2c\alpha}{c_0}} - 2c\alpha \right\},$$

which is the monopoly value. At $t = 0$ this value takes

$$\sigma_u^F = \sigma_u^M = \sqrt{\frac{2}{\pi}} \left(\sqrt{\frac{2c\alpha}{c_0}} - \frac{2c\alpha}{p_1 - c_0} \right), \tag{21}$$

where σ_u^F is the first-best value of σ_u.

Equation (21) shows that the value of σ_u is the same in both the mono-poly and the first-best cases. However, this does not mean that the replace-ment investment that maximizes social welfare is optimally chosen even when there is monopoly. The level of technical inefficiency depends both on the speed of replacement investment and on the level of production, as shown in equation (14); the social surplus also depends on the speed of replacement investment and on the level of production. Therefore, the level of technical efficiency that maximizes social surplus under the competitive output level does not maximize social surplus under the monopolistic profit maximization condition (15).

Indeed the discounted sum of social surplus under the monopolistic output level schedule (15) is

$$\frac{p_1 - c_0}{8ar}\left[(p_1 - c_0)\left(3 - \frac{2\alpha c_0}{av}\right) - \frac{6\alpha c_0}{r}\right] - \frac{vc}{r},$$

which is maximized when v is

$$v^S = \left(\frac{p_1 - c_0}{2a}\right)\left(\sqrt{\frac{c_0\alpha}{c}}\right). \tag{22}$$

Here we denote this second-best value of v as v^S. The second-best value of σ_u is

$$\frac{1}{p_1 - c_0}\left\{[p_1 - c_0(1 - \alpha t)]\sqrt{\frac{c\alpha}{c_0}} - c\alpha\right\},$$

and this value takes

$$\sigma_u^S = \sqrt{\frac{2}{\pi}}\left(\sqrt{\frac{c\alpha}{c_0}} - \frac{c\alpha}{p_1 - c_0}\right) \tag{23}$$

at $t = 0$.

The relationship among the speeds of replacement investment for the three cases is

$$v^M < v^S < v^F,$$

and for the levels of technical efficiency,[21]

$$\sigma_u^M = \sigma_u^F > \sigma_u^S.$$

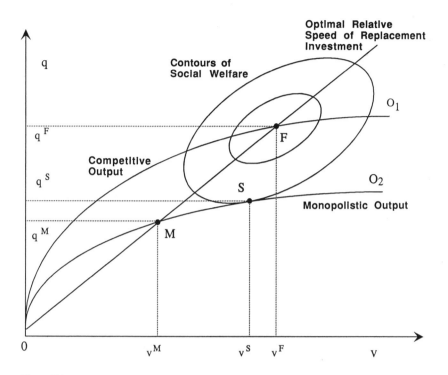

q

Optimal Relative
Speed of Replacement
Investment

Contours of
Social Welfare

O_1

q^F F

Competitive
Output

q^S S O_2

Monopolistic Output

q^M M

0   v^M v^S v^F V

Figure 2.1

Figure 2.1 illustrates this relationship. Social welfare is determined by both the level of output and the speed of replacement investment, and it is maximized at point F where $(v, q) = (v^F, q^F)$. This first-best case is attained when the level of output is determined competitively (curve OFO_1) and the speed of replacement investment is set v^F/q^F. The monopolistic output (curve OMO_2) is lower than competitive output for each level of v. In this case a monopolist chooses the point M at which v/q is the same as v^F/q^F on curve OMO_2. On the other hand, the social welfare is maximized at point S conditional on the curve OMO_2. At point S, $q^S/v^S < q^F/v^F$, which means that $\sigma_u^S < \sigma_u^M$. This relation implies that though the level of technical efficiency of monopoly is the same as that of first best, the speed of replacement investment chosen is lower than that of second best, which maximizes social welfare under the monopolistic output level constraint. Monopoly's absolute level of replacement investment is slower than under first best, but this does not directly imply a lower level of technical efficiency because the level is determined by speed and output level.

In Cournot-Nash competition we get the ith firm's conduct simply by replacing p_0 by $p_1 - a\sum_{j \neq i} q_j$. Therefore

$$\pi_{ti} = \left(p_1 - a\sum_{j \neq i} q_j - aq_i\right)q_i - c_0 q_i\left(1 - \alpha t + \frac{\alpha q_i}{2v_i}\right) - cv_i,$$

and ith firm's level of production at time t is the solution of:

$$p_1 - a\sum_{j \neq i} q_j - 2aq_i - c_0\left(1 - \alpha t + \frac{\alpha q_i}{2v_i}\right) = 0.$$

Summing up these N equations, and assuming a symmetrical equilibrium, we get

$$q^N = \frac{p_1 - c_0(1 - \alpha t)}{a(N + 1) + (c_0\alpha/2v)},$$

where q^N is the equilibrium output level when there are N firms. Similarly the speed of replacement investment is determined by

$$v^N = \frac{p_1 - (N - 1)q^N - c_0(1 - \alpha t)}{2a}\sqrt{\frac{\alpha c_0}{2c}},$$

where v^N is the equilibrium speed of replacement investment. Since σ_u is $\alpha q/v \cdot \sqrt{2/\pi}$, the technical efficiency and the output levels at $t = 0$ are determined by the equations

$$aq^N(N + 1) + \frac{c_0 \sigma_u^N}{2} = p_1 - c_0,$$

$$\sigma_u^N = \frac{4aq^N}{p_1 - (N - 1)q^N - c_0}\sqrt{\frac{\alpha c}{\pi c_0}}. \tag{24}$$

Here σ_u^N exhibits the level of technical efficiency when there are N firms.

The level of technical efficiency of (23) monotonically decreases when N increases. That is, $\sigma_u^{N+1} < \sigma_u^N$. We provide a proof of this proposition in appendix B. Unfortunately, it is not clear how the number of firms affects social welfare, as is shown by this example (parameters set are $p_0 = 10$, $c_0 = 1$, $c = 1$, $a = 1$, $\alpha = 0.02$, and $t = 0$):

N	q^N	Q	σ_u^N	W
1	4.402	4.402	0.1957	29.27
2	2.936	5.871	0.1936	34.73
3	2.202	6.606	0.1917	36.46
4	1.762	7.048	0.1898	37.07
5	1.469	7.343	0.1880	37.25
7	1.102	7.714	0.1846	37.06
10	0.802	8.018	0.1798	36.32
20	0.421	8.413	0.1670	33.26
50	0.174	8.684	0.1420	25.01
100	0.088	8.793	0.1192	14.26

In most cases welfare increases as N increases when N is small, and decreases when N is large. The increase of welfare when N is small is due to the increase of production. When N becomes large, that effect is exhausted, and excessive replacement investment reduces welfare. Thus increased technical efficiency does not always imply increased social welfare especially when the number of firms is large. However, when the number of firms is small, it is quite possible that increased technical efficiency mean increased social welfare.

Because α and c do not appear in the first equation of (24), it is clear from the second equation of (24) that technical efficiency decreases as α and c increase. Faster growth means more rapid obsolescence, so technical efficiency declines. As c increases, so does the cost of replacement. With firms reluctant to replace plants, technical efficiency is reduced.

The limit of application of the preceding model analyses B lies in the assumption of continuously replaceable assets. In those models plants are assumed so small that they can be replaced continuously. Even if plants are thought of as machines, this assumption is too strong to apply to atomistic industries.

The situation in which the size of plants or machines is large relative to the size of firms is expressed in the type of cost function of replacement investment. If the cost of replacement is proportional to the size of capacity replaced, there is no problem with divisibility of replacements. However, when the size of firms is small, we have to consider the indivisibility of assets. In this section an extreme case is considered in which every firm is so small that it has only one asset.

As in preceding models, technological progress reduces production cost at a constant rate α. The level of production cost at time 0 is c_0, therefore the production cost at time t is $c_0 \exp(-\alpha t)$. A firm can produce any level of output at this constant $MC = AC$ cost if its plant was built at time t. It takes a fixed cost K to make replacement investment. This fixed cost K represents lumpiness of asset replacement; if we assume that the cost depends on the capacity replaced, this model comes to have the properties of the continuous replacement model. Technological progress is also assumed in this replacement cost, so K decreases by the same rate α. There are N firms in this market. The market inverse demand function is $p = p_1 - a \sum q_i$. The level of production is determined by Cournot-Nash competition in quantities.

In this type of model it is known that time intervals of investments are the same, as demonstrated by Førsund and Hjalmarsson (1987, 46, thm. 2.1). This model is a simplified, modified version of Førsund and Hjalmarsson, so we can easily demonstrate the same result. We set these intervals as Δt, so that the ith firm's cost level at the beginning of time $N\Delta t$ is $c_0 \exp(-\alpha i \Delta t)$ $(i = 0, 1, \ldots, N - 1)$. Because each firm can operate only one plant, the firm that possesses the oldest and the highest-cost plant makes the next replacement. Therefore at the end of time $N\Delta t$ the 0th firm that had a plant with cost c_0 builds a new plant that achieves cost level $c_0 \exp(-\alpha N\Delta t)$. This firm decides on replacement by comparing the discounted cash flows of undertaking replacement with not undertaking it.

If this firm does not make the replacement, N firms with cost $c_0 \exp(-\alpha i \Delta t)$ $(i = 0, 1, \ldots, N - 1)$ compete each other. By the Cournot-Nash assumption the ith firm's output level is the solution of

$$p_1 - a \sum_{j \neq i} q_j - 2aq_i = c_0 \exp[-\alpha(i - 1)\Delta t].$$

Summing up N equations, we get

$$\sum q_j = \frac{Np_1 - c_0[1 - \exp(-\alpha N\Delta t)]/[1 - \exp(-\alpha \Delta t)]}{a(N + 1)},$$

$$p = \frac{p_1 + c_0[1 - \exp(-\alpha N\Delta t)]/[1 - \exp(-\alpha \Delta t)]}{N + 1}.$$

From this the discounted cash flow is

$$\frac{1}{ar}\left\{\frac{p_1 + c_0[1 - \exp(-\alpha N\Delta t)]/[1 - \exp(-\alpha\Delta t)]}{N + 1} - c_0\right\}^2.$$

Similarly the discounted cash flow, when this firm chooses to replace, is

$$\frac{1}{ar}\left\{\frac{p_1 + c_0\exp(-\alpha\Delta t)[1 - \exp(-\alpha N\Delta t)]/[1 - \exp(-\alpha\Delta t)]}{N + 1}\right.$$

$$\left. - c_0\exp(-\alpha\Delta tN)\right\}^2.$$

The firm elects to replace the asset when the difference between these cash flows exceeds the cost of replacement investment. The condition is

$$\frac{2(p_1 - c_0)c_0 N^2\alpha\Delta t}{a(N + 1)^2 r} > K.$$

We use the same approximation method as in former sections which neglects α^2 to deduce this equation. The replacement interval for each firm is then

$$N\Delta t = \frac{a(N + 1)^2 K}{2(p_1 - c_0)c_0 N\alpha},$$

which corresponds to q_i/v_i in model analysis A, since q_i/v_i is also an average speed of replacement investment.[22] Therefore σ_u is expected to be

$$\sigma_u = \sqrt{\frac{2}{\pi}}\alpha \cdot N\Delta t = \left(\sqrt{\frac{2}{\pi}}\right)\left[\frac{a(N + 1)^2 K}{2(p_1 - c_0)N}\right], \tag{25}$$

which is apparently an increasing function of N contrary to the preceding result. In the model of continuous replacement, as N increases, competitive pressure forces firms to hasten replacement investments, which pulls up technical efficiency. However in this model, firms are assumed to be so small that they should refrain from replacement investments because the cost is proportionate to the frequency of replacement.

The model of continuous replacement is more suitable in the case where the number of firms is small enough that every firm has several plants or productive assets. Then technical efficiency is an increasing function of the number of firms. On the other hand, the model of discontinuous replacement is applicable when the size of firms is small and the assets are lumpy.

In those circumstances technical efficiency is a decreasing function of the number of firms. As a whole the relationship between technical efficiency and the number of firms is considered to be inverted U-shaped so that an intermediate level of N maximizes efficiency.

Equation (25) also implies that technical efficiency decreases as the cost of replacement increases, which is the same result as the last section. However, the speed of technological growth α does not affect technical efficiency in this case. Faster growth again means more rapid obsolescence, but at the same time faster technological growth makes replacement investments more profitable. Therefore the total effect becomes neutral.

Model Analysis C: A Managerial Model of Technical Inefficiency

The model of technical inefficiency just presented depends on properties of technology. However, it is more natural to regard inefficiency as originating in managerial failure, control loss, or loss due to opportunism in ways explained by Williamson. Here we consider these types of inefficiency.

First, a parameter that indicates the level of efficiency is defined. If $x = 0$, the firm operates at technically ideal minimum costs (perfectly efficient). If $x > 0$, some inefficiency pushes the cost level upward by multiples of $\exp(x)$.

Two assumptions are employed. First, managerial opportunism tends to increase each firm's costs at rate γ, where γ is a constant expressing the rate of cost increase. In other words, in a very small time interval Δt, unit cost is multiplied by $1 + \Delta t \cdot \gamma$. Thus, if the level of inefficiency increases by Δx in that time interval, then $\Delta x = \Delta t \cdot \gamma$. Second, firms can reform their inefficient states by appropriate managerial action. For each firm the probability of reform is proportional to its level of inefficiency. In this case a firm's probability of reform is θx, where θ is a parameter reflecting managerial effort and x is as defined above. In general, the higher the inefficiency level, the more adverse are its consequences and the less likely are managers to continue to overlook it. This assumption could take another form. The alternative is to suppose that this probability is independent of the current level of inefficiency. Then the probability to reform is θ, and we obtain a different distribution of inefficiency. In either case we suppose that inefficiency is eliminated by reform.

Using these assumptions, we can analyze the asymptotic probability density of firms' levels of inefficiency. For $x > 0$ and $t \geq 0$, we define $\rho(x, t)$

as the density function that represents a firm's probability to be at inefficiency level x at time t. No firm's inefficiency level is stationary. In the very small time interval Δt, with probability $\theta x \Delta t$ the level becomes 0, and otherwise $(1 - \theta x \Delta t)$ the level increases by $\gamma \Delta t$.

Therefore

$$\rho(x + \Delta x, t + \Delta t) = \rho(x)(1 - \theta x \Delta t).$$

Expanding this equality, we get

$$\rho(x, t) + \frac{\partial \rho}{\partial x} \Delta x + \frac{\partial \rho}{\partial t} \Delta t = \rho(x, t) - \rho(x, t) \theta x \Delta t.$$

Next we consider the asymptotic distribution. We define $\rho(x)$ as the asymptotic distribution of $\rho(x, t) : t \to \infty$, which is defined in the range $0 < x < \infty$. Thus $\partial \rho / \partial t$ is 0, and

$$\frac{\partial \rho}{\partial x} = -\frac{\theta x}{\gamma} \rho(x)$$

because $\Delta x / \Delta t$ is γ by the assumption. We can easily solve this differential equation, obtaining

$$\rho(x) = C_1 \exp\left(-\frac{\theta}{2\gamma} x^2\right),$$

where C_1 is a constant.

Until now we have excluded the case of $x = 0$ in the definition of $\rho(x, t)$. In Δt length of time interval

$$\int_0^\infty \rho(x) \theta x \Delta t \, dx = \int_0^\infty C_1 \exp\left(-\frac{\theta}{2\lambda} x^2\right) \theta x \Delta t \, dx = C_1 \Delta t \gamma,$$

plants are reformed. Their current levels of efficiency are dispersed in interval $[0, \gamma \Delta t]$, so the probability density around $x = 0$ is $C_1(\Delta t \gamma / \Delta t \gamma) = C_1$. This value is equivalent to $\rho(x)$ defined above at $x = 0$. Therefore we can expand the definition of ρ for $x \geqq 0$ continuously.

Because ρ is a probabilistic density function,

$$\int_0^\infty \rho(x) \, dx = C_1 \int_0^\infty \exp\left(-\frac{\theta}{2\gamma} x^2\right) dx = C_1 \sqrt{\frac{\pi \gamma}{2\theta}} = 1.$$

Then $C_1 = \sqrt{2\theta/\pi\gamma}$, and

$$\rho(x) = \sqrt{\frac{2\theta}{\pi\gamma}} \exp\left(-\frac{\theta}{2\gamma}x^2\right).$$

This is the probabilistic density function of technical inefficiency of the half-normal type:

$$\sqrt{\frac{2}{\pi}}\left(\frac{1}{\sigma_u}\right)\exp\left(-\frac{1}{2\sigma_u^2}u^2\right),$$

where σ_u is $\sqrt{\gamma/\theta}$. As demonstrated above, the level of technical inefficiency is proportional to the square root of the speed of obsolescence, and inversely proportional to the level of effort to restore the efficiency. In the putty-clay type of vintage model in model analysis A, the half-normal distribution is approximated by a rectangular distribution. In this section no approximation is used and the half-normal distribution of efficiency is developed directly.[23]

If we choose the variant assumption that reform is independent of the current inefficiency level,

$$\rho(x + \Delta x, t + \Delta t) = \rho(x)(1 - \theta\Delta t).$$

By expanding this and following the same procedure, we get the differential equation:

$$\frac{\partial\rho}{\partial x} = -\frac{\theta}{\gamma}\rho(x).$$

The solution is

$$\rho(x) = C_2 \exp\left(-\frac{\theta}{\gamma}x\right),$$

where C_2 is a constant.

In Δt length of the time interval,

$$\int_0^\infty \rho(x)\theta\Delta t\, dx = \int_0^\infty C_2 \exp\left(-\frac{\theta}{\gamma}x\right)\theta\Delta t\, dx = C_2\Delta t\gamma$$

plants are reformed. Then we can expand the definition of ρ for $x \geqq 0$ continuously because the probability around $x = 0$ is C_2, which is equivalent to $\lim_{x \to 0} \rho(x)$. After normalization, we get

$$\rho(x) = \frac{\theta}{\gamma} \exp\left(-\frac{\theta}{\gamma} x\right).$$

This is the distribution function of technical inefficiency of the exponential type. Here σ_u, the standard deviation of inefficiency, is $\sqrt{\gamma/\theta}$. Again, the level of technical inefficiency is proportional to the square root of the speed of obsolescence and inversely proportional to the level of effort to reform the firm's inefficiency.

Model Analysis D: Optimal Managerial Effort and Technical Inefficiency

Now we turn to the relationship between technical inefficiency in model analysis C and market structure. The notation in this analysis is

$c(\theta, Q) =$ management's cost of reforming productive inefficiency,

$\theta =$ a parameter reflecting the level of managerial effort,

$Q =$ firm's level of production,

$c_0 =$ production cost of the most efficient plant,

$X =$ production cost (probabilistic variable).

Three assumptions are employed. First, θ is defined as the speed of restoring efficiency as in model analysis C. This managerial action incurs a cost that depends on the degree of effort and the production level. That is, the more intensely the management monitors productivity, and the larger the scale of production, the larger the managerial cost becomes. We denote this function as $c(\theta, Q)$, where Q is the production level, and $C_\theta > 0$, $C_Q > 0$, and $C_{\theta\theta} > 0$. Second, the production cost of the most efficient plants is c_0, and the probability that the cost falls $c_0 \exp(u)$ is

$$\left(\sqrt{\frac{2}{\pi}}\right) \frac{1}{\sigma_u} \exp\left(-\frac{1}{2\sigma_u^2} u^2\right) \qquad \text{for } u \geqq 0.$$

We denote $c_0 \exp(u)$ as X. Third, we assume that firms do not know the exact efficiency levels of their plants, only the distribution of productivity. Because the parameters of this distribution depend on the degree of effort θ, and there is a cost c for that effort, they choose only the optimal level of effort, which would be the level that maximizes the expected profit. Their subjective demand function is $p = p_0 - aQ$, where p_0 and a are constants.

The probabilistic density function of X is

$$\left(\sqrt{\frac{2}{\pi}}\right)\frac{1}{X\sigma_u}\exp\left[-\frac{1}{2\sigma_u^2}\left(\log\frac{X}{c_0}\right)^2\right].$$

We denote this function as $\psi(X; \sigma_u)$. A firm's profit is total revenue minus production cost XQ and managerial cost $c(\theta, Q)$. Thus, because the choice of Q does not depend on the unknown cost X, the expected profit is

$$\int_{c_0}^{\infty} [Q(p_0 - aQ - X) - c(\theta, Q)]\psi(X; \sigma_u)\, dX$$

$$= [Q(p_0 - aQ) - c(\theta, Q)] - Q\int_{c_0}^{\infty} X\psi(X)\, dX$$

$$= [Q(p_0 - aQ) - c(\theta, Q)] - c_0 Q \cdot \phi(\sigma_u), \tag{26}$$

where

$$\phi(\sigma_u) = \frac{2}{\sqrt{\pi}}\int_{-\infty}^{\sigma_u/\sqrt{2}} \exp(-t^2)\, dt \cdot \exp\left(\frac{\sigma_u^2}{2}\right).$$

We can easily ascertain that $\phi' > 0$ and $\phi'' > 0$.

To obtain the optimal θ and Q, we use the relation $\sigma_u = \sqrt{\gamma/\theta}$ of model analysis C. However, in this analysis we treat γ as a constant. Substituting this for σ_u, we can represent the firm's profit as a function of Q and θ. Differentiating equation (26) by Q and θ, we get the conditions for optimality as

$$-2aQ + p_0 - c_Q(\theta, Q) - c_0\Phi(\theta) = 0,$$

$$c_\theta(\theta, Q) = -c_0 Q \cdot \Phi'(\theta), \tag{27}$$

where $\Phi(\theta) = \phi(\sqrt{\gamma/\theta})$. Then $\Phi' < 0$, and $\Phi'' > 0$. If c is proportional to production level Q, equation (27) shows that the optimal θ is independent of Q. Otherwise, from (27)

$$\frac{d\theta^*}{dQ} = -\frac{\tilde{c}_{\theta Q}(\theta^*, Q)}{c_0\Phi''(\theta^*) + (c_{\theta\theta}/Q)}, \tag{28}$$

where θ^* is the optimal level of effort and $\tilde{c}$ is C/Q managerial cost per output. Since equation (27) does not include a parameter for demand conditions, a full analysis of comparative statistics is not necessary.

From equation (28) we can deduce the relationship between the technical inefficiency and market structure. We consider N firms in the market. As N increases, the market become more competitive, and each firm's Q decreases. If $\tilde{c}_{\theta Q} > 0$, that is, if the marginal cost of effort per output is an increasing function of output, optimal level of effort is a decreasing function of Q. Thus the more competitive the industry, the higher is its efficiency, which is essentially due to diseconomies of scale in managerial control. This setting is similar to that of Leibenstein's X-inefficiency. On the other hand, if $\tilde{c}_{\theta Q} < 0$, that is, if the marginal cost of effort is a decreasing function of output, the optimal level of effort decreases as Q decreases. Then the more competitive is an industry, the less efficient it becomes. This is the case of economies of scale in managerial control.

2.3.2 Determinants of Technical Inefficiency

In model analyses A and B the degree of technical inefficiency was shown to be proportional to the rate of technological progress and to the inverse of the relative rate of replacement of outdated plants. The relationship between the concentration ratio and technical efficiency is inverted U-shaped. That is, there is a level of concentration that maximizes efficiency. When the number of firms in the market is relatively small, the efficiency level increases as the number of firms increases, which is mainly due to competition forcing firms to produce more efficiently. When the number of firms is relatively large, the efficiency level decreases as the number of firms increases, and this is due to indivisible replacement investment. As the replacement cost increases, making the firm reluctant to replace plants, technical efficiency decreases.

The Lee-Tyler average technical efficiency predicted from the vintage model by equation (14) is

	Average intervals of replacement investment (years)			
α	5	10	15	20
0.005	0.984	0.969	0.954	0.939
0.010	0.969	0.939	0.911	0.884
0.015	0.954	0.911	0.871	0.834
0.020	0.939	0.884	0.834	0.789
0.025	0.925	0.859	0.800	0.747
0.030	0.911	0.834	0.767	0.709

In Japan α and investment intervals are estimated to be 0.013 and 13.7, respectively.[24] In this case average technical efficiency is about 90 percent. That is, about one-third of technical inefficiency can be explained from these vintage models.

The result of model analyses C and D should be intuitively clear, so a mathematical model is not necessary. The larger the firm with diseconomies of scale in managerial cost, the greater is its inefficiency. In contrast, the larger the firm with economies of scale in managerial control, the less inefficiency it experiences. The value of the mathematical models lies in deriving the half-normal or exponential shape of the distribution of inefficiency.

It should be noted that the models in subsection 2.3.1 explain only certain aspects of technical inefficiency that have important implications for the relation between structural factors and technical efficiency. Other factors could affect the technical inefficiency level. Some operate through the optimal choices of economic agents, others through irrationality in the economic sense, or both. In this section we discuss these possibilities. Precise definitions of variables used in this section are provided in appendix C.

HI: Herfindahl index

HISQ: HI^2

HI is an index of market concentration. In model analysis B we showed inefficiency to be an inverted U-shaped function of the concentration ratio. In model analysis D we found inefficiency to be an increasing or decreasing function according to the shape of the managerial cost function. The observed level of inefficiency is a mixture of these inefficiencies which are affected differently by exogenous variables. Therefore we will test a quadratic relation between inefficiency and HI.

There are still other factors related to competitive pressures on firms' performances which are discussed in Caves and Barton (1990, 68–70) that may influence the level of the technical efficiency. They are (1) slack within the plant or firm due to an absence of competitive pressure and threats to survival, (2) more numerous experiments with resource deployment and faster diffusion of the results associated with more firms participating in the market, and (3) oligopolistic rivalry and effects on resource use of nonprice competition. Unlike the vintage effect discussed earlier, these effects predict monotonic relations with the inefficiency level, that is, competitive pressure reduces sources of inefficiency.

We use HI as the concentration measure because it reflects both the number and size distribution of sellers and takes all firms into account. Average efficiency is the average discrepancy from the production frontier for all firms in the market. This discrepancy exists for every input level or every input intensity (K/L) on the production possibility set. The concentration index accordingly should include information on all sellers in the market.

IMPT: Ratio of imports to industry shipments

EXPT: Ratio of exports to industry shipments

TARF: Height of tariff barrier

SUBS: Ratio of government subsidy to gross value added

TARSUB = TARF + SUBS: Effective rate of protection

VIO: Number of violations of antimonopoly law

IMPT and EXPT correct the competitiveness implied by domestic producers' concentration for overseas market competition. In Japan exporting activity is extensive and may be an important source of increased competitive pressure. Both IMPT and EXPT contribute to competitiveness, which is expected to decrease inefficiency.[25] Likewise protection by tariffs is thought to reduce the competitive pressure from foreign firms. Tariffs are not the only source of protection from import competition; Shōda (1981) calculated an index of effective rates of protection in Japanese food industries incorporating government subsidies and disadvantageous effects on inputs caused by protection of other industries. Here we take account of the effect of subsidies. TARF and SUBS are treated separately, but their combined effect is also examined. VIO is an index of collusive behavior, which may have a negative association with competitiveness.

The vintage effect of concentration on technical inefficiency is a combined consequence of the relative sizes of firms and competitive pressure, and its relationship is expected to be curvilinear. On the other hand, variables introduced here affect competitiveness separately from size distribution of firms, and they are related to factors analyzed in Caves and

Barton. Although competitive pressure affects the working of the vintage model, the relationship between competitiveness represented by these variables and technical inefficiency is expected not to be curvilinear but to monotonically decrease inefficiency.

K: Average tangible assets per plant

TYPK: Tangible assets of typical plant

KSHI: Fixed cost of replacement investment

RSIZ: Ratio of median plant size to market size

In model analysis B efficiency was analyzed as a decreasing function of the cost of replacing old capacity with new plants. Here we approximate this cost by the average value of tangible assets per plant. The model of efficiency discussed in model analysis D also raised this possibility. Capital cost also has significance as an entry barrier. This role will strengthen the effect mentioned above by reducing potential competition. Thus we expect a negative relation between K and efficiency.

While K is a simple arithmetic average of tangible assets per plant, TYPK is the value of tangible assets of the plant that supplies the median unit of industry output when plants are sorted by shipment size. TYPK is considered to have the same role as K has, but it can perform differently as an explanatory variable if industries' size distributions of plants are irregular.

In the model analysis of lumpy assets the role of fixed cost in replacement investment was found to lower efficiency when the number of firms is large. The existence of this fixed cost makes small enterprises reluctant to undertake replacement investment in order to achieve the lowest production cost. This analysis is parallel to the argument of Caves and Barton (1990, ch. 7) as to why technical inefficiency is lower in the small plants than in the large plants in U.S. industries.[26] The variable KSHI represents this indivisibility of capital cost. This variable is the t-statistic of the intercept c_0 of a regression analysis:

Value of tangible assets$_i = c_0 + c_1 \cdot$ (total shipment$_i$),

where $i = 1, \ldots, N$ designates plants in each industry. This equation is a kind of cost function, and this simple form may possibly exclude relevant exogenous variables. In such cases the OLS estimator of c_0 will be biased upward. Therefore the t-statistic is employed here, not the estimator c_0. The null hypothesis $c_0 = 0$ is not rejected when the t-statistic is high, implying the plausibility of the existence of indivisibility of capital cost.[27] This variable is expected to have a negative effect on technical efficiency.

The fourth variable RSIZ is the relative size of the median plant. This variable also represents discontinuity in the process of replacement. A large value of RSIZ could make replacement difficult if firm size is fixed, so this variable is expected to depress technical efficiency. In some analyses RSIZ is used as an index of minimum efficient scale of plant and thus of the height of barriers to entry. Therefore it may also affect efficiency negatively through the competitive environment. In Caves and Barton (1990), RSIZ (RSIZE) or a similar variable PSIZE (median plant size) is used as an index of the prevalence of large-scale plants or the absence of small ones. They found strong positive effects on technical efficiency.

PRGM: Growth rate of productivity

R&D: Ratio of company-financed research expenditure to value of shipments

The analysis based on putty-clay implies that the productivity growth rate is negatively correlated with efficiency. High productivity growth makes older plants obsolete. The model assumes that productivity growth is exogenous in the determination of efficiency. However, the rate of technological growth may have some dependence on static efficiency. Caves and Barton (1990, ch. 8) have detailed this possibility. They reported a weak positive association between these variables in the determination of productivity growth. If this also holds in Japan, simultaneous analysis may be necessary, a possibility investigated in subsection 2.3.4.

The R&D variable has a meaning similar to PRGM in one respect. Very high rates of innovation can cause inefficiency. A rapidly changing environment can bring about unequal disturbances to an industry's members. However, this link between R&D and efficiency assumes that R&D operates to expand the frontier. If R&D functions to foster efficient production, the relationship should be the opposite. Model analysis C is applicable in this case if managerial cost is replaced by R&D expenditure. The proportional relationship between efficiency-restoring effort and the discrepancy from the frontier predicts a half-normal type of distribution of inefficiency, and the standard deviation of that distribution similarly would be inversely proportional to the R&D effort, making efficiency positively correlated with R&D expenditure.

If R&D is taken as an index of dynamic efficiency, it would be desirable to treat R&D as endogenous. For decades the relationship between market structure and R&D has drawn the attention of researchers. It is necessary to estimate a simultaneous model to investigate the relationship between static and dynamical efficiency.

GRWT: Growth ratio of total shipments

GRVC: variance of demand

Unanticipated increases in demand lead to discrepancies between expected and actual demand, affecting existing production capacity. Unanticipated high use of existing production capacity delays the scrapping of older plants and can cause inefficiency. Demand growth rates are used to predict windfall profits in analyses of market performance, and thus expected profits influence the construction of plants with new technology. In circumstances of expanding demand, the variable GRWT would be correlated positively with efficiency. In general, however, its sign cannot be predicted.

Five years preceding the year examined (1978), there occurred the first energy shock, which affected the conduct of firms in numerous ways. We employ GRVC to represent the magnitudes of shocks in demand conditions. Using a simple regression analysis, this variable is calculated as the coefficient of variation of deviations from the trend:

$$\log(\text{total shipments in the market}) = c_0 + c_1 \text{ time.}$$

Severe fluctuations in demand could require firms to accommodate flexibly. Failures in these adjustments can cause technical inefficiency. Therefore GRVC is expected to have negative effect on technical efficiency.

ADV: Ratio of advertising expenditures to shipments

The ADV variable is used as a proxy of the level of product differentiation. Segmentation of markets by product differentiation has the same effect as RSIZ. Such heterogeneity in the market also brings about an increase in the variance of profitability, although its effect on the asymmetrical variance is ambiguous, as Caves and Barton (1990, 75) have observed.

ICOV: Proportion of shipments of industry's products made by plants classified to the industry

The ICOV variable includes the absence of competition from other industry plants. Recently many studies have pointed out that industry boundaries are becoming more blurred by technological progress. ICOV captures this tendency, which is thought to have a negative association with efficiency. However, as Caves and Barton (1990, 80) have argued, if outsiders are inefficient operators of an industry's plants, this variable could have a positive effect on the measure of efficiency.

SPE4: Proportion of shipments by plants classified to a four-digit industry that consists of products classified to the industry

The relationship between the SPE4 variable and the technical inefficiency index depends on the cause of diversification. Studies investigating the relation between performance and levels of diversification of industries have reported a negative relationship, noting that diversification was used for survival. When there is excessive diversification, efficiency might suffer in plants if the parent firms is preoccupied by diversified activities.

MULT: Share of shipments by multiple plants within an industry

According to model analysis A, as a firm's relative production scale increases, older plants are likely to be kept in operation, causing inefficiency. Thus efficiency is expected to be lower in industries with high MULT. Nevertheless, a problem emerges for testing this hypothesis because the variable MULT is not purely exogenous. In model analysis A the firm's multiplant strategy stems from endogenous determination of optimal firm size relative to plant size. It is not the cause of inefficiency but a phenomenon determined simultaneously with the level of inefficiency. Therefore this variable is treated as endogenous in the simultaneous model (subsection 2.3.4).

The next four variables are used to explain productivity in estimating the production frontier function, but they may also serve to explain asymmetrical deviations from the frontier.

SUBC: Ratio of subcontracting payments to total material costs

According to Uekusa (1982), when a contractor has both monopolistic and monopsonistic power, cost reductions by subcontractors increase profits of the contractor. The rate of gain capture varies according to the price strategies of the contractor. Following Uekusa's model, cost reductions by the subcontracting industry should appear as cost reductions in the contractors's industry. This effect is particularly evident in industries that depend on the subcontracting system. Generally speaking, subcontractors' activities are very competitive, or rather atomistic. In atomistic industries the spread of new technology is relatively slow; it emphasizes the differences in performances and deteriorating levels of technical efficiency. If two industries have no subcontracting system between themselves, the retarded technology transfers affect technical efficiency not only of the supplier's industry but also of the purchaser's industry because in some major sectors supplied components account for large proportions of purchasers' material costs (sectoral mean values are shown in table 2.9). When a subcontracting agreement is concluded, the purchaser promotes rapid transfer of new technology among subcontractors because of the gain flowing to the purchaser. A positive relationship between efficiency indexes and SUBC is predicted by this hypothesis.

SPE7:   Index of specialization within plants in seven-digit products

SPE7 also supplies us information about the heterogeneity of products of the four-digit industries analyzed in this study. If this variable is high, the industry can be homogeneous, or it can be finely fragmented. Therefore SPE7 is a kind of index of aggregation, and with aggregation the observed inefficiencies are likely to increase. A low SPE7 indicates heterogeneous outputs within plants. The plants' output mixtures could be diverse, but they could instead be similar, so the four-digit classification would be appropriate. With plants' product mixtures similar to each other, they are free from the biases that could be caused by aggregation. Thus a negative relationship between SPE7 and efficiency is possible, as well as the more obvious positive one.

ENER: Ratio of energy cost to total material cost

PRWR: Ratio of production workers to total employees

The two variables ENER and PRWR refer to inputs likely to be required in fixed proportions for an industry's output. The higher their values, the fewer will be the variances in plants' productivity levels. These variables are therefore correlated positively with the level of efficiency.

Table 2.9
Mean values of selected variables indicating technology structures, by two-digit industry

Two-digit code	Industry	ENER	SUBC	PRWR	SPE7
18/19	Food, beverage, and tobacco	0.052	0.007	0.737	0.842
20	Textiles	0.140	0.158	0.838	0.846
21	Textile products	0.135	0.304	0.882	0.890
22	Wood and wooden products	0.060	0.033	0.816	0.774
23	Furniture and fixtures	0.031	0.100	0.809	0.889
24	Pulp and paper products	0.138	0.046	0.770	0.824
25	Printing and publishing	0.049	0.320	0.591	0.770
26	Chemical products	0.092	0.015	0.619	0.770
27	Petroleum and coal products	0.082	0.004	0.612	0.440
28	Rubber products	0.083	0.095	0.786	0.727
29	Leather and leather products	0.047	0.137	0.841	0.912
30	Earthen and related products	0.256	0.050	0.767	0.870
31	Iron and steel	0.159	0.045	0.776	0.601
32	Nonferrous metals	0.060	0.089	0.743	0.805
33	Fabricated metal products	0.062	0.205	0.745	0.833
34/38	Mechanical machinery	0.045	0.250	0.706	0.756
35	Electrical machinery	0.070	0.229	0.767	0.830
36	Transport equipment	0.034	0.137	0.760	0.774
37	Precision equipment	0.098	0.261	0.805	0.840
39	Other	0.061	0.133	0.759	0.865
	Light industries	0.135	0.095	0.777	0.841
	Heavy industries	0.081	0.114	0.710	0.717
	Materials industries	0.126	0.057	0.713	0.732
	Process/assembly industries	0.068	0.181	0.772	0.818

Note. The industries were grouped as follows:
Light industries: 18/19, 20, 21, 22, 23, 24, 25, 28, 29, 30
Heavy industries: 26, 27, 31, 32, 33, 34/38, 35, 36, 37
Materials industries: 24, 26, 27, 30, 31, 32, 33
Process/assembly industries: 18/19, 20, 21, 22, 23, 25, 28, 29, 34/38, 35, 36, 37

For example, high levels of subcontracting (SUBC) suggest that technologies used in an industry are diverse and nonstandardized, complicating the relation between the contractor (principal) and subcontractor (agent). The practice of subcontracting, as was noted, serves as an intermediate form of organization. This type of organization is assumed to circumvent agency problems in the market while retaining its efficiency. If the products subcontracted were easily standardized, they could be bought in the market.

Table 2.9 shows the averages of these variables for two-digit industries and industry groups: so-called light and heavy industries, materials industries, and processing/assembly industries. For example, ENER is high in materials industries and low in processing/assembly industries. These four variables seem to proxy heterogeneities in the technologies of four-digit industries, a status that may affect or explain their coefficients in the regression analysis.

DREG: Dummy for regulation

DTARSUB: DREG*TARSUB

PART: Proportion of part-time production workers

UNION: Proportion of production workers who are union members

We use DREG and DTARSUB to examine the effects of government intervention on efficiency. Large parts of Japanese industries were subject to some kind of regulation in 1978. These variables indicate regulation that in some way controls the entry of firms. Such regulation often helps preserve inefficient operation of plants and encourages collusive conduct. Nevertheless, such regulation can promote intraindustry homogeneity which increases technical efficiency. Thus DREG can be used to measure an intercept shift, and DTARSUB to measure a slope shift when industry protection and regulation coincide (note that TARSUB is expected to have a high correlation with DREG).

As Caves and Barton (1990) have reported, PART, the share of part-time workers in production, has a significant positive effect on efficiency. Caves and Barton argued that flexibility and adaptability are enhanced by the optimal use of part-time employees. Davies and Caves (1987) found that a significant part of difference of technical efficiency between the United States and the United Kingdom can be associated with differences in unionization of workers. However, the function of unions in Japan may be different from the way unions operate in these two countries. Muramatsu (1984) argued that in 1977 the fraction of union members was closely associated with net value added per employee, invoking the view of Brown and Medoff (1978) and Freeman and Medoff (1979) of the trade union as a "collective voice." However, in a comment on Muramatsu's paper, Freeman (1984) claimed that similar findings could be obtained in the United States. In Japan, however, the average value of the unionization ratio is expected to be less than 0.5, so among firms the extent of unionization varies. If unionization does contribute to productivity, technical efficiency will have a negative relationship to the extent of unionization.

TCHMSAL: Ratio of payments for technology import to sales

TCHXSAL: Ratio of receipts from technology export to sales

The effect of imported technology, or TCHMSAL, is considered to have enabled Japanese industries to attain high growth rates. Suzuki and Miyagawa (1986) reported that about 10 percent of total production of Japanese industries rested on imported technology in 1960. If these imported technologies are distributed unequally among firms according to license contracts, they can be a source of technical inefficiency.

TCHXSAL, on the other hand, is used to examine the relationship between efficiency and technological advancement. Rather than a determinant of technical efficiency, TCHXSAL deals with attained technology. Although a high rate of technological growth can be a source of inefficiency, TCHXSAL can have a positive effect on efficiency because it represents mature technology.

PCMA: Price-cost margin, all plants classified to an industry

PCML: Price-cost margin, larger plants accounting for half of industry's output

PCMS: Price-cost margin, smaller plants accounting for other half of industry's output

PCMD: (PCML − PCMS)/PCML

Dual structures have long prevailed in Japanese industries. In comparison with their large counterparts, small enterprises have suffered from low productivity, average wages, and value added per capita, mostly due to suboptimal capital–labor ratios. Despite the dual structure small enterprises have contributed substantially to Japan's rapid growth, a contribution appreciated only recently. Hence it is important to analyze the performance of small enterprises, or size-related heterogeneity of performance, in Japan.

When we examine the data on price-cost margins, the distinction between the performance levels of the large-plant and small-plant sectors is not obvious. The simple correlation coefficients and descriptive statistics are

	PCMA	PCML	PCMS
PCML	0.9872		
PCMS	0.8007	0.7086	
PCMD	0.3159	0.4358	− 0.2438

	Maximum	Minimum	Mean	Standard deviation
PCMA	0.5801	0.0745	0.2400	0.0768
PCML	0.5915	0.0706	0.2411	0.0805
PCMS	0.5592	0.0729	0.2353	0.0742
PCMD	0.6088	− 1.704	− 0.0182	0.2886

The average difference is negative and statistically insignificant ($t = 1.14$, while for the test of the hypothesis of PCML = PCMS, $t = 0.96$). The range and standard deviation of PCMD show that the difference in the price-cost margin varies enormously from industry to industry. The causes and effects of these differences are interesting problems.

One way we can use PCMD is to indicate the extent of inefficiency due to differences in large and small firms' choice of capital–labor (K/L) ratio, which is driven by different factor prices. To examine this, we calculated the differences between K/L ratios for large- and small-plant halves of industries, as well as the relation between the differences in the price-cost margins and the K/L ratios. They are not closely related and the correlation is in fact negative, though insignificant.

We can also use the information in PCMD to determine the elasticity of the industry's cost structure. When PCMD > 0, economies of scale are assumed to prevail, and when PCMD < 0, diseconomies of scale. Our objective is to find what the relationship is between these differences and the aveage level of productivity. Since the outcome for the market price level depends on an industry's competitive circumstances, and the competitiveness of its market on relative cost differences between larger and smaller production units, the question we attempt to answer is: In what case is the price level kept high and in what case is it held to a competitive price level? When PCMD > 0, the smaller units will suffer a low price-cost margin, the larger units will enjoy high margins, or both. When PCMD < 0, the results will be reversed.

The two regression equations that follow present a simple, conventional structure-performance analysis. Most of the variables have been defined already. PCMA is the dependent variable, HI measures concentration, K, RSIZ, and R&D represent barriers to entry, GRWT stands for windfall profit, IMPT and EXPT for overseas competition, ADV for product differentation, SPE4 for absence of diversification, and K/S is the ratio of capital to total shipments (to control for capital rentals included in PCMA):

$$PCMA = 0.070 + 0.154**HI + 2.224**R\&D + 0.002*GRWT$$
$$\qquad\quad (2.20) \qquad\;\; (2.34) \qquad\qquad (3.72)$$

$$+ 0.413RSIZ - 0.000K - 0.110*IMPT - 0.128*EXPT$$
$$\quad (1.30) \qquad\quad (1.50) \qquad (3.47) \qquad\qquad (3.64)$$

$$+ 1.824*ADV + 0.122*SPE4 + 0.133*K/S,$$
$$\quad (3.50) \qquad\qquad (2.81) \qquad\qquad (3.22)$$

$$\bar{R}^2 = 0.181, \quad N = 326,$$

$$PCMA = 0.060 + 0.177*HI + 2.134**R\&D + 0.001*GRWT$$
$$\qquad\quad (2.70) \qquad\;\; (2.41) \qquad\qquad (3.21)$$

$$+ 0.843*RSIZ - 0.000K - 0.134*IMPT - 0.106*EXPT$$
$$\quad (2.80) \qquad\quad\; (1.63) \qquad (4.50) \qquad\qquad (3.24)$$

$$+ 1.712*ADV + 0.128*SPE4 + 0.144*K/S + 0.093*PCMD,$$
$$\quad (3.54) \qquad\qquad (3.18) \qquad\qquad (3.74) \qquad\quad (7.07)$$

$$\bar{R}^2 = 0.291, \quad N = 326.$$

Here t-statistics appear in parentheses; * = significant in a two-tailed test at 0.01, and ** = significant in a two-tailed test at 0.05.

We will not discuss these results in detail. Except for K, most of the signs and significance levels of the coefficients agree with theory and previous studies. We have included PCMD as an explanation variable for PCMA, which takes a highly significant positive coefficient. It enlarges the correlation of the dependent variable with the set of independent variables by 11 percentage points without affecting their significance.[28]

By construction, PCMD is positively correlated with PCML and negatively correlated with PCMS. PCMD is positively correlated with the average level of the price-cost margin. That is, when the difference in price-cost margins is such that small plants have lower and large plants higher margins, the large plants enjoy high margins rather than the small plants earning suboptimal margins. For PCMD < 0, as happens not infrequently, the reverse occurs. That is, in industries whose small plants earn higher margins, the large plants' margins are somehow compressed rather than the small plants' margins being abnormal. This interpretation is supported by the descriptive statistics for PCML and PCMS, which show that the variance of PCML among industries is larger than that of PCMS.

The price-cost margins for industries subdivided by plant size cannot be determined independently of competitive conditions, so the preceding observation about the relation between PCMD and PCMA needs more theoretical analysis to be fully understood. For example, an umbrella model with an oligopolistic core and competitive fringes might explain the pattern.

What we know of the PCMA variable is important for an analysis of technical inefficiency. We know that overall profits to the industry increase with PCMD; they consist mainly of rents to larger units. However, such high values of PCMD can also make small units appear to be technically inefficient. That is, some part of the difference in margins can be explained by differences in the level of technical efficiency. As a result the relationship between the efficiency level and PCMD would be the same as that between PCMA and PCMD, and this demonstrates that in some industries a difference in margins is partly due to the variance in technical efficiency.

2.3.3 Result of Multiple Regression Analysis

The dependent variables LTF, LTE, $\hat{\sigma}_u$ (denoted SDU), and skewness (denoted SKW) are analyzed in this subsection. Because correlations between variables estimated by different methods are high, we use only the results of EWD.

First we provide an overview with the following equation which presents the result of a backward-elimination method of selecting regressors that utilized all variables introduced in subsection 2.3.2.

LTF = 0.436 + 1.38*HI − 2.45**HISQ − 0.093*PCMD − 0.279**SPE7
            (3.63)   (2.08)   (2.98)   (2.21)

    + 0.393*PRWR − 0.011*KSHI + 5.63**R&D − 0.179*MULT
     (3.96)   (3.34)   (2.51)   (3.43)

    + 0.393*TCHXSAL + 0.181**SPE4 − 0.123**ICOV
     (3.29)   (1.99)   (2.45)

    − 0.002*GRWT − 1.71ADV,
     (2.77)   (1.48)

$\bar{R}^2 = 0.511, \quad N = 108$

Every regressor that had a definite expected sign for its coefficient (HI, HISQ, KSHI, MULT, ICOV, ADV) takes the predicted sign, and most of these coefficients are significant. This estimated equation also includes the two variables R&D and MULT which require some further remarks. If R&D were to represent dynamic efficiency, this equation should be a part of a system of simultaneous equations, because ordinary least square (OLS) estimators can have biases. Similarly, because MULT can be an endogenous variable, its inclusion as a regressor would make the OLS method unsuitable.

Core Model

When there are a large number of independent variables, there can be no clear hierarchical ordering among variables. Therefore we limit our independent variables to a core group consisting of HI, HISQ, GRWT, PCMD, K, PRWR, and KSHI; these variables seem to have rather stable significance levels and little effect on other variables' coefficients. The result is

$$LTF = 0.340 + 1.59^*HI - 3.38^{**}HISQ - 0.003^*GRWT - 0.082^{**}PCMD$$
$$\quad\quad\quad (3.77) \quad\quad (2.60) \quad\quad\quad\quad (3.42) \quad\quad\quad\quad (2.49)$$

$$\quad - 0.000000068^{**}K + 0.288^*PRWR - 0.0120^*KSHI,$$
$$\quad\quad (2.48) \quad\quad\quad\quad\quad (2.93) \quad\quad\quad\quad (3.92))$$

$\bar{R}^2 = 0.346, \quad N = 116$

All of the hypotheses underlying these variables are supported by this result. Coefficients of HI and HISQ indicate that a value of HI around 0.2 maximizes efficiency, and so the inverted U-shaped relation with concentration is confirmed, consistent with both effects predicted in model analysis B. K and KSHI exhibit significant relations that are as predicted, by deterring the preservation of efficiency by means of timely replacement. GRWT reduces efficiency, consistent with a rapid growth rate making room for the survival of inefficient plants.

PCMD has a negative association with the level of efficiency. The cases of positive PCMD, which means that PCML > PCMS, include three possible situations: PCML is high, PCMS is low, or both conditions

Table 2.10
Correlations and other descriptive statistics of efficiency (LTF) in small and large
establishments, and related variables

| | Variables | | | | |
Measure	LTF	LTFL	LTFS	PCMD	PCMA
LTF	1.0000	0.6718	0.7909	−0.1963	0.1892
LTFL		1.0000	0.4694	−0.0528	0.0287
LTFS			1.0000	−0.1318	−0.0986
PCMD				1.0000	0.3159
PCMA					1.0000
Maximum	1.0000	0.9708	0.9110	0.6088	0.5801
Minimum	0.4295	0.4633	0.4654	−1.7040	0.0745
Mean	0.6407	0.6578	0.6599	−0.0182	0.2400
Standard deviation	0.0988	0.0852	0.1055	0.2886	0.0768
Number	113	86	59	346	346

prevail. The positive association between PCMD and PCMA observed in
the last section rules out the second case, so the price-cost margin of large
plants should be high. The negative association between efficiency and
PCMD implies that the relatively high performance of large plants is not
due to a high efficiency level. On the contrary, even when the inefficiency
level rises large plants are able to preserve their high price-cost margin, as
is indicated by the positive relation between PCMA and PCMD. Direct
estimation of the inefficiency level by plant size could help in the identification of this mechanism. However, there are only a small number of industries that contain enough plants and that can avoid both type I and type
II failures. Table 2.10 offers some relevant statistics. The two variables in
the table which we have not yet defined are

LTFL = adjusted Lee-Tyler estimator of average efficiency for
large-plant sector of industry,

LTFS = adjusted Lee-Tyler estimator of average efficiency for
small-plant sector of industry.

In the table the weak negative correlation between LTFS and PCMD
implies that in some industries technical inefficiency depresses the productivity of small-plant industries. It also contributes to the difference in
price-cost margins, the third possibility in the relation between PCMA and
PCMD. However, this possibility is ambiguous. As noted previously, from

the relation between PCMD and PCMA we can deduce only that a positive PCMD is due to high value of PCML. At this stage we conjecture, but cannot determine, that positive PCMD is associated with a low value of PCMS, so we need more information to determine the level of PCMS (see chapter 10 in this book for a further analysis).

Another possibility inferred from the relationship of PCMD with PCMA and LTF is that, when large plants have the advantage in productivity, the overall price-cost margin can be set high, making room for inefficiency. When the large plants lose their advantage, their industry's price-cost margin becomes low. Therefore close competition between large and small plants enforces a high level of efficiency.

PRWR's positive association with LTF is the expected direction. However, as was noted previously, this relationship should be examined again with the other variables, SUBC, ENER, and SPE7.

Competitive Conditions

Table 2.11 shows the results of adding other variables to the core model, including those that describe competitive conditions. The effect of imports is negative and significant contrary to expectation (equation 1, 3). One reason is that because the concentration index HI is not adjusted for import share, HI is overestimated in industries in which imported goods have large shares. The estimated value of HI that maximizes efficiency according to the core model is 0.234, which is larger than the average value of HI. Therefore in those industries the effect of HI is also overestimated, and IMPT has a negative sign to adjust this bias. Another reason is that IMPT and TARF, or IMPT and TARSUB are highly correlated. ρ(IMPT, TARF) = 0.372, and ρ(IMPT, TARSUB) = 0.378, where ρ is simple correlation coefficient. This indicates a clear intention to protect by means of a tariff. TARF and TARSUB have strong negative associations with efficiency (equations 4, 6). Thus the positive effect of IMPT on efficiency, if it exists, can be biased by a negative effect running through tariff protection, which deteriorates efficiency. Therefore, when IMPT is accompanied with TARSUB in equation 7, the negative association becomes insignificant. Overseas competition represented by EXPT has a positive but insignificant effect on efficiency.

TARF has an independent, negative, significant effect on efficiency (equation 4); SUBT also has a negative effect, but it is not significant (equation 5). The combined effects of protection deter efficiency as ex-

Table 2.11
Regression analysis of determinants of interindustry differences in technical efficiency: additions to core model

Equation number	Equation	R^2	$\bar{R}^2$	Degrees of Freedom
1	−0.199**IMPT (2.56)	0.400	0.354	112
2	+0.094EXPT (1.51)	0.376	0.328	112
3	−0.198**IMPT + 0.091EXPT (2.56) (1.52)	0.414	0.362	112
4	−0.614*TARF (3.09)	0.422	0.378	114
5	−0.375SUBT (0.875)	0.390	0.344	116
6	−0.491*TARSUB (2.94)	0.417	0.373	114
7	−0.120IMPT − 0.459**TARSUB (1.46) (2.54)	0.437	0.386	111
8	+0.00105VIO (0.214)	0.386	0.340	116
9	0.333 + 1.54*HI − 3.28**HISQ (3.67) (2.52) −0.003*GRWT − 0.083**PCMD (3.36) (2.50) +0.297*PRWR − 0.011*KSHI (3.01) (3.71) −0.000000007**TYPK (2.27)	0.380	0.340	116
10	−0.969RSIZ (1.33)	0.395	0.350	116
11	−0.006**PRGM (2.06)	0.409	0.365	116
12	+5.42**R&D (2.34)	0.409	0.364	113
13	−0.957GRVC (0.93)	0.378	0.329	111
14	−1.39ADV (1.16)	0.386	0.339	116
15	+7.29*R&D − 2.70**ADV (3.00) (2.18)	0.436	0.386	113
16	−0.123**ICOV (2.44)	0.376	0.328	112
17	−0.109SPE4 (1.37)	0.422	0.377	111

Table 2.11 (continued)

Equation number	Equation	R^2	$\bar{R}^2$	Degrees of Freedom
18	−0.305**SPE7 (2.59)	0.422	0.379	116
19	−0.142**MULT (2.11)	0.410	0.366	116
20	+0.112SUBC (1.42)	0.397	0.352	116
21	+0.155**ENER (2.00)	0.408	0.363	116
22	−0.321*SPE7 + 0.168**ENER (2.78) (2.23)	0.448	0.401	116
23	−0.049**DREG (2.42)	0.417	0.374	116
24	−0.334**DTARSUB (2.14)	0.396	0.350	114
25	−0.226PART (0.360)	0.386	0.340	116
26	−0.0000006UNION (0.135)	0.386	0.340	116
27	+0.152*TCIMPT (3.25)	0.441	0.399	116
28	+0.302**TCEXPT (2.38)	0.416	0.373	116
29	+0.224TCEXPT + 0.133*TCIMPT (1.77) (2.80)	0.457	0.411	116
30	+0.122**TCIMPT + 3.82R&D (2.49) (1.63)	0.443	0.394	113
31	+0.346*TCEXPT + 6.12*R&D (2.80) (2.71)	0.451	0.403	113

Note: Variables of the core model (intercept, HI, HISQ, GRWT, K, PCMD, PRWR, KSHI) were included in each equation but not reported. The t-statistics appear in parentheses. Significance levels are * = 1 percent in the two-tailed test, and ** = 5 percent in the two-tailed test.

pected, but these effects stem mainly from the tariff (compare the results of equations 4, 6). VIO does not show a definite effect on efficiency (equation 8). Probably this is due to the insufficient capacity of VIO to represent collusive activity within industries.

Size of Assets

K and KSHI appear in the core model as indexes of the cost of replacement. Their correlation is surprisingly low: $\rho(K, KSHI) = -0.0438$. It indicates there is no relation between the absolute value of assets per plant and indivisibility, so K and KSHI can play independent roles as proxies of replacement cost and indivisibility. TYPK has so high a correlation with K that there is no difference between estimated equations that use K or TYPK (equation 9).

Caves and Barton (1990) have shown that in the United States, RSIZ has a positive and very significant correlation with efficiency. In Japan this relation is negative but not significant (equation 10). Because PCMD, which represents the relative profitability of large-plant sectors of industries, and K have roles similar to RSIZ, the presence of PCMD and K may affect the significance of the coefficient of RSIZ. However, even if we exclude PCMD or both PCMD and K, the sign of coefficient of RSIZ does not change, as indicated in following estimated equations:

LTF = 0.308 + 1.79*HI − 3.82*HISQ − 0.003*GRWT
           (4.12)   (2.85)   (3.48)

         − 0.000000058**K + 0.333*PRWR
           (2.04)   (3.35)

         − 0.0010*KSHI − 0.907RSIZ,
           (3.17)   (1.22)

$\bar{R}^2 = 0.318,\quad N = 116,$

LTF = 0.305 + 1.64*HI − 3.41**HISQ − 0.003*GRWT
           (3.78)   (2.54)   (3.16)

         + 0.340*PRWR − 0.0099*KSHI − 1.15RSIZ,
           (3.37)   (2.95)   (1.54)

$\bar{R}^2 = 0.298,\quad N = 116.$

The different results for the United States and Japan imply different effects of the large plants on technical efficiency.

Productivity Growth and Growth of Demand

PRGM's negative association with efficiency is as expected (equation 11). On the other hand, R&D's positive association indicates that R&D plays a different role from PRGM although they are both indexes of dynamic efficiency (equation 12). Contrary to our expectation, the correlation of these variables is not positive: $\rho(\text{PRGM, R\&D}) = -0.3350$. R&D's positive association can be interpreted as consistent with its role of pre-serving the maximum efficiency. The role of R&D will be analyzed further in the next section by the method of simultaneous equations.

GRWT has been shown to have negative association with efficiency. GRVC's coefficient is negative as expected but not significant (equation 13). This is due to multicollinearity between GRWT and GRVC, that is, $\rho(\text{GRWT, GRVC}) = 0.5367$, although GRVC is the coefficient of variation. Therefore in the regression equations GRWT also has no significance (t-statistic is -1.71). When their effect is combined with the GRWT * GRVC variable, the coefficient is significant but not superior to the core equation:

$$\text{LTF} = 0.312 + 1.66\text{*HI} - 3.68\text{*HISQ} + 0.293\text{*PRWR} - 0.0126\text{*KSHI}$$
$$\phantom{\text{LTF} = 0.312 + }(3.79)\phantom{+ 1.66\text{*HI}}(2.73)\phantom{- 3.68\text{*H}}(2.86)\phantom{+ 0.293\text{*PR}}(3.37)$$

$$- 0.000\text{K} - 0.76\text{**PCMD} - 0.03\text{**GRWT} * \text{GRVC},$$
$$(1.42)(2.14)\phantom{- 0.03\text{**GR}}(2.13)$$

$\bar{R}^2 = 0.298, \quad N = 111.$

Advertisement and Diversification

ADV has a negative coefficient as implied by the product differentiation hypothesis, but it is not significant (equation 14). When R&D is also included in the model (equation 15), the coefficient of ADV is both negative and significant. However, its negative significance could be due to a simul-taneous equations bias, since R&D can be affected by technical efficiency. When an instrumental-variables method is employed, ADV is no longer significant. This effect of ADV will be reexamined in the next section.

So-called inbound diversification measured by ICOV has a negative and significant coefficient (equation 16), and this supports the hypothesis based on the effect of interindustrial competition. However, SPE4 does not show the same sign as in the stepwise regression, and the coefficient is insignificant (equation 17). On the other hand, SPE7 has a negative, significant coefficient that agrees with the stepwise regression result (equation 18). Considering the sign of the SPE7 effect, this variable could serve as an index of heterogeneity in a four-digit industry. When SPE7 is high, the industry should be subdivided into narrower industries. SPE4's negative effect on efficiency could be caused by SPE4's close association with SPE7, $\rho(\text{SPE4, SPE7}) = 0.6215$. SPE4's effect on efficiency will be examined in next section.

Multiplant Operation, Subcontracting, and Intensive Energy Usage

As was mentioned earlier, MULT can impair the regression result because it is highly correlated with variable K that is, $\rho(\text{MULT, K}) = 0.304$. It nevertheless has a significant, negative coefficient, which is consistent with model analysis A (equation 19), and as a result the t-statistic of K's coefficient drops. Because the coefficient of MULT may be sensitive to application of the simultaneous equations method, discussion of its properties will be deferred to the next section.

SUBC's relationship with LTF is positive, which is consistent with our earlier hypothesis, but insignificant (equation 20). ENER has a positive, significant coefficient (equation 21), and this illustrates that even when the shocks caused by the energy crisis have not fully abated, the affected industries showed relatively high efficiency. Partly this effect can be explained by the hypothesis stated earlier, and partly it could be due to the enormous cost of adjusting to the energy-price increase.

SPE7, SUBC, and ENER's coefficients should be examined as to whether their relationship can be explained by the hypothesis or whether it can be explained by the difference in the fundamental properties of the industries, as was argued in the last section. If SPE7's negative association stems from this effect, coefficients of PRWR and SPE7 should have the same sign, since they are both high in heavy or process/assembly industries. If both variables are included in a regression equation, a multicollinearity problem could arise but does not: in equation 22 their signs are opposite, and no problem from multicollinearity would be detected. Since SUBC takes a high value in heavy or process/assembly industries while ENER is high in light or material industries, if SUBC and ENER reflect only the difference in the technology used, they would take opposite signs. However, in our case they have the same sign.

Intervention by Government and Labor Relations

DREG has a negative, significant effect on efficiency (equation 23), and this effect is viewed as an intercept shift; it does not strengthen the effect of government protection of industries (compare equations 6 and 24). Industries that are regulated seem similar to those being protected, for ρ(DREG, TARSUB) = 0.5799. Thus the effect of DREG is the same as that of protection, and there may be a bias in the coefficient of DREG.

Neither PART nor UNION has a significant effect on efficiency (equations 25, 26), unlike the case of the United States. Both variables lack any significant correlation with the core model, which implies that there is no influence from multicollinearity. This result could be due to the homogeneity of Japanese labor compared to that of the United States.

Trade of Technology

TCHMSAL does not have the expected negative sign but a positive and significant association with the level of efficiency (equation 27). One explanation is that imported technology is relatively mature and standardized. Using imported, mature technology would mitigate heterogeneity in an industry. Prior to 1977 annual payments for new programs of technology imports had not been increasing. Moreover their ratio to total payment for technology imports in manufacturing industries was only 7.5 percent in 1977.[29] The following data show the trends in total industry payments and payments for new programs (million yen):

Year	Total	New programs
1971	134,543	15,642
1972	173,916	14,462
1973	173,309	19,522
1974	159,832	14,635
1975	169,131	13,300
1976	177,302	17,860
1977	190,066	16,888
1978	192,058	38,183
1979	240,984	26,808
1980	239,529	27,675
1981	259,632	24,911
1982	282,613	44,439

Another possible explanation involves the effect of R&D. R&D efforts have a positive effect on efficiency in Japan, and technology imports may require complementary R&D efforts.[30] Until early in the 1970s total R&D expenditure and payments for technology imports were highly correlated. In our data set the correlation between R&D and TCHMSAL also is positive: 0.3516 in over all Japanese industries ($n = 349$), and 0.3216 in industries for which the LTF index is available ($n = 113$). They confirm a complementary relationship between R&D and technology imports. Comparison of equations 27 and 30 suggest that some part of the effect of TCHMSAL may be explained by high R&D effort to catch up to the technology frontier.

TCHXSAL also has positive association with efficiency. R&D and TCHXSAL are uncorrelated: -0.0354 for all 349 industries, and -0.1268 for 113 industries with LTF estimated. Technology exports are related not to the current technology flow but to the stock of knowledge.[31] A large stock of knowledge could already have diffused or spilled to most domestic firms, leading to heightened efficiency.

Other Indexes of Efficiency as Alternative Measures

Table 2.12 gives the results of core regression models in which the dependent variable was replaced by unadjusted LTE, SDU, SDV, SKW, and λ. Replacing LTF by LTE, we found that the explanation power of the regression equations declines by more than one-half, and that the t-values diminish as well,[32] but the signs of the coefficients remained the same.

SDU is not a function of $\hat{\sigma}_u$ but of the σ_u estimator. Because LTE is a monotonically decreasing function of σ_u, the choice between them makes no difference in principle. Note that the σ_u estimator is an index of inefficiency, so the signs of the regression coefficients are reversed. Its adjusted $\bar{R}^2$ is slightly higher but without substantial difference.

When skewness and λ are employed as dependent variables, they show no significant regression coefficients and can be considered failures (R^2 values are low). In Japanese industries the symmetrical error term σ_v is low relative to the σ_u estimator, and skewness and λ are functions of the ratio of these estimators (σ_u/σ_v). The low value of σ_v and its variability can make the skewness estimator very noisy and also obscure the relationship between skewness (or λ) and structural factors.[33]

The number of industries that can be used in an analysis of LTF is about 110, which is small compared to the maximum number available (352).

Table 2.12
Effects of alternative dependent variables on interindustry differences in technical efficiency

Equation	R^2	$\bar{R}^2$	Degrees of Freedom
LTE = 0.434 + 0.795**HI − 1.91HISQ − 0.0003GRWT	0.169	0.125	138
(2.01) (1.54) (0.343)			
− 0.055PCMD + 0.269*PRWR			
(1.70) (2.82)			
− 0.006KSHI − 0.000000004**K			
(1.81) (2.05)			
SDU = 1.164 − 2.24**HI + 5.15HISQ + 0.002GRWT	0.170	0.128	146
(2.32) (1.70) (0.948)			
+ 0.119PCMD − 0.630PRWR			
(1.51) (2.74)			
+ 0.010KSHI + 0.000000013*K			
(1.41) (2.71)			
SKW = −0.410 + 6.87**HI − 14.0HISQ + 0.0067GRWT	0.046	0.026	340
(2.53) (1.85) (0.960)			
− 0.116PCMD − 0.927PRWR			
(0.56) (1.35)			
+ 0.019KSHI − 0.000000003K			
(0.824) (0.578)			
λ = −5.06 − 93.8HI + 204HISQ + 0.048GRWT	0.100	0.054	146
(1.05) (0.73) (0.239)			
− 0.840PCMD + 12.2PRWR			
(0.116) (0.575)			
− 1.61**KSHI + 0.0000013*K			
(2.38) (2.92)			
EXSDU = 0.75 − 4.78**HI + 9.19HISQ − 0.0038GRWT	0.047	0.027	340
(2.87) (1.87) (0.886)			
+ 0.063PCMD − 0.060PRWR			
(0.493) (0.143)			
+ 0.003KSHI − 0.000000002K			
(0.275) (0.578)			
EXLTE = 0.80 + 3.22*HI − 5.98HISQ + 0.002GRWT	0.052	0.032	340
(2.95) (1.85) (0.633)			
− 0.026PCMD − 0.205PRWR			
(0.321) (0.739)			
+ 0.002KSHI + 0.000000008K			
(0.197) (0.441)			

Note: Significance levels are * = 1 percent in the two-tailed test, and ** = 5 percent in the two-tailed test.

Thus the results pertain only to industries whose technical inefficiency levels are measurable by composed error with half-normally distributed inefficiency. We could have tried another strategy such as that mentioned in the previous section where we expanded the definition of the estimator mathematically to cover the range of type I or type II failures. However, that would have complicated the regression analysis. The problem is the discontinuity in the transformation from the third moment to the σ_u estimator at skewness $= 0$. Table 2.13 shows the distribution of these extended σ_u estimators and LTE. The discontinuities in the distributions occur at $\sigma_u = 0$ and LTF $= 1.0$. EXSDU and EXLTE in table 2.12 gave the result of these regressions. EXSDU is a index of the extended σ_u estimator, which we calculated from the same source ignoring the restriction $\hat{\sigma}_v^2 \geq 0$; EXLTE is the index transferred from EXSDU by the same procedure from σ_u to LTE. In this case no variable exerts a significant influence on the extended estimator.

2.3.4 A Simultaneous Equations Analysis

When simultaneous equations are used to model industrial organization, the usual procedure is to consider some structural factors as endogenous. Concentration ratios and advertising intensities are often treated as endogenous. A fuller treatment would make the model too large to handle. In our study the number of observable truly exogenous variables was so limited that it was difficult for us to maintain enough instrumental variables. The simultaneous equations model we developed is small as a result of this. We limited it to an analysis of the relation between static and dynamic efficiency. For static efficiency, we included LTF and PCMA (price-cost margin), and for dynamic efficiency R&D. These are all endogenous variables. MULT was included as an endogenous variable that influences LTF. The model is

$$\text{LTF} = f_1(\text{R\&D, MULT, HI, HISQ, GRWT, PCMD, PRWR, KSHI,} $$
$$\text{ICOV, SPE4, SPE7, TCHXSAL, TARSUB, ADV}),$$

$$\text{MULT} = f_2(\text{HI, GRWT, K, SPE4}),$$

$$\text{PCMA} = f_3(\text{LTF, R\&D, } K/S, \text{ HI, GRWT, K, SUBC, PCMD, RSIZ,}$$
$$\text{ADV, VIO, SPE4, IMPT, EXPT}),$$

$$\text{R\&D} = f_4(\text{LTF, PCMA, HI, HISQ, SPE7, EXPT, TCHMSAL}).$$

Table 2.13
Distributions of extended estimators of σ_u and LTF

Range	Value of extended σ_u estimator	Range	Value of extended LTF
−0.9−−0.8	2	2.3−2.4	1
−0.8−−0.7	6	2.2−2.3	1
−0.7−−0.6	6	2.1−2.2	3
−0.6−−0.5	19	2.0−2.1	1
−0.5−−0.4	19	1.9−2.0	4
−0.4−−0.3	18	1.8−1.9	3
−0.3−−0.2	14	1.7−1.8	4
−0.2−−0.1	4	1.6−1.7	14
−0.1−0.0	1	1.5−1.6	8
0.0−0.1	1	1.4−1.5	15
0.1−0.2	4	1.3−1.4	16
0.2−0.3	10	1.2−1.3	14
0.3−0.4	21	1.1−1.2	4
0.4−0.5	24	1.0−1.1	1
0.5−0.6	21	0.9−1.0	4
0.6−0.7	34	0.8−0.9	11
0.7−0.8	24	0.7−0.8	45
0.8−0.9	28	0.6−0.7	69
0.9−1.0	20	0.5−0.6	74
1.0−1.1	16	0.4−0.5	28
1.1−1.2	8	0.3−0.4	21
1.2−1.3	9		
1.3−1.4	7		
1.4−1.5	3		
1.5−1.6	3		
1.6−1.7	5		
1.7−1.8	5		
1.8−1.9	3		
1.9−2.0	1		
2.0−2.1	4		
2.1−2.2	0		
2.2−2.3	1		

We use the same model to determine the level of LTF as we did in the last section, that is, a core equation with some additional variables. However, we exclude K because it was shown to affect efficiency through the vintage effect in multiplant operation. We keep KSHI because its effect on efficiency is through indivisibility of assets which does not involve multiplant operation. In our ordinary least squares analysis R&D affected the LTF estimator positively, and MULT affected it negatively.

MULT is defined by HI and K according to model analysis B. In this case MULT is a monotonically increasing function of HI (we neglect the result of the lumpy asset case of model analysis B). GRWT can affect multiplant operation because, when demand exceeds the anticipated rate, older plants need to be kept in operation. Diversification which is represented by SPE4 can be a cause of multiplant operation. Therefore GRWT is expected to have a positive coefficient, and SPE4 a negative one.

The level of technical efficiency affects the price-cost margin, because differences in the distribution of productivity in an industry bring about different supply structures. The heterogeneity of the supply structure affects the competitive process and the market outcome. But in which direction is the correlation between these two indexes of static efficiency? Intuitively a high level of efficiency suggests high level of performance. However, this situation can only occur when the equilibrium output and prices are the same for different levels of technical efficiency. In general, the relation between the efficiency level and market output is not fixed; it depends on the competitive circumstances of the market. Suppose, for example, that markets have the same demand structures but different technical efficiency levels. In circumstances where the competitive condition ensures that the marginal suppliers' performance level is the same in the two equilibria, lower technical efficiency corresponds to higher productivity at the frontier. Thus the average price-cost margin can be higher in an industry with low technical efficiency.

A simple market model can further explain this situation. Consider a market whose demand structure is expressed by an inverse demand function $p = p_0 - aQ$, where p indicates price, Q quantity, and p_0 and a are constants. The supply structure is assumed to be $c = c_0 + kQ$, where c is the marginal suppliers' cost, and c_0 and k are constants. In this model suppliers are atomistically small, and their production costs are uniformly distributed along the supply function. The aggregate supply is provided by decreasingly efficient suppliers at the margin. In the context of technical efficiency, c_0 expresses the position of the frontier and k indicates the level of inefficiency. The greater k is, the greater the inefficiency is.

When suppliers act as a cartel, the market equilibrium is reached when $p_0 - 2aQ = c_0 + kQ$, which corresponds to $MR = MC$ in textbook model of monopoly. In equilibrium $p*$ and $Q*$ are denoted the price and supply, so $p* = p_0 - a[(p_0 - c_0)/(k + 2a)]$, $Q* = [(p_0 - c_0)/(k + 2a)]$. The price-cost margin is

$$\frac{\int_0^{Q*} [p* - (c_0 + kQ)]\, dQ}{p*Q*} = \frac{p_0 - c_0}{2[p_0 - a(p_0 - c_0)/(k + 2a)]}$$

It should be noted that the price-cost margin defined in this model is somewhat different from Lerner's index of concentration. Since every firm's cost is different, it is difficult to determine marginal cost. The price-cost margin in this model is calculated as the average margin, and it corresponds to the definition of the variable PCMA. In the preceding equation the price-cost margin at equilibrium is a decreasing function of k. This means that the more efficient the supply condition, the larger is the price-cost margin.

Consider now a market where competition prevails and products are supplied until the marginal supplier's cost is equal to the market price: $p_0 - aQ = c_0 + kQ$, which corresponds to $P = MC$. Then $p* = p_0 - a[(p_0 - c_0)/(k + a)]$, and $Q* = [(p_0 - c_0)/(k + a)]$. The price-cost margin is

$$\frac{1}{2} - \frac{c_0}{2[p_0 - a(p_0 - c_0)/(k + a)]},$$

which is an increasing function of k. In this case the more technically efficient the market is, the smaller is the price-cost margin.

Under competitive market circumstances differences in productivity among firms are necessary for the price-cost margins to be positive. If all firms were identical and atomistic, their prices could not exceed their uniform cost level. Therefore, when the level of technical efficiency is high, the price-cost margin is correspondingly low, because rents to firms with high performance are transferred to consumers. On the other hand, when the market is monopolistic or collusive, a larger part of rents due to high efficiency is retained by the suppliers, and the part transferred to consumers is rather small, so that higher efficiency directly corresponds to higher margins. The outcome runs in opposite directions depending on the competitiveness of the market. Because of this we cannot determine the sign of the coefficient of LTF on PCMA before hand.

The effect of R&D on PCMA is somewhat controversial. For Japanese industries many researchers have pointed out that barriers to entry have resulted from the hoarding of imported technology through licensing and company-financed research, especially in periods of high growth. Therefore in Japan R&D can be viewed as an important anticompetitive factor. In this sense R&D has a positive influence on PCMA.

Other determinants of PCMA need no elaboration. K is in some respect a barrier to entry. RSIZ, as a proxy for the ratio of minimum efficient plant scale to market size, is also barrier to entry. Intensive subcontracting suggests "don't make but buy," so this variable would affect PCMA negatively.

R&D in turn is affected by both indexes of static efficiency. By supplying ample funds, high PCMA opens up the opportunity of investing in R&D. There is, however, no ex ante information to determine the effect of LTF. Static efficiency in firms could coincide with the initiative to undertake R&D, or technological growth might emerge in more chaotic circumstances because of greater need for improvement.

HI and HISQ are the market-structure factors determining R&D in this study. In Japan the Galbraith-Schumpeter hypothesis has received much attention in research. Uekusa (1973) reported quadratic or cubic relationships between the firm size and R&D intensity, implying that the relationship between concentration and R&D intensity could not be linear. In this study we utilize a quadratic form of this relationship.

The relationship between EXPT and R&D can run from EXPT to R&D, and vice versa. Competitiveness in world product markets is to some extent determined endogenously and may depend on R&D outlays. Nevertheless, it is difficult to explain competitiveness in overseas markets of products, so the relationship between R&D and EXPT should be regarded as causally ambiguous. As argued in the last section, technology imports call forth complementary R&D efforts, indicating a positive coefficient for TCHMSAL. SPE7 is included in this equation because diversification encourages R&D, indicating a negative coefficient.

The equations estimated by 2SLS (two-stage least squares) are

$$LTF = 0.481 + 2.84R\&D - 0.279MULT + 1.54HI - 2.77HISQ$$
$$(0.54) \quad (2.80) \quad (3.58) \quad (2.08)$$

$$- 0.002GRWT - 0.335SPE7 - 0.088PCMD + 0.425PRWR$$
$$(2.63) \quad (2.42) \quad (2.66) \quad (3.47)$$

$$- 0.010KSHI - 0.286TARSUB - 0.103ICOV + 0.207SPE4$$
$$(2.69) \quad (1.32) \quad (1.85) \quad (2.07)$$

$$+ 0.331TCHXSAL - 0.812ADV,$$
$$(2.55) \quad (0.53)$$

$$MULT = 0.191 + 0.327HI + 0.001GRWT + 0.140SPE4 + 0.00000003K,$$
$$(1.60) \quad (1.06) \quad (1.27) \quad (6.99)$$

$$PCMA = -0.127 - 0.961R\&D + 0.213LTF - 0.060HI + 0.001GRWT$$
$$(0.36) \quad (2.36) \quad (0.61) \quad (1.33)$$

$$+ 1.95RSIZ - 0.058SUBC - 0.001VIO + 0.131PCMD$$
$$(3.53) \quad (1.00) \quad (0.38) \quad (5.57)$$

$$- 0.148IMPT - 0.017EXPT + 1.76ADV + 0.157SPE4$$
$$(2.88) \quad (0.29) \quad (2.00) \quad (2.87)$$

$$+ 0.296K/S + 0.000000001K,$$
$$(5.41) \quad (0.72)$$

$$R\&D = 0.021 - 0.007PCMA - 0.008LTF + 0.053HI - 0.155HISQ$$
$$(0.98) \quad (1.54) \quad (3.02) \quad (2.96)$$

$$- 0.011SPE7 + 0.015EXPT + 0.003TCHMSAL.$$
$$(2.73) \quad (5.50) \quad (1.45)$$

Although in the preceding ordinary least squares analysis LTF is affected positively by R&D, the relationship now loses its significance. MULT significantly diminishes efficiency, as expected. For other core variables the results are little changed. TARSUB and ICOV have lost their significance. ADV's negative coefficient is quite insignificant, and so its significance in equation 15 of table 2.11 could come from a simultaneous equations bias through R&D. On the other hand SPE4 shows the positive significant coefficient predicted by the hypothesis of overdiversification.

The expected positive effect of HI on MULT is insignificant, and the same holds for GRWT. K strongly increases MULT, but SPE4's positive association is unexpected. It could be due to a misdefinition of SPE4, which is an index of specialization of plants, not firms (no index of specialization of firms was available).

Technical efficiency enlarges the price-cost margin, consistent with monopolistic conduct prevailing in the market and precluding the transfer of efficiency increases to consumers. R&D's effect on PCMA is negative but not significant, and HI loses its explanatory power. Compared to the equation estimated to illustrate the relationship between PCMA and PCMD, this equation seems to correct the overestimation of the role of R&D or HI. However, that is doubtful because the sample is restricted to those industries whose level of the technical inefficiency is explained by composed error with half-normally distributed inefficiency. These number only 106, about one-third of the observations in the previous regression. If that specification is estimated for the present sample, we obtain

$$PCMA = -0.041 + 0.034HI + 2.557R\&D + 0.0002GRWT$$
$$\qquad\qquad (0.336) \quad (1.32) \qquad\quad (0.327)$$

$$+ 2.026RSIZ - 0.000K + 0.103PCMD - 1.182IMPT$$
$$\quad (3.27) \qquad\quad (0.034) \quad (4.14) \qquad\quad (3.25)$$

$$- 0.067EXPT + 0.929ADV + 0.191SPE4 + 0.338K/S.$$
$$\quad (1.35) \qquad\quad (1.04) \qquad\quad (3.21) \qquad\quad (5.50)$$

The reduced sample is a sufficient explanation for the loss of significance by R&D and HI.

RSIZ becomes significant, whereas K loses significance. SUBC takes the expected sign but is not significant. PCMD again shows a positive association with PCMA, as does ADV. Foreign competition can have a more severe effect on the price-cost margin in the domestic market through imports than on exports in overseas markets. A positive coefficient of SPE4 could indicate overdiversification.

PCMA shows no significant effect on R&D intensity, which in this case does not depend on current performance. LTF has a negative but insignificant relationship with R&D, despite the positive simple correlation coefficient between these variables, 0.235 for 108 industries. In Japan relatively inefficient industries can be heterogeneous with active R&D. The effect of concentration on R&D activity takes an inverted U-shape whose peak occurs at about 0.25, interestingly similar to the relationship between LTF and HI, although R&D and LTF are unrelated. The negative coefficient of SPE7 suggests that diversification fosters R&D activity. The export ratio strongly increases R&D intensity, while the import ratio has no effect.

2.4 Summary

We have examined the properties of estimators of technical efficiency for Japanese manufacturing industries. We started with the corrected ordinary least square (COLS) estimator which we found to be robust even when translog production functions were employed, though its efficiency was somewhat impaired, mainly due to difficulties in estimating the third moment of residuals. Very often in our estimates we observed type I failures, in which the skewness of deviations from production frontier is positive and cannot be predicted from composed error term assumption, and type II failures, in which skewness is too large in the negative direction. These failures were shown to cause biases in the estimators, though under certain conditions these biases could be adjusted. We have set aside as a future task to devise an estimator by a method that uses information about the restriction of the feasible range of estimators.

Using an adjusted estimator of σ_u, we have obtained a low value of 64 percent for average efficiency in Japanese manufacturing industries. This is lower than the average value of the Lee-Tyler estimator of average efficiency which is about 70 percent. However, these values do not prove that Japanese industries waste about one-third of their resources. Some of this inefficiency is inevitable because, even if firms make optimal investment decisions, they must cope with old and inefficient plants which are still in operation alongside new and efficient plants. Inefficiency that can be explained by a vintage model is about 10 percent in Japan. Not all of this 10 percent is inevitable, however. Monopolistic power can deter firms from making renewal investments, and this depresses efficiency. In general, the vintage model presented in this chapter predicts an inverted U-shaped relation of efficiency to concentration. When the market is oligopolistic, increases in competitive pressure force firms to hasten replacement investment, which improves efficiency. On the other hand, when the market is atomistic and indivisibility of investments deters firms from preserving currently efficient technology, efficiency may increase with concentration. However, the relationship between the level of efficiency and welfare is ambiguous.

This and other hypotheses about the determination of the level of technical efficiency are tested for Japanese manufacturing industries. The inverted U-shaped relation of efficiency to concentration ratio proved to be highly robust. Other factors thought to retard investment, proxies for the fixed part of investment cost, in fact decrease technical efficiency. Efficient productivity is sacrificed when there is accelerated growth of demand, or accelerated technological progress, for inefficient plants must be made to accommodate production. Multiplant operation and diversification decrease efficiency. Overseas competition has no effect on efficiency, but tariff protection depresses it. Using the method of ordinary least squares we also found R&D effort to raise efficiency, but in the simultaneous equations model we found no relationship.

This chapter has yielded only limited conclusions about the relative efficiency of large and small plants. When the large-plant sector of an industry earns higher price-cost margins than the small-plant sector, the difference is not due to high technical efficiency in large plants. However, we cannot tell whether it is due to low efficiency level of the small-plant sector. On the other hand, the simultaneous equations model indicates that technical efficiency increases price-cost margins, implying that savings in production cost due to high efficiency are not transferred to consumers through lower prices.

2.5 Appendix A: Data on Individual Establishments

The source of data was on individual establishments was the 1978 Census of Manufactures. The establishments investigated were those employing no less than 30 workers. Four-digit industries were taken as the basis for cross-sectional analysis. Variables were defined as follows:

VA = shipments − (total material costs − increments in inventories of materials and fuel − increments in inventories of work in progress).

K = initial tangible fixed assets + (acquisition of tangible fixed assets − removal of tangible fixed assets − depreciation of tangible fixed assets)/ 2 + (initial total inventory + final total inventory)/2.

L = total compensation for workers.

Z_1 = number of production workers/total employees.

Z_2 = (fuel cost + electricity cost)/total materials costs.

Z_3 = (initial total inventory + final total inventory)/2/K.

Z_4 = shipment of the largest seven-digit product/shipments.

Z_5 = payments for subcontracting work/total materials costs.

2.6 Appendix B: Proof of Negative Relationship between Technical Efficiency and Number of Firms in Cournot-Nash Competition

In this appendix we provide a proof for the proposition that the solution of σ_u^N in equations (15),

$$aq^N(N + 1) + \frac{c_0 \sigma_u^N}{2} = p_1 - c_0, \tag{B1}$$

$$\sigma_u^N = \frac{4aq^N}{p_1 - (N - 1)q^N - c_0} \sqrt{\frac{\alpha c}{c_0 \pi}}, \tag{B2}$$

decreases as N increases. First, we define q^0 and q^1 as the solutions of

$$aq^0(N + 2) + \frac{c_0 \sigma_u^N}{2} = p_1 - c_0, \tag{B3}$$

$$\sigma_u^N = \frac{4aq^1}{p_1 - aNq^1 - c_0} \sqrt{\frac{\alpha c}{c_0 \pi}}. \tag{B4}$$

Here σ_u^N is the solution of (B1) and (B2). From (B1) and (B3),

$$q^N(N + 1) = q^0(N + 2).$$

Therefore

$$q^0 = \frac{N + 1}{N + 2} q^N. \tag{B5}$$

On the other hand, from (B2) and (B4),

$$\frac{4aq^N}{p_1 - a(N - 1)q^N - c_0} = \frac{4aq^1}{p_1 - aNq^1 - c_0}.$$

From this we get

$$q^1 = \frac{(p_1 - c_0)q^N}{p_1 - c_0 + aq^N}.$$ (B6)

By (B1), (B5), and (B6),

$$q^1 = \frac{p_1 - c_0}{p_1 - c_0 + aq^N}q^N = \frac{aq^N(N+1) + c_0\sigma_u^N/2}{aq^N(N+2) + c_0\sigma_u^N/2}q^N$$

$$> \frac{aq^N(N+1)}{aq^N(N+2)}q^N = \frac{N+1}{N+2}q^N = q^0.$$ (B7)

By the way, σ_u^{N+1} and q^{N+1} are the solutions of

$$aq^{N+1}(N+2) + \frac{c_0\sigma_u^{N+1}}{2} = p_1 - c_0$$ (B8)

$$\sigma_u^{N+1} = \frac{4aq^{N+1}}{p_1 - aNq^{N+1} - c_0}\sqrt{\frac{\alpha c}{c_0\pi}}.$$ (B9)

If we assume that $\sigma_u^{N+1} > \sigma_u^N$, from (B4) and (B9),

$$\frac{4aq^1}{p_1 - aNq^1 - c_0} < \frac{4aq^{N+1}}{p_1 - aNq^{N+1} - c_0},$$

then $q^{N+1} > q^1$. From (B3) and (B8),

$$aq^{N+1}(N+2) < aq^0(N+2),$$

then $q^{N+1} < q^0$. Therefore we get $q^0 > q^1$, which contradicts (B7). Thus we have demonstrated that $\sigma_u^{N+1} < \sigma_u^N$.

2.7   Appendix C: Definitions of Variables in Interindustry Regression Analysis

HI   Herfindahl index of concentration of shipments of firms (Census of Manufactures 1978), calculated during the estimation of frontier production function (hereafter denoted as CEFPF).

HISQ HI^2, 1978, CEFPF.

K   Average tangible assets per plant, 1978, CEFPF (see appendix A).

TYPK   Value of tangible assets of plant accounting for the median
            unit of industry shipments, 1978, CEFPF.

RSIZ   Ratio of median plant size measured by shipments to total
            supply of the market, 1978, CEFPF.

KSHI   Index of indivisibility of investment: ith firm's tangible
            assets K_i are regressed on its shipments S_i, that is,
            $K_i = a_0 + a_1 S_i$; KSHI is defined as the t-statistic of
            coefficient a_0, 1978, CEFPF.

PRGM   Growth rate of productivity: estimated coefficient of a
            simple regression model in which ratio of shipments to total
            material cost is regressed on time for 1969–78 (Census of
            Manufactures 1978).

R&D   Ratio of total company-financed research expenditure in
            the industry to the total domestic product, Input-Output
            Tables, 1980.

GRWT   Growth ratio of total shipments: estimated coefficient of a
            simple regression model in which log (industries' total
            shipments) is regressed on time for 1969–78 (Census of
            Manufactures 1978).

GRVC   Variance of demand: ratio of standard error of the
            coefficient of regression estimating GRWT to the average
            value of total shipments.

ADV   Ratio of total advertising expenditures in the industry to
            the total domestic product, Input-Output Tables, 1980.

ICOV   1 − (proportion of shipments accounted for by plants
            belonging to enterprises classified to another industry),
            1978, CEFPF.

VIO   Number of decrees of antimonopoly law violation for
            1969–78, from Kōsētorihiki-Iinkai Nenji Hōkoku.

SPE4   Index of specialization (four-digit level): ratio of sum of
            shipments of commodities classified to the SIC industry to
            total shipments by establishments classified to the industry,
            1978, CEFPF.

IMPT   Ratio of total imports to total final demand of the industry,
            Input-Output Tables, 1980.

EXPT   Ratio of total exports to total final demand of the industry,
            Input-Output Tables, 1980.

TARF   Ratio of customs duties to total imports, Input-Output
            Tables, 1980.

SUBT   Ratio of current subsidies to gross value added, Input-
            Output Tables, 1980.

TARSUB   TARF + SUBT, 1980, denominator adjusted.

DREG   Dummy for intensity of regulation set equal to 2 if
            regulation affects both entry (by permission or license) and
            more than one of equipment, price, and quantity; 1 if
            regulation affects both entry (by registration) and more than
            one of equipment, price, and quantity; and 0 otherwise,
            1978.

DTARSUB   DREG * TARSUB.

MULT   Share of shipments accounted for by firms that operate
            multiple plants, 1978, CEFPF.

SUBC   Ratio of payment for subcontracting to total materials
            cost (see definition of Z_5 in appendix A), 1978, CEFPF.

SPE7   Index of specialization by seven-digit product within plants
            (see definition of Z_4 in appendix A), 1978, CEFPF.

ENER   Ratio of energy cost to total material cost (see definition of
            Z_2 in appendix A), 1978, CEFPF.

PRWR   Ratio of production workers to total workers (see definition
            of Z_1 in appendix A), 1978, CEFPF.

TCHMSAL   Ratio of payments for technology imports to total sales,
            1978, Kagaku-Gijutsu Chōsa Hōkoku, Sōrifu.

TCHXSAL   Ratio of receipts from technology exports to total sales,
            1978, Kagaku-Gijutsu Chōsa Hōkoku, Sōrifu.

UNION   Ratio of number of unionized workers to total employees;
            number of unionized workers, Rōdō-Kumiai Kihon
            Chōsa (Labor Union Basic Survey), 1978, Ministry of
            Labor.

PART   Ratio of payment to part-time workers to total employee
            compensation, 1978, CEFPF.

PCMA   Industry price-cost margin, measured by (value added −
              total compensation for workers)/shipments, 1978.

PCMD   (PCML − PCMS)/PCML.

PCML   Price-cost margin of large plants that are greater than the
              median plant.

PCMS   Price-cost margin of small plants that are smaller than the
              median plant.

Notes

I am deeply indebted and grateful to Richard E. Caves, Harvard University, and Masu
Uekusa, University of Tokyo, for continual support, guidance, and advice. I am also grateful
to Hideki Yamawaki, Catholic University of Louvain, and other participants at the Conference on Technical Efficiency for helpful comments.

   Much of the work on this chapter was done during my visit at Harvard University which
was funded by Denkitsūshin Fukyū Zaidan, Tokyo. I would like to thank the university and
the foundation for facilitating my stay in Cambridge. Part of this work is also supported by
Seimeikai in Tokyo. Finally, I am also grateful to the Ministry of International Trade and
Industry, Japan, for access to the Census of Manufactures data.

1. Førsund and Hjalmarsson (1987, 79) called such a frontier an "ex ante frontier."

2. Førsund and Hjalmarsson (1987) have pointed out that "From a static point of view a
dispersed structure may seem non-optimal, but is nevertheless part of an optimal dynamic
development" (p. 54).

3. Caves and Barton (1990, 65–66) identify four sets of technically inefficient circumstances
that are consistent with economic equilibrium: incomplete contracts, incomplete diffusion of
information, imperfect competition, and regulatory constraint.

4. This condition ensures positive estimators of σ_u and σ_v. From equation (2) we show the
condition to be

$$\sqrt{\frac{2}{\pi}}\left(\frac{\pi - 4}{\pi}\right)\left(\frac{\pi}{\pi - 2}\hat{\mu}_2\right)^{3/2} < \hat{\mu}_3 < 0.$$

5. For example, D'Agostino and Person (1973) reported the results of simulations for i.i.d.
samples. White and MacDonald (1980) and Pierce and Gray (1982) analyzed the case of
regression residuals.

6. These tests were detailed in Pierce and Gray (1982).

7. By using information about the basic asymptotic distribution reported in the appendix of
OSW (pp. 80–82), we could calculate the asymptotic distributions of estimators.

8. The size is somewhat larger than the average sample size of Japanese four-digit industries,
where the average sample size is 143.7 and the median is 83.

9. See Uekusa and Torii (1985, fig. 4, pp. 12–13) for distributions of estimated indexes of
technical inefficiency.

10. For details of the properties of translog production function, see Christensen, Jorgenson,
and Lau (1973).

11. See chapter 10 of this book for this point.

12. The standard usage of the translog production function is

$\ln(VA) = a_0 + a_1 \cdot \log(K) + a_2 \cdot \log(K)^2 + a_3 \cdot \log(L) + a_4 \cdot \log(L)^2 + a_5 \cdot \log(K) \cdot \log(L)$.

The approximation of equation (7) helps us to examine homotheticity or the constancy of the elasticity.

13. See Caves and Barton (1990) for the consequences of using gross output as the dependent variable of the production function.

14. Different levels of σ_i will generate different patterns of estimator bias as noted in subsection 2.2.2. The estimator biases for various σ_i are discussed in the next section.

15. The threshold value of λ depends on sample size. Moreover Caves and Barton (1990, 58–62) have reported that the bias dependent on sample size is inversely proportional to the square root of the sample size.

16. The numbers stated in the regressions are the numbers of cells in the Monte Carlo study that meet the qualifications. The number of industries whose estimator of the technical inefficiency meets the condition is 112 when skewness < -0.2.

17. The discrepancy is due to a failure in estimating the production function in the cement industry (SIC 3021), where the multicorrelations among independent variables preclude the computation of the inverse matrix with Z_i.

18. The absolute levels of this efficiency index between the United State and Japan are compared in chapter 11.

19. In chapter 11 an attempt is made to explain the difference in efficiency levels between U.S. and Japanese industries, and the result might be useful in assessing the validity of the efficiency index.

20. More precisely, to neglect α^2 in the preceding transformations we would have to examine the magnitude of q_i/v_i relative to α because q_i and v_i are endogenously determined and we neglected $(\alpha q_i/v_i)^2$. In the transformation we approximate $\exp(-\alpha t)[\exp(\alpha q_i/v_i) - 1]/(\alpha/v_i)$ by $1 - \alpha t + (\alpha q_i/2v_i)$. q_i/v_i is the replacement interval, and it was estimated to be about 13.7 years on average by Suzuki and Miyagawa (1986, p. 44, table 2-4) for Japanese manufacturing industry from 1975 to about 1979. α was estimated to be about 1.13 percent by Takenaka (1984, p. 117, table 5-5) for 1975 to about 1978. In this case the discrepancy between $\exp(-\alpha t)[\exp(\alpha q_i/v_i) - 1]/(\alpha/v_i)$ and $1 - \alpha t + (\alpha q_i/2v_i)$ is 0.00165 when $t = 10$, which guarantees a good approximation.

21. Since equations (21) and (23) use an approximation that neglects α^2, the sizes of σ_u would be ambiguous. If we use $(p_0 - c_0)/(2a + c_0 \alpha/v)$ as the monopolistic output schedule in place of approximation (15), we get

$$\sigma_u^M = \frac{\sqrt{2c/\alpha c_0}}{1 + \sqrt{2c\alpha c_0}/(p_1 - c_0)}$$

and

$$\sigma_u^S = \frac{\sqrt{c/\alpha c_0}}{1 + \sqrt{c\alpha c_0}/(p_1 - c_0)},$$

and we can clearly see that $\sigma_u^M > \sigma_u^S$.

22. Because approximations are employed, the value of the equation depends on the absolute value of c_0, which means that replacement intervals depend on the initial value of production cost. However, when N is sufficiently large, $p_1 \gg c_0$ is assumed. If we change time 0 to another period, K and c_0 change proportionally by construction. Therefore for the small firm case, constant replacement intervals are ensured.

23. If we employ the assumption in model analysis A that plants are replaced at a rate that is proportional to the level of inefficiency, the discrepancy between production cost of the newest technology and the current cost of the plant, then the distribution of efficiency becomes half-normal. The structure of model fairly resembles to the model analysis C.

24. See note 19.

25. Many researchers incorporate the share of imported goods as an adjustment to concentration ratios. In this analysis the import factor is treated separately. Chapter 11 provides a comparative analysis of U.S. and Japanese efficiency in which an imports adjusted concentration ratio is used.

26. An analysis of Japanese industries subdivided by size is presented in chapter 10. The effect of PCMD is discussed later in this section.

27. We ignore the difference in degrees of freedom in this case.

28. PCMA is determined as a weighted average of PCML and PCMS. Since PCML has a larger variance than PCMS, PCML's weight is larger than PCMS's, as indicated by the following regression equation:

$$PCMA = -0.003 + 0.21PCMS + 0.80PCML,$$
$$(37.7) (156.7)$$

$$\bar{R}^2 = 0.995, \quad N = 346.$$

This imbalance may cause a bias in the coefficient of PCMD. If PCMS and PCML were independent of each other, $PCMD = (PCML - PCMS)/PCML$ and $0.8 \cdot PCML + 0.2 \cdot PCMS$ would show a positive correlation. If $(PCML - PCMS)/(PCML + PCMS)$ were used in replace of $(PCML - PCMS)/PCML$, this correlation would increase. This is why $(PCML - PCMS)/(PCML + PCMS)$ is not employed here. The problem could be avoided by replacing PCMA with $(PCML + PCMS)/2$; then the properties of the regression result will not change:

$$PCMA = 0.062 + 0.140^{**}HI + 2.117^{**}R\&D + 0.001^*GRWT + 0.887^*RSIZ$$
$$(2.17) (2.43) (2.86) (2.99)$$

$$- 0.000K - 0.127^*IMPT - 0.102^*EXPT + 1.641^*ADV$$
$$(1.76) (4.33) (3.15) (3.44)$$

$$+ 0.125^*SPE4 + 0.148^*K/S + 0.036^*PCMD,$$
$$(3.15) (3.90) (2.78)$$

$$\bar{R}^2 = 0.206, \quad N = 326.$$

Thus PCMD has a positive and significant association with the absolute value of the price-cost margin.

29. This tendency changed later. After 1978 payments under new programs increased more rapidly than did total payments, due to active interchange in high-technology industries.

30. Blumenthal (1976, 245–255) reported this relation.

31. Those exports flow mainly to developing countries. From *Kagaku-gijutsu Chōsa Hōkoku* (1978), North America and Europe's share in exports of technologies was only 23.1 percent, while their share in imports was 99.4 percent. The export-intensive industries are synthetic fiber (0.345 percent = receipts/total sales), earthen products (0.241 percent), and steel mills (0.198 percent).

32. When other variables are included in regression equations, SUBC and MULT take increased *t*-statistics. In these equations SUBC and MULT have the significant relations predicted by the hypotheses.

33. This result is contrary to what Caves and Barton (1990, p. 109, table 6.6) observed for the United States; they found only small differences in the estimated equation. The difference here is due to the magnitude of σ_v. The average value of λ in Japan is 3.84, and in the United States 0.808.

References

Aigner, D. J., C. A. K. Lovell, and P. J. Schmidt. 1977. On the estimation of production frontiers: Maximum likelihood estimation of the parameters of discontinuous density function. *International Economic Review* 17: 377–396.

Blumenthal, T. 1976. Japan's technological strategy. *Journal of Development Economics* 3: 245–255.

Brown, C., and J. L. Medoff. 1978. Trade unionism in the production process. *Journal of Political Economy* 86: 355–378.

Caves, R. E., and D. R. Barton. 1980. *Efficiency in U.S. Manufacturing Industries*, Cambridge: MIT Press.

Caves, R. E., and M. Uekusa. 1976. *Industrial Organization in Japan*. Washington: Brookings Institution.

Christensen, L. R., D. W. Jorgenson, and L. J. Lau. 1973. Transcendental logarithmic production frontiers. *Review of Economics and Statistics* 55: 28–45.

Davies, S. W., and R. E. Caves. 1987. *Britain's Productivity Gap*. Cambridge: Cambridge University Press.

D'Agostino, R. B. and E. S. Person. "Tests for departure from normality: Empirical results for the distribution of b_2 and $\sqrt{b_1}$. *Biometrika* 60: 613–622.

Farrell, M. J. The measurement of productive efficiency. *Journal of the Royal Statistical Society* A120: 253–81.

Førsund, F. R., and L. Hjalmarsson. 1987. *Analyses of Industrial Structure: A Putty-Clay Approach*. Stockholm: Almqvist & Wiksell International.

Frantz, R. S. 1988. *X-Efficiency: Theory, Evidence and Applications*. Norwell, MA: Kluwer Academic Publishers.

Freeman, R. B. 1984. De-mystifying the Japanese labor market. In M. Aoki, ed., *The Economic Analysis of Japanese Firms*, Amsterdam: North-Holland.

Freeman, R. B., and J. L. Medoff. 1979. The two faces of unionism. *Public Interest* (Fall): 69–93.

Lee, L. F., and W. G. Tyler. The stochastic frontier production function and average efficiency: An empirical analysis. *Journal of Econometrics* 7: 385–390.

Muramatsu, K. 1984. Trade unions and productivity in Japanese manufacturing industries. In M. Aoki, ed., *The Economic Analysis of Japanese Firms*. Amsterdam: North-Holland.

Meeusen, W., and J. van den Broeck. 1977. Efficiency estimation from Cobb-Douglas production functions with composed error. *International Economic Review* 18: 435–444.

Olson, J. A., P. Schmidt, and D. M. Waldman. 1980. A Monte Carlo study of estimators of stochastic production functions. *Journal of Econometrics* 13: 67–82.

Pierce, D. A., and R. J. Gray. 1982. Testing normality of errors in regression models. *Biometrika* 69: 233–236.

Schmidt, P., and T. Lin. 1984. Simple test of alternative specifications in stochastic frontier models. *Journal of Econometrics* 24: 349–361.

Schmidt, P. 1985–86. Frontier production functions. *Econometric Reviews* 4: 289–328.

Shōda, Y. 1981. Syokuryōhin sangyō no sangyō-chōsei (Regulation of the food industry). In S. Sekiguchi, ed., *Nihon no Sangyō-Chōsei (Regulation in Japan)*. Tokyo: Nihon-Keizai Sinbunsha.

Suzuki, K., and T. Miyagawa. 1986. *Nihon no kigyo toshi to kenkyukaihatsu senryaku (Investments in Japanese Corporation and R&D Strategy)*. Tokyo: Toyokeizai Shinposha.

Takenaka, H. 1984. *Kenkyukaihatsu to Setsubitoshi no keizaigaku (Economics of R&D and Investment)*. Tokyo: Toyokeizai Shinposha.

Uekusa, M. 1973. *Sangyososiki to Inovation (Industrial Organization and Innovation)*. Tokyo: Nihonkeizaisinbunsha.

Uekusa, M. 1982. *Sangyososikiron (Industrial Organization)*. Tokyo: Chikumasyobo.

Uekusa, M., and A. Torii. 1985. Stochastic production frontier wo mochiita nihon no seizōgyō ni okeru gi jutsuhikouritsudo no keisoku (An estimation of technical inefficiency in Japanese manufacturing industries based on the stochastic production frontier model). *Keizaigaku Ronsyū (Journal of Economics)* 51: 2–23.

White, H., and G. B. MacDonald. 1980. Some large-sample tests for non-normality in the linear regression model. *Journal of the American Statistical Association* 75: 16–27.

3 Technical Efficiency in Korea

Seong Min Yoo

3.1 Introduction

Technical efficiency is an important aspect of market performance that has received little attention in Korea until recently. The reason is that traditional microeconomic theory had simply assumed away any form of inefficiency in production.[1] Today, however, research efforts have been devoted to answering such questions as: To what extent do technical inefficiencies exist in the production activities of firms and plants? What factors account for the level of inefficiency found and explain the interindustry differences in technical inefficiency? Are there any significant international differences in the levels of technical efficiency and, if so, how can we reconcile these results with the observed pattern of international trade? And so on.

This chapter attempts to answer the first two questions in the context of Korea's manufacturing industries.[2] In doing so, we borrow heavily from existing findings on the concept of technical efficiency, on the options of econometric modeling and appropriate methods of estimating technical efficiency, and on desirable ways to construct a suitable data base. The starting point for the present analysis was studies done for the United States by Caves and Barton (1990) and for Japan by Uekusa and Torii (1985). We sought to make the results comparable to these studies as much as possible.

We start by clarifying the relationships among the various concepts of efficiency—allocative efficiency, factor-price efficiency, technical efficiency, Leibenstein's X-efficiency, and scale efficiency.[3] It becomes clear that unless, ceteris paribus, certain assumptions are satisfied, our estimates of technical inefficiency are related to input price inefficiency as well.

The empirical model employed is what is called a *stochastic frontier production function*. It divides the stochastic term into two components—one with a symmetric distribution for pure white noise and the other with an asymmetric distribution for technical inefficiency. A translog production function is assumed for the functional relationship between input and output and is estimated by the corrected ordinary least squares method. The second and third sample moments of the regression residuals are then used to yield estimates of four types of measures for technical (in)efficiency suggested in previous studies.

The estimation of technical efficiency requires the use of plant-level data for each of the five-digit KSIC (Korea Standard Industrial Classification) industries available from the Census of Manufactures. Therefore the findings of this chapter constitute empirical evidence of technical efficiency in Korea's manufacturing industries at the most disaggregated level. This chapter also presents results of a cross-sectional analysis of the determinants of technical efficiency in Korea: market characteristics, including competitive conditions, product differentiation and heterogeneity, occurrence of change and innovation, and organizational and/or institutional influences. Although we designed the analysis to support an international comparison that is responsive to the reasons for expecting considerable differences in the evidence between Korea and other economies, it opens the way to formulating theoretical hypotheses that have greater relevance to Korea.

There is yet another important question which we should address: How does the level of technical efficiency change over time? Evidence on the stability of efficiency over time is not only important in itself but also provides us with a criterion to evaluate the robustness of efficiency estimates to the passage of time. Efficiency estimates for different years allow us to expose and explain any time trends. The stability of efficiency may differ among national economies. For the Korean economy, one of the most dynamic in the world, dynamic aspects of technical efficiency hold special interest.[4]

3.2   The Measurement of Technical Efficiency

When we estimate a production function by employing the conventional regression method, the observations will exhibit both positive and negative residuals from the fitted function. The fact that some plants or firms have positive residuals contradicts the theoretical definition of a production function as an envelope of production possibilities. This statistically irrelevant problem constitutes a starting point for an economic inquiry into technical inefficiency at the plant or firm level.

Existing literature on technical efficiency has defined a "frontier production function" as an empirical counterpart of the theoretical production function.[5] Thus the frontier production function lies above the so-called average production function, which is conventionally fitted to actual data points, unless all the plants or firms in the sample are indeed technically efficient.[6] The gap between the frontier and the average production functions then defines technical inefficiency empirically, and the major task in estimating the level of technical efficiency devolves to estimating the frontier production function.

In this section we review the concept of technical efficiency, the methods employed in estimating the production frontier, and the measures of technical efficiency.

3.2.1 Technical Efficiency and Other Concepts of Efficiency

The theoretical concept of technical efficiency in a firm's or plant's production activities was defined by Farrell (1957) in conjunction with price efficiency. According to Farrell, there exists price inefficiency when the ratio of marginal product to factor input price differs among production inputs, given their relative prices. Thus, even a point on the isoquant (in the input space) can be price inefficient unless it satisfies the condition for an optimal combination of factor inputs. The concept of technical inefficiency refers to another type of suboptimality—the failure of a production unit to yield the maximum attainable output from given amounts of factor inputs. Therefore any input-output combination not on the isoquant is technically inefficient.

These two types of inefficiencies are easily distinguished theoretically but not empirically, since actual observations would normally involve both types. For those observations lying below the production frontier, the question is how we separate these two from each other with the information available to us. Early writers on technical efficiency, Carlsson (1972), for example, thought that they could not be distinguished empirically. Later studies by Schmidt and Lovell (1979, 1980) showed that the distinction could be effected by making use of the duality between production and cost functions.[7] As pointed out by Caves and Barton (1990), however, the job of estimating technical inefficiency separately from price inefficiency would require detailed information on factor demand and input prices, which is seldom available.

Although the term *efficiency* is one of the most frequently used words in economic jargon, it may refer to different concepts in different situations. Thus we often need to clarify the relationship among different names for efficiency, as we have done for technical and price inefficiencies in the preceding paragraphs.

First of all, the overall inefficiency, which refers to the combined effect of technical and price inefficiencies, should represent Leibenstein's X-inefficiency.[8] Any plant or firm producing below the production frontier is X-inefficient.[9] Production inefficiency or cost inefficiency, on the other hand, is said to exist whenever production does not occur at the lowest point of the long-run average cost function. Thus the chances that production (cost) inefficiency would exist are greater than for X-inefficiency in that the former takes into account another dimension, the scale of production. It is in this context that Siegfried and Wheeler (1981) decomposed production (cost) inefficiency into three components: X-inefficiency, inefficiency of suboptimal capacity, and that of excess capacity. The relationship between scale inefficiency and X-inefficiency is then made clearer.

These various concepts of (in)efficiency are all applicable to the production activities of a plant or firm. However, the concept of allocative inefficiency, the central concern in industrial organization, applies to a market situation. That is, the market power of a monopolist or an oligopolist allows it to set the price at a level higher than one a competitive market would set. This will in turn provide wrong signals on the trade-offs among commodities, reducing consumer welfare and causing allocative inefficiencies. According to Carlsson (1972), the allocative inefficiency or the cost of resource misallocation estimated by Harberger (1954) could be far less significant than the production inefficiency often found in monopolies and oligopolies.[10] Allocative inefficiency has often been called price inefficiency in the literature on technical efficiency, although a price-efficient monopolist can create allocative inefficiency in the market context.

3.2.2 The Stochastic Production Frontier and Its Estimation

Research on technical efficiency that utilizes the concept of the frontier production function is classified according to the econometric model assumed and the estimation method employed. As regards the econometric model, assumptions imposed on the production frontier seem to be the most important. Let $y = f(x)$ represent the theoretical production function, where y and x denote the amounts of output and inputs, respectively. Since most of the actual observations on y and x would not satisfy this functional relationship, the following deterministic frontier production function is suggested:[11]

$$y = f(x) \cdot \exp(-u), \qquad u > 0. \tag{1}$$

The essence of the model given in equation (1) is that since the production frontier $f(x)$ is deterministic, the actual observations on y will always lie below the frontier due to the assumption that $u > 0$. Although the model is useful in recovering the production frontier, it has a critical weakness when applied to real world data. As pointed out by Caves and Barton (1990), the requirement of one-sided residuals causes the position of the estimated frontier to depend on a small number of outliers that might be inaccurately measured or otherwise abnormal. Modeled as in equation (1), the term u will include not only pure technical inefficiency but also the effects of measurement errors and other exogenous factors.

For the case where the frontier itself is stochastic, a stochastic frontier production function (SFPF) decomposes the disturbance term into two components, one for the pure white noise and the other for technical inefficiency, as follows:[12]

$$y = f(x) \cdot \exp(v - u)$$

$$= f(x) \cdot \exp(\varepsilon), \qquad \varepsilon = (v - u), \quad u > 0. \tag{2}$$

We assume again that the term u has a one-sided distribution in order to represent the technical inefficiency, and we assume that v has a symmetric distribution in order to allow the production frontier $f(x) \cdot \exp(v)$ to be stochastic due to white noise, measurement error, and other exogenous factors beyond the plant's or firm's control.

Although the model in equation (2) is still criticized for various defects, we adopt it for estimating the production frontier. The weak points associated with the stochastic frontier production function are the following: First, there exist no a priori criteria to specify the distributions of u and v, and so the choice is usually made on an ad hoc basis. Second, once we succeed in estimating the deterministic kernel $f(x)$, it is not possible to decompose the difference between y and $f(x)$ into u and v, respectively. Thus only the average technical inefficiency for an industry can be calculated, and it is impossible to obtain estimates of technical inefficiency for a single firm or plant.[13] Third, the estimated extent of technical inefficiency will include input price inefficiency as well. However, this is not a problem of the model itself because the input demand frontier could be estimated simultaneously but for the lack of data on factor input prices.

Given a parametric functional form for $f(x)$ and certain distributional assumptions on u and v, the model in equation (2) can be estimated either by maximum likelihood estimation method or the so-called corrected ordinary least squares (COLS) method.[14] Olson et al. (1980) showed that the COLS estimators have statistical properties at least as desirable as those of the maximum likelihood estimators. In addition to the advantage of the COLS estimators in simplifying the computations, we adopt the COLS method for maximum comparability to other studies employing the method.

We briefly introduce the COLS method by rewriting equation (2) in logarithms. Denoting $\mu \equiv E(u) > 0$, we have

$$\ln(y) = \ln[f(x)] + (v - u)$$

$$= -\mu + \ln[f(x)] + (v - u + \mu). \tag{3}$$

We assume that u and v are independently and identically distributed and that the disturbances are also independent of x, so equation (3) satisfies all the assumptions for the usual OLS regression model except for the normal distribution condition on $v - u + \mu$. Furthermore, we assume that the expression $\ln[f(x)]$ is linear in the parameters, so the OLS regression of equation (3) will yield the best linear unbiased estimators of the parameters except for the constant term, denoted α_0, for which the bias will be $-\mu$. In other words, the OLS regression gives an unbiased estimator of $(\alpha_0 - \mu)$.

The estimation of the SFPF by the OLS method involves finding a consistent estimator of μ by making use of the following distributional assumptions on u and v, thus obtaining consistent estimators for all the parameters.[15]

$$v \sim N(0, \sigma_v^2),$$

$$u \sim |N(0, \sigma_u^2)|. \tag{4}$$

Weinstein (1964) obtained the expression for μ from the probability density function of $\varepsilon = (v - u)$ under the assumptions given in (4):

$$E(\varepsilon) = E(-u) = -\mu = -\sigma_u \sqrt{\frac{2}{\pi}}. \tag{5}$$

The consistent estimator of μ can then be found if we simply replace σ_u in equation (5) by its consistent estimator, and it can be shown that expressions for the second and third central moments of ε, denoted $m_2(\varepsilon)$ and $m_3(\varepsilon)$, give rise to the following.

$$\sigma_u^2 = \left[\sqrt{\frac{\pi}{2}} \cdot \left(\frac{\pi}{\pi - 4} \right) \cdot m_3(\varepsilon) \right]^{2/3},$$

$$\sigma_v^2 = m_2(\varepsilon) - \left(\frac{\pi - 2}{\pi} \right) \cdot \sigma_u^2. \tag{6}$$

The consistent estimators for σ_u^2 and σ_v^2 are obtained by replacing $m_2(\varepsilon)$ and $m_3(\varepsilon)$ in equation (6) with their sample counterparts $\hat{m}_2$ and $\hat{m}_3$, which in turn should yield a consistent estimator of μ from equation (5).[16]

3.2.3 Measures of Technical Efficiency

Before introducing the measures of technical (in)efficiency, we should first deal with the two cases in which the estimation of the SFPF by COLS fails to yield satisfactory estimators. The first type of failure, called *type I failure*, exists when the third sample moment $\hat{m}_3$ takes on a nonnegative value so that σ_u^2 cannot be defined.[17] Because the probability of type I failure increases as the third central moment approaches zero, it follows that the smaller the σ_u^2, the greater is the probability of type I failure. Since a small value of σ_u^2 implies, other things being equal, that the gap (equivalent to $\sigma_u\sqrt{2/\pi}$) between the average production function and the production frontier is also small, the chances are that type I failure may occur in relatively efficient industries.[18] We treat $\hat{\sigma}_u = 0$ when type I failure occurs.

The second type of failure, called *type II failure*, will be encountered when the second sample moment is so small relative to the estimate of σ_u^2 that it results in a negative value of σ_v^2. As opposed to type I failure, this constitutes an extreme case in which the estimate of σ_u^2 takes on a relatively large value, which implies that type II failure is likely to occur in relatively inefficient industries. We treat $\hat{\sigma}_v = 0$ when type II failure occurs.

The discussions on the two types of failures imply that we should be careful when interpreting estimates of the following four measures of technical (in)efficiency, as suggested in many existing studies and employed by Caves and Barton (1990). Since there cannot exist an a priori criterion to determine which measure to use, we simply adopt all of them and report their estimates in this chapter.[19]

$$\text{EFF} = 2 \cdot \exp\left(\frac{\sigma_u^2}{2} \right) \cdot [1 - \Phi(\sigma_u)], \tag{7}$$

$$\text{ATI} = \frac{\sigma_u\sqrt{2/\pi}}{\overline{\ln(y)} + \sigma_u\sqrt{2/\pi}}, \tag{8}$$

$$\lambda = \frac{\sigma_u}{\sigma_v}, \tag{9}$$

$$S = \frac{m_3(\varepsilon)}{[m_2(\varepsilon)]^{3/2}}. \tag{10}$$

Lee and Tyler (1978) proposed the use of EFF (efficiency) as a measure of technical efficiency. The expression for EFF, as given in (7), is the expected value of the ratio of $f(x) \cdot \exp(v - u)$, the actual observation of y, to $f(x) \cdot \exp(v)$, the SFPF in equation (2). Thus, as the actual observation of y approaches the SFPF, EFF approaches 1. On the other hand, ATI (average technical inefficiency) measures the gap between the average production function and the production frontier (the numerator), normalized by the mean of the production frontier measured on the y axis (the denominator). Thus, ATI should serve as a measure of technical inefficiency.[20] When type I failure occurs, EFF = 1 and ATI = 0. Otherwise, the two measures are constrained to lie in the (0, 1) interval.

In contrast to EFF and ATI, the other two measures use information on both σ_u and σ_v. Since we assumed a half-normal distribution for u and a normal distribution for v, the third measure λ tells us the degree of asymmetry in the distribution of $\varepsilon = (v - u)$. Representing a measure of technical inefficiency (σ_u) normalized by the degree of variation in the SFPF (σ_v), this measure of technical inefficiency indirectly exhibits whether the gap between y and $f(x)$ comes from u or v. The fourth measure S (skewness) is closely related to λ and is defined to be a measure of skewness in the distribution of ε. As the degree of negative skew increases with the level of technical inefficiency, S is used as a measure of technical efficiency. The exact relationship between λ and S is determined from the two equations in (6).[21] When type I failure occurs, λ is equal to 0. In the case of type II failure, λ is not defined. However, S always exists regardless of the two types of failures.

The last important issue in the estimation of the SFPF concerns which specific functional form we should impose on the production function $f(x)$. Following Caves and Barton (1990), we employ the translog form for $\ln[f(x)]$. We discuss the issue in greater detail in the next section, where three alternative specifications of the translog production function are suggested for estimation.

3.3   Analysis of Estimation Results

Estimation of the SFPF in equation (2) using the COLS method requires, first of all, an appropriate data set containing information on the output y and the inputs x. We choose individual establishments instead of firms as the unit of observation in our empirical analysis. Since the data should conform to this requirement, we used the data tape of the Census of Manufactures for the year 1978, which contains raw data on various attributes of individual establishments in manufacturing industries.[22]

We employ 389 KSIC (Korea Standard Industrial Classification) five-digit industries (the most disaggregated level) as our initial sample of industries. The five-digit level of the KSIC system corresponds roughly to the four-digit industries of the U.S. SIC. Although some of the KSIC five-digit industries contain an insufficient number of establishments and will therefore be omitted from the final sample, we thought that industries disaggregated at this level would best match the theoretical concept of an industry.

In this section we first explain how the variables for outputs and inputs are constructed, and then decide upon alternative specifications of the translog production function to be estimated. We also discuss the criteria used for editing the raw data and report the effects of these criteria. Estimation results are then presented, and the estimates of technical (in)efficiency are evaluated.

3.3.1   Variable Definitions and Regression Equations[23]

Output is measured by the following two variables: GO (gross output) and VA (valued added). See the appendix for definitions of the various items included in the following formulas for output and input variables:[24]

$$GO = S + INV1b - INV1a,$$

$$VA = GO2 - MC.$$

Labor input is measured either by the total number of employees N or by equivalent production-worker hours L. Thus L is defined to be the sum of production-worker hours LP and non-production-worker hours LNP. The other important variables for input are the stock of capital K and materials purchased M.

$L = LP + LNP,$

where

$LP = LPHR \cdot NP,$

$LNP = LNPHR \cdot NNP,$

$K = 0.5 \cdot (ASSETa + ASSETb) + 0.5 \cdot (INVa + INVb),$

$M = MC - (INV2b - INV2a) - (WPb - WPa).$

The following variables are used as additional explanatory variables to control for the possible effects of other sources of heterogeneity among the establishments classified into an industry.

$X1 = \dfrac{NNP}{N},$

$X2 = \dfrac{MCFE}{MC},$

$X3 = 0.5 \cdot \dfrac{INVa + INVb}{K}.$

With these variables we specify three forms of translog production functions for estimation.

$$\ln\left(\frac{GO}{N}\right) = a_0 + a_1 \ln\left(\frac{K}{L}\right) + a_2 \ln\left(\frac{M}{L}\right) + a_3 \ln(N) + a_4 \left[\ln\left(\frac{K}{L}\right)\right]^2$$

$$+ a_5 \left[\ln\left(\frac{M}{L}\right)\right]^2 + a_6 [\ln(N)]^2 + a_7 \left[\ln\left(\frac{K}{L}\right)\right]\left[\ln\left(\frac{M}{L}\right)\right]$$

$$+ a_8 \left[\ln\left(\frac{K}{L}\right)\right][\ln(N)] + a_9 \left[\ln\left(\frac{M}{L}\right)\right][\ln(N)]$$

$$+ \sum_{i=1}^{3} a_{i+9} X_i + v - u, \tag{11}$$

$$\ln\left(\frac{VA}{L}\right) = a_0 + a_1 \ln\left(\frac{K}{L}\right) + a_2 \ln(L) + a_3 \left[\ln\left(\frac{K}{L}\right)\right]^2 + a_4 [\ln(L)]^2$$

$$+ a_5 \left[\ln\left(\frac{K}{L}\right)\right][\ln(L)] + \sum_{i=1}^{3} a_{i+5} X_i + v - u, \tag{12}$$

$$\ln\left(\frac{VA}{L}\right) = a_0 + a_1 \ln\left(\frac{K}{L}\right) + a_2 \ln(L^*) + a_3 \left[\ln\left(\frac{K}{L}\right)\right]^2 + a_4[\ln(L^*)]^2$$

$$+ a_5 \left[\ln\left(\frac{K}{L}\right)\right][\ln(L^*)] + \sum_{i=1}^{3} a_{i+5}X_i + v - u. \qquad (13)$$

We see that the differences between equation (11) and equation (12) lie in, first, whether we use gross output (per employee) or value added (per unit of labor hour) as the dependent variable, second, whether we include the materials input in the set of explanatory variables, and, third, whether we use N or L as the labor input. Following Caves and Barton (1990), we report the estimation results for both specifications in this chapter. The third specification in equation (13) is similar to the one suggested by Uekusa and Torii (1985), and we include it for a comparison with their study on Japanese industries. It differs from equation (12) only in that we use total labor compensation (L*, which is defined as the sum of LNPPAY and LPPAY), instead of L, as the labor input.

3.3.2 Editing the Raw Data

Estimates of technical efficiency will be very sensitive to any errors made in compiling the raw data because all four measures of technical (in)efficiency critically depend on information about the empirical distribution of regression residuals. This explains why it is important to edit the raw data so as to exclude those observations (establishments) that seem likely to cause measurement errors. We need to be very careful, however, in deciding upon the editing rules because the estimates of technical efficiency will be biased if the rules exclude outliers which are in fact very (in)efficient.

Table 3.1 lists the rules adopted for editing the raw data, as well as the number of establishments excluded when we apply the rules. Since our procedure for estimating technical efficiency makes sense only for those establishments that operated normally during the time period under consideration, the establishments reporting zero values for output and/or inputs should be excluded as in rules (1) through (9). Also excluded are establishments reporting extraordinarily high or low values for certain measures, as in rules (10) through (12).

The last two rules in table 3.1 are introduced in order to exclude establishments reporting very high values for the two key variables GO/N and VA/L. In particular, the COLS method is designed in such a way that the

Table 3.1
Editing rules and the number of observations excluded

	Editing rules	Establishments excluded
(1)	$N < 5$	67
(2)	$NP = 0$	173
(3)	$LPHR = 0$	3,986
(4)	$S = 0$	3,714
(5)	$GO = 0$	3,671
(6)	$LPPAY = 0$	173
(7)	$MC = 0$	21
(8)	$K = 0$	116
(9)	$VA = 0$	179
(10)	$LPHR > 4,500$	56
(11)	$GO/N > MEAN(GO/N) + 4.5 \cdot SD(GO/N)$	175
(12)	$VA/L > MEAN(VA/L) + 4.5 \cdot SD(VA/L)$	180
(1)–(12)	Simultaneously applied	7,677

Note: For definitions of variables, see the text or the appendix. $MEAN(\cdot)$ and $SD(\cdot)$ denote sample mean and sample standard deviation, respectively.

probability of type I and II failures increases with the number of establishments reporting abnormally high or low values for these variables. Out of the 12 rules, (3), (4), and (5) play the most significant role. When we apply all the editing rules simultaneously, 7,677 establishments (26 percent of total establishments in the manufacturing sector) are excluded.

After editing the raw data as in table 3.1, we additionally excluded industries with less than 15 observations (establishments) in order to secure the necessary degrees of freedom to estimate the translog production function for each industry. The final result is summarized in table 3.2, which also reports the results for each of the two-digit industries. Thus the final data set for our estimation included 21,298 establishments classified into 242 five-digit industries.

As can be seen in table 3.2, the procedure of omitting industries with less than 15 establishments excluded as many as 124 industries, while the major effect of imposing the 12 editing rules is the significant reduction in the number of establishments. Although there can be many ways to explain the structural differences between the industries retained in our final data set and those excluded, one obvious explanation is that the latter group of industries is highly concentrated. That is the case,[25] but these industries are also small, accounting for 31.9 percent of industries but only 19.5 percent of value added and 5.9 percent of employment.

Table 3.2
Summary of data for analysis

KSIC two-digit	Total (A)	Editing rules	Below 15 observations[a]	Retained (B)	B/A (%)
		Exclusion basis			
31	4,448 (46)	1,282 (5)	86 (14)	3,080 (27)	69 (59)
32	7,990 (57)	2,719 (1)	109 (14)	5,162 (42)	65 (74)
33	2,388 (20)	368 (1)	62 (8)	1,958 (11)	82 (55)
34	2,001 (25)	455 (2)	46 (5)	1,500 (18)	75 (72)
35	2,737 (62)	475 (4)	190 (27)	2,072 (31)	76 (50)
36	2,314 (28)	869 (2)	35 (7)	1,410 (19)	61 (68)
37	835 (13)	130 (0)	18 (2)	687 (11)	82 (85)
38	6,123 (116)	1,105 (5)	306 (41)	4,712 (70)	77 (60)
39	1,028 (22)	274 (3)	37 (6)	717 (13)	70 (59)
Total	29,864 (389)	7,677 (23)	889 (124)	21,298 (242)	71 (62)

Note: The first numbers apply to establishments and those in the parentheses to industries.
a. We rule out those industries with less than 15 establishments.

Table 3.3
Number of industries with successes and failures in estimating technical efficiency, by estimating equation

Equation used	Type I failure	Type II failure	Success industries	Total
Equation (11)	85	29	128	242
Equation (12)	83	25	134	242
Equation (13)	88	26	128	242

3.3.3 Failure versus Success Industries

COLS estimations of the three equations (11), (12), and (13) allow us to classify the 242 industries into two groups: the "failure" industries suffering from either type I or type II failure and the remaining "success" industries.[26] Table 3.3 reports the number of industries classified in this way for the three regression equations, and table 3.4 reports the distribution of type I and type II failures for each of the two-digit KSIC industries. The number of type I failure industries is consistently and considerably greater than that of type II failures. The result presents a sharp contrast to Torii (subsection 2.2.7), who reports a greater number for type II failure in the case of Japan, and Mayes and Green (subsection 4.1.5), who report approximately equal numbers for the two types of failures in the case of the United Kingdom.

Table 3.4
Number of industries with successes and failures in estimating technical efficiency, by
industrial sector

		Equation (11)			Equation (12)		
KSIC	Total	Type I	Type II	Success	Type I	Type II	Success
31	27	7	1	19	9	1	17
32	42	12	9	21	14	7	21
33	11	3	1	7	3	2	6
34	18	10	1	7	7	2	9
35	31	13	0	18	10	4	17
36	19	6	2	11	6	1	12
37	11	4	1	6	5	1	5
38	70	24	12	34	20	5	45
39	13	6	2	5	9	2	2
Total	242	85	29	128	83	25	134

These findings, however, cannot be interpreted as implying that Korean industries are relatively more efficient. To prove that assertion, we would require, among other things, strong empirical evidence to support the theoretically sound hypothesis associating type I failure with technical efficiency. Paradoxically the framework of the present study makes it impossible to find independent evidence because all the available information is already used in the regression analysis.[27]

Caves and Barton (1990) argued that differences in the minimum-to-maximum range of the dependent variable are closely related to the distinction between failure and success industries. That is, industries showing small ranges in output are likely to result in type I failure, while those with great variations are likely to be type II failures. The success industries are then somewhere in between. The evidence presented in table 3.5 tells us that to a certain extent the conjecture holds true for Korea, although the result is less vivid than for the united States.[28]

3.3.4 Overall Extent of Technical Efficiency

In table 3.6 we report the summary statistics of the four measures of technical (in)efficiency estimated by means of the three regression equations. The overall extent of technical (in)efficiency can be read from the means of EFF and ATI. ATI indicates about 3 percent of technical inefficiency in equation (11) and 68 percent in equation (12).[29] EFF implies 78 percent of technical efficiency in equation (11) and 67 percent in equation

Table 3.5
Intraindustry range of plants' productivity levels, by cases of success and failure in estimation of technical efficiency

Maximum/minimum of GO/N[a]	Type I failure	Success industries	Type II failure	Total
0–15	33 (38.8)	41 (32.0)	2 (6.9)	76 (31.4)
15–50	41 (48.2)	53 (41.4)	7 (24.1)	101 (41.7)
Above 50	11 (13.0)	34 (26.6)	20 (69.0)	65 (26.9)
Total	85 (100)	128 (100)	29 (100)	242 (100)

Note: The first figure represents the number of industries; figures in parentheses are percentages within each column.
a. Maximum and minimum values of GO/N for each industry.

Table 3.6
Summary statistics of efficiency measures

Measure	Number of observations	Mean	Standard deviation	Minimum	Maximum
Equation (11): GO/N					
EFF	128	0.783	0.075	0.481	0.932
	(242)	(0.835)			
ATI	128	0.032	0.014	0.007	0.100
	(242)	(0.026)			
λ	128	1.849	1.310	0.454	8.680
	(213)	(1.111)			
S	242	−0.265	0.785	−5.479	1.451
Equation (12): VA/L					
EFF	134	0.672	0.089	0.492	0.864
	(242)	(0.761)			
ATI	134	0.680	0.189	0.206	0.994
	(242)	(0.460)			
λ	134	2.552	6.233	0.363	71.895[a]
	(217)	(1.576)			
S	242	−0.280	0.646	−4.129	1.152
Equation (13): VA/L					
EFF	128	0.679	0.095	0.443	0.890
	(242)	(0.772)			
ATI	128	0.683	0.179	0.240	0.994
	(242)	(0.449)			
λ	128	2.539	4.434	0.322	42.051[a]
	(216)	(1.505)			
S	242	−0.268	0.664	−3.972	1.191

Note: For EFF, ATI, and λ we first report the statistics for the success industries. The numbers in the parentheses apply to entire industries, but type II failures are still excluded for λ.
a. In the case of value added, maximum values of λ seem unexpectedly high. These numbers are thought to be abnormal because the second highest values of λ are 12.276 for equation (12) and 24.230 for equation (13).

Table 3.7
Percentile values for efficiency measures

	Percentiles				
	0%	25%	50%	75%	100%
EFF(GO)	0.481	0.738	0.790	0.835	0.932
EFF(VA)	0.492	0.597	0.673	0.739	0.864
ATI(GO)	0.007	0.022	0.029	0.039	0.100
ATI(VA)	0.206	0.518	0.692	0.838	0.994
λ(GO)	0.454	1.067	1.485	2.070	8.680
λ(VA)	0.363	1.077	1.674	2.652	71.895
S(GO)	−5.479	−0.484	−0.180	0.175	1.451
S(VA)	−4.129	−0.585	−0.169	0.117	1.152

Note: For EFF, ATI, and λ we included only the success industries (128 for GO/N and 134 for VA/L). For S the percentile distribution is for the entire sample of 242 industries.

(12).[30] The equation with GO/N as the dependent variable yields higher estimates of technical efficiency for all four measures. The summary statistics for equation (13) closely resemble those for equation (12), as expected. Thus we omit efficiency measures based on equation (13) from the following analysis. The percentile values of efficiency estimates in table 3.7 depict the distribution of the estimates.

Table 3.8 summarizes the mean values of the efficiency measures for the two-digit KSIC industries.[31] Rankings for the 9 two-digit industries in terms of the observed value of technical (in)efficiency are not closely correlated between the efficiency measures nor between the two regression equations.[32] The observation raises concerns about the robustness of our estimates of technical (in)efficiency that will be checked on disaggregated data.

3.3.5   Correlations between Different Measures

Table 3.9 reports the Spearman correlation coefficients between possible pairs of efficiency measures. When we employ equation (11) with GO/N as the dependent variable, all the correlation coefficients between measures of technical efficiency are high and statistically significant, relieving our concern about robustness of estimates in table 3.8. Thus we can conclude that all four measures of technical efficiency are almost equally qualified, as long as they are obtained from equation (11). The choice of a particular efficiency measure as the dependent variable in the ensuing cross-sectional analysis should not affect the result in a fundamental way.

Table 3.8
Mean values of efficiency measures by industrial sector

KSIC	Equation (11): GO/N				Equation (12): VA/L			
	EFF	ATI	λ	S	EFF	ATI	λ	S
31	0.765	0.035	1.623	−0.318	0.667	0.685	1.809	−0.344
32	0.782	0.032	2.015	−0.369	0.672	0.607	1.902	−0.379
33	0.807	0.028	1.403	−0.267	0.714	0.626	1.344	−0.250
34	0.791	0.031	1.221	−0.211	0.702	0.654	1.542	−0.309
35	0.773	0.031	1.997	−0.389	0.646	0.673	1.930	−0.383
36	0.821	0.025	1.292	−0.227	0.658	0.648	2.252	−0.457
37	0.791	0.028	2.642	−0.387	0.612	0.716	2.193	−0.479
38	0.782	0.032	1.879	−0.357	0.678	0.742	3.895	−0.400
39	0.746	0.039	3.048	−0.581	0.749	0.473	1.622	−0.340

Note: For all four measures the mean values are calculated only for the success industries (128 for GO/N and 134 for VA/L).

Table 3.9
Spearman correlations between efficiency measures

	EFF	ATI	λ	S	OBS[a]
Equation (11): GO/N					
EFF	1.00	−0.989	−0.758	0.758	−0.235
	(0.00)	(0.0001)	(0.0001)	(0.0001)	(0.0076)
ATI		1.00	0.748	−0.748	0.242
		(0.00)	(0.0001)	(0.0001)	(0.0059)
λ			1.00	−1.00	0.084
			(0.00)	(0.00)	(0.345)
S				1.00	−0.084
				(0.00)	(0.345)
OBS					1.00
					(0.00)
Equation (12): VA/L					
EFF	1.00	−0.351	−0.853	0.853	−0.0079
	(0.00)	(0.0001)	(0.0001)	(0.0001)	(0.9275)
ATI		1.00	0.332	−0.332	0.128
		(0.00)	(0.0001)	(0.0001)	(0.141)
λ			1.00	−1.00	−0.056
			(0.00)	(0.00)	(0.519)
S				1.00	0.056
				(0.00)	(0.519)
OBS					1.00
					(0.00)

Note: The correlation coefficients are obtained for the success industries. The numbers in the parentheses are the levels of significance.
a. OBS refers to the number of establishments in each industry utilized to estimate the SFPF.

Table 3.10
Spearman correlations between EFF estimates based on different estimating equations

	EFF(GO)	EFF(VA)	EFF(13)[a]
EFF(GO)	1.00	0.071	0.279
	(0.00)	(0.5512)	(0.0187)
EFF(VA)		1.00	0.850
		(0.00)	(0.0001)
EFF(13)			1.00
			(0.00)

Note: The correlation coefficients are obtained for the success industries. We have 72 industries for {EFF(GO), EFF(VA)}, 71 industries for {EFF(GO), EFF(13)}, and 113 industries for {EFF(VA), EFF(13)}.
a. EFF(13) is EFF based on equation (13).

The same conclusion holds when we employ equation (12) with VA/L as the dependent variable as the basis for obtaining the three measures EFF, λ, and S. However, a kind of dichotomy exists between ATI and the other three efficiency measures.[33] These findings present a striking contrast to Caves and Barton (1990), who found an obvious dichotomy existing between (EFF, ATI) and (λ, S) for both specifications of the regression equation.[34]

We also need to consider correlations between measures based on different specifications of the production function. Table 3.10 presents them for EFF estimated for three different equations. The correlation between EFF(GO) and EFF(VA) or EFF(13) is low and insignificant, while the correlation between EFF(VA) and EFF(13) is high as expected. Thus the issue of validity and robustness of efficiency estimates is raised once again. In sum, our estimation procedure and the data employed do not yield any reliable basis for choosing among different regression equations.

3.3.6   Effect of Establishment Size: An Experiment

One could argue that small-sized establishments are likely to be more technically inefficient. To observe the technical efficiency of small units, we excluded all the establishments with less than 20 employees from our data set, then reestimated the SFPF by the same method to obtain efficiency estimates EFF(20), ATI(20), λ(20), and S(20).[35]

In table 3.11 we report the correlations between the original efficiency estimates and the new ones. The diagonal elements of the two correlation

Table 3.11
Correlations between measures of technical efficiency estimated with small establishments included and excluded

	EFF	ATI	λ	S
Equation (11): 61 industries				
EFF(20)	0.441	−0.398	−0.142	0.131
	(0.0004)	(0.0015)	(0.2742)	(0.3137)
ATI(20)	−0.484	0.471	0.170	−0.173
	(0.0001)	(0.0001)	(0.1896)	(0.1813)
λ(20)	−0.022	0.007	0.169	−0.089
	(0.8653)	(0.9597)	(0.1940)	(0.4936)
S(20)	−0.003	0.035	−0.189	0.099
	(0.9835)	(0.7911)	(0.1448)	(0.4460)
Equation (12): 74 industries				
EFF(20)	0.555	−0.181	−0.261	0.349
	(0.0001)	(0.1233)	(0.0246)	(0.0023)
ATI(20)	−0.018	0.686	0.025	0.044
	(0.8766)	(0.0001)	(0.8353)	(0.7069)
λ(20)	−0.310	0.085	0.550	−0.313
	(0.0072)	(0.4717)	(0.0001)	(0.0066)
S(20)	0.410	−0.176	−0.347	0.449
	(0.0003)	(0.1329)	(0.0024)	(0.0001)

Note: The correlation coefficients are obtained for the success industries. The numbers in the parentheses are the levels of significance.

matrices are particularly noteworthy since they represent the effect of excluding the small establishments on a particular measure of efficiency. The correlations are significant in most cases but not high, implying that the small-sized establishments achieve different levels of technical efficiency. Table 3.12 shows that the revised data excluding the small-sized establishments yield higher levels of technical efficiency. Thus the small-sized establishments are, on average, less efficient.[36]

3.4 Interindustry Determinants of Technical Efficiency

We now turn to address the second question mentioned at the outset: What factors account for the observed levels of inefficiency and explain interindustry differences in technical efficiency? This important question is, in principle, a theoretical one that warrants a rigorous theoretical analysis. However, no theoretical model of technical efficiency has emerged that is strong enough in its formal underpinnings. Lacking an orthodox theory of

Table 3.12
Mean values of measures of technical efficiency estimated with small establishments included and excluded

	Equation (11): 61 observations	Equation (12): 74 observations
EFF	0.776	0.669
EFF(20)	0.789	0.681
ATI	0.032	0.696
ATI(20)	0.030	0.646

Note: For the case of equation (11) out of 61 industries there are 33 industries for which EFF(20) > EFF and 35 industries for which ATI(20) < ATI. Thus the comparison of mean values in the table does not suffice to give us strong evidence on the positive effect of establishment size on efficiency. However, in the case of equation (12), there are 42 industries (out of 74) for which EFF(20) > EFF and 51 industries for which ATI(20) < ATI.

technical efficiency, empirical research is likely to rely liberally on educated guesses.

For Korean manufacturing industries the situation is somewhat more complicated. We first need to consider if the existing hypotheses about the interindustry determinants of technical efficiency, however soundly based, hold similar implications for Korean industries and plants. We also need to identify hypotheses that bear specifically on the Korean context. The two sets of hypotheses, once established, will not be mutually exclusive since both deal with an essentially identical question.[37] We incorporate as many as possible of the explanatory variables that have been used in previous research on market structure, plus any additional ones found in research on technical efficiency.[38] However, we try to refurbish existing hypotheses wherever possible in order to adapt them to the Korean context.

Before we introduce the variables and hypotheses, we should consider exactly what our efficiency estimates represent in order to avoid entanglement with hypotheses inappropriate to the efficiency estimates. The discussion follows Caves and Barton (1990). First, the estimates will not directly reflect the prevalence of plants that operate at inefficiently small scales but minimize costs of those scales. Caves and Barton (1990) explain that this limitation results mainly from our assumption of a translog production function that allows for variations in productivity with scale. The point is related to our discussion in the preceding section on the effect of establishment size on technical efficiency. One way to overcome this problem could be to control for the effect of size as in table 3.12. This, however, does not tell us whether the difference in efficiency estimates comes solely from suboptimal capacity, since other possibilities also exist. Second, the theoretical distinction between technical inefficiency and input price inefficiency is not implemented, although a positive correlation is expected between an inefficient choice of factor proportions and technical inefficiency. Third, the estimation method, which depends only on the shape of the empirical distribution of output, cannot detect industries consisting of uniformly inefficient plants. These points set the boundaries within which we propose hypotheses and interpret the results.

3.4.1 Competitive Conditions[39]

Many hypotheses relate the competitive conditions of a market to the suppliers' technical efficiency. As surveyed in Caves and Barton (1990), they included the extent of slack within the plant or firm, the amount of economic experimentation and information flows, and the degree of imperfect competition and different ways of using resources.

Although the explanations based on these factors have been widely accepted in general microeconomic theory, the last point deserves special attention in the Korean context since Korean industries in 1978 were highly protected from competitive pressures, domestic as well as from abroad. The degree of imperfect competition and the extent of distortion in resource allocation may have been enlarged and consequently the level of technical efficiency lowered. It was the Korean government's trade and industrial policies in the 1970s that played a key role in this process. Tariff and nontariff barriers sheltered domestic suppliers from foreign competition, and the government's regulatory functions, including its licensing and permit systems, protected the domestic incumbents from the threat of entry. The government's industrial policy measures induced investment in excess capacity in some industries.[40]

It is not appropriate, however, to assume that protection had only negative effects on Korea in 1978. The ultimate objective of the protectionist policies was to make the implementation of the export-led economic growth strategy more effective, which Korea did do, so the net effect of competitive conditions on technical efficiency seems less clear. As can be argued for any country exposed to international trade, the existence of opportunities for Korean producers to sell in export markets must have made Korean industry more efficient and competitive. To the extent that protection of the domestic market and the incumbent producers served the purpose of rapidly expanding exports, the protectionist policy regime cannot be blamed for having made Korean industries technically inefficient. Thus protection may have fostered allocative inefficiency rather than technical inefficiency.

The following variables are defined and used to indicate the competitive conditions of an industry.

CR3 = percentage of shipments accounted for by the three largest firms in 1978 (source: calculated from the Bureau of Statistics, Economic Planning Board (hereafter EPB), *Census of Manufactures*, commodity and enterprise data tapes, 1978).

HI = Herfindahl-Hirschman index of market concentration, based on shipments, 1978 (source: see CR3).[41]

MS = imports divided by the sum of industry shipments and imports, 1978 (source: KDI trade tape, 1978; originally from Trade Statistics, Customs Office).[42]

XS = exports divided by industry shipments, 1978 (source: see MS).

EPR1 = effective rate of protection based on the Balassa method, 1978 (source: Kim and Hong 1982).

EPR2 = effective rate of protection based on the Corden method, 1978 (source: see EPR1).[43]

NN = number of establishments in the industry, 1978 (source: see CR3; calculated during the estimation of SFPF).[44]

3.4.2 Heterogeneity, Occurrence of Change, and Innovation

In contrast to an industry's competitive conditions, hypotheses relating technical efficiency to product heterogeneity and to change and innovation focus on the dispersion of plant productivity levels. Whenever possible, we distinguish whether the hypothesized effect applies to v or u in our composed-error model of SFPF. Hypotheses should be phrased in terms of the net effect on the inefficiency component u.

A good example is the extent of structural product differentiation in an industry, which is expected to increase the variance of the gross profit rates of its firms. However, it is not clear whether the greater variance is associated with apparent technical inefficiency. The following variable is used to control the effect of product differentiation.

ADS = the ratio of purchased advertising services to industry shipments, 1978 (source: Bureau of Statistics, EPB, *Census of Manufactures*, 1978).[45]

Because the method for estimating technical efficiency depends on the shape of the empirical distribution of plants in the input-output space, any change that affects plants asymmetrically can alter its shape. Besides product differentiation, other candidates are

RDS = ratio of research and development spending to industry shipments, 1978 (source: see ADS).

SDKL = standard deviation of the ratio of adjusted capital stock to adjusted labor input, plants classified by industry, 1978 (source: Bureau of Statistics, EPB, *Census of Manufactures*, establishment data tape, 1978; calculated during the estimation of SFPF).[46]

FUELS = cost of fuels divided by industry shipments, 1978 (source: see ADS).

KVINT = acquisition of new machinery, equipment, tools and furniture, vehicles, ships and transport equipment, summed over the period 1975–78, divided by the total value of the corresponding category of fixed assets at the end of the year 1978 (source: Bureau of Statistics, EPB, *Census of Manufactures*, 1975–77).[47]

We note that the variable SDKL is likely to indicate the existence of input price inefficiency, which pretends to be technical inefficiency according to our efficiency estimates, since it is closely related to differences in input combinations among plants in the industry. Other factors may affect SDKL such as capital market imperfections, poor managerial decisions, and vintage effects. In the case of the variables RDS and FUELS, it is again unclear whether they affect the distribution of plants asymmetrically.

In comparison to the variables indicating competitive conditions, we do not find among these five variables anything particularly Korean. However, ADS and RDS may not have the same effects in Korea as in the mature industries of developed countries. This doubt, coupled with suspected errors in the measurement of ADS, RDS, and KVINT, leads to a low expectation of their significance in explaining technical efficiency.

3.4.3 Organizational Influences

Another important group of variables proposed by Caves and Barton (1990) is designed to test the effects of organizational and/or institutional differences between production units on technical efficiency. The following institutional features and size-related variables are considered:

KCOV = shipments of products classified under the industry by enterprises classified under the industry, divided by total shipments of products classified under the industry, 1978 (source: Bureau of Statistics, EPB, *Census of Manufactures*, commodity and enterprise data tapes, 1978).

KSPEC = shipments of products classified under the industry by enterprises classified under the industry, divided by total shipments of enterprises classified under the industry, 1978 (source: see KCOV).

KMULT = shipments of products classified under the industry by multiplant enterprises, divided by total shipments of products classified under the industry, 1978 (source: see KCOV, commodity, establishment and enterprise data tapes, 1978).

COSIZE = industry shipments multiplied by CR3, 1978 (source: see CR3).

PSIZE = approximate shipments of the plant accounting for the median unit of industry shipments, 1978 (the median is found by identifying the employment size class containing median shipments) (source: see KCOV).

RSIZE = PSIZE divided by the industry shipments, 1978 (source: see KCOV).

We note that the first three variables, designed to indicate the level of enterprise specialization (KCOV and KSPEC) and the extent of multiplant operation (KMULT), are defined in a manner different from their corresponding counterparts, as used by Caves and Barton (1990). Besides, the first two being measures of specialization rather than diversification, they are calculated from product rather than establishment shipments.

To make our analysis comparable to Uekusa and Torii (1987), we also include the following two control variables:

MEANK = industry average of the adjusted capital stock per plant, plants classified by industry, 1978 (source: see SDKL; calculated during the estimation of SFPF).

SUBCON = industry average of the payment for subcontracting work divided by total materials cost, plants classified by industry, 1978 (source: see SDKL; calculated during the estimation of SFPF).

3.4.4 Evidence on Interindustry Determinants of Technical Efficiency

There remains the important issue of how we choose the dependent variable to be explained from the alternative measures of technical efficiency. In subsection 3.3.5 we showed that the choice of a particular measure should matter little given the underlying regression equation from which it is derived. We first choose EFF based on GO/N as our dependent variable and then look into what effects the choice of different efficiency measures and different specifications of the production function might have.

Another procedural issue of concern is how we should treat the type I and type II failure industries in our cross-sectional analysis. If the theoretical hypothesis associating type I failure with high levels of efficiency and type II with extensive inefficiency is indeed true empirically, then any analysis including only the success industries fails to utilize the full body of information available. In this case we should include type I industries with their EFF values set equal to one, because a regression model treating type I failure industries as being censored at 1 would be a more appropriate choice than the more conventional ones.[48] Unfortunately, however, we still do not have evidence strong enough to confirm this hypothesis and thus exclude the type I failure industries from our cross-sectional analysis.

A number of experiments were conducted with different specifications for the regression equation before we obtained the following result, which is robust and has moderate statistical power to explain the relationship between EFF based on GO/N and selected explanatory variables. This result is fortunate since EFF, the ratio of actual output to the production frontier, can be regarded as the most direct and theoretically sound measure of efficiency.

$$EFF(GO) = 0.635 + 0.485HI - 0.607HI^2 - 0.012SDKL + 0.399 \text{ FUELS}$$
$$(10.857) \quad (2.707) \quad (2.079) \quad (1.777) \quad (1.250)$$

$$- 0.051KCOV + 0.144KSPEC - 0.119KMULT$$
$$(1.160) \quad (2.182) \quad (1.483)$$

$$+ 3.445RSIZE - 0.620SUBCON,$$
$$(3.709) \quad (1.848)$$

$R^2 = 0.223$, d.f. $= 147$, $F = 4.696$;

t-values appear in parentheses.

There are several points worthy of note. First, our results are rather similar to Caves and Barton (1990) in terms of the most robust set of explanatory variables. RSIZE, DIV (sum of COVE and SPECE), SDKL, and NOBS included in the study by Caves and Barton find their counterparts in RSIZE, KCOV, KSPEC, SDKL, and HI of our study.[49] The coefficients of RSIZE, KSPEC, SDKL, and HI obtain the right signs. However, the t-values of coefficients for these variables are much lower than those reported by Caves and Barton, and in the case of KCOV, the hypothesized positive effect on EFF(GO) is reversed. It is also interesting to note from our experiments that the negative effect of KCOV on EFF(GO) becomes more significant when we include KSPEC in the set of explanatory variables.

A plausible explanation for this result arises from the difference between KCOV and KSPEC. A high value of KSPEC implies that firms classified to the industry concentrate on production activities primary to that industry. On the other hand, a high value of KCOV implies that products classified to the industry are produced mostly as main products, not by-products, of all firms producing those products. Thus KSPEC has a direct interpretation as being a measure of specialization (diversification), while KCOV is less clearly associated with specialization in the industry at hand.[50] In sum, the evidence on the interindustry determinants of technical efficiency in Korean manufacturing industries is similar to the evidence on U.S. manufacturing industries but less strong.

The second point of interest is the difference in the set of variables with robust results. The capital-vintage dispersion, R&D, and part-time employment serve as additional important variables in Caves and Barton (1990), the first two of which are found insignificant determinants of EFF(GO) for Korean industries.[51] Instead, we report that FUELS, KMULT and SUBCON are relatively important variables although their t-values are not high enough to achieve statistical significance. It is interesting to observe a negative effect of SUBCON, since it is contrary to the hypothesis set forth by Uekusa and Torii (1987). The hypothesis of Uekusa and Torii of a positive effect of SUBCON on technical efficiency seems to depend on an efficient contracting system, usually ascribed to Japanese manufacturing industries. We do not think that Korean industries in 1978 utilized such an efficient system.

Third, the positive effect of establishment size on efficiency reported in table 3.12 parallels the positive and significant effect of RSIZE on EFF(GO), but the messages are different. In table 3.12 we found that omitting small-sized plants (those with less than 20 employees) results in an increase in average estimated efficiency, a finding on the effect of plant size on efficiency within industries. On the other hand, the positive effect of RSIZE on EFF(GO) provides us with cross-industry evidence on the effect of relative plant size, that is, the size of a representative (median) plant relative to the industry size. These findings, when combined, support a general positive relationship between plant size and efficiency. One explanation could be that Korean factor markets price capital and labor differently for small and large firms, as was the case for Japan.

Fourth, the insignificant and negative effect of MS on EFF(GO) is contrary to the usually hypothesized positive effect of import competition on efficiency and constitutes one of the major differences from Caves and Barton (1990).[52] So are the effects of XS, EPR1 and EPR2 on efficiency, although the results for these variables are not reported here due to the statistical insignificance of their coefficients. Besides the measurement errors in constructing data for MS, this seemingly discouraging result can be explained by the role of imports in Korea's industrial development. In Korea, imports of raw materials including oil and intermediate production goods had far exceeded imports of consumption goods until the latter recently began to rise sharply due to market opening measures in the 1980s. This fact explains why in most industries imports could not play the role of enhancing market performance by increasing competitive pressures. By testing a system of simultaneous equations for Korean manufacturing industries in 1983, Yoo (1988) showed that imports do not affect profitability.[53] This, combined with our result for MS, constitutes strong evidence on the lack of effect of imports on market performance, either allocative or technical efficiency. The main function of imports, as Yoo (1988) pointed out, was to promote exports in an export-led economy like Korea.

The fifth point of interest is that our result verifies the expected nonlinear influence of HI on EFF(GO). The coefficient of HI becomes much more significant when we add HI^2 to express the relationship in a quadratic form. Thus the result gives strong evidence for the hypothesis that technical efficiency is maximized in moderately concentrated industries. It is interesting to find similar conclusions in Uekusa and Torii (1987) and Caves and Barton (1990).

The last point of note is concerned with the quality of data. All the explanatory variables reported to have robust and relatively significant effects on technical efficiency are based on data directly available under the five-digit KSIC codes. For variables that required the conversion of industry codes into the KSIC system, it is uncertain whether their insignificant effects stem from measurement errors due to inaccurate code matching or the absence of behavioral relations.

3.4.5   Results for Alternative Dependent Variables

We conduct a further analysis of the robustness of our findings by employing the same set of regressors for different measures of technical efficiency. Table 3.13 summarizes the regression results for the eight models. We can evaluate the results in table 3.13 in two ways. First, we can observe the effect of selecting alternative measures of technical (in)efficiency by making comparisons among EFF, ATI, λ, and S with the choice between gross output and value added fixed. Thus, by comparing the columns for EFF(GO), ATI(GO), λ(GO), and S(GO), we can see that all the explanatory variables exhibit consistent directions of effect on the respective dependent variable, with minor exceptions. The extent of robustness of the regression results to changes in efficiency measures indicates that the model for EFF(GO) can be accepted as a good reference point in our analysis. Although the significance levels of the regression coefficients differ, the runs for EFF(GO) and ATI(GO) indicate that the significance levels are fairly stable, while the ones with S(GO) and λ(GO) show less significant coefficients.[54] All these results are in fact expected from the simple correlation test presented in table 3.9.

Second, by focusing on a particular measure of technical inefficiency, we can see the effect of the choice between gross output and value added. The difference between the runs for EFF(GO) and EFF(VA) obviously lies in the significance levels of regression coefficients for each individual explanatory variable. That is, the switch from gross output to value added significantly reduces the significance level of coefficients for most variables. Similar observations can be made for the other three cases, as well. This is opposite to the result found in Caves and Barton (1990), but consistent with the simple correlation test between EFF(GO) and EFF(VA) as presented in table 3.10.

3.5   Summary and Conclusions

In this chapter we attempted to answer some questions about the technical efficiency of Korea's manufacturing industries. We started by clarifying the

Table 3.13
Effect of alternative dependent variables on estimated determinants of interindustry differences in technical efficiency

Exogenous variable	Measures of efficiency				Measures of inefficiency			
	EFF(GO)	EFF(VA)	S(GO)	S(VA)	ATI(GO)	ATI(VA)	λ(GO)	λ(VA)
HI	0.485	−0.163	2.348	0.647	−0.101	−0.506	1.994	−2.609
	(2.707)	(0.899)	(1.875)	(0.712)	(2.347)	(1.794)	(0.770)	(0.250)
HI^2	−0.607	0.328	−2.164	−0.514	0.113	0.946	−3.078	−7.320
	(2.079)	(1.088)	(1.061)	(0.339)	(1.619)	(2.014)	(0.762)	(0.434)
SDKL	−0.012	−0.008	0.032	−0.017	0.002	0.003	−0.062	−0.440
	(1.777)	(0.926)	(0.666)	(0.415)	(1.381)	(0.204)	(0.625)	(0.853)
FUELS	0.399	0.068	1.704	0.543	−0.090	−0.887	−4.227	−9.271
	(1.250)	(0.183)	(0.763)	(0.291)	(1.176)	(1.534)	(0.928)	(0.452)
KCOV	−0.051	0.028	−0.053	−0.047	0.010	0.002	−0.339	2.073
	(1.160)	(0.536)	(0.174)	(0.178)	(0.993)	(0.023)	(0.560)	(0.682)
KSPEC	0.144	0.062	0.371	0.419	−0.031	−0.071	−0.728	−4.077
	(2.182)	(0.814)	(0.808)	(1.092)	(2.001)	(0.597)	(0.759)	(0.890)
KMULT	−0.119	−0.142	−1.353	−0.174	0.040	−0.068	0.070	7.290
	(1.483)	(1.646)	(2.405)	(0.403)	(2.070)	(0.508)	(0.056)	(1.426)
RSIZE	3.445	0.347	11.704	−2.017	−0.629	0.533	5.301	−13.635
	(3.709)	(0.324)	(1.804)	(0.374)	(2.836)	(0.319)	(0.418)	(0.207)
SUBCON	−0.620	0.072	−3.802	−0.297	0.146	−0.585	2.937	3.670
	(1.848)	(0.176)	(1.624)	(0.144)	(1.824)	(0.912)	(0.617)	(0.149)
Constant	0.635	0.589	0.409	−0.906	0.063	0.822	2.576	5.330
	(10.857)	(7.903)	(2.740)	(2.416)	(4.539)	(7.078)	(3.039)	(1.241)
R^2	0.223	0.048	0.126	0.015	0.187	0.042	0.040	0.037
Degrees of freedom	147	149	147	149	147	149	118	124

relationship among the various concepts of efficiency and found that our estimates of technical efficiency are in fact related to factor-price efficiency as well. We employed an empirical model, called the stochastic frontier production function, that divides the disturbance term into two compo-nents—one with a symmetric distribution for pure white noise and the other for technical inefficiency with an asymmetric distribution. A translog production function was assumed for the functional relationship between inputs and output, and it was estimated by the corrected ordinary least squares method.

The data from the Census of Manufactures for 1978 were refined in order to exclude unsuitable plants and industries. For the industries per-mitting successful estimation of technical efficiency we sought robust and consistent relationships among alternative measures of technical efficiency and between different specifications of the production function. The pro-duction function turns out to be the sensitive choice.

A cross-sectional analysis was carried out of the interindustry deter-minants of technical efficiency, yielding points of both similarity and difference between the cross-sectional evidence on Korea's manufacturing industries and that on U.S. and Japanese industries, as discussed in detail in section 3.4. The evidence becomes consistently stronger when we use the efficiency estimates based on gross output instead of value added. The empirical evidence obtained on the interindustry determinants of technical efficiency provides a counterpart to the findings of Caves and Barton (1990) on the U.S. case and those in Uekusa and Torii (1987) and chapter 2 on the Japanese case. The regressors were chosen and hypotheses were posed to make our results comparable to those studies. Therefore one could suspect that we have not made sufficient efforts to develop hypoth-eses and to find evidence on peculiarly Korean determinants of technical efficiency. Many of the hypotheses relating technical efficiency to competi-tive conditions, heterogeneity, the occurrence of change and innovation, organization influences, size, and so forth, have proved applicable to Ko-rean industries to some extent. Nevertheless, new hypotheses can be de-veloped in a Korean context. They are associated with rapid development and establishments embodying different degrees of modernization, the effects of the presence of *chaebol* (big business conglomerates in Korea) in many industries, and other Korea-specific institutional conditions. The evidence we found on the effect of size is related to the degree of moderniza-tion to the extent that it varies with the size of establishments. The effects of the *chaebol* are also partly related to our findings about organizational influences. Issues associated with the rapid growth of Korean industries must be dealt with in a dynamic setting and will thus be analyzed in chapter 8.

Also on the research agenda are new variables to capture unexplored effects of Korea-specific institutions. The study of Lee (1986) deserves special attention for introducing a new variable, credit allocated to each industry, in addition to familiar ones like effective protection and economies of scale, in analyzing the technical and allocative efficiencies of Korean industries.[55] We did a similar experiment by regressing EFF(GO) and EFF(VA) on the effective rate of protection (EPR1 or EPR2), scale economies (average shipments of larger establishments accounting for 50 percent of industry shipments divided by industry shipments), and subsidized credit (the amount of bank loans and foreign loans, divided by value added). Only the positive effect of scale economies on technical efficiency proved significant, but data problems may have obscured the effect of credit.[56]

Appendix.   Variables Used in Stage 1

S   Value of shipments.

INV1a   Finished goods inventories, beginning of the year.

INV1b   Finished goods inventories, end of the year.

GO2   Shipments plus net addition of inventories of finished goods, semifinished goods and work in progress.

MC   Direct production costs.

LPHR   Average working hours per day times annual number of days operated per production worker.

NP   Number of production workers.

LNPHR   LPHR × (LNPPAY/LPPAY), where LNPPAY and LPPAY are total annual compensations of nonproduction and production workers, respectively.

NNP   N − NP.

ASSETa   Tangible fixed assets, beginning of the year.

ASSETb   Tangible fixed assets, end of the year.

INVa   Total inventories, beginning of the year.

INVb   Total inventories, end of the year.

M   MC minus net additions of inventories of raw materials and work in progress.

MCFE   Fuels and electricity purchased.

The average working hours per day are obtained by dividing the data for the sum of 12 monthly average production-worker-hours per day by 12. The annual number of days operated are the sum of 12 monthly numbers of days operated. Since the number of total employees N is slightly different from the sum of the number of working proprietors and unpaid family workers A, the number of operatives B, and the number of administrative and other workers C, NP is defined as $N \times (A/A + B + C)$.

Notes

I received useful comments from Joon-Kyung Park and Ji-Hong Kim of the Korea Development Institute, and also from Richard Caves. I am deeply grateful and indebted to Jae-Hyung Lee, Inn-Chan Lee and Hyunduk Son for their invaluable assistance in handling data. My thanks also extend to the Bureau of Statistics, Economic Planning Board of Korea, for allowing me access to the data, and to the Korea Development Institute for financial support.

1. Empirical research in industrial organization has placed its main emphasis on allocative inefficiency arising from distorted allocation of resources, as related to market structure and firms' business conduct. This tradition, however, had not been found in Korea until recently as Korean economists began to recognize the importance of research on the issue. See Yoo (1988).

2. Further research remains to be done on the third question—the question on accounting for any international differences in technical efficiency. However, one must be very careful in devising the method of cross-national comparison.

3. In contrast to previous literature on the various concepts of efficiency, we try to distinguish factor-price efficiency from allocative efficiency, although the two are analogous to each other.

4. We deal with the question of the stability of technical efficiency over time in chapter 8.

5. The concept of the frontier production function has been applied to many different data sets by many researchers to obtain estimates of technical efficiency and link them with certain characteristics of plants or firms. Some of the studies focused more on improving the econometric model or the method of estimation. More recently, studies including Caves and Barton (1990) attempted to explain the interindustry differences in technical efficiency.

6. In the ensuing paragraphs, however, the additional condition of so-called price efficiency is required for any points on the production frontier.

7. Schmidt and Lovell (1979, 1980), who extended the previous works of Aigner et al. (1977) and Meeusen and van den Broeck (1977) on the stochastic frontier production function, contrasted the case in which cost minimization is achieved and technical inefficiency is the only type of inefficiency, with another case in which both types of inefficiencies exist and cost

is not minimized. They showed that the estimated stochastic frontier cost functions for these two cases allow us to distinguish between technical inefficiency and price inefficiency.

8. See Leibenstein (1966). In a reply to Schwartzman (1973), Leibenstein (1973) treated his concept of X-inefficiency as identical to Farrell's technical inefficiency. However, later writers including Carlsson (1972), Førsund et al. (1980), Siegfried and Wheeler (1981), and Schmidt (1985–86) treated X-inefficiency as comprised of both technical and price inefficiencies.

9. By quoting Schmidt and Lovell (1979) who say that "If a firm is technically inefficient, it operates beneath its stochastic production frontier, and if a firm is input price inefficient, it operates off its least cost expansion path," Siegfried and Wheeler (1981) gave the impression that any technically efficient points will lie on the production frontier. However, the condition Schmidt and Lovell assumed for the above statement is that "the firm seeks to minimize the cost of producing its desired level of output, subject to a stochastic production frontier constraint."

10. The discussion raises another important question on what effect the monopolistic market structure might have on technical inefficiency, which was indeed the central concern of Leibenstein (1966). We deal with this in the subsequent analysis of interindustry determinants of technical inefficiency.

11. Førsund et al. (1980) classified the econometric models for estimating the frontier production function according to the following: first, whether one treats the production frontier as a parametric function of inputs of production or as a nonparametric function; second, what functional relationship is to be specified between the production frontier and the actual output; and third, whether one assumes the production frontier to be deterministic or stochastic.

12. The model in equation (2), often called *composed error model*, was proposed by Aigner et al. (1977) and Meeusen and van den Broeck (1977).

13. Jondrow et al. (1982) showed that the conditional distribution of u given $\varepsilon = (v - u)$ can be utilized to decompose ε into v and u.

14. In the case of maximum likelihood estimation, the probability distributions assumed on u and v define the likelihood function, which in turn yields the maximum likelihood estimators. For the asymptotic properties of maximum likelihood estimators thus obtained, see Aigner et al. (1977) and Olson et al. (1980). The COLS method was first proposed by Richmond (1974) and named by Førsund et al. (1980).

15. The assumption of normal and half-normal distributions for v and u as in (4) is of course subject to many criticisms. However, changes in the distributional assumptions will not affect the result in a significant way, insofar as we assume a symmetric distribution for v and a one-sided distribution for u.

16. Let e_i, $i = 1, 2, \ldots, N$, denote the regression residuals as we estimate equation (3) by the OLS method. Then the second and third sample central moments, $\hat{m}_2$ and $\hat{m}_3$, are calculated using the following formulas, where N is the sample size and k is the number of regressors including the constant term:

$$\hat{m}_2 = \frac{1}{N - k} \sum_{i=1}^{N} e_i^2,$$

$$\hat{m}_3 = \frac{N - k + 1}{(N - k)(N - k - 1)} \sum_{i=1}^{N} e_i^3.$$

17. Given the assumptions in (4), the third central moment is always negative in the population.

18. Many prerequisites will be necessary for this problematic statement to be true. We will discuss this in greater detail in chapter 8.

19. For a detailed explanation of the four measures of technical (in)efficiency, see Caves and Barton (1990). In equation (7), $\Phi(\cdot)$ denotes the standard normal distribution function. In equation (8), $\overline{\ln(y)}$ denotes the mean of $\ln(y)$.

20. When we actually calculate ATI, we use the absolute value of $\overline{\ln(y)}$, $|\overline{\ln(y)}|$, in order to correct for the error that is made for negative values of $\overline{\ln(y)}$.

21. Uekusa and Torii (1985) showed that λ and S have a negative relationship in the interval $(-0.9968, 0)$.

22. For 1978 the data tape contains 29,864 establishments for 389 KSIC five-digit industries. Access to the data was made possible under the permission of the Bureau of Statistics, the Economic Planning Board of the Government of Korea.

23. Most of the variables used and methods of construction are similar to those in Caves and Barton (1990). However, we need to formulate some variables in a different way due to characteristics peculiar to Korean data.

24. Most of the items are directly available from the data tape of the Census of Manufactures. Otherwise, we give explanations in the appendix on how we calculate them.

25. In fact we find that the two groups of industries exhibit a significant divergence in average concentration ratios.

	Number of industries	CR3	HI
Retained	242	0.466	0.129
Excluded	150	0.802	0.400

Note: CR3 is the percentage of shipments accounted for by the three largest firms. HI is the Herfindahl-Hirschman index. We use individual commodity data in order to obtain better measures of concentration.

26. Caves and Barton (1990) called the two groups NA industries and TI industries, respectively.

27. The changes of efficiency estimates over time will give us important evidence in this regard. If type I failure is closely related to a high level of efficiency within industries over time, it will constitute evidence in favor of the theoretical claim. See chapter 8.

28. The case of equation (12) where VA/L is the dependent variable exhibits somewhat weaker evidence.

29. These remarkable differences between the means of ATI for the two equations mainly come from the difference in the means of GO/N and VA/L.

30. When we say "percent," it should be understood in terms of the definitions of EFF and ATI given in equations (7) and (8).

31. The mean values are simple averages of the sample industries, such as those in table 3.6. However, one can argue for an average weighted by the number of establishments in each industry, because the estimate of technical efficiency for an industry represents average efficiency for all its establishments.

32. The only exception is the correlation between EFF and ATI based on gross output (the first two columns in table 3.8). The Spearman correlation coefficient between these two estimates is -0.9106, with a significance level of 0.0006.

33. Obviously the underlying source of this dichotomy is the average of $\ln(VA/L)$ which is included in the denominator of the formula for ATI.

34. Table 3.9 also includes the correlations between each efficiency measure and the number of establishments in an industry, denoted OBS. Although the coefficients are low and insignificant, the variable OBS exhibits a trend of being positively correlated with {ATI, λ} and negatively correlated with {EFF, S}. As OBS is expected to have a relationship with the competitive conditions in an industry, this trend becomes a subject for further analysis.

35. There is no particular reason why we choose the cutoff point at 20 employees. However, the number of industries to be included for analysis in table 3.11 and table 3.12 would be sharply reduced if we increase the cutoff point.

36. Among possible explanations the small-sized units could employ different production technology, and input price inefficiency could exist.

37. The present study claims by no means to present a comprehensive set of "Korea-specific" hypotheses, if any do indeed exist. See section 3.5.

38. Most of the variables are also found in Caves and Barton (1990) and Uekusa and Torii (1987).

39. In defining the explanatory variables, we borrow heavily from Caves and Barton (1990) in our notations and formulas.

40. See Lee (1986) and Kim (1990) for further details.

41. CR3 and HI used for the present analysis are somewhat different from what can be computed directly from the enterprise data tape of 1978 Census of Manufactures. We include only the shipments of commodities classified to the industry to focus more closely on product competition.

42. We had to match commodity-based CCCN codes with KSIC industries. The concordance table, however, was written in terms of the new KSIC code revised in 1984, which required an additional step of converting the new KSIC into the old classification. Thus measurement errors are deemed to be significant for MS and XS.

43. Kim and Hong (1982) provide EPR1 and EPR2 computed for 163 manufacturing industries. Thus, for certain KSIC industries, we applied a single number.

44. NN counts only the establishments included in the data set edited for the estimation of SFPF.

45. Data on ADS found in the Census of Manufactures are not entirely reliable since for many large conglomerate enterprises in Korea, advertising outlays are spent by the headquarters office of the entire business group and are thus not captured accurately for each industry. Data on RDS available from the Census suffer from similar measurement errors.

46. Adjusted capital stock and labor input are K and L, respectively, as defined in section 3.3.

47. Without appropriate data on the age structure of capital stock by industry, we use KVINT as a proxy variable to represent the capital-vintage effect. The rationale for using KVINT is based on the following relationship.

$$K_T = K_0 + \sum_{t=1}^{T} I_t - \sum_{t=1}^{T} D_t, \qquad t = 1, 2, \dots, T.$$

where K_t is the capital stock at the end of year t, I_t is the acquisition of new fixed assets in year t, and D_t is depreciation of capital in year t. However, the data available provide only the sum of I_t for the period 1975–78, and no reliable information was available for D_t and the age of K_0.

48. This argument appears to be particularly important when we consider the large proportion of type I failure industries in our sample. For further discussion, see chapter 8.

49. Note that HI should be the counterpart to NOBS (square root of the number of plants), since both are related to the seller distribution in a market.

50. The formulas for KCOV and KSPEC have the same numerator, implying that a high correlation would exist between these two variables. However, the Pearson correlation coefficient between KCOV and KSPEC is 0.2876, which is low enough to make the two variables free of any multicollinearity problem. See Lee et al. (1984, ch. 3) for further details.

51. We do not have a variable in our analysis equivalent to part-time employment. Remember that we might have significant measurement errors in KVINT and RDS as explained before.

52. See Caves and Barton (1990, table 6.1).

53. The model tested in Yoo (1988) consists of four equations, with profitability, exports, imports, and the market concentration ratio jointly determined in the system. See Yoo (1988, table 4).

54. We can make similar observations on the differences between the runs for EFF(VA), ATI(VA), λ(VA), and S(VA).

55. According to Lee (1986), credit rationing is an important form of market distortion and a probable determinant of technical efficiency in Korea. Since access to subsidized credit was the best path to business success in Korea, there are important incentives for rent-seeking activities, which could generate technical inefficiencies. Lee also maintains that the firms receiving more subsidized credit may not use it as economically as those that pay the market-clearing rate, constituting another form of technical inefficiency.

56. Lee's method of estimating technical efficiency differed from ours. Also converting the data on subsidized credit (available from the Bank of Korea's Financial Statements Analysis) into KSIC five-digit industries must have created serious measurement errors.

References

Aigner, D. J., C. A. Knox Lovell, and P. Schmidt. 1977. Formulation and estimation of stochastic frontier production function models. *Journal of Econometrics* 6: 21–37.

Carlsson, B. 1972. The measurement of efficiency in production: an application to Swedish manufacturing industries, 1968. *Swedish Journal of Economics* 74: 468–485.

Caves, R. E., and D. R. Barton. 1990. *Efficiency in U.S. Manufacturing Industries*. Cambridge. MIT Press.

Farrell, M. J. 1957. The measurement of productive efficiency. *Journal of the Royal Statistical Society A* 120: 253–282.

Førsund, F. R., C. A. Knox Lovell, and P. Schmidt. 1980. A survey of frontier production functions and of their relationship to efficiency measurement. *Journal of Econometrics* 13: 5–25.

Harberger, A. C. 1954. Monopoly and resource allocation. *American Economic Review* 44: 77–87.

Jondrow, J., C. A. Knox Lovell, I. S. Materov, and P. Schmidt. 1982. On the estimation of technical inefficiency in the stochastic frontier production function. *Journal of Econometrics* 19: 233–238.

Kim, K. S. 1990. Industrial policy and trade regimes in Korea: Past, present and future. Paper presented at the Workshop on Korea's Political Economy. Honolulu, August.

Kim, K. S. and S. D. Hong. 1982. *Long-Term Trend of Real and Nominal Rates of Protection in Korea* (in Korean). Seoul: Korea Development Institute.

Lee, J. M. 1986. Market performance in an open developing economy: Technical and allocative efficiencies of Korean industries. *Journal of Industrial Economics* 35: 81–96.

Lee, K. U., J. H. Lee, and J. H. Kim. 1984. *Market and Market Structure* (in Korean). Research Report 84-06. Seoul: Korea Development Institute.

Lee, L.-F., and W. G. Tyler. 1978. The stochastic frontier production function and average efficiency: An empirical analysis. *Journal of Econometrics* 7: 385–389.

Leibenstein, H. 1966. Allocative efficiency vs. *X*-efficiency. *American Economic Review* 56: 392–415.

Leibenstein, H. 1973. Competition and *X*-efficiency: Reply. *Journal of Political Economy* 81: 763–777.

Meeusen, W., and J. van den Broeck. 1977. Efficiency estimation of Cobb-Douglas production functions with composed error. *International Economic Review* 18: 435–444.

Olson, J. A., P. Schmidt, and D. M. Waldman. 1980. A Monte Carlo study of estimators of stochastic frontier production functions. *Journal of Econometrics* 13: 67–82.

Richmond, J. 1974. Estimating the efficiency of production. *International Economic Review* 15: 515–521.

Schmidt, P. 1985–86. Frontier production functions. *Econometric Reviews* 4: 289–328.

Schmidt, P., and C. A. Knox Lovell. 1979. Estimating technical and allocative inefficiency relative to stochastic production and cost frontiers. *Journal of Econometrics* 9: 343–366.

Schmidt, P., and C. A. Knox Lovell. 1980. Estimating stochastic production and cost frontiers when technical and allocative inefficiency are correlated. *Journal of Econometrics* 13: 83–100.

Schwartzman, D. 1973. Competition and efficiency: Comment. *Journal of Political Economy* 81: 756–764.

Siegfried, J. J., and E. H. Wheeler. 1981. Cost efficiency and monopoly power: A survey. *Quarterly Review of Economics and Business* 21: 25–46.

Uekusa, M., and A. Torii. 1985. An estimation of the level of technical inefficiency in Japanese industries by use of stochastic production frontier (in Japanese). *Papers on Economics* 51: 1–23.

Uekusa M., and A. Torii. 1987. The determinants of the level of technical inefficiency in Japanese industries (in Japanese). Mimeo.

Weinstein, M. A. 1964. The sum of values from a normal and a truncated normal distribution. *Technometrics* 6: 104–105.

Yoo, S. M. 1988. An empirical analysis on the international linkages of Korea's industrial organization (in Korean). *Korea Development Review* 10: 65–94.

4 Technical Inefficiency in U.K. Manufacturing Industry

David G. Mayes and Alison Green

4.1 Introduction

This chapter presents results from the study of technical inefficiency in 19,023 establishments in 151 sectors of the manufacturing industry in the United Kingdom, as part of the wider project comparing inefficiency in the manufacturing industry across the countries described in this book.

The analysis follows the common framework set out in earlier chapters of estimating measures of technical inefficiency, as defined by Michael Farrell (1957), for each industry from the residuals obtained by fitting stochastic translog frontier production functions to the data. The nature of the data, definition of variables, specification of the production functions, and the measures of inefficiency used may vary in details but these results, based on data drawn from the U.K. *Annual Census of Production* for 1977, are comparable with those used in the other country studies.

The program of research has three phases, estimation, explanation, and international comparison. We have set out the characteristics of the estimates elsewhere (Green and Mayes 1991) and discussed the theoretical details in a comparison with the Australian results in Green, Harris, and Mayes (1989). The third phase is the comparison among countries, of which this book is the first step. This chapter therefore is concerned with the second phase, the explanation of why technical inefficiency occurs and why it varies across industries in United Kingdom. The methodology and the resulting measures are summarized in the first section of this chapter.

Technical inefficiency can vary between industries for a variety of reasons, and we are concerned here to investigate some of the best-known hypotheses. We have classified them into five groups: competitive conditions, product differentiation, rate of change, spatial disparities, and organizational influences. The basic hypotheses are simple.

1. The harsher the competitive environment, the less scope there is for inefficiency. Inefficient firms will go out of business rapidly.

2. The more differentiated the products of the industry, the more efficiency can vary. In part this is a comment on the inappropriateness of estimating a single frontier production function for the sector.

3. The faster the rate of change in a sector, the more we can expect behavior to vary. This applies whether the industry is contracting, expand-

ing, or innovating, although we cannot expect to see exactly the same spread of behavior in each case.

4. In the same way that increased variation in performance is possible, the more variety there is in the product, the more geographically diverse is the market, and the more variety there is in production, the more performance can vary.

5. In many respects organization and management of the firm is the archetypal source of residual or X-inefficiency. Once we have taken account of all the identifiable factors relating to the quality of inputs and other items set out in hypotheses 1 through 4, the only option left lies in how the firm is run. However, we have treated this differently and tried to identify explicit organizational differences, for example, the greater the number of plants in a firm, the greater is the chance of heterogeneity and weaker control.

In sections 4.3 through 4.7 we explore each hypothesis in turn and draw general conclusions in section 4.8. However, the relationships that we use are not independent and our model is a multivariate one that takes into account all of the above factors simultaneously.

4.2 Technical Inefficiency in Manufacturing Industry

The manufacturing sector in the United Kingdom is mature and well established and accounts for 20 to 25 percent of employment and output. However, with the exception of a period in the 1980s, its proportion of employment and output and contribution to economic activity has been falling since the 1950s. Manufactured goods are readily tradable, and since over half of the United Kingdom's trade is not subject to tariff, the success of the industry is largely dependent on maintaining international competitiveness. The importance of trade is increasing. Exports accounted for 20 percent of U.K. manufacturing sales in the mid-1950s, rising to over 30 percent by 1980. Manufactures accounted for 80 percent of exports of goods in the 1950s, and in 1980 they still accounted for 75 percent despite the development of North Sea oil.

Although the declining share of manufacturing in economic activity is paralleled by the experience of the other advanced countries, the United Kingdom's performance was generally worse than that of its competitors until the second half of the 1980s. Given the importance of manufacturing in the balance of payments, the performance of this sector has been central in explaining the problems for the economy as a whole. Not surprisingly therefore U.K. manufacturing performance has been the subject of considerable research.

The research undertaken has been varied, frequently focusing on macroeconomic issues with little attention given to microeconomic organization and plant-level efficiency. Microeconomic work has tended to utilize relatively small samples of firms or industry-level data (e.g., OECD 1986). Broader studies using large numbers of firms have generally been precluded because of a lack of data. Most of the data that do exist relate to financial performance (e.g., Dun and Bradstreet, ICC, and EXSTAT) and not to the major variables necessary for explaining economic performance.

Comparisons have been made at industry level of productivity differences between counties, either for labor (Davies and Caves 1987) or for total factor productivity (Baldwin and Gorecki 1986). But the use of industry-level data tends to obscure many of the fundamental issues behind U.K. performance. It is, for example, frequently argued that the best U.K. firms are competitive with the best in the world. Hence, if U.K. productivity is lower, it is either because there is much more inefficiency within the rest of manufacturing industry or because the United Kingdom has a concentration of activity in low productivity industries. The second point can be covered in part by examining the data at the industry level. However, low productivity might have also occurred because plant size tends to be smaller in the United Kingdom (Pratten 1971). Our analysis therefore seeks to fill this gap by looking at the individual establishment and assessing its efficiency *given* its industry's size and inputs of capital and labor.

The approach used in this study builds on a straightforward decomposition of the sources of productivity variation among countries:

1. They might be using different technologies.

2. The distribution of activity among industries might differ.

3. They might operate at different scales.

4. Having allowed for all these, they might still obtain different levels of output from the same level of inputs.

The last condition means that there must be some inefficiency in the production process. Several sources of this inefficiency can be described, but a well-known and widely used approach following Farrell (1957) categorizes them as allocative and technical inefficiencies. *Allocative ineffi-ciency* is defined as a failure to choose the optimal combination of inputs (i.e., at the given input-price ratio to use the smallest total value of input). *Technical inefficiency* is the failure to achieve maximum output from the chosen combination of inputs. Our study concentrates on technical inefficiency, as this has previously been the most difficult component to quantify. In addition technical inefficiency appears to be a cause of under-performance. Daly et al. (1985) suggest that the major discrepancy between U.K. and German productivity is not a lack of capital, in the form of plant and machinery, but an inability to exploit that capital due to poor skills of both operatives and management. Technical inefficiency therefore embodies all the managerial and organizational sources of inefficiency, what Leibenstein (1966) refers to as *X-inefficiency*.

For any given level of inputs a range of outputs is achieved by different establishments. To determine how inefficient an establishment is we have to ascertain what constitutes efficient production at the level of inputs. This could be a reflection of the *best* performances actually achieved in an industry, or it could be a construct of the maximum output theoretically attainable based on the technology of the production process. Such tech-nological constructs are difficult to establish for many industries, where variations in the quality of inputs or differentiated products are possible. Thus suitable calculations could be made for, say, electricity generation but not for many other processes. Best actual performance is usually therefore the chosen route. Initial studies preferred a programming ap-proach to estimating such performance, and more recent work, such as that by Thiry and Tulkens (1989), shows it to good effect.

There are, however, two drawbacks to this approach that might lead us to prefer yet a different method. The first is simply that the best-perfor-mance case does not translate readily to economic decision making by the firm. There is no behavioral explanation of how inputs are transformed into these maximal outputs. The second is that it assumes a degree of homogeneity and similarity of establishments in the same industry that likely exceeds what actually prevails. We would expect in practice that various minor sources of variation affect the efficient output that any particular firm can attain at any particular time. To accommodate the first drawback, we can use a functional relationship between inputs and output, and to allow for the second, the relation can include random residual variation. These two can be combined by using a stochastic production function to estimate the relation. It enjoys a clear basis in economic theory for the chosen behavior and yet admits of variation for various particular and largely random rather than identifiable reasons. This property enables us to avoid defining the best as some unusual outlier and permits the determination of a frontier of efficient behavior that is attained in practice.

The frontier production function assumes that for any technology in an industry, it is possible to represent the locus of efficient production by some readily expressible function that relates output to inputs. For a given technology the production frontier is the theoretical maximum output that can be achieved using each of the possible combinations of inputs. In practice many firms operate inside that frontier because of the presence of some inefficiency.

4.2.1 The Stochastic Production Frontier Model

The idea behind the stochastic frontier model is that the standard production function $Q = f(K, L, Z)$—where Q is a measure of output, K and L the capital and labor inputs, Z a vector of other influences, and f the functional form—is augmented by a residual e. This residual has two elements; a symmetric random component, as is common in economic behavioral relations, and a nonsymmetric component that represents technical inefficiency. Thus the specification can be written as

$$Q = f(K, L, Z) + e, \tag{1}$$

where

$$e = v + u,$$

defining u as the random residual, v as the asymmetric measure of inefficiency with v and u independent. The u component has a symmetric distribution, whereas $v \leq 0$, reflecting the fact that each firm's output must lie on or below the frontier after allowing for purely random variations. This enables efficient firms to be randomly distributed around the frontier and inefficient firms to be spread out inside the frontier but also subject to the same random influences. The actual shape of the two distributions is open to debate, and there is a considerable problem to be resolved in deciding how to split the residual into its two components.

Under this definition of inefficiency deviations from the frontier are the result of factors that lie within the firm's control, such as technical and economic inefficiency due to firm-specific knowledge (Page 1980), the will and efforts of the producer and employees (Aigner, Lovell, and Schmidt 1977; Lee and Tyler 1978), and work stoppages and disruptions to production (Lee and Tyler 1978). But the frontier itself is a random variable varying across firms and, over time, for any given firm. The random component u is assumed to be distributed symmetrically, since it represents both positive and negative effects on the production process such as luck, weather (Aigner, Lovell, and Schmidt 1977; Schmidt and Sickles 1984), or measurement errors on the levels of output (Aigner, Lovell, and Schmidt 1977).

4.2.2   Specification and Estimation

The resulting estimates of inefficiency depend upon the choice of specification for the production frontier and the functional forms assumed for the two components of the residual. Clearly several widely used forms of production function could be estimated and then tests undertaken to determine which fits best in each instance. In view of the size of our data set and the heterogeneity of industries involved, we opted for a very general formulation, namely, the transcendental logarithmic (translog) form (a discussion of it is contained in Harris 1989). The basic specification for the equation can be written as

$$\ln Q = a_0 + a_1 \ln L + a_2 \ln K + a_3(\ln L)^2 + a_4(\ln K)^2 + a_5(\ln L \cdot \ln K)$$

$$+ \Sigma_i a_{i+5} X_i + e, \tag{2}$$

where $e = u + v$, with u and v defined as above and the X_i variables being the identified components of the vector Z.

The additional X variables were chosen to try to eliminate as many differences between the nature of inputs and outputs within the particular industry as could be identified from the *Annual Census of Production*.[1] The rationale for the inclusion of these variables is discussed by Griliches and Ringstad (1971) and Caves and Barton (1990).

X_1 = proportion of plant and machinery in total capital stock,

X_2 = number of production workers as percent of total employees,

X_3 = cost of goods purchased for resale as a percent of total material costs,

X_4 = cost of fuel and electricity as a percent of total material costs,

X_5 = exports as percent of total deliveries,

X_6 = inventories as percent of total capital stock,

X_7 = degree of product specialization,

X_8 = annual hours worked per production worker,

X_9 = annual income of nonproduction workers.

These variables were tested for the U.S. version of the study (Caves and Barton 1990) and were reproduced as far as possible in our research. However, data were not available for X_4, X_5, X_7, and X_8, so they had to be excluded. The variables allow for differences in the nature of inputs and outputs in the industry to affect the form of the production function. X_1 and X_6 give a decomposition of capital, allowing for the fact that buildings, plant and machinery, and inventories play rather different roles in the production process. Similarly X_2 and X_9 provide a decomposition of the labor input, first distinguishing those involved directly in the production process and then obtaining a crude estimate of the level of skills in the labor force through per capita wage levels. Lastly, goods for resale X_3 are separated out as they do not require the same amount of transformation in their production.

The X variables used in the U.K. study therefore were

X_1 = plant and machinery as a percentage of capital,

X_2 = number of production workers as a percent of labor,

X_3 = cost of goods for resale as percent of material costs,

X_4 = wages and salaries per head of production workers,

X_5 = wages and salaries per head of nonproduction workers.

The definition of capital stock used is discussed below.

Data were obtained from the Annual Census of Production (ACOP) on 151 minimum list heading (MLH) industries. This information is collected annually by the Business Statistics Office (BSO) from each establishment. The information is then aggregated by the BSO and published in the form of ACOP summary tables at industry level. Our research used data at establishment level, with the BSO itself conducting the statistical analysis in order to protect confidentiality. We were then provided with results from the regression model for the 151 industries. The year 1977 was chosen because it was a benchmark year and would provide a direct comparison with the U.S. study for the same year.

Information is available from ACOP on acquisitions and disposals of capital items under three headings of buildings, plant and machinery, and vehicles, and for firms employing more than 100 people, expenditure on rent and leasing of equipment were also recorded. It is therefore possible to construct a rather crude estimate of the capital stock from this, given information about the plausible length of life of assets in each class. It is important to include leased and rented capital because production possibilities depend on the capital available for use regardless of its ownership. However, on average, in about 40 percent of cases no renting or leasing information was available, and it was necessary to scale up the own capital stock estimates in these cases by assuming the ratio of owned to leased assets is the same as the average for all firms in the industry for which the information exists.

These estimates are rather crude, since they are based on only a year's investment data. A more reliable method would be to use a series of several years' data from ACOP. This approach would smooth out any lumpiness in investment expenditure, but it would also be a complex and expensive task, well beyond the resources of this project.

Denoting assets A, disposals D, and life lengths l, for the three categories of capital—land and buildings, plant and machinery, and vehicles—for which there are data i ($i = 1, 2, 3$), we have as an estimate for owned capital K_1 of each establishment

$$K_1 = \sum_{i=1}^{3} \frac{(A_i - D_i)l_i}{2},$$

which allows for a uniform rate of depreciation. Data on leasing and hiring for large firms can also be incorporated to obtain K_2 of

$$K_2 = K_1 + \frac{H}{r + 1/l_4} + \frac{R}{r + 1/l_5},$$

where

H = expenditure on hiring, leasing, or renting of plant, machinery, or vehicles,

R = rent paid for industrial or commercial buildings,

r = rate of interest.

Assuming that for small firms the ratio of leased and hired assets to owned assets is the same as for large firms,

$$K_2 = \frac{K_1}{k^*},$$

where

$$k^* = \frac{1}{n} \sum_{j=1}^{n} \frac{K_1}{K_2}.$$

k^*, the average proportion of the capital stock of large firms in the industry owned by them, is estimated for $j = 1, \ldots, n$ large firms in the industry. On the basis of life lengths assumed by the CSO the following estimates were used:

l_1 (land and buildings) = 50 years,

l_2 (plant and machinery) = 12–21 years depending upon industry,

l_3 (vehicles) = 7 years,

l_4 (leased plant and machinery) = 12 years,

l_5 (rented buildings) = 30 years.

Although small firms form a relatively small proportion of total employment and output, they account for between a third and a half of the observations.

A pilot study was conducted on six industries in order to establish whether the methods used by Caves and Barton (1990) in the United States could successfully be applied to the U.K. data and, if so, to establish the form of the production frontier model to be applied in the full study for the first phase of the project. Because of the absence of data on hours worked by establishment, it was not possible to use a scaled equation of the form specified by Caves and Barton. Therefore two separate forms of the equation were used, with unscaled and scaled numbers employed.

A range of measures of output is also available from ACOP, and five variables were used as dependent variables in the equation: gross output, gross value added, gross output per head, gross value added per head, and net output per head.[2] Unfortunately, while giving some pointers, the results of the pilot study did not provide a clear indication of how to proceed with the study. It was necessary to make the decisions on the basis of the limited evidence from the U.K. pilot sample and from the experience of the U.S. and Australian studies. However, it became clear that the equations using gross output and gross output per head as the dependent variables were not successful, so we omitted them from the main study. We then took a simple pragmatic approach and selected gross value added as the dependent variable for the main study in order to make the results directly comparable with those obtained from the Australian project; direct comparability with the United States was impossible because of the lack of data on hours worked.

Choosing the functional forms for the two components of the residual is more contentious. Assuming that the stochastic component is normal follows convention, but there is little previous hard empirical evidence on the shape of the distribution of inefficiency. The half-normal distribution assumes that the likelihood of inefficiency diminishes as one moves away from the frontier. An alternative assumption is to retain the normal shape but truncate the distribution somewhere other than the mean. Truncating above the mean allows the distribution of inefficiency to have a maximum inside instead of on the frontier. In Green, Harris, and Mayes (1989) we discuss how the appropriate truncation point can be estimated, along with the production frontier itself, by maximum likelihood (see chapter 5 for an application).

Even if we accept the hypothesis of continuously diminishing inefficiency below the frontier the half-normal is not the only possible form. Others have used the exponential (see Harris 1989 for a discussion). The results are sensitive to the form chosen but the basis of choice is rather arbitrary. We have therefore opted for the simplest solution, the half-normal, which also has the great advantage of comparability with the results for the other countries in the study.

One of the great advantages of the half-normal formulation is that it is possible to obtain estimates of the standard deviations of the decomposed residuals σ_u and σ_v from the moments of the residuals of an ordinary least regression estimate of (2). (σ_v is not the standard deviation of v but of the complete normal distribution from which the half normal distribution of v is taken; see Green, Harris, and Mayes 1989.)

4.2.3   A Drawback

For our method to be calculable in practice the distribution of actual residuals calculated from the regression has to be compatible with our assumptions about their skewness. There are therefore circumstances in which the standard deviations of u and v cannot be calculated because they would involve the square root of a negative number. The first instance occurs when the skewness of the overall residuals is positive, and the second when the implied variance of v is greater than the variance of the total residual, e. (We label these type I and type II failures in the subsequent discussion.) A positive skew means that the longer tail of the distribution lies outside rather than inside the frontier. Thus in some sense establishments in that industry are extremely efficient rather than inefficient (Caves and Barton 1990 offer a number of suggestions for the causes of this finding in particular industries). The second quirk of the method is that the estimated spread of inefficiency can be so great that $\sigma_v^2 > \sigma_e^2$, implying that $\sigma_u^2 < 0$ which is infeasible. In practice this rarely occurs.

4.2.4   Measures of Technical Inefficiency

Given that σ_u and σ_v can be calculated, several measures of inefficiency can be computed for each industry. Those in normal use are set out below.

1.   The standard error of the residuals from the regression σ_e can always be calculated and makes no assumptions about the shapes of the distributions of u and v. This gives a measure of the variation of behavior of the industry.

2.   Mean inefficiency $\sigma_v\sqrt{(2/\pi)}$, is referred to as *average technical inefficiency* (ATI), which is the expected value of v. With a log regression the residuals have a direct interpretation in terms of percentage deviations from the fitted frontier.

3.   One of the simplest measures of inefficiency available is λ, the ratio of the two standard deviations,

$$\lambda = \frac{\sigma_v}{\sigma_u}. \tag{5}$$

This ratio compares the inefficiency under the control of management to the external sources of variation in efficiency u.

4.   ATE, average technical efficiency, is $2\exp(\sigma_v^2/2)[1 - F(-\sigma_v)]$, where F is the distribution function of v. This provides a measure of the average of the ratio of actual output to frontier output (i.e., a comparison of what is achieved with what could be).

5. A second measure that can be calculated is skewness s of the overall residuals. A large variance of the random component belies the notion that asymmetry represents technical inefficiency. Skewness of the overall residuals takes account of this and hence can be used as a measure of inefficiency.

4.2.5   Estimation of the Results

Following the exploratory stage, the analysis proceeded for all 151 industries, with gross value added as the independent variable. A uniform approach was required because the Statistics of Trade Act prevented us from having direct access to data. In running the regressions, we therefore had to make use of the Business Statistics Office.

The most prominent outcome was the numerous cases for which the residuals could not be satisfactorily decomposed, as can be seen from table 4.1.[3] Of the 151 industries in the U.K. study, 48 (32 percent) showed positive skewness of the combined residuals (type I failure). Of the remaining 103 industries, a further 31 (20 percent) showed type II failure ($\sigma_v^2 > \sigma_u^2$). Thus full results were available for 72 out of 151 industries (48 percent). The number of failures might lead one to question the methodology, but such a large number is to be expected from the estimation method. Uekusa and Torii (1985) have shown that if $\sigma_u = \sigma_v = \lambda = 1$, then for a sample of size 100, type I failures are to be expected on 29 percent of occasions, whereas for a sample of size 200, the number falls to 21 percent. In our study the average sample size is 130, but the true value of λ is unknown. So while we can say that on this limited evidence our results appear consistent with experience, more evidence is required. However, Uekusa and Torii also show that the expected number of type II failures is approximately zero at sample sizes of 100 and 200. Therefore we clearly have a problem in this regard. In practice it appears that many industries do not show any great inefficiency. There in fact are others where it is apparent that the statistical classification does not identify a single industry but a group of similar industries. In future research we hope to establish whether it is the definitional problem or the great inefficiency which is the cause of the failure.

The large numbers of type I and type II failures led us to survey the traits of the industries in which they occur. Neither the subgroup subject to type I failure nor that subject to type II failure contained a particularly high quantity of very large or very small industries. They seem to be distributed

Table 4.1
Distribution of estimated inefficiency levels and estimation failures among subindustries, by major industry

	Industry heading	Number of subindustries	Type I failure (%)	ATI below mean[a] (%)	ATI above mean[a] (%)	Type II failure (%)
21, 22, 23	Food, drink, and tobacco	14	36	7	36	21
26	Coal and petroleum products	3	33	0	0	67
27	Chemicals	16	31	25	31	13
31	Iron and steel	3	0	33	33	33
32	Aluminium and other metals	3	0	67	33	0
33, 34	Mechanical engineering	21	38	14	29	19
35	Instrument engineering	4	50	25	0	25
36	Electrical engineering	11	27	27	27	18
37	Shipbuilding	1	100	0	0	0
38	Vehicles	6	50	0	17	33
39	Metal goods not elsewhere specified	11	45	27	27	0
41, 42	Textiles	16	19	31	31	19
43	Leather and fur	3	33	0	0	67
44, 45	Clothing and footwear	9	56	11	11	22
46	Building materials	7	43	43	14	0
47	Timber and furniture	6	0	0	17	83
48	Paper and printing	8	13	50	25	12
49	Other manufactures	9	11	22	44	22

a. Mean ATI = 0.320.

fairly evenly throughout the whole sample, rather than being concentrated in any particular one of the broader SIC industry classifications shown in table 4.1. The only exception to this is the Timber and Furniture group (MLH 4170–4790), in which five out of the six industries showed type II failures. It may be that the furniture industry generally is inefficient, or more likely that the industry possesses other characteristics that make the fitting of a single production function inappropriate.

Although the findings indicate that some caution should be taken in drawing conclusions from the results, enough information is available for us to attempt to explain apparent differences in efficiency levels between industries. The failure to decompose the residuals in nearly half of all cases did pose problems, and these industries deserve particular attention in the next phase of the project. Caves and Barton (1990, ch. 7) suggest that it may be more appropriate to divide industries into large and small establishments and to fit several different production functions. On the whole, however, numbers of establishments within many industries are sufficiently small to make decomposition by size difficult. In any event Caves and Barton were able to estimate satisfactory measures of inefficiency using the whole set of establishments in most cases. Division into large and small for separate estimation 'merely' improved the explanation.

The use of stochastic frontier production functions with a decomposed residual to measure technical inefficiency has been criticized, particularly for the half-normal assumption for v. However, evidence from the Australian study (Harris 1989) shows that using a different distribution for v actually makes relatively little difference to the spread of the results. Our study and the results obtained have shown interesting differences between industries, and the next step is to analyze these differences and seek explanations of them. Whatever criticisms may be leveled at the half-normal assumption, it is always possible to work with skewness, which does not depend on the decomposition of the residuals and permits all industries to be retained for analysis.

4.3   Competitive Conditions

The basic argument is straightforward. Perfect competition in an industry precludes inefficiency because perfect competition entails a large number of firms of the same size, using the same technology and producing a homogeneous product where both purchasers and suppliers have full information about market conditions. Almost all real world markets differ from this paradigm in every respect. Our task therefore is to measure these departures and estimate their relation to observed inefficiency. Where competitive pressures are lower, firms will tend to operate at lower levels of inefficiency.

The best-known and most widely studied example is that where the number of firms in the industry is small or where production is concentrated in the hands of a few large producers. In these circumstances the large companies can exercise market power by restricting the ability of smaller companies to compete. However, it was not always possible to identify effective concentration from our data. Since our industries are defined by statistical categories and not in homogeneous economic terms the industry could be characterized by two somewhat separate markets: one composed of small specialized producers who face little competition in their small segments, and the other composed of a small number of volume producers competing for a range of more standarized products.

Our first measure of competitive conditions in therefore concentration. There is considerable argument about how concentration should be measured, whether the chosen variable should be value added or sales, whether it should include all firms as in the case of the Herfindahl index or only the largest ones. These factors are important but the question is academic because only one measure is available, namely, the five-firm concentration ratio based on the gross output of the five largest firms in the industry recorded in the *Annual Census of Production*, divided by output in the industry as a whole. This measure introduces an extra link in the analysis because market competition occurs among firms (enterprises), whereas our analysis is based on establishments (plants).

The five-firm concentration ratio, referred to as CONC1 in our list of variables (in the appendix), can be misleading because it treats the market as if only domestic output mattered. This approach is mistaken in two respects, first, because the concentration of domestic suppliers becomes irrelevant if the U.K. market is dominated by importers and, second, because the domestic market could be fragmented and the large firms mainly export oriented. There are two ways to deal with the problem. The first is to expand the definition of the market to include imports, which we do:

$$\text{CONC2} = \text{CONC1}\left(\frac{\text{sales}}{\text{sales} + \text{imports}}\right).$$

The second is to measure the openness of the industry to foreign trade as a separate issue from concentration, as we also consider below.

We have the advantage that the U.S. and Japanese studies have already examined concentration. Their results are mixed. According to Caves and Barton (1990) there is no *linear* relation between efficiency and concentration but a significant curvilinear one does exist: efficiency *rises* with concentration up to a four-firm concentration ratio of 35 percent. Thereafter

Table 4.2
Distribution of estimates of ATI by industries' producer concentration ratios

Five-firm concentration ratio (%)	Industries Number	Percent	Type I failures	ATI below mean	ATI above mean	Type II failures
0–24	25	17	19	26	12	10
25–49	59	39	38	48	30	41
50–74	39	26	23	13	36	33
75–100	28	19	21	13	21	18
Total	151	100	100	100	100	100
Number of cases			48	31	33	39

it falls away again. These results are replicated in the Japanese case (chapter 2).

Our findings are somewhat different. The greatest frequency of concentration ratios falls between 25 and 49 percent (table 4.2). Using the five measures of inefficiency, skewness, standard error (σ_e), average technical inefficiency (ATI), the Lee-Tyler measure of average technical efficiency (ATE), and the ratio of the standard deviation of the inefficiency component of the residuals to that of the symmetric, stochastic residual λ, we observe that for skewness there is a linear negative relation between inefficiency and concentration (table 4.3). (To ease exposition, we refer to all the measures in terms of inefficiency, which involves implicit reversal of the signs for ATE and skewness.) This relation applies whether the concentration ratio includes or excludes imports. It should be recalled that while the skewness and variance measures can be estimated for all industries (151), the remaining measures relate only to those 72 industries where the residuals were decomposable. As only the relation with the ATI measure is also marginally significant, we might speculate that concentration is related to the causes of inability to measure inefficiency. In the full model (see tables 4.4 through 4.8) the relation prevails across all the measures of inefficiency. Concentration is not rejected in the final model although the regression coefficients are only marginally significant. In general the greater the concentration, the greater is the inefficiency (less the efficiency in the case of the ATE measure), but the sign is sometimes the opposite.

The curvilinear relation is less clearly borne out with significant coefficients only in the case of ATI and ATE (our preferred specifications) although it is also not rejected in the case of λ. All have the same form with

Table 4.3
Associations between inefficiency and concentration, measured by coefficient of determination r^2

Inefficiency measure	CONC1	CONC2	Number of industries
Skewness	0.06**	0.06**	151
σ_e	0.00	0.00	151
ATI	0.03	0.04*	72
ATE	0.03	0.03	72
λ	0.01	0.01	72

Note: * indicates significance at the 10 percent level; ** indicates significance at the 5 percent level.

a diminishing effect of concentration as the level rises. This relation was modeled by including the square of concentration in the regression, CONSQ1 and CONSQ2 corresponding to CONC1 and CONC2.

In a purely numerical sense, the smaller the industry, the more likely it is to be concentrated. Conversely, the more firms in the industry, the greater the chance that some of them will diverge greatly from the industry norm. This was not only observed empirically for the U.S. data (though not the Japanese) but was justified by Caves and Barton (1990) in theoretical terms in a deterministic model. We therefore looked simply at the hypothesis that inefficiency is related to the number of plants, CASES in the list of variables. This is borne out only for the skewness measure, although it is also weakly significant in the σ_e and λ models. However, in the case of σ_e inefficiency is negatively correlated with the number of cases not positively as in the American case, which leads us to question its generality.

To explore the relation between concentration and efficiency, we cross-tabulated the two measures in table 4.2. We see here the two effects, first, the relation between concentration and inefficiency and, second, the way in which the concentration measures themselves are concentrated in the 25 to 49 percent and to a lesser extent 50 to 74 percent ranges.

As we mentioned earlier, the extent of competition can be measured by the openness of the market to imports, not in potential terms, but in terms of actual market share: imports/sales (designated IMPORTS). In theory the more the market is open to foreign competition, the smaller the opportunity for inefficiency. However, a high import ratio could indicate that the

Table 4.4
Explanations of inefficiency using σ_e as the dependent variable

Exogenous variable	Equation number				
	(1)	(2)	(3)	(4)	(5)
WORKRAT	0.1344	0.1298	0.1197	0.1122	0.1267
	(1.86)	(1.89)	(1.76)	(1.65)	(1.88)
PROD	0.2276	0.2384	0.2351		
	(1.08)	(1.16)	(1.23)		
EXPORTS	−0.0012	−0.0005			
	(−0.76)	(−0.78)			
GEOG	−0.0018	−0.0017	−0.0019	−0.0018	−0.0016
	(−2.14)	(−2.11)	(−2.28)	(−2.23)	(−2.00)
CASES	−0.0002	−0.0002	−0.0002	−0.0002	−0.0002
	(−1.91)	(−2.03)	(−1.83)	(−1.78)	(−1.74)
ENTRY	−0.0093	−0.0097	−0.0092	−0.0091	−0.0078
	(−2.53)	(−2.77)	(−2.64)	(−2.62)	(−2.30)
CHANGEK	−0.0002				
	(−0.55)				
SPECIAL	0.0041	0.0041	0.0036	0.0035	0.0040
	(2.42)	(2.43)	(2.22)	(2.14)	(2.52)
EMP	0.0753				
	(0.22)				
ESTENT	0.0012	0.0012	0.0013	0.0013	
	(1.29)	(1.36)	(1.49)	(1.46)	
KINTENSE	−0.1800	−0.1740	−0.1658	−0.1711	−0.1803
	(−3.60)	(−3.65)	(−3.53)	(−3.65)	(−3.86)
IMPORTS	0.0060				
	(0.52)				
CONC1	−0.0039	−0.0041	−0.0019	−0.0017	−0.0017
	(−1.59)	(−1.67)	(−2.92)	(−2.73)	(−2.69)
CONCSQ	−0.0001	−0.0000			
	(−0.85)	(−0.92)			
CONSTANT	0.3322	0.3279	0.3130	0.3779	0.3186
	(1.77)	(1.80)	(1.73)	(2.18)	(1.88)
R^2	0.2867	0.2833	0.2736	0.2643	0.2512
$\bar{R}^2$	0.2054	0.2154	0.2183	0.2148	0.2075
DF	113	116	118	119	120

Note: t-values are shown in parenthesis, and each model is adjusted for heteroskedasticity.

Table 4.5
Explanations of inefficiency using SKEW as the dependent variable

Exogenous variable	Equation number					
	(1)	(2)	(3)	(4)	(5)	(6)
WORKRAT	−0.3202 (−1.14)	−0.3058 (−1.12)	−0.2858 (−1.09)	−0.2698 (−1.03)		
PROD	0.6250 (0.76)	−0.6411 (−0.79)	−0.5486 (−0.69)			
EXPORTS	−0.0029 (−0.47)	−0.0031 (−1.22)	−0.0032 (−1.26)	−0.0032 (−1.27)	−0.0031 (−1.24)	
GEOG	0.0040 (1.17)	0.0041 (1.25)	0.0042 (1.30)	0.0038 (1.19)		
CASES	−0.0001 (−1.36)	−0.0006 (−1.52)	−0.0006 (−1.53)	−0.0005 (−1.45)	−0.0006 (−1.67)	−0.0006 (−1.59)
ENTRY	0.0165 (1.15)	0.0157 (1.12)	0.0135 (0.99)			
CHANGEK	−0.0008 (−0.59)	−0.0008 (−0.61)				
SPECIAL	−0.0034 (−0.51)	−0.0028 (−0.43)				
EMP	−1.8105 (−1.34)	−1.8582 (−1.39)	−1.8169 (−1.38)	−1.6771 (−1.29)	−2.0801 (−1.65)	
ESTENT	−0.0032 (−0.90)	−0.0032 (−0.90)	−0.0035 (−1.03)	−0.0025 (−0.77)		
KINTENSE	−0.0277 (−1.94)	−0.0291 (−2.12)	−0.0268 (−2.04)	−0.0258 (−1.98)	−0.0202 (−1.63)	−0.0161 (−1.32)
CONC1	0.0083 (0.81)	0.0042 (1.62)	0.0045 (1.77)	0.0043 (1.72)	0.0034 (1.42)	0.0041 (1.70)
CONSQ	−0.0004 (−0.41)					
IMPORTS	−0.0027 (−0.06)					
CONSTANT	−0.1095 (−0.15)	−0.0718 (−1.00)	−0.4109 (−1.26)	−0.5137 (−1.77)	−0.5304 (−2.57)	−0.6111 (−3.06)
R^2	0.1818	0.1805	0.1766	0.1659	0.1454	0.1202
$\bar{R}^2$	0.0777	0.0927	0.1043	0.1083	0.1095	0.0984
DF	110	112	114	116	119	121

Note: t-values are shown in parentheses. Multiple regression estimates include adjustment for heteroskedasticity.

industry has many inefficient firms rather than that foreign competition drives them out of business.

One should perhaps therefore look at the industry's ability to export: exports/sales (labeled EXPORTS). The greater the ability of an industry to export, then prima facie the greater its international competitiveness. However, this hypothesis ignores the existence of intraindustry trade, which increasingly tends to characterize trading patterns. Under these circumstances it is possible to specialize within market segments. Hence we would see both higher imports and exports consistent with continuing inefficiency simply because the market is segmented. We therefore employed two further measures, NETTRADE = (imports − exports)/sales and GROSSTRADE = (exports + imports)/(sales + imports), which would be positively correlated with inefficiency insofar as they show the existence of intraindustry trade.

Much to our surprise these variables are rather poorly correlated with inefficiency except for the λ measure. However, in the final specifications of the full model, imports and exports are included in the ATI equation (table 4.6, with imports negative and exports positive) and the ATE equation (table 4.7, with the opposite signs, as this is a measure of efficiency; exports alone is included in the λ equation, table 4.8, with a positive coefficient). This therefore is somewhat of a conundrum. Higher imports do appear to be associated with high levels of efficiency, but not all the inefficient firms appear to have been driven out of business. However, higher exports also coincide with higher inefficiency (the same signs are observed in the σ_e and skewness equation although the coefficients are not significantly different from zero). The U.S. results show the same pattern in relation to imports and exports, but Caves and Barton (1990) attribute the effect of exports to their concentration in a relatively small proportion of establishments.

As is clear from our earlier discussion, part of this confusion may occur because trade is a static, or snapshot, measure of a changing environment. (We consider dynamic factors specifically in section 4.5.) If high imports drive out inefficient domestic producers, we need to know the history of imports to know whether that process of driving out has only just begun or is long established. Caves and Barton (1990, ch. 8) found that productivity growth increases with the growth rate of import penetration. An alternative means of examining this phenomenon is to measure it directly by looking at the number of firms leaving and entering an industry. Highly competitive industries tend to show high levels of both entry and exit. Lack

Table 4.6
Explanations of inefficiency using ATI as the dependent variable

Exogenous variable	Equation number					
	(1)	(2)	(3)	(4)	(5)	(6)
WORKRAT	0.1451	0.1504	0.1432	0.0966	0.0746	
	(1.57)	(1.69)	(1.70)	(1.30)	(1.02)	
EXPORTS	0.0037	0.0038	0.0040	0.0035	0.0039	0.0040
	(2.29)	(2.43)	(2.61)	(2.47)	(2.83)	(2.89)
CONC1	0.0046	0.0047	0.0042	0.0029		
	(1.46)	(1.56)	(1.44)	(1.21)		
CONCSQ	−0.0004	−0.0005	−0.0004	−0.0003	−0.0001	−0.0001
	(−1.76)	(−1.84)	(−1.75)	(−1.60)	(−1.60)	(−2.04)
ENTRY	0.0021	0.0022				
	(0.58)	(0.63)				
GEOG	−0.0011	−0.0012	−0.0013	−0.0012		
	(−1.13)	(−1.25)	(−1.42)	(−1.35)		
CHANGEK	0.0001					
	(0.00)					
PROD	0.0852					
	(0.31)					
EMP	1.0009	1.0063	1.0528	0.9363	0.9897	1.0030
	(2.68)	(2.75)	(2.96)	(2.79)	(2.95)	(3.07)
ESTENT	−0.0005	−0.0006				
	(−0.72)	(−0.73)				
CASES	0.0001	0.0001	0.0001			
	(0.73)	(0.79)	(0.72)			
SPECIAL	0.0026	0.0026	0.0024	0.0024	0.0025	
	(1.45)	(1.45)	(1.56)	(1.52)	(1.55)	
KINTENSE	0.0045	0.0047	0.0050			
	(0.90)	(1.02)	(1.08)			
IMPORTS	−0.0289	−0.0298	−0.0309	−0.0278	−0.0297	−0.0297
	(−2.25)	(−2.46)	(−2.60)	(−2.51)	(−2.73)	(−2.73)
CONSTANT	−0.0820	−0.0671	−0.0366	0.0779	0.1045	0.3711
	(−0.35)	(−0.31)	(−0.18)	(0.45)	(0.62)	(18.18)
R^2	0.3600	0.3586	0.3492	0.3299	0.2965	0.2641
$\bar{R}^2$	0.1733	0.2047	0.2240	0.2306	0.2211	0.2134
DF	48	50	52	54	56	58

Note: t-values are shown in parentheses. Multiple regression estimates include adjustment for heteroskedasticity.

Table 4.7
Explanations of inefficiency using ATE as the dependent variable

Exogenous variable	Equation number					
	(1)	(2)	(3)	(4)	(5)	(6)
WORKRAT	−0.1263	−0.1317	−0.1286	−0.0884		
	(−1.60)	(−1.74)	(−1.76)	(−1.40)		
EXPORTS	−0.0030	−0.0031	−0.0032	−0.0029	−0.0034	−0.0033
	(−2.17)	(−2.31)	(−2.42)	(−2.36)	(−2.88)	(−2.83)
CONC1	−0.0039	−0.0041	−0.0029	−0.0027		
	(−1.47)	(−1.58)	(−1.44)	(−1.36)		
CONCSQ	0.0004	0.0004	0.0003	0.0003	0.0001	0.0001
	(1.80)	(1.90)	(1.77)	(1.76)	(1.58)	(2.03)
ENTRY	−0.0017	−0.0017				
	(−0.55)	(−0.59)				
GEOG	0.0011	0.0012	0.0012	0.0012		
	(1.32)	(1.46)	(1.53)	(1.58)		
CHANGEK	0.0000					
	(0.008)					
PROD	−0.0861					
	(−0.37)					
EMP	−0.8170	−0.8223	−0.8537	−0.7673	−0.8838	−0.8361
	(−2.57)	(−2.64)	(−2.82)	(−2.69)	(−3.14)	(−2.99)
ESTENT	0.0005	0.0005	0.0003			
	(0.75)	(0.76)	(0.58)			
CASES	−0.0001	−0.0001				
	(−0.58)	(−0.64)				
SPECIAL	−0.0026	−0.0022	−0.0024	−0.0020	−0.0015	
	(−1.46)	(−1.46)	(−1.69)	(−1.50)	(−1.19)	
KINTENSE	−0.0035	−0.0037	−0.0036			
	(−0.82)	(−0.94)	(−0.94)			
IMPORTS	0.0238	0.0248	0.0259	0.0231	0.0259	0.0251
	(2.18)	(2.40)	(2.57)	(2.45)	(2.78)	(2.69)
CONSTANT	1.0457	1.0310	1.0072	0.9160	0.7994	0.6650
	(5.28)	(5.49)	(5.84)	(6.17)	(7.01)	(38.05)
R^2	0.3604	0.3850	0.3492	0.3337	0.2752	0.2571
$\bar{R}^2$	0.1739	0.2045	0.2240	0.2350	0.2116	0.2059
DF	48	50	52	54	57	58

Note: t-values are shown in parentheses. Multiple regression estimates include adjustment for heteroskedasticity.

Table 4.8
Explanations of inefficiency using LAMBDA as the dependent variable

Exogenous variable	Equation number						
	(1)	(2)	(3)	(4)	(5)	(6)	(7)
WORKRAT	-0.3295 (-0.21)						
EXPORTS	0.0528 (1.95)	0.0521 (1.99)	0.0564 (2.23)	0.0542 (2.15)	0.0471 (2.03)	0.0313 (2.45)	0.0269 (2.18)
CONC1	0.0717 (1.38)	0.0751 (1.52)	0.0705 (1.46)	0.0664 (1.39)	0.0454 (1.07)		
CONCSQ	-0.0006 (-1.45)	-0.0007 (-1.61)	-0.0006 (-1.58)	-0.0006 (-1.53)	-0.0005 (-1.48)	-0.0001 (-1.26)	
ENTRY	0.0139 (0.23)	0.0129 (0.21)					
GEOG	0.0037 (0.21)						
CHANGEK	0.0063 (0.96)	0.0060 (0.96)	0.0059 (0.97)				
PROD	8.5104 (1.83)	8.2000 (1.85)	8.0181 (1.85)	7.2249 (1.70)	7.7942 (1.85)	8.8829 (2.18)	8.5545 (2.11)
EMP	7.6210 (1.19)	7.5042 (1.20)	7.9716 (1.32)	8.4512 (1.40)	5.9108 (1.07)	5.9212 (1.07)	
ESTENT	-0.0100 (-0.74)	-0.0101 (-0.81)					
KINTENSE	0.0795 (0.93)	0.0863 (1.14)	0.0938 (1.27)	0.0664 (0.97)			

Table 4.8 (continued)

Exogenous variable	Equation number						
	(1)	(2)	(3)	(4)	(5)	(6)	(7)
SPECIAL	0.0342	0.0364	0.0322	0.0330	0.0395	0.0416	0.0475
	(1.11)	(1.35)	(1.29)	(1.32)	(1.62)	(1.72)	(2.04)
CASES	0.0028	0.0028	0.0028	0.0023			
	(1.03)	(1.13)	(1.12)	(0.96)			
IMPORTS	−0.2045	−0.2029	−0.2263	−0.2020	−0.1609		
	(−0.96)	(−0.97)	(−1.11)	(−1.00)	(−0.86)		
CONSTANT	−5.3618	−5.6717	−5.1552	−4.5093	−3.8502	−3.2241	−4.0621
	(−1.31)	(−1.61)	(−1.87)	(−1.68)	(−1.48)	(−1.30)	(−1.70)
R^2	0.2908	0.2896	0.2797	0.2658	0.2406	0.2155	0.1738
$\bar{R}^2$	0.0702	0.1082	0.1326	0.1337	0.1384	0.1429	0.1295
DF	45	47	49	51	52	54	56

Note: t-values are shown in parentheses. Multiple regression estimates include adjustment for heteroskedasticity.

of competition on the other hand is often characterized by barriers to entry that attenuate the turnover of firms. Furthermore, where the costs of exit are high, firms will be reluctant to leave. Baldwin (chapter 7) shows that in the case of Canada it tends to be the less productive plants that exit. Furthermore small firms are more prone to exit as a result of normal market fluctuations insofar as they are capital constrained.

We could not investigate the role of turnover directly from the ACOP data because all that the official source provides is net entry in the form of the average annual change in the number of enterprises over 1973–76 (ENTRY). We did utilize a private source of information (S. Toker, London Business School) on entry and exit that is available for these same years. Unfortunately, they match the ACOP industry categories even less well than the trade data, but they do pertain to 116 industries. Using these data, we can observe not just the number of entries and exits but their average sales as well. This enables us to create four variables:

$$\text{ENT1} = \frac{\text{average number of entrants} - \text{average number of exits, 1973–76}}{\text{number of establishments}},$$

$$\text{ENT2} = \frac{\text{average sales of entrants} - \text{average sales of exits, 1973–76}}{\text{average industry sales, 1973–76}},$$

$$\text{PENTS} = \frac{\text{average sales of entrants, 1973–76}}{\text{average industry sales, 1973–76}},$$

$$\text{PEXITS} = \frac{\text{average sales of exits, 1973–76}}{\text{average industry sales, 1973–76}}.$$

These variables indicate not just how many firms are changing but what their importance is to the industry as a whole. We also considered the sum of entrants and exits as a measure of the extent of change.

We had no success with any of these variables based on Toker's data, although there is a limited correlation between ENT2 and σ_e. ENTRY, however, has a clear negative relation with σ_e and a weaker one with ATI. For σ_e it forms part of our preferred model (table 4.4) indicating clear evidence of the relation between competition and efficiency.

These measures are of course indicators of the extent to which the industry is contested, rather than contestable (Baumol et al. 1982). An industry does not have to be contested to be efficient, merely contestable in the sense that the incumbent firms believe that others will enter if they are inefficient and hence pursue efficiency to deter entry. This again provides problem of interpretation as actual entry will be low (1) where there are effective barriers to entry, in which case incumbents may indulge in efficiency, and (2) where the incumbents are so efficient that potential entrants see little gain from entry. We can only distinguish industries in category (1) from those in category (2) if we utilize an independent measure of barriers to entry. Use of a single measure might confuse the two influences. Entry and exit also reflect the industry's position in the product life cycle.

The dynamic forces of competition are modeled explicitly in section 4.5, so problems observed here with the use of variables related to entry and exit may be relieved to some extent by the more direct measures of change in the industries discussed in that section.

4.4   Product Differentiation and Heterogeneity

The second major market characteristic that can lead to the existence of technical inefficiency is heterogeneity of the product. This can take two forms. The first is the pursuit of product differentiation such as through the use of brand names. Although in practice branded products can be highly substitutable—like different brands of baked beans, instant coffee, or washing powder—producers are able to build up considerable brand loyalty that enables them to charge higher prices and yet keep market share. Put another way, they can manage to reduce the cross-price elasticities to low levels. Once this is done, producers can increase margins or decrease control over costs and yet still remain competitive. Insofar as firms have varying successes in achieving this, futher variety in performance would be observed. One form that inefficiency might take is high-level advertising or other promotional costs in order to maintain the brand image.

All this falls properly within the scope of the discussion of technical inefficiency. However, the second possible source of heterogeneity is simply that an industry classification comprises a very wide range of products. Diversity appears in a wildly heterogeneous group such as mainframe computers and portable electric typewriters coming under the same heading of office equipment, but also lesser examples such as machine tools, where it is possible to define several major types. Not only does the unit value range from just a few pounds for minor components to several millions for major systems for the motor car industry, but also the precision required and the degree of automation possible in its production vary enormously. Hence producers will select diverse combinations of labor and capital inputs even if they are equally efficient in their own product segments. To some extent therefore we question the appropriateness of fitting a single production function to the data. The departures from common behavior could be random and hence picked up in the random components of the residual of the production function; systematic tendencies would be picked up in the skewed residual and treated as technical inefficiency. We thus have to appreciate that technical inefficiency can assume a wider meaning in these circumstances. What is in fact variance, a component of the second moment of the residuals, will be picked up in measures of the third and higher moments.

Advertising expenditure may therefore be the best method of detecting product differentiation. Bain (1956) suggested that it is the most important source. Advertising and branding tend to be firm specific rather than plant specific, hence it need neither be clearly related to plant efficiency nor be correctly allocated to the appropriate industry. Advertising creates effective barriers to entry because it takes many years to establish new brands; existing incumbents always have the option to try to match the new entrant's expenditure, and hence they make the task harder. Matching is less effective where the new entrant is already established in a different part of the market and hence already has a brand image. Under these circumstances, as is shown by Comanor and Wilson (1967), advertising can provide stability for an existing informal cartel.

Advertising expenditure is not measured as part of ACOP, but as a result of good fortune, a major survey of advertising expenditure was taken in 1977 by the Mirror Group. This did not cover all industries and did not match exactly with our industry classification (see the appendix). The variable we used, ADVERT = advertising expenditure/sales, can therefore only be incorporated in a regression with the loss of some observations. This subset of data is not random; it relates mainly to industries where advertising is important. The results were nowhere significant.

Heterogeneity, on the other hand, can be measured for all industries, albeit crudely, by simply counting the number of five-digit product categories in each three-digit industry. This very arbitrary measure at least gives some indication of the variability of the product structure. A second and more helpful ratio is that of total sales of products primary to the industry to total sales of all goods produced and work done (designated

Table 4.9
Distribution of industries' plant–specialization ratios

Specialization (%)	Number of industries	Percent of industries
90–100	87	62
80–89	39	27
70–79	11	8
60–69	5	4
Total	142	100

Table 4.10
Distribution of inefficiency estimates (number and percent of industries) by level of industry specialization

Specialization (%)	Type I failure	ATI below mean	ATI above mean	Type II failure
90–100	25 (57)	18 (56)	26 (66)	18 (68)
80–89	15 (34)	11 (34)	7 (18)	7 (25)
70–79	4 (9)	1 (3)	2 (5)	1 (4)

SPECIAL). The variable ranges between 60 percent and 100 percent, with most industries falling between 80 percent and 100 percent (table 4.9). Unfortunately, although derived from ACOP, it is available for only 142 of the 151 industries. From table 4.10 it appears that there is a tendency for greater specialization to be associated with greater inefficiency. Correlations are weak on a bivariate basis, but in the full model the variable is significant in all cases except skewness.

4.5   Change and Efficiency

We argued earlier that dynamic factors can have as important an influence upon efficiency as static characteristics of the industry. A simple example is rapid growth of demand. If an industry is growing rapidly, capacity will tend to be insufficient to meet demand, making room for all in the market including the inefficient. The range of efficiency may also widen as firms invest and expand capacity. Those with new plants will be at high levels of efficiency compared with those with older plants, particularly where they are using marginal capacity to meet the high levels of demand. However, this relation is two sided due to the delay in bringing new equipment to full efficiency. Indeed in some industries it is unusual for the learning curve to have leveled off with one set of products or technology before the next is implemented, and a firm's position on the learning curve itself generates a competitive advantage.

It is therefore appropriate to look for indicators of this rate of change. Theoretical options include the rate of change of the production function for the industry. However, this option is not open to us, nor can technical change be measured directly. What we can measure is the effort to achieve such change by means of R&D expenditures or indicators of the output of innovations (registration of patents or the numbers of significant innovations).

There are problems with both approaches. R&D expenditure is a notoriously inaccurate indicator: Research could be unsuccessful, and technical success in generating new products or processes might not yield commercial success. Therefore innovative effort might not be a good measure of the amount of technical change in the industry. As has been shown by Buxton, Mayes, and Murfin (1990) some industries are more research intensive but not more innovative than others. Research might merely be an extremely expensive process, such as in the case of pharmaceuticals where there is need for extensive clinical trials. Diverse efficiency levels might not only appear from innovators' varying successes. The innovator is the firm that first meets the difficulties and works to put them right. The companies that follow can learn from the innovator's mistakes. In some cases the main gain may be by the followers, not the innovator. These issues were discussed with specific examples in Ray (1984).

We used RSALES = R&D expenditure/sales as a measure in the regression analysis. Again we lack data for some industries due to classificatory problems. Unfortunately, little useful relationship appeared. A similar story was unfolded when we tried an output measure of innovation, namely, the average numbers of patents per establishment over the years 1973–76. These data were also supplied by Toker, who used data collected by the Science Policy Research Unit at the University of Sussex. The variable was available for 115 industries and was defined as

$$\text{INNSIZE} = \frac{\text{average number of patents, 1973–76}}{\text{number of establishments}}.$$

It worked little better than RSALES, but on empirical grounds, we could not justify the inclusion of either of these two variables in the final specification. Patenting is more commonly used to protect innovations in some industries; this calls INNSIZE into question (see Ray 1984).

We therefore resorted to more indirect measures of change. The simplest were the change in employment in the industry, EMP = average change in employment 1973–77, and productivity, PROD = rate of change in net output per head 1973–77. Our initial prejudice favored PROD because the strong cyclical movements that occur in productivity are directly related to efficiency, with efficiency rising in upturns and falling in downturns. However, the relation, certainly at the bivariate level, was closer with EMP; skewness, ATI, and ATE show significant bivariate relations at the 5 percent level. In our preferred equations this pattern was repeated (tables 4.4 through 4.6), but the relationship was positive in each case: The faster the growth of employment, the greater was the level of inefficiency.

It is easy to provide a justification for these results. Where an industry is in trouble, it not only has inefficiency but a falling work force. In this case the perceived correlation is the result of common cause rather than from employment change causing efficiency, which is the implicit structure of the model. In the LAMBDA equation both EMP and PROD are included because it is possible to distinguish their effects. Inefficiency is only observed when some firms react more successfully than others to difficult conditions. A comparison with other countries of such inefficient industry wide behavior would not be picked up by our measures.

We felt that capital would also have a role to play in dynamic efficiency. Where capital–labor ratios are high, there are considerable sunk costs to inhibit change. Thus the greater the capital–labor ratio, the more inefficiency we might expect. We unfortunately had no direct measure of capital stock and so have to be content with the investment–labor ratio:

$$\text{KINTENSE} = \frac{\text{capital expenditure} + \text{hiring and leasing of plant and machinery} + \text{acquisitions} - \text{disposals}}{\text{total wage bill}}.$$

In four cases out of five KINTENSE did indeed have positive coefficients. However, in the remaining case not only was the relationship much more significant but also it was of the opposite sign. This result may reflect our initial argument about the influence of technology. An industry that is increasing its efficiency rapidly will also be investing more heavily, or at any rate cutting surplus labor.

4.6 The Effect of Spatial Disparities

Spatial factors can influence efficiency in two main ways: through dispersion of production and through dispersion of demand. The first occurs where inputs, particularly materials, are locally based and vary across the country. This applies to food manufacturing and to other resource processing. Quality of inputs can vary considerably. Insofar as labor markets are not homogeneous, skills can also vary across the country. This applies not just to the direct labor input but also to purchased services. The general quality of business services could be higher in the main business centers, for example. Thus the sheer dispersion of production across the country would give an opportunity for differences in efficiency because of differences in productive conditions.

The second effect of geographical dispersion occurs if demand is very localized or market size is limited because of the need for freshness or closeness to the producer, as is the case for agricultural products and many business and consumer services. Here competitive conditions can vary considerably. Near-monopoly would exist in rural areas, while there would be considerable competition in the larger cities. Countrywide measures of competition would be misleading because they are calculated on the assumption that the appropriate market definition is the whole country. The more fragmented the market, the more likely is any given national measure to overstate competitive pressures.

We were able to get suitable data only on the first of these phenomena, namely, the dispersion of production. The measure available from ACOP is

GEOG = percent of industry output concentrated in the largest
       production area.

This variable performed moderately well in three cases, σ_e, ATI, and ATE, with the expected sign, namely, the greater the geographical spread of production the greater the level of inefficiency (the lower the efficiency). The same relation was observed for skewness but more weakly.

4.7 Managerial and Organizational Influences

Once we have taken into account all the other factors affecting heterogeneity of inputs—technology and products, and the competitive pressures in the market—the main source of variation lies in how the plant is organized and managed. We have by no means incorporated all other influences, such as variations in skill levels. Some problems of management relate to competence, which is difficult to measure, but others occur for structural reasons. A simple one is that the more diverse the firm, the more difficult it is to manage all activities successfully. Those in peripheral industries might suffer.

This organizational problem can be replicated within the industry. If a firm has many plants, it could find it more difficult to run all of them efficiently compared with the firm that only has one or a few plants. Fortunately ACOP provides data on enterprises as well as establishments, so we were able to incorporate the establishment–enterprise ratio ESTENT into the analysis. Only in the case of σ_e was the result significant, and here it appears that rises in the ratio, implying increasing concentration, are correlated with the level of inefficiency. The usefulness of the ESTENT variable is greatly attenuated by the long tail of single establishment enterprises. A better measure, if it were obtainable, would concentrate only on the larger firms.

4.8   The Characteristics of Inefficiency

Taking these five factors together, table 4.11, we can see that over the five inefficiency measures each has the expected influence but with some apparently perverse results and considerable differences among the five inefficiency measures.

To account for missing values in some of the explanatory variables and to eliminate outliers, some adjustments had to be made before estimation. These involved either elimination of the industry from the analysis or replacement by an average value for a more aggregated sector containing the specific industry for a small number of cases (see Green, Harris, and Mayes 1992). The resulting simple correlations are shown in table 4.12 together with the eventual sample size. The regressions were also corrected for heteroskedasticity of the residuals for the results shown in tables 4.4 through 4.8 by weighting the observations according to the number of firms in each industry.

Skewness is clearly the most difficult measure of inefficiency to explain. The fullest explanation accounts for only 11 percent of the total variation.

Table 4.11
Summary of multiple regression results on relations between industry characteristics and inefficiency

Exogenous variable	Endogenous variable				
	σ_e	Skew[a]	ATI	ATE[a]	λ
CONC1	− − −	−	+	+	+
CONSQ1			− − −	−	−
SPECIAL	+ + +		+		+ + +
ENTRY	− − −	(−)			
ESTENT		(+)			
EXPORTS		+	+ + +	+ + +	+ + +
WORKRAT	+ +	+	+	+	
GEOG	− − −	−	−	−	
KINTENSE	− − −	+ +	+		+
EMP		+	+ + +	+ + +	+
PROD	+	+			+ + +
INNSIZE					
CASES	− −	+			+

Note: Number of pluses and minuses indicate the following: one, coefficient > standard error; two, 10 percent significance level; three, 5 percent level. Parentheses indicate excluded from preferred regression.
a. Signs are reversed for comparability.

Table 4.12
Correlations of inefficiency measures and exogenous variables

Exogenous variables	Inefficiency measures					
	SKEW	NEWSKEW	σ_e	ATI	ATE	λ
BIGNO	0.257	0.304	−0.015	−0.202	0.199	−0.137
KINTENSE	−0.083	−0.201	−0.269	−0.144	−0.150	0.051
SPECIAL	0.001	−0.055	0.100	0.133	−0.129	0.216
EMP	0.013	−0.117	0.085	0.324	−0.318	0.048
PROD	0.100	0.009	0.086	0.135	−0.144	0.185
GEOG	0.055	0.033	−0.164	−0.144	0.163	−0.079
CHANGEK	−0.075	0.029	0.021	0.075	0.077	0.036
ENTRY	0.039	0.014	−0.182	0.148	−0.141	0.030
ESTENT	−0.100	−0.052	0.126	−0.043	0.050	−0.091
IMPORTS	0.032	−0.082	−0.038	−0.144	0.146	−0.150
EXPORTS	−0.043	−0.085	−0.039	0.022	−0.017	−0.263
TRADE	0.044	0.084	0.039	−0.045	0.040	−0.272
CASES	−0.240	−0.259	−0.081	0.140	−0.122	0.141
WORKRAT	0.010	−0.017	0.169	0.155	−0.064	−0.114
n	125	125	128	63	63	60

Although the equation includes concentration, capital intensity, change in employment, number of firms, and exports, none of the individual coefficients is significantly different from zero. The collinearity is sufficient that in effect there is little source of systematic variation other than concentration, which alone explains nine percent of the total variation. Of the remaining four measures the level of explanation for lambda was also low, at around 13 percent, while the others lay in the range 20 to 25 percent. This is a lower level of explanation than in the U.S. case (Caves and Barton 1990) where about 30 percent the variance was explained, but in the context of cross-sectional analysis this is still a reasonable result.

One of the problems of the decomposed residual method of estimating inefficiency is that it requires the inefficiency to be the unusual behavior. If, on the other hand, there are just a few efficient establishments and the bulk of the industry is inefficient, then this bulk of establishments will dominate the positioning of the estimated production frontier, and the resulting residuals will be positively skewed. Such an industry will then be omitted from consideration under inefficiency measures which require decomposition of the residuals. However, if the average behavior of the skewed part of the residuals represents the frontier of efficient behavior, we can reverse the sign of the measure of skewness in these cases to obtain a measure of inefficiency. Thus the measure NEWSKEW referred to in table 4.12 is defined as

$$NEWSKEW = SKEW \qquad SKEW \leq 0,$$

$$= SKEW(-1) \qquad SKEW > 0.$$

This therefore turns skewness into another measure of inefficiency that can be estimated for all industries. However, it is also clear from table 4.12 that this transformation was not particularly successful in terms of correlation with the hypothesized characteristics of inefficiency. The results from the multiple regression model of NEWSKEW are therefore not reported. Work on the Australian data reported in chapter 6 shows that the mean efficiency of the positively skewed values is significantly greater than the mean of the negatively skewed ones, also implying that the NEWSKEW transformation is probably not an appropriate way of coping with this problem.

Only σ_e among the other measures covers all of the industries. In the preferred regression, omitting variables not significant at least at the 10 percent level, and following the pattern shown in table 4.4, we obtain the equation[5]

$\sigma_e = 0.50 \quad - 0.21\text{KINTENSE} - 0.010\text{ENTRY} + 0.0022\text{SPECIAL}$
$(4.21) \: (-5.63) (-3.70) (1.75)$

$ - 0.0015\text{CONC1} - 0.0005\text{CASES} + 0.0024\text{ESTENT},$
$ (-2.87) (-1.78) (3.22)$

$\bar{R}^2 = 0.286, \quad N = 131.$

As expected, these results show that greater competition in the form of entry into the industry increases efficiency. The rest of the findings are more contentious. The more specialized, less capital intensive and less concentrated the industry, and the smaller the number of establishments and the number of establishments per enterprise, the greater is the inefficiency.

The difference in the structure of the significant relationships in the equations for the other three measures of inefficiency makes comparison difficult. The ATI model does not show significant relationship with KINTENSE, ENTRY, CASES, or ESTENT. However, it does add EXPORTS, IMPORTS, and EMP to the list (and marginally GEOG). (Note also that in these specifications we added a variable WORKRAT, the ratio of operatives to total employment in the industry, as a measure of difference of structure of employment, not captured by the original production function.) Thus we see in this case the expected relation with respect to concentration, that is, increasing concentration being associated with increasing inefficiency but only up to a point. Beyond that inefficiency falls with further increases in concentration. Here it is the trade relationships that seem counterintuitive. The higher import ratios are associated with lower inefficiency, which could be taken as showing that import competition increases efficiency. However, the export ratio is positively associated with inefficiency. We argued earlier that this might be a measure of intraindustry specialization, but the combination of the signs on these two variables is a little surprising for that. The ATE equations (table 4.7) are similar (with the signs reversed as the dependent variable relates to efficiency). The lambda equations confirm the trade picture but also confirm the association of faster growth with greater measured inefficiency, which we expected to emerge from the increased opportunity for variety in behavior.

Taken together, these results are promising but not without problems. We can explain some of the variation in inefficiency in U.K. manufacturing industry by variables related to competition, product differentiation, the rate of change, spatial variation, and the organizational structure of firms. However, the spatial factor is weak in its influence, product differentiation seems negatively related to inefficiency. The other three main categories of influence show some confusion in their results. Nevertheless, greater competition does seem to be related to lower inefficiency. In common with U.S. and Japanese experience there is a maximum to the adverse impact of concentration. The more rapidly changing industries, with fewer establishments per enterprise, do appear to be more efficient.

Ironically, while having the benefit of covering the whole of manufacturing industry and hence being generalizable, this analysis also suffers from being comprehensive. There are more problems with data quality and compatibility than there would be with specialized studies of individual industries. But while the results do not come up to the quality of Førsund and Hjalmarsson (1979) as a treatment of individual industries they provide a first attempt to cover the whole of manufacturing and provide a rich source of information for further study. Initial comparisons between the U.K. and Australia (Green, Harris, and Mayes 1989) and the U.S. and Japan (chapter 11) show that there are common elements to their experience. In the next phase of the study this international comparison may show further light on inefficiency in the United Kingdom, its sources, and the way its manufacturing competitiveness differs from that of its competitors.

Appendix: Sources of Data and Definition of Variables

Unless stated otherwise, variables are from 1977 *Annual Census of Production*. LBS indicates data supplied by S. Toker from the industry data base at the London Business School.

ADSALES   Advertising expenditure/sales 1977 (Mirror Group Publication).

BIGEMP   Percentage of employment accounted for in an industry by the five largest producers 1977.

CASES   Number of enterprises in the industry 1977.

CHANGEK	Rate of change in capital equipment expenditure 1973–77.
CONC 1	Percentage of net output produced by the five largest producers in the industry 1977.
CONC 2	CONC1 × [total sales/(value of imports + total sales)], 1977.
COSIZE	CONC1 × SALES 1977.
COVERAGE	IMPORTS/EXPORTS.
EMP	Rate of change in employment 1973–77.
ENTRANTS	Average number of entrants to the industry 1973–76, LBS.
ENTRY	Change in the number of enterprises 1973–77.
ENTSIZE	ENTRANTS/CASES.
ENT1	(ENTRANTS − EXITS)/CASES.
ENT2	(SALESENT − SALESEX)/total industry sales.
ESTENT	Rate of change in the ratio of establishments to enterprises 1973–76, LBS.
EXITS	Average number of exits from the industry 1973–76, LBS.
EXPORTS	Value of exports/total sales 1977 (World Trade Statistics).
EXSIZE	EXITS/CASES.
GEOG	Percentage of output concentrated in largest geographical production area 1977.
IMPORTS	Value of imports/total sales 1977.
INNOV	Total number of innovations (patents) 1973–76, LBS.
INNSIZE	INNOV/CASES.
KINTENSE	Capital expenditure/labor cost 1977.
NEWTRADE	IMPORTS + EXPORTS.
OPWAGPH	Wages of operatives per head 1977.
OTHWAGPH	Wages of nonoperatives per head 1977.
PENTS	SALESENT/total industry sales, LBS.

PEXITS   SALESEX/total industry sales, LBS.

PROD   Rate of change in net output per head 1973–77.

RSALES   Expenditure on research and development/sales 1979
                (CSO R&D Expenditure Occasional Publication).

SALESENT   Sales of entrants to the industry 1973–76, LBS.

SALESEX   Sales of exiters from the industry 1973–76, LBS.

SIZENT   SALESENT/ENTRANTS, LBS.

SIZEEX   SALESEX/EXITS, LBS.

SPECIAL   Percentage of production of six-digit product 1977.

TRADE   IMPORTS – EXPORTS.

WORKRAT   Ratio of operatives to total employment.

Notes

This research would not have been possible without the help of the Business Statistics Office and Bernard Mitchell. We are grateful to Nicholas Oulton, George Ray, and participants at the European Production Study Group meeting in Paris on 1–3 November 1989 and the conference at Harvard on Technical Inefficiency in September 1990 for comments, and to Paul Geroski and S. Toker at the London Business School for data. However, our major debt is to Richard Caves for his comments and encouragement throughout. The project was supported by the ESRC Grant No. R000231195. Work on the original estimation was financed by the National Economic Development Office and involved Anne Hickling and Michael Bramson. An earlier version on this chapter was circulated as National Institute of Economic and Social Research Discussion Paper No. 173, March 1990.

1. The term "plant" following the definitions used in the U.K. *Annual Census of Production* refers to equipment *not* buildings.

2. Although the words used for most of these variables are common across English-speaking countries, the definitions may not be. *Gross output* is calculated by adjusting the value of total sales and work done by the change during the year of work in progress and goods on hand for sale. *Net output* is calculated by deducting from gross output the cost of purchase of materials for use in the production and packaging and fuel and purchases of goods for merchanting or factoring, the cost of industrial services received, and it is adjusted for net duties and levies, etc., where applicable. Purchases are adjusted for changes during the year of stocks of materials, stores, and fuels. *Gross value added* (at factor cost) is calculated by deducting from net output the cost of nonindustrial services received, rates (property taxes), and the cost of licensing of motor vehicles. Per head values are calculated by dividing by employment.

3. There are five measures for each of 151 industries. The full table of results is available in Green, Harris, and Mayes (1992).

4. We are grateful to K. Field for this suggestion.

5. We have a full set of observations on three more industries that can be included in the regression when this more limited set of variables is used.

6. The same process of omitting variables insignificant at the 10 percent level is followed in each of tables 4.4 through 4.8.

References

Aigner, D. J., C. A. K. Lovell, and P. Schmidt. 1977. Formulation and estimation of stochastic frontier production function models. *Journal of Econometrics* 6: 21–37.

Bain, J. S. 1956. *Barriers to New Competition.* Cambridge: Harvard University Press.

Baldwin, J. R., and P. K. Gorecki. 1986. The relationship between plant scale and product diversity in Canadian manufacturing industries. *Journal of Industrial Economics* 34: 373–388.

Buxton, A., D. G. Mayes, and A. Murfin. 1990. R&D, innovation and trade performance. In B. Dankbaar, J. Groenewegen and H. Schenk, eds., *Perspectives in Industrial Organisation.* Dordrecht: Kluwer.

Caves, R. E. and D. R. Barton. 1990. *Efficiency in U.S. Manufacturing Industries.* Cambridge: MIT Press.

Comanor, W. S., and T. A. Wilson. 1967. Advertising, market structure, and performance. *Review of Economics and Statistics* 49: 423–440.

Daly, A., D. M. W. N. Hitchens, and K. Wagner. 1985. Productivity, machinery and skills in a sample of British and German manufacturing plants. National Institute Economic Review No. 111.

Davies, S. W., and R. E. Caves. 1987. *Britain's Productivity Gap.* Cambridge: Cambridge University Press.

Farrell, M. J. 1957. The measurement of productive efficiency. *Journal of the Royal Statistical Society A* 120: 253–290.

Førsund, F. R., and L. Hjalmarsson. 1979. Generalised Farrell measures of efficiency: An application to milk processing in Swedish dairy plants. *Economic Journal* 89: 294–315.

Green, A. J., and D. G. Mayes. 1991. The measurement of technical inefficiency of UK manufacturing industry. *Economic Journal* 10: 523–538.

Green, A. J., C. Harris, and D. G. Mayes. 1989. The estimation of technical inefficiency of manufacturing industry. Mimeo. University of Exeter.

Green, A. J., C. Harris, and D. G. Mayes. 1992. *Inefficiency in Industry.* Hemel Hempstead: Harvester-Wheatsheaf, forthcoming.

Griliches, Z., and V. Ringstad. 1971. *Economies of Scale and the Form of the Production Function: An Econometric Study of Norwegian Manufacturing Establishment Data.* Amsterdam: North-Holland.

Harris, C. M. 1989. Technical inefficiency of Australian manufacturing industry. Bureau of Industry Economics, Occasional Paper No. 4. Canberra: Bureau of Industry Economics, Department of Industry Trade and Commerce, 1989.

Lee, L.-F., and W. G. Tyler. 1978. The stochastic frontier production function and average efficiency: An empirical analysis. *Journal of Econometrics* 7: 385–389.

Leibenstein, H. 1966. Allocative Efficiency vs. *X*-efficiency. *American Economic Review* 56: 392–415.

Leibenstein, H. 1973. Competition and *X*-efficiency: Reply. *Journal of Political Economy* 81: 765–777.

OECD. 1986. R&D, invention and competitiveness. OECD Science and Technology Indicators, No. 2.

Page, J. M. 1980. Technical efficiency and economic performance: Some evidence from Ghana. *Oxford Economic Papers* 32: 319–339.

Pratten, C. F. 1971. *Economies of Scale in Manufacturing Industry.* Cambridge: Cambridge University Press.

Ray, G. F. 1984. *The Diffusion of Mature Technologies.* Cambridge: Cambridge University Press.

Schmidt, P., and R. C. Sickles. 1984. Production frontiers and panel data. *Journal of Business and Economic Statistics* 2: 367–374.

Thiry, B., and H. Tulkens. 1989. Productivité, efficacité et progres technique. In H. Tulkens, ed., *Efficacite et Management.* Charleroi: Centre Interuniversitaire de formation Permanente.

Uekusa, M., and A. Torii. 1985. Stochastic production functions: An application to Japanese manufacturing industry (in Japanese). *Keizaigaku Ronsyu* (*Journal of Economics*) 51: 2–23.

5 Technical Efficiency in Australia: Phase 1

Chris M. Harris

5.1 Introduction

Although it is difficult to compare productivity levels between countries, there is a widely held view that Australian manufacturing plants are generally less productive than similar plants overseas. Various reasons put forward to explain such differences include inefficient work and management practices; the age, technology, flexibility, and utilization of the capital stock; lack of economies of scale; poor training and skill formation; government regulation; bad industrial relations and inadequate quality control.

The objective of this chapter is to contribute to the productivity debate by analyzing the technical efficiency of Australian manufacturing industries. In general, *technical efficiency* refers to the extent to which a plant produces maximum output from its inputs. This efficiency concept therefore is one component of broader measures of efficiency that relate the average productivity of Australian plants to those abroad. Improvements in technical efficiency can be considered to be an intermediate target of policy because they are one means by which productivity growth and living standards can be enhanced.

5.2 Efficiency

Economic efficiency is a concept which expresses the degree to which observed performance approaches its potential and indicates the success with which economic resources are utilized. Efficiency therefore requires that a standard of performance be established against which the success of economic units is assessed. Establishing such a standard requires the specification of a behavioral goal or objective for the economic units under consideration. For example, revenue maximization might be assumed as the objective for economic units with a given set of inputs and given production technology.

Having established an objective for the economic units, optimization with respect to that objective yields the locus of constrained maximum or minimum values, which is known as a *frontier*. It is a set of best attainable positions. In the case of a firm, a *production function frontier* identifies maximum obtainable outputs given available factor inputs and existing production technologies. The proximity of units to the frontier is used to derive a measure of technical efficiency (or inefficiency). Although units may be observed below the production frontier, producing less than maximum outputs given input and technology constraints, none should be observed above the production frontier.

The technical efficiency measures derived in this study are relative to the best practices observed in the sample of plants in Australia, and not generally to the best practices that might be observed in a more extensive sample that included data from other countries. It follows that any assessment of firm or industry technical efficiency in an international context can be partitioned into an analysis of technical efficiency relative to the best practice domestically, and of the technical efficiency of the best practice domestically relative to the global best practice.

The analysis presented in this chapter is limited to the first category. The analysis of Caves (1984) falls into the second category, in that the productivity of Australian manufacturing industries was assessed relative to their counterparts in the United States. Subsequent research by the Bureau of Industry Economics is examining in microeconomic detail the important factors that influence productivity differences between Australian and overseas producers in selected industries (BIE 1990, 1991).

5.2.1 The Measurement of Technical Efficiency

The most general of the alternative methods for the derivation of an efficiency frontier and the computation of a technical efficiency measure is currently the stochastic frontier model pioneered by Aigner, Lovell, and Schmidt (1977) and Meeusen and van den Broeck (1977a, 1977b). This model is not subject to some of the statistical and empirical shortcomings of earlier approaches.

According to the stochastic production frontier approach, the model and error structure respectively for the ith of N units within a given industry can be written:

$$\ln(y_i) = \ln f(x_i; \beta) + e_i, \qquad i = 1, \dots, N, \tag{1}$$

where y_i is the output obtained by unit i from x_i, a vector of nonstochastic inputs, and β is the unknown parameter vector. e_i is the composed error:

$$e_i = v_i - u_i, \qquad u_i \geq 0, \tag{2}$$

where v_i and u_i are independent, unobservable random errors. The v_i are assumed to have a symmetric distribution, whereas the u_i are assumed to be truncated below at zero.

Estimation of (1) employs data on the quantities of output and inputs only. Because information on prices is not used, the analysis cannot be used to examine price efficiency, which refers to the utilization of inputs in proportions that minimize costs. The aim of the analysis is thus to obtain information only on the technical efficiency of units individually and in aggregate relative to the stochastic production frontier, via the output-based measure discussed below.

The first component v of the composed error e is assumed to be distributed symmetrically. It represents

1. random variations in the economic environment facing production units, reflecting luck, weather, machine breakdown, variable input quality and other events beyond the control of the units (Aigner, Lovell, and Schmidt 1977; Schmidt and Sickles 1984);

2. measurement, observation, and reporting errors by the economic units on the levels of output (Aigner, Lovell, and Schmidt 1977); and

3. "unimportant" variables omitted from the functional form $f(x_i; \beta)$ (Corbo and de Melo 1983).

This component is typically assumed to be normally distributed with mean zero and variance σ_v^2. The assumption can be justified by the central limit theorem (Schmidt and Lovell 1979) and the random nature of the events that v represents (Lee 1983).

The second component u of the composed error is assumed to be distributed asymmetrically. It represents a variety of features that reflect inefficiency. These features include

1. firm-specific technical knowledge (Page 1980);

2. the will, skills, and effort of management and employees (Aigner, Lovell, and Schmidt 1977; Lee and Tyler 1978); and

3. work stoppages, material bottlenecks, and other disruptions to production (Lee and Tyler 1978).

The shape of the distribution selected for u shows an a priori picture of the distribution of efficiency below the possible maximum. Although the selection of a distribution should be based on the economic mechanisms that generate the inefficiency (Van den Broeck et al. 1980), theory provides little guidance on picking a distribution for u (Schmidt and Lovell 1979; Lee 1983). Researchers in this area have generally selected either the half-normal (Aigner, Lovell, and Schmidt 1977) or exponential (Aigner, Lovell, and Schmidt 1977; Meeusen and van den Broeck 1977a, 1977b) distributions for u. These distributions have a mode at zero, which means that the likelihood of inefficient behavior monotonically decreases for increasing levels of inefficiency.

Stevenson (1980) suggested that characteristics such as degree of educational training, intelligence, persuasiveness, and other factors that relate to managerial efficiency are not likely to be distributed over the population with such a monotonically declining density function. He considered that the possibility of a nonzero mode for the density of u was a more tenable presumption and generalized the half-normal and exponential specifications for the dual cost function ($e = v + u$). The generalization permits a nonzero mode for the density function of u and enables the relevance of the special case of a zero mode to be tested. The analysis for the stochastic production frontier model and a truncated-normal distribution for u is presented below. This formulation was employed in the derivation of the results presented in section 5.4.

The stochastic frontier approach differs in several respects from that employed by Farrell (1957) in his pioneering work. First, the stochastic frontier approach is a parametric technique because the frontier is modeled explicitly using the functional form summarized by the notation $f(x_i; \beta)$. Second, the approach allows the frontier itself to be stochastic via the symmetric error term v. That is, the production by each unit is bounded above by a stochastic frontier SPF_i:

$$SPF_i = \ln f(x_i; \beta) + v_i, \qquad\qquad (3)$$

which is the value attained in (1) by $\ln(y_i)$ when inefficiency and u_i are zero. The presence in (3) of v_i means that the frontier is stochastic, as the placement of the frontier can vary randomly across units with the same vector of inputs x_i (Schmidt and Lovell 1979). That is, the SPF represented by (3) expresses maximal output for a unit, given some set of inputs, as a distribution $\ln f(x_i; \beta) + v_i$ that varies randomly about a deterministic kernel $\ln f(x_i; \beta)$. The notion of a production frontier that is stochastic alleviates the major shortcoming of earlier approaches. Methodologies that omit the v_i component employ a deterministic frontier, which means that random events would be lumped together with inefficiency. The nonnegative component u_i permits firms to be technically inefficient relative to their own frontier, rather than to some sample norm:

$$\ln(y_i) = \text{SPF}_i - u_i, \qquad u_i \geq 0, \tag{4}$$

on substituting (2) and (3) in (1). The condition that u_i be nonnegative ensures that all observations lie on or beneath their SPF (Førsund et al. 1980).

The stochastic production frontier model does have a number of potential disadvantages. First, functional forms must be specified for $f(x_i; \beta)$ and the components of the error term because the method is parametric. Second, it is assumed generally that the selected functional form is valid over the complete range of the observations, whereas it is preferable that the restrictions imposed by this assumption are tested for the sample.

Third, the results for measured technical efficiency and inefficiency are sensitive to the functional form selected (Corbo and de Melo 1983). For example, Kopp and Smith (1980) and Huang and Bagi (1984) reported that the measured technical efficiency for an industry increased with the flexibility of the functional form specified for $f(x_i; \beta)$. These findings indicate that a misspecification of the functional form can lead to error that is incorrectly considered to be a component of measured technical inefficiency. The reason is that the evidence of technical inefficiency is negative skewness of the regression error term, and such skewness can reflect both inefficiency and misspecification of the functional form.

Finally, there can be another statistical problem. Schmidt and Sickles (1984) noted that if a firm knew its level of technical inefficiency, for example, this should affect its input choices. It would then be invalid to assume that inefficiency was independent of the regressors. In addition there can be the more usual problem of simultaneity bias, which occurs if the levels of certain inputs are correlated with the overall error term. However, the potential applicability of these points extends to all statistical frontiers, not just to the stochastic frontiers.

5.2.2 The Production Function

Efficiency is measured in this study in terms of a production rather than a cost function because the data on output and input quantities are more readily available than the corresponding prices. Since ordinary least squares (OLS) estimates of the production function coefficients can be best, linear unbiased, and consistent, except for the constant term, we are justified in drawing on earlier results with average production functions to select an appropriate, functional form.

The transcendental logarithmic (translog) specification of the production function was selected for the empirical work. The specification can be viewed as a second-order Taylor series expansion of the underlying log output function in terms of the logs of factor inputs (Christensen, Jorgenson, and Lau 1970, 1973; Barnett 1985). That is, the first- and second-order partial derivatives of the translog approximation equal those of the twice differentiable reference function at the point of expansion (Denny and Fuss 1977).

Given its general form, the translog does not impose prior restrictions on the underlying production structure, unlike the Cobb-Douglas and CES specifications. For example, the elasticity of output with respect to an input is not restrained to be invariant with the levels of the reference input or of other inputs. This generality reduces the possibility that a misspecification of the functional form could lead to error that is incorrectly considered to be technical inefficiency (Kopp and Smith 1980, Huang and Bagi 1984).

The translog approximation to the unknown gross output function can be written

$$\ln(GO) = a_0 + a_1 \ln(K) + a_2 \ln(L) + a_3 \ln(M) + \frac{a_4[\ln(K)]^2}{2}$$

$$+ \frac{a_5[\ln(L)]^2}{2} + \frac{a_6[\ln(M)]^2}{2} + a_7 \ln(K)\ln(L)$$

$$+ a_8 \ln(K)\ln(M) + a_9 \ln(L)\ln(M) + e_1. \tag{5}$$

The gross output GO of the production process depends on the flows of capital K, labor L, and material M services. The derivation of GO, K, L, and M is explained in BIE (1988, appendix 3). e_1 is an error term, and the symmetry constraints have been imposed on the functional form (Denny and Fuss 1977). All the variables (GO, K, L, M) are indexed around an expansion point. It is the sample geometric mean (arithmetic mean of the logged variable) in the current study.

Equation (5) can be estimated by OLS if it is assumed that the levels of inputs are uncorrelated with the error term. A basis for this approach is the assumption that firms maximize expected profit (Zellner, Kmenta, and Dreze 1966). That is, firms do not know the impact of the disturbance [e_1 in (5)] earlier than when they select the levels of input services.

An alternative is to employ a translog approximation to the unknown value added function, which can be written

$$\ln(VA) = b_0 + b_1 \ln(K) + b_2 \ln(L) + \frac{b_3[\ln(K)]^2}{2} + \frac{b_4[\ln(L)]^2}{2}$$

$$+ b_5 \ln(K)\ln(L) + e_2, \tag{6}$$

where VA is the value added by the production process. e_2 is an error term, and the symmetry constraints have been imposed on the functional form (Denny and Fuss 1977). All the variables are indexed around the sample geometric mean in this case too.

An argument in favor of the selection of (6) over (5) could be made as follows: The levels of gross output and materials input are likely to be determined by the production unit within the one-year period to which our data apply. Estimation by OLS would yield inconsistent estimates of the parameters.[1] Estimation of (6) could avoid such a simultaneity problem and would increase the degrees of freedom in the regression equation. In the absence of evidence on the simultaneity issue, both (5) and (6) are employed in the analysis and the results are compared in section 5.4.

5.2.3 Estimation

The method of corrected OLS (COLS) was employed in this study to estimate the stochastic production frontier. The approach is as follows: First, estimate the parameter vector β using OLS. Conditional on the values of the independent variables, OLS provides a best linear unbiased and consistent estimate of β (except for the intercept term). Given a specific distribution for e, the parameters of this distribution can be estimated consistently from the sample moments of the OLS residuals, provided that the parameters of the distribution can be derived from its higher-order (second-, third-, etc.) central moments. In this case the COLS method provides consistent estimates of all the parameters of the frontier (Olson, Schmidt, and Waldman 1980).

Given the assumption of a truncated-normal/normal error structure, the second (μ_2), third (μ_3), and fourth (μ_4) moments of the OLS residuals are functions of σ_v^2, σ_u, and μ (BIE 1988, app. 2):

$$\mu_2 = \sigma^2 - \frac{\mu\sigma_u f(\mu/\sigma_u)}{F(\mu/\sigma_u)} - \frac{\sigma_u^2 f^2(\mu/\sigma_u)}{F^2(\mu/\sigma_u)}, \tag{7}$$

$$\mu_3 = \frac{\sigma_u(\sigma_u^2 - \mu^2)f(\mu/\sigma_u)}{F(\mu/\sigma_u)} - \frac{3\mu\sigma_u f^2(\mu/\sigma_u)}{F^2(\mu/\sigma_u)} - \frac{2\sigma_u^3 f^3(\mu/\sigma_u)}{F^3(\mu/\sigma_u)}, \tag{8}$$

$$\mu_4 = 3\sigma^4 - \frac{\mu\sigma_u(\mu^2 + 3\sigma^2 + 3\sigma_v^2)f(\mu/\sigma_u)}{F(\mu/\sigma_u)}$$

$$- \frac{2\sigma_u^2(2\mu^2 + \sigma^2 + 2\sigma_v^2)f^2(\mu/\sigma_u)}{F^2(\mu/\sigma_u)} - \frac{6\mu\sigma_u^3 f^3(\mu/\sigma_u)}{F^3(\mu/\sigma_u)}$$

$$- \frac{3\sigma_u^4 f^4(\mu/\sigma_u)}{F^4(\mu/\sigma_u)}, \tag{9}$$

where $\sigma^2 = \sigma_u^2 + \sigma_v^2$, and $f(\cdot)$ and $F(\cdot)$ are the standard normal density and distribution functions, respectively. The three equations are not linear in the three parameters, so a closed form solution does not exist. In this study the system of nonlinear equations was solved iteratively using the IMSL routine ZSYSTEM (International Mathematical and Statistical Libraries 1980).

There are two cases in which the COLS estimator of the generalized error term parameters does not exist in a meaningful form. The first arises in data for which the estimated σ_u is negative. It occurs frequently for industries with a positive third moment of the residuals—that is, in cases for which the residuals are skewed in the "wrong" direction for a stochastic production frontier. Following Olson et al. (1980) this phenomenon is known as a type I failure of the COLS method.

The second problem with the COLS method and the generalized error specification arises in cases for which the value of μ/σ_u selected by the iterative routine is persistently less than -5. In such cases the magnitude of $F(\mu/\sigma_u)$ tends to zero; the magnitudes of the calculated second, third, and fourth moments of the residuals become unbounded, and the ZSYSTEM subroutine aborts. This phenomenon is defined to be a type III failure.

It is not necessary to solve a system of nonlinear equations if the parameter μ is set to zero and the half-normal/normal error structure is adopted.

In this case, (7) through (9) simplify to

$$\mu_2|_{\mu=0} = \sigma_u^2\left(1 - \frac{2}{\pi}\right) + \sigma_v^2, \tag{10}$$

$$\mu_3|_{\mu=0} = \sigma_u^3\left(\frac{2}{\pi}\right)^{1/2}\left(1 - \frac{4}{\pi}\right), \tag{11}$$

$$\mu_4|_{\mu=0} = 3\sigma_v^4 + 6\left(1 - \frac{2}{\pi}\right)\sigma_u^2\sigma_v^2 + \left(3 - \frac{4}{\pi} - \frac{12}{\pi^2}\right)\sigma_u^4. \tag{12}$$

From (11) the standard error parameter of the half-normal error term is estimated consistently by

$$\sigma_u = \frac{\mu_3^{1/3}\pi^{1/2}}{2^{1/6}(\pi - 4)^{1/3}}. \tag{13}$$

The phenomenon of a positive μ_3 is known as a type I failure (Olson et al. 1980). The implied σ_u is negative in such circumstances because the residuals are skewed in the wrong direction for a stochastic production frontier. Waldman (1982) has shown that the OLS slope estimates and the value of σ_u equal to zero represent a local maximum of the likelihood function for such data, while the empirical evidence in Olson et al. (1980) suggests that this point is a global maximum.

From (13) and (10) the variance of the normal error term is estimated consistently by

$$\sigma_v^2 = \begin{cases} \mu_2 - \dfrac{(\pi - 2)\mu_3^{2/3}}{2^{1/3}(\pi - 4)^{2/3}} & \text{if } \mu_3 \leq 0, \\[2mm] \mu_2 & \text{if } \mu_3 > 0. \end{cases} \tag{14}$$

As defined by Olson et al. (1980) a type II failure occurs if the estimated value of σ_v^2 implied by (14) is negative. Equation (14) can be rearranged to show that such failures occur if

$$s = \frac{\mu_3}{\mu_2^{3/2}} < \frac{(\pi - 4)2^{1/2}}{(\pi - 2)^{3/2}} = -0.9953, \tag{15}$$

where s is the skewness of the OLS residuals. Olson et al. (1980) reported that there appears to be no comparable problem with estimation by the method of maximum likelihood ML. Finite maxima for σ_u and σ_v^2 always appeared to exist, and they had the correct, positive signs.

As noted above, theory provides little guidance on picking a distribution for u. It follows that the choice and evaluation of particular distributions are based on statistical methods. Two approaches have been suggested in the literature, and they are dealt with in turn.

The first approach follows from the notion that the stochastic frontier model is a generalization of the standard OLS model, with the additional feature of a one-sided error component u. It follows that a test for the existence of a frontier can be based on the OLS residuals, noting that the null hypothesis is that the errors are independently and identically normally distributed.

Schmidt and Lin (1984) suggested that the test be based on the sample skewness of the residuals, given that the most obvious difference between a normal and the sum of a normal and a one-sided error is the skewness of the latter. Two means of performing the test were outlined. The first was based on the 5 percent and 1 percent critical values for skewness reported in the Biometrika Tables for Statisticians. It is quite straightforward to apply and the results for the current study are discussed in section 5.4. The second means was to transform the skewness variable to a form that is approximately standard normal. The authors noted that the COLS estimate of σ_u in the half-normal/normal error structure is a simple function of μ_3 [see (13)], so for large samples the skewness test is equivalent to testing whether the COLS estimate of σ_u is significantly different from zero.

A more general test for normality than those based solely on the skewness of the OLS residuals is that suggested by Jarque and Bera (1980). This asymptotic test makes use of information on both the skewness and kurtosis of the OLS residuals, just as COLS estimation of the truncated-normal/normal error structure employs data on the second, third, and fourth sample moments of the residuals. Results for the current study with this test too are discussed in section 5.4.

The second approach to the choice and evaluation of particular distributions employs asymptotic Lagrange multiplier tests based on the Pearson family of truncated distributions (Lee 1983). Tests were derived explicitly for the half-normal and truncated-normal distributions. The method was not feasible for our analysis, because only the sample moments of the residuals for each industry regression could be made available to us by the Australian Bureau of Statistics due to a confidentiality constraint.

After the stochastic production frontier has been estimated, the average technical efficiency of the industry can be determined using the approach suggested by Afriat (1972). Using (1) and (2), the technical efficiency of the ith observation within a given industry is

$$\text{TE}_i = \frac{y_i}{f(x_i; \beta)\exp(v_i)}. \tag{16}$$

Thus the average technical efficiency (ATE) of the industry is

$$\text{ATE} = E[\exp(-u)] = \int_0^\infty \exp(-u)g(u)\,du$$

$$= \frac{\exp[\sigma_u^2/2 - \mu]F(\mu/\sigma_u - \sigma_u)}{F(\mu/\sigma_u)}, \tag{17}$$

where $g(u)$ is the density function for u. The ATE of the industry can be estimated consistently, but with an upward bias, by substituting the estimates of the parameters in (17).

An alternative and perhaps more obvious efficiency measure is the average of the distribution of the one-sided disturbance, u_i (Schmidt and Lovell 1979). From (1) and (2),

$$u_i = v_i - \ln\left[\frac{y_i}{f(x_i; \beta)}\right]. \tag{18}$$

Thus the average technical inefficiency (ATI) of the industry is

$$\text{ATI} = E[u]$$

$$= \int_0^\infty ug(u)\,du$$

$$= \mu + \frac{\sigma_u f(\mu/\sigma_u)}{F(\mu/\sigma_u)}. \tag{19}$$

The ATI of the industry can be estimated consistently, but with an upward bias, by substituting the estimates of the parameters in (19). The measure can be made independent of the level of factor inputs to the industry by dividing it by the mean of the dependent variable in the regression. This approach was adopted in the current study.

Two features of these average measures should be noted. First, they provide no information on the level of price efficiency in the industry, or on the extent to which plants in the industry are of optimal scale. This is

because a plant is counted as inefficient only to the extent that it falls short
of what is estimated to be the output attainable in a plant of its own factor
proportions and scale. Second, the measures are essentially an unweighted
average of the technical efficiencies and inefficiencies of the production
units.

5.3 Exploratory Analyses

In this section we describe the sources of data and the exploratory analyses
undertaken to determine the procedures that would be adopted in the full
study. These exploratory analyses were necessary because neither theory
nor the limited number of empirical studies that have employed the stochastic production frontier method provided a strong basis for choosing
between the available alternatives.

5.3.1 Source of Data

The unit of analysis in this study was the individual manufacturing establishment, classified by four-digit ASIC class. This level of disaggregation is
in line with the suggestion of Meeusen and van den Broeck (1977b) that
two-digit industries are too heterogeneous and that at least three-digit,
and preferably four-digit, observations are required. Data for individual
manufacturing establishments are not made available by the Australian
Bureau of Statistics (ABS) due to confidentiality requirements. For this
study the ABS estimated the regression equations and passed the processed results to the Bureau of Industry Economics for further analysis.

Most of the data used in this study were drawn from the 1977–78 Census
of Manufacturing Establishments. Manufacturing, as specified in Division
C of the Australian Standard Industrial Classification (ASIC), broadly
relates to the physical or chemical transformation of materials or components into new products, whether the work is performed by power-driven
machines or by hand. The raw data generally relate to establishments
which operated at any time during 1977–78. The same year was selected
for analysis of manufacturing industries in the United States by Caves and
Barton (1990).

In accordance with the ASIC, the establishment is in general a unit
covering all the operations carried on under the ownership of one enterprise (business) at a single physical location. The exceptions relate to

locations where the subsidiary activities exceeded $A 2.4 million in terms of sales and transfers out of goods and services during the year. These locations are treated for statistical purposes as two or more establishments corresponding to the various kinds of activity carried on. The establishment statistics also include data relating to separately located administrative offices and ancillary units serving the establishments and forming part of the enterprise that owns and operates the establishments.

Only employment and wages and salaries data are collected from single establishment manufacturing enterprises with fewer than four persons employed. These small enterprises contribute only marginally to statistical aggregates other than the number of establishments, so they were excluded from subsequent analysis. The records for all other establishments number more than 26,000. These establishments had an average total employment of around 1.1 million persons and turnover in excess of $A 48,000 million in 1977–78.

The raw data employed in the study differ from published data in two respects: In-scope establishments of out-of-scope enterprises were excluded from subsequent analysis because there was no parent enterprise record from which to reallocate capital stock data.[2] Central ancillary units are included in published data but were excluded from our analysis, essentially because their production functions are likely to differ from those of other establishments. The derivation of the data is explained in BIE (1988, app. 3).

5.3.2   Quality Variables

In addition to the standard production variables outlined in section 5.2, a range of additive X_i variables was included in the exploratory regressions. The rationale for inclusion of the latter set of variables was discussed by Griliches and Ringstad (1971, ch. 3) and Caves and Barton (1990, ch. 3). All of the X_i variables are compositional variables, of the general form X_i equals $z_2/(z_1 + z_2)$ If z equals $(z_1 + z_2)$ is an aggregate variable and z^* equals $z_1 + (1 + d)z_2$ is the "correct" aggregate, then z^* equals $z(1 + dX_i)$. The use of $\ln(z)$ in an equation linear in logs of the variables amounts to excluding $\ln(1 + dX_i)$ from the regression. Griliches and Ringstad suggested that as X_i is less than unity, the term $\ln(1 + dX_i)$ could be approximated by dX_i for small d. That is, the implicit premium d can be estimated by including the variable X_i in the relevant regression.

$$X_1 = \frac{BVP}{K}.$$

X_1 was included in the exploratory regressions as a check on the weight accorded to the owned plant component (BVP) of the capital input (K).

$$X_2 = \frac{NP}{N}.$$

X_2 was included in the exploratory regressions as a check on the weight accorded to the nonproduction worker component (NP) of average total employment (N).

$$X_3 = \frac{GR}{TMC}.$$

X_3 was included in the exploratory regressions as a check on the weight accorded to the goods purchased for resale component (GR) of total purchases, transfers in and selected expenses (TMC). By definition, goods purchased for resale are processed differently to the other components of TMC.

$$X_4 = \frac{EF}{TMC}.$$

X_4 was included in the exploratory regressions as a check on the weight accorded to the electricity and fuels (EF) energy component of TMC.

$$X_5 = \frac{INV}{K}.$$

X_5 was included in the exploratory regressions as a check on the weight accorded to the inventories (INV) component of the capital input.

$$X_6 = \frac{AOR}{T}.$$

X_6 was included in the exploratory regressions as a check on the weight accorded to the all other operating revenue (AOR) component of turnover (T).

$$X_7 = \frac{LEAS}{K}.$$

X_7 was included in the exploratory regressions as a check on the weight accorded to the leased (LEAS) component of the capital input.

$$X_8 = \frac{PCS}{TMC}.$$

X_8 was included in the exploratory regressions as a check on the weight accorded to the payments for commission and subcontract work component (PCS) of TMC.

The 15 industries employed in the exploratory regressions were selected in an attempt to represent industries with a range in number of establishments, and in degree of product differentiation, that would enable the model specification to be tested and simplified (BIE 1988, ch. 3).

The exploratory series of regressions used either gross output (GO) or value added (VA) as the dependent variable. The explanatory variables were those of the corresponding translog production functions, with and without the additive X_i variables. The full set of additive variables (X_1 to X_8) was employed in the GO regressions, whereas the VA regressions employed (X_1, X_2, X_5, X_7)—that is, the additive variables which relate to GO or materials were excluded.

With GO as the dependent variable, X_1 and X_4 were significant in the regressions for six and seven industries, respectively. With one exception these coefficients were positive. The findings indicate that the weights accorded to the owned plant component of the capital input and the electricity and fuels component of total purchases, transfers in and selected expenses tended to be understated in around 40 percent of the exploratory industries. X_1 and X_4 were retained in the full series of GO regressions.

With VA as the dependent variable, X_1 and X_5 were significant in the regressions for six and five industries, respectively. The corresponding coefficients were positive in each case and indicate that the weights accorded to the owned plant and inventories components of the capital input tended to be understated in around 40 percent of the exploratory industries. X_1 and X_5 were retained in the full series of VA regressions.

On the basis of these exploratory results for the sample of 15 industries, we decided to estimate two versions of the stochastic production frontier for each industry that contained sufficient plant observations. The frontiers would be based on gross output and value added as alternative dependent variables. Each specification would include two additive X_i variables as well as the variables in the standard translog form.

5.3.3 Initial Results for the Full Data Set

With gross output as the dependent variable, estimates of ATI were secured for only 46 (33 percent) of the full set (140) of four-digit ASIC classes. They were calculated assuming a half-normal/normal error structure, using the method of corrected ordinary least squares. Of the 94 industries in the data set for the Australian manufacturing sector that failed to yield an estimate of ATI with gross output as the dependent variable, 92 were characterized by a type I failure in which the third moment of the OLS residuals is positive. Such a situation is likely to occur for industries where most of the variance of the composed error is due to randomness (σ_v^2) rather than inefficiency (σ_u^2) (Olson et al. 1980).

The other two industries were characterized by a type II failure, in which the implied variance of the symmetric component (σ_v^2) of the composed error term is negative. This is most likely to occur when most of the error variance is due to inefficiency rather than randomness. In effect the residuals for these industries are skewed too strongly overall in either the right or wrong direction for a stochastic production frontier, due to one or more outlying observations that might reflect erroneous data.

A higher success rate was achieved in the regressions with value added as the dependent variable. Estimates of ATI were secured for 79 of the 140 industries, a success rate of 56 percent. Of the other 61 industries, the residuals for 37 were skewed in the wrong direction, whereas 24 were characterized by type II failure.

To exclude those establishments that were unsuitable for analysis, certain editing criteria were applied to the primary census of establishments data before the stochastic production frontiers were estimated (BIE 1988, app. 3). For example, establishments that reported zero values for the input or output variables were excluded, both because this suggested some peculiarities in their production activities and because it was required by the logarithmic formulation of the production frontier. In addition establishments were excluded that reported data lying far enough from the industry mean to suggest errors in reporting.

However, the confidential nature of the census data for individual establishments precluded inspection by the Bureau of Industry Economics of the actual observations within each industry. Hence the possibility remained that the data set used in calculating the estimates of ATI presented above included instances of measurement or reporting error. This phenomenon could have contributed to the failure of some industries to yield an estimate of ATI. It would also have resulted in inconsistent parameter estimates (Johnston 1984, sec. 10–6).

As an initial step to investigating this possibility, plots of residuals against observed values for the dependent variable of the regressions were examined. Many of the industries for which satisfactory estimates of ATI could not be obtained seemed to contain a small number of outliers that could have strongly influenced the regression plane. However, the regression residuals alone are not a sufficient diagnostic tool for the identification of influential observations (Belsley, Kuh, and Welsch 1980, ch. 2). This tool fails to show directly what the estimated model would be if a subset of the data were deleted, and the extent to which the presence of erroneous observations affects the estimated coefficients, standard errors and test statistics.

Belsley et al. (1980) reported a number of techniques for diagnosing influential data points that avoid some of these weaknesses. The diagnostic measures used in this study were the studentized residuals (RSTUDENT), the covariance matrix (COVRATIO), the change in fit (DFFITS), and the hat matrix (HAT). In general, these statistics, respectively, indicate observations that are influential in the determination of large residuals, changes in the covariance matrix of the estimated coefficients, changes in the fit to the dependent variable, and multivariate outliers.

For each industry regression the following critical values of the diagnostic measures were used to identify influential observations:

$$RSTUDENT > 2,$$

$$1 + \frac{3p}{n} > COVRATIO > 1 - \frac{3p}{n},$$

$$DFFITS > 2\left(\frac{p}{n}\right)^{1/2},$$

$$HAT > \frac{2p}{n},$$

where p is the number of parameters in the regression model and n the number of observations. An observation was considered to be highly influential if it jointly exceeded at least three of the four criteria.

Having identified the highly influential observations, it was then necessary to investigate the possibility that measurement errors were present. To this end, the raw data on the basic variables (gross output, value added, capital stock, persons employed, and material inputs) for the individual establishments in question were inspected by officers of the Australian Bureau of Statistics (ABS). It was found that one variable in particular frequently aroused suspicions of measurement error, namely, the reported capital stocks. The next most frequent explanation for the finding that an observation was influential was that the figures had been imputed by the ABS in cases where an establishment had not supplied the relevant data.

As a result of this examination of the raw data, roughly half the highly influential observations were diagnosed as being most probably attributable to measurement error. The corrective action taken was to delete the offending observations. In all, 281 (or 1.3 percent) of the total number of observations were deleted. The other influential observations were retained, so the information on potentially inefficient establishments in an industry was available for extraction by our analysis.

5.4   Evaluation of Efficiency Measures

We first discuss the results with a conventional half-normal/normal error structure.[3] This facilitates comparison with the findings of other studies that have employed the COLS method of estimation.

5.4.1   Half-normal/Normal Error Structure

With gross output as the dependent variable, estimates of ATI are secured for only 29 percent (40) of the 140 industries, a decrease of 4 percentage points from that obtained before the deletion of erroneous observations. All failures (100 out of 140) are type I, with the residuals skewed in the wrong direction for a stochastic production frontier. The net decrease in the number of successes occurs because 19 successes become type I failures, and this change outnumbers the 12 type I and 1 type II failures that become successes. There are no type II failures after the deletion of erroneous observations. This result is consistent with the notion that type II failures could result from measurement or reporting error in some observations.[4]

There is an increase in the success rate secured from the final regressions with value added as the dependent variable. Estimates of ATI are secured for 91 of the 140 industries (65 percent) an increase of 9 percentage points over that obtained before the deletion of erroneous observations. As is the case with the gross output data set, all failures are type I with the residuals skewed in the wrong direction for a stochastic production frontier. The net increase in the number of successes occurs because the 10 type I and 16 type II failures that become successes outnumber the 14 successes that become type I failures. The 24 type II failures are removed by the deletion of erroneous observations, although 8 become type I failures.

It might seem that the removal of erroneous observations results only in a small increase in the success rate of the value-added regressions, and a decrease in the success rate of the gross output regressions. But it is important to take into account the point that the observations removed were both erroneous and highly influential, so the previous estimates of the model parameters and ATI would have been erroneous.

The summary statistics for the estimates of ATI in Australian manufacturing industries with the half-normal/normal error structure are presented in table 5.1. The most efficient two-digit subdivisions on average, according to the ATI measure with gross output as the dependent variable, are nonmetallic mineral products (ASIC 28) and transport equipment (ASIC 32). Basic metal products (ASIC 29) and food, beverages, and tobacco (ASIC 21) have the highest mean levels of measured inefficiency.

The mean estimates of ATI for Australian manufacturing industries with value added as the dependent variable are much larger than those obtained with the gross output set. The most efficient industry subdivision according to the value-added data has a higher mean level of ATI than that of the most inefficient industry in the gross output data. Note that the same industry subdivision is being referred to here, basic metal products (ASIC 29). Thus it seems that the ATI estimates are very sensitive to the form of the dependent variable.

The most efficient two-digit subdivisions on average, according to the ATI measure with value added as the dependent variable, are basic metal products (ASIC 29) and textiles (ASIC 23). At the other end of the spectrum, miscellaneous manufacturing (ASIC 34), transport equipment (ASIC 32), and food, beverages, and tobacco (ASIC 21) have the highest mean levels of measured inefficiency. However, it is important to bear in mind that these efficiency measures are relative to the best practices observed in the sample. That is, they do not generally reflect the best practices that

Table 5.1
Means and standard deviations of ATI estimates by two-digit ASIC subdivision, half-normal/normal error structure

ASIC code	Description	Gross output		Value added	
		ATI	Number of observations	ATI	Number of observations
21	Food, beverages, and tobacco	0.113 (0.066)	3	0.362 (0.121)	13
23	Textiles	0.085 (0.035)	4	0.239 (0.170)	5
24	Clothing and footwear	0.106 (0.021)	4	0.277 (0.046)	6
25	Wood, wood products, and furniture	0.099 (0.036)	3	0.330 (0.073)	7
26	Paper, paper products, printing, and publishing	0.105 (0.031)	3	0.271 (0.119)	7
27	Chemical, petroleum, and coal products	0.073 (0.018)	3	0.301 (0.153)	6
28	Nonmetallic mineral products	0.038 (0.000)	1	0.301 (0.068)	7
29	Basic metal products	0.119 (0.029)	4	0.235 (0.042)	5
31	Fabricated metal products	0.108 (0.024)	4	0.296 (0.091)	9
32	Transport equipment	0.065 (0.048)	3	0.369 (0.121)	4
33	Other machinery and equipment	0.092 (0.034)	6	0.244 (0.056)	15
34	Miscellaneous manufacturing	0.096 (0.038)	2	0.391 (0.070)	7

Source: BIE (1988, table 4.2).
Note: Standard deviations are in parentheses.

might be observed in a more extensive sample that included data from other countries, such as Japan, the United States, and Germany.

5.4.2 Generalized Error Structure

The conventional assumption for the technical inefficiency component of the composed error is that the elements of u are independently and identically distributed as half-normal, which is equivalent to assuming a truncated-normal distribution with zero mode. The assumption implies that the likelihood of inefficient behavior monotonically decreases for increasing levels of inefficiency. This restrictive error structure is relaxed in section 5.2 for the production frontier, following the generalization by Stevenson (1980) for the cost frontier. The method allows the elements of u to be distributed as a truncated-normal, with the mode μ determined by the data.

The results from estimation with the generalized error structure are now discussed.[5] With gross output as the dependent variable, estimates of ATI are secured for 46 percent (65) of the 140 industries, an increase of 17 percentage points from that obtained with the half-normal/normal error structure. Sixty-six of the failures are type I, while there are 9 type III failures. The net increase in the number of successes occurs because the 33 type I failures that become successes outnumber the 8 successes that become type I and type III failures. Sixty-four type I failures remain in that category, while 3 transfer to become type III failures.

The fact that estimates of ATI could be derived with the generalized error structure for some of the industries with the residuals skewed in the wrong direction appears to reflect two factors. The first is the use made by the generalized model of information contained in the fourth moment of the regression residuals, which is not used in the COLS method with the half-normal/normal error structure. The second is the failure of the estimated parameters to solve exactly the three nonlinear equations for the second to fourth moments of the residuals; in particular, the sample third moments are positive while the estimated moments are nonpositive by construction.

The selection of the generalized error structure for the value added data leads to little change in the success rate with which ATI can be measured. Estimates of ATI are secured for 90 of the 140 industries, versus the 91 obtained with the half-normal/normal error structure. Forty-one of the failures are type I, while there are 9 type III failures. The unit decrease in the number of successes occurs because the 5 type I failures that become successes are outnumbered by the 6 successes that become type I and type III failures. Forty type I failures remain in that category, while 4 transfer to become type III failures.

The summary statistics for the estimates of ATI in Australian manufacturing industries with the truncated-normal error structure are presented in tables 5.2 and 5.3 for the gross output and value added frontiers, respectively. The most efficient two-digit subdivisions on average, according to the ATI measure for the gross output frontiers, are wood, wood products and furniture (ASIC 25), and miscellaneous manufacturing (ASIC 34). Chemical, petroleum, and coal products (ASIC 27) and food, beverages, and tobacco (ASIC 21) have the highest mean levels of measured inefficiency. Of the individual four-digit ASIC classes, wine and brandy (ASIC 2188) and synthetic resins and rubber (ASIC 2753) have the highest levels of measured inefficiency and are located within the ASIC subdivisions identified above.

The mean estimates of ATI for the value-added frontiers (table 5.3) are much larger than those obtained for the gross output frontiers (table 5.2). Indeed the most efficient industry subdivision according to the value added frontiers has a higher mean level of ATI than that of the most inefficient industry according to the gross output frontiers. This finding that the ATI estimates are very sensitive to changes in the dependent variable was noted also in discussion of the results with a half-normal/normal error structure.

The most efficient two-digit subdivisions on average, according to the ATI measure for the value-added frontier, are fabricated metal products (ASIC 31), clothing and footwear (ASIC 24), and textiles (ASIC 23). Other machinery and equipment (ASIC 33) and food, beverages, and tobacco (ASIC 21) have the highest mean levels of measured inefficiency. Of the individual four-digit ASIC classes, photographic and optical goods (ASIC 3341) and fruit products (ASIC 2131) have the highest levels of measured inefficiency and are located within the ASIC subdivisions identified above.

5.4.3 Statistical Significance of Efficiency Estimates

Information on the second, third, and fourth moments of the OLS residuals is available for each regression with either gross output or value added as the dependent variable. These data enable tests to be undertaken for the statistical significance of the estimates for ATI against the null

Table 5.2
Summary statistics for ATI estimates by two-digit ASIC subdivision, truncated-normal/normal error structure, gross output frontiers

ASIC code	Description	Minimum	Maximum	Mean	Standard deviation	Number of observations
21	Food, beverages, and tobacco	0.006	0.631	0.133	0.173	11
23	Textiles	0.060	0.147	0.107	0.039	5
24	Clothing and footwear	0.015	0.132	0.081	0.057	5
25	Wood, wood products, and furniture	0.017	0.090	0.047	0.038	3
26	Paper, paper products, printing, and publishing	0.061	0.126	0.095	0.026	6
27	Chemical, petroleum, and coal products	0.062	0.463	0.173	0.194	4
28	Nonmetallic mineral products	0.038	0.105	0.067	0.034	3
29	Basic metal products	0.086	0.106	0.097	0.010	4
31	Fabricated metal products	0.038	0.431	0.121	0.153	6
32	Transport equipment	0.057	0.131	0.087	0.039	3
33	Other machinery and equipment	0.010	0.211	0.072	0.060	9
34	Miscellaneous manufacturing	0.040	0.103	0.062	0.023	6

Source: BIE (1988, table 4.7).

Table 5.3
Summary statistics for ATI estimates by two-digit ASIC subdivision, truncated-normal/normal error structure, value-added frontiers

ASIC code	Description	Minimum	Maximum	Mean	Standard deviation	Number of observations
21	Food, beverages, and tobacco	0.080	0.889	0.426	0.234	14
23	Textiles	0.023	0.443	0.233	0.162	6
24	Clothing and footwear	0.194	0.309	0.230	0.060	5
25	Wood, wood products, and furniture	0.162	0.465	0.288	0.091	7
26	Paper, paper products, printing, and publishing	0.047	0.666	0.290	0.207	6
27	Chemical, petroleum, and coal products	0.169	0.415	0.252	0.115	4
28	Nonmetallic mineral products	0.160	0.364	0.236	0.076	7
29	Basic metal products	0.156	0.558	0.370	0.146	5
31	Fabricated metal products	0.103	0.320	0.221	0.071	9
32	Transport equipment	0.124	0.354	0.250	0.103	5
33	Other machinery and equipment	0.123	0.995	0.452	0.307	13
34	Miscellaneous manufacturing	0.051	0.543	0.329	0.141	9

Source: BIE (1988, table 4.8).

hypothesis that the errors are independently and identically normally distributed. The analysis is based on the regression residuals because the COLS method of estimation was employed by this study. A test for the statistical significance of the ATI estimates would have been much more straightforward had the Australian Bureau of Statistics been able to undertake maximum likelihood estimation. In that case an appropriate procedure would have been to test for the joint significance of the estimates for σ_u and μ.

The first test used here is based on the sample skewness of the residuals, given that the most obvious difference between a normal and the sum of a normal and a one-sided error is the skewness of the latter.[6] Forty-one of the 140 skewness values derived from regressions with gross output as the dependent variable are significant at the 10 percent level (two-tail test). However, just two of these values are for industries with the residuals skewed in the direction that is appropriate for a stochastic production frontier. That is, the results obtained from the gross output regressions do not lend much support to the model of technical inefficiency on which the analysis is based.

Analysis of the value-added data yields more positive results. Thirty-five of the 140 skewness values are significant at the 10 percent level (two-tail test). Twenty-seven of the 35 values are negative, which is the appropriate sign for a stochastic production frontier. The results suggest that 27 (30 percent) of the 91 nonzero values of ATI (with the half-normal/normal error specification) differ significantly from zero.

The Jarque-Bera (1980) statistic is a more general test for normality than that based on skewness because it makes use of information on both the skewness and kurtosis of the OLS residuals.[7] The statistic indicates that the hypothesis of normality is rejected at the 10 percent significance level for 64 of the 140 industries, with gross output as the dependent variable. This sample of 64 includes 39 of the 41 industries selected by the skewness statistic, plus 25 additional industries for which the deviation from normality is predominantly due to kurtosis rather than skewness. Fifteen industries in the sample have negative skewness values, so the results suggest that 15 (38 percent) of the 40 nonzero values of ATI (with the half-normal/ normal error specification) differ significantly from zero. The number of significant estimates for ATI declines to 11 with the truncated-normal/ normal error specification due to two type I and two type III failures.

Analysis of the value-added data indicates that the hypothesis of normality is rejected at the 10 percent significance level for 64 of the 140 industries. This sample of 64 includes 30 of the 35 industries selected by the skewness statistic, plus 34 additional industries for which the deviation from normality is predominantly due to kurtosis rather than skewness. Thirty-four industries in the sample have negative skewness values, so the results suggest that 34 (37 percent) of the 91 nonzero values of ATI (with the half-normal/normal error specification) differ significantly from zero. The number of significant estimates for ATI declines to 31 with the truncated-normal/normal error specification, due to one type I and two type III failures.

5.4.4 Sensitivity of Efficiency Estimates to the Definition of Output

As noted above for the data grouped by two-digit ASIC, the range of the efficiency estimates derived for the value-added frontiers (table 5.3) is considerably larger than that for the gross output frontiers (table 5.2) with a generalized error structure. Caves and Barton (1990, ch. 4) report a parallel finding for U.S. manufacturing industries. Against this background we examine patterns in the estimates for efficiency and the symmetric error in the case of the 50 Australian manufacturing industries for which estimates could be derived for both the gross output and value-added frontiers. The results are presented in table 5.4.

The value-added data set suggests significantly higher levels of inefficiency and randomness than those obtained with the gross output data set. Possible reasons for the apparent sensitivity of the ATI measure to model specification include the invalidity of the estimates derived from the gross output regressions, due to correlation between the level of material inputs and the error term, and the much larger range of the ratio between the maximum and minimum values for the dependent variable in the value-added regressions relative to those for the gross output regressions (Caves and Barton 1990, ch. 4).

Further evidence on the relationship between the estimates of ATI is obtained by regressing the linear and logarithmic forms of the efficiency estimates using a gross output frontier on the analogous estimates using a value-added frontier. The data are shown in figures 5.1 through 5.4, and the regression results are given in table 5.5.

In no case is there a significant linear relationship between the efficiency estimates derived using gross output or value added frontiers (table 5.5).

Table 5.4
Summary statistics for ATI and symmetric error, industries for which ATI could be
estimated for both gross output and value-added frontiers, generalized error structure

	Gross output		Value added	
Variable	ATI	σ_v	ATI	σ_v
Minimum	0.006	0.015	0.023	0.001
Maximum	0.631	0.237	0.995	0.534
Mean	0.101	0.120	0.355	0.206
Standard deviation	0.100	0.056	0.202	0.129
t-statistic for difference between the means	8.00	4.33		

Source: BIE (1988, tables 4.7 and 4.8).

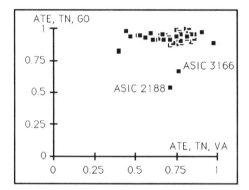

Figure 5.1
Relationship between the estimates for ATE derived with a generalized error structure, gross
output, and value-added frontiers (source: BIE 1988, tables 4.7 and 4.8)

This conclusion holds good whether or not the data sets include the
outliers (ASIC 2188, 3166) evident in figures 5.1 through 5.4. On this basis
one might expect to obtain quite different statistical explanations for interindustry differences in efficiency, depending on whether gross output or
value-added frontiers had been employed with a generalized error structure.

These results can be compared with those for the sample of 35 industries
for which estimates could be derived with a half-normal error structure for
both the gross output and value-added frontiers. The patterns in the
estimates are summarized in table 5.6. As is the case for the generalized
error structure, the value-added data set suggests significantly higher levels

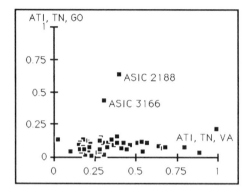

Figure 5.2
Relationship between the estimates for ATI derived with a generalized error structure, gross output, and value-added frontiers (source: BIE 1988, tables 4.7 and 4.8)

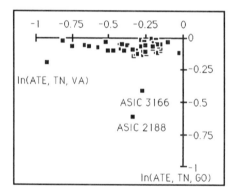

Figure 5.3
Relationship between the estimates for ln(ATE) derived with a generalized error structure, gross output, and value-added frontiers (source: BIE 1988, tables 4.7 and 4.8)

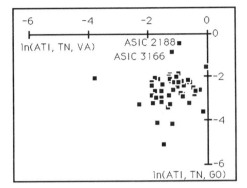

Figure 5.4
Relationship between the estimates for ln(ATI) derived with a generalized error structure, gross output, and value-added frontiers (source: BIE 1988, tables 4.7 and 4.8)

Table 5.5
The relationship between efficiency estimates derived with gross output and value-added frontiers, generalized error structure

Data set	Estimated data[a]		
	Slope coefficient[b]	Degrees of freedom	R^2
ATE	0.037	48	0.004
	(0.43)		
ATE ASIC 2188, 3166 excluded	0.036	46	0.015
	(0.84)		
ATI	0.038	48	0.006
	(0.53)		
ATI ASIC 2188, 3166 excluded	0.033	46	0.028
	(1.15)		
ln(ATE)	0.024	48	0.002
	(0.33)		
ln(ATE) ASIC 2188, 3166 excluded	0.030	46	0.021
	(0.98)		
ln(ATI)	0.108	48	0.008
	(0.62)		
ln(ATI) ASIC 2188, 3166 excluded	0.074	46	0.005
	(0.48)		

a. Very similar results were obtained using White's (1980) correction for an unknown form of heteroskedasticity.
b. *t*-ratios are in parentheses.

Table 5.6
Summary statistics for ATI, industries for which ATI could be estimated for both gross output and value-added frontiers, half-normal error structure

Variable	Gross output	Value added
Minimum	0.032	0.142
Maximum	0.182	0.591
Mean	0.100	0.326
Standard deviation	0.035	0.105
t-statistic for difference between the means	12.08	

Source: BIE (1988, table 4.2).

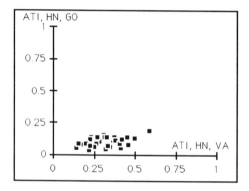

Figure 5.5
Relationship between the estimates for ATI derived with a half-normal error structure, gross output, and value-added frontiers (source: BIE 1988, table 4.2)

of inefficiency (table 5.6, figure 5.5) than those obtained with the gross output data set.

Further information on the relationship between the ATI estimates is obtained by regressing the linear and logarithmic forms of the estimates using a gross output frontier on the analogous estimates using a value-added frontier. The data are shown in figures 5.5 and 5.6 and the regression results are given in table 5.7. In each case there is a significant linear relationship between the efficiency estimates derived using gross output or value-added frontiers. On this basis one might expect there to be a degree of similarity between the statistical explanations for interindustry differences in efficiency, based on either gross output or value-added frontiers with a half-normal error structure. This conclusion is of some interest,

Table 5.7
The relationship between ATI estimates derived with gross output and value-added frontiers, half-normal error structure

Data set	Estimated data[a]		
	Slope coefficient[b]	Degrees of freedom	R^2
ATI	0.146	33	0.194
	(2.82)		
ln(ATI)	0.489	33	0.166
	(2.56)		

a. Very similar results were obtained using White's (1980) correction for an unknown form of heteroskedasticity.
b. t-ratios are in parentheses.

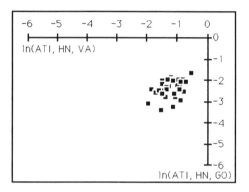

Figure 5.6
Relationship between the estimates for ln(ATI) derived with a half-normal error structure, gross output, and value-added frontiers (source: BIE 1988, table 4.2)

given the apparent absence of a linear relationship between the efficiency estimates derived using the less restrictive, generalized error structure.

5.4.5 Sensitivity of Efficiency Estimates to the Error Structure

It is of interest to compare the efficiency estimates obtained with the half-normal/normal and truncated-normal/normal error structures because this study is one of the first to apply the COLS version of both methods to a substantial number of industries.

There are 32 gross output frontiers for which estimates of ATI are secured if the half-normal or truncated-normal distribution is selected for

Table 5.8
Summary statistics for efficiency estimates, industries for which ATI could be estimated with both truncated-normal and half-normal errors

Data set		Estimated data			
Frontier	Distribution for u	Minimum	Maximum	Mean	Standard deviation
Gross output	Truncated-normal	0.038	0.631	0.126	0.114
	Half-normal	0.032	0.182	0.101	0.036
Value added	Truncated-normal	0.080	0.995	0.336	0.188
	Half-normal	0.060	0.591	0.303	0.103

Source: BIE (1988, tables 4.2, 4.7, and 4.8).

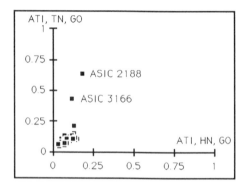

Figure 5.7
Relationship between the estimates for ATI derived with a generalized and half-normal error structure, gross output frontiers (source: BIE 1988, tables 4.2 and 4.7)

the inefficiency error term u. The summary statistics for the ATI values estimated for this sample are presented in table 5.8, and the data are shown in figure 5.7. Although the minimum and mean[8] estimated values of ATI are similar for each specification, the maximum value and the standard deviation of the truncated-normal sample are substantially larger than the corresponding variables for the half-normal sample. Inspection of the data (figure 5.7) indicates that the latter findings are due largely to the magnitudes of two ATI estimates in the truncated-normal sample: 0.631 and 0.431 for ASIC classes 2188 and 3166. A distinguishing feature of these estimates is that their magnitude is due largely to the size of μ, the estimated mode of the truncated-normal distribution. It is this parameter that is restricted to zero by the half-normal specification for u.

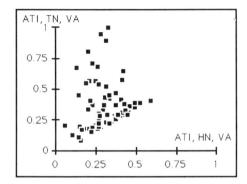

Figure 5.8
Relationship between the estimates for ATI derived with a generalized and half-normal error
structure, value-added frontiers (source: BIE 1988, tables 4.2 and 4.8)

There are 85 value-added frontiers for which estimates of ATI are
secured if the half-normal or truncated-normal distribution is selected for
the inefficiency error term u. The summary statistics for the ATI values
estimated for this sample are presented in table 5.8 and the data are shown
in figure 5.8. The results do not differ greatly from those obtained for the
gross output data. Although the minimum and mean[9] values of ATI are
similar for each specification of u, the maximum value and standard deviation of the truncated-normal sample are substantially larger than the
corresponding variables for the half-normal sample. Further information
on the relationship between the ATI estimates is obtained by regressing the
linear and logarithmic forms of the estimates obtained using a truncated-
normal error term on the analogous estimates obtained using a half-
normal error term. The data are shown in figures 5.7 though 5.10, and the
regression results are given in table 5.9.

There is a significant linear relationship between the efficiency estimates in
three of the four cases. The exception is the value-added frontiers with ATI
entering the regression in linear form. The t-statistics for the restriction
that the slope coefficient in the log–log regressions equals unity suggests
that the ATI estimates tend to move in a fixed proportion for the gross
output data, and that there is a less than proportional movement for the
value-added data. However, this hypothesis is no longer supported for the
gross output data set once the two outliers evident in figures 5.7 and 5.9
are excluded from the regression (table 5.9). On this basis one might expect

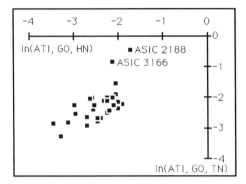

Figure 5.9
Relationship between the estimates for ln(ATI) derived with a generalized and half-normal error structure, gross output frontiers (source: BIE 1988, tables 4.2 and 4.7)

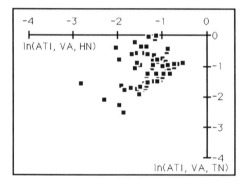

Figure 5.10
Relationship between the estimates for ln(ATI) derived with a generalized and half-normal error structure, value-added frontiers (source: BIE 1988, tables 4.2 and 4.8)

Table 5.9
The relationship between ATI estimates derived with truncated-normal and half-normal
errors, gross output and value-added frontiers

Frontier	Dependent variable	Estimated data[a]			
		Slope coefficient[b]	t (slope $= 1$)	Degrees of freedom	R^2
Gross output	ATI	1.691 (3.44)	NA[c]	30	0.283
	ln(ATI)	0.795 (4.22)	-1.09	30	0.372
Value added	ATI	0.267 (1.34)	NA[c]	83	0.021
	ln(ATI)	0.410 (2.97)	-4.27	83	0.096
Gross output	ATI ASIC 2188, 3166 excluded	0.559 (3.43)	NA[c]	28	0.296
	ln(ATI) ASIC 2188, 3166 excluded	0.546 (4.35)	-3.61	28	0.403

a. Very similar results were obtained using White's (1980) correction for an unknown form of
heteroskedasticity.
b. t-ratios are in parentheses.
c. Not applicable.

there to be a degree of similarity between the statistical explanations for
interindustry differences in efficiency, based on gross output frontiers with
either a truncated-normal or a half-normal error structure. This conclusion is less sustainable for the efficiency estimates derived from the value-
added frontiers, given the apparent weakness of the linear and logarithmic
relationships between those estimates.[10]

As noted above, theory provides little guidance on picking a distribution
for u. It follows that the choice and evaluation of particular distributions
are based on statistical methods. The preferred approach with COLS
estimation is to employ the explicit, Lagrange multiplier tests for the
half-normal and truncated-normal distributions, based on the OLS residuals (Lee 1983). The method was not feasible for this analysis because
of the confidentiality constraints on the data that could be made available
by the Australian Bureau of Statistics. In the absence of such information,
the choice between the efficiency estimates derived using the truncated-
normal and half-normal error structures can be made only on the basis of
the restrictions imposed by each specification. Because the truncated-

normal specification does not restrict the likelihood of inefficient behavior to decrease monotonically for increasing levels of inefficiency, it is preferred overall to the less general half-normal specification.

5.5 Concluding Remarks

The most general of the alternative methods for the derivation of an efficiency frontier and the computation of a technical efficiency measure is currently the stochastic frontier model. This model is not subject to some of the statistical and empirical shortcomings of earlier approaches. In common with most earlier approaches, however, it yields efficiency measures that do not reflect the operation of plants at scales that are too small or too large, or of plants with input combinations that are inefficient at prevailing input prices.

According to the stochastic production frontier approach, the error structure of the regression model contains two components. The first component is assumed to be distributed symmetrically. It represents random variations in the economic environment facing production units. The second component is assumed to be distributed asymmetrically. It represents a variety of features that reflect inefficiency. These features include firm-specific technical knowledge, the will, skills, and effort of management and employees, and work stoppages, material bottlenecks, and other disruptions to production.

The shape of the distribution selected for the asymmetric component shows an a priori picture of the distribution of efficiency below the possible maximum. Although the selection of a distribution should be based on the economic mechanisms that generate the inefficiency, theory provides little guidance on picking an appropriate distribution. In this study both the half-normal distribution and the less restrictive truncated-normal distribution are employed. The latter distribution means that the likelihood of inefficient behavior does not necessarily decrease monotonically for increasing levels of inefficiency.

The estimation of stochastic production frontiers for more than 100 Australian manufacturing industries is a substantial task. In the absence of a time or budget constraint, it would have been desirable to test the estimated models with a range of diagnostic procedures and to refine the models so as to ensure that the results were statistically adequate.[11] For example, it would have been of considerable interest to assess whether the same frontier was appropriate for small as well as large plants, and then to examine whether the technical efficiency of the small-plant sector differed from that of the large-plant sector.[12] Information could also have been obtained on the extent of returns to scale in the range of industries and on the degree to which inputs were substitutable for or complementary to each other. Such areas remain for further study.

The results for the complete set of four-digit industries (140) are only moderately successful in terms of the number of industries that support the estimation of a stochastic production frontier. Estimates of average technical inefficiency (ATI) are secured for only 40 (29 percent) of the 140 gross output frontiers with a half-normal distribution for inefficiency. A higher success rate (65 percent) is achieved for the value-added frontiers. If the stochastic frontier methodology is plausible, one would expect to find inefficiency present in a substantial majority of Australian manufacturing industries. On this basis the results for the gross output frontiers should be regarded with some scepticism.

The next step in the analysis was to allow the distribution of inefficiency for each industry to be determined by the data rather than by the methodology. That is, inefficiency was assumed to be distributed as a truncated-normal with the mode determined by the data rather than set at zero (which is a half-normal distribution). A comparison between the values of ATI obtained with the half-normal and truncated-normal distributions of inefficiency yields a significant linear relationship between the efficiency estimates derived from the gross output frontiers. However, the relationship is much weaker for the value-added frontiers. Thus one would have little confidence that similar explanations would be found for interindustry differences in efficiency derived from value-added frontiers but with different distributions of efficiency.

Theory provides little guidance on picking a distribution for inefficiency, so the choice is generally based on statistical methods. However, the absence of suitable data meant that explicit tests for the half-normal and truncated-normal distributions could not be performed in this study. On this basis the results with the truncated-normal distribution for inefficiency are preferred to those obtained with the half-normal distribution because the truncated-normal case allows the distribution of inefficiency for each industry to be determined by the data. Data were available that enabled tests to be undertaken for the statistical significance of the efficiency estimates. The results obtained with the more general of two tests indicate that just 11 of the ATI estimates for the gross output frontiers differ significantly from zero, while the number of significant estimates increases to 31 for the value-added frontiers. Thus one would favor the value-added measures as the basis for any analysis of interindustry differences in efficiency.

Additional research is necessary on reasons for the apparent sensitivity of estimated technical efficiency to model specification. Part of the reason for the relatively low success rates in the estimation of efficiency for Australian manufacturing industries could reflect a limitation of the current specification. An efficiency estimate cannot be derived using the existing stochastic production frontier methodology in cases where comparatively few plants in the industry are technically efficient. This deficiency might be remedied in subsequent work by the use of a distribution for inefficiency that can have either negative or positive skewness.

Considerable caution must be exercised in deriving implications for policy from the efficiency estimates presented here. Apart from the statistical limitations of the results, the estimates are derived from a single cross section of data for a particular year, whereas the pursuit of efficiency is a dynamic problem. It remains for subsequent research to examine hypotheses concerning the determinants of interindustry differences in technical efficiency and to extend the analysis to include the issue of the efficiency of the best practice in Australia relative to that abroad. The latter issues are taken up in chapter 6.

Notes

This chapter is based on research with Robert W. Phillips. We are grateful to officers of the Australian Bureau of Statistics for their support and to Richard E. Caves, Michael J. Bramson, and David G. Mayes for their advice and encouragement.

1. The role of materials in production is discussed in detail by Griliches and Ringstad (1971, ch. 5).

2. An establishment is in scope if it falls within the scope of the census—that is, if it is defined as an establishment mainly engaged in manufacturing.

3. The detailed results are presented in BIE (1988, ch. 4).

4. Caves and Barton (1990, ch. 3) comment in a similar vein that the possibility of not being able to estimate ATI is closely associated with a finding of extreme values for the residuals.

5. The detailed results are presented in BIE (1988, ch. 4).

6. Skewness is defined as $\mu_3/\mu_2^{3/2}$, where μ_2 and μ_3 are, respectively, the second and third moments of the regression residuals. The test for significance was based on the critical values reported in the Biometrika Tables for Statisticians.

7. μ_4/μ_2^2 equals three for the normal distribution, where μ_4 is the fourth moment of the regression residuals. Deviations from three by this ratio of moments are said to reflect kurtosis of the distribution.

8. The t-statistic for the restriction that the means are identical has a value of 1.16.

9. The t-statistic for the restriction that the means are identical has a value of 1.39.

10. A priori there are few grounds for selecting either ATE or ATI as a preferred measure of efficiency. One might also consider selecting the logarithmic transforms of these variables, which have different bounds to those of the untransformed variables. The choice between these four alternatives should be based on the data, obtained by statistical decision-making methods (McAleer 1984; Sargan 1984) with appropriate diagnostic checking (Pagan and Hall 1983). An in-depth discussion of this is beyond the scope of this work.

11. Relevant test procedures would include tests for incorrect functional form and omitted variables (Ramsey 1969; Anscombe 1961), heteroskedasticity (Breusch and Pagan 1979), and parameter stability (Chow 1960).

12. Caves and Barton (1990, ch. 7) examine the latter issue.

References

Afriat, S. N. 1972. Efficiency estimation of production functions. *International Economic Review* 13: 568–598.

Aigner, D. J., C. A. K. Lovell, and P. Schmidt. 1977. Formulation and estimation of stochastic frontier production function models. *Journal of Econometrics* 6: 21–37.

Anscombe, F. J. 1961. Examination of residuals. *Proceedings of the Fourth Berkeley Symposium on Mathematical Statistics and Probability*, vol. 2, 433–436.

Barnett, W. A. 1985. The minflex-Laurent translog flexible functional form. *Journal of Econometrics* 30: 33–44.

Belsley, D. A., E. Kuh, and R. E. Welsch. 1980. *Regression Diagnostics*. New York: Wiley.

Breusch, T. S., and A. R. Pagan. 1979. A simple test for heteroscedasticity and random coefficient variation. *Econometrica* 47: 1287–1294.

Bureau of Industry Economics. 1988. Technical efficiency in Australian manufacturing industries. Occasional Paper No. 4. Canberra: Bureau of Industry Economics.

Bureau of Industry Economics. 1990. International productivity differences in manufacturing—Photographic paper. Research Report No. 34. Canberra: AGPS.

Bureau of Industry Economics. 1991. International comparisons of plant productivity—Domestic water heaters. Research Report No. 38. Canberra: AGPS.

Caves, R. E. 1984. Scale, openness and productivity in Australian manufacturing industries. In R. E. Caves and L. B. Krause, eds., *The Australian Economy: A View from the North*. Washington: Brookings Institution, pp. 313–345.

Caves, R. E., and D. R. Barton. 1990. *Efficiency in U.S. Manufacturing Industries*. Cambridge: MIT Press.

Chow, G. C. 1960. Tests for equality between sets of coefficients in two linear regressions. *Econometrica* 28: 591–605.

Christensen, L. R., D. W. Jorgenson, and L. J. Lau. 1971. Conjugate duality and the transcendental logarithmic function. *Econometrica* 39: 255–256.

Christensen, L. R., D. W. Jorgenson, and L. J. Lau. 1973. Transcendental logarithmic production frontiers. *Review of Economics and Statistics* 55: 28–45.

Corbo, V., and J. de Melo. 1983. Measuring technical efficiency: A comparison of alternative methodologies with census data. *Working Memorandum*. RPO 672–85. World Bank.

Denny, M., and M. Fuss. 1977. The use of approximation analysis to test for separability and the existence of consistent aggregates. *American Economic Review* 67: 404–418.

Farrell, M. J. 1957. The measurement of productive efficiency. *Journal of the Royal Statistical Society A* 120: 253–290.

Forsund, F. R., C. A. K. Lovell, and P. Schmidt. 1980. A survey of frontier production functions and of their relationship to efficiency measurement. *Journal of Econometrics* 13: 5–25.

Griliches, Z., and V. Ringstad. 1971. *Economies of Scale and the Form of the Production Function: An Econometric Study of Norwegian Manufacturing Establishment Data*. Amsterdam: North-Holland.

Huang, C. J., and F. S. Bagi. 1984. Technical efficiency on individual farms in northwest India. *Southern Economic Journal* 51: 108–116.

International Mathematical and Statistical Libraries Inc. 1980. *Reference Manual*, vol. 3. 8th ed. International Mathematical and Statistical Libraries Inc.

Jarque, C. M., and A. K. Bera. Efficient tests for normality, homoscedasticity and serial independence of regression residuals. *Economics Letters* 6: 255–259.

Johnston, J. 1984. *Econometric Methods*. 3d ed. New York: McGraw-Hill.

Kopp, R. J., and V. K. Smith. 1980. Frontier production function estimates for steam electric generation: A comparative analysis. *Southern Economic Journal* 47: 1049–1059.

Lee, L.-F. 1983. On maximum likelihood estimation of stochastic frontier production models. *Journal of Econometrics* 23: 269–274.

Lee, L.-F., and W. G. Tyler. 1978. The stochastic frontier production function and average efficiency, an empirical analysis. *Journal of Econometrics* 7: 385–389.

McAleer M. 1984. Specification tests for separate models. In M. L. King and D. E. A. Giles, eds., *Specification Analysis in the Linear Model*. London: Routledge and Kegan Paul.

Meeusen, W., and J. van den Broeck. 1977a Technical efficiency and dimension of the firm: Some results on the use of frontier production functions. *Empirical Economics* 2: 109–122.

Meeusen, W., and J. van den Broeck. 1977b. Efficiency estimation from Cobb-Douglas production functions with composed error. *International Economic Review* 18: 435–444.

Olson, J. A., P. Schmidt, and D. M. Waldman. 1980. A Monte Carlo study of estimators of stochastic frontier production functions. *Journal of Econometrics* 13: 67–82.

Pagan, A. R., and A. D. Hall. 1983. Diagnostic tests as residual analysis. *Econometric Reviews* 2: 159–218.

Page, J. M. 1980. Technical efficiency and economic performance: Some evidence from Ghana. *Oxford Economic Papers* (new series) 32: 319–339.

Ramsey, J. B. 1969. Tests for specification errors in classical linear least squares analysis. *Journal of the Royal Statistical Society B* 31: 350–371.

Sargan, J. D. 1984. Wages and prices in the United Kingdom: A study in econometric methodology. In D. F. Hendry and K. F. Wallis, eds., *Econometrics and Quantitative Econometrics* Oxford: Basil Blackwell.

Schmidt, P., and T.-F. Lin. 1984. Simple tests of alternative specifications in stochastic frontier models. *Journal of Econometrics* 24: 349–361.

Schmidt, P., and C. A. K. Lovell. 1979. Estimating technical and allocative inefficiency relative to stochastic production and cost frontiers. *Journal of Econometrics* 9: 343–366.

Schmidt, P., and R. C. Sickles. 1984. Production frontiers and panel data. *Journal of Business and Economic Statistics* 2: 367–374.

Stevenson, R. E. 1980. Likelihood functions for generalized stochastic frontier estimation. *Journal of Econometrics* 13: 57–66.

Van den Broeck, J., F. R. Forsund, L. Hjalmarsson, and W. Meeusen. 1980. On the estimation of deterministic and stochastic frontier production functions. *Journal of Econometrics* 13: 117–138.

Waldman, D. M. 1982. A stationary point for the stochastic frontier likelihood. *Journal of Econometrics* 18: 275–279.

White, H. 1980. A heteroskedasticity-consistent covariance matrix estimator and a direct test for heteroskedasticity. *Econometrica* 48: 817–838.

Zellner, A., J. Kmenta, and J. Dreze. 1966. Specification and estimation of Cobb-Douglas production functions. *Econometrica* 34: 784–795.

6 Determinants of Technical Efficiency in Australia

Richard E. Caves

6.1 Introduction

This chapter reports an investigation of the determinants of technical efficiency in Australian manufacturing industries in 1977; it is based on the efficiency measures calculated by Harris (1988; see also chapter 5). Australia represents a strategic case for a fundamental issue in the application of stochastic frontier production functions: Can a meaningful efficiency frontier be defined by establishments in this small, geographically isolated nation? True, Australia enjoys high levels of income per capita and productivity. However, its overall economic structure confines the manufacturing sector to import-competing status. The structures of Australian industries are further affected by a long-standing policy of heavy tariff protection as well as other important controls and restrictions. Australia depends heavily for productivity gains and improvements on innovations imported from abroad.

These structural traits make the explanation of technical efficiency in Australia an interesting task for two reasons. The first is the possibility of testing novel hypotheses about how the country's distinctive structure and policies affect technical efficiency. The second is the insight that the testing process should provide on whether to infer an efficient frontier for Australian producers who represent such a distinctive fragment of a given manufacturing industry worldwide.

Investigation of the latter issue is eased by building on a previous study (Caves 1984) of the determinants of average productivity in Australian manufacturing industries relative to their counterparts in the United States. Assume that measured productivity in the matched U.S. industries is an unbiased estimate of the "true" world efficiency frontier. Assume also that the efficiency attainable by each Australian industry can be predicted from its U.S. counterpart's productivity level, the quantities and qualities of inputs used by the Australian industry, and perhaps other factors. The inefficiency of each Australian industry would then be an omitted component when the relation is tested on actual outputs and inputs of Australian industries, a hypothesis that now becomes testable.

We first develop and test hypotheses about the determinants of technical efficiency in Australia's context; then we address the interrelation of these findings with the determinants of average efficiency.

6.2   Determinants of Technical Efficiency

Theory does not provide a compact model of the determinants of technical inefficiency, but a strategy for identifying them has been developed in other studies. That strategy locates theoretical determinants of inefficiency in (1) suboptimal organization and agency relationships within the firm, (2) suboptimal oligopoly bargains and related competitive factors within the industry, (3) interventions of public policy, and (4) structural factors (e.g., product differentiation) that create variance in the revenue-productivity levels of competing producers that do not (automatically) carry the stigma of inefficiency. The subsections that follow take up particular sources of inefficiency that fit within one or another category.

6.2.1   Producer Concentration and Competition

Hypotheses about the effect of noncompetitive markets on efficiency are complex at the outset, and grow more so in a setting such as Australia where domestic producers' concentration is affected by the national market's small size and the heavy protection long given to them. We take up the general problem first. Small numbers of competitors can permit or foster inefficiency through at least three mechanisms (Caves and Barton 1990, 65–72): (1) the likely absence of strong competition among sellers permits inefficient firms to survive, (2) imperfect competition generates its own forms of inefficiency when partial collusive bargains in oligopoly induce rent-seeking forms of nonprice competition, (3) the fewer the market's participants, the fewer independent experimenters seek better ways to carry out the industry's activities. All three mechanisms are consistent with efficiency decreasing monotonically with the concentration of producers, although the second mechanism raises the possibility that minimum efficiency occurs in moderately concentrated industries (because the oligopoly bargains in highly concentrated industries are fairly complete and rent-seeking outlays averted). The empirical results for both the United States and Japan are consistent with efficiency declining with concentration above a threshold, but they also find low levels of efficiency in unconcentrated industries.[1]

The structure of Australia's economy injects further complications because the manufacturing sector is heavily protected and serves a small, mainly domestic market. Quite apart from the effect on efficiency of competitive conditions *given* concentration, concentration itself depends on factors likely to affect technical efficiency. The delivered price of imports in such a market sets a limit price for domestic producers. Although that price can constrain them to pure competition on the fringe of a large (world) market, it can also supply a collusive focal point for domestic producers who are few in number and whose minimized costs lie below the limit price. Such focal-point pricing can in turn promote suboptimal-scale entry of domestic producers, reducing the industry's cost efficiency without increasing its price competitiveness.[2] Scale inefficiency, though, is not necessarily technical inefficiency because excessively numerous or suboptimal-scale entrants could be producing efficiently at their own too-small activity levels. Scale efficiency and technical efficiency may or may not interact.

Previous research provides some useful background. At times, such as during the 1950s, high-concentration levels have persisted in many industries unperturbed except by horizontal mergers (Brown and Hughes 1970; Karmel and Brunt 1962, 60–62).[3] Competition policy has been essentially passive. No barriers have been imposed on mergers to restrict competition (Bushnell 1961; Sheridan 1974), and at least until 1974 there were no effective restraints on collusive price fixing and other such restrictive agreements (Nieuwenhuysen and Norman 1976). The specific consequences for pricing have not been researched, but the adjustment of prices following disturbances was found to be retarded in concentrated industries (Dixon 1983).

This conjunction of circumstances makes it unclear a priori whether concentrated industries have earned excess profits. If not, one possible explanation is that potential monopoly rents have been dispersed in technical inefficiency. More than in any other industrial country, studies of the profits–concentration relation fail to show any robustly significant relation (e.g., Round 1976, 1979; Leech and Grant 1978). Plenty of room remains for explanations based on inefficiency, including both inefficient scale (small-scale entry under price umbrellas) and technical inefficiency. Caves (1984) found support for the scale-inefficiency hypothesis: The lower the overall productivity of an Australian industry, the lower is its concentration relative to a benchmark defined by minimum efficient scale in the U.S. counterpart industry (where market-size constraints on efficient plant scales should be minimal).

Accepting this conclusion about overall productivity does not automatically yield a hypothesis about concentration and technical efficiency. This mechanism could simply depress the effective efficient frontier in the Australian industry without affecting the distribution of actual efficiency levels. That possibility is better checked empirically than addressed on a priori grounds. We make use of the simple producer–concentration ratio,

C4 = share of turnover accounted for by the industry's four largest enterprises, 1973[4],

and an adjusted form that was used in Caves (1984),

C4AJ = residuals from a regression of C4 on CDRU, EFF, and MESU,

where CDRU is an inverse measure of the productivity disadvantage of small-scale production units in the U.S. counterpart industry,[5] EFF is the effective rate of tariff protection of the Australian market, and MESU is shipments by the plant in the U.S. industry accounting for the median unit of output (when plants are ranked from largest to smallest) divided by industry output, 1977. The C4AJ measure spotlights markets in which concentration is low relative to the level warranted by production scale economies observed in the United States, with the market-enlarging effects of protection controlled. The reason for including Australia's effective rate of protection is discussed below. Technical efficiency should increase with C4AJ.[6] The hypothesis turns on the direct implications of concentration for efficient scales and puts aside any effect on efficiency of oligopolistic rivalry among of domestic producers.

6.2.2 International Competition

If competition from domestic rivals can affect technical efficiency, so should potential competition from foreign rivals. The well-known efficiency of free trade and inefficiency of tariff protection are of course general-equilibrium effects with no necessary connection to technical efficiency, which is a partial-equilibrium concept. However, the literature on developing economies contains abundant empirical evidence of the technical inefficiency of protected production. Tariff protection itself has no statistical effect on efficiency in the United States, but import competition does prove a spur to technical efficiency among the more concentrated domestic industries. Furthermore changes in imports' penetration of the domestic market are positively associated with the domestic industry's rate of productivity growth, after controlling for technological opportunities.[7]

In Australia protection might be expected to wield more influence on efficiency relative to observed import levels. Made-to-measure protection is an established tradition. Also the high variance of Australian tariff rates causes them to be negatively correlated with imports-shipments ratios, whereas tariffs and import penetration commonly are positively correlated for other countries (Industries Assistance Commission 1980, app. 2.3).

Statistical measures can represent either the trade that survives or the tariffs that restrict it. We can assume that trade restrictions matter only for the trade that they exclude, so their influence is controlled by

IMP = imports (net of re-exports) divided by value of industry shipments.[8]

Alternatively, the effect can be represented by the height of protection supplied to the domestic industry. For a geographically remote land like Australia substantial protection comes from natural transportation costs as well as artificial trade barriers, so we employ two measures:

EFF = effective rate of tariff protection, 1977,

TRAN = ratio of c.i.f. (cost, insurance, freight) delivered value of imports to their f.o.b. value, 1974.

In terms of the wedges that they drive between the world price and the delivered price of imports within Australia, TRAN − 1 and EFF should be directly comparable. Their behavioral effects could differ, however, if the policy mechanism that picks EFF should respond to the actual level of efficiency (as when made-to-measure protection guarantees that domestic producers can cover their costs).

Giving heavy protection to manufacturing industries is a long-standing tradition in Australia. In 1977, the year of our analysis, the average effective rate in manufacturing was 26 percent. It had in fact fallen from 36 percent in 1968 due to an across-the-board cut of one-fourth in 1973. That reduction, however, was promptly eroded by reversals and exceptions for many industries, so the standard deviation of industries' rates of protection was in fact rising. It had been 30 percent in 1968, fell to 23 percent in 1973, and then rose to 34 percent by 1977 (Industries Assistance Commission 1980). Structural comparisons with other economies confirm that participation in international trade has been correspondingly low and grew less during 1962–73 than in other industrial nations (Industries

Assistance Commission 1976b; Robertson 1978). Because of Australia's strong comparative advantage in resource-based exports, manufacturing industries' exports have been low except in resource-processing sectors. Intraindustry trade is two-thirds that of Canada and much lower than in most industrial countries (Industries Assistance Commission 1977a). The short-run insulation of the manufacturing industries has been considerable. Gregory (1978) found that the effect of import prices on domestic prices is quite weak, although Dixon (1983) concluded that the adjustment of prices to domestic labor and materials costs is faster in industries more exposed to import competition.

Because we test the influence of protection on efficiency in cross section with various market-structure elements controlled, it is important to consider whether industries' levels of protection are themselves systematically related to market structures. Research on this topic has been abundant (Conybeare 1978; Anderson 1980; Gregory and Pincus 1982; Aislabie 1988), as has policy-making activity. Protection has favored labor-intensive, low-skill industries, which accordingly are unconcentrated. It seems to have benefited mainly slow-growing sectors, and there is a long tradition of made-to-measure protection despite the effort through the Industries Assistance Commission starting in the 1970s to reduce the variance and stabilize the levels of rates of protection.[9] The Commission itself (1975, 38–40) espoused the view that import competition increases technical efficiency and made-to-measure protection impairs it.

Because of its structure-related and expedient character, tariff protection might have a stronger effect on industrial efficiency than the truly exogenous natural protection supplied by Australia's remoteness. Conlon (1979) reported that manufacturing industries' median nominal rate of protection based on international transport costs was 14.4 percent, compared to a nominal tariff of 22.9 percent. Because transport-cost protection (contrary to tariffs) tends to decline with the degree of fabrication of goods, the median effective rate of transport-cost protection (10.3) is a good deal less than the median effective tariff (32.0).[10]

6.2.3 Regional Dispersion

The Australian economy is not only small overall but also fragmented geographically. Most of the population and nonprimary production activity is located in roughly a half-dozen metropolitan areas dotted around the continent's perimeter (Vipond 1978). Internal transportation costs have long been high (Webb 1978), so home-market products that face high transportation costs are subject to further fragmentation. A variety of state-level policies toward transportation and the promotion of development have encouraged inefficient spatial location patterns (Industries Assistance Commission 1976a). Although small-scale production units are not necessarily inefficient given their scales of operation, the combination of local market power and fragmented scales seems likely to produce inefficiency. Round (1981) found that concentrated industries' profits are pulled down by the extent of their multiplant operations, consistent with rent-seeking dispersion of plants. Earlier, Bushnell (1961) had taken note of what appeared to be strategic geographic-expansion mergers, and Karmel and Brunt (1962, 100) observed the use of geographic market division as a form of collusion. Thus any inefficiency associated with geographic dispersion is likely to reflect strategic behavior and public policy as well as natural conditions. The variable used is

REGH = Herfindahl index of concentration of the industry's
       employment among states, 1979.

The greater the REGH, the more concentrated is the industry geographically, and the more efficient is it expected to be.

6.2.4 Scales of Operation

Concentration affects efficiency through the manner and extent of competition among producers. However, it is also related to the scales of operation of domestic producers, which can in turn be related to technical efficiency if we assume that a managerial cost must be incurred to sustain (or restore) efficiency and that this cost is not proportional to the plant's output. Torii (chapter 2, subsection 2.3.1) shows that the half-normal distribution of technical inefficiency can in fact be derived from a mechanism by which plants tend to drift exogenously into inefficiency but can be reformed by an outlay of managerial effort. Efficiency would increase (decrease) with concentration if scale economies (diseconomies) exist in the managerial pursuit of efficiency. Plant size can also affect efficiency through its effect on incentives to replace old plants in an industry where embodied technological change is occurring. Torii finds a negative relation between an industry's efficiency and two measures of its capital stock or fixed cost per plant. The absence of plant-level capital-stock data in Australia causes us to formulate the variable as follows:

PLSZ = average size (value added) of the largest plants accounting for
   50 percent of industry shipments, 1977.

Torii finds a negative effect consistent with the replacement-cost model or
with diseconomies of scale in management. No sign is predicted a priori.

   Torii's replacement-cost model has a clear affinity for the institutional
evidence on Australia. The possible link between excessive regional dispersion and small production scales was just noted. The Bureau of Industry
Economics (1981) voiced concern that efficient small firms find it difficult
to finance their expansion externally. It is not clear that this self-finance
constraint on small firms is tighter in Australia than elsewhere, but the
scales of business organizations do seem small compared to other countries, even with differences in economic geography controlled (Johns,
Dunlop, and Sheehan 1978). Finally, it was noted above that the combination of effective price collusion and small market size can promote
suboptimal-scale entry.

   Suboptimal-scale units need not be technically inefficient at their chosen
scales. Scale efficiency and technical efficiency become related, however, if
the diversity of plant sizes found in an industry is due to some set of
constraints (not otherwise controlled) on managers' abilities to achieve
what they regard as long-run efficient scales. The technical inefficiency then
devolves from units operating in what may for them be constrained short-
run but not long-run optimal configurations. The following variable measures the heterogeneity of plant sizes:

GINI = Gini coefficient measure of inequality of plant sizes, 1980.

Efficiency should decrease with inequality and thus with GINI.

6.2.5   Organization of Industry

Several aspects of the industry's organization can affect its efficiency. One
of potential importance in Australia is the prevalence of foreign-controlled
establishments. Companies generally operate multinationally to capture
rents to some proprietary asset or skill that has come into the possession
of the parent firm, and for successful multinationals these rents turn up
(transfer prices permitting) as high productivity in their foreign-subsidiary
establishments. If the foreign-subsidiary members of an industry define the
efficient frontier due to rent components in their revenues unavailable to
their domestic competitors, the industry's apparent efficiency level will be
reduced.[11] The prediction is not clear-cut, however. A small number of

profitable subsidiaries in an industry dominated by domestic firms could give rise to positive skewness in the production-function residuals and a type I failure in the estimation of technical efficiency, inviting the interpretation that the industry actually harbors little or no inefficiency (Harris 1988, 124–129). In any case the profitability of foreign subsidiaries has been found to exceed that of domestic enterprises (Sheridan 1975), and Brash (1960) documented examples of rent-yielding advantages that may or may not be open to emulation or capture by domestic firms. During the decade preceding the year of our analysis, however, a falloff of foreign subsidiaries' rents was noted and attributed to increasing numbers of multinational competitors (Johns 1967; Roach Ward Guest & Co. 1976).

The influence of foreign investors' presence is measured simply by

FSE = share of industry shipments accounted for by companies deemed to be under foreign control, 1973.

Its influence should be positive if efficient foreign subsidiaries tend to define the industry's efficiency frontier, but that condition need not be satisfied even if the hypothesis of foreign efficiency advantages is correct.[12]

Other aspects of business organization that could affect efficiency notably include diversification. Efficient diversification can achieve full utilization of lumpy, multiple-use assets attached contractually to the firm, an arrangement congenial to economic efficiency. In the United States, however, considerable evidence supports the proposition that corporate diversification was overextended in the 1960s and 1970s, leading in the 1980s to an extensive retrenchment of firms' activities around their primary businesses. Caves and Barton (1990) found that in the United States in 1977 technical efficiency decreased with enterprise diversification, especially the extent to which plants in an industry are controlled by enterprises based in other industries.

The measures of diversification available for Australian manufacturing industries parallel those used in the U.S. study

COV = employment in establishments classified to this industry that are controlled by enterprises classified to this industry, divided by employment in all establishments classified to this industry, 1977

SPEC = employment in establishments classified to this industry and controlled by enterprises classified to this industry, divided by employment in all establishments controlled by enterprises classified to this industry, 1977.

If Australian enterprises followed the U.S. lead in overextending corporate diversification, efficiency should increase with both variables and with their sum (DIV = COV + SPEC).

The evidence on business organization in Australia does not point toward a result parallel to the U.S. finding. The largest enterprises are smaller than their counterparts in the United States and probably did not push diversification so far. The dispersion of shareholding has not proceeded so far and thus may have provoked less slippage in the principal-agent relation between owners and managers (Lawriwsky 1978). The market for corporate control seems to select takeover targets properly (Lawriwsky 1984). On the other hand, the trend toward the diffusion of corporate control parallels those in other countries, and incentive compensation seems to play a smaller role for Australian executives (Lawriwsky, 1982).

Heterogeneous organization of business can give rise to apparent technical inefficiency in a way related to the prevalence of nonproduction workers in an industry's labor force. A firm's nonproduction activities can be located either under the same roof with production activities or in separate establishments. They also may be spun off contractually to other enterprises. Because nonproduction workers' compensation differs from (often exceeds) that of production workers, their uneven distribution among an industry's establishments increases the variance of plant efficiencies. Caves and Barton (1990) were able to utilize an appropriate measure of heterogeneous organization—the variance among plants of the ratio of nonproduction to total employees—and found it to exert a negative effect on efficiency. Of course the variance of nonproduction activities cannot have this effect except where nonproduction activities are important on average. Torii (subsection 2.3.3) finds a positive effect on efficiency of the Japanese industry's average production-worker intensity. We test the hypothesis in the form

NPW = ratio of nonproduction employees to total employees, 1978.

6.2.6 Incidence of Disturbances

Technical efficiency as measured is likely to pick up various dynamic disturbances that increase the dispersion of units' apparent levels of efficiency even though they lack normative implications. The inflated dispersion may or may not also enlarge the one-sided residuals that signal technical inefficiency. Caves and Barton (1990) found that an industry's research and development activity increases the one-sided residuals and inflates apparent inefficiency. They could isolate the effect in the different amounts of innovative rents accruing to establishments depending on the extent and success of their innovative activities. They found no influence of the industry's rate of productivity growth as such. With Australia serving mainly as an importer rather than a producer of new technology (Johns 1978) and apparently performing the absorption function efficiently, domestic R&D levels seem unlikely to have the same effect as in the United States.[13] The possible effect of the rate of output growth can be tested using

GROW = ratio of industry turnover in real terms, 1979, to its value in 1969.

A difficulty with GROW is that efficiency may suffer temporarily from rapid change of any type, whether it is growth or shrinkage. We can of course transform GROW to test that hypothesis. However, a more focused approach also seems desirable. That is especially so because of the squeeze that the manufacturing sector experienced as a result of the expansion of exports from the minerals sector starting in the mid-1960s,[14] so that manufacturing's share of GDP at factor cost shrank from 27 percent in 1962–63 to 23 percent in 1973–74 (Industries Assistance Commission 1977b, table 1.1). This occurred in a period when Australia's population was growing rapidly and GDP per capita slowly compared to other countries, and the 1973 energy shock was followed by an increase of unemployment larger than elsewhere (Gruen 1986).

Contraction seems most likely to affect efficiency when it forces a reduction in the industry's employment, as producers (and unions) seek to ward off at least temporarily the doleful consequences of losing valued workers (Mangan and Regan 1983). We form

EMP = ratio of industry employment in 1979 to industry employment in 1969 when that ratio < 1, one otherwise.

Several other variables were used in an effort to expose the effect of economywide adjustments on industries' levels of efficiency in 1977. We explain the strategy of investigation below rather than define the various measures in advance.

Certain hypotheses are omitted from the model because data are not adequate to test them. An important omission is the divisive state of labor relations in Australia. The sources of technical inefficiency in restrictive work rules and the incidence of strikes are clear enough. However, no data were published at the industry level that serve adequately to represent interindustry differences.[15] Another variable that proved a significant determinant of technical efficiency in the United States was the dispersion of capital vintages for each industry. Dixon (1985) provided evidence that the aggregate age of equipment (though not structures) had been rising for some time up to 1977.

Table 6.1 provides details on the sources of the exogenous variables that have been defined and summarizes the predictions about their signs.

6.3   Determinants of Technical Efficiency: Results

6.3.1   Dependent Variables and Their Properties

Harris (1988) reported four measures of technical efficiency that could be used as dependent variables in this analysis: average technical inefficiency estimated on the assumption that inefficiency follows the half-normal distribution (ATIN), average technical inefficiency based on a truncated-normal distribution of inefficiency (ATIT), average technical efficiency (ATE); and skewness (SKEW).[16] These differ in their correlations with one another as well as in the number of industries for which estimates could be computed.

First, we consider the numbers of observations. ATIT, ATIN, and ATE are available for 93 industries—a seemingly ample number that in fact erodes seriously in regressions on exogenous variables with missing observations[17]. Skewness, however, is available for 146 industries, being defined whether the residuals from the stochastic frontier production function are positively or negatively skewed, whereas (roughly speaking) the standard technical-inefficiency measures depend on negative skewness. Whether the probability that an industry exhibits no technical inefficiency increases with SKEW over its positive range is an empirical question (the U.S. findings were reasonably supportive). This consideration plus its advantage in number of observations keeps SKEW in the analysis.

Table 6.1
Expected determinants of technical efficiency: summary of hypotheses and data sources

Variable	Expected sign	Source
C4	−	*Enterprise Statistics, 1977–78*, public user tape
C4AJ	−	Residuals from regression of C4 on CDRU, EFF, and MESU, where MESU calculated from U.S. Bureau of the Census, *1977 Census of Manufactures*, vol. 1; see entries for C4 and EFF
COV	+	Australian Bureau of Statistics, *Enterprise Statistics: Details by Industry Class, Australia, 1972–73*, catalog no. 8103.0
EMP	+	See GROW for 1969 data; Australian Bureau of Statistics, *Manufacturing Establishments: Details of Operation by Industry Class, Australia, 1979–80*, catalog no. 8203.0
EFF	−	Industries Assistance Commission, public user tape
FSE	?	Australian Bureau of Statistics, *Foreign Ownership and Control in Manufacturing Industry, 1972–73*, catalog no. 5315.0
GROW	−	Commonwealth Bureau of Census and Statistics, *Manufacturing Establishments: Details of Operations by Industry Class, Australia, 1968–69*, reference no. 12.29; Australian Bureau of Statistics, *Manufacturing Establishments: Details of Operation by Industry Class, Australia, 1977–78*, catalog no. 8203.0; Australian Bureau of Statistics, *Key between the 1978 and 1969 Editions of ASIC*, catalog no. 1209.0
IMP	+	For imports, Industries Assistance Commission; for value of shipments, Australian Bureau of Statistics, *Manufacturing Establishments: Details of Operations by Industry Class, Australia, 1977–78*, catalog no. 8203.0
NPW	−	Australian Bureau of Statistics, *Manufacturing Establishments: Details of Operation by Industry Class, 1977–78*, catalog no. 8203.0
PLSZ	?	Calculated from Australian Bureau of Statistics, *Manufacturing Establishments: Details of Operation by Industry Class, 1977–78*, catalog no. 8203.0
REGH	+	Australian Bureau of Statistics, *Census of Manufacturing Establishments: Details of Operations by Industry Class, 1979–80*, catalog nos. 8201.1–8201.6
SPEC	+	See COV
TRAN	−	Industries Assistance Commission, public user tape

Examination of the correlations among these measures shows that ATE and ATIT are so highly correlated (-0.993) that nothing is gained by analyzing both. The other correlations are lower: SKEW and ATIN, -0.642; SKEW and ATIT, -0.218; ATIN and ATIT, 0.151. The last is not statistically significant. If divergent messages are received about the empirical determinants of efficiency, we expect ATIT to be the outlier. In the event SKEW and ATIN yield quite similar results while ATIT could not (with one conspicuous exception) be explained at all. Therefore the following report focuses on SKEW and ATIN.

6.3.2 Regression Results

Because of the limited degrees of freedom and weak theoretical foundations for the analysis, we sought to build a core empirical model consisting of the most likely regressors and then to explore more speculative hypotheses (and those poorly embodied in the available exogenous variables). The attempt to establish a core model was, we feel, fairly successful and not open to the charge of data mining. Among the fringe hypotheses, however, enough sifting occurred to deter giving much credence to coefficients of marginal statistical significance.

The preceding section of this chapter and previous empirical results for Japan and United States led us to expect that the core influences would be seller concentration (C4), absolute plant scales (PLSZ), regional fragmentation (REGH), and protection from external competition (EFF, TRAN). The results of testing those hypotheses are summarized in table 6.2. Concentration does not have a significant influence when entered as a linear variable, but as in previous studies proves significant in a quadratic form C4 and C4SQ) for SKEW (equation 2.1). Furthermore the level of concentration at which efficiency is at a maximum corresponds closely to the levels found for other countries, a 47 percent combined share for the leading four firms in equation 2.1. The significance of the quadratic relation holds up when other variables are added if one-tail tests are thought appropriate (see equation 2.3 and the tables that follow), and the position of the efficiency-maximizing concentration ratio is quite stable. With ATIN as the dependent variable the same relation appears, with inefficiency minimized in the neighborhood of C4 = 50 percent, but the coefficients are not significant at much more than 10 percent. Thus we are prone to accept the conclusion that efficiency declines as concentration increases beyond the level at which where oligopolistic interdependence starts

Table 6.2
Determinants of technical efficiency: core model and effects of protection

Equation	Regression model	$\bar{R}^2/DF$
2.1	SKEW $= -1.055 + 2.300$C4 $- 2.430$C4SQ $+ 0.046$PLSZ (4.32) (2.38) (2.39) (2.10) $+ 1.130$REGH (2.63)	0.226 56
2.2	ATIN $= 0.562 - 0.471$C4 $+ 0.452$C4SQ $+ 0.010$PLSZ (4.91) (1.34) (1.28) (0.50) $- 0.610$REGH (2.02)	0.057 31
2.3	SKEW $= -0.911 + 1.735$C4 $- 1.963$C4SQ $+ 0.049$PLSZ (3.44) (1.66) (1.80) (2.09) $+ 1.325$REGH $- 0.150$PROT (2.52) (1.51)	0.211 47
2.4	ATIN $= 0.607 - 0.346$C4 $+ 0.364$C4SQ $+ 0.003$PLSZ (5.31) (0.95) (1.06) (0.10) $- 0.931$REGH $+ 0.070$PROT (2.82) (2.00)	0.146 26

strongly to influence producers' behavior; it also appears to decline in highly fragmented (competitive) industries. Given the endogeneity of concentration, we consider below whether forces other than oligopoly behavior are likely to account for the result.

With concentration controlled, efficiency (SKEW) increases with the absolute size of the industry's typical plant (PLSZ), consistent with the assumption that maintaining or restoring plant-level efficiency entails scale economies or a fixed cost. This relation proves quite robust for SKEW but does not hold at all for ATIN (or ATIT). According to the model for SKEW the effect is not very large.[18] The effect of the regional dispersion of activity (measured inversely by REGH) is significantly to diminish efficiency according to both SKEW and ATIN. The effect is substantial: According to equation 2.2, an industry concentrated in one state would exhibit 1.69 standard deviations less inefficiency (ATIN) than one dispersed equally among the states.

Protection from international competition arises from both effective tariffs (EFF) and transport costs (TRAN). We found that their effect on efficiency is negative and best predicted by the sum of the two (PROT)— see equations 2.3 and 2.4. Because EFF and TRAN both exhibit strong collinearity with other regressors, their coefficients and significance levels

Table 6.3
Determinants of technical efficiency: scale-efficiency factors

Equation	Regression model	$\bar{R}^2/DF$
3.1	$SKEW = 0.921 + 1.727C4 - 1.952C4SQ + 0.049PLSZ$ $(3.43)\quad(1.63)\quad\quad(1.78)\quad\quad\quad(2.06)$ $+ 1.339REGH - 0.145PROT + 1.006SCL$ $(2.52)\quad\quad\quad\quad(1.44)\quad\quad\quad(0.35)$	0.196 46
3.2	$ATIN = 0.615 - 0.289C4 + 0.327C4SQ - 0.005PLSZ$ $(5.40)\quad(0.79)\quad\quad(0.95)\quad\quad\quad(0.17)$ $- 0.955REGH + 0.070PROT - 1.242SCL$ $(2.90)\quad\quad\quad\quad(1.99)\quad\quad\quad(1.12)$	0.154 25
3.3	$SKEW = -0.925 + 1.761C4 - 1.963C4SQ + 0.049PLSZ$ $(1.94)\quad(1.35)\quad\quad(1.78)\quad\quad\quad(2.04)$ $+ 1.323REGH - 0.148PROT - 0.027C4AJ$ $(2.50)\quad\quad\quad\quad(1.31)\quad\quad\quad(0.03)$	0.194 46
3.4	$ATIT = -0.434 + 1.165C4 + 0.583C4SQ + 0.004PLSZ$ $(1.69)\quad(1.67)\quad\quad(1.10)\quad\quad\quad(0.08)$ $- 0.088REGH + 0.110PROT - 1.495C4AJ$ $(0.17)\quad\quad\quad\quad(1.55)\quad\quad\quad(4.19)$	0.402 25

vary a good deal with the model's specification. If one-tail tests are deemed appropriate (as we believe), PROT's coefficient is usually significant at 5 percent with ATIN and at 10 percent with SKEW. Actual import competition has no significant effect (IMP, not shown).

Table 6.3 takes up the question whether the scale-inefficiency problem previously found to affect Australian industries interacts with their levels of technical efficiency. Table 6.2's results already imply that technical inefficiency increases once the number of competitors grows large enough, but that need not result from diseconomies of small scale. We tried deleting C4 and C4SQ from the model and replacing them with variable C4AJ, which seeks to identify divergences between actual concentration and the level that would maximize scale efficiency. It is insignificant in models thus specified, suggesting that the effect of C4 and C4SQ is behavioral and does just proxy technical efficiency associated with scale factors. We therefore proceeded by adding to equations 2.3 and 2.4 several complex variables devised to capture the idea that scale inefficiency occurs where (1) inefficiently small operating scales are viable due to high protection, and (2) technical scale economies are substantial but not so severe that they preclude suboptimal-scale units. SCL, defined for this purpose in Caves (1984), obtains the right signs in equations 3.1 and 3.2 but is not significant.

Table 6.4
Determinants of technical efficiency: business organization

Equation	Regression model	$\bar{R}^2/DF$
4.1	SKEW = $-0.987 + 2.564$C4 $- 2.879$C4SQ $+ 0.004$PLSZ (3.36) (1.92) (2.20) (1.43) $+ 0.955$REGH $- 0.117$PROT $+ 0.001$FSE (1.38) (0.80) (0.42)	0.230 34
4.2	ATIN = $0.651 - 0.345$C4 $+ 0.331$C4SQ $+ 0.004$PLSZ (5.52) (0.71) (0.80) (1.06) $- 1.194$REGH $+ 0.104$PROT $- 0.001$FSE (3.29) (2.59) (1.00)	0.299 18
4.3	SKEW = $-0.988 + 1.831$C4 $- 2.369$C4SQ $+ 0.047$PLSZ (3.39) (1.73) (2.12) (2.02) $+ 1.222$REGH $- 0.126$PROT $- 0.045$COV (2.33) (1.23) (0.04) $+ 0.999$SPEC (1.66)	0.227 45
4.4	ATIN = $0.620 - 0.239$C4 $+ 0.257$C4SQ $+ 0.001$PLSZ (4.58) (0.60) (0.64) (0.03) $- 0.881$REGH $+ 0.063$PROT $- 0.341$COV (2.42) (1.70) (0.91) $+ 0.009$SPEC (0.04)	0.106 24

C4AJ is also insignificant when SKEW or ATIN is the dependent variable (see equation 3.3). The result is quite different for ATIT, however, as shown in equation 3.4. Although ATIT is not significantly related to any Australia-based variable used in the regression analysis, it has a highly significant negative relation to the extent of plant-scale economies inferred from U.S. data, and therefore to any complex scale-economies variable that includes U.S. minimum efficient scale as a component. One is unsure what conclusion to draw. With the quadratic relation to C4 controlled, no other statistical link appears between scale inefficiency and technical inefficiency. On the other hand, a t-statistic of 4.19 is hard to ignore.

Table 6.4 takes up hypotheses about technical efficiency and business organization. In equations 4.1 and 4.2 the prevalence of foreign subsidiaries in Australian markets (FSE) proves statistically insignificant. Equations 4.3 and 4.4 seek to replicate the U.S.-based finding that efficiency decreases with the extent of enterprise diversification. Greater specialization has a weakly significant positive influence on efficiency (SKEW) and coverage a much weaker negative influence on inefficiency (ATIN), but

Table 6.5
Determinants of technical efficiency: dynamic disturbances

Equation	Regression model	$\bar{R}^2/DF$
5.1	SKEW = $-0.831 + 1.715$C4 $- 2.039$C4SQ $+ 0.048$PLSZ (3.06) (1.64) (1.88) (2.06) $+ 1.269$REGH $- 0.093$PROT $- 0.197$EMP (2.42) (0.85) (1.18)	0.217 46
5.2	ATIN = $0.609 - 0.350$C4 $+ 0.371$C4SQ $+ 0.003$PLSZ (5.10) (0.93) (1.02) (0.09) $- 0.939$REGH $+ 0.070$PROT $+ 0.004$EMP (2.63) (1.91) (0.07)	0.112 25
5.3	SKEW = $-0.763 + 1.983$C4 $- 2.250$C4SQ $+ 0.046$PLSZ (2.75) (1.90) (2.07) (1.99) $+ 1.292$REGH $- 0.179$PROT $- 0.113$DPLSZ (2.50) (1.80) (1.57)	0.234 46
5.4	SKEW = $-0.735 + 1.847$C4 $- 2.033$C4SQ $+ 0.049$PLSZ (2.58) (1.69) (1.73) (2.06) $+ 1.320$REGH $- 0.174$PROT $- 0.035$DPLUP (2.44) (1.60) (0.09) $- 0.127$DPLDN $- 0.304$DP (1.68) (0.68)	0.221 44
5.5	ATIN = $0.617 - 0.551$C4 $+ 0.596$C4SQ $+ 0.001$PLSZ (5.63) (1.51) (1.69) (0.01) $- 0.110$REGH $+ 0.096$PROT $+ 0.044$DPLSZ (3.35) (2.63) (1.82)	0.216 25
5.6	ATIN = $0.582 - 0.552$C4 $+ 0.632$C4SQ $- 0.002$PLSZ (5.62) (1.63) (1.84) (0.08) $- 0.840$REGH $+ 0.048$PROT $+ 0.252$DPLUP (2.66) (1.30) (2.58) $+ 0.027$DPLDN $- 0.123$DP (1.16) (1.00)	0.365 23

the null hypothesis must be accepted for enterprise diversification. The importance of nonproduction workers to an industry has no significant effect (not shown).

Because of the general-equilibrium squeeze on Australia's manufacturing sector in the 1970s, we experimented extensively with measures of the extent and character of adjustments that had affected each industry prior to 1977 (see table 6.5). The industry's real rate of growth (GROW, not shown) exerts no significant effect. The extent to which employment has contracted (EMP) has a weak negative effect on SKEW but none on ATIN (equations 5.1 and 5.2). In the spirit of EMP, we formed several other measures of the change that had occurred in the previous decade in plant scale or productivity. Equations 5.3 through 5.6 report the most revealing of these. DPLSZ is the change in average plant size between 1968 and 1977, measured by the ratio of employees per plant in 1977 to employees per plant in 1968. In equations 5.3 and 5.5 reductions in employment per plant seem to increase efficiency (reduce inefficiency) but at marginal levels of statistical significance. Was this association due to the squeeze-out of employment in industries under pressure to contract? In 5.4 and 5.6 we let DPLSZ take a different coefficient in industries whose total number of plants increased (DPLUP) and decreased (DPLDN) (DP represents an intercept shift). With SKEW (equation 5.4) we apparently do see efficiency gains associated with a squeeze-out. With ATIN, however, inefficiency reductions seem to come from employment reductions in growing industries. There are hints of the importance of dynamic effects, but we cannot claim to have captured them in any robust way.

With ATIT largely immune to explanation (see equation 3.4 and discussion), we formed the variable ATIT − ATIN, the difference between inefficiency inferred from the truncated and half-normal distributions, and searched for structural factors that might explain it. The variance of this difference is due much more to ATIT (correlation is 0.858) than to ATIN (−0.379). The difference is in fact significantly (positively) correlated with several dimensions of market structure in Australia. They include C4 (0.277, significant at 5.1 percent), FSE (0.244, significant at 4.9 percent) and PLSZ (0.248 significant at 4.8 percent). The extra inefficiency exposed by the truncation procedure thus seems to increase with producer concentration and other variables that are closely associated with it. This finding makes ATIT's strong association with scale-economies measures derived from United States data (equation 3.4) seem much less of a freak occurrence.

Finally, we notice that the explanatory power of models with SKEW as the dependent variable almost always beats that of comparably specified models with ATIN. This pattern merits some thought because ATIN (and ATE) have superior theoretical standing as measures of technical efficiency. Two tests were performed. First, does SKEW's explanatory performance depend just on the greater number of degrees of freedom that it affords, or is it (statistically) a superior measure of efficiency? We found that when we constrain any given model so that SKEW has available the same set of observations as ATIN, their levels of explanatory power are about the same. Second, we wondered whether positive and negative values of SKEW are equally well explained. If positive values contain less (or no) information about degrees of inefficiency, they should have larger squared residuals. The mean squared residual for positive observations on SKEW (equation 2.3) is indeed 48 percent larger, but the difference is not statistically significant. If the single largest outlier (a negative value) is removed, the difference increases to 108 percent and is significant. Thus, SKEW does not appear to be a superior measure, but it roughly matches the technical-efficiency measure on a common sample of industries and does provide a substantial advantage in the access to additional degrees of freedom. Positive values of SKEW seem to provide some information about efficiency, but the signal is noisier than for negative values.

6.4 Technical Efficiency and Average Efficiency

6.4.1 Framework for Analysis and Dependent Variable

If technical efficiency is measured with some accuracy, it should bear a predictable relation to realized average efficiency or productivity. Suppose that we possessed an ideal measure V_{Ai} of total factor productivity for each Australian manufacturing industry, and also a measure V_{Fi} of total factor productivity attainable at a maximally efficient world frontier. V_{Ai} can fall short of V_{Fi} for two reasons: because the efficient frontier that can be reached in Australia (V_{Ai}^*) lies beneath the world frontier and because average productivity in Australia lies below the attainable frontier due to technical efficiency. That is, $V_{Fi} - V_{Ai}^*$ should depend on factors constricting the frontier realizable in Australia, such as lags in the absorption of foreign technology, systemic limits on managerial and organizational capacities, "climatic" factors that limit the local productivity of particular industries (Ricardian comparative advantage), policies that systematically impair efficiency, and the like. The other component, $V_{Ai}^* - V_{Ai}$, is of course related to the technical efficiency already analyzed. Indeed, if average technical inefficiency were calculated from size-weighted establishment data, it would be exactly this difference.

These considerations point to strategies for extending the analysis of technical efficiency. One could test hypotheses about $V_{Fi} - V_{Ai}^*$ by using ATIT or ATIN to adjust V_{Ai} upward to approximate V_{Ai}^* and then proceed with the test using that proxy for the Australian frontier. One could put the technical-efficiency measures aside and analyze $V_{Fi} - V_{Ai}$ as a function of the determinants of both differences between the Australian and world frontiers and technical inefficiency in Australia.

We proceed to approximate the first of these strategies, but the project is restricted by at least two major constraints. First, V_{Fi} is of course unknown and must be proxied. The assumption can be made that productivity in industries in some actual country, such as the United States, lies closer to the unobserved frontier than for any other observable production experience. On this assumption previous studies developed a method for analyzing in cross section factor productivity in industries matched between the United States and a foreign country's standard industrial classifications (see Caves, Porter, and Spence 1980, 257–274; Davies and Caves 1987, ch. 2). The method has a number of tactical limitations, but cogent findings in its application to Australian manufacturing industries (Caves 1984) support its reuse here.

The second constraint grows from these tactical limitations interacting with limitations of the method of frontier production functions, and it centers on scarce degrees of freedom. Standard industrial classifications can seldom be completely matched between countries. Not only are many industries usually lost, but the losses tend to be nonrandom in that each major division either mostly matches and is included, or mostly fails to match and is lost. The method of frontier production functions fails to yield an efficiency measure for any industry that incurs a type I or type II failure. These losses (plus sundry others, e.g., industries with too few plants to analyze) bring the proportion of industries with usable estimates of technical efficiency down toward half of the total. Should losses from failure to match industries also approach one-half, and the two sources of loss are uncorrelated, the usable sample sinks to a nonrandom one-quarter of the total industries.

These constraints force the researcher to retreat from idealized designs to a simple approach that respects the limitations of the data. We proceed in that spirit, focusing on the analysis of relative productivity in matched industries. We start with the problems of measuring physical between labor productivity and total-factor productivity. As the preceding analysis of technical efficiency shows, the two simple ways to model the value productivity of factors employed in a national industry producing internationally traded goods are both wrong. It depends neither on a closed-economy demand-supply equilibrium nor on a common world price. Both theory and evidence (especially for Australia) tell us that domestic prices of traded goods diverge from world prices due to tariffs, transport costs, and perhaps patterns of seller competition.

The approach used in some previous studies assumes that national traded-goods prices are set at levels dictated by the delivered world prices of importables (i.e., the world price plus the tariff). On that assumption the desired internationally comparable measure of relative physical (labor) productivity is obtained for each industry as follows:

$$\frac{V_A}{V_U} = \frac{VP_A(1 + t_U)}{VP_U(1 + t_A)}.$$

Here industry subscripts are omitted, V_A and V_U are physical labor productivity in Australia and the United States, VP_A and VP_U are labor value productivities measured in domestic prices, and t_A and t_U are effective rates of tariff protection. The assumption of pricing up to the tariff is of uncertain accuracy, especially for the United States but even for Australia's import-competing manufacturing sector. We can check it against the alternative of assuming a random relation between domestic prices and tariffs and therefore omitting the $(1 + t)$ adjustment.

6.4.2 Structure of Model

Given this approach to measuring relative labor productivity, we proceed to take account of other inputs. One expects a producer to employ labor, capital, and other inputs so as to minimize the cost of output subject to the industry's production function and the relevant prices. We lack the statistical leverage to estimate a separate production function for each industry, but we can at least frame the cross-sectional (interindustry) analysis so that it is roughly consistent with the presumption of distinct industry production functions. Following Davies and Caves (1987) assume that every industry (in either country) operates on the same Cobb-Douglas production function, written in terms of net output, capital, and labor. Divide through by labor input so that value added (net output) per unit of labor input is related to the capital–labor ratio. Control for the possibility that returns to scale at the plant level are not constant (i.e., the output elasticities of the Cobb-Douglas function do not sum to 1.0) by allowing value added per unit of labor input to depend on the size of the typical plant as well as the capital–labor ratio and the intercept, a catchall efficiency term.

Now divide the equation for the Australian industry by that for its U.S. counterpart. For the ith industry one has

$$VPW_i = (EFF_i)(CAP_i)^\alpha (TP_i)^{\alpha+\beta-1},$$

where VPW_i is value added per employee in the Australian industry divided by value added per employee in the U.S. counterpart, CAP_i is assets per employee in the Australian industry divided by assets per employee in the counterpart, TP_i is median plant size in the Australian industry divided by median plant size in the counterpart, and EFF_i is the ratio of the two efficiency terms, accounting for all labor-productivity differences between the two countries not due to capital inputs or scale economies.[19]

This model provides an attractive starting point for the interindustry analysis of the determinants of relative productivity. The role of relative plant size, important for Australia, enters directly through TP_i, and in empirical estimation EFF_i can be made a function of the determinants of relative frontier efficiency. With a disturbance term added, the model is readily estimated in logarithms.

At this point the model has the unattractive feature of assuming that all industries in both countries share the same Cobb-Douglas production function. The restriction can be relaxed although not removed. Suppose that all industries in Australia shared the same Cobb-Douglas production function, as did all industries in the United States, but that the Australian and U.S. functions differed. That difference could be tested by adding two terms—the logarithmic values of TP and CAP for Australia alone (TPA and CAPA). Regression coefficients for the Australian terms would indicate the differences between the Australian and U.S. values of α and β. Suppose that each industry's Australian and U.S. branches shared the same production function but that the coefficients for some industries differed from the common values of α and β. Slope shifts could accommodate any industries thought to differ from typical patterns of factor intensity and scale economies.

The capital incorporated in the model should include not only the productive physical capital that appears on the firm's books but also human capital possessed by employees. Because estimating a single commensurable stock of physical and human capital is unattractive, Davies and Caves (1987) proposed an approach based on the simple assumption that an industry's proportion of nonproduction workers in total employees describes its utilization of human capital adequately. Then the difference between the percentage of nonproduction workers in the Australian industry and its U.S. counterpart becomes the appropriate component of the model.

The factors that might depress the efficiency frontier attainable in Australia below its U.S. counterpart were pursued in detail in a previous study and will be summarized briefly here. Attention centered on the conjunction of small market size with heavy protection and imperfect competition that could on certain assumptions intensify the problem of suboptimal scales, the setting in which we expected that Australia's intrinsic cost disadvantages of small market size and remoteness might not have minimized. Two complex variables were formed to capture this possibility (for details, see Caves 1984, 333–336). One, SCL, captures the hypothesis that Australian productivity is depressed by the conjunction of high protection, small market size, and diseconomies of small scale moderate enough to make suboptimal-scale production viable. The other is C4AJ, introduced above, which looks at actual rather than potential congestion of small-scale units in Australian markets in terms of the influences on Australian producer concentration. Both variables were found to have statistically significant influences.

6.5   Determinants of Relative Productivity: Results

Because of the present study's problem with degrees of freedom we put aside the scale-economy variables just mentioned. Their significance was documented before, and each proved to exact a heavy cost in degrees of freedom. Another compromise made at the start was to forego adjusting the U.S. component of the dependent variable for the effect on U.S. prices of tariff protection. Not only does it compound the problem of missing observations, but also the assumption of pricing up to the tariff is much less appealing for U.S. than for Australian industries.

In the event the data did not support the assumption of pricing up to the tariff in Australia. In table 6.6, equation 6.1 retains the assumption while equation 6.2 drops it and employs an alternative dependent variable (VPW*) that is simply the logarithm of value added per employee in the Australian industry divided by that for its U.S. counterpart, adjusted for the exchange rate. Notice equation 6.2's considerable gain in explanatory

Table 6.6
Determinants of relative productivity

Equation	Regression model	$\bar{R}^2/DF$
6.1	VPW = 1.952 + 0.062CAP − 0.193CAPA − 0.423CAPL (2.48) (0.71) (2.08) (3.20) + 0.094TP − 0.046TPA + 1.308NPW (2.82) (0.76) (2.36)	0.305 49
6.2	VPW* = 1.360 + 0.175CAP − 0.040CAPA − 0.242CAPL (2.47) (2.92) (0.61) (2.91) + 0.094TP − 0.072TPA + 1.262NPW (4.02) (1.74) (3.29)	0.513 58
6.3	VPW = 2.049 + 0.060CAP − 0.185CAPA − 0.404CAPL (2.57) (0.65) (1.97) (3.01) + 0.094TP − 0.057TPA + 1.278NPW (2.83) (0.93) (2.30) + 0.088SKEW (0.84)	0.300 48
6.4	VPW* = 1.568 + 0.164CAP − 0.036CAPA − 0.245CAPL (2.87) (2.79) (0.56) (3.03) + 0.098TP − 0.089TPA + 1.180NPW (4.27) (2.14) (3.14) + 0.144SKEW (2.02)	0.538 57

power. In both equations relative productivity increases with relative capital intensity, plant size, and the utilization of nonproduction workers. All three coefficients are significant at the 1 percent level in 6.2, only the latter two in 6.1. The coefficient of CAP in 6.2 is a reasonable estimate of α, as is the estimate of scale economies (9 percent) implied by the coefficient of TP.

The negative coefficient of CAPA implies that the output elasticity of capital is lower and that of labor higher in Australia than in the United States; it is significant for VPW although not for VPW*. Similarly the negative coefficient of TPA implies that Australian producers, adapted to operating in a small market, have learned to minimize their productivity disadvantage in industries subject to economies of scale; however, its coefficient is not significant for VPW, significant only at 10 percent (two-tailed) for VPW*. Finally, CAPL allows a slope shift for the output elasticity of capital in a group of highly labor-intensive industries

Now we consider whether technical efficiency in Australia accounts for part of the difference between average Australian and U.S. productivity. SKEW is added to equation 6.2 to obtain 6.3, and ATIN is added to 6.2 to obtain 6.4. In equation 6.3 the coefficient of SKEW is indeed appropriately positive and significant. In equation 6.4, however, the coefficient of ATIN is inappropriately positive and takes a t-statistic of appreciable magnitude. If VPW is the dependent variable both t-statistics fall somewhat, and SKEW is no longer significant (not surprising in light of SKEW's dependence on PROT, which is used to construct VPW). Thus equation 6.3 taken by itself confirms the maintained hypothesis, but the robustness problem exposed by equation 6.4 and the weakened results with VPW preclude strong claims.[20]

6.6   Summary and Conclusions

We find that technical efficiency in Australia increases with industries' plant sizes and with the regional concentration of economic activity, declines with protection from international competition (artificial and natural), and also declines with producer concentration beyond a moderate level. Technical efficiency probably does not interact with the problem of scale efficiency stressed in previous research on Australia. Aside from plant size, it is not related to features of business organization (foreign ownership, diversification). The general-equilibrium squeeze on the manufacturing sector in the 1970s yielded only hints of effects on efficiency.

Although positive findings about the determinants of efficiency were not overwhelmingly numerous, they certainly provide some basis for believing that a national efficiency frontier is a meaningful concept for industries in a country such as Australia. The study supports the hypothesis that the skewness of production-function residuals provides a decent measure of technical efficiency, notable in those industries for which the standard measures of efficiency cannot be computed.

Finally, the study is not particularly encouraging about the usefulness of international comparisons in research on technical efficiency. The problems are tactical and center on the paucity of degrees of freedom remaining after industries are lost in matching industrial classifications, failures to estimate technical efficiency, and other sources. One's initial hope that the methodology of technical efficiency might contribute to the ever-present interest in international competitiveness and comparative national performance are not crushed by any great conceptual flaw but nibbled to death by small problems of implementation.

Notes

I am grateful to the Division of Research, Harvard Business School, for research support and for help in organizing the data base used for this project. Denise Neumann provided valued research assistance, and Chris Harris offered helpful comments

1. That pattern is consistent with Torii's theoretical models of the effect of competition in the context of capital vintages and lumpy replacement investment. See chapter 2, subsection 2.3.1.

2. Round (1980) found that little of the variance of industries' concentration levels in Australia is explained by plant scale economies observed in the United States.

3. The average four-firm concentration ratio for Australian manufacturing industries is at least 78 percent higher than their U.S. counterparts (Caves 1984, 321–322). Although large, the difference is a good deal less than proportional to the size difference of the two economies because Australian firms and plants are small (Caves 1984, 316–317).

4. Exogenous variables were collected for 1977 when available, but we commonly had to utilize other years if variables were not published annually or considerations of data quality demanded.

5. Net output per employee in the smallest plants accounting for one-half of the U.S. counterpart industry's output divided by net output per employee in the large plants accounting for the rest, 1977. The higher the CDRU, the less we assume do diseconomies of small plant scale discourage the operation of small-scale firms.

6. C4AJ amounts to a backhanded recognition that concentration in Australia is endogenous in this setting and, with a richer data set, would be treated in a simultaneous equations design as in Caves, Porter, and Spence (1980).

7. Caves and Barton (1990, 92–94, 142–144). The conclusion about productivity growth must be discounted somewhat for sensitivity to the model's specification.

8. In a purely competitive market, what would matter is the elasticity of world excess supply of imports and not the realized import share, which is endogenous. The more readily observed variable IMP, used here as in other studies, can be justified if manufactured goods are generally heterogeneous and differentiated. IMP then indicates the likelihood that the typical domestic producer's output will face an imported close substitute, as well as the extent to which potential foreign competitors have incurred the fixed cost of establishing a presence in Australia and thus becoming actual competitors.

9. In our data base protection increases significantly with an industry's labor intensity and regional concentration and decreases with its producer concentration, rate of market growth, and extent of transport-cost protection. A case can certainly be made for treating protection (like concentration) as endogenous in the model

10. In our data base nominal rates of tariff and transport protection show a negative correlation (-0.23) significant at 5 percent (86 industries). Of course transport costs also contribute to precluding Australian industries from integration with world markets through exports (Sampson and Yeats 1977).

11. Caves (1984) confirmed a corollary of this proposition, namely, that the scales of Australian plants relative to minimum efficient scale estimated from U.S. data increase with the prevalence of foreign investors.

12. Like tariffs, multinational enterprises inject multicollinearity into the analysis because their prevalence (FSE) can be predicted by various underlying elements of market structure such as the importance of intangible assets originating in research and development and sales promotion. See Parry (1978) on Australia.

13. During the 1970s concern was expressed that productivity growth in Australia was running toward the low end of the industrial countries' experience (Industries Assistance

Commission 1976b). However, no defects are evident in the country's efficiency at absorbing new technology from abroad, once the intrinsic limitations of remoteness and small market size are acknowledged (Department of Trade and Industry 1972).

14. Robert Gregory first called attention to this general-equilibrium effect in Australia. See Smith (1978) for an account.

15. Gordon's (1975) analysis employed a coarse sector-by-region analysis. Also see Mitchell's (1984) survey. Bureau of Industry Economics (1990) is an intensive case study that documents the productivity-impairing effects of craft demarcations, closed-shop restrictions, and the compression of skill-based pay differentials; it also shows the effects of small operating scales and small lot sizes.

16. The underlying production functions utilize value added as the dependent variable. The efficiency measures are taken from tables 4.2 (ATIN) and 4.8 (SKEW, ATIT, ATE) in Harris (1988).

17. Because of the small number of producers in some Australian industries, it is fairly common for basic data to be suppressed in census publications because of disclosure. This problem is in addition to the one that arises in the following section: observations lost in matching the Australian and U.S. standard industrial classifications.

18. Doubling an industry's plant sizes would raise its value of SKEW by 0.13 standard deviations The other variable proposed to capture plant-size effects, the dispersion of an industry's plant sizes (GINI), proved not at all significant.

19. Monetary values are converted to a common currency. Typical plant size, here measured by employment, summarizes the size distribution of each industry's plants. Davies and Caves showed that a suitable approximation is the size of the plant accounting for the fiftieth percentile of output when plants are ranked by size.

20. It is quite reasonable to suppose that the error structure of the model calls for estimating the coefficient of SKEW or ATIN by two-stage least squares. That has not been done, partly because tables 6.2 through 6.5, which contain the obvious candidates for instruments, do not register sufficient explanatory power to make the step look very promising.

References

Aislabie, C. 1988. Economic incentives and the pattern of the Australian tariff. *Australian Economic Papers* 27: 20–32.

Anderson, K. 1980. The political market for government assistance to Australian manufacturing industries. *Economic Record* 56: 132–144.

Brash, D. T. 1966. *American Investment in Australian Industry.* Cambridge: Harvard University Press.

Brown, P., and H. Hughes. 1970. The market structure of Australian manufacturing industry, 1914 to 1963–4. In C. Forster, ed., *Australian Economic Development.* London: Allen & Unwin, pp. 169–207.

Bureau of Industry Economics. 1981. Finance for small business growth and development. Research Paper No. 10. Canberra: Australian Government Publishing Service.

Bureau of Industry Economics. 1990. International productivity differences in manufacturing—Photographic paper, Research Report No. 34. Canberra: Australian Government Publishing Service.

Bushnell, J. A. 1961. *Australian Company Mergers, 1946–1959.* Melbourne: Melbourne University Press.

Caves, R. E. 1984. Scale, openness, and productivity in manufacturing industries. In R. E. Caves and L. B. Krause, eds., *The Australian Economy: A View from the North.* Washington: Brookings Institution, pp. 313–347.

Caves, R. E., and D. R. Barton. 1990. *Efficiency in U.S. Manufacturing Industries.* Cambridge: MIT Press.

Caves, R. E., M. E. Porter, and A. M. Spence. 1980. *Competition in the Open Economy.* Cambridge: Harvard University Press.

Committee to Advise on Policies for Manufacturing Industry. 1975. *Policies for Development of Manufacturing Industry: A Green Paper,* vol. 3. Parliamentary Paper No. 160/1975.

Conlon, R. M. 1979. Transport costs as barriers to Australian trade. Centre for Applied Economic Research. Paper No. 8. Kensington: University of New South Wales.

Conybeare, J. 1978. Public policy and the Australian tariff structure. *Australian Journal of Management* 3: 49–64.

Davies, S., and R. E. Caves. 1987. *Britain's Productivity Gap.* National Institute of Economic and Social Research. Occasional Paper No. 40. Cambridge: Cambridge University Press.

Department of Trade and Industry, Office of Secondary Industry. 1972. *A Study of the Rate of Diffusion of New Technology within Australian Industry.* Canberra: Australian Government Publishing Service.

Dixon, R. 1983. Industry structure and the speed of price adjustment. *Journal of Industrial Economics* 32: 25–38.

Dixon, R. 1985. Indices of the average age of structures and equipment in Australia 1955/56–1982/83. *Economic Record* 61: 564–566.

Gordon, B. 1975. A ninety-sector analysis of industrial disputes in Australia. *Journal of Industrial Relations* 17: 240–254.

Gregory R. G. 1978. Determination of relative prices in the manufacturing sector of a small open economy: The Australian experience. In Kasper and Parry (1978), pp. 219–238.

Gregory, R. G., and J. J. Pincus. 1982. Industrial assistance. In Webb and Allan (1982), ch. 6.

Gruen, F. H. 1986. How bad is Australia's economic performance and why? *Economic Record* 62: 180–193.

Harris, C. M. 1988. Technical efficiency in Australian manufacturing industries. Bureau of Industry Economics. Occasional Paper No. 4. Canberra: Bureau of Industry Economics.

Industries Assistance Commission. 1975. Implications of the commission's approach to the development of industries (1975). In Committee to Advise on Policies for Manufacturing Industry (1975), pp. 29–68.

Industries Assistance Commission. 1976. *Annual Report, 1975–76.* Canberra: Australian Government Publishing Service.

Industries Assistance Commission. 1977a. *Annual Report, 1976–77.* Canberra: Australian Government Publishing Service.

Industries Assistance Commission. 1977b. *Structural Change in Australia.* Canberra: Australian Government Publishing Service.

Industries Assistance Commission. 1980. *Trends in the Structure of Assistance to Manufacturing.* Approaches to General Reductions in Protection, Information Paper No. 1. Canberra: Australian Government Publishing Service.

Johns, B. L. 1967. Private overseas investment in Australia: Profitability and motivation. *Economic Record* 43: 233–261.

Johns, B. L. 1978. The production and transfer of technology. In Kasper and Parry (1978), pp. 239–253.

Johns, B. L., W. C. Dunlop, and W. J. Sheehan. 1978. *Small Business in Australia: Problems and Prospects*. Sydney: Allen & Unwin. 1978.

Karmel, P. H., and M. Brunt. 1962. *The Structure of the Australian Economy*. Melbourne: P. W. Cheshire.

Kasper, W., and T. G. Parry, eds. 1978. *Growth, Trade and Structural Change in an Open Australian Economy*. Kensington: Centre for Applied Economic Research.

Lawriwsky, M. 1978. Ownership and control of Australian corporations. Occasional Paper No. 1. Transnational Corporations Research Project. University of Sydney.

Lawriwsky, M. L. 1982. Objectives and internal organizations of firms. In Webb and Allan (1982), ch. 2

Lawriwsky, M. L. 1984. Some tests of the influence of control type on the market for corporate control in Australia. *Journal of Industrial Economics* 32: 277–291.

Leech, S. A., and J. McB. Grant. 1970. Profitability and concentration in Australian manufacturing industries 1970–71 to 1972–73; A further examination. *Economic Record* 54: 397–400.

Mangan, J., and P. Regan. 1983. A note on organisational slack and market power in Australian manufacturing. *Australian Economic Papers* 22: 356–363.

Mitchell, D. J. B. 1984. The Australian labor market. In R. E. Caves and L. B. Krause, eds. *The Australian Economy: A View from the North*. Washington: Brookings Institution, pp. 127–193.

Nieuwenhuysen, J. P., and N. R. Norman. 1976. *Australian Competition and Prices Policy: Trade Practices, Tariffs, and Price Justification*. London: Croom Helm.

Parry, T. G. 1978. Structure and performance in Australian manufacturing, with special reference to foreign-owned enterprises. In Kasper and Parry (1978), ch. 8.

Roach Ward Guest & Co., Syntec Economic Services Pty. Ltd. 1976. Financing manufacturing: Past trends and the current crisis. In Committee to Advise on Policies for Manufacturing Industry (1976), pp. 69–114.

Robertson, D. H. 1978. Australia's growth performance; An assessment. In Kasper and Parry (1978), ch. 4.

Round, D. K. 1976. Price-cost margins in Australian manufacturing industries, 1971–72. *Australian Journal of Management* 1: 85–95.

Round, D. K. 1979. Concentration and the level and variability of rates of return in Australian manufacturing industries. *Antitrust Bulletin* 24: 573–594.

Round, D. K. 1980. Plant size, scale economies, and "optimum" concentration levels in Australian manufacturing industries. *Weltwirtschaftliches Archiv* 116: 341–352.

Round, D. K. 1981. Concentration, plant size, and multiple plant operations of large firms in Australian manufacturing industries. *Nebraska Journal of Economics and Business* 20: 573–594.

Sampson, G. P., and A. H. Yeats. 1977. Tariff and transport barriers facing Australian exports. *Journal of Transport Economics and Policy* 11: 141–154.

Sheridan, K. 1974. *The Firm in Australia: A Theoretical and Empirical Study of Size, Growth and Profitability*. Melbourne: Thomas Nelson.

Sheridan, K. 1975. Business performance of American and British affiliated firms in Australia. *Economic Record* 51: 549–563.

Smith, B. 1978. Australian minerals development, future prospects for the mining industry, and effects on the Australian economy. In Kasper and Parry (1978), ch. 6.

Vipond, J. 1978. The regional consequences of structural change and the scope for regional adjustment policies. In Kasper and Parry (1978), pp. 348–368.

Webb, G. R. 1978. Transport, growth and trade. In Kasper and Parry (1978), pp. 372–383.

Webb, L. R., and R. R. Allan, eds. 1982. *Industrial Economics: Australian Studies.* Sydney: Allen & Unwin.

7 Industry Efficiency and Plant Turnover in the Canadian Manufacturing Sector

John Baldwin

7.1 Introduction

Most studies of industry performance fail to recognize the diversity of productivity attributes of firms within an industry. For example, productivity growth is generally measured at the industry level with almost complete disregard for the underlying production entities. This habit is probably the result of the widespread acceptance of the concept of a representative or average firm. As Reid (1987) has pointed out, in industrial organization the Vinerian concept of the representative firm has dominated the more complex notion of the diversity of firm performance stressed by Marshall. As a result the mainstream of industrial organization has had trouble in coming to grips with the reality of heterogeneity of firms.

One of the few strands of applied industrial economics to face the existence of firm heterogeneity is the literature on X-inefficiency. On the one hand, economists such as Leibenstein (1966) have argued, from observation, that this phenomenon deserved attention. On the other, economists such as Stigler (1976) have argued that profit maximization makes it unlikely that inefficiency can exist for long, therefore claims to observe the phenomenon must be based on incorrect measurement. Despite this existential debate econometricians who were working on the estimation of frontier production functions began to investigate how the error structure of these production functions could be used to characterize the degree of efficiency in an industry. The resulting literature has now developed an impressive body of empirical evidence on the nature and correlates of efficiency (see Caves and Barton 1990 for a summary of the literature).

Many articles have focused on methodology. Most empirical applications have been limited to a small number of industries, until the recent work of Caves and Barton (1990) that looked at a broad cross section of U.S. manufacturing industries in the 1970s. But until now there have been few studies that would allow an assessment of how fleeting the phenomenon is—thereby answering one of Stigler's criticisms—or the causes of changes in the level of efficiency over time that result from more efficient firms replacing the less efficient. This study uses a longitudinal panel of Canadian manufacturing firms in the 1970s to investigate both issues.

7.2 The Measurement of Efficiency

Measures of efficiency have typically been divided into two categories: technical and allocative. Technical efficiency arises when a firm makes the best use of its inputs. Allocative efficiency occurs when a firm employs its inputs in the correct proportions. Like the majority of previous studies, this chapter focuses on technical efficiency. Inefficiency implies that the same amount of resources, if reallocated from the least productive to the most productive plants, could yield increased output.

Recent work in measuring efficiency has estimated production functions from plant and firm data. This approach attempts to correct for differences in output that are caused by the use of different input combinations and differences in the size of the production unit. The residuals are then utilized to produce an "average" measure of efficiency.

The same concept of efficiency is adopted here, but a simpler measurement technique is used. Efficiency is measured as the ratio of actual output to potential output. Potential output is calculated as the efficient level of output per person multiplied by the level of employment in each establishment, summed over all producing establishments. As such, the measure of efficiency used here is size weighted. The efficient level of output per person is defined as the sum of output divided by the sum of all employment in the most productive establishments accounting for a specified percentage of total output—10, 20, 30, or 40 percent.

This method is more direct although less elegant than those that estimate efficiency from the residuals derived from a production function. It may be the more efficient research strategy for several reasons. First, it is not obvious that utilizing the production function is the correct strategy. Estimating the average level of efficiency from a production function presumes that it is appropriate to correct for differences in productivity that result from differing establishment sizes or from different factor proportions. But if the cause of inefficiency is the existence of suboptimal-sized plants, then part of the estimated inefficiency is being eliminated by the use of a production function.

The measure employed here will avoid some of these problems. By focusing directly on output per worker, it presumes that our goal should be to maximize product per worker and that firms setting the lead in this area can and should be emulated. Whether this view is justified depends on the extent to which intraindustry differences in factor proportions and plant sizes are efficient. It might be argued that different factor proportions within an industry are justifiable in terms of different factor prices. If differences in capital–labor ratios are optimal because of different factor costs, or because of different vintage effects, inefficiency as measured here will be overstated. It also might be argued that small inefficient firms provide externalities that compensate for their inefficiencies and make their existence desirable—that these firms provide external discipline on large firms and that it is this group that provides the next generation of large efficient firms.

These views are very much akin to the view that the concept of efficiency is misplaced. Stigler (1976) voiced the opinion that the search for optimum techniques that leads to dispersions in firms' efficiency levels is costly—just like the search for the best price or the most suitable occupation; these costs are as legitimate as costs associated with the static use of factor inputs. As such, the term inefficiency is a misnomer.

This is not the place to try to resolve the issue. But the parallel between search and input costs can be used to justify interest in the dispersion of relative productivity among plants within an industry—irrespective of the term applied to the phenomenon. Materials inputs are a cost, and the economics profession has increasingly come to recognize that productivity improvements can also be had by economizing on these inputs. Similarly, to the extent that the productivity levels in less productive plants can be brought up to levels in the most productive plants, productivity gains will ensue. How this occurs and the process that generates it has been poorly documented and warrants further investigation (see Downie 1958 for one such attempt).

This study then makes no apologies for the topic pursued. It is more modest about the efficiency measure adopted, for the use of production functions to estimate efficiency measures has become widespread. As a practical matter, none of the potential problems in the use of the specific measure adopted here—failure to correct for differing factor proportions or firm size—could be very important if the measure used closely correlates with others. Unfortunately, there are no studies that provide a comparative analysis of how closely this measure relates to others. But there is an increasing body of evidence to suggest that alternate measures of efficiency in general are highly correlated (Caves and Barton 1990, 53) and that the use of different measures has a relatively minor effect on isolating the determinants of efficiency (Caves and Barton 1990, 107–110). In this respect it has been observed that skewness measures of efficiency—from which the measure used here is derived—are closely correlated to other efficiency measures derived from the residuals of production functions.

There are several additional reasons to adopt the measure used here. First, its interindustry variance is relatively unaffected by the choice of industry sample that is used to define optimal output-per-person ratios. The measure is not greatly affected by outliers and is less likely to be affected by the number of observations used to estimate it than are most measures that are derived from the production function approach. Second, as a subsequent section demonstrates, it is correlated with many of the variables found in previous studies to be correlated with alternative inefficiency measures. Its interindustry variability therefore appears to be closely related to the more complex and more costly measures of efficiency that are derived from production functions.

7.3   Efficiency in the Canadian Manufacturing Sector

7.3.1   Choice of Sample

When industry efficiency is defined using output per person of the most productive plants, as it is here, some subset must be chosen to define maximum potential productivity. If the interindustry variability is sensitive to the sample chosen, then choice of the subset becomes critical. To examine this issue, different cutoff points based on the percentage of industry shipments covered were used to define the plants considered to be efficient, frontier output per person was calculated for plants above each cutoff point, and the correlations between the various efficiency estimates associated with each cutoff were calculated. The sample chosen for the exercise was the four-digit level of the Canadian manufacturing sector, which subdivides manufacturing into some 167 industries. The years chosen were 1970 and 1979. Data on all plants reporting to the Canadian Census of Manufactures were used. Output per person was defined alternately as shipments per worker and as value added per worker. For the first measure (EFF1) the efficient output per person was defined as the sum of output over the sum of labor input of the most productive plants that accounted for 10 percent of output. Alternative levels of 20, 30, and 40

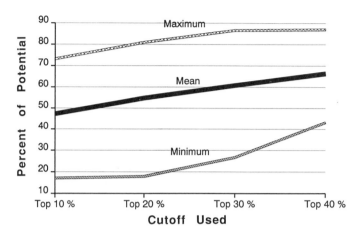

Figure 7.1
Industry efficiency measures by cutoff point for 1970

percent of industry output were also used, yielding the efficiency measures EFF2, EFF3, and EFF4, respectively.

The level of efficiency on average differs substantially for the different cutoff points. Figure 7.1 plots the mean value of efficiency for each cutoff point, as well as its upper and lower bounds for 1970 using value added as the output measure. When the most productive plants that account for 10 percent of value added are used to define maximum potential output per person, production is only 47 percent of potential. This increases to 55, 61, and 66 percent when the top most productive plants accounting for 20, 30, and 40 percent of value added, respectively, are used for the cutoff. Comparable measures using shipments per worker are 44, 52, 57, and 63 percent. Since there is little difference in the value added and the shipments-based measures, only the former are subsequently reported herein.[1]

In light of the number of different methodologies for measuring efficiency and a lack of agreement on the most appropriate one, comparisons among countries of the *level* of inefficiency are hazardous. Nevertheless, they are made. Caves and Barton (1990) summarize several studies that use the stochastic production function technique and that find efficiency estimates ranging upward from 50 to 90 percent for such disparate countries as Colombia, Indonesia, and France. Caves and Barton themselves report mean values for efficiency in the U.S. manufacturing sector as different as

63 and 99 percent, using the stochastic production frontier approach but two different techniques (p. 50). The differences in these values indicates the degree to which estimates of *levels* of efficiency are sensitive to the technique used.

Although large differences in the level of efficiency are generated for the United States in the Caves and Barton study, the cross-industry variability of the two main estimates is quite similar. The partial correlation coefficient of the two main measures is 0.96, and the regressions that examine the relationship between an industry's efficiency and its characteristics using each of these measures tell the same story.

This is also the case for the measures of efficiency that are derived here for the Canadian manufacturing sector. While the mean value of the efficiency measures differs for the four cutoff points used, the interindustry variability of the measures is closely related. The correlation matrix for the four 1970 measures derived using the 10, 20, 30, and 40 percent cutoff points is presented in table 7.1. The correlations are all high and for adjacent cutoff points are about 0.90. This pattern suggests that the choice of cutoff will not be critical because the nature of interindustry variability and changes therein is of great import. This supposition was tested and confirmed by using several values of the efficiency measure at subsequent stages of the analysis. The conclusions were generally the same, irrespective of the cutoff chosen to generate the inefficiency measure. Results based on the measure that uses value added and that corresponds to the 40 percent cutoff point will be reported in this chapter.

Table 7.1
Correlations between alternative efficiency estimates for 1970, and between 1970 and 1979 estimates

| | 1970 estimates | | | | |
	EFF1	EFF2	EFF3	EFF4	1979
EFF1	1.0	0.91	0.82	0.77	0.61
EFF2		1.0	0.89	0.84	0.51
EFF3			1.0	0.92	0.55
EFF4				1.0	0.52

Source: Special tabulations, Business and Labour Market Analysis Group, Statistics Canada.
Note: All correlations are significantly different from zero; for definitions of the variables, see text; the correlations for 1979 are between the 1970 and 1979 estimate of efficiency that uses the same cutoff point.

7.3.2   Characteristics of the Efficiency Measure

The efficiency estimates vary considerably among the 167 industry sample, as the upper and lower bounds attached to the mean value in figure 7.1 indicate. The efficiency value is 53 percent for the industry at the tenth percentile and increases to 77 percent at the ninetieth percentile. The preferred efficiency measure in the Caves and Barton study ranged from 46 percent at the tenth percentile to 81 percent at the ninetieth percentile (p. 51).

The interindustry differences in efficiency change over time. The last column of table 7.1 contains the estimates of the correlation of the efficiency estimates in 1970 and 1979. Correlations between 0.5 and 0.6 indicate that while patterns of cross-industry efficiency differentials persist, they are not immutable. Figure 7.2 plots the mean value of both the 1970 and the 1979 efficiency estimates based on the decile ranking of the 1970 estimates. There is a certain tendency for industries to regress toward the mean—or at least for those with high efficiency values in 1970 to decrease over the decade.

What is most striking is the increase in the dispersion of industries that were grouped in the same decile in 1970. The bottom line shows the range in 1970 (of course, small by construction). The range in 1979 for each of the industries in a particular 1970 decile (second bottom line) is much greater. The increase in variability is particularly large for the industries

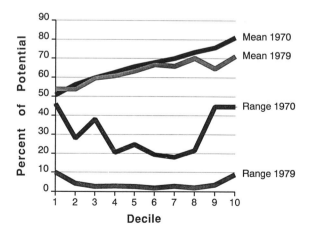

Figure 7.2
Comparison of ranges of efficiency measures for 1970 versus 1979

that were most efficient in 1970. The world does not stand still. Industries where most firms have moved close to the maximum potential output are those where something, perhaps new technology, is likely to result in some firms gaining an advantage over others in the future.

7.4 Industry Characteristics Associated with Inefficiency

The industry characteristics associated with efficiency are important both for the light they shed on the reasons for interindustry differences in efficiency and for the verification they provide on the usefulness of the efficiency measure adopted herein. Because this measure is not identical to others, it is important to ask whether it is related in much the same way to industry characteristics found to be important determinants of efficiency in other countries.

To provide this comparison, the taxonomy developed by Caves and Barton for their extensive U.S. study is used. Industry characteristics are divided into six broad groups. In the first group are competitive conditions such as concentration and exposure to international trade that are posited to produce centripetal pressures that reduce firm heterogeneity. The second group consists of product differentiation characteristics that are used to control for the likelihood that efficiency is measured with error. Efficiency measures are generally based on value of shipments or value added—variables that combine both output and price. It is normally assumed that prices are reasonably similar across firms. If there are differences in the prices buyers pay, some of the measured differences in efficiency will actually be due to differences in rents accruing to firms. Product differentiation variables control for this possibility. The third group of variables captures the occurrence of change and therefore the centrifugal forces that might allow plants' productivity levels to diverge. The fourth group encompasses characteristics that permit heterogeneity due to dissimilar geographic markets. The fifth group includes organizational influences that are postulated to exert pressures on management—the extent of diversification, of multiplant operation, of large plant size, and certain labor characteristics such as the degree of unionization and the use of full as opposed to part-time workers. Finally, a group of variables serves to control for omitted influences. Some of these variables, such as the vintage of capital or the variation in capital–labor ratios, proxy factors that have been missed in estimating a simplified production function.

Other variables, such as the number of observations on which the production function was based, are used to account for the bias that arises because of a purely statistical factor. Technical efficiency, as defined in most studies, depends inversely on the highest observed value of a distribution. The theory of order statistics suggests that the larger the number of observations drawn (i.e., plants in an industry), the greater the range will be, and thus the lower will be measured efficiency (Caves and Barton 1990, 58–62). Since the efficiency measure used in this study is size weighted, this problem is hypothesized to be less important here.

The correlations between industry characteristics for 1970 and the measure of efficiency for the same year are reported in table 7.2.[2] Correlation rather than regression analysis was used because the prime objective was to depict the relationship between each characteristic and efficiency, not to sort out the relative importance of each. The variables that were used are

Table 7.2
Correlations between efficiency estimates and industry characteristics

Variable	Correlation	Probability value
CONC	−0.10	0.18
XC	−0.20	0.01
MS	−0.04	0.60
XS	−0.03	0.67
COMP	−0.08	0.27
ADS	−0.19	0.01
R&D	−0.07	0.36
SD(M/L)	−0.18	0.02
N5D	−0.12	0.14
SD(HERF)	0.04	0.65
SD(SIZE)	0.07	0.36
CVTOP8	−0.08	0.24
SUBOPT	−0.08	0.28
KL	−0.26	0.01
REG	−0.02	0.81
COVE	−0.13	0.09
MULT1	−0.11	0.14
MULT2	−0.18	0.03
RPSIZE	−0.04	0.59
RFSIZE	−0.03	0.69
UNION	−0.12	0.12
FULL	−0.18	0.02
NOBS	0.08	0.29

Source: Special tabulations, Business and Labour Market Analysis Group, Statistics Canada.
Note: For definitions of variables, see the appendix.

listed in the appendix. They were defined as carefully as possible to resemble those used in the U.S. study (see Baldwin and Gorecki 1987 for discussion of data base and definitions).

The correlations between efficiency and industry characteristics produce a story similar to that reported by Caves and Barton for the United States. Several of what were classified as core variables in the U.S. analysis have high correlations with the Canadian efficiency measure. As was the case for the United States, the higher the proportion of an industry's sales that are controlled by firms with their main interests elsewhere (COVE), the lower is efficiency. Similarly the greater the diversity of the inputs available to work with labor—SD(M/L)—the lower is efficiency. In the Canadian case several other variables that capture the heterogeneity in the industry—variables that reflect the mechanism that might cause variations in productivity and thus lower efficiency levels—were also employed. The number of products classified to the industry (N5D), the variation in the plants' level of specialization (SD[HERF]), and the standard deviation in the plant–specialization ratio (SD[SPEC]) were all included. None of these was significantly correlated with efficiency at the 5 percent level. Also included in the core set of U.S. explanatory variables was a labor-conditions variable—the importance of full-time workers (FULL). As with the U.S. results Canadian efficiency was positively related to the use of part-time workers.

In the U.S. case the importance of competitive conditions proved difficult to discern. By itself, concentration was not significant, but when it was entered in a nonlinear fashion, an effect was found. Efficiency first rose and then fell as concentration increased. In Canada the concentration ratio is negatively correlated with efficiency. This is not inconsistent with the U.S. finding because the level of concentration in most Canadian industries is higher than their U.S. counterparts. As was the case for the U.S. study, export and import intensity in Canada are not closely related to industry efficiency. Nominal and effective tariff variables also are insignificant. Similarities between the Canadian and U.S. results extend to the set of relationships outside the core variables. In both countries geographic market heterogeneity has no robust effect, product differentiation is strongly associated with lower efficiency, and the labor-market variable (UNION) has a negative effect on efficiency that is only weakly significant.

An attempt was made to ascertain whether the strongly negative effect of concentration might be related to economies of plant scale, as opposed to multiplant operation. To this end, the average plant size of the top four firms divided by market size was included (RPSIZE), as well as excess concentration (XC). The former proxies the concentration effect due to plant scale economies and the latter the concentration effect due to multiplant activity. The former is not significant, while the latter is negatively correlated with efficiency. It is the multiplant aspect of concentration that appears most harmful. Additional variables that captured the multiplant nature of the industry (MULT1 and MULT2) also exhibit negative correlations with industry efficiency. Diversification across industries has a negative effect on efficiency; so too does horizontal expansion within an industry by multiplant operations.

While the two analyses contain many similar results, there are two important differences. First, the number of observations is inversely related to efficiency in the U.S. study because of the "order" effect. This was posited and found to be less of a problem with the measure used for the Canadian study. The number of observations is not significantly correlated with efficiency in Canada. Second, the U.S. study found that research and development intensity was negatively correlated with efficiency. This too is not the case for Canada. One of the reasons for the difference may be the truncated nature of research and development in Canada. To test for this phenomenon, a variable that consisted of technology payments made abroad divided by sales was used both alone and in conjunction with domestic expenditures on R&D divided by sales. The latter, like the employee-based measure that was used above, continues to be insignificantly correlated with efficiency; the former is positively correlated with efficiency but only marginally significant.

Industry efficiency, expressed in log-odds form, was regressed on the industry characteristics. The results of the regression are reported in equation (1), which includes only the most significant regressors (values in second parentheses are significance probabilities):

$$EFF4 = 2.61 - 4.77ADS - 0.378XC - 0.001N5D$$
$$ (2.74) \quad\ (2.98) \quad\ (2.18)$$
$$ (0.004) \quad (0.031) \quad (0.085)$$

$$- 0.768FULL - 0.001UNION - 0.005SD(M/L), \qquad (1)$$
$$(1.75) \qquad\quad (1.70) \qquad\qquad (1.80)$$
$$(0.092) \qquad\quad (0.023) \qquad\quad (0.074)$$

$$R^2 = 0.16, \quad DF = 143, \quad \text{prob } F = 0.0001.$$

Simultaneous consideration of industry characteristics once more confirms the importance of the core set of U.S. variables. Product differentiation (ADS), labor-market conditions (FULL, UNION), and variability of the factor input ratio (SD[M/L]) decrease efficiency. Concentration due to multiplant activity (XC) and the diversity of products produced in industry (N5D) do so as well.

Consideration of the various industry characteristics jointly in a regression may run afoul of multicollinearity. This problem is compounded here by the fact that some of the variables measure industry characteristics— such as competitive conditions—that are hypothesized to affect efficiency; others capture the mechanism by which inefficiency may develop—such as the degree of suboptimal capacity or the degree of diversity within an industry. The latter also beg explanation and may themselves be related to basic industry characteristics like product differentiation, research and development activity, the state of industry competition, and organizational traits.

To sort out the relative importance of the determinants of interindustry efficiency levels, a principal component analysis was performed on the set of industry characteristics, and the components were used in a regression, producing the results reported in equation (2). Principal component analysis permits us to characterize the joint effects of the industry characteristics, since each of the components generated by the analysis is constructed as a weighted average of the original variables. Examining which of the original variables are heavily weighted in a component that significantly affects industry efficiency provides greater insight into how various industry characteristics tend to work together. Table 7.3 reports the weights of the original variables for the components that proved to be significant in the regression.

$$EFF4 = 0.70 - 0.098VAR2 + 0.061VAR3 - 0.056VAR4 - 0.061VAR5$$
$$\quad\quad\quad\quad (2.75) \quad\quad (1.94) \quad\quad (1.82) \quad\quad (1.82)$$
$$\quad\quad\quad\quad (0.01) \quad\quad (0.05) \quad\quad (0.07) \quad\quad (0.07)$$

$$\quad - 0.079VAR9 + 0.060VAR10 - 0.079VAR18, \quad\quad\quad (2)$$
$$\quad\quad (2.57) \quad\quad\quad (1.97) \quad\quad\quad (2.52)$$
$$\quad\quad (0.01) \quad\quad\quad (0.05) \quad\quad\quad (0.01)$$

$$R^2 = 0.166, \quad DF = 143.$$

Table 7.3
Principal component analysis of industry characteristics

Eigenvectors

	VAR1	VAR2	VAR3	VAR4	VAR5	VAR6	VAR7	VAR8	VAR9
CONC	0.47	−0.09	−0.09	−0.01	0.12	−0.02	0.06	0.05	−0.07
ADS	0.02	−0.02	−0.29	0.20	−0.10	−0.36	0.43	0.12	0.28
COMP	0.16	0.24	0.32	−0.11	−0.15	−0.09	−0.06	−0.49	0.04
RD	0.18	−0.16	0.12	0.30	−0.03	−0.28	−0.15	0.09	0.30
MULT1	0.28	0.37	0.01	0.14	0.16	−0.14	−0.05	−0.01	−0.14
MULT2	0.29	0.27	−0.14	0.10	0.31	−0.13	0.04	−0.23	0.00
COVE	0.20	0.13	0.16	−0.04	−0.16	0.35	−0.17	0.39	−0.23
NSD	−0.10	0.01	0.15	0.56	0.00	−0.09	−0.14	0.09	0.12
REG	−0.08	0.23	−0.04	−0.31	−0.07	−0.25	−0.04	0.15	0.37
XS	0.19	0.01	0.39	0.16	−0.36	0.19	0.13	−0.37	0.09
MS	0.02	−0.33	−0.07	0.38	0.05	0.21	−0.23	−0.23	0.08
CVTOP8	0.44	−0.11	−0.02	−0.04	0.08	−0.12	0.06	0.02	−0.03
XC	0.02	0.48	−0.16	0.16	0.13	0.15	0.08	−0.06	−0.05
NOBS	−0.24	0.19	0.15	0.02	−0.22	−0.25	−0.26	−0.07	0.16
FULL	0.13	0.18	0.03	0.06	0.25	0.27	−0.41	0.21	0.44
SUBOPT	−0.16	0.05	−0.20	0.37	−0.03	0.27	0.39	0.03	−0.08
UNION	0.06	−0.10	−0.21	−0.23	0.07	0.42	0.15	−0.24	0.55
RPSIZE	0.30	−0.41	0.06	−0.12	−0.02	−0.12	−0.02	0.08	−0.01
SDML	0.19	0.15	0.24	0.04	−0.33	0.15	0.35	0.43	0.19
SDHERF	−0.16	−0.08	0.43	−0.02	0.40	−0.08	0.27	0.06	0.02
SDSPEC	−0.13	−0.05	0.42	−0.02	0.50	0.06	0.20	0.07	0.09

Table 7.3 (continued)

Eigenvectors

	VAR10	VAR11	VAR12	VAR13	VAR14	VAR15	VAR16	VAR17	VAR18
CONC	0.13	0.04	-0.10	0.09	0.06	0.07	0.13	0.24	0.11
ADS	-0.40	0.12	0.19	0.39	-0.11	0.25	0.08	-0.02	-0.10
COMP	-0.33	0.15	0.08	0.04	0.25	-0.20	0.20	0.26	0.32
RD	-0.03	0.29	0.15	-0.65	0.23	0.14	-0.16	-0.02	-0.04
MULT1	0.15	-0.11	-0.03	0.04	0.10	0.03	0.09	0.03	-0.63
MULT2	0.04	0.03	-0.03	0.12	0.02	-0.21	-0.40	-0.59	0.26
COVE	-0.08	0.20	0.44	0.27	0.37	0.21	-0.05	-0.16	0.04
N5D	0.05	-0.55	0.23	0.16	0.18	-0.35	0.13	0.10	0.09
REG	0.56	0.29	0.29	0.14	-0.07	-0.29	0.12	0.08	0.02
XS	0.12	0.10	0.03	0.07	-0.32	0.02	-0.06	-0.12	-0.39
MS	0.29	0.23	0.11	0.24	-0.23	0.19	0.13	-0.06	0.25
CVTOP8	0.22	-0.18	-0.12	0.04	-0.01	0.21	0.03	0.28	0.17
XC	0.10	-0.03	0.12	-0.21	-0.15	0.33	0.16	0.19	0.21
NOBS	0.16	-0.05	-0.43	0.29	0.29	0.46	-0.24	0.02	0.08
FULL	-0.36	0.19	-0.35	0.11	-0.18	-0.14	0.16	0.07	-0.07
SUBOPT	0.18	0.39	-0.32	0.03	0.38	-0.26	-0.08	0.20	-0.05
UNION	0.06	-0.32	0.12	-0.04	0.38	0.14	-0.03	-0.07	-0.13
RPSIZE	0.01	0.04	-0.16	0.21	0.15	-0.20	-0.03	0.02	-0.08
SDML	0.08	-0.20	-0.23	-0.12	-0.20	-0.05	-0.08	-0.14	0.28
SDHERF	0.11	0.08	-0.12	-0.01	0.17	0.17	0.54	-0.37	0.02
SDSPEC	-0.01	0.03	0.19	0.14	-0.13	0.06	-0.52	0.38	-0.02

Each of the significant components is heavily weighted on one of the variables that was previously found to be important, but there are other variables that come into play. The addition of these variables considerably enriches the interpretation of the process at work. The first component has a positive, though insignificant, effect on efficiency. It is the plant scale portion of concentration—weighting both the four-firm concentration ratio (CONC) and the relative plant size (RPSIZE) positively. The second component has a negative effect on efficiency that is significant. It represents the multiplant nature of the industry with XC, MULT1, and MULT2 heavily weighted.[3] Relative plant size (RPSIZE) is negatively weighted, and the regional variable is positively weighted in this component. Thus inefficiency here is associated with multiplant ownership where plants are small relative to the market and where production is dispersed regionally.

The third component has a positive effect on efficiency; it positively weights both comparative advantage (COMP) and export intensity (XS) but negatively weights advertising intensity. This component can be interpreted as representing the resource-based industries that export a significant proportion of their production and that do little advertising. The fourth component has a negative effect on efficiency: import intensity (MS), advertising (ADS), and number of products (N5D) are included in this component with positive weights. In addition suboptimal capacity (SUBOPT) has a positive weight. This component represents import-competing industries with a large number of products that are intensively advertised. The signs and significance of the coefficients of both components indicate that trade matters—a conclusion that the earlier partial analysis missed. Export industries are relatively efficient; import-competing industries are less efficient.

The fifth component has a negative effect on efficiency: It combines a negative weight on export intensity and a positive weight on both the use of full-time employees and multiplant activity. Here as elsewhere, it is a combination of factors that contributes to inefficiency.

Both the ninth and tenth components represent regional industries but have opposite effects on efficiency. In both the effect of advertising intensity and the use of full-time workers is to decrease productivity. The ninth component, which has a negative effect on efficiency, represents regional industries with intensive advertising, suboptimal capacity, high unionization, and few part-time workers. The tenth component represents regional industries with little advertising and more part-time workers. The difference between the two components lies primarily in the existence of suboptimal capacity in the component that has a negative effect on efficiency.

The use of principal components of industry characteristics confirms and extends the picture drawn by the simple correlation analysis and regression analysis. Advertising is deleterious not so much as an unconditional force giving rise to differential rents but in conjunction with other factors that set the context for advertising—high import intensity, suboptimal capacity, and a large number of products. Export and import intensity both matter. Labor conditions also affect efficiency but primarily in regional industries.

7.5 Turnover and Industry Efficiency

Most empirical studies of industries' efficiency have used single-period cross-sectional regressions as was done in section 7.4 and have not provided size-weighted measures. This methodology can miss the manner in which efficiency changes and the extent of the change. Changes in relative efficiency levels are important as the evidence on the correlation between the estimates for 1970 and 1979 presented in table 7.1 indicated. This section briefly outlines the forces that cause them. The next section investigates the determinants of the strength of these forces and relates them to the same industry characteristics that were found to be important in the cross-sectional analysis.

7.5.1 The Nature of Turnover and Its Relationship to Productivity Growth

Changes in efficiency will occur as the productivity levels of individual establishments and their market shares change. With market shares held constant, changes in the level of industry efficiency will be a function of the extent to which productivity growth is spread evenly across establishments. The value of the efficiency measure does not change if productivity gains are spread equally across all establishments. Efficiency can increase if those firms that are less productive make greater productivity gains over the period. Efficiency will decrease if the most productive plants make the greatest productivity gains.

When productivity changes are not spread equally across establishments, changes in the efficiency measure depend on the initial positions of the gainers and their associated share changes. If firms already at the frontier make the greatest productivity gains, then skewness in the distribution of productivity becomes greater. Since our efficiency measure involves both skewness and relative shares of units at the frontier, it will decrease unless the productivity gainers also increase market share. The productivity gain and the market share gain in these firms have opposite effects on the measure of industry efficiency. The larger the gain in market share, the greater the likelihood of gains in efficiency.

The nature of the relationship between turnover and relative productivity performance therefore is of crucial importance. Turnover in the Canadian manufacturing sector for the period 1970–79 has been detailed elsewhere by Baldwin and Gorecki (1989, 1991) using a longitudinal panel that links plants to firms and tracks both over time. Market-share gains and losses, based on comparisons of 1970 and 1979 plant shipments, were calculated for the categories that are listed in table 7.4. More than one category was used because of the heterogeneity of the underlying plant population and the belief that there were differences—both in size and productivity—in the various categories.

Turnover, as measured by market-share changes within four-digit industries between 1970 and 1979, was substantial. In 1970 plants that were to close by 1979 accounted for 22.7 percent of industry shipments on average. The largest component of plant closedowns (18.1 percent of 1970 ship-

Table 7.4
Categories of plants for which changes in combined market shares between 1970 and 1979 are calculated

A Plants that gained market share over the period 1970–79	
SHARE23	1979 share of plants that were opened since 1970 by new firms (greenfield entry)
SHARE13	1979 share of plants newly constructed since 1970 by firms that continued in the industry between 1970 and 1979 (other births)
SHAREU	Share gain between 1970 and 1979 of continuing plants—those in existence in 1970 and 1979—that gained market share over the decade (the gainers)
B Plants that lost market share over the period 1970–79	
SHARE34	1970 share of plants closed by 1979 that were owned by firms exiting the industry (closedown exit)
SHARE14	1970 share of plants closed by 1979 that were owned by firms that continued in the industry throughout the period (other exits)
SHARED	Share loss between 1970 and 1979 of continuing plants that lost market share over the period (the losers)

ments) was the category of plants owned by firms that were to exit the industry. Some 4.6 percent of 1970 shipments were in plants that were to be closed by 1979 by firms that would continue production in some other facility in the same industry. The third category where market share was lost—losers that continued over the decade—saw their market share decline by some 14 percent.

Gains in market share are spread across three categories. First, greenfield entrants accounted for some 16.1 percent of market share in 1979. Second, new plants of continuing firms account for 5.2 percent. The division of plant openings between new and continuing firms is similar to that for plant closedowns between exiting and continuing firms. Finally, gaining continuing plants acquired some 15.8 percent of share over the period.

All of this indicates that a considerable proportion of market share was transferred over the decade of the 1970s as a result of plant entry and exit, growth, and expansion. In total, some 37 percent of market share was lost due to plant closedown and decline.

Market-share turnover among continuing plants was accompanied by substantial changes in relative productivity, defined in terms of output per worker (see Baldwin and Gorecki 1990b). In 1970 the mean ratio of the productivity of plants that were subsequently to gain market share to those that were subsequently to lose share was 0.98, not significantly different from one. By 1979 the mean relative productivity of gainers to losers was 1.34 (standard error of mean = 0.09). Gains in market share and changes in relative productivity then went hand in hand in such a way that the transfer of market share among continuing firms contributed substantially to productivity growth.

A similar conclusion holds true for entrants and exits. Figure 7.3 depicts the productivity of exiting plants relative to continuing plants as of 1970, and of entrants relative to continuing plants in 1979. Plants that enter and exit are divided into those belonging to continuing firms and to entering/exiting firms. Closedown exits are approximately 79 percent as productive as all continuing plants in 1970. Greenfield entrants are about 4 percent more productive than all continuing plants in 1979. The closed plants of continuing firms are 96 percent as productive as the continuing population in 1970, but new plants of continuing firms are 16 percent more productive in 1979 (see Baldwin and Gorecki 1990b, table 3).

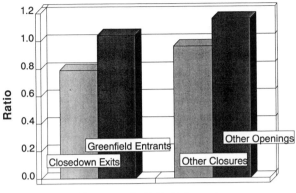

Entry and Exit Categories

Figure 7.3
Productivity of plant openings and plant closings relative to continuing plants

7.5.2 Turnover and Changes in Efficiency

The pattern of market-share turnover was also associated with changes in efficiency. The efficiency of each of the turnover categories is reported in table 7.5.[4] Plants closed by exiting firms were less efficient than plants started by new firms. Plants closed by continuing firms were less efficient than new plants opened by continuing firms. In 1970 the continuing plants that were to gain market share differed very little in terms of efficiency from either those about to lose market share over the subsequent decade or the industry average. But this situation had changed dramatically by 1979. Market-share losers had become much less efficient than plants that had gained market share. This pattern accords with the previous finding (Baldwin and Gorecki 1990b) that continuing plants' changes in productivity and market share were positively correlated.

The contribution to the change in efficiency made by each of the new-plant categories and of the continuing plants that gained market share will depend upon the pattern of replacement. Each percentage point of market share gained by one of the categories of panel A in table 7.4 comes at the expense of one or other category of losers of panel B. The contribution made to efficiency change by each of the gainers will depend upon how much share is given up by each category displaced and the difference in efficiency between the two classes.

Table 7.5
Efficiency of each component of plant turnover expressed as a percentage of potential efficiency

1970			1979
Plant category	Relative efficiency	Relative efficiency	Plant category
Closedown exits	57.6 (1.6)	62.0 (1.5)	Greenfield births
Other exits	65.6 (2.2)	71.2 (2.9)	Other births
Plants gaining share, 1970–79	66.7 (0.9)	67.7 (0.9)	Plants gaining share, 1970–79
Plants losing share, 1970–79	69.0 (0.9)	56.7 (1.2)	Plants losing share, 1970–79
Mean	66.3	62.8	Mean

Source: Special tabulations, Business and Labour Market Analysis Group, Statistics Canada.
Note: These estimates make use of the efficiency estimate used to derive EFF40 and EFF49. The standard errors of the means are in parentheses.

The replacement pattern was estimated by calculating the components of gain and loss for all manufacturing industries and then by regressing each of the market share changes in the gaining categories on the market share losses in the three loss categories across the 167 industry sample. The resulting coefficients estimate the extent to which market share gain is derived from the different loss categories (see Baldwin and Gorecki 1990c for a discussion of this procedure). Figure 7.4 shows the percentage of each of the gainers that come from each of the losers. Greenfield entrants primarily replaced closedown exits but took about one-third of their gains from declining plants. Continuing plants that gained market share took most of their gain from closedown exits. New plants of continuing firms obtained most of their market share from declining plants and the remainder from plants that they themselves closed.

The turnover process clearly contributes to changes in efficiency. Greenfield entrants were more efficient than both categories that they replaced—closedown exits and declining plants. In 1979 they were approximately 5 percentage points more efficient than closedown exits were in 1970; they were also about 5 percentage points more efficient in 1979 than the remaining incumbent plants that had lost market share since 1970. The same pattern holds for the replacement process accompanied by the opening of

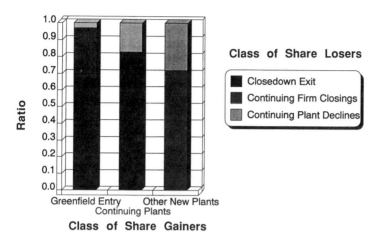

Figure 7.4
Percentage of share gains from each class of losers

new plants by continuing firms—which replaced closed plant in 1970 (about 5 percentage points less efficient) and continuing plants (in 1979, about 15 percentage points less efficient). Finally, the turnover associated with the replacement of declining continuing plant by those continuing plants that gained market share would also have increased efficiency.

Despite the replacement of the less efficient with the more efficient, the mean level of efficiency fell over the period. Continuing plants gaining share retained about the same level of efficiency, while those losing share declined substantially. Among other things, it was the failure of the gainers to make greater efficiency gains as a group and to take away even more market share from the losers that was one force contributing to the decline in average efficiency levels.

Nevertheless, the fundamental conclusion is that the turnover of market share associated with the competitive process contributed substantially to efficiency gains. Without this turnover there would have been even greater declines in efficiency. With certain information an estimate of the joint impact of all the turnover categories on efficiency can be made. Market share is transferred as a result of turnover and the effect of this transfer on our size-weighted measures was calculated. The first requirement for this estimate is knowledge of the replacement pattern. This was provided above. The second requirement is an assumption about the level of efficiency as of 1979 that would have existed for plants in the two exit categories, SHARE34 and SHARE14 in table 7.4, had they not been replaced. It will be assumed that the efficiency of each category of plant exit would have been the same in 1979 as it was in 1970 relative to continuing plants that lost market share over the decade. This is a conservative assumption because exiting plants fared even worse than declining plants over the decade. The latter just lost market share; the former had to close down.

Then the contribution that one of the entry or growth categories i made to efficiency by displacing category j ($DEFF_{ij}$) is calculated by

$$DEFF_{ij} = SHARE_i \cdot P_{ij} \cdot (EFF_i - EFF_j)$$

where

$SHARE_i$ = the increase in market share of the ith entry or growth category,

P_{ij} = the proportion of the ith entry or growth category to come from the jth exit or decline category,

EFF_i, EFF_j = the efficiency of the ith entry or growth category or the jth exit or decline category in 1979.

The total effect of each entry or growth category is the sum of its effects across all exit and decline categories of panel B in table 7.4. The effect of all entry categories is then the sum of the effects of the categories of panel A. The importance of each of these categories is expressed as a proportion of the total and reported in Table 7.6. Without turnover, efficiency levels would have been 58.7 percent rather than 62.8 percent. Greenfield entry

Table 7.6

Contribution of turnover to efficiency	Percent
Mean industry efficiency level, 1979	62.8
Mean industry level without turnover, 1979	58.7
Contribution of turnover category to difference	
Greenfield births	34
Other births	15
Continuing plants gaining	51

Source: Special tabulations, Business and Labour Market Analysis Group, Statistics Canada.

contributed almost 34 percent of this; other plant births some 15 percent and gains in market shares in continuing plants contributed 51 percent.[5]

7.6 The Determinants of Turnover

Efficiency then is affected, among other things, by plant turnover—replacement by the efficient of the inefficient. Ultimately the determinants of that process should affect the level of industry efficiency. If more efficient entrants displace less efficient exits, industry efficiency will increase.

The relationship between the intensity of turnover and the level of efficiency is complex because opposing forces are at work. The rate of technical progress and the dispersion of capacities to adopt new processes will determine the rate at which late adopters of new technology fall behind. The rate of turnover will then determine the extent to which the latter are eliminated and efficiency is maintained in equilibrium. In a world where efficiency does not vary, the two forces will be in balance. But equilibrium does not always prevail. Exogenous shocks may come in coordinated waves that cause efficiency levels across a wide variety of industries to change. In turn, turnover may intensify while efficiency is being restored to its previous levels. The intensity of turnover in the latter case affects the speed of adjustment to exogenous shocks.

This tendency was at work in Canada during the decade of the 1970s. Caves and Barton postulated that growth in productivity would produce a disequilibrating force yielding lower levels of efficiency. There is support for this proposition in the experience of Canada. Between 1970 and 1979, the change in efficiency across four-digit industries was negatively correlated with growth in real output per worker (−0.25, significant at the 90 percent level). This suggests that some changes in efficiency are brought about by the external shocks that lead to growth spurts. Just as revealing is the fact that the change in industry efficiency and the change brought about by market-share turnover reported in table 7.6 were negatively and significantly correlated (−0.24: significant at the 99 percent level). Similarly the share of greenfield entrants was significantly negatively correlated with the change in efficiency. Thus, where efficiency was falling, turnover was larger than elsewhere and productivity gains were higher. Turnover would appear to be part of an equilibrating process associated with rapid technological change.

Because the intensity of the turnover process affects both the level of efficiency and its adjustment path, it follows that the determinants of turnover may be expected to affect both and that these determinants may differ somewhat from the determinants of industry efficiency at a point in time.

7.6.1 Modeling the Turnover Process

Several problems must be resolved in modeling the determinants of the turnover process. First, the process has more than one component: three on the expansion and three on the contraction side, respectively. The resulting system of equations produces a large number of coefficients that have to be evaluated in order to estimate the net effect of the various determinants of efficiency. This problem is handled here by estimating an overall turnover equation—the sum of the share changes in the various entry and growth categories (GAIN). Since the turnover categories have different effects on changes in efficiency, weights were applied to each category. These weights reflected the contribution that a 1 percent gain in that category had on changes in efficiency. They were calculated using the same assumptions employed for the estimates reported in table 7.6.

The determinants of the turnover process are broken into three groups. The first set includes those variables that have already been hypothesized to affect industries' efficiency levels. This set includes some variables that engender change and others that tend to dampen that change. Caves and Porter (1978) stressed these two groups as the determinants of changes in the market shares of incumbent firms. It is of interest here to discover the extent to which the various forces that affect efficiency also influence the turnover process.

The second set of variables contains those traditionally used in entry and exit studies but not captured in the original set of variables used to explain efficiency.[6] These variables, with the exception of foreign ownership, can be classified as inducement variables that attract entry or reduce exit (see Baldwin and Gorecki 1986, app. A, for definitions of the variables). They are

GROW = rate of growth of real shipments between 1970 and 1979,

VAR = variability of output around the trend growth line,

PROF = rate of profitability of the industry in 1970 and 1979,

PROFG = rate of growth of profitability, 1970–79,

FOR = proportion of shipments accounted for by foreign-controlled establishments, 1979.

The third set of determinants consists of relative productivity variables. It has been demonstrated that the turnover process replaces the less efficient with the more efficient, the less productive with the more productive. The differences in productivity between the various categories are taken here to represent the technological opportunities available to new participants. These variables are taken to proxy basic technological conditions that favor one or other form of turnover. For example, the market share captured by entrants is postulated to be a function of the productivity advantage that entrants possess over units that exit and over their prospective competitors: continuing plants that are growing and new plants of continuing firms.

Several measures are required to represent the various factors at work. The first captures the extent to which the 1979 productivity of continuing plants that gained market share was higher than those losing market share:

RLUD = productivity of continuing plants in 1979 that gained market share between 1970 and 1979 divided by the productivity in 1979 of continuing plants that lost market share over the decade.

Another set of variables compare the 1979 productivity of the two entrant categories to the continuing plant of gainers and losers:

RLGU = productivity in 1979 of greenfield entrants relative to continuing plants that gained market share,

RLGD = productivity in 1979 of greenfield entrants relative to continuing plants that lost market share,

RLNU = productivity in 1979 of new plants of continuing firms relative to continuing plants that gained market share,

RLND = productivity in 1979 of new plants of continuing firms relative to continuing plants that lost market share.

The next three measures provide similar comparisons for 1970 of the gainers and the two plant-closing categories to the continuing plants that lost market share over the decade. These are

RLUD = productivity in 1970 of continuing plants that gained market share between 1970 and 1979 divided by the productivity in 1970 of continuing plants that lost market share over the decade,

RLCD = productivity in 1970 of closedown exits of the continuing plants that were to lose market share over the decade divided by the productivity in 1970 of continuing plants that lost market share over the decade,

RLDD = productivity in 1970 of plants closed by firms that continued over the decade divided by the 1970 productivity of the continuing plants that were to lose market share over the decade.

Finally, three variables represent the progress that resulted from the replacement of closedown exits by greenfield entrants, other exits by other births, and declining but continuing plants with gaining, continuing plants.[7]

RLUDDIF = growth in productivity of gainers relative to losers over the decade (RLUD for 1979 minus RLUD for 1970),

RLGDIF = productivity of greenfield entrants in 1979 relative to continuing plant market-share losers in 1979 minus the productivity of closedown exits in 1970 relative to market share losers in 1970,

RLODIF = productivity of other plant births in 1979 relative to continuing plant market share losers in 1979 minus the productivity of other plant deaths in 1970 relative to market-share losers in 1970.

The correlations between these various measures are presented in table 7.7. The degree of progress that is made in continuing plants (RLUDDIF) is the basic indicator of technological rivalry—of the potential for rivalrous behavior without the creation of new plant. It is more highly correlated with RLGDIF than with RLODIF. Situations in which technological conditions lead some continuing plants to outstrip others are also situations where new plants of entrants are substantially more productive than the closed plants of exiting firms.

The plant replacement process for continuing firms (SHARE13 and SHARE34 in table 7.4) is enhanced in situations where new technology may not be as adaptable to old plant. Productivity growth associated with the replacement process in continuing firms (RLODIF) is not as closely correlated with productivity differences that arise in continuing plants (RLUD) as it is with gains associated with the greenfield entry and close-

Table 7.7
Correlations between measures of differential productivity growth and productivity growth

	RLGU	RLGD	RLNU	RLND	RLUD	RLCD	RLDD	RLUDDIF	RLGDIF	RLODIF
RLGU	1.0	0.37	0.28	0.37	−0.14	−0.01	−0.05	−0.10	0.81	0.34
		a	a	a	(0.07)	(0.96)	(0.59)	(0.19)	a	a
RLGD		1.0	0.12	0.35	0.85	0.05	−0.04	0.85	0.95	0.44
			(0.20)	a	a	(0.55)	(0.62)	a	a	a
RLNU			1.0	0.82	−0.22	0.12	0.14	−0.18	0.05	0.70
				a	(0.01)	(0.19)	(0.16)	(0.05)	(0.55)	a
RLND				1.0	0.33	0.09	0.10	0.29	0.27	0.85
					a	(0.30)	(0.28)	a	a	a
RLUD					1.0	0.02	−0.05	0.98	0.81	0.33
						(0.77)	(0.51)	a	a	a
RLCD						1.0	0.18	−0.05	−0.27	−0.05
							(0.05)	(0.51)	a	a
RLDD							1.0	−0.05	−0.09	−0.43
								(0.60)	(0.30)	a
RLUDDIF								1.0	0.84	0.38
									a	a
RLGDIF									1.0	0.84
										a

Source: Special tabulations, Business and Labour Market Analysis Group, Statistics Canada.
Note: The probability value is listed below each correlation estimate. The letter a represents a value of 0.001 or less.

down process (RLGDIF). This difference indicates that the latter also partially reflects the need for new technology to be embedded in new plant. Thus large differences in productivity between greenfield entrants and closedown exits occurs both when technological rivalry is manifesting itself in the continuing plant population and when technological improvements are associated with the construction of new plants. Entry is a multifaceted phenomenon.

Other indications exist that similar but not identical technical opportunities are at work across industries. A positive correlation between the productivity of greenfield entrants relative to losers (RLGD) and the disparity that develops in the continuing sector (RLUD) can be seen, as well as a negative relationship between the productivity of greenfield entrants relative to the gainers (RLGU) and RLUD. Thus, when productivity differentials are developing within the continuing sector, entrants do relatively well compared to those being displaced, but poorly, relative to the gainers. When new technology can be embodied very successfully in existing plant, entrants are not excluded from doing well, but they do not do quite as well as continuing plants that are gaining market share.

To distinguish the ways in which the various technological characteristics are combined within industries, the principal components of the relative productivity variables were derived and are reported in table 7.8. The first component positively weights most of the variables. The second component represents situations where both RLGU and RLNU are high but RLUD is low. It denotes industries where new plants for both entrants and continuing firms do relatively well compared to the continuing plants that

Table 7.8
Principal component analysis of productivity variables

| | Eigenvectors | | | | | | |
	PROD1	PROD2	PROD3	PROD4	PROD5	PROD6	PROD7
RLGU	0.39	0.40	0.51	−0.24	−0.18	0.44	0.39
RLNU	0.36	0.46	−0.51	0.18	−0.15	0.34	−0.48
RLCD	−0.04	0.48	0.31	0.25	0.74	−0.19	−0.16
RLDD	−0.26	0.30	0.07	0.70	−0.47	−0.19	0.29
RLGDIF	0.53	−0.17	0.42	0.09	−0.28	−0.49	−0.44
RLODIF	0.56	−0.00	−0.42	0.07	0.22	−0.37	0.57
RLUD79	0.24	−0.53	0.13	0.58	0.23	0.50	0.03

Source: Special tabulations, Business and Labour Market Analysis Group, Statistics Canada.

are gaining share, but where productivity differentials do not develop within the continuing sector. The third component resembles the second, except in that greenfield entrants alone do well. RLGU and RLGDIF both have positive weights, but RLNU and RLODIF have negative weights. This component represents situations in which technological advantage is related to new plant construction by new firms, but is not as readily available to other plants, perhaps because patents matter more.

The fourth component represents situations conducive to the adaptation of new technology within existing plants, reflected in the productivity differential between continuing plants (RLUD). The fifth component designates situations in which the relative productivity of closedown exits is high (RLCD). This suggests causes of exits other than the productivity disadvantages measured here.

The sixth component positively weights internal productivity differences (RLUD) and the relative success of new plants (RLGU, RLNU). It differs from the first component in that negative weights are attached to the growth in relative productivity of each of the corresponding plant exit and entry categories (RLGDIF, RLODIF), but a positive weight is given to the development of emerging productivity differences in the continuing plant sector (RLUD). This component indicates situations in which dramatic change is occurring in relative productivity within the continuing plant population and new plant of both kinds does relatively well, but exiting plants are not particularly inefficient at the beginning of the period. In such industries turnover should be more closely related to rapid technical change over the period than to the elimination of laggards in efficiency at the beginning of the period. This represents technological rivalry that is felt in both the continuing and the new sector.

The seventh component, like the third, positively weights greenfield entrants' success (RLGU), negatively weights continuing firms' new plant success (RLNU), and disregards productivity differentials that develop in the continuing sector (RLUD). The primary difference between the seventh and the third component is that RLODIF is negatively weighted in the third component, while RLGDIF is negatively weighted in the seventh component. The seventh component represents situations in which greenfield entrants are doing well relative to continuing plants that are gaining share and continuing firms are making productivity gains with investment in new plant (RLODIF) but are still disadvantaged relative to entrants (RLNU).

Most studies of entry and exit or turnover in the continuing firm population have ignored the exogenous influence of changing technology and
its influence on the turnover process. To characterize the process at work,
the correlations were calculated between the total unweighted share gain
(GAIN), the proportion of this total accounted for by each of the components outlined in table 7.4 (GAIN23, GAIN13, GAINU, LOSS34,
LOSS14, and LOSSD) and the relative productivity components. Overall,
market-share change (GAIN) is most closely associated with components
two and three. These components represent situations in which no substantial differences in productivity in the continuing plant population
emerge and new plant does well relative to continuing plant. The proportion of market-share gains taken by greenfield entrants (GAIN23) is
primarily related to component six. The proportion taken by gaining
continuing plants (GAINU) is negatively correlated with this same
component. The proportion taken by new plants of continuing firms
(GAIN13) is positively related to the catchall first component but negatively related to the second.

7.6.2 The Total Turnover Equation

Because the industry characteristics available in the three sets of determinants are numerous, the principal components of each set were derived and
used in the subsequent regression analysis. The components of the main
set of industry characteristics (VAR1 to VAR18) were presented previously
in table 7.3, and the productivity components (PROD1 to PROD7) were
presented in table 7.8. The principal components of the inducement variables (WEL1 to WEL5) are presented in table 7.9.

Table 7.9
Principal component analysis of inducement variables

| | Eigenvectors | | | | |
	WEL1	WEL2	WEL3	WEL4	WEL5
GROW	0.70	−0.14	−0.15	−0.08	−0.68
VAR	0.04	0.62	0.53	0.52	−0.25
PROFG	0.18	−0.67	0.23	0.65	0.19
FOR	0.42	0.37	−0.60	0.35	0.44
PROF	0.55	0.06	0.53	−0.41	0.49

Source: Special tabulations, Business and Labour Market Analysis Group, Statistics Canada.

The results of the regression are reported in table 7.10. To enable comparison to the determinants of efficiency, column 1 contains the signs of the components of the industry characteristics, mainly those found to be significant in equation (2). Column 2 contains the main regression results for the weighted turnover regressand (GAIN).

The inducement and the productivity components represent the disequilibrium forces that cause turnover. Four variables in these two groups affect turnover. The third inducement component, with a positive coefficient, positively weights both average profitability over the decade and variability in demand. The fifth inducement component has a negative but less significant coefficient; it negatively weights growth and positively weights profitability. The third and sixth productivity components positively affect turnover. Both of these components represent situations in which new plants are relatively productive compared to the continuing sector. The sixth was described as the general technological rivalry variable.

Five components from the industry characteristics components affect turnover. Concentration associated with larger plant size (component 1) has a negative effect on turnover. Multiplant activity associated with low export intensity but a wide variability in plant diversification across different products (component 5) has a negative effect. Union activity associated with the lack of part-time workers, inward bound diversification and plant suboptimality (component 6) positively affects turnover.

The only component entering with the same sign into both the turnover equation (column 2) and the efficiency equation is component 5. However, this formulation does not allow for interaction effects. It may be that the effect of the industry characteristic was to reduce the impact of the technological conditions represented by the productivity variables. This possibility was examined by entering interaction effects between the relative productivity components 3 and 6 and the components that had a negative effect on efficiency—2, 4, 5, 9, and 18. Individual terms entered on their own showed significance, but because of multicollinearity this was not the case when several were entered simultaneously. In the end, components 2, 4, and 5 were summed and used interactively with the third productivity component to form the variable INTER. The results with INTER added are reported in column 4. In this formulation the productivity component itself loses some of its significance, but the interaction term is significant and becomes even more so if the productivity component is removed—

Table 7.10
Determinants of plant turnover

Exogenous variable (1)	Effect on efficiency (2)	Equations explaining turnover		
		Coefficient (3)	Coefficient (4)	Coefficient (5)
Wel3		0.025 (2.0)[a] (0.048)	0.027 (0.075)	0.023 (0.066)
Wel5		−0.018 (1.7)[a] (0.097)	−0.25 (0.038)	−0.021 (0.071)
Var1	+	−0.025 (2.1)[a] (0.038)	−0.31 (0.011)	−0.034 (0.006)
Var2	−			
Var3	+			
Var4	−			
Var5	−	−0.020 (1.8)[a] (0.078)	−0.021 (0.053)	−0.023 (0.040)
Var6	+	0.046 (4.0)[a] (0.0001)	0.048 (0.0001)	0.050 (0.0001)
Var9	−			
Var10	+			
Var11				
Var16	−	−0.021 (1.8)[a] (0.063)	−0.016 (0.156)	−0.020 (0.078)
Var18	−	0.024 (2.0)[a] (0.051)	0.019 (0.110)	0.019 (0.109)
Prod3		0.021 (1.9)[a] (0.055)	0.017 (0.098)	
Prod6		0.021 (2.0)[a] (0.047)	0.022 (0.041)	0.022 (0.033)
Inter			−0.011 (0.032)	−0.012 (0.018)
R^2		0.41	0.435	0.42
Prob > F		0.001	0.0001	0.0001

Source: Special tabulations, Business and Labour Market Analysis Group, Statistics Canada.
Note: The interpretation of the principal components can be read from tables 7.3, 7.8, and 7.9. Probability measures and t-statistics are in parentheses.
a. t-statistics.

column 5. The important conclusion is that the multiplant component 2, the import-advertising, suboptimal-capacity component 4 along with component 5 serve to reduce the effect of productivity on turnover. These are the same characteristics found in industries with lower levels of efficiency.

7.7 Conclusion

Analysis of the turnover process can contribute in important ways to our understanding of the nature of the competitive process. First, it can be used to provide a measure of the intensity of the competitive process. The extent to which market shares are changing provides an alternate and more direct measure of the intensity of the competitive process than do concentration measures. Second, an examination of the links between turnover and productivity change serves to emphasize the connection between productivity progress and the extent to which the new supplant the old.

This chapter adds another dimension to our understanding of the turnover process. It has shown that turnover directly contributes to improvements in industry efficiency and that it is affected by many of the same sets of variables that influence the level of industry efficiency. To this extent our study provides a bridge between two different sets of studies.

Until now, the literature on efficiency has relied mainly on cross-sectional studies at one point in time. It was therefore difficult to ascertain whether the variables that were found to be related to efficiency were chance correlates. One method of contributing to this debate is to attempt to replicate the results for similar economies. This was done in the first section of this chapter where it was demonstrated that efficiency in Canadian and U.S. manufacturing industries in the 1970s was related to many of the same industry characteristics.

Even more important is the link between turnover and efficiency that is provided. If the causes of efficiency are to better understood, the forces that cause some firms to move ahead and others to fall behind need examination. When technical change instigates this process, efficiency falls if the less efficient are not eliminated. This chapter has documented how important this turnover process is in reducing inefficiencies that develop. More important, it has demonstrated that the same forces that lead some industries at a point in time to be less efficient are contained in the set of forces that reduce the amount of turnover. That they can also be found to restrain the turnover process that has been demonstrated to reduce the level of inefficiency lends credence to the cross-sectional results.

Appendix: Exogenous Variables Used in the Analysis

Competitive Conditions

CONC   Percentage of shipments accounted for by the four largest firms, 1970.

XC   The excess concentration ratio defined as CONC minus the share that the largest four firms would have if they each operated one plant equal to MES. MES is defined as the average plant size of those largest plants accounting for the top 50 percent of shipments.

MS   Import intensity: imports divided by domestic disappearance (domestic production minus exports plus imports), 1970.

XS   Export intensity: exports divided by domestic production, 1970.

COMP   Comparative advantage: exports less imports divided by exports plus imports, 1970.

Product Differentiation

ADS   Inputs of advertising services divided by value of industry shipments, 1971.

Occurrence of Heterogeneity and Change

R&D   Ratio of research and development personnel to all wage and salary earners, 1975.

SD(M/L)   Standard deviation of the ratio of materials and energy expenses to the number of wage and salary workers, 1970.

N5D   Number of five-digit ICC (industrial commodity classification) commodities per four-digit SIC industry.

SD(HERF)   Standard deviation of the plant level of product specialization. The latter is defined using a Herfindahl index of the proportion of the plant's shipments classified to the Nth four-digit ICC commodity, 1970.

SD(SIZE)   Standard deviation of average plant size based on salaried and production workers, 1970.

SD(SPEC)   Standard deviation of the plant specialization ratio (proportion of plant's output classified to same industry as the plant).

CVTOP8   Coefficient of variation of shipments by the top eight firms, 1970.

SUBOPT   Percentage of industry sales made by plants smaller than the average U.S. plant size of those plants accounting for the top 50 percent of sales, 1970.

KL   Capital–labor ratio for the industry, 1970.

Geographic Market Heterogeneity

REG   Dummy variable for an industry classified as being regional.

Organizational Influences

Enterprise Diversification
COVE   Sales of plants belonging to enterprises classified to other industries divided by sales by all establishments classified to this industry, 1970.

Multiplant Operation
MULT1   Sales by plants belonging to companies that are multiplant operators in this industry divided by sales of all establishments classified to the industry, 1970.

MULT2   Number of plants per enterprise, 1970.

Size of Production Units
RPSIZE   Average plant size of the largest plants that account for the top 50 percent of shipments divided by industry shipments, 1970.

RFSIZE   Average firm size of the largest firms that account for the top 50 percent of shipments divided by industry shipments, 1970.

Labor Relations

UNION   Proportion of production workers who were union members, 1971.

FULL   Importance of full-time workers as measured by the number of person-hours worked by production workers divided by the number of production workers, 1970.

Other

NOBS   Number of plants on which the efficiency measure was based, 1970.

Notes

1. The similarities between the measures extended beyond the mean values reported here. Cross-industry correlations of the various measures were very high. Correlations of the measures with industry characteristics were similar.

2. The correlations were estimated both for the entire sample for which observations were available and for a reduced sample that eliminated those industries that provided extreme values of the efficiency measure. Generally, the sign and the significance levels were very similar, suggesting that errors in observation may exist but that they are relatively unimportant. The correlations for all available four-digit industries are reported in table 7.2.

3. VAR18 reiterates the conclusion about the effect of MULT1.

4. These efficiency levels use the potential output-per-person ratios derived from the value-added 40 percent cutoff levels for the entire industry plant distribution.

5. The contribution that each turnover category made to productivity growth can be usefully compared to these estimates. The detailed calculations are described in Baldwin and Gorecki (1990c). Almost half of productivity growth in the 1970s arose from turnover. Some 21 percent came from the greenfield entry category, some 7 percent from other new plants, and about 19 percent from gains in market share of continuing plants.

6. See Geroski and Masson (1987) for a general discussion of such models and Baldwin and Gorecki (1987) for a specific application to the Canadian situation along with more detailed definitions of the variables used here.

7. While these replacement assumptions distort reality slightly, using them makes the description of the ongoing replacement process much simpler.

References

Baldwin, J. R., and P. K. Gorecki. 1986. *The Role of Scale in Canada–U.S. Productivity Differences in the Manufacturing Sector, 1970–1979*. Toronto: University of Toronto Press.

Baldwin, J. R., and P. K. Gorecki. 1987. Plant creation versus plant acquisition. *International Journal of Industrial Organization* 5: 25–41.

Baldwin, J. R., and P. K. Gorecki. 1989a. Measuring the dynamics of market structure. *Annales d'Economie et de Statistique* 15/16: 316–332.

Baldwin, J. R., and P. K. Gorecki. 1990b. Productivity growth and the competitive process: The role of firm and plant turnover. Research Paper #23e. Analytic Studies Branch. Statistics Canada. Forthcoming in P. Geroski and J. Schwalbach, eds., *Entry and Market Contestability: An International Comparison.* Oxford: Basil Blackwell, 1991.

Baldwin, J. R., and P. K. Gorecki. 1990c. Measuring entry and exit to the Canadian manufacturing sector: Methodology. In A. C. Singh and P. Whitridge, eds., *Analysis of Data in Time.* Proceedings of a Conference sponsored by Statistics Canada, Carleton and Ottawa Universities. Ottawa: Statistics Canada.

Baldwin, J. R., and P. K. Gorecki. 1991. Firm entry and exit in the Canadian manufacturing sector, 1970–1982. *Canadian Journal of Economics* 24: 300–323.

Caves, R. E., and D. R. Barton. 1990. *Technical Efficiency in U.S. Manufacturing Industries.* Cambridge: MIT Press.

Caves, R. E., and M. E. Porter. 1978. Market structure, oligopoly, and stability of market shares. *Journal of Industrial Economics* 26: 289–313.

Downie, J. 1958. *The Competitive Process.* London: Duckworth.

Geroski, P. A., and R. T. Masson. 1987. Dynamic market models in industrial organization. *International Journal of Industrial Organization* 5: 1–13.

Leibenstein, H. 1966. Allocative efficiency vs. "X-efficiency." *American Economic Review* 56: 392–415.

Reid, G. 1987. *Theories of Industrial Organization.* Oxford: Basil Blackwell.

Stigler, G. J. 1976. The Xistence of X-inefficiency. *American Economic Review* 66: 213–216.

Timmer. C. P. 1971. Using a probabilistic frontier production function to measure technical efficiency. *Journal of Political Economy* 79: 775–795.

II EXTENSIONS IN TIME AND SPACE

8 Technical Efficiency over Time in Korea, 1978–88: Exploratory Analyses

Seong Min Yoo

8.1 Introduction

Most empirical studies of technical efficiency in the production activities of plants or firms have employed data for a single year; none have attempted to gather evidence on the behavior of technical efficiency estimates over time. Furthermore, the empirical evidence in diverse studies varies by country and by the chosen points in time. As a result we are not yet fully persuaded of the validity and robustness of existing measures of technical efficiency. This uncertainty extends to other important questions as well, such as whether the existing econometric models are reasonably designed for estimating technical efficiency and whether the methods of estimating technical efficiency and the underlying assumptions are appropriate.

In this chapter we attempt to add new evidence on technical efficiency by looking into the changes in technical efficiency in Korea's manufacturing industries over time; thus we will complement the findings in chapter 3. The questions to be addressed are straightforward. How stable is technical efficiency over time among and within industries? If substantial trends exist for some industries, what accounts for them?[1] A study on the interannual stability of technical efficiency not only holds great interest in itself but also provides important evidence on whether the conventional measures of technical efficiency yield reliable estimates.

We first deal with a specification of the production function that is consistent for different years so as to enable an intertemporal comparison of technical efficiency. We then use the estimation process of chapter 3 applying it to data for different years. Thus the discussion in chapter 3 will be a reference point throughout this chapter. The efficiency estimates obtained will be analyzed to expose the time patterns across industries as well as within industries. We hope that the discussion and analysis in this chapter will provoke studies of the intertemporal behavior of technical efficiency in other countries as well.

8.2 Considerations Governing Initial Choices

To make our efficiency measures comparable between years, we review the available data on output and input variables. Then we choose a particular specification of the production function to be estimated. We set aside alternative econometric models and estimation methods and simply esti-mate the stochastic frontier production function by the corrected ordinary least squares method as in chapter 3.

8.2.1 Data Availability and Functional Specification

The data set used for the present analysis comes from the Census of Manufactures for 1978, 1983, and 1988 and from the Annual Survey of Manufactures for 1978 to 1988.[2] To draw firm and unbiased conclusions about the stability of our efficiency estimates, we found it necessary to include all the years in our data set instead of selecting a few sample years.

For the first important issue of what variables to include in estimating the production function, we employ two criteria: First, we use the three alternative specifications of the production function given in subsection 3.3.1 as our reference point, and second, we minimize the number of input variables in order to maximize degrees of freedom in estimating the trans-log production function.

We note that the correlation coefficients reported in table 3.9 for equa-tion (12) exhibit a dichotomy between ATI and the other three efficiency measures. We thus start with equation (11) in chapter 3. Because the data for labor input measured in work hours (L) are not available for every year, we can only use the total number of employees (N) to measure labor inputs.[3] These considerations result in the following form of the translog production function to be estimated from annual data.[4]

$$\ln\left(\frac{GO}{N}\right) = a_0 + a_1 \ln\left(\frac{K}{N}\right) + a_2 \ln(N) + a_3 \ln\left(\frac{M}{N}\right) + a_4\left[\ln\left(\frac{K}{N}\right)\right]^2$$

$$+ a_5[\ln(N)]^2 + a_6\left[\ln\left(\frac{M}{N}\right)\right]^2 + a_7\left[\ln\left(\frac{K}{N}\right)\right][\ln(N)]$$

$$+ a_8\left[\ln\left(\frac{K}{N}\right)\right]\left[\ln\left(\frac{M}{N}\right)\right] + a_9[\ln(N)]\left[\ln\left(\frac{M}{N}\right)\right]$$

$$+ a_{10}X_1 + a_{11}X_2 + a_{12}X_3 + v - u. \tag{1}$$

8.2.2 Editing the Raw Data

The new specification of the production function allows us to apply a simplified set of editing rules to the annual data (variables were defined in chapter 3):

N < 5,

NP = 0,

S = 0,

K = 0,

GO = 0,

MC = 0,

LPPAY = 0,

(GO/N) > MEAN(GO/N) + 4.5·SD(GO/N),

(K/N) > MEAN(K/N) + 4.5·SD(K/N),

(M/N) > MEAN(M/N) + 4.5·SD(M/N).

In addition we exclude industries with less than 15 establishments in order to secure enough degrees of freedom to estimate the translog production function. Table 8.1 summarizes the number of establishments and industries retained in this editing process. The degree to which less strict criteria would result in more establishments and industries is shown in subsection 3.3.2 for 1978. In table 8.1 note that the year 1980 exhibits a significant shrinkage of the entire manufacturing sector, which is consistent with the negative growth of the economy that year.

Table 8.1
Number of establishments and industries available for analysis

| | | After exclusion due to | |
| | | | |
Year	Raw data	Editing rules	Observations < 15[a]
1978	29,864 (389)	24,471 (367)	23,657 (252)
1979	31,804 (389)	27,379 (375)	26,460 (248)
1980	30,823 (389)	19,268 (369)	18,304 (232)
1981	33,431 (392)	27,915 (382)	27,087 (266)
1982	36,799 (393)	29,933 (379)	29,071 (263)
1983	39,243 (507)	31,544 (484)	30,376 (321)
1984	41,549 (506)	33,759 (488)	32,714 (341)
1985	44,039 (506)	35,280 (488)	34,230 (341)
1986	50,063 (512)	39,554 (489)	38,516 (348)
1987	54,389 (512)	42,960 (491)	42,012 (362)
1988	59,928 (512)	47,395 (498)	46,448 (373)

Note: The first number in each entry indicates establishments, and the number in the parentheses indicates industries.
a. Refers to the number of establishments in each industry.

The sudden jump in the number of industries in 1983 is due to the revision of the KSIC (Korea Standard Industrial Classification) system in that year. This creates a serious problem because efficiency estimates must be presented under a common industrial classification system over the entire time period in order to permit a test of the intertemporal stability of technical efficiency. The alternate ways of resolving this difficulty are to reclassify the new KSIC industries for the years 1983 to 1988 under the old system or to do the converse for the earlier years. We choose the former approach because the revision commonly involved disaggregating the old-code industries into several new ones. As will be shown, the reclassification requires us to calculate a weighted average of the efficiency estimates for the years 1983 to 1988 so that a single number can be obtained to represent the efficiency of an old code industry.[5]

8.3   Exploratory Analyses of Estimation Results

In table 8.2 we summarize the numbers of failures and successes in estimating the stochastic frontier production function for each year and industry. Note that the first column in table 8.2 gives the least common denominator (LCD) of the number of industries included in our sample at least once. Thus for the years 1978 to 1982 (the old KSIC period), 285 industries appear at least once in our samples, whereas 391 industries are represented

Table 8.2
Numbers of industries yielding failures and successes in estimation of stochastic frontier production functions

Year	LCD[a]	Sample	Type I failure	Type II failure	Successes
1978	285	252	95	34	123
1979	285	248	87	53	108
1980	285	232	84	42	106
1981	285	266	111	51	104
1982	285	263	90	58	115
1983	391	321	122	49	150
1984	391	341	121	67	153
1985	391	341	114	76	151
1986	391	348	122	62	164
1987	391	362	176	64	122
1988	391	373	172	65	136

a. Least common denominator (see text).

for the years 1983 to 1988 (the new KSIC period). These counts will be referred to when we consolidate the efficiency estimates for the 11 years into a single data set.

8.3.1   Stability of Correlation between Efficiency Measures

Before we deal with the intertemporal stability of the efficiency estimates, we ascertain whether the correlation between different measures of technical efficiency is stable over time. Table 8.3 gives this information, and it can be thought of as a dynamic extension of table 3.9 (subsection 3.3.5). We find that over time the values of the correlation coefficients are quite stable in all but a few exceptional years. We also note that the correlations are high enough to make irrelevant the issue of choice among different measures of efficiency. This conclusion reflects a similar one noted in chapter 3 for the static analysis.

8.3.2   Pooling Efficiency Estimates, 1978–88

To analyze the stability of technical efficiency over time, we need to combine the efficiency estimates for each year into a single set of data. As mentioned earlier, we rearranged the efficiency estimates to coincide with a uniform system of industrial classification over these 11 years; this task

Table 8.3
Spearman correlations between measures of technical efficiency

Year	Measures of technical efficiency					
	(EFF, ATI)	(EFF, λ)	(EFF, S)	(ATI, λ)	(ATI, S)	(λ, S)
1978	−0.995	−0.789	0.871	0.767	−0.858	−1.00
1979	−0.886	−0.705	0.798	0.587	−0.679	−1.00
1980	−0.942	−0.767	0.872	0.692	−0.788	−1.00
1981	−0.953	−0.807	0.882	0.737	−0.835	−1.00
1982	−0.951	−0.768	0.879	0.752	−0.846	−1.00
1983	−0.944	−0.773	0.861	0.719	−0.815	−1.00
1984	−0.941	−0.757	0.829	0.670	0.752	−1.00
1985	−0.959	−0.759	0.829	0.681	−0.769	−1.00
1986	−0.949	−0.738	0.861	0.640	−0.811	−1.00
1987	−0.970	−0.732	0.858	0.649	−0.822	−1.00
1988	−0.980	−0.792	0.900	0.718	−0.869	−1.00

Note: In computing the coefficients, we excluded industries with type I failures. If the correlation involved λ, we also excluded industries with type II failures. Thus the number of industries included is different for each cell in the matrix.

was accomplished by converting the classifications of new industries back to the old ones. Thus we applied the following procedure to each measure of technical efficiency:

1. For 285 industries in table 8.2, we pooled the efficiency estimates for 1978–82 to construct a 285 × 5 matrix with missing observations.

2. For 391 industries in table 8.2, we pooled the efficiency estimates for 1983–88 to construct a 391 × 6 matrix with missing observations.

3. For each old KSIC code we identified the new KSIC code(s).[6]

4. We classified the 285 old KSIC industries into two groups: *problematic industry* if an industry contains at least one missing observation in the five-year period (1978–82) or if the time trend of the number of establishments for the 11 years indicates that the code-matching procedure in 3 is problematic, and *satisfactory industry* otherwise.

5. For satisfactory industries we converted the efficiency estimates for 1983–88 into values consistent with the old KSIC codes by calculating a weighted average of estimates. For the old and new industries that did not have a one-to-one relationship, we calculated the weighted average of two or more efficiency estimates. In this case we used the number of establishments as the weight because an efficiency estimate does not take into account the shipments of individual establishments; it rather represents the average level of technical efficiency of establishments in an industry.[7]

6. We omitted those industries that had at least one missing observation in 1983–88.

This procedure yielded 201 industries with efficiency estimates for the 11 years. Table 8.4 reports the summary statistics of EFF for each year.

8.3.3 Stability of Technical Efficiency across Industries

To investigate further the question of stability, we distinguished for each industry the years in which type I failures occurred from the rest of the 11 years, and then found the mean of EFF for only the years that are not type I failures.[8] We did this because, as expressed in subsection 3.4.4, the exact relationship between type I failure and technical efficiency is uncertain. We instead counted the number of type I failure years for each industry and used this count in our analysis.[9]

Table 8.4
Summary statistics of EFF

Year	Number of industries[a]	Mean	Standard deviation	Minimum	Median	Maximum
1978	123	0.731	0.114	0.463	0.743	0.959
1979	131	0.701	0.109	0.373	0.703	0.947
1980	134	0.702	0.123	0.377	0.719	0.958
1981	121	0.716	0.139	0.377	0.742	0.961
1982	138	0.727	0.117	0.434	0.735	0.963
1983	138	0.722	0.122	0.370	0.741	0.963
1984	143	0.700	0.114	0.429	0.709	0.962
1985	153	0.703	0.118	0.411	0.697	0.943
1986	146	0.699	0.126	0.385	0.713	0.939
1987	124	0.723	0.123	0.460	0.729	0.903
1988	122	0.716	0.122	0.365	0.733	0.937

a. Excludes type I failures.

Table 8.5 reports the Spearman correlation coefficients between EFF vectors of different years. Table 8.6 reports the Spearman correlations between the mean vector of EFF calculated for the years that do not involve type I failures (denoted MEAN in table 8.6), the EFF vectors of individual years, and the vector of the number of years with type I failures (denoted NFYR in table 8.6).[10]

What are the conclusions? It is surprising to find in table 8.5 that our efficiency estimates, at least those of EFF based on GO/N, reveal low rank correlations between any two consecutive years of the 11-year period. The pairs (1978, 1979) and (1980, 1981) show no correlation. But how can we use the evidence in table 8.5 on the interannual instability of technical efficiency to evaluate the robustness and validity, if any, of our efficiency estimates? Can we believe that an industry's ranking in terms of technical efficiency really changes that much year to year? Or is it that our measures of technical efficiency have serious defects?

Although we cannot give definitive answers to these questions at this stage, it is unlikely that the numbers in table 8.5 exhibit the true intertemporal behavior of technical efficiency in Korean manufacturing industries. Since our measures of technical efficiency are fundamentally based on the shape of the distribution of plants in the input–output space, we want to relate the evidence given in table 8.5 to the factors causing abrupt changes in the shapes of such distributions. The data in table 8.5 also have implications for the interindustry determinants of technical efficiency. The

Table 8.5
Spearman correlation coefficients between values of EFF for adjacent years

	1978–79	1979–80	1980–81	1981–82	1982–83	1983–84	1984–85	1985–86	1986–87	1987–88
Spearman correlation coefficients	0.066	0.292	0.050	0.296	0.235	0.333	0.298	0.343	0.347	0.281
Significance levels	0.542	0.005	0.652	0.004	0.019	0.001	0.001	0.0002	0.001	0.010
Number of industries free of type I failures	89	92	85	94	99	103	114	115	95	84

Table 8.6
Spearman correlations between mean EFF and annual EFF values

	EFF78	EFF79	EFF80	EFF81	EFF82	EFF83	EFF84	EFF85	EFF86	EFF87	EFF88	NFYR
Spearman correlation coefficients	0.4838	0.4837	0.4692	0.5441	0.5159	0.5777	0.5692	0.6519	0.6366	0.6634	0.6058	0.4235
Significance levels	0.0001	0.0001	0.0001	0.0001	0.0001	0.0001	0.0001	0.0001	0.0001	0.0001	0.0001	0.0001
Number of industries free of type I failures	123	131	134	121	138	138	143	153	146	124	122	201

observed instability of technical efficiency over time naturally leads us to question the stability over time of the cross-sectional evidence developed in subsection 3.4.

In table 8.6 are the results of another experiment where we calculated the rank correlations between the EFF vector for each year and the MEAN vector (arithmetic means of the EFFs over years without type I failures). The higher correlation coefficients in table 8.6, as compared to those of table 8.5, reveal that the average ranking of an industry's level of technical efficiency is maintained with modest stability that increased somewhat during the period under consideration. It is interesting that in table 8.6 the MEAN vector has positive, though not very high, correlation with the number of type I failure years (NFYR). Since the average ranking of technical efficiency during the period is fairly stable, this result weakly supports the hypothesis associating type I failure with the absence of inefficiency.

8.3.4   Time Trend of Technical Efficiency: Stability within Industries

The preceding analyses were based on simple correlations between time-dependent variables; they do not provide information on any time trend of technical efficiency within industries. To provide complementary evidence, we use a simple score function.[11]

$$D_{it} = \begin{cases} 1 & \text{if } S_{it} > S_{it-1}, \quad \text{for all } i = 1, 2, \ldots, 201, t = 2, 3, \ldots, 11, \\ -1 & \text{otherwise,} \end{cases}$$

where S_{it} is the value of S (skewness) for industry i at time t.

$$D_i = \frac{1}{10} \sum_{t=2}^{11} D_{it} \quad \text{for all } i.$$

Table 8.7
Grouped distribution of indicator of trends in efficiency (D_i)

Size classes of D_i	Number of industries
$-0.45--0.25$	14
$-0.25--0.05$	42
$-0.05-0.05$	81
$0.05-0.25$	52
$0.25-1.45$	12
Total	201

Table 8.7 gives a grouped distribution of D_i. Over time only a small number of industries are relatively monotonic. This is consistent with what we observed in table 8.5.

8.4 Nature of Efficiency Measures and Stability

The findings of the preceding section and the ensuing questions about the stability of our efficiency estimates can be analyzed further in at least two ways. First, as mentioned before, factors that over time change the shape of the distribution of plants in the input–output space could help explain the dynamic instability of the efficiency estimates. To permit a test, these factors must be observable yearly for each industry; the issue here is instability among, as well as within, industries over time.[12] Second, if we reflect on the method we used in estimating technical efficiency, we could gain a better understanding of why and how our efficiency estimates exhibit instability over time.

8.4.1 Behavior of Efficiency Measures over Time

This subsection takes the second approach; we examine the nature of our efficiency measures with relation to their dynamic instability. Recall that the four measures of technical (in)efficiency introduced in chapter 3 are all based on the estimation of the stochastic frontier production function by the corrected OLS method, and also that the skewness or asymmetry of the empirical distribution of regression residuals determines the level of technical efficiency, which in turn depends on $\hat{\sigma}_u$ and $\hat{\sigma}_v$.[13]

The distribution of the error term ε of the stochastic frontier production function, $\varepsilon = v - u$, always has its mode at zero, although its mean is $-\sigma_u\sqrt{2/\pi}$. In a dynamic context it is also important to note that for any year t, it is the extent of the skewness and asymmetry of the empirical distribution of regression residuals that determines the estimated level of efficiency. In other words, it does not matter for efficiency whether the deterministic kernel $\ln[f(x)]$ of the stochastic production frontier $\ln[f(x)] + v$ moves upward or downward between t and $t + 1$. What matters for estimated efficiency are changes over time in the shape of the empirical distribution.

Figure 8.1 illustrates the argument that the estimates of technical efficiency at different points of time are not affected by movements of the

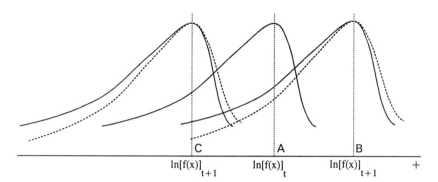

Figure 8.1
Estimates of technical efficiency versus position and shape of empirical distribution of regression residuals

production frontier but by changes in the shape of the empirical distribution. In the figure the empirical distributions of regression residuals at times t and $t + 1$ are assumed to be unimodal, continuous curves with the estimated production frontiers as their modes. The solid line curve with its mode at $\ln[f(x)]_t$ (point A) is regarded as the empirical distribution at time t; it would yield the efficiency estimate EFF_t. Suppose now that the empirical distribution at time $t + 1$ is either one of the two solid-lined curves with modes at points B and C. Then EFF_{t+1} is equal to EFF_t as long as the new curves exhibit the same degree of skewness and asymmetry. However, EFF_{t+1} will be greater than EFF_t if the distribution at time $t + 1$ is represented by either one of the dotted curves.

Thus upward or downward movements of production frontiers do not affect estimated efficiency if they do not change the shapes of the empirical distributions. Therefore an important message is that over time measures of technical efficiency that depend solely upon the shape of the empirical distribution of regression residuals should not vary systematically with movements of the production frontier caused by such factors as technological progress and changes in factor-market conditions. These efficiency measures are better used for static analyses because they ignore the intertemporal relationship between the best practices at time t and $t + 1$.

8.4.2 Further Evidence on ATI

It is fortunate, however, that one of the four measures of technical (in)efficiency is defined so that the intertemporal shifts of production frontiers can be captured in estimated efficiency. Compared to the other three measures of technical (in)efficiency, ATI [defined in equation (8)] takes into account the average level of output in its denominator. Thus it can be shown that ATI at time $t + 1$ is lower than ATI at time t if $\ln[f(x)]$ moves upward from t to $t + 1$, other things being equal.[14]

It remains to be seen to what extent the estimates of ATI prove more stable over time than did those of EFF. Tables 8.8 and 8.9 report evidence on the stability of estimates of ATI. The results are at once a disappointment and an encouragement. The bad news is that the interannual correlations, as well as those between MEAN and other annual vectors, are still low. The good news is that the correlation coefficients in tables 8.8 and 8.9 are consistently higher than corresponding ones in tables 8.5 and 8.6, which confirms the conjecture based on the nature of our efficiency measure in a dynamic context.

8.5 Future Research Directions

This chapter has presented our exploratory analyses on the stability of technical efficiency estimates in Korea's manufacturing industries. Though the method of testing stability that we used in this chapter is not comprehensive, we could not find strong evidence that our efficiency estimates are stable over time. This outcome is both surprising and disappointing. We could show that the instability of technical efficiency over time is partly explained by the way we constructed our measures of efficiency. Measures of efficiency that depend only upon the shape of the empirical distribution of regression residuals do not systematically reflect movements of the production frontier over time, so technical efficiency could increase with a downward movement of the production frontier over time. Efficiency measures that take into account the shifts of the production frontier over time, as well as distributional changes, exhibit increased stability and are more appropriate for use in a dynamic context.

Otherwise, the instability of technical efficiency over time was not explained satisfactorily in this chapter. Among the many ways to look further into the question of stability, we propose the following approach for future investigations: A proper methodology for testing the stability of technical efficiency will involve not only devising appropriate testing techniques but also determining what factors, if any, should be controlled when

Table 8.8
Spearman correlation coefficients between values of ATI for adjacent years

	1978–79	1979–80	1980–81	1981–82	1982–83	1983–84	1984–85	1985–86	1986–87	1987–88
Spearman correlation coefficients	0.079	0.337	0.156	0.346	0.262	0.410	0.397	0.390	0.401	0.338
Significance levels	0.462	0.001	0.153	0.0006	0.009	0.0001	0.0001	0.0001	0.0001	0.0016
Number of industries free of type I failures	89	92	85	94	99	103	114	115	95	84

Table 8.9
Spearman correlations between mean ATI and annual ATI values

	ATI78	ATI79	ATI80	ATI81	ATI82	ATI83	ATI84	ATI85	ATI86	ATI87	ATI88	NFYR
Spearman correlation coefficients	0.3984	0.6197	0.5661	0.6169	0.5656	0.5434	0.6883	0.6678	0.6354	0.6689	0.6101	−0.4454
Significance levels	0.0001	0.0001	0.0001	0.0001	0.0001	0.0001	0.0001	0.0001	0.0001	0.0001	0.0001	0.0001
Number of industries free of type I failures	123	131	134	121	138	138	143	153	146	124	122	201

we test for stability. We believe that the factors to be controlled are any time-dependent components of the output and inputs that may not be associated with technical efficiency but affect the level of our efficiency estimates. Any factors that over time change the shape of the distribution of plants in the input–output space must be considered seriously in explaining the intertemporal discrepancies of our efficiency estimates. The interindustry determinants of technical efficiency introduced in chapter 3 will become important again in a new dynamic context.

Notes

I express deep appreciation to Hyunduk Son for his assistance and patience in handling data.

1. Unfortunately, our research has not been sufficiently developed to answer the second question. Future research will address related questions.

2. The 1988 Census of Manufactures was the most recent census available for use.

3. The average number of total employees was available for the eleven years under consideration.

4. Note that this specification differs from equations (11) and (12) in chapter 3. We need to show how close the efficiency estimates obtained from this regression equation are to those for the previous equations. We compared efficiency estimates based on equation (11) of chapters 3 with those from our equation (1). The Spearman correlation coefficient is 0.4510, with a significance level of 0.0001. This correlation is lower than expected due to differences between the two chapters in data-editing rules and in the ways of constructing input variables. For the definition of variables and notation, see table 3.1 and the appendix of chapter 3. We use the same notation in this chapter.

5. The method of reclassifying old industries under the new KSIC system presents a problem because there is as yet no procedure for converting the efficiency estimates of an old industry into comparable measures of new industry.

6. We referred to Economic Planning Board (1984) in constructing the conversion table.

7. We did not use the values of efficiency measures EFF or ATI associated with type I failure. We also excluded type II failure in the case of λ. Although we included all estimates of S, the converted industry will continue to be a type I failure if all the new KSIC industries under consideration exhibit type I failures.

8. For example, industry 31113 exhibits type I failures (EFF = 1) in five years. Thus the summary statistics are calculated only for the six remaining years.

9. The number of type I failure years has a mean of 3.6716 and a standard deviation of 2.3349.

10. The term vector is used to emphasize that all the variables included in the correlations analyses are 201 × 1 vectors whose elements are individual industries.

11. We used data on S instead of EFF because we encountered difficulty in handling industries with EFF = 1.

12. We have not yet pursued this. It involves laborious computations, so we leave it on our agenda for future research.

13. See chapter 3 for notation, definition, and other details.

14. According to equation (8) of chapter 3, $\widehat{ATI}$, the estimator of ATI, is defined as follows:

$$\widehat{\text{ATI}} = \frac{\hat{\sigma}_u\sqrt{2/\pi}}{\overline{\ln[f(x)]}},$$

since

$$\overline{\ln(y)} = \overline{\ln[f(x)]} - \hat{\sigma}_u\sqrt{\frac{2}{\pi}}.$$

Note that $\overline{\ln[f(x)]}$ is the estimated production frontier.

References

Economic Planning Board. 1984. *Korean Standard Industrial Classification.*

9 The Intraindustry Dispersion of Plant Productivity in the British Manufacturing Sector, 1963–79

Sheryl D. Bailey

9.1 Introduction

This chapter reports an analysis of the dispersions of productivity levels of British manufacturing establishments between 1963 and 1979, in context of the question of how technical efficiency behaves over time. The data set, inherited from another project, suffers from some peculiar properties. It can be used neither to estimate technical efficiency nor, strictly speaking, to observe how technical efficiency behaves over time. It does, however, permit a close look at a question that is important, closely related, and not previously investigated: How variable over time is the dispersion of an industry's plant productivity levels, and what factors determine that variability? First, in relating this question to the research on static levels of technical efficiency, it becomes apparent that this research leaves open a number of questions that can be pursued effectively only by observing variation over time in plants' productivity levels and in static summary measures of productivity dispersions.

Interindustry analyses of static technical efficiency for Great Britain, the United States, Japan, and Australia have confirmed a number of hypotheses about the determinants of technical efficiency. These confirmations tend to validate the efficiency measure itself, but they still leave our confidence seriously qualified. Only the U.S. study has obtained a strong preponderance among industries of the negative skewness values that indicate technical inefficiency. For other countries the manufacturing industries divide rather evenly between those with positive and negative skewness of the production-function residuals, leaving room for doubt that theoretical technical efficiency measures really capture what they seek. Analysis of the intertemporal churning of plants' productivity dispersions provides another avenue into the underlying data and basis for judgment as to what is really being observed.

Another feature of the cross-sectional studies that underlines the importance of a dynamic approach is the prevalence of dynamic determinants of technical efficiency. Capital vintages are an obvious example. In the United States the dispersion of an industry's equipment vintages was found to be a significant determinant of technical efficiency, implying that technical efficiency would change over time with the rate of renewal of the equipment stock. Similarly research intensity enlarges apparent technical efficiency, implying that it should expand and contract over time as innovation waxes and wanes in an industry. Another depressant of U.S. efficiency is the extent of exporting activity, which could rest on either the uneven distribution of exporting among plants or the high incidence of disturbances encountered in the international marketplace. Again the analysis of intertemporal patterns is needed to clarify the extent and significance of these static patterns.

Economists skeptical about the concept of technical efficiency have commonly argued that it is inconsistent with the assumption that value-maximizing production units are being observed in static equilibrium. Even if one rejects this position and believes that cogent bases do exist for conceptualizing equilibrium inefficiency, it seems true that market forces tend over time to eliminate technical inefficiency by forcing the inefficient from the scene, just as they tend to erode the rents that make some firms and establishments appear to be "superproductive." Static analyses of technical efficiency cannot tell us anything directly about the strength and speed of these equilibrating forces, or by implication the role of transitory relative to permanent forces in accounting for technical inefficiency. The analysis of technical efficiency and other measures of intraindustry productivity dispersion over time are needed to address this question of the extent and speed of adjustment.

9.2   Properties of the Data

9.2.1   Source and Contents

The data used in this study were obtained from the National Economic Development Office of London (NEDO). The Business Statistics Office (BSO) prepared the data set for NEDO using the returns of the Census of Production for the years 1963, 1968, 1973 and each year of 1975 through 1979. The BSO, as authorized by the Statistics of Trade Act of 1947, surveyed all establishments employing 20 or more persons that were operating at any time during the calendar year. The returns from these surveys of the United Kingdom's manufacturing sector form the basis of the data set used in this analysis. The BSO also made estimates for the smaller establishments exempt from the surveys each year. However, this information was not included in the data base because it is considered to be "less securely based" (U.K. Department of Industry 1973, 6) and therefore less reliable.

The Statistics of Trade Act 1947 expressly prohibits the disclosure of information relating to an individual firm or establishment without the previous consent in writing of the person carrying on the undertaking. Hence data on individual establishments supplied by NEDO are grouped according to the size of net output per head (NOPH) in order to suppress information relating to individual undertakings and thereby avoid the disclosure problem. Hence, for each four-digit minimum list head (MLH) industry, information is reported for specific size classes within each industry, with the size classes organized by NOPH. For a given industry and year, the size classes are not uniform in either range of NOPH or number of establishments included, but they are large enough to avoid disclosure.

This form of grouping is somewhat troublesome because the focus of this study is the analysis of plant differences in productivity inferred primarily from net output per head. This variable cannot be used as the dependent variable in any regression equations because the data are grouped by NOPH and hence the resulting estimates would be seriously biased, inconsistent, and inefficient. Therefore fitting production functions using NOPH as the dependent variable was out of the question.

Despite these limitations the data do offer a chance to analyze how intraindustry dispersions of NOPH vary over time. The grouping procedure does not preclude estimation of the intraindustry distributional parameters. Thus the primary measures used are the intraindustry dispersion of plant-level productivity and the variation over time in these productivity dispersions.

BSO uses the establishment as the statistical unit for the census and requests information from individual plants where production takes place. Information relating to departments not engaged in production is excluded. Details relating to head offices that were primarily engaged in the administration of the production units surveyed by the census were included. The head office administrative information of multiplant firms was apportioned among the relevant establishments. In general, firms operating in more than one area or more than one establishment in the same area were listed as two or more separate establishments.

The industrial classification is based on the U.K. Standard Industrial Classification, which follows the general principles of the International Standard Industrial Classification of all Economic Activities of the United

Nations Statistical Office. This study embraces two versions of the standard industrial classification, 1968 and 1973. The 1968 SIC was adopted here to define industries because the 1973 SIC is more disaggregated than the corresponding 1968 SIC. Hence the 1973 industries were aggregated into their 1968 MLH definitions in order to identify industries comparable throughout the period.

The following variables are included in the basic data set:

Number of establishments per size class

Total employment

Employment—operatives

Employment—administrative, technical, and clerical (ATC)

Wages and salaries—operatives

Wages and salaries—ATC

Total sales and work done

Gross output

Total net output

Net output per head

Total gross value added at factor cost (available only for the 1970s)

Gross value added per head (available only for the 1970s)

Net capital expenditure

Total stock and work in progress at year end

The focus of the current analysis is NOPH.[1] However, some of the other variables in the data set are used to examine the various features of the intertemporal behavior of the dispersion of plant productivity.

9.2.2 Selection Rules

Of the 143 available industries, only 15 were excluded from the analysis. These industries were omitted either because data were missing for some years or because too few observations were reported for some years (three or fewer size classes).[2] The remaining 128 industries are summarized by order class in the tables presented subsequently.

The underlying data collected by the Business Statistics Office are said to be subject to careful editing and rechecks to eliminate reporting errors that give rise to internal inconsistencies in individual establishments' returns. Therefore no adjustments were made to the data supplied by NEDO.

9.3   Evaluation of Measures of the Intertemporal Behavior of Productivity Dispersion

The focus of this analysis is the behavior over time of the intraindustry dispersion of plants' levels of NOPH. In a perfectly competitive industry, surrounded by competitive factor and product markets, the individual plants would each achieve the common equilibrium level of net output per head, and they would adjust uniformly to any disturbance that affected their realized revenue-productivity level. Hence no intraindustry dispersion in plant productivity would be expected at any point in time except as random noise, and any dispersion would not persist over time. However, broader theoretical considerations as well as empirical research steers one to expect that a number of factors—including imperfectly competitive markets, product differentiation, capital-vintage effects, diversification, and research and development activities—would give rise to variation of the realized revenue-productivity levels of plants within an industry. Moreover some of these factors would likely cause the dispersion to persist as well as to churn over time. This study seeks to identify the patterns and the determinants of the variation over time of productivity dispersion.

9.3.1   Dispersion in Plant-Level Productivity within Industries

To describe the intraindustry dispersion in plant productivity at any one point in time, a measure is sought that will communicate the degree of variation in individual plants' productivity levels as well as be comparable among different industries and time periods. The within-industry coefficient of variation fulfills these criteria and thus was adopted to represent the intraindustry dispersion in plant productivity. This measure of dispersion forms the basis for all subsequent calculations.

From the grouped dated provided by NEDO, the parameters of the distribution of productivity across size classes were calculated for each industry and year using the standard weighting procedure for grouped data (i.e, the class midpoints were multiplied by their respective frequencies). Thus eight sets of basic descriptive statistics are available for each industry, corresponding to the eight years examined here. The within-industry coefficient of variation of NOPH was calculated for each industry and year using the respective estimated standard deviations and means.

The grouping procedure employed in the construction of this data set was a cause for significant research and deliberation. The class intervals were created to avoid the disclosure of the information pertaining to individual plants. As a result the class intervals employed varied across industries and among years for the same industry. In general, the estimates of mean and variance derived from grouped data are biased, inconsistent, and inefficient. Yet the inconsistencies and inefficiencies of simple parameter estimates are usually minor. Moreover, when the same grouping procedure is used across the sample and the estimates are used in cross-sectional analysis, the individual biases are not cause for concern since all units of the sample have been treated comparably.

However, the focus of this analysis is the intertemporal variation of productivity dispersion, and the variation in the grouping procedures over time does warrant some consideration. The usual method of counteracting the effects of grouping, Sheppard's correction, is inappropriate in this case. In particular, Sheppard's correction requires that (1) the population distribution is of finite range and there is high-order contact at the terminals of the range, or (2) the grouping intervals are located at random on the range. Also Sheppard's correction assumes constant interval widths and bounded derivatives.

The correction procedure breaks down completely when neither the condition for high-order contact nor the requirement of random location of grouping is achieved. That is the case for a distribution abruptly truncated at zero, such as the distribution of net output per head. Under such conditions the correction procedure will likely add additional error to the parameter estimates. Moreover the disclosure principle created uneven size classes for most industries and years in the data set of this study. Hence application of Sheppard's correction in this case would exacerbate any errors resulting from the use of the grouped data.[3]

Inasmuch as the focus of this analysis is the interindustry determinants of the intertemporal behavior of productivity dispersions and all estimated distributional parameters are employed in cross-sectional analysis, the primary concern is whether particular industries were treated any differently than the others. Since the universal grouping rule (i.e., avoid disclosure) was applied evenly to all industries in the sample, it was concluded

Table 9.1
Distribution of the dispersion of plant productivity levels (CVNOPH), by year

Year	Minimum[a]	Mean[b]	Maximum[c]	Coefficient of variation[d]
1963	0.212	0.479	1.724	0.347
1968	0.227	0.450	0.773	0.237
1973	0.252	0.480	0.956	0.290
1975	0.223	0.502	1.234	0.340
1976	0.189	0.491	1.176	0.287
1977	0.266	0.490	1.136	0.254
1978	0.247	0.478	1.044	0.269
1979	0.255	0.464	0.883	0.254

Note: Observations were taken on 128 industries for each year. See the text for the derivation of CVNOPH.
a. Minimum value of observations of stated variable.
b. Unweighted mean over 128 industries of the observations for stated variable.
c. Maximum value of observations of stated variable.
d. Coefficient of variation of basic observations of stated variable.

that any variations due to minor modifications in group intervals would probably have a negligible effect on the cross-sectional results. Hence no adjustments were administered to the estimated basic descriptive statistics.

Table 9.1 presents the basic descriptive statistics of the within-industry coefficients of variation, CVNOPH, by year. The yearly mean of CVNOPH tends to decrease during 1963–68 to a minimum in 1968, increase during 1968–75 to a maximum in 1975, then decline again during 1976–79. Yet only the minimum of 1968 and the next lowest value of 1979 differ from the means of the other years by enough to approach statistical significance.[4]

Although the gaps in the data between 1963, 1968, 1973, and 1975 conceal details on the pattern during those years, it seems very likely that the maximum average CVNOPH of 1975 is partly attributable to the oil price run-up after the 1973 oil embargo. Expectedly, a broad macro disturbance would lead to a short-term increase in the intraindustry dispersion of productivity as individual plants respond differently to the unexpected shock. Note, however, that the maximum average CVNOPH of 1975 is only significantly different from the two lowest values of 1968 and 1979. Also, while the percentage variation of CVNOPH among industries is higher for 1975 than the surrounding years, the greatest (absolute) percentage deviation is the low value in 1968, which has no obvious explanation.

The aforementioned pattern displayed in the aggregate was not found to be germane to the individual industries. If it were, a quadratic time trend should fit the time series of observations for the typical industry. An exploratory analysis revealed that a quadratic time trend is not statistically significant for 96 percent of the industries. Hence macroeconomic factors do not seem to explain the variations in the individual industries' CVNOPH values, leaving room for the microeconomic factors investigated in what follows.

9.3.2 Intertemporal Behavior of Productivity Dispersion

Measures were sought that would capture all relevant aspects of the behavior over time of the intraindustry dispersion in productivity for each industry. Six alternative variables were derived from the set of eight within-industry coefficients of variation for each industry. Each of these variables will be discussed in turn.

Intertemporal Variation in Productivity Dispersion

The core concept to be captured is the degree of variation over time of the within-industry dispersion of plant productivity. The most direct measure is the normalized standard deviation of the annual dispersion measures: the coefficient of variation across time of the within-industry coefficients of variation for each industry. Again the coefficient of variation was chosen because it is a relative measure of variation that is comparable among industries. The intertemporal coefficient of variation does not, however, consider the existence of any systematic trend in the intraindustry dispersions or any difference in the speed with which a perturbed intraindustry dispersion returns to an equilibrium level. Alternative measures were developed to capture these aspects of intertemporal behavior, and they will be addressed below.

Table 9.2 presents the basic descriptive statistics of the intertemporal coefficient of variation (INTCV) by two-digit order classification. The mean intertemporal coefficient of variation for all industries is 16 percent, ranging from a minimum of 3 percent up to a maximum of 67 percent. As can be seen in table 9.2, the range for INTCV is generally much lower within the two-digit order classifications than it is for the manufacturing sector as a whole. Also, INTCV varies approximately 54 percent across the 128 industries studied.

Table 9.2
Distribution of the intertemporal coefficient of variation of the dispersion of plant productivity levels (INTCV), by two-digit standard industrial classification industry

	Industry	Number of four-digit industries	Minimum[a]	Mean[b]	Maximum[c]	Coefficient of variation[d]
3	Food, drink, and tobacco	13	5.376	13.335	24.150	46.191
4	Coal and petroleum	1	26.970	26.970	26.970	NA
5	Chemicals and allied industries	16	10.534	18.112	31.201	33.440
6	Metal manufacture	6	6.990	13.896	20.444	45.512
7	Mechanical engineering	15	4.340	15.454	32.970	45.199
8	Instrument engineering	2	7.060	9.344	11.628	34.571
9	Electrical engineering	9	7.229	15.427	26.174	36.082
10	Shipbuilding and marine engineering	1	66.680	66.680	66.680	NA
11	Vehicles	4	6.605	27.999	46.540	58.698
12	Metal goods not elsewhere specified	10	3.403	12.606	23.771	50.358
13	Textiles	14	7.483	14.517	27.706	45.932
14	Leather, leather goods, and fur	3	12.579	19.771	30.217	46.825
15	Clothing and footwear	9	11.759	17.927	29.730	31.501
16	Bricks, pottery, glass, and cement	5	7.460	11.829	18.607	36.570
17	Timber and furniture	6	6.856	12.602	19.980	42.392
18	Paper, printing, and publishing	7	5.307	10.621	16.530	32.644
19	Other manufacturing industries	7	7.156	14.297	22.659	39.058
	Total industries	128	3.403	15.630	66.676	53.667

a. Minimum values of observations of stated variable.
b. Unweighted mean over relevant number of industries for stated variable.
c. Maximum value of observations of stated variable.
d. Coefficient of variation of basic observations of stated variable.

Linear Trend Coefficient

A linear trend was fitted to the eight within-industry coefficients of variation for each industry to determine the extent of any long-term trends in
the dispersions of productivity. Given the uneven gaps between the years
studied, the time variable was defined as $t = 0, 5, 10, 12, 13, 14, 15$, and 16
in order to correspond to the years 1963, 1968, 1973, and 1975–79.

The estimated slope coefficients measure the extent and the direction of
any systematic time trend in the intraindustry dispersion of plant productivity. Although many of the linear trends fitted to the within-industry
dispersions are not significant (only 31 of the trend slope coefficients are
significant), it is assumed that even nonsignificant coefficients may be
regarded as best guesses that may contain useful information. Therefore all
of the trend coefficients were used in order to capture whatever information they contain on the direction and the extent of change over time in
the intraindustry dispersion measures. Table 9.3 presents the descriptive
statistics of the linear trend coefficients, LINCOEF1, by two-digit order
classification. On average the within-industry dispersions exhibit a very
small upward linear time trend of 0.10 percent, ranging from a minimum
of −5.38 percent up to a maximum of 2.31 percent. In general, the average
time trend within a two-digit order classification is an upward trend, yet
seven order classes have negative means of the trend coefficients.

The absolute value of the linear trend coefficient, LINCOEF2, is also
employed in order to show the extent of long-run trends in the productivity
dispersions, regardless of direction. This measure would reveal any forces
that are changing industries' interplant productivity dispersions persistently but not unidirectionally. Table 9.4 presents the descriptive statistics
of the absolute value of the linear trend coefficients, by two-digit order
classification. On average the within-industry dispersions exhibit a very
small linear trend of 0.62 percent, ranging from a minimum of 0.01 percent
to a maximum of 5.38 percent.

Standard Error around the Linear Trend

Related to the linear trend coefficient LINCOEF1, the standard error
around the trend (STANDERR) was used to represent the residual variation of the productivity dispersions not accounted for by the fitted trends.
Each standard error was standardized by dividing by the mean within-
industry coefficient of variation for each industry to make the measures

Table 9.3
Distribution of the linear trend coefficient (LINCOEF1), by two-digit standard industrial classification industry

	Industry	Number of four-digit industries	Minimum[a]	Mean[b]	Maximum[c]
3	Food, drink, and tobacco	13	−0.0067	0.0023	0.0194
4	Coal and petroleum	1	0.0225	0.0225	0.0225
5	Chemicals and allied industries	16	−0.0172	−0.0002	0.0146
6	Metal manufacture	6	−0.0126	0.0021	0.0129
7	Mechanical engineering	15	−0.0094	0.0017	0.0115
8	Instrument engineering	2	0.0007	0.0026	0.0044
9	Electrical engineering	9	−0.0064	0.0003	0.0190
10	Shipbuilding and marine engineering	1	−0.0538	−0.0538	−0.0538
11	Vehicles	4	−0.0091	0.0034	0.0128
12	Metal goods not elsewhere specified	10	−0.0108	0.0003	0.0097
13	Textiles	14	−0.0216	−0.0006	0.0113
14	Leather, leather goods, and fur	3	−0.0009	0.0039	0.0109
15	Clothing and footwear	9	−0.0061	0.0085	0.0231
16	Bricks, pottery, glass, and cement	5	−0.0018	0.0034	0.0087
17	Timber and furniture	6	−0.0017	0.0029	0.0095
18	Paper, printing, and publishing	7	−0.0135	−0.0035	0.0029
19	Other manufacturing industries	7	−0.0160	−0.0016	0.0049
	Total industries	128	−0.0538	0.0010	0.0231

a. Minimum value of observations of stated variable.
b. Unweighted mean over relevant number of industries for stated variable.
c. Maximum value of observations of stated variable.

Table 9.4
Distribution of the absolute value of the linear trend coefficient (LINCOEF2), by two-digit standard industrial classification industry

	Industry	Number of four-digit industries	Minimum[a]	Mean[b]	Maximum[c]
3	Food, drink, and tobacco	13	0.0006	0.0055	0.0194
4	Coal and petroleum	1	0.0225	0.0225	0.0225
5	Chemicals and allied industries	16	0.0002	0.0064	0.0172
6	Metal manufacture	6	0.0003	0.0063	0.0129
7	Mechanical engineering	15	0.0001	0.0041	0.0115
8	Instrument engineering	2	0.0007	0.0026	0.0044
9	Electrical engineering	9	0.0003	0.0064	0.0190
10	Shipbuilding and marine engineering	1	0.0538	0.0538	0.0538
11	Vehicles	4	0.0014	0.0087	0.0128
12	Metal goods not elsewhere specified	10	0.0008	0.0049	0.0108
13	Textiles	14	0.0004	0.0063	0.0216
14	Leather, leather goods, and fur	3	0.0009	0.0045	0.0109
15	Clothing and footwear	9	0.0014	0.0099	0.0231
16	Bricks, pottery, glass, and cement	5	0.0007	0.0041	0.0087
17	Timber and furniture	6	0.0005	0.0040	0.0095
18	Paper, printing, and publishing	7	0.0001	0.0047	0.0135
19	Other manufacturing industries	7	0.0004	0.0048	0.0160
	Total industries	128	0.0001	0.0062	0.0538

a. Minimum value of observations of stated variable.
b. Unweighted mean over relevant number of industries for stated variable.
c. Maximum value of observations of stated variable.

comparable among industries. This particular measure is related to INTCV, except that it describes the intertemporal variation in the intra-industry productivity dispersions after the time trend has been removed. Table 9.5 presents the descriptive statistics of STANDERR, by two-digit order classification. The mean of STANDERR across all industries is 14 percent, ranging from a minimum of 3 percent up to a maximum of 52 percent. The mean value of STANDERR is slightly lower than that for INTCV, 16 percent, and its range is narrower, indicating that the long-term linear trends did account for some of the intertemporal variation observed in the productivity dispersions. INTCV and STANDERR should be closely related, however, because of the paucity of significant trends.

Average Interannual Variation

The variables developed above measure different aspects of the inter-temporal behavior of productivity dispersion over the entire sample period (i.e., the variation over the entire period or the long-run trend over the entire period). Also of interest is the average annual variation of the intraindustry dispersion of plant productivity. That is, the amount by which productivity dispersion varies from year to year can reveal the operation of forces that propel or restrict short-run changes in the dispersion. Hence two measures of average interannual variation were developed to examine the yearly aspect of the variation of the interplant dispersion of productivity.

Normally only one measure would be needed to delineate the average annual variation. However, given the unevenly spaced years of observation, two variants were developed that encompass alternative assumptions regarding the effect of the multiperiod gaps in the data. The assumptions can be regarded as alternative limiting cases of the possible effect of time on the dispersion of productivity. First, it can be assumed that the change in the within-industry coefficient of variation of NOPH (CVNOPH) observed between any two data points more than one year apart is the cumulation of equal annual changes that occurred in the unobserved years. That is, the change in CVNOPH taken between two points that are five years apart is five times the unobserved annual changes. Hence the change taken over the five-year period should be divided by five in order to get an estimate of the annual change for that period.

Alternatively, since the change in CVNOPH measures a change in dispersion, it can be assumed instead that uneven time gaps do not affect

Table 9.5
Distribution of the standard error around the linear trend (STANDERR), by two-digit standard industrial classification industry

	Industry	Number of four-digit industries	Minimum[a]	Mean[b]	Maximum[c]	Coefficient of variation[d]
3	Food, drink, and tobacco	13	3.694	12.614	25.788	55.949
4	Coal and petroleum	1	24.912	24.912	24.912	NA
5	Chemicals and allied industries	16	11.190	17.398	30.112	32.604
6	Metal manufacture	6	5.345	11.868	19.492	43.018
7	Mechanical engineering	15	3.689	14.897	32.167	47.329
8	Instrument engineering	2	7.579	9.392	11.204	27.293
9	Electrical engineering	9	6.681	13.823	20.868	5.694
10	Shipbuilding and marine engineering	1	52.999	52.999	52.999	NA
11	Vehicles	4	6.594	26.056	48.755	68.569
12	Metal goods not elsewhere specified	10	3.260	11.642	23.861	57.057
13	Textiles	14	5.537	12.228	27.21	46.733
14	Leather, leather goods, and fur	3	8.115	18.086	32.656	71.331
15	Clothing and footwear	9	8.601	14.770	29.470	39.551
16	Bricks, pottery, glass, and cement	5	6.683	11.098	16.458	37.348
17	Timber and furniture	6	7.047	11.923	20.182	45.580
18	Paper, printing, and publishing	7	4.797	8.780	11.088	29.285
19	Other manufacturing industries	7	7.060	13.404	24.482	42.110
	Total industries	128	3.260	14.215	52.999	55.358

a. Minimum values of observations of stated variable.
b. Unweighted mean over relevant number of industries for stated variable.
c. Maximum value of observations of stated variable.
d. Coefficient of variation of basic observations of stated variable.

the interpretation that is given to the difference between two dispersion readings. In particular, it can be supposed that the unobserved changes in dispersion during a five-year interval represent random vibrations that are in the limit as large as the change in dispersion between two observations that are one year apart. That is, the amount of time separating the observed time periods does not affect the change in dispersion between those points. Under this hypothesis no compensation is needed for the multiperiod gaps in the data.

Alternative assumptions that lie between these two bounds could be devised if additional information were available from a longer time series. However, these two limiting cases will be examined here.

On the basis of the first assumption, the variable INTANN1 was computed with adjustments for the time gaps in the sample data. The change in CVNOPH was calculated for each adjacent pair of observations, and then divided by the number of years separating the two data points. The adjusted differences were squared and normalized by the average CVNOPH for each interval to produce seven estimates of the annual percentage variation of CVNOPH. INTANN1 is the simple average of these annual percentage variation estimates.

The second interannual variation variable, INTANN2, follows the same procedure for INTANN1, except that the change in CVNOPH was not divided by the number of years separating each pair of data points. Based on the second assumption above, no adjustment was made for the multiperiod time gaps.

Table 9.6 presents the descriptive statistics of INTANN1 by two-digit order classification. The mean of INTANN1 across all industries is 1.10 percent, ranging from a minimum of 0.02 percent up to a maximum of 10.90 percent. The descriptive statistics of INTANN2 are presented in table 9.7 by two-digit order classification. The mean and range across all industries are greater for INTANN2, with a mean of 2.24 percent, a minimum of 0.10 percent, and a maximum of 24.49 percent. The higher mean of INTANN2 shows the effect of not dividing by the size of the interval. However, the variation over the sample is about the same for both INTANN1 and INTANN2 at 141 percent.

Speed of Adjustment of Productivity Dispersions

In analyzing the intertemporal behavior of the intraindustry dispersions of productivity, another aspect of interest is the rate at which the intra-

Table 9.6
Distribution of the average interannual variation with compensation for time gaps
(INTANN1), by two-digit standard industrial classification industry

Industry	Number of four-digit industries	Minimum[a]	Mean[b]	Maximum[c]	Coefficient of variation[d]
3 Food, drink, and tobacco	13	0.078	0.803	2.090	84.677
4 Coal and petroleum	1	4.370	4.370	4.370	NA
5 Chemicals and allied industries	16	0.244	1.434	7.149	119.436
6 Metal manufacture	6	0.175	0.681	1.477	73.679
7 Mechanical engineering	15	0.670	0.954	2.815	80.915
8 Instrument engineering	2	0.261	0.664	1.067	85.912
9 Electrical engineering	9	0.164	1.066	3.357	102.383
10 Shipbuilding and marine engineering	1	1.432	1.432	1.432	NA
11 Vehicles	4	0.127	4.299	10.899	107.871
12 Metal goods not elsewhere specified	10	0.024	0.636	3.223	150.367
13 Textiles	14	0.104	0.903	3.793	120.014
14 Leather, leather goods, and fur	3	0.222	3.268	8.862	148.460
15 Clothing and footwear	9	0.188	1.20	4.648	103.162
16 Bricks, pottery, glass, and cement	5	0.194	0.741	2.149	110.816
17 Timber and furniture	6	0.034	0.763	2.490	116.945
18 Paper, printing and publishing	7	0.118	0.337	0.487	43.804
19 Other manufacturing industries	7	0.131	0.609	1.462	68.871
Total industries	128	0.024	1.100	10.899	141.138

a. Minimum value of observations of stated variable.
b. Unweighted mean over relevant number of industries for stated variable.
c. Maximum value of observations of stated variable.
d. Coefficient of variation of basic observations of stated variable.

Table 9.7
Distribution of the average interannual variation without compensation for time gaps (INTANN2), by two-digit standard industrial classification industry

Industry	Number of four-digit industries	Minimum[a]	Mean[b]	Maximum[c]	Coefficient of variation[d]
3 Food, drink, and tobacco	13	0.166	1.876	4.744	86.352
4 Coal and petroleum	1	7.433	7.433	7.433	NA
5 Chemicals and allied industries	16	0.539	2.915	7.753	77.946
6 Metal manufacture	6	0.255	1.203	2.193	65.354
7 Mechanical engineering	15	0.098	1.858	5.102	73.418
8 Instrument engineering	2	0.418	0.924	1.430	77.436
9 Electrical engineering	9	0.537	2.187	5.308	77.473
10 Shipbuilding and marine engineering	1	24.485	24.485	24.485	NA
11 Vehicles	4	0.249	7.488	19.408	113.518
12 Metal goods not elsewhere specified	10	0.103	1.289	5.358	124.163
13 Textiles	14	0.334	1.512	4.473	88.033
14 Leather, leather goods, and fur	3	0.397	4.019	10.467	139.267
15 Clothing and footwear	9	0.524	2.376	7.714	97.241
16 Bricks, pottery, glass, and cement	5	0.244	0.982	2.239	86.677
17 Timber and furniture	6	0.440	1.318	3.169	74.494
18 Paper, printing and publishing	7	0.254	0.654	1.052	44.370
19 Other manufacturing industries	7	0.556	1.766	4.621	82.161
Total industries	128	0.098	2.240	24.485	140.720

a. Minimum value of observations of stated variable.
b. Unweighted mean over relevant number of industries for stated variable.
c. Maximum value of observations of stated variable.
d. Coefficient of variation of basic observations of stated variable.

industry dispersions when displaced adjust over time to an equilibrium level. A measure of the speed at which the observed dispersions adjust over time is desirable.

After extensive experiments in fitting various autoregressive models, it was determined that the estimates derived are too sensitive to minor shifts in procedure to be worth using in the structural analysis. Two factors inhibit the successful estimation of a speed-of-adjustment measure using the data set at hand. First, only eight observations are available for each industry, which limits the number of coefficients that can be estimated in an autoregressive model. In addition the uneven spacing of the eight observations puts additional methodological demands on the preciously few degrees of freedom available for estimation. It is thus unsurprising that the estimates are highly unstable.[5]

9.3.3   Comparison of Measures of Intertemporal Behavior

As a result of the estimation procedures described above, six measures are available to characterize the intertemporal behavior of the intraindustry dispersion in plant productivity. The six measures are summarized in table 9.8. Some overlap between these six variables is expected since they are all

Table 9.8
Descriptive statistics of alternative dependent variables

Variable	Minimum[a]	Mean[b]	Maximum[c]	Coefficient of variation[d]
Intertemporal coefficient of variation (INTCV)	3.4026	15.6300	66.6760	53.6660
Linear trend coefficient (LINCOEF1)	−0.0538	0.0010	0.0231	NA
Absolute linear trend coefficient (LINCOEF2)	0.0001	0.0062	0.0538	106.1937
Standard error around linear time trend (STANDERR)	3.2603	14.2145	52.9991	55.3583
Average interannual variation 1 (INTANN1)	0.0243	1.1002	10.8985	141.1377
Average interannual variation 2 (INTANN2)	0.0983	2.2403	24.4845	140.7196

Note: Observations were taken on 128 industries for each variable. See the text for the derivation of each dependent variable.
a. Minimum value of observations of stated variable.
b. Unweighted mean over 128 industries of the observations for stated variable.
c. Maximum value of observations of stated variable.
d. Coefficient of variation of basic observations of stated variable.

evaluating the same fundamental phenomenon. However, each of these variables does emphasize somewhat different features of the variation of productivity dispersion over time. In general, they fall into three classes: (1) the intertemporal instability of productivity dispersion as reflected in INTCV and STANDERR, (2) the average short-run variation as evaluated by INTANN1 and INTANN2, and (3) the measures of systematic long-run intertemporal movement, LINCOEF1 and LINCOEF2. In particular, INTCV and STANDERR appraise the variation in productivity dispersion over the entire sample period, whereas INTANN1 and INTANN2 gauge the average year-to-year variation. Moreover the four INTANN and LINCOEF measures are affected by the temporal sequence of the observations, while INTCV and STANDERR overlook this effect.

Table 9.9 reports the simple correlation coefficients between the six variables. As is expected, INTCV and STANDERR are closely related. In addition both INTANN1 and INTANN2 are highly correlated with INTCV and STANDERR, indicating that the average short-run and long-run variations are strongly associated. Significant correlations also exist between LINCOEF2 and each of the variables in the other classes. However, LINCOEF1 has an irregular pattern of correlation with the other measures.

Each of these six variables will be used as the dependent variable in the subsequent analysis as the determinants of the intertemporal behavior of productivity dispersion are explored.

9.3.4 Intertemporal Behavior of the Basic Components of Productivity

The productivity measure NOPH is comprised of two basic components, total net output and total employment. These two components are exam-

Table 9.9
Simple correlation coefficients between alternative measures of the intertemporal behavior of the intraindustry dispersion of plant productivity

	INTCV	LINCOEF1	LINCOEF2	STANDERR	INTANN1	INTANN2
INTCV	1.000	−0.134	0.727*	0.912*	0.643*	0.897*
LINCOEF1		1.000	−0.187**	−0.046	0.238*	−0.178**
LINCOEF2			1.000	0.442*	0.205**	0.595*
STANDERR				1.000	0.742*	0.905*
INTANN1					1.000	0.725*
INTANN2						1.000

Note: Using two-tail tests of significance, * = 1 percent and ** = 5 percent.

ined in order to explore the forces that drive the intertemporal behavior of productivity dispersion. The intertemporal stability of the dispersion of both total net output and total employment will be related to the structural determinants used in the analysis of NOPH. This procedure will yield insight on the relationships between productivity dispersion, its basic components and the structural determinants.

It is important to note the specific features of the data set as it relates to this line of inquiry. As indicated earlier, the data are grouped into size classes by NOPH for each industry and year. The information on total employment and total net output are reported in the form of interval totals for each NOPH size class within an industry. That is, the employment figure reported is the sum of the total employment across all plants that fall within that interval, and likewise for the net output figure. The value reported for NOPH for each size class is the ratio of these two group sums. Thus an analysis of the total employment and net output grouped data series is equivalent to an analysis of the components of the NOPH grouped data series. Using the number of establishments per size class, the within-industry mean, standard deviation, and coefficient of variation are computed for total employment and total net output as well as for NOPH from the grouped data.

It would be preferable to analyze the basic components of NOPH from data on individual establishments. As is the case in the NOPH analysis, the estimates derived from the grouped data will be used in cross-sectional analysis. Hence it is expected that the biases resulting from the grouped data will not distort the results significantly. Therefore the patterns identified from the grouped data will be used as indicators of the patterns that reside at the individual plant level.

Measures were developed to represent the intertemporal stability of the within-industry dispersion of both total employment and net output. Following the procedure employed for the development of INTCV above, the coefficient of variation over time of the within-industry coefficients of variation were calculated for both total net output and total employment: INCVNO and INCVEMP, respectively. These two measures will be used in the ensuing analysis of the determinants of the intertemporal behavior of productivity dispersion.

Table 9.10 presents the simple correlation coefficients among the intertemporal variation of the dispersions of productivity, total net output, and total employment. Both INCVNO and INCVEMP are significantly asso-

Table 9.10
Simple correlation coefficients between the intertemporal variation of the dispersions of productivity, total net output and total employment

	INTCV	INCVNO	INCVEMP
INTCV	1.000	0.265*	0.192*
INCVNO		1.000	0.703*
INCVEMP			1.000

Note: Using two-tail tests of significance, * = 1 percent and ** = 5 percent.

ciated with INTCV. Moreover INCVNO and INCVEMP are strongly related to each other.

9.4   Interindustry Determinants of the Intertemporal Behavior of Productivity Dispersion

Research that has been done so far on the determinants of technical efficiency and of the intraindustry dispersions of plants' productivity levels shows that a number of factors cause these inefficiencies and dispersions to arise and persist over time. Some of these causal factors are stable and imply nothing about the intertemporal turnover of efficiency levels; examples are the prevalence of product differentiation and the extent of spatial isolation of producers in markets with high transport costs. Other determinants of efficiency or dispersion imply both a static scattering of plants' productivity levels and an intertemporal churning of the distribution. These include capital-vintage effects, the importance of research and development, and the extent of enterprise diversification (in the United States).[6]

In seeking explanations for the intertemporal behavior of intraindustry productivity dispersions, it is generally assumed that an industry's dispersion at any point in time depends on these various static and dynamic forces. It then becomes evident how to identify theoretically the factors that should determine the intertemporal variability of productivity levels of individual plants, and thus of the industrywide dispersion of productivity levels. It is useful to state two general propositions that will assist in identifying and classifying the expected determinants of intertemporal behavior:

1.   The greater the incidence of disturbances to the realized revenue-productivity levels of individual units and thus to the intraindustry disper-

sion, the less intertemporal stability there is. Examples of forces having this effect are the dynamic disturbances already identified. If high levels of research and innovation spread out the realized productivity levels of an industry's plants, the random successes of innovative efforts and the displacement of established product configurations by new ones should cause churning and intertemporal instability in an industry's productivity dispersion. Similarly in a capital-intensive industry with durable equipment and vintage effects, individual plants' productivity levels slip down through the ranks as their equipment ages, eventually to be restored when major replacement or renewal investments are made (Shen 1970). Intertemporal stability should thus decrease with capital intensity and the importance of capital-vintage effects.

2.   The less that the typical plant's productivity can be displaced from its equilibrium level and the quicker it returns once displaced, the greater is the intertemporal stability of productivity dispersion. As was noted previously, a plant's level of net output per head has a theoretical optimal value, given factor and product prices and the production function that it utilizes. In a perfectly competitive industry surrounded by competitive factor and product markets and free of adjustment costs, by construction a plant's productivity level would never depart from that optimum and no intertemporal variability would be observed. The greater the sunkenness of plants' input combinations, and the greater the incentive to delay the completion of adjustment to new conditions, the farther out of equilibrium can be the individual plant's productivity level, and the wider the intra-industry dispersion.[7] In particular, costs of adjustment can lengthen the period for which disequilibrium productivity levels persist. Thus, given the incidence of disturbances striking the productivity levels of an industry's production units, intertemporal instability should increase with the degree to which producers' input and activity decisions are sunk and irreversible, and with the cost of adjustment per period of time. Capital stocks and skilled nonproduction specialists, for example, represent resource commitments that are not readily changed and largely independent of the unit's short-run marginal cost. If that assumption is correct, industries that utilize fixed capital and specialist nonproduction labor heavily should exhibit more intertemporal instability, once the incidence of shocks to the productivity distribution is controlled.

As the various substantive classes of variables investigated as potential determinants of intertemporal stability are discussed, it will be shown how they fit into these two categories of sources of disturbance and regulators of the speed (extent) of optimal adjustment to disturbance.

9.4.1 Competitive Conditions

Producer concentration is a perennially favorite variable to explore in any interindustry analysis such as this one. It must be handled with care. It is expected that concentration regulates the conduct patterns of firms in the market, which in turn affect their productivity dispersions.[8] In addition, however, concentration also is caused by (and thus correlated with) a number of other elements of market structure, which have their own standing as either sources of disturbances or regulators of the speed of adjustment. The initial focus is on the consequences of concentration for conduct that affects the productivity dispersion and its stability.

It is useful to identify three reference cases. (1) Nash behavior by definition rules out any instability of producers' revenue-productivity levels due to the cut and thrust of oligopolistic rivalry; in that sense industries competitive enough to lack systematic recognition by rivals of their strategic interdependence should show little intertemporal instability. (2) A perfect cartel could by assumption optimize the reactions of all producers to disturbances that affect the joint-profit-maximizing set of resource allocations, eliminating productivity disturbances due to strategic interactions to the same degree as Nash behavior but through an entirely different mechanism. (3) Between these cases lie all the possible types of oligopoly markets in which strategic interactions among sellers can take place.

The primary emphasis here is the effect of these strategic interactions on the intertemporal stability of productivity dispersions. Oligopolistic but incompletely collusive industries can display intertemporal instability for at least three reasons. First, breakdowns of quasi agreements are themselves a source of disturbance to plants' revenue-productivity levels, in ways identified by the processes of cheating, reversion, and the revival of cooperation much studied in the recent literature on supergames. Second, a strong empirical tradition in industrial organization holds that oligopolies are more successful at cooperating on price than on nonprice forms of rivalry. Strategic interaction in these nonprice lines—advertising and promotion, product quality and innovation, brand proliferation, and the like—should clearly increase the intertemporal instability of productivity dispersions as it waxes and wanes over time.[9] Finally, insofar as oligopoly markets provide some excess profits to their typical members, they permit the survival of less than optimally efficient units and tolerate slow adjustment (they may or may not cause this tardiness).[10] Thus oligopolistic conditions can increase intertemporal instability both through injecting disturbances and by permitting retarded adjustment to whatever disturbances occur.

These considerations lead to the problem of predicting relations between intertemporal stability and variables related to producer concentration. The specific variable used for Britain is CONC, the average percentage of shipments accounted for by the five largest firms, 1970–79.[11] What relation exists between intertemporal stability and concentration depends on one's beliefs about the empirical distribution of the three categories of market conduct just defined. Suppose that consistent with much empirical research on industrial organization, perfect cartels are rarely observed in industrial markets, there exists a wide range of unconcentrated and moderately concentrated industries exhibiting Nash behavior, and oligopolistic interaction is found in an upper tail of concentrated industries.[12] This assumption implies a monotonic increase of instability with concentration. Such a pattern would be consistent with studies of the determinants of technical efficiency, which have regularly found maximum efficiency at a moderate level of concentration, presumably still in the Nash orbit, and with efficiency declining for more highly concentrated industries.[13] On the other hand, cartel-like stabilization of conduct at the highest observed levels of concentration cannot be ruled out because a number of studies have found the incidence of nonprice competition and of market-share instability to be maximized at concentration levels lower than the highest ones observed.[14] Therefore diverse expectations exist about the relation between intertemporal stability and concentration. Stability might decrease monotonically with concentration, or there might be an internal minimum followed by an increase in stability at the highest concentration levels.

Changes in and variability of concentration raise their own questions about intertemporal stability. Changes in concentration within the oligopolistic orbit themselves imply changes in firms' modes of behavioral interaction involving decreased intertemporal stability. The variables used are CONCCHG, the percentage change in concentration over the period 1970 to 1979, and CONCABS, the absolute value of the percentage change in concentration over the same period.

Changes in concentration presumably result from internal market forces or some outside disturbance such as market growth, import competition and innovation. It is expected that industries will vary in the extent to which these disturbances induce changes in competitive behavior. Although such disturbance sources will be addressed specifically by the inclusion in the analysis of certain exogenous variables, the interindustry differences in the responses to such disturbances will be reflected at least partly in changes in concentration.

With regard to any long-run trends in concentration, the ultimate effect of such basic structural changes on the stability of the dispersion in productivity will depend on a number of factors. The beginning level of concentration in the industry—as well as the direction, degree, and speed of any long-run change in concentration—will determine the extent to which the behavioral interactions between the plants are affected and thereby the extent of the effect on the intertemporal stability in productivity dispersion. The source will also be important: Compare a change in concentration due to market growth or shrinkage to one due to changing optimal sizes of firms or plants. A number of possible scenarios emanate from the combination of these factors. Therefore there are a diverse mix of expectations about the relation between intertemporal stability and long-run changes in concentration, and no definite theoretical sign predictions.

9.4.2 International Competition

Imports

The level of imports as a percentage of industry shipments reflects the degree to which the plants in an industry are exposed to various sources of disturbance that originate outside the domestic market. Such external disturbances would include exchange rate fluctuations, changes in tariffs, new product introductions, and the introduction of new technologies. Assuming that each plant is operating at its optimum level of productivity and that all products, both domestic and foreign, are homogeneous, it is expected that all of the plants within an industry would be affected similarly by any disturbance emanating from abroad. Hence the stability in the productivity dispersion would not be affected. Suppose, more realistically, that both the foreign and domestic products are heterogeneous, which is consistent with many findings of empirical research on industrial organization and international (especially intraindustry) trade (Caves 1981, 1988). This assumption implies that the effect of the disturbances associated with imports on the individual plants within an industry will be uneven. Moreover the same heterogeneity should extend to the costs of adjustment per period faced by each plant. Hence the plants are expected to have varied responses to such global disturbances and differences in the speeds of adjustment. Instability in the dispersion of plant productivity should increase with the level of imports. The variable used is IMP, the average level of imports as a percentage of total output plus imports, averaged over 1970–75.

Exports

The level of exports as a percentage of industry shipments also reflects the degree to which plants within an industry are directly exposed to global market disturbances, but the mechanisms at work should differ slightly from those of imports. Not all plants within an industry participate in foreign markets, and there is uneven participation among those that do export. Larger plants are more likely to export than smaller plants because of the higher fixed costs of exporting than of distribution into domestic commerce. In addition the small plants that do export are likely to export large percentages of their production. Hence plants' diverse degrees of participation in export markets imply diverse consequences of export disturbances for plants' productivity levels.[15] To the extent that individual plants participate in global markets, each will be exposed to many possible market disturbances, including demand changes, changes in various government policies, technological changes, and exchange rate fluctuations. Such external disturbances will affect plants unequally according to their diverse patterns of participation in export markets. Furthermore, assuming heterogeneity in both domestic and foreign products, the exporting plants are expected to vary in their responses to any global disturbances and differences in their speeds of adjustment. As a result the instability in the dispersion in plant productivity should increase with the industry's level of exports. The variable used to test this effect is EXP, the average level of exports as a percentage of total output for 1970–75.

9.4.3 Business Organization

The internal organization of firms within an industry may affect the intertemporal stability of the dispersion in plant productivity. All firms in a perfectly competitive industry (surrounded by competitive factor and product markets) are expected to have similar organizational profiles, given a standardized product and corresponding production functions. However, more realistically, with heterogenous products, imperfectly competitive interactions of varying degrees, variations in the vintages of capital employed, differences in the patterns of diversification, and the like, it is expected that the plants within an industry would offer variegated profiles of organizations. This discussion seeks to identify the influences that the organizational elements have on the intertemporal stability of productivity dispersion.

Diversification

The degree to which an individual plant focuses on the production of the products of a certain industry reflects the extent to which that specific plant has developed particular expertise in the successful production and marketing of those products. This distinctive expertise may manifest itself in more uniform recognition of the quantitative and qualitative dimensions of changes in both consumer demand and factor supply, and thus in speed or extent of adjustment.

Moreover, the more specialized the plant, the less will be its exposure to disturbances in other markets. For various reasons, including product heterogeneity and diversity in the assets controlled by firms, managers of individual plants within an industry will adopt disparate patterns of diversification into other industries. Let us further assume that disturbances are market specific and randomly distributed among markets. The more diversified the plants classified to an industry, the greater is their exposure to the disturbances emanating from other markets and thus the greater is the intertemporal instability in productivity dispersion. Additionally diversification increases the likelihood of dissimilar types or vintages of capital being employed by the plants within an industry, hence augmenting the asymmetry in the rates of adjustment to any particular disturbance. Consequently the more specialized are the plants within an industry, the more will they be shielded from disturbances arising in other markets, and the less diverse will be their individual rates of adjustment. Hence intertemporal stability is expected to increase with the level of plant specialization. The specific variable employed is SPEC, the percentage of total industry output produced by establishments classified to the main industry group, averaged over the period 1963–79.

Concentration of Production in Large Plants

Small establishments are not miniature versions of large establishments. Production processes are generally different in different sized plants. In particular, empirical research has found that capital intensity increases with plant size (Davis 1956; Shen 1965; Caves and Pugel 1980). This relationship implies that large plants have more sunken input combinations and therefore have slower rates of adjustment to any changed conditions. Moreover the individual plants are expected to employ a diverse pattern of capital vintages. As a result intertemporal stability is expected to decrease with the proportion of production produced by large plants, particularly in the sense of retarded adjustment to disturbances. The variable used is LGESTB, the average share of industry employment in establishments employing 1,000 or more workers, 1972–77.

Multiplant Operations of Leading Firms

Leading firms in some industries operate multiple plants supplying a similar selection of products. With multiplant operations, a number of plants are consolidated under one administrative direction. Assume that information on how to raise or optimize productivity in an industry, possessed by the manager of one plant, percolates more quickly to managers of other plants when they are controlled by the same enterprise than when they are independent. The assumption requires nothing more than a manager's incentive to keep profit-increasing tricks secret from competitors unless they can be efficiently licensed. With one management team directing the activity of a number of plants, instead of a totally separate management team directing each different plant, the responses of plants to any particular disturbance should be more similar.[16] The variance in plants' rates of adjustment is expected to diminish as the extent of multiplant operations increases. As a result the intertemporal stability in productivity dispersion is expected to increase with multiplant operations. The variable used is MULTI, the average number of plants operated by the five leading firms in an industry, 1972–77. MULTI emphasizes the multiplant development of the leading firms only, consistent with the evidence that multiplant operation increases with both plant and firm size.

9.4.4 Innovation and Occurrence of Change

The plants within an industry are subject to a number of dynamic forces that disturb their realized revenue-productivity levels. As stated earlier, the greater the incidence of such disturbances, and the more irregularly they affect individual plants, the less stable over time is the dispersion in productivity. The sources and effects of the dynamic incursions on the intertemporal stability of plant productivity are considered below.

Research and Development Intensity

The intensity of the research and development activities of the firms reflects the magnitude of technological opportunity and change experienced within their industry. Because of uneven success rates, high levels of R&D imply increased dispersion in the productivity levels realized by plants within the industry. Also innovative efforts are expected to have random patterns of payoffs over time in the achievement of new technological processes, new product introductions, and improvements in existing products.[17] Therefore intertemporal instability in productivity dispersion is expected to also increase with R&D intensity. The variable used is RD, the average level of R&D expenditures as a percentage of total sales for the years 1975 and 1978.

Work Stoppages

Work stoppages by employees are a source of disturbance to the revenue-productivity level of a plant, and the more days lost per year, the more contentious are management-labor relations and the more is plant productivity likely to be impaired. Moreover union activity in the United Kingdom is rather parochial, being localized around individual plants. Therefore the disturbances due to work stoppages are expected to affect an industry's plants unevenly. Besides, contentious management-labor relations tend to inject internal coordination issues that constrain the rate at which a plant adjusts to any new circumstances. In particular, research has found that unionized labor in the United Kingdom has been more resistent to technological changes than workers in the same industries in other countries. Hence the unions require a number of impact studies and review

procedures before any adjustments can be made to the production process.[18] These encumbering procedures and negotiations naturally retard
the speed at which any plant can modify its operations in response to any
new conditions. Consequently, contentious management-labor relations
predict both a greater incidence of disturbances experienced by the individual plants and greater variation in the rates of adjustment among
plants. Thus the intertemporal instability in plant productivity is expected
to increase with days lost due to work stoppages. The variable used is
LOST, the average number of days lost annually per 1,000 employees due
to work stoppages in the industry for the period of 1970–75.

Growth in Output

A rapid growth in output that is due to increasing demand puts pressure
on the capacity of the individual plants in an industry. Each plant must
therefore consider whether its individual capital expenditure plans provide
the optimal capacity to meet current and expected future growth in
demand. A checkerboard configuration is expected to prevail in the vintages of capital employed by the individual plants. Each of them will have
different levels of capacity utilization and will be at different points in their
respective plans for capital renewal and expansion.[19] Consequently each
plant will respond differently and at a different rate to an increase in
demand that induces growth in industry output. Moreover high rates of
growth are probably associated with higher rates of various qualitative
changes that would produce churning in individual plants' revenue-
productivity positions. With high growth optimal capacity may be less predictable, so more plants in a given year wind up out of equilibrium because
they guessed wrong.[20] Thus the intertemporal instability in productivity
dispersion is expected to increase with the growth rate in output. The
specific variable used is OPCHG, the average annual percentage change
in net output, 1970–79.

Net Entry

There is a good chance that both the mean and dispersion of productivity
levels of new plants entering an industry diverge from those of established
plants. A steep learning curve may be faced by each new plant that enters
an industry. Until the plant smooths out its operations and its internal
coordination, as well as refines its perception of conditions in the product

and factor markets, its productivity level is expected to lie somewhat outside the range of productivity of the veteran plants.[21] Also suppose that potential entrepreneurs know only the average level of managerial ability in the populace and not their own position, and that they can discover how good they are only by entering and trying (Jovanovic 1982). The productivity levels of new plants will then be more diverse than those of the established ones because of those fated not to succeed. Therefore, the greater is the turnover of plants in an industry, the greater is the intertemporal variability in productivity dispersion. Data on the gross turnover in plants are unavailable, yet it is possible to calculate the net change in plants in each industry. The variable used is PLANTABS, the absolute value of the percentage change in the number of plants during the period of 1963 to 1979.

9.4.5   Level and Costs of Inputs

As indicated in the introduction of this section, an industry's combination of inputs can affect its intertemporal stability through the size and persistence of divergences of establishments' actual from normal net output per head. Some input-choice decisions may also be considered sources of disturbance.

Given all input and product prices and the production technology used in the industry, there exists an equilibrium value-maximizing level for NOPH. Any disturbance to input or output markets, technology, product characteristics, and so forth, pushes the plant's NOPH to a new value out of equilibrium. The manager is induced to reoptimize the plant's activities to the new situation, which may involve reconfiguring its inputs and activities. The reconfiguring changes may entail substantial divestments and investments, each with its transaction or adjustment cost. In general, adjustment is spread optimally over time, quite possibly more than a year.

Input adjustment costs affect both the sizes and the intertemporal stability of the intraindustry dispersions of NOPH. The greater the adjustment costs facing plants in an industry, given the magnitude of disturbances striking it, the longer does it take the intraindustry dispersion to resume an equilibrium value. The degree of autoregression seen in year-to-year movements of the intraindustry dispersion should be especially affected.

If adjustment costs were independent of the input mix, no interindustry differences could be predicted. Independence, however, is improbable because of differences in the properties of inputs and their terms of employment. Each input source will be examined in terms of its projected effect on the intertemporal stability of productivity dispersion.

Capital Intensity

Capital-expenditure decisions clearly involve substantial planning and construction lags, and these perpetuate out-of-equilibrium NOPH values. The more capital intensive is an industry, the larger are the proportional distortions (windfall gains/losses) that enter into NOPH in the short run, and the greater is the intertemporal variability of industry NOPH as disturbances and adjustments run their course.[22] This can be measured by the variable KL68, defined as the capital–labor ratio for 1968. A broader measure of capital intensity that encompasses the entire period studied would be preferred. However, capital stock data are available only for 1968. The one-period observation should be highly correlated with an average level for the whole period.

Sunkenness of Capital

It is probably reasonable to assume that the specificity and sunkenness of an industry's fixed capital if anything increases with the capital-intensity of its production process, so KL68 reflects the sunkenness as well as the importance of capital commitments in an industry. Ideally sunkenness would be measured independently. Although no direct measures exist, an indirect measure is available in the importance of rented capital in an industry. For capital to be rented at arm's length without being frustrated by transaction-cost and agency problems between owner and user, it must presumably have alternative uses (not be highly specialized) and be capable of physical separation from the user's plant without exorbitant removal costs. The importance of rental capital should therefore offset the negative effect of capital intensity on intertemporal stability and thus exert a positive influence on stability. The variables employed are RENT, expenditures on rented capital expenditures as a percentage of the value of output for the period 1972 to 1979, and RENTCHG, the percentage change in the proportion of expenditures on rented capital for the same period.

Net Capital Expenditures

KL68 and RENT pick up the influence of an industry's long-run or equilibrium capital input, but they omit information that is available on the interannual variation of actual expenditures on plant and equipment. Although the average scale of annual capital expenditures is related to equilibrium capital intensity (given the depreciation rate, rate of market growth, and other such factors), the interannual variation of the rate of capital expenditure is an independent source of intertemporal instability that can be controlled. Moreover the average level of annual capital investment expenditures indicates the extent to which new technology is flowing into an industry, thereby broadening the spectrum of technologies that are employed in an industry at the same time. The greater is this vintage effect, the greater should be the intertemporal variation of productivity dispersion.[23] Hence stability should decrease with the variable NKXAVG, the average level of annual net capital expenditures as a percentage of total output for 1963 to 1979, and with the variable, INCVNKX, the intertemporal variation of the interplant dispersion of net capital expenditures for the same period. INCVNKX should be correlated with the intertemporal variability of the typical plant's expenditure.

Nonproduction Workers

The literature on labor hoarding implies adjustment costs (the recruitment and training of replacements) discourage the instantaneous downward adjustment of labor input following a disturbance. The labor force is probably not homogeneous with regard to adjustment costs. Therefore, although measures of labor hoarding can be developed, attention is directed instead to the interindustry differences in labor adjustment associated with the composition of an industry's labor input. An industry's intertemporal variability should increase with the nonproduction-worker component of its workforce, for two reasons. First, white-collar workers seem subject to greater costs of recruitment and effective integration into the organization. Second, they typically perform overhead-type activities that (it is assumed) do not vary in scale so long as the plant remains in operation, while the services of production workers are used in current output. That is, production workers' wages enter into marginal cost while nonproduction workers' salaries do not. Then the greater the proportion of employees who are nonproduction workers, the greater are the proportional disturbances that can occur to NOPH, and the greater is the intertemporal variability of NOPH as (again) disturbances and adjustments run their course.[24] The specific variable used is NPW, the average share of total employment allocated to nonproduction workers, 1963–79.

Material Inputs

The productivity measure NOPH of course omits materials inputs, so disturbances to materials-inputs markets and usage do not automatically affect NOPH in any particular way. Nonetheless, there may be a mechanism by which intertemporal stability decreases with the importance of materials inputs in total cost. Suppose that each industry buys the same primary input, whose price is stochastic with a known mean and variance. Production functions differ, with some industries using much of this input and some little relative to all other inputs (capital and labor). Assume that market prices of industries' outputs adjust to variations in input prices only with a lag. Then the higher the proportion of materials inputs in an industry's total costs, the greater will be the variance of NOPH, because a larger variance is entering into a smaller total of value-added opportunity costs. The variable used to test this effect is PURCH, the average level of total material inputs as a percentage of total output, 1963–79.

Inventories

The holding of inventories, especially finished-good inventories, may affect intertemporal stability. Optimal inventory holdings serve as a buffer between the rate of output and the random arrival of demand. On the one hand, they permit smoothing the plant's rate of output over time, and in that sense a higher level of inventories should correspond to greater intertemporal stability. Optimal inventories also reflect the expected incidence of disturbances, however. The greater the churning of inventories —buildup and drawdown over time—the greater should be both the (unobserved) incidence of various relevant disturbances and the short-term variation of plants' output rates and NOPH levels. The variables used are STKAVG, the average level of inventories as a percentage of total industry output, 1963–79, and INCVSTK, the intertemporal variation of the intra-industry dispersion of inventory holdings. INCVSTK indicates indirectly the variability of inventories for the typical establishment because off-setting changes are surely important within industries. Other buffers play a role parallel to inventories, such as order backlogs in production-to-order industries, but cannot be controlled directly due to lack of data.

Resale Goods

The composition of the plants' activities may affect the intertemporal stability of productivity dispersion. In particular, variations in the percentage of sales accounted for by resale transactions will affect the intra-industry dispersion of plant productivity levels. Most inputs to the plant (except the purchased goods) must be independent of the level of resale transactions. Any fluctuations in the volume of resales will translate themselves into magnified changes in NOPH, unlike demand disturbances that require the application of more of all inputs including workers. Hence intertemporal instability should increase with the level of resale transactions. The variable used to test this effect is GOOD, the percentage of total sales accounted for by resale goods, averaged over 1970 to 1979.

The variables discussed in this section will be used as the exogenous variables in the following analysis of the determinants of the intertemporal behavior of productivity dispersion. Table 9.11 presents the basic descriptive statistics of these variables, and their sources are identified in the appendix at the end of this chapter.

9.5   Report of Statistical Results

The hypotheses developed in section 9.4 are now tested and the results reported. The process of confronting theory with evidence in this case is complicated by a number of factors that preclude a strictly classical approach. The principal ones are

1.   The theoretical foundation just laid consists not of one monolithic, widely accepted model but a number of somewhat independent conjectures. Each is plausible on the basis of standard theory and empirical evidence from other contexts, but none is compelling in the sense of identifying uniquely important influences on behavior well supported in other contexts by previous research.

2.   The successful empirical test of a hypothesis requires not just that the theory be correct but also that the data pick up disturbances that will put the theoretical mechanism into play. The hypotheses about sources of disturbances could lack confirmation simply because no disturbing changes in the exogenous variables took place (even if the conditional effects of their occurrence were correctly predicted).

3.   The market-structure variables available to embody the theoretical effects inevitably represent something short of ideal, so one's judgment about provisional empirical results demands some allowance for the qual-

Table 9.11
Descriptive statistics for regressors

Symbol	Minimum[a]	Mean[b]	Maximum[c]	Coefficient of variation[d]
CONC	8.000	47.856	92.000	45.809
CONCCHG	−137.079	−1.423	75.342	NA
CONCABS	0.000	12.254	137.079	129.900
EXP	0.126	53.835	1013.356	232.206
GOOD	0.987	8.634	52.874	90.523
IMP	0.032	19.651	93.823	107.720
INCVNKX	11.208	32.789	89.397	42.730
INCVSTK	11.491	28.725	72.078	37.615
KL68	0.704	11.812	98.654	170.757
LGESTB	0.000	31.518	87.510	78.225
LOST	2.600	425.644	3422.167	139.369
MULTI	1.000	4.891	37.500	100.866
NKXAVG	−9.061	3.391	12.911	69.575
NPW	11.165	26.616	51.362	37.975
OPCHG	−6.461	13.81	118.259	NA
PLANTABS	0.791	35.911	161.074	NA
PURCH	25.532	54.141	178.942	28.520
RD	0.025	1.217	18.595	195.981
RENT	0.174	0.752	6.270	76.708
RENTCHG	−156.597	22.064	200.000	NA
SPEC	45.333	88.180	99.167	9.888
STKAVG	0.65	14.158	66.049	72.931

Note: Observations were taken on 128 industries for each variable. See the appendix for the source for each exogenous variable.
a. Minimum value of observations of stated variable.
b. Unweighted mean over 128 industries of the observations for stated variable.
c. Maximum value of observations of stated variable.
d. Coefficient of variation of basic observations of stated variable.

ity of the statistical embodiment as well as the conceptual tightness of the hypothesis.

4. Market-structure variables used in interindustry analyses are notoriously prone to multicollinearity of a predictable sort. Econometric procedures for dealing with this multicollinearity are generally not very helpful unless a particular partial relationship is the center of attention, which is not the case here.

5. There are several dependent variables (set forth in section 9.3), not just one. To avoid cluttering section 9.4, only sporadically were the hypotheses about intertemporal stability tied to one particular measure thereof. Some

discriminations can be made, however, about which intertemporal measure is best aligned with any given hypothesis. Attention will be paid to that issue in reporting and evaluating the results.

6. The economic behavior measured by the dependent variables is sufficiently important and unexplored that one does not rely solely on received economic theory to identify all structural correlates of possible interest. For example, if the intraindustry dispersions of NOPH in certain types of industries have been systematically expanding or contracting, that knowledge is valuable even if a theoretical explanation does not fall readily to hand.

The combined force of these considerations is to support an approach to the testing of hypotheses that is long on pragmatism and emphasizes the robustness of particular partial relations as well as their survival of the standard tests of statistical significance in single-equation tests.

Table 9.12 outlines the empirical results. The most satisfactory equation after filtering on the above criteria is reported for each of the dependent variables. Some strong associations have manifested themselves that are consistent with the hypotheses and the findings of other empirical work. Also some interesting relationships have been discovered that point to the need for additional inquiry. Each of the four broad categories will be discussed separately.

9.5.1 Intertemporal Variation in Productivity Dispersion

The primary focus of this analysis is the intertemporal stability of the productivity dispersion and testing the theoretical factors that should govern the variation over time of the dispersion in plant productivity. Of the dependent variables examined, the one that measures this concept most straightforwardly is INTCV, the intertemporal coefficient of variation of the productivity dispersion (see section 9.3 for details on its derivation). INTCV is an unadjusted measure that captures the total variation over time in the dispersion in plant productivity. As seen in table 9.12, seven exogenous variables have been found significantly related to the intertemporal stability of productivity dispersion as measured by INTCV and the adjusted R^2 is 0.331.

Changes in the competitive conditions of an industry significantly affect the stability of the dispersion in productivity, as measured by the variable CONCABS. The results indicate that the greater is the change in concen-

Table 9.12
Results on the interindustry determinants of the intertemporal behavior of productivity dispersion

Equation	Regression model
1	$INTCV = 9.584^{aa} + 0.137^{aa}CONCABS + 0.066^{b}IMP - 0.182^{c}MULTI$

1 $INTCV = 9.584^{aa} + 0.137^{aa}CONCABS + 0.066^{b}IMP - 0.182^{c}MULTI$
       (4.305)   (3.296)   (2.090)   (1.389)
       $+ 0.005^{a}LOST - 4.168^{a}RENT + 0.114^{b}INCVSTK + 0.178^{b}GOOD$
        (4.853)   (3.530)   (1.972)   (2.056)
   Adjusted $R^2 = 0.331, DF = 120$

2 $STANDERR = 6.581^{aa} - 0.095^{bb}CONCABS + 0.039IMP - 0.188^{c}MULTI$
       (3.02)   (2.424)   (1.281)   (1.515)
       $+ 0.005^{a}LOST + 0.041^{c}KL68 - 3.214^{a}RENT$
        (5.131)   (1.324)   (2.844)
       $+ 0.158^{a}INCVSTK + 0.195^{b}GOOD$
        (2.896)   (2.345)
   Adjusted $R^2 = 0.320, DF = 119$

3 $INTANN1 = -0.218 + 0.014^{b}IMP + 0.001^{a}LOST - 0.397^{c}RENT$
       (0.509) (2.216)   (3.67)   (1.640)
       $+ 0.024^{b}INCVSTK + 0.037^{b}GOOD$
        (1.947)   (2.045)
   Adjusted $R^2 = 0.138, DF = 122$

4 $INTANN2 = -0.700 + 0.069^{aa}CONCABS + 0.002^{a}LOST + 0.017^{c}KL68$
       (0.933) (4.613)   (5.609)   (1.493)
       $- 1.281^{a}RENT + 0.047^{b}INCVSTK + 0.066^{b}GOOD$
        (2.983)   (2.281)   (2.091)
   Adjusted $R^2 = 0.388, DF = 121$

5 $LINCOEF1 = -0.001 + 0.00007^{cc}CONCCHG + 0.0008^{b}RD - 0.0001^{c}KL68$
       (0.533) (1.825)   (2.350)   (1.616)
       $- 0.00002^{c}RENTCHG + 0.0002^{a}INCVNKX$
        (1.404)   (2.915)
       $- 0.003^{a}STKAVG + 0.003^{a}GOOD$
        (4.394)   (2.950)
   Adjusted $R^2 = 0.221, DF = 120$

6 $LINCOEF2 = 0.006^{aa} - 0.0001^{aa}CONCABS + 0.000002^{b}LOST$
       (3.595) (4.086)   (1.687)
       $+ 0.00003^{b}PLANTABS - 0.004^{a}RENT - 0.001^{b}NPW$
        (1.750)   (3.854)   (2.173)
       $+ 0.001^{c}STKAVG + 0.002^{b}GOOD$
        (1.385)   (2.299)
   Adjusted $R^2 = 0.254, DF = 120$

Note: The t-value for each regression coefficient is denoted below the coefficient. Where one-tail tests of significance are appropriate, a = 1 percent, b = 5 percent, and c = 10 percent; where two-tail tests of significance are appropriate, aa = 1 percent, bb = 5 percent, and cc = 10 percent.

tration (regardless of direction) the greater will be the intertemporal variation in the productivity dispersion. This outcome conforms to the a priori hypothesis that individual firms and thus plants will be affected differently by alternations in competitive conditions and will adjust at different rates to these disturbances.

International competition is also found to affect the intertemporal stability of the productivity dispersion. The variable IMP is found to have a significantly positive effect on the intertemporal variation of productivity dispersion. This result corresponds to the a priori hypothesis that exposure to global disturbances affects individual plants unevenly. Moreover the variable EXP has a significantly positive coefficient when substituted for the imports variable, indicating that participation in foreign markets also increases the exposure of exporting plants to external disturbances. However, EXP is not significant if IMP is also present in the regression. IMP is the stronger of the two variables and is therefore included in the most satisfactory regression in table 9.12.

Of the organizational features examined, only one proves significant in the empirical tests: the extent of multiplant operations by the leading five firms, MULTI. This organizational property is found to increase significantly the intertemporal stability of productivity dispersion, which corresponds to the a priori hypothesis that the multiplant operations of firms decrease the variance in the rates of adjustment across plants. As a result the productivity dispersion is more stable over time. The degree of industry specialization and the proportion of employment in large plants (1,000 plus employees) are found to have insignificant effects.

The number of days lost due to work stoppages, LOST, is the only element of innovative activity and change that is found to have a significant impact on the intertemporal variation of productivity dispersion. This variable has the expected positive coefficient. Hence antagonistic management-labor relations affect the incidence of disturbances and the rate of adjustment of individual plants, such that the dispersion in plant productivity is less stable over time.

The other elements of change, namely, R&D expenditures, output growth, and net entry, do not have significant effects on the intertemporal variation of productivity dispersion.

Three input variables are found to have significant effects on the stability of productivity dispersion. The intertemporal churning in inventory dispersion and the percentage of resale goods each has the expected positive effect on the intertemporal variation of productivity dispersion. The percentage of rented capital employed has the expected negative.

The intertemporal churning of inventory dispersion, INCVSTK, is found to have a destabilizing effect on productivity dispersion. Corresponding with the hypothesis, the fluctuations in the dispersion of inventory levels appear to reflect the incidence of disturbances, which augment the short-term variation of plants' output rates and NOPH levels.[25]

The level of resale goods (GOOD) has a significantly positive association with the intertemporal variability of productivity dispersion. The greater are the variations in the revenue of individual plants, as represented by this variable, the greater will be the observed instability.

The level of rental capital is found to contribute significantly to the stability productivity dispersion. As an inverse measure of the sunkenness of capital commitments in an industry, the level of rental capital indicates the importance of less specialized equipment in an industry.

The other variables related to the level and costs of inputs (capital intensity, net capital expenditures, material inputs, and nonproduction workers) are not found to have stable, significant coefficients.[26]

9.5.2   Standard Error around the Linear Trend

The dependent variable STANDERR is by construction closely related to the intertemporal coefficient of variation, except that STANDERR describes the percentage variation over time in productivity dispersion after a linear trend has been removed (see section 9.3 for details on its derivation). The multiple regression results should parallel those for the intertemporal coefficient of variation, which they do with one notable addition.

Equation 2 of table 9.12 indicates the most satisfactory regression for STANDERR based on the analytical criteria listed above. The adjusted R^2 for this regression is 0.320, and eight exogenous variables are found to be significant. Seven of these variables also appear in the best fitting regression for INTCV above and have the same sign in both equations: CON-CABS, IMP, MULTI, LOST, RENT, INCVSTK and GOOD.[27] One additional factor, however, exerts some influence (10 percent significance) on the detrended intertemporal variation in productivity dispersion, capital intensity of an industry (KL68). Thus, as expected in the a priori hypothesis, the more capital intensive is an industry, the larger are the proportional distortions that enter NOPH in the short run, and the greater is the intertemporal variability of industry NOPH as disturbances and adjustments run their course.

9.5.3   Average Interannual Variation

To gain perspective on the year-to-year sequence of changes in productivity dispersion, two measures of average interannual variation are used, INTANN1 and INTANN2 (see section 9.3 for their derivations). These variables measure the average annual percentage variation in productivity dispersion, with INTANN1 taking into account the gaps between years in the sample and INTANN2 ignoring the differing time gaps. They emphasize the temporal sequence of changes, which is ignored by INTCV and STANDERR.

Equation 3 of table 9.12 indicates the most informative regression for INTANN1, as does equation 4 for INTANN2. The results for the two variables are similar, and both models agree with the results derived for INTCV and STANDERR above. All of the coefficients have the expected signs. However, the adjusted R^2's for these regressions reveal that INTANN1 is less well explained than INTANN2 or INTCV and STANDERR. Moreover all of the significant variables in the regressions for INTANN1 and INTANN2 are also significant in the regressions for INTCV and/or STANDERR. The interpretations are basically the same for the average annual variation in productivity dispersion as they are for the average variation over the entire sample period; hence they will not be repeated in detail here.[28]

The model for INTANN1 contains five significant exogenous variables, IMP, LOST, RENT, INCVSTK, and GOOD. This is the only model in which concentration is not a significant factor. In the investigation of alternative models for INTANN1, the variable CONC was the strongest of the concentration measures, whereas CONCABS appeared in the previous regressions. The estimated coefficient for CONC was always positive and oftentimes was greater than its standard error, but it never proved significant. This evidence weakly indicates that the average interannual variation in productivity dispersion increases with the average concentration level, consistent with hypotheses dealing with both oligopoly behavior and the structural foundations of concentration.

Six exogenous variables are significant in the model for INTANN2 (equation 4). LOST, RENT, INCVSTK, and GOOD are repeated from the regression for INTANN1. In addition CONCABS and KL68 are significant in the INTANN2 regression. Overall, the results for INTANN2 correspond very closely to the results for INTCV and STANDERR, with each of the significant variables here appearing in one or both of equations 1 and 2. The only variables that proved significant in the INTCV and STANDERR regressions that are not retained in the INTANN2 regression are IMP and MULTI.[29] Also the explanatory power of the INTANN2 regression is greater than that for the INTCV and STANDERR regressions.

As can be seen from equations 1 through 4 of table 9.12, the factors that influence the long-run variation in productivity dispersion also drive the short-run variation (with one exception). This result is not surprising given that INTANN1, INTANN2, INTCV, and STANDERR are highly correlated with each other (table 9.9). However, the evidence we have from equation 4 indicates that the identified determinants account for a greater proportion of the short-run variation than of the long-run variation. Hence the temporal sequence of changes in productivity dispersion is more strongly linked to the disturbances and adjustment costs associated with the identified determinants.

9.5.4 Linear Trend Coefficient

Two versions of the linear trend coefficient are examined. The first, LINCOEF1, measures the direction and the magnitude of any time trend in the dispersion of plant productivity. The absolute value of the linear trend coefficient, LINCOEF2, measures the magnitude of any time trend in productivity dispersion, regardless of direction.[30]

The theoretical sources of interannual stability or variability delineated in section 9.4 should give rise to period-long trends only under special conditions, such as permanent disturbances that give rise to substantial but very slow adjustments. More plausibly time trends reflect changes over time in the structural variables that determine the equilibrium levels of productivity dispersion and efficiency. As a result the trend is expected to be related to changes in structural variables that determine the level of dispersion. Moreover, given the importance of productivity dispersions and the limited knowledge of their behavior, it is desirable to investigate the associations between the trends and the structural characteristics of industries, even if no obvious causal hypothesis predicts them.

Equation 5 of table 9.12 reports the results for LINCOEF1. Seven exogenous variables prove to be significantly related to the linear trend coefficient. Also the explanatory power of the model for LINCOEF1 is less than that for INTCV, STANDERR, and INTANN2 above, with an adjusted R^2 of 0.221. The changes in the industry's competitive conditions, as measured by CONCCHG, positively affect the linear trend coefficient. The result implies that the greater is the percentage increase in concentration, the larger will be the upward trend in productivity dispersion. This finding is consistent with one of the initial hypotheses of intertemporal instability increasing with concentration and with the results for INTANN1 above, as well as a finding of Mayes and Green (chapter 4) about the effect of concentration on the level of efficiency.

The level of innovative activity as measured by RD is found to have a significant positive association with the linear trend coefficient, implying that the greater the intensity of research and development ventures, the larger will be the upward trend in productivity dispersion. This result seems related to the hypothesis that innovative activity has a destabilizing effect on the intraindustry dispersion of plant productivity, but it is not obvious why a high and stable research orientation would lead to an ever-increasing dispersion.

The remaining five significant exogenous variables in equation 5 reflect the impact of the composition of inputs, and the results are mixed. The capital–labor ratio (KL68) and the average level of year-end inventories (STKAVG) are found to have significant negative effects on the trend in the dispersion of productivity. These findings contradict the a priori hypotheses as well as the previous results regarding capital intensity and inventories.[31]

The intertemporal churning of the dispersion of net capital expenditures and the average level of resale goods (INCVNKX and GOOD, respectively) each exerts a significant positive effect on the trend in productivity dispersion. The percentage change in the proportion of rented capital (RENTCHG) has a significant negative effect on the trend. These outcomes seem related to the a priori hypotheses that the composition of inputs affects the adjustment costs facing plants in an industry which is reflected in the intertemporal behavior of the dispersion of productivity.[32]

Equation 6 reports the regression for LINCOEF2. This dependent variable measures the long-run trend in productivity dispersion, regardless of direction. LINCOEF2 addresses the question of long-run stability rather than the direction of any trends. It is also more highly correlated with INTCV, STANDERR, INTANN1, and INTANN2 than is LINCOEF1, although LINCOEF2 does not directly measure short-run variations in productivity dispersion.

As seen in equation 6, seven exogenous variable are found to be related significantly with the absolute value of the linear trend coefficient. The LINCOEF2 regression performs slightly better than the LINCOEF1 regression but less well than those for INTCV, STANDERR, and INTANN2 above. Also, of the two linear trend measurements, the results for LINCOEF2 correspond more closely to the results of INTCV, STANDERR, and INTANN2, with one unexpectedly signed coefficient.

CONCABS, LOST, RENT, and GOOD have significant coefficients with the expected signs. The results for these exogenous variables parallel those in the models for INTCV, STANDERR, and INTANN2 above. Moreover CONCABS is much more significant for LINCOEF2 than is CONCCHG for LINCOEF1, tending to confirm the importance of disturbances in competitive conditions without regard to the sign of the exogenous structural change.

The average level of inventories (STKAVG) is significant in this model with the expected positive sign, whereas the intertemporal churning of inventory dispersion (INCVSTK) has proved significant in previous models where an inventory variable has appeared. As posited in the a priori hypotheses, the holding of inventories appears to reflect the incidence of disturbances and thus indicates the presence of destabilizing effects on the dispersion in plant productivity. Although it is expected that higher levels of inventories will be associated with greater variation in productivity dispersion, it is unclear why higher levels of inventories are related to a monotonic, long-run trend (up or down) in productivity dispersion.

Plant turnover, PLANTABS, also is found to have a positive significant effect on the absolute value of the linear trend coefficient. This effect, in common with CONCABS, indicates that sustained changes in an industry's population of plants or firms are associated without regard to sign with cumulative changes in productivity dispersion.

The proportion of nonproduction workers (NPW) appears significant for the first time in this model. However, contrary to the a priori hypothesis, the coefficient is negatively signed, indicating that the long-run trend in productivity dispersion decreases as the proportion of nonproduction workers increases.

The proportion of nonproduction workers is expected to have the same impact on the variation of productivity dispersion as fixed capital. Hence this unexpected result was analyzed further. The simple correlation coefficient between LINCOEF2 and NPW is also negative, so the negative regression coefficient is not due to multicollinearity. In addition NPW does not have a consistent correlation pattern with the other dependent variables in this study, as does the other major exogenous variables in the analysis. Therefore whatever drives the NPW result in equation 6, a corresponding robust relation does not exist through the data set.

A number of insights have been gained from the analysis of the linear trend coefficients. In general, the results for the LINCOEF1 and LINCO-EF2 models tend to correspond to the results for the models for INTCV, STANDERR, and INTANN above. However, some questions still remain regarding the unexpected signs of the coefficients of STKAVG and KL68 in the LINCOEF1 model. These perverse signs are not present in any of the other models. Moreover, in reviewing the simple correlation coefficients among the exogenous and endogenous variables, the perverse results can not be attributed to multicollinearity. Attention therefore is directed toward the strength of the linear coefficient measure as a dependent variable (only 24 percent of the coefficients are significant) and the appropriateness of the algebraic measure, LINCOEF1. The results for the absolute measure, LINCOEF2, are generally more consistent with those of the other models in the study, but they suggest that apparent trends may result in most cases from nothing but large transient disturbances striking at the beginning or end of the period of observation. Hence it can be concluded that given the information available in the linear trend coefficients, the absolute measure is the stronger version of the variable, but even it adds little.

9.5.5 Intertemporal Behavior of the Basic Components of Plant Productivity

The components of net output per head, total net output, and total employment are examined in order to explore further the intertemporal behavior of productivity dispersion. The purpose of this decomposition of productivity is to investigate in another way the forces that drive the intertemporal churning of the dispersion of plant productivity. To this end, the relation of the intertemporal churning of the dispersion of the two basic components to the structural determinants is examined. Companion measures to INTCV were developed for these two components: the intertemporal coefficient of variation of the dispersion of total net output,

Table 9.13
Results on the interindustry determinants of the intertemporal behavior of the basic components of productivity dispersion

Equation	Regression model
1	$INTCV = 9.583^{aa} + 0.231^{b}INCVNO + 0.010INCVEMP$
	(4.037) (2.114) (0.098)
	Adjusted $R^2 = 0.055, DF = 125$
2	$INCVNO = 0.010 + 0.001^{b}CONC + 0.007^{a}RD + 0.001^{a}INCVNKX$
	(0.447) (2.254) (2.420) (2.783)
	$+ 0.001^{b}STKAVG + 0.005^{a}INCVSTK$
	(2.153) (8.830)
	Adjusted $R^2 = 0.524, DF = 122$

Note: The t-value for each regression coefficient is denoted below the coefficient. Where one-tail tests of significance are appropriate, a = 1 percent and b = 5 percent; where two-tail tests of significance are appropriate, aa = 1 percent.

INCVNO, and the intertemporal coefficient of variation of the dispersion of total employment, INCVEMP (see section 9.3 for details on their estimation).

To determine the relevant importance of the two components on the intertemporal behavior of productivity dispersion, INTCV was regressed on INCVNO and INCVEMP. The results are presented in equation 1 of table 9.13. It is found that only INCVNO has a significant coefficient. Hence the focus of the subsequent analysis is directed toward INCVNO.

An investigation was made of the structural determinants of the intertemporal variability of total net output, parallel to those for INTCV and the other productivity measures. Here industrial performance is being reviewed in the form of net output, instead of as net output per head. Although "output per unit of resource employed" is the appropriate measure for an analysis of productivity and efficiency, an examination of the structural determinants of the stability of output performance will indicate some of the mechanisms that generate the instability of productivity dispersion.

The relationships between the structural determinants and the intertemporal stability of the dispersion of net output are expected to be analogous to those posited for productivity dispersion in section 9.4 above. The regression was developed inductively and the patterns discovered are reported.

Equation 2 of table 9.13 reports the regression for INCVNO. Five variables are found to be related significantly to the intertemporal variation of the dispersion of net output. The average level of concentration, the level of research and development expenditures, the intertemporal variation of the dispersion of capital expenditures, the average level of inventories, and the intertemporal variation of inventory dispersion (CONC, RD, STKAVG, INCVNKX, and INCVSTK, respectively) are all found to have positive effects on the intertemporal stability of net output dispersion. These results conform to the a priori hypotheses of section 9.4 for productivity dispersion, and they parallel those derived for the net output per head models above. Therefore some of the structural forces that contribute significantly to the variation of productivity dispersion also contribute significantly to the variation of the dispersion of total net output.

It is also notable that the input-composition variables (e.g., KL68, GOOD, and RENT) are not found to be significant determinants of the stability of net output dispersion as they proved to be in the productivity dispersion models. This result is expected since these variables do not operate directly through demand-side disturbances. Thus, although most variation in NOPH comes from the output side, some forces do operate through variations in inputs.

Unlike the previous models, this regression has an adjusted R^2 greater than 50 percent, indicating that the structural variables explain a substantial proportion of the variation in INCVNO. Of the five significant exogenous variables, INCVSTK is the strongest variable, accounting for approximately 40 percent of the explanation of the variation of INCVNO. Hence the churning in inventory dispersion is a major predictor of the instability of net output dispersion. The variation of inventory dispersion is also significant in explaining the instability of productivity dispersion, yet the effect is not as strong.

Appendix: Sources of Exogenous Variables

CONC   Average percentage of shipments accounted for by the five largest firms, 1970–79. (Source: Business Statistics Office, *Report on the Census of Production*, 1971–79.)

CONCCHG   Percentage change in concentration, 1970–79. (Source: See CONC.)

CONCABS   Absolute value of the percentage change in concentration, 1970–79. (Source: See CONC.)

EXP   Exports divided by total sales and work done, averaged
               over 1970–75. (Source: Great Britain, Business Statistics
               Office, *Overseas Trade Analysed in Terms of Industries*,
               Business Monitor M10, 1975, and *Report on the Census
               of Production*, 1971–75.)

GOOD   Goods merchanted and factored divided by total sales
               and work done, averaged over 1970–79. (Source: Business
               Statistics Office, *Report on the Census of Production*,
               1971–79.)

IMP   Imports divided by total sales and work done plus
               imports, averaged over 1970–75. (Source: Great Britain,
               Business Statistics Office, *Overseas Trade Analysed in
               Terms of Industries*, Business Monitor M10, 1975, and
               Report on the Census of Production, 1971–75.)

INCVNKX   Intertemporal variability of the intraindustry dispersion
               of net capital expenditures, 1963–79; calculated as the
               coefficient of variation across time of the within-industry
               coefficients of variation for each industry. (Source:
               National Economic Development Office data tape [based
               on returns of the *Census of Production*, 1963–79].)

INCVSTK   Intertemporal variability of the intraindustry dispersion
               of total year-end inventories, 1963–79; calculated as the
               coefficient of variation across time of the within-industry
               coefficients of variation for each industry. (Source:
               National Economic Development Office data tape [based
               on returns of the *Census of Production*, 1963–79].)

KL68   Capital–labor ratio, 1968. (Source: Ian Elliott,
               Disaggregation of 1968 gross fixed capital stock data to
               MLH level—revision and testing of estimates [National
               Economic Development Office, 1976], and Business
               Statistics Office, *Report on the Census of Production*, 1972.)

LGESTB   Share of industry employment in establishments
               employing 1,000 or more workers, averaged over
               1972–74. (Source: Business Statistics Office, *Report on the
               Census of Production*, 1972 and 1977.)

LOST   Average number of days lost due to work stoppages per
               1,000 employees, 1970–75. (Source: C. T. B. Smith, et al.,

	Strikes in Britain: *A Research Study of Industrial Stoppages in the United Kingdom*, Department of Employment, Manpower Paper No. 15, London: HMSO, 1978.)
MULTI	Average number of plants operated by the five leading firms, 1972–77. (Source: Business Statistics Office, *Report on the Census of Production*, 1972–77.)
NKXAVG	Net capital expenditures as a percentage of total sales and work done, averaged over 1963–79. (Source: Business Statistics Office, *Historical Record of the Census of Production*, 1972, and *Report on the Census of Production*, 1971–79.)
NPW	Share of total employment allocated to non-production workers, averaged over 1963–79. (Source: Business Statistics Office, *Historical Record of the Census of Production*, 1972, and *Report on the Census of Production*, 1971–79.)
OPCHG	Average annual percentage change in net output, 1970–79. (Source: Business Statistics Office, *Historical Record of the Census of Production*, 1972, and *Report on the Census of Production*, 1971–79.)
PLANTABS	Absolute value of the percentage change in the number of plants in an industry, 1963–79. (Source: Business Statistics Office, *Historical Record of the Census of Production*, 1972, and *Report on the Census of Production*, 1971–79.)
PURCH	Level of total purchases as a percentage of total sales and work done, averaged over 1963–79. (Source: Business Statistics Office, *Historical Record of the Census of Production*, 1972, and *Report on the Census of Production*, 1971–79.)
RD	Average level of R&D expenditures as a percentage of total sales, 1975–78. (Source: Great Britain, Business Statistics Office, *Industrial Research and Development Expenditure and Employment*, Business Monitor-MOH, London: HMSO, 1980.)

RENT   Expenditures on rented capital as a percentage of total
            sales and work done, averaged over 1972–79. (Source:
            Business Statistics Office, *Report on the Census of
            Production, 1972–79.*)

RENTCHG   Percentage change in the proportion of expenditures on
            rented capital, 1972–79. (Source: See RENT.)

SPEC   Percentage of total output produced by establishments
            classified to the main industry, averaged over 1963–79.
            (Source: Business Statistics Office, *Historical Record of
            the Census of Production*, 1972, and *Report on the Census
            of Production, 1971–79.*)

STKAVG   Level of finished goods and work in progress at year end
            as a percentage of total sales and work done, averaged
            over 1963–79. (Source: Business Statistics Office,
            Historical Record of the Census of Production, 1972, and
            Report on the Census of Production, 1971–79.)

Notes

The basic data for this research were made available by the National Economic Development Office, London, with special assistance provided by Derek J. Morris and David G. Mayes. Additional data were provided by the PICA Data Project of Harvard Business School. I have benefited tremendously from the counsel of Zvi Griliches on this research project. Most notably, distinct thanks are due Richard E. Caves for his insightful suggestions, continued encouragement, and financial research support.

1. Gross output is defined as the value of total sales and work done, adjusted for changes in the stocks of work in progress and goods on hand for sale. Total net output is defined as gross output less the cost of purchases (adjusted for changes in the stock of materials), the cost of industrial services received (i.e., payments for work given out to other firms and for transport provided by other organizations), and net duties (where applicable). Total gross value added at factor cost is defined as net output less the cost of nonindustrial services (rent of buildings, hire of plant, machinery and vehicles, commercial insurance premiums, bank charges and costs of professional services, etc.), rates, and the cost of licensing motor vehicles (U.K. Department of Industry 1978).

2. The 15 excluded industries are sugar; margarine; British wines, cider, and perry; tobacco; coke ovens and manufactured fuel; mineral oil refining; photographic chemical materials; miscellaneous (nonelectrical) machinery; industrial (including process) plant and steelwork; photographic and document copying equipment; watches and clocks; wheeled tractor manufacturing; miscellaneous metal manufactures; production of artificial fibers; and cement.

3. See Kendall and Stuart (1977, 1: 47, 77–82; 1979, 2: 77–78, 551–555). Lindley (1950) derived the maximum likelihood grouping correction which coincides with the Sheppard correction when applied to the estimation of the parameters of a normal distribution. Maximum likelihood estimation of distributional parameters using grouped and censored data was explored in detail for the normal case by Gjeddebæk (1949–61), Kulldorff (1958a, 1958b),

Swan (1969), and Wolynetz (1979). Maximum likelihood estimation using various types of incomplete data were examined in a general sense (with no specific distributional assumption) in Turnball (1974, 1976) and Dempster et al. (1977). A number of issues arise with regard to maximum likelihood estimation, including the appropriate distributional assumption, the extent of truncation and censoring, the number of sample observations and convergence of the algorithm. This complex matrix of issues makes the maximum likelihood approach multifarious and laborious as applied to the eight years of data for the 128 industries of this study, whereas the expected adjustment to the parameter estimates would be relatively small. Moreover the primary objective of this investigation is the cross-sectional analysis of the structural determinants of the behavior of productivity dispersions over time.

4. Based on a two-tailed test, the yearly means are significantly different at the 1 percent level for the pairs 1968–75, 1968–76, and 1968–77; at the 5 percent level for the pairs 1975–79; and at the 10 percent level for the pairs 1968–73, 1968–78, 1976–79, and 1977–79.

5. See Bailey (1991) for a discussion of the methodology employed; the analysis might be more successful if applied to a longer-time series.

6. See Caves and Barton (1990) for a thorough analysis of the determinants of technical efficiency in U.S. manufacturing. Mayes and Green (chapter 4) conduct a similar study for the British manufacturing sector. Nelson (1980) provided a broad survey of productivity research. Ball and Skeoch (1981) investigated interplant differences in productivity and earnings for 15 British manufacturing industries. Also Klotz, Madoo, and Hansen (1980) analyzed high- and low-productivity establishments for 191 U.S. manufacturing industries.

7. Shen (1970) termed this the *Penrose effect*: Plants find it advantageous to delay changes in their fixed equipment because of previous investment in relatively invariable equipment as well as organizational problems associated with various swift changes.

8. Klotz, Madoo, and Hansen (1980) found that there is a significant positive relation between concentration and the interquartile dispersion in plant productivity.

9. For a discussion of advertising rivalry in oligopolistic industries, see Fellner (1949), Simon (1970), Schmalensee (1972), Lambin (1976), and Comanor and Wilson (1974, 1979). Product variety, quality and durability were examined in Scherer (1979), Schmalensee (1978a, 1978b, 1979), and Spence (1976). Innovation and market structure were investigated in Kamien and Schwartz (1975), Scherer (1965, 1967), Comanor (1967), and Grabowski and Baxter (1973).

10. See Thomadakis (1977), Ravenscraft (1983), Leibenstein (1966), Carlsson (1972), and Esposito and Esposito (1974).

11. The number of years covered by the exogenous variables are always maximized subject to data availability constraints. In some instances the time periods used for the exogenous variables are conditioned by the change in census taking and publication procedures brought on by the BSO in 1970.

12. See Shepherd (1982) for a discussion of the changes in the pattern of competition in the U.S. economy over the period 1939–80.

13. See Caves and Barton (1990) and Swann et al. (1974). Although Mayes and Green (chapter 4) had mixed results, they also found a weak curvilinear relationship between efficiency and concentration in some of the models they tested.

14. See Lambin (1976) and Comanor and Wilson (1979).

15. See Auquier (1980) and Caves (1986). Also Caves and Barton (1990) found that exporting activity affected disproportionately the efficiency of large and small plants, that it has a greater negative impact on the efficiency of larger plants.

16. Although research indicates that managerial economies are slight for multiplant operations, this assumption does not require significant administrative economies, only a coordinated management team overseeing multiple plants (Scherer et al. 1975).

17. See Mansfield (1968), Jewkes et al. (1968), and Kamien and Schwartz (1975). The returns to research and development expenditures for the individual firm are examined by Griliches (1980), Mansfield (1980), and Nadiri and Bitros (1980). In addition Caves and Barton (1990) found that research and development intensity has an uneven effect on the efficiency of large and small plants, that it has a greater negative effect on the efficiency of small plants. They also found that the level of research and development activities contributes significantly to the differences between the efficiency levels in large and small plants.

18. See Pratten (1976a, 1976b), Caves (1980), Jones and Prais (1978), and Freeman and Medoff (1979).

19. See Salter (1966), Gregory and James (1973), Nelson (1981), and Klotz, Madoo, and Hansen (1980).

20. In addition Klotz, Madoo, and Hansen (1980) found that output growth does influence the intraindustry differentials in plant productivity.

21. See Mansfield (1962), Hause and Du Rietz (1984), and Dunne, Roberts, and Samuelson (1988).

22. Klotz, Madoo, and Hansen (1980) also found that capital intensity is a significant determinant of the interquartile differences in the productivity of plants in the same industry.

23. In their examination of capital expenditures, Klotz, Madoo, and Hansen (1980) found significant correlations between average productivity and average capital expenditures, but low correlations between variations in relative capital expenditures and variations in relative productivity. They presumed that the low correlations resulted from the fact that capital expenditures also reflect various transitory effects and that only one year of capital expenditures (1967) was used in their analysis.

24. Klotz, Madoo, and Hansen (1980) found that the variation in the relative productivity of top-quartile plants is highly correlated with the variation in the relative proportion of nonproduction workers. However, the bottom-quartile plants did not exhibit the same relationship.

25. The intertemporal variation of inventory dispersion (INCVSTK) is not expected to be an endogenous variable and empirical tests confirm this expectation. When INCVSTK is regressed on all six dependent variables, none is found to be significant.

26. Net capital expenditure does have a significantly positive coefficient when included with the other variables in the model for INTCV in table 9.12, which is consistent with the a priori hypothesis. However, the estimated coefficient for net capital expenditure is not stable, changing sign as different variables are included in the regression. Moreover the simple correlation between INTCV and NKXAVG is negative, whereas a positive coefficient is most often obtained. The instability in the coefficient estimate for NKXAVG appears to be due primarily to multicollinearity, since NKXAVG is highly collinear with many of the other exogenous variables in the model. The other input variables, KL68, PURCH, and NPW never proved significant in the regressions for INTCV.

27. EXP also has a significantly positive coefficient when substituted for IMP in the model for STANDERR, with the explanatory power of the regression staying about the same. EXP is not significant, however, when IMP is also present. IMP is reported in the model for STANDERR because it is the stronger of the two foreign competition measures.

28. All of the significant variables for INTANN1, INTANN2, INTCV, and STANDERR had the expected signs. Although the coefficients of some of the other exogenous variables had perverse or unstable signs, none proved significant except as indicated for the individual models.

29. IMP, when included in the model for INTANN2, has a positive estimated coefficient that exceeds its standard error but is not significant. The estimated coefficient for MULTI, while negative as in previous regressions, never exceeds its standard error.

30. Note from table 9.8 that LINCOEF1's mean is just about zero and that LINCOEF2's mean is very small.

31. The anomalous signs of the estimated coefficients for KL68 and STKAVG do not appear to result from multicollinearity. Both variables are negatively correlated with LINCOEF1. Moreover the estimated coefficients are always negative regardless of which exogenous variables are included in the model.

32. The intertemporal variation of the dispersion of net capital expenditures (INCVNKX) is not found to be an endogenous variable. None of the six dependent variables is significant when INCVNKX is regressed on them. Additionally the abnormal sign of the estimated coefficient for KL68 in the LINCOEF1 regression cannot be attributed to multicollinearity as a result of a significant correlation between KL68 and INCVNKX.

References

Auquier, A. A. 1980. Size of firm, exporting behavior, and the structure of French industry. *Journal of Industrial Economics* 29 (December): 203–218.

Bailey, S. D. 1991. The interindustry dispersion of plant productivity and wages in the British manufacturing sector, 1963–1979. Ph.D. Dissertation. Harvard University.

Ball, J. M., and N. K. Skeoch. 1981. *Inter-plant Comparisons of Productivity and Earnings*. London: Department of Employment, Unit of Manpower Studies.

Carlsson, B. 1972. The measurement of efficiency in production: An application to Swedish manufacturing industries, 1968. *Swedish Journal of Economics* 74 (December): 468–485.

Caves, R. E. 1980. Productivity differences among industries. In R. E. Caves and L. B. Krause eds., *Britain's Economic Performance*. Washington: Brookings Institution, pp. 135–198.

Caves, R. E. 1981. Intraindustry trade and market structure in the industrial countries. *Oxford Economic Papers* 33 (July): 203–223.

Caves, R. E. 1986. Exporting behaviour and market structure: Evidence from the United States. In H. W. de Jong and W. G. Shepherd, ed., *Mainstreams in Industrial Organization*. Dordrecht: Kluwer Academic, pp. 189–210.

Caves, R. E. 1988. Trade exposure and changing structures of U.S. manufacturing industries. In M. Spence and H. A. Hazard eds., *International Competitiveness*. Cambridge, MA: Ballinger, pp. 1–26.

Caves, R. E., and D. R. Barton. 1990. *Efficiency in U.S. Manufacturing Industries*. Cambridge: MIT Press.

Caves, R. E., and T. A. Pugel. 1980. *Intraindustry Differences in Conduct and Performance: Viable Strategies in U.S. Manufacturing Industries*. Monograph Series in Finance and Economics No. 1980-2. New York: Graduate School of Business Administration, New York University.

Comanor, W. S. 1967. Market structure, product differentiation, and industrial research. *Quarterly Journal of Economics* 81 (November): 639–657.

Comanor, W. S., and T. A. Wilson. 1975. *Advertising and Market Power*. Cambridge: Harvard University Press.

Comanor, W. S., and T. A. Wilson. 1979. The effect of advertising on competition: A survey. *Journal of Economic Literature* 17 (June): 453–476.

Davis, H. S. 1956. Relation of capital–output ratio to firm size in American manufacturing: Some additional evidence. *Review of Economics and Statistics* 38 (August): 286–293.

Dempster, A. P., N. M. Laird, and D. B. Rubin. 1977. Maximum likelihood from incomplete data via the EM algorithm. *Journal of the Royal Statistical Society* 39: 1–38.

Dixit, A., and V. Norman. 1978. Advertising and welfare. *Bell Journal of Economics* 9 (Spring): 1–17.

Dunne, T., M. J. Roberts, and L. Samuelson. 1988. Patterns of firm entry and exit in U.S. manufacturing industries. *Rand Journal of Economics* 19 (Winter): 495–515.

Esposito, F. F., and L. Esposito. 1974. Excess capacity and market structure. *Review of Economics and Statistics* 56: 188–194.

Fellner, W. 1949. *Competition among the Few.* New York: Knopf.

Freeman, R. B., and J. L. Medoff. 1979. The two faces of unionism. *The Public Interest* 57 (Fall): 69–93.

Gjaddebæk, N. F. 1949. Contribution to the study of grouped observations, I: Application of the method of maximum likelihood in the case of normally distributed observations. *Skandinavisk Aktuarietidskrift* 32: 135–159.

Gjaddebæk, N. F. 1956. Contribution to the study of grouped observations, II: Loss of information caused by grouping of normally distributed observations. *Skandinavisk Aktuarietidskrift* 39: 154–159.

Gjaddebæk, N. F. 1957. Contribution to the study of grouped observations, III: The distribution of estimates of the mean. *Skandinavisk Aktuarietidskrift* 40: 20–25.

Gjaddebæk, N. F. 1959a. Contribution to the study of grouped observations, IV: Some comments on simple estimates. *Biometrics* 15 (September): 433–439.

Gjaddebæk, N. F. 1959b. Contribution to the study of grouped observations, V: Three-class grouping of normal observations. *Skandinavisk Aktuarietidskrift* 42: 194–207.

Gjaddebæk, N. F. 1961. Contribution to the study of grouped observations, VI. *Skandinavisk Aktuarietidskrift* 44: 55–70.

Grabowski, H. G., and N. D. Baxter. 1973. Rivalry in industrial research and development: An empirical study. *Journal of Industrial Economics* 21 (July): 228–233.

Gregory, R. G., and D. W. James. 1973. Do new factories embody best practice technology? *Economic Journal* 83: 1133–1155.

Griliches, Z. 1980. Returns to research and development expenditures in the private sector. In J. W. Kendrick and B. N. Vaccara, eds., *New Developments in Productivity Measurement and Analysis.* Chicago: University of Chicago Press, pp. 419–461.

Hause, J. C., and G. Du Rietz. 1984. Entry, industry growth, and the microdynamics of industry supply. *Journal of Political Economy* 92 (August): 733–757.

Jewkes, J., D. Sawers, and R. Stillerman. 1968. *The Sources of Innovation,* rev. ed. New York: St. Martin's.

Jones, D. T., and S. J. Prais. 1978. Plant-size and productivity in the motor industry: Some international comparisons. *Oxford Bulletin of Economics and Statistics* 40 (May): 131–152.

Jovanovic, B. 1982. Selection and the evolution of Industry. *Econometrica* 50 (May): 649–670.

Kamien, M. I., and N. L. Schwartz. 1975. Market structure and innovation: A survey. *Journal of Economic Literature* 8 (March): 1–37.

Kendall, M., and A. Stuart. 1977. *The Advanced Theory of Statistics.* Vol. 1: *Distribution Theory.* 4th ed. London: Charles Griffin.

Kendall, M., and A. Stuart. 1979. *The Advanced Theory of Statistics.* Vol. 2: *Inference and Relationship.* 4th ed. London: Charles Griffin.

Kulldorff, G. 1958a. Maximum likelihood estimation of the mean of a normal random variable when the sample is grouped. *Skandinavisk Aktuarietidskrift* 41: 1–17.

Kulldorff, G. 1958b. Maximum likelihood estimation of the standard deviation of a normal random variable when the sample is grouped. *Skandinavisk Aktuarietidskrift* 41: 18–36.

Klotz, B., R. Madoo, and R. Hansen. 1980. A study of high and low labor productivity. In J. W. Kendrick and B. N. Vaccara, eds., *New Developments in Productivity Measurement and Analysis*. Chicago: University of Chicago Press, pp. 239–292.

Lambin, J. J. 1976. *Advertising, Competition and Market Conduct in Oligopoly over Time*. Amsterdam: North-Holland.

Leibenstein, H. 1966. Allocative efficiency vs. *X*-efficiency. *American Economic Review* 56 (June): 392–412.

Lindley, D. V. 1950. Grouping corrections and maximum likelihood equations. *Proceedings of the Cambridge Philosophical Society* 46: 106–110.

Mansfield, E. 1968. *Industrial Research and Technological Innovation*. New York: Norton.

Mansfield, E. 1962. Entry, Gibrat's law, innovation and the growth of Firms. *American Economics Review* 52 (December): 1023–1151.

Mansfield, E. 1980. Basic research and productivity increase in manufacturing. *American Economic Review* 70 (December): 863–873.

Mayes, D. G., and A. Green. 1992. Technical efficiency in U.K. manufacturing industry. In R. E. Caves, ed., *Industrial Efficiency in Six Nations*. Cambridge: MIT Press.

Nadiri, M. I., and G. C. Bitros. 1981. Research and development expenditures and labor productivity at the firm level: A dynamic model. In J. W. Kendrick and B. N. Vaccara, eds., *New Developments in Productivity Measurement and Analysis*. Chicago: University of Chicago Press, pp. 387–417.

Nelson, R. 1981. Research on productivity growth and productivity differences: Dead ends and new departures. *Journal of Economic Literature* 19 (September): 1029–1164.

Pratten, C. F. 1976a. *A Comparison of the Performance of Swedish and U.K. Companies*. Cambridge: Cambridge University Press.

Pratten, C. F. 1976b. *Labour Productivity Differentials within International Companies*. Cambridge: Cambridge University Press.

Ravenscraft, D. J. 1983. Structure-profit relationships at the line of business and industry level. *Review of Economics and Statistics* 65 (February): 22–31.

Salter, W. E. G. 1966. *Productivity and Technical Change*. 2d ed. Cambridge: Cambridge University Press.

Scherer, F. M. 1965. Firm size, market structure, opportunity and the output of patented inventions. *American Economic Review* 55 (December): 1097–1125.

Scherer, F. M. 1967. Market structure and the employment of scientists and engineers. *American Economic Review* 57 (June): 524–531.

Scherer, F. M. 1975. *The Economics of Multi-plant Operation: An International Comparisons Study*. Cambridge: Harvard University Press.

Scherer, F. M. 1979. The welfare economics of product variety: An application to the ready-to-eat cereals industry. *Journal of Industrial Economics* 28: 113–134.

Schmalensee, R. 1972. *The Economics of Advertising*. Amsterdam: North-Holland.

Schmalensee, R. 1978a. A model of advertising and product quality. *Journal of Political Economy* 86 (June): 485–504.

Schmalensee, R. 1978b. Entry deterrence in the ready-to-eat breakfast cereal industry. *Bell Journal of Economics* 9 (Autumn): 305–327.

Schmalensee, R. 1979. Market structure, durability and quality: A selective survey. *Economic Inquiry* 17 (April): 177–196.

Shen, T. Y. 1968. Economies of scale, expansion path, and growth of plants. *Review of Economics and Statistics* 50 (February): 293–310.

Shen, T. Y. 1970. Economies of scale, Penrose effect, growth of plants and their size distribution. *Journal of Political Economy* 78 (July–August): 702–716.

Shepherd, W. G. 1982. Causes of increased competition in the U.S. economy, 1939–1980. *Review of Economics and Statistics* 64 (November): 614–620.

Simon, J. L. 1970. *Issues in the Economics of Advertising.* Urbana, IL: University of Illinois Press.

Spence, M. 1976. Product differentiation and welfare. *American Economic Review* 66 (May): 407–414.

Swan, A. V. 1969. Computing maximum likelihood estimates from parameters of the normal distribution from grouped and censored data. *Applied Statistics* 18: 63–39.

Swann, D., D. P. O'Brien, W. P. J. Maunder, and W. S. Howe. 1974. *Competition in British Industry: Restrictive Practices Legislation in Theory and Practice.* London: Allen and Unwin.

Thomadakis, S. B. 1977. A value based test of profitability and market structure. *Review of Economics and Statistics* 59 (May): 179–185.

Turnball, B. W. 1974. Nonparametric estimation of a survivorship function with doubly censored data. *Journal of the American Statistical Association* 69 (March): 169–173.

Turnball, B. W. 1976. The empirical distribution function with arbitrarily grouped, censored and truncated data. *Journal of the Royal Statistical Society* 38: 290–295.

U.K. Department of Industry, Business Statistics Office. 1973–79. Introductory note. In *Report on the Census of Production.* Business Monitor PA1001.

Wolynetz, M. S. 1979. Maximum likelihood estimation from confined and censored normal data. *Applied Statistics* 28: 185–194.

10 "Dual Structure" and Differences of Efficiency between Japanese Large and Small Enterprises

Akio Torii

10.1 Introduction

Japanese small- and medium-scale enterprises (denoted SME) have almost always been treated as a reflection of the economy's structure. Although there are many versions of the concept of "dual structure," in Japanese manufacturing it is typically represented by the stylized fact that productivity and average wage levels differ between large and small enterprises.[1]

Most studies on the difference in productivity focus on the comparison of value added per worker in small-scale firms with that of the largest-scale firms. In Caves and Uekusa (1976) this ratio was reported as 1.71, which was compared to 1.16 for the United States (1967). Most countries exhibit the same positive relation between firm scale and value added per worker, although the discrepancy has been known to be by far largest in Japan.[2] In 1978 the ratio was 1.85, measured by gross value added per worker in firms with 500 or more employees relative to firms with 20 to 499 employees, compared to 1.32 in the United States, 1.25 in the United Kingdom, 1.23 in West Germany.[3]

As in productivity, considerable differences have been observed in the average wage, the capital–labor ratio, and capital cost.[4] These discrepancies are thought to be related to each other. Shinohara (1961) has claimed that the discrepancies in productivity and wage levels are due to differences in the labor–equipment ratio, which in turn stem from imperfections in financial markets. These discrepancies manifest themselves in the dual structure. However, Koike (1987) carried out extensive studies that led him to express doubt that a dual structure can be deduced solely from wage differentials by size of firm.[5] He suggested that the discrepancy in wage levels might simply reflect the difference in work force composition between large and small firms rather than wage differentials. The dependence of inefficiency on imperfections in financial markets has been the subject of some research, but no other definite conclusions have emerged.[6] The observed capital–labor ratio differences could be explained in a neoclassical manner as a reflection of factor market heterogeneity. There also is reason to believe that a precise relationship exists between discrepancies in value added per worker and in capital–labor ratios. However, the difficulty of investigating relationships in Japanese factor markets precludes a direct empirical analysis of them.

The observed discrepancies in wages and productivity have attracted attention from concern that small-scale industry has remained under-developed, with low productivity which reflects inefficiency. Obviously inefficiency in this context consists of not only inefficiency in factor alloca-tion but also technical inefficiency. Now that an index of the level of technical efficiency is available, the possible shortcoming in the level of technical efficiency in Japanese SMEs can be investigated. Caves and Barton (1990) (hereafter denoted CB) found the efficiency of larger enter-prises is slightly higher than that of smaller ones in manufacturing indus-tries in the United States, and they analyzed factors that determine the discrepancy. Their findings may help to explain Japan's dual structure. Differences in levels of technical efficiency related to scale, their contribu-tion to differences of productivity, and their relation to profitability are problems that concern this report.

We estimated the levels of technical efficiency in four-digit industries which we subdivided by establishment size (employees) into smaller and larger sectors, each accounting for one-half of the industry's employment. Production frontiers are estimated for these separate sectors. Because of a technical problem we could not directly apply the COLS method. With the COLS method one obtains the estimator in the course of fitting the pro-duction function, which requires substantial number of degrees of freedom. Type I and type II failures, which result from relatively large variances of COLS estimators, hampered our estimation of efficiency, so only 19 indus-tries would have yielded efficiency indexes for both large and small sectors by the COLS method.

We avoided this difficulty by introducing a kind of Bayesian COLS estimator. This index is an extension of the COLS estimator that yields values for type I and type II failure cases with some accuracy. This method was responsive to the problems mentioned above and enabled us to pro-ceed with the analysis.

Our study, however, was not exactly an examination of dual structure. Research on this subject has focused on the relation between the absolute scales of firms and other variables. Generally, the SME sector of an indus-try, which is defined by an absolute scale, and the smaller sector of the industry distinguished in this chapter, which is defined as the small estab-lishments accounting for one-half of an industry's employment, do not coincide. Nevertheless, an analysis of relative size may fit well into an investigation of plants operated at suboptimal scales.[7] The problem with the dual structure is nothing less than the problem of suboptimality, so the method of dividing industries into halves should contribute to the analysis of SMEs.

10.2   A Modified COLS Estimator

There are two deterrences to employing COLS estimators for interindustry cross-sectional analyses. One is the relatively high variance of skewness estimators compared with variance estimators. This occurs because the calculation of COLS estimators utilizes the third moments of residuals. The other is caused by this large variance of estimators. Because σ_u and σ_v in the model must be nonnegative, the second and the third moments (μ_2 and μ_3) of the regression residuals have restrictions on their feasible sets. The estimators of σ_u and σ_v are calculated by

$$\hat{\sigma}_u = \sqrt[3]{\sqrt{\frac{\pi}{2}} \frac{\pi}{\pi - 4} \hat{\mu}_3},$$

$$\hat{\sigma}_v = \sqrt{\hat{\mu}_2 - \frac{\pi - 2}{\pi} \left(\sqrt{\frac{\pi}{2}} \frac{\pi}{\pi - 4} \hat{\mu}_3 \right)^{2/3}}, \tag{1}$$

so μ_3 must be negative and μ_2 has both upper and lower bounds. When μ_2 and μ_3 of the regression residuals have large variances, they do not fall into the feasible set and estimates of σ_u and σ_v cannot be calculated. These cases are called type I and type II failures by Olson, Schmidt, and Waldman (1980) (OSW). Because of their frequency such failures prevent the data set from supplying enough usable observations[8] and cause biases in estimators. The biases in turn can cause serious problems when they are used in cross-industry analyses.[9]

The problem is mainly with the high variance of μ_3 estimators. We could rather rely on information in the μ_2 of the residuals, which is expected to have much less variance. Note that the σ_u estimator of COLS depends only on μ_3. In chapter 4 Mayes and Green employ the relatively effective estimator of variance or $\hat{\mu}_2$ as an index of technical efficiency. By using ML estimators in place of the derivatives from the third moment of residuals as COLS estimators to obtain efficiency indexes, we can avoid type I failures. When the COLS estimator incurs a type I failure, the ML estimate of $\lambda (= \sigma_u/\sigma_v)$ also will be 0, as OSW have reported.[10] This fact will make the distribution of estimates across industries discontinuous at the point where σ_u equals 0 or average efficiency equals 100 percent. This discontinuity in the distribution function makes subsequent interindustry cross-sectional analyses difficult, but a more serious problem may be the reliability of assumptions that assign 100 percent efficiency to a considerable proportion of sample industries. In the analysis of putty-clay type vintage models in chapter 2, we find that so long as the speed of replacement investment is finite, some positive level of observed technical inefficiency is inevitable, and that part of inefficiency does not always imply the existence of inefficiency in a normative sense. In Japan this part of inefficiency is approximately 10 percent. Our preference for COLS over MLE mainly rests on the ease of calculating the estimator shown fairly efficient by OSW, and the economic interest in finding the causes of negatively skewed residuals from the production frontier, which have a simple intuitive meaning.

One way to use the presumption that σ_u and σ_v should not be negative is to employ a Bayesian type of estimator,[11] using posterior probability to develop indexes of technical efficiency. There is no information on the prior distributions of (σ_u, σ_v) other than that they are not negative. We do not know that they are distributed normally around certain values of $(\bar{\sigma}_u, \bar{\sigma}_v)$. Therefore a uniform distribution on a rectangular subset Ω of the nonnegative orthant of two-dimensional euclidean space $\mathbf{R}_+$ is assumed here. That is,

$$\Omega = ((x, y) | \max(\tilde{\sigma}_u - K, 0) \le x \le \tilde{\sigma}_u + K,$$

$$\max(\tilde{\sigma}_v - K, 0) \le y \le \tilde{\sigma}_v + K),$$

where $(\tilde{\sigma}_u, \tilde{\sigma}_v)$ are COLS estimator that have been set as

$$(\tilde{\sigma}_u, \tilde{\sigma}_v) = (0, \sqrt{\hat{\mu}_2}) \qquad \text{at type I failure,}$$

$$(\tilde{\sigma}_u, \tilde{\sigma}_v) = \left(\sqrt{\frac{\pi}{\pi - 2} \hat{\mu}_2}, 0 \right) \qquad \text{at type II failure,}$$

and K is a sufficiently large constant. When the number of sample enterprises is large enough, the probability that $(\hat{\mu}_2, \hat{\mu}_3)$ of OLS residuals take values apart from $\check{\sigma}_v^2 + (\pi - 2/\pi)\check{\sigma}_u^2, \sqrt{(2/\pi)}(1 - 4/\pi)\check{\sigma}_v^3$ decreases rapidly as the distance between them increases, where $(\check{\sigma}_u, \check{\sigma}_v)$ is the true value of (σ_u, σ_v). Experimentation indicates that, when K is set to be 3.0, the possibility falls well below 10^{-15} order at the boundaries. From this observation the prior density of (σ_u, σ_v), $f(\sigma_u, \sigma_v)$, is

$$f(\sigma_u, \sigma_v) = \begin{cases} 0 & \text{when } (\sigma_u, \sigma_v) \in \Omega, \\ \dfrac{1}{L}, & \text{when } (\sigma_u, \sigma_v) \notin \Omega, \end{cases}$$

where $L \equiv \int_\Omega d\sigma_u \, d\sigma_v$.

The conditional probability that a certain value of (μ_2, μ_3) is observed when the true value of (σ_u, σ_v) equals $(\breve{\sigma}_u, \breve{\sigma}_v)$ is denoted as $P(\mu_2, \mu_3 | \breve{\sigma}_u, \breve{\sigma}_v)$. For this probability the asymptotic distribution of $(\hat{\mu}_2, \hat{\mu}_3)$ which is presented in OSW[12] is assumed here:

$$P(\mu_2, \mu_3 | \breve{\sigma}_u, \breve{\sigma}_v) = \frac{1}{2\pi\sqrt{|\mathbf{Q}|}} \exp\left[-\frac{(m - \gamma)' \mathbf{Q}^{-1}(m - \gamma)}{2} \right],$$

where $m \equiv (\mu_2, \mu_3)'$, $\gamma \equiv \left(\breve{\sigma}_v^2 + \dfrac{\pi - 2}{\pi} \breve{\sigma}_u^2, \sqrt{\dfrac{2}{\pi}}\left(1 - \dfrac{4}{\pi}\right)\breve{\sigma}_v^3 \right)'$, and

$$\mathbf{Q} \equiv \frac{1}{N} \begin{pmatrix} m_2 & m_5 - 4m_2 m_3 \\ m_5 - 4m_2 m_3 & m_4 - m_2^2 \end{pmatrix}.$$

In this definition N is the sample size and

$$m_2 = \breve{\sigma}_v^2 + \frac{\pi - 2}{\pi} \breve{\sigma}_u^2,$$

$$m_3 = \sqrt{\frac{2}{\pi}}\left(1 - \frac{4}{\pi}\right)\breve{\sigma}_u^3,$$

$$m_4 = 3\breve{\sigma}_v^4 + 6\frac{\pi - 2}{\pi}\breve{\sigma}_v^2 \breve{\sigma}_u^2 + \left(3 - \frac{4}{\pi} - \frac{12}{\pi^2}\right)\breve{\sigma}_v^4,$$

$$m_5 = 10\sqrt{\frac{2}{\pi}}\left(1 - \frac{4}{\pi}\right)\breve{\sigma}_v^2 \breve{\sigma}_u^3 + \sqrt{\frac{2}{\pi}}\left(7 - \frac{20}{\pi} - \frac{16}{\pi^2}\right)\breve{\sigma}_u^5.$$

By Bayes's theorem the posterior probability density is

$$P(\sigma_u, \sigma_v | \hat{\mu}_2, \hat{\mu}_3) = \frac{P(\hat{\mu}_2, \hat{\mu}_3 | \sigma_u, \sigma_v) f(\sigma_u, \sigma_v)}{\int_\Omega P(\hat{\mu}_2, \hat{\mu}_3 | \sigma_u, \sigma_v) f(\sigma_u, \sigma_v) \, d\sigma_u \, d\sigma_v}.$$

The estimator tested in this chapter is the expected value using this posterior probability:

$$\hat{\sigma}_i = \int_\Omega \sigma_i P(\sigma_u, \sigma_v | \hat{\mu}_2, \hat{\mu}_3) \, d\sigma_u \, d\sigma_v, \qquad i = u, v.$$

So long as the estimators of the moments of residuals are consistent, these estimators are consistent. As the sample size increases, the posterior probabilistic distribution function asymptotically converges to Dirac's δ function, and this estimator converges to the ordinary COLS estimator (hereafter the COLS estimator is denoted the ordinary COLS, whereas this newly introduced estimator is called the modified COLS estimator).

Table 10.1 shows results of a Monte Carlo experiment into the properties of the modified COLS estimator. This experiment is quite parallel to the experiment reported in chapter 2, tables 2.4b and 2.4c, examining the properties of ordinary COLS estimators. These tables show that the estimator introduced here can provide somewhat improved estimates especially for σ_u in the relatively wide range of cases investigated. Except when λ is quite high, the new estimates come nearer to the true values; variances diminish, but precision is not ensured for large departures from the true values. Note that the statistics here pertain to the full number of experiments. That is, while the statistics of the ordinary COLS method bear on the numbers of observations that avoid type I or type II failures, the statistics of modified COLS pertain to the same (100) experiments, thanks to the method's evasion of failures.

The pattern of discrepancies between the true values of (σ_u, σ_v) and the means of estimates indicate an area where the value of λ is low and the recovery of true values by some linear transformation of observed estimates seems to be infeasible. This area was also seen in the Monte Carlo experiment for the ordinary COLS estimator. Although for ordinary COLS estimators their relationship appeared to be linear where the value of λ was high, in this case the linearity seems to be lost. A bias-correcting method of omitting cases with low values of observed λ was employed in chapter 2. The correction based on the estimate of λ seems to enhance the accuracy because biases appear related to the estimates of λ. However, that might not be the appropriate method to use in this chapter for the following reason: This distribution of σ_v is expected to be random, so the exclusion of cases with low values of λ means that cases with low values of σ_u are purged with higher probability than those with high values of σ_u. A bias might affect our comparison of the efficiency of industry sectors because, if the larger sectors showed greater efficiency than the smaller ones, the large-difference industries are excluded with higher probabilities. Therefore we introduce another correction here, that allows us to omit cases with problematically high values of the σ_v estimate. This approach produces no

Table 10.1
Monte Carlo experiments on properties of modified COLS estimators (average values and standard deviations of estimates)

True value of σ_v	True value of σ_u				
	0.1	0.5	1.0	2.0	4.0
σ_u, sample size 50					
0.1	0.0971	0.3964	0.7623	1.5460	3.1792
	(0.0246)	(0.0892)	(0.1573)	(0.2975)	(0.6597)
0.5	0.3978	0.4908	0.8004	1.5385	3.3022
	(0.0904)	(0.1263)	(0.2225)	(0.3889)	(0.7728)
1.0	0.7531	0.8303	1.0296	1.5085	3.2602
	(0.1780)	(0.2256)	(0.2702)	(0.4968)	(0.8664)
2.0	1.5513	1.5041	1.6206	1.9456	3.2160
	(0.3463)	(1.6195)	(0.2589)	(0.5720)	(1.1454)
3.0	2.0563	2.0413	2.2456	2.3606	3.2902
	(0.7387)	(0.7105)	(0.8550)	(0.9579)	(1.5156)
4.0	2.5617	2.6975	2.3686	2.9462	3.2689
	(1.3046)	(1.3890)	(1.2454)	(1.5419)	(1.9729)
σ_v, sample size 50					
0.1	0.0887	0.1830	0.3449	0.6522	1.3066
	(0.0134)	(0.0297)	(0.0505)	(0.0848)	(0.1977)
0.5	0.3862	0.4414	0.5299	0.8053	1.3330
	(0.0610)	(0.0593)	(0.0743)	(0.1106)	(0.1970)
1.0	0.7925	0.8065	0.8287	1.0816	1.5092
	(0.1107)	(0.1238)	(0.1263)	(0.1749)	(0.2061)
2.0	1.5909	1.6195	1.6119	1.7727	2.1175
	(0.2408)	(0.2496)	(0.2589)	(0.3237)	(0.4361)
3.0	2.4980	2.4670	2.4988	2.6654	2.9156
	(0.4497)	(0.4655)	(0.4442)	(0.4689)	(0.7041)
4.0	3.3806	3.3586	3.5097	3.3644	3.7736
	(0.7268)	(0.6866)	(0.7283)	(0.7454)	(0.8121)
σ_u, sample size 100					
0.1	0.0959	0.4378	0.8752	1.7310	3.5283
	(0.0266)	(0.0693)	(0.1195)	(0.2321)	(0.4574)
0.5	0.3590	0.4463	0.8055	1.7344	3.5068
	(0.1043)	(0.1272)	(0.2102)	(0.3333)	(0.4873)
1.0	0.6770	0.7329	0.9492	1.6852	3.4245
	(0.1758)	(0.2007)	(0.2643)	(0.3824)	(0.5852)
2.0	1.2807	1.3952	1.4132	1.8214	3.5410
	(0.3058)	(0.3882)	(0.3128)	(0.5332)	(0.9655)
3.0	1.8782	1.9488	1.9112	2.2886	3.3352
	(0.6702)	(0.5751)	(0.6797)	(0.8553)	(1.3230)
4.0	2.3065	2.4886	2.5301	2.6688	3.4743
	(1.1591)	(1.1957)	(1.2768)	(1.3370)	(1.8142)

Table 10.1 (continued)

True value of σ_v	True value of σ_u				
	0.1	0.5	1.0	2.0	4.0
σ_v, sample size 100					
0.1	0.0911	0.1529	0.2749	0.5459	1.0504
	(0.0131)	(0.0262)	(0.0427)	(0.0824)	(0.1521)
0.5	0.4244	0.4636	0.5220	0.6611	1.1014
	(0.0603)	(0.0658)	(0.0932)	(0.1217)	(0.1589)
1.0	0.8455	0.7329	0.9065	1.0174	1.3434
	(0.1020)	(0.1060)	(0.1319)	(0.1784)	(0.2687)
2.0	1.7287	1.6891	1.7659	1.8588	1.9147
	(0.1953)	(0.2042)	(0.2024)	(0.2526)	(0.4160)
3.0	2.5832	2.5970	2.6375	2.6918	2.9079
	(0.3507)	(0.3399)	(0.3879)	(0.4104)	(0.6040)
4.0	3.5522	3.4748	3.4986	3.6175	3.8027
	(0.5334)	(0.5527)	(0.6210)	(0.6008)	(0.8113)
σ_u, sample size 200					
0.1	0.0843	0.4657	0.9395	1.8377	3.6613
	(0.0295)	(0.0446)	(0.0829)	(0.1611)	(0.3432)
0.5	0.2936	0.4325	0.9220	1.9018	3.7500
	(0.0741)	(0.1483)	(0.1839)	(0.2155)	(0.3459)
1.0	0.6178	0.6126	0.8375	1.8602	3.6760
	(0.1767)	(0.1580)	(0.2475)	(0.3904)	(0.4990)
2.0	1.1410	1.2021	1.2958	1.6868	3.5273
	(0.3447)	(0.3120)	(0.3847)	(0.5427)	(0.8277)
3.0	1.8019	1.7596	1.8184	2.0114	3.6230
	(0.5803)	(0.5776)	(0.6352)	(0.7135)	(1.1912)
4.0	2.1695	2.1619	2.1652	2.3613	3.1686
	(0.9540)	(0.8331)	(0.9678)	(1.0117)	(1.4025)
σ_v, sample size 200					
0.1	0.0971	0.1276	0.2187	0.4370	0.8543
	(0.0124)	(0.0221)	(0.0269)	(0.0634)	(0.1256)
0.5	0.4607	0.4871	0.4793	0.5520	0.9022
	(0.0366)	(0.0675)	(0.0998)	(0.1002)	(0.1196)
1.0	0.8863	0.9350	0.9777	0.9472	1.1360
	(0.0862)	(0.0788)	(0.1017)	(0.1964)	(0.2112)
2.0	1.8045	1.8099	1.8450	1.9769	1.9900
	(0.1685)	(0.1590)	(0.1693)	(0.2299)	(0.4325)
3.0	2.6601	2.7024	2.6944	2.8383	2.8112
	(0.2386)	(0.2644)	(0.2916)	(0.3163)	(0.5525)
4.0	3.6205	3.6725	3.6713	3.7323	3.9969
	(0.3775)	(0.3238)	(0.3755)	(0.3821)	(0.5527)

systematic bias in the analysis of differences in efficiency because its effect is symmetrical with respect to the value of σ_v.

After several experiments we obtained the following regression equation which we found to be the most suitable for implementing the bias correction (t-value in parentheses). We estimated it over the set of true and estimated values of σ_u in cases where $\sigma_v \leq 0.3$.

$$\sigma_u = 0.0091 + 1.0989\hat{\sigma}_u,$$
$$(29.61) \qquad\qquad\qquad\qquad (2)$$

$$R^2 = 0.9932, \quad \bar{R}^2 = 0.9921.$$

If there were more information about the prior distributions of σ_u and σ_v than that they are positive, we could have obtained more efficient estimators. The advantage of using this type of Bayesian estimator depends on a priori information, but we could impose very little restriction on the prior distribution of estimated parameters. However, unlike the ordinary COLS estimator, this estimator can be calculated for all observations. Therefore, although the modified COLS estimator adds little sophistication to ordinary COLS, since it depends on information in the second moment of the regression residuals, it makes an important gain in avoiding type I and II failures.

Table 2.1 in Chapter 2 indicated that when the value of λ is less than 1, about half of the observations incur type I failures, and the frequency of this failure seems to have little association with the absolute value of σ_u. Therefore, when λ is low, the usefulness of estimated skewness as an index of technical inefficiency could suffer. This is consistent with the fact that not all the cases subject to type I failures have high estimates of σ_u. When the third moment of the residual becomes positive, this estimator is determined by the magnitude of the second moment. Because a high value of the second moment expands the possible values of σ_u, it also accompanies higher values of the estimate of σ_u.

Neither COLS nor related estimators of the composed inefficiency term is of particularly high quality. Modified COLS is not an exception. Our main concern about the quality of estimators should lie with their variance. However, the critical point for applications to empirical studies is not the absolute value of the variance of estimators but its magnitude relative to the dispersion of the observed distribution of these indexes. Even when the estimator is not very efficient and the estimated variance of estimator is high, the wide spread of that index among industries will alleviate problems in employing the estimator. The main concern about the properties of some estimator of indexes in a cross-sectional study should be how fully the relations between the index and the set of exogenous variables are preserved in using that index.

This qualification depends on how fully the relationship between true values of σ_u and its estimates is preserved. On this point the modified COLS method supplies us an estimator with enough efficiency for comparative analyses. Consider two variables X and Y. X_i is distributed by standard deviation $\bar{\sigma}$, and Y_i is the estimate of σ_u on condition that σ_u takes the value of X_i. If a regression equation $Y_i = c_0 + c_1 X_i + \varepsilon_i$ is estimated, $\hat{c}_1$ is expected to be unity, $\hat{c}_0$ to be zero, and R^2 is $\bar{\sigma}^2/(\bar{\sigma}^2 + s^2)$, where s is the standard deviation of ε. Thus the ratio of explained variance to total variance depends on the ratio of the variance of estimator to the variance of distribution of the true value.

In the case of Japan the dispersion of the COLS estimates of σ_u is about 0.22 to 0.24, and the mean is about 0.55 to 0.60. The variance is estimated to be about 0.10 in these circumstances according to the preceding Monte Carlo experiment. Thus the variance of the estimate is less than half of the variance of the distribution of that index. More than 80 percent of the variance of estimates of σ_u is expected to be explained by the variance of the distribution of true values of σ_u. This relation is easily examined by another Monte Carlo experiment in which parameters are preset to the mean values in Japan. The coefficient of correlation between the true values and the modified COLS estimates exceeds 0.9 as predicted above. Therefore this method supplies us an estimator efficient enough for comparative studies.

How different are the values that this new estimator can supply? According to the results in the preceding Monte Carlo experiments, this estimator exhibits somewhat smaller variance and somewhat less bias. Table 10.2 gives the results of similar Monte Carlo experiments with preset values of σ_u and σ_v fixed to the mean values observed in Japan using COLS: $\sigma_u = 0.5814$, $\sigma_v = 0.2777$, and sample size = 114. These experiments yielded less bias and variance in favor of ordinary COLS, and this is consonant with the relatively high mean value of λ in Japan. The bias can be corrected by equation (2) at the expense of degrees of freedom. The statistics of this revised estimator appear in the third and the fourth columns of the table. Ordinary COLS with bias correction follows the

Table 10.2
Results of Monte Carlo experiment using average values for Japanese industries

Variables	Ordinary COLS	Modified COLS	Ordinary COLS bias adjusted	Modified COLS bias adjusted
Mean	0.5498	0.4909	0.6078	0.6432
Standard deviation	0.1212	0.1338	0.0951	0.1148
Number of successful cases	956	1000	827	581

Note: $\sigma_u = 0.5814$, $\sigma_v = 0.2777$, sample size $= 114$.

method used in chapter 2. By applying the bias correction, we reduce the variance for the modified COLS, although the bias is still larger than that of the ordinary COLS with a corrected bias. These bias corrections are at the expense of degrees of freedom. In the experiments reported above, the bias-corrected ordinary COLS supplied more degrees of freedom than the bias-corrected modified COLS. However, while the chance of encountering type I and type II failures depends on the ratio of σ_u/σ_v, the availability of a bias correction depends on the absolute value of σ_v. Therefore for Japanese industries, which apparently have low values of σ_v, the modified COLS can supply us with enough cases to be investigated in cross section. In addition, for cases that avoided both type I and type II failures in this experiment, the simple correlation coefficient of ordinary COLS estimates and the modified COLS estimates is 0.9805, which ensures that the modified COLS is a close extension of ordinary COLS.

To summarize, the modified COLS estimator is not so superior to the ordinary COLS estimator that it relieves the problem of high variance of the estimator. However, this approach can provide an estimator at least as accurate as ordinary COLS even for cases that incur type I or type II failures, and a sufficient amount of information about the true distribution of σ_u is retained in the distribution of estimates of σ_u. Considering that about half of Japanese industries incur type I or type II failures and exhibit relatively low values of σ_v, the modified COLS method can provide more degrees of freedom, even after bias correction; in fact it yields enough degrees of freedom to permit the comparison of efficiency levels of large- and small-enterprise sectors reported in the following sections. Yet the relative accuracy revealed in the second Monte Carlo experiment supports the use of the ordinary COLS method, which supplied a sample only barely adequate for the analysis in chapter 2.

10.3   Comparison of Efficiency between Large and Small Enterprises

10.3.1   Result of Modified COLS

Table 10.3 shows some basic statistics of estimated Lee-Tyler average efficiency obtained by ordinary and modified COLS. The mean values of these indexes do not differ much between ordinary and modified COLS despite the number of degrees of freedom which were 2.5 times larger for modified COLS. The dispersion is somewhat increased, however. As expected, even when the bias correction is implemented, the degrees of freedom available for modified COLS exceed those for ordinary COLS.

The means of the modified COLS estimates are 0.843 for 89 cases that met with type I failure, 0.547 for 106 case with type II failure, and 0.696 for 146 cases that avoided both failures. Thus cases with type I failure have higher estimated efficiency than others, but the maximum value is below 100 percent (0.938). This fact is consistent with the implication of putty-clay type vintage model in chapter 2.

For industries that avoid both type I and type II failures, the two methods yielded quite close estimates (the simple correlation coefficient, hereafter denoted as ρ, is 0.9553, shown in table 10.3a), and this similarity was retained when possible biases were corrected. The high correlation before bias correction supports the assumption that modified COLS can be used as an extension of ordinary COLS to the cases of type I and type II failures, while the high correlation after correction confirms that in

Table 10.3a
Measures of efficiency (Lee-Tyler average efficiency) in Japanese industries using modified COLS estimator: whole industries

Variables	Ordinary COLS	Modified COLS	Ordinary COLS bias adjusted	Modified COLS bias adjusted
Mean	0.6839	0.6880	0.6289	0.6241
Standard deviation	0.0944	0.1361	0.1012	0.1321
Number of successful cases	138	341	116	203
Simple correlation coefficients				
Ordinary COLS		0.9553	0.8657	0.9662
Modified COLS			0.8798	0.9999
Ordinary COLS bias adjusted				0.8749

modified COLS the bias can be corrected linearly from the estimates for industries with low values of σ_v.

The gain in degrees of freedom with modified COLS enables a meaningful efficiency comparison between large- and small-scale enterprises. When ordinary COLS is used, indexes for both the larger and smaller sectors are available for only 19 industries. This shortage of degrees of freedom precludes analysis of the difference. The modified COLS secures 74 industries, a number that is not large but seems adequate for further analysis. Table 10.3b shows that the large gain in degrees of freedom brings little change to the mean absolute efficiency levels or differences in efficiency between smaller and larger sectors of industries obtained by ordinary COLS.

10.3.2 Descriptive Analysis of Differences in Technical Efficiency

First, the means of estimated technical efficiency are compared between the smaller and larger plants of industries. In their analysis of U.S. industries CB reported a statistically significant 6.6 percent difference of means. As for Japan, although a 3.6 percent discrepancy is detected using ordinary COLS, it is not statistically significant ($t = 1.46$). With modified COLS the means are almost same ($t = -0.01$) as are the medians. When the mean differences of efficiency indexes for individual industries are tested for significant difference from zero, this result does not change (in ordinary

Table 10.3b
Measures of efficiency (Lee-Tyler average efficiency) in Japanese industries using modified COLS estimator: large and small plants

Variables	Ordinary COLS bias adjusted			Modified COLS bias adjusted		
	Large	Small	Difference	Large	Small	Difference
Mean	0.6465	0.6165	0.0078	0.6497	0.6498	−0.0038
Median	0.6409	0.6186	0.0016	0.6354	0.6252	−0.0003
Standard deviation	0.0912	0.0880	0.0968	0.1251	0.1297	0.1409
Number of successful cases	83	55	19	127	106	74
Simple correlation coefficients						
Ordinary COLS						
Large		0.0341	0.7080	0.7921	0.0640	0.2315
Small			−0.6817	0.1808	0.7674	−0.2857
Difference				0.7561	−0.7783	0.9923
Modified COLS						
Large					0.3802	0.5478
Small						−0.5655

COLS, $t = 0.35$, in modified COLS, $t = -0.23$). Thus no overall difference
of efficiency levels is found. Of course, there are some industries with levels
of technical efficiency considerably higher in larger plants. The maximum
value of the difference of efficiency levels is 0.3134. At the other extreme
smaller plants in one industry are 37 percent more efficient.

Could the 74 industries be unrepresentative of the whole data set? In this
set of industries, clear discrepancies in productivity associated with dual
structure are evident. Productivity measured by value added per worker is
27 percent higher in larger plants than in smaller plants. The means are
significantly different ($t = 4.28$), and the mean difference is significantly
different from 0 ($t = 9.03$). Thus dual structure is present in this set of
industries, and the 74 industries are representative in this sense.

Procedures for correcting bias can cause some distortions in the data set.
However, for estimates of σ_u before bias correction the mean of the larger
sector is slightly larger than that of the smaller sector (0.565 for 214
industries and 0.557 for 194 industries, respectively). Note that σ_u should
be considered an index of inefficiency. The t-statistic testing the difference
of the means is 0.24, so the hypothesis of equal values of the means cannot
be rejected. The mean of differences is 0.014 and its t-statistic is 0.44, which
is also insignificant.

The correlations between the estimated efficiencies of the small-plant
and large-plant halves of industries are surprisingly low. They are 0.034 in
ordinary COLS and 0.064 in modified COLS, seemingly almost independent. However,

$$\rho(\text{LTF, LTFS}) = 0.71, \qquad \rho(\text{LTF, LTFL}) = 0.61,$$

and

$$\text{LTF} = -0.0359 + 0.5223\text{LTFL} + 0.4798\text{LTFS},$$
$$\qquad\qquad\quad (12.88) \qquad\qquad (12.03)$$

$$\bar{R}^2 = 0.8750, \quad N = 71,$$

where LTF is the level of technical efficiency of the industry as a whole,
LTFS of its smaller sector, and LTFL of its larger sector. In Japan the
efficiency level of an industry seems to be approximately the average
efficiency of its sectors; in other words, contrary to the U.S. case reported
in CB, there is no significant difference between coefficients. Incidentally
no correlation appears between the difference LTFL − LTFS and LTF
($\rho = 0.010$).

Table 10.4
Efficiency levels and small and large-plant differences in efficiency of two-digit industries

Industry	LTF	LTFL	LTFS	DF1	DF2	Number of four-digit industries
Food, beverages, and tobacco	0.475	0.505	0.597	−0.021	−0.023	8
Textiles	0.616	0.699	0.642	0.085	0.068	6
Textile products	0.613	0.626	0.621	0.006	0.004	3
Wood and wood products	0.514	0.541	0.506	0.014	0.009	5
Furniture and fixtures	0.551	0.581	0.611	0.017	0.015	1
Pulp and paper products	0.530	0.561	0.648	0.029	0.024	1
Printing and publishing	0.649	0.648	0.648	0.029	0.024	2
Chemical products	0.517	0.797	0.511	0.288	0.231	1
Petroleum and coal products	NA	NA	NA	NA	NA	0
Rubber products	0.620	0.655	0.649	0.005	0.004	2
Leather and leather products	0.802	0.621	NA	NA	NA	0
Earthen and related products	0.639	0.647	0.644	−0.015	−0.010	6
Iron and steel materials and products	0.760	0.620	0.627	0.073	0.062	2
Nonferrous metal materials and products	0.508	0.665	0.649	NA	NA	0
Fabricated metal products	0.573	0.579	0.610	−0.041	−0.026	8
Ordinary machinery	0.586	0.613	0.661	−0.056	−0.042	12
Electrical machinery	0.597	0.607	0.623	0.024	0.019	7
Transport equipment	0.561	0.578	0.621	−0.119	−0.095	4
Precision equipment	0.703	0.713	0.704	NA	NA	0
Other	0.576	0.583	0.588	−0.010	−0.013	6

The observed indexes are aggregated to two-digit-level industries in table 10.4. In the table DF1 is defined as LTFL − LTFS, and DF2 is defined as (LTFL − LTFS)/(LTFL + LTFS), following CB. The table shows that the chemical products industry's large plants have a much higher efficiency level than the small ones, although that two-digit sector includes only one four-digit industry with indexes available for both small and large plants. Other industries with seemingly more efficient large plants are textiles and iron and steel materials and products. Ordinary machinery industries and transport equipment industries seem to have relatively efficient small plants.

Differences within these two-digit industries could prove to be statistically significant in some cases. Using the estimated standard deviation of

Table 10.5
Statistics of estimated σ_v

Statistic	Whole industry	Large plants	Small plants	Difference
Mean	0.2604	0.2682	0.2817	−0.0088
Standard deviation	0.1138	0.1061	0.1376	0.1435
Number of successful case	338	211	186	182
Simple correlation coefficients				
Whole industry		0.6922	0.4592	0.0746
Large plants			0.3386	0.4191
Small plants				−0.7124

$\hat{\sigma}_u$, 0.095, the difference measured by index DF1 is not significant in any industry. The t-statistic is 2.19 in textile industries, −2.04 in ordinary machinery, and −2.48 in transport equipment industries, but for no industry is the statistic significant at 5 percent in a two-tailed test. The t-statistics for equality of the means of LTFL and LTFS are 1.37 (textiles), −1.53 (ordinary machinery), and −0.74 (transport equipment). Again none of these statistics are significant. If the standard deviation estimated in the Monte Carlo experiment is replaced by the larger dispersion of the estimates in four-digit industries, these t-statistics become smaller. Overall, there is no evidence that significant discrepancies in technical efficiency exist even in two-digit industries.

Finally, table 10.5 examines differences among σ_v estimates. There are a number of reasons why we should expect relatively large variances in small plants. First, as Kusuda et al. (1979) showed, both the entry and the exit rates are negatively correlated with firm size in manufacturing industries. For example, the ratio of entrants to total number of firms during 1969–71 was 19.2 percent in enterprises with 1 to 3 workers, 14.6 percent with 20 to 29 workers, and 9.8 percent with 200 to 299 workers. The ratio of exits to total number of firms during 1966–71 was, respectively, 13.9 percent, 9.2 percent, and 7.8 percent for each category. Clearly, since the small-plant category includes more firms in disequilibrium, the observed dispersion is greater in that group. Second, in Japan's subcontracting system, it is often said that small subcontractors are used as buffers for large oligopolistic firms. Business cycle disturbances therefore can have a greater effect on small plants, and this should be reflected in the random noise term. Third is the fact that this tendency can be inferred indirectly from CB (their results for λ and the level of average efficiency).

The mean of σ_v estimates for the small plants is larger by 5 percent, as expected, but the difference is not significant ($t = 1.08$). The sign of the mean difference of these estimates indicates that smaller plants have larger dispersions, though their t-statistic is also insignificant ($t = -0.828$). If ordinary COLS estimates are employed in place of modified COLS, this result does not change ($t = -0.07$). Therefore we find no evidence of difference in either the technical efficiency level or the symmetrical component of composed residuals.

10.4 Determinants of Efficiency Discrepancy

In this section and the next, using regression analysis, we analyze the relationship between technical efficiency level and productivity and between technical efficiency and the price-cost margin. The technical efficiency level depends on the structural variables identified by CB and appearing in chapters 2 through 7. If there exists a mutually dependent system of relationships, the structure is considered recursive. The efficiency level is determined by exogenous variables and in turn affects productivity or the price-cost margin, or both. If the disturbance terms of these equations are independent, OLS of course can provide estimators with desirable properties.[13] However, the disturbance terms in the determinants of technical efficiency levels and productivity (or the price-cost margin) can be correlated because of any determinants omitted from the model. Many technical factors that are difficult to proxy can be excluded or neglected, and these omitted factors can cause residuals to be correlated.

To avoid the biases and inconsistencies that can result from correlated disturbances, an iterative least squares method is employed. That is, we use the estimate of technical efficiency to determine productivity and the price-cost margins. Here we analyze the determinants of the difference in efficiency levels—this is in itself an interesting problem. In chapter 2 we considered the possible determinants of interindustry differences in efficiency. Determinants of variation in levels among industries could well be different from the determinants of efficiency discrepancies between the small and large plants. Some factors have different effects on small and large sectors; others affect them equally. We apply the findings of chapter 2 for the modified COLS estimator to industries' two sectors. Next, we develop some hypotheses about the determinants of efficiency differences.

Since most of the determining variables have been introduced in earlier chapters, and their effects have been analyzed, we omit discussion of the mechanisms at work and the definitions of these variables.

10.4.1 Determinants of the Levels of Technical Efficiency for Large and Small Establishments

The core model for determining interindustry differences in technical efficiency given in section 2.3 includes six explanatory variables: HI, the Herfindahl index; GRWT, the rate of growth; PCMD, the difference in the price-cost margins between larger and smaller plants; K, the absolute size of tangible assets; PRWR, the ratio of production workers in total employees; and KSHI, the index of inflexibility of fixed capital.

In analyzing the modified COLS estimates of efficiency, we encountered a problem because the increase in degrees of freedom due to the new set of industries analyzed brought more multicollinearity with it. Some changes in the core model hence are required. First, KSHI was eliminated and K replaced by log(K). KSHI and K are different kinds of indexes of capital fixity. Fortunately there was no correlation detected in the industry set analyzed in chapter 2, but positive correlation now arises with the index of absolute capital size. Second, PRWR was replaced by ENER, which represents the intensity of energy use. They both show industry specific factors besides expressing fixity in the production processes. PRWR is higher in light than in heavy industries and in process/assembly than in material industries, while ENER is higher in heavy industries and in material industries.[14] This change is also due to a multicollinearity problem. Third, PCMD was eliminated because its original function no longer applies. PCMD was included in the regression analysis because it was thought to control for difference in performance between the large and small plants. Now that effect may be analyzed directly.[15] Finally, GRWT was eliminated; it lost significance due to high correlation with HI.

Then new core model becomes a very simple one:

$$LTF = 0.8459 + 1.921*HI - 3.728*HI^2 - 0.0328*\log(K)$$
$$ (4.70) \qquad (3.14) \qquad (3.66)$$

$$+ \ 0.251**ENER$$
$$ (2.45)$$

$$\bar{R}^2 = 0.169, \quad N = 202,$$

where *t*-statistics appear in parentheses, * indicates significance in a two-tailed test at 0.01 and ** at 0.05. The effects of other exogenous variables are summarized in table 10.6. Although it does not offer as comprehensive analysis as chapter 2, it does show the effect of adding each of several variables one at a time to the core equation just reported. One major change in the regression results is in the coefficient of RSIZ (relative size of typical enterprise measured by the size total tangible assets). For the United States CB found a positive association between RSIZE (RSIZ) and EFF (Lee-Tyler average efficiency), indicating relatively efficient performance in industries dominated by large scale plants. For Japan we observed an insignificant negative coefficient in our analysis in chapter 2. Now, however, the modified COLS estimates of efficiency indicate a positive association with RISZ. A possible explanation of this change is correlation with eliminated independent variables such as KSHI or K, although this posed no problem in chapter 2.

The variables that have not changed are the significant negative coefficients of TARF (protection by tariff barrier), TARSUB (effective protection by tariff and governmental subsidies), DREG (dummy of governmental regulation), PCMD (difference in price-cost margins between large and small plants), and the significant positive coefficient of SUBC (a subcontracting index). We obtained expected signs but insignificant coefficients as before for ADV (advertising intensity) and IMPT (adjustment term of concentration with imports). The signs of PRGM (growth ratio of productivity), R&D (R&D intensity), and ICOV (inbound diversification) are the same as in the previous study and consistent with our hypotheses, but their significance levels have somewhat been reduced. We need to use simultaneous equations to analyze more fully PRGM and R&D because they could be dependent on the technical efficiency level. ICOV is significant when industries are divided by plant size[16]

We applied the core model to small and large plants to obtain these regression equations:

$$LTFL = 0.7773 + 2.146*HI - 4.387**HI^2 - 0.024 \log(K)$$
$$\qquad\qquad\quad (3.49) \qquad (2.30) \qquad\quad (-1.78)$$
$$\qquad + 0.288**ENER,$$
$$\qquad\quad (2.34)$$

$$\bar{R}^2 = 0.150, \quad N = 127;$$

Table 10.6
Regression analysis of determinants of technical efficiency in whole industries, large and small plants: coefficients of variables added to core model

	LTF	$\bar{R}^2(N)$	LTFL	$\bar{R}^2(N)$	LTFS	$\bar{R}^2(N)$
ADV	−1.89	0.176(201)	−1.73	0.154(127)	−2.49	0.023(105)
	(1.68)		(1.27)		(1.38)	
RSIZ	1.61**	0.189(202)	7.80*	0.195(127)	12.15*	0.103(106)
	(2.44)		(2.78)		(3.28)	
IMPT	−0.039	0.165(201)	−0.071	0.145(127)	−0.127	0.013(105)
	(0.507)		(0.440)		(0.905)	
TARF	−0.691*	0.204(202)	−0.495	0.161(127)	−0.529	0.036(106)
	(3.11)		(1.62)		(1.75)	
TARSUB	−0.658*	0.206(202)	−0.444	0.163(127)	−0.448	0.031(106)
	(3.20)		(1.72)		(1.61)	
PRGM	−0.001	0.188(201)	−0.002	0.144(127)	−0.010	0.031(106)
	(0.290)		(0.31)		(1.59)	
R&D	1.405	0.165(201)	4.33	0.163(127)	7.78**	0.051(105)
	(0.499)		(1.69)		(2.20)	
ICOV	−0.099	0.170(197)	−0.20**	0.184(124)	−0.253**	0.038(103)
	(1.59)		(2.47)		(2.19)	
DREG	−0.069*	0.199(202)	−0.085**	0.188(127)	−0.052	0.032(106)
	(2.92)		(2.57)		(1.61)	
SUBC	0.200*	0.192(202)	0.161	0.166(127)	0.230**	0.057(106)
	(2.59)		(1.82)		(2.30)	
PCMD	−0.313**	0.181(202)	−0.168	0.147(127)	−0.215	0.012(106)
	(2.00)		(0.72)		(0.72)	
GRWT	−0.0002	0.165(202)	−0.0006	0.144(127)	−0.0006	0.008(106)
	(0.278)		(0.383)		(0.328)	
SPE4	0.020	0.160(197)	−0.273**	0.175(124)	0.102	−0.006(103)
	(0.203)		(2.18)		(0.591)	

Note: For definition of variables, see chapter 2, appendix. Coefficient of variables in the core model (intercept, HI, HI^2, log(K), ENER) has been omitted from this table. t-statistics are in parentheses. Levels of significance (in two-tailed tests) are * = 1 percent, ** = 5 percent.

$$\text{LTFS} = 0.8839 + 0.977\text{HI} - 1.63\text{HI}^2 - 0.028\log(K)$$
$$\phantom{\text{LTFS} = 0.8839 +} (1.31) \qquad (0.74) \qquad (1.72)$$
$$\phantom{\text{LTFS} = 0.8839} + 0.155\text{ENER},$$
$$\phantom{\text{LTFS} = 0.8839 +} (0.76)$$

$\bar{R}^2 = 0.017, \quad N = 106.$

The result for small plants is weak, while the result for the large plants resembles those for industries as a whole. Although no signs have been changed, no coefficient is significant at 5 percent in a two-tailed test.

The expected inverted U-shaped relation between HI and LTF rests on two related hypotheses. Highly concentrated industries lack the incentive to install new technology, whereas renewal investments in relatively atomistic industries are hindered by the lumpiness of capital. In small plants only the latter effect ought to appear because the expected value of concentration at which the level of technical efficiency is maximized is relatively high and because small firms seldom can participate in oligopolistic behavior. Consequently the technical efficiency levels of small plants appear to increase monotonically with the degree of concentration:

$$\text{LTFS} = 0.9080 + 0.4933\text{HI} - 0.027\log(K),$$
$$\phantom{\text{LTFS} = 0.9080 +} (1.68) \qquad (-1.75)$$

$\bar{R}^2 = 0.024, \quad N = 106.$

Both coefficients are significant at 5 percent in one-tailed tests, and the coefficient of HI does not reject the hypothesis. However, the relation is not particularly robust. Increases of significance occur when some other variables such as R&D or ICOV are included.

The effects of most other structural variables undergo no changes in the two industry sectors, as shown in table 10.6. The variables whose coefficients experience the same changes between the entire industry and its two sectors are RSIZ, TARF (or TARSUB), ICOV, and PCMD. RSIZ and ICOV show increases in significance; TARF and PCMD decreases. PCMD represents the differential effect of scale on margins. The negative significant coefficient of PCMD applied to the entire industry could indicate that factors other than different technical efficiency levels affect the price-cost margin, and this is consistent with the variable's loss of significance in divided industries. On the other hand, asymmetric effects are detected in the divided industries in coefficients of PRGM, R&D, DREG,

SUBC, and SPE4. PRGM, R&D, and SUBC have stronger effects on the small sectors of industries than DREG and SPE4. This asymmetric effect is investigated in the next section.

10.4.2 Determinants of Differences in Efficiency

The differentiated effects in divided industries just shown could be among the factors that cause differences in efficiency between industries' large and small plants. Additional factors are suggested by the results of CB, who found that the main variables exerting significant effects were R&D, RSIZ, GRWT, the ratio of exports to shipments, and indexes of diversification. Of these variables, R&D and plant-level diversification index were shown in table 10.6 to have different effects on divided industries. The R&D pattern of Japan is the reverse of that of the United States. In the U.S. case R&D was found to widen the efficiency gap, implying that greater risks are experienced by small plants in innovative industries (thus the negative association between efficiency and R&D intensity). In Japanese case, however, R&D was positively associated with overall efficiency, although it had no significant effect in the simultaneous equations analysis. This difference in the direction of R&D's effect could indicate the R&D activities differ. The negative association for R&D expenditures in the United States suggests that innovative activity functions as a disturbance while the positive association for R&D in Japan suggests that absorption of current technology enhances the level of efficiency.[17] As a determinant of the difference in efficiency between the United States and Japan, R&D turned out to be negative (see chapter 11).

The asymmetric effect of R&D shown in table 10.6 is consistent with this function of R&D activities. A fixed-cost component in R&D expenditures discourages small firms from engaging in R&D activities. This tendency is stronger in industries with low rates of R&D spending because small firms spend no money for R&D in industries in which R&D activities are not crucial to survival. In Japan the number of firms conducting R&D activities was only 13.1 percent in 1978 of the total number of firms for manufacturing firms with 1 to 299 employees, while the ratio was 91.8 percent for firms with no less than 1,000 employees.[18] Therefore a negative correlation was observed between the absolute value of R&D intensity and the differences between the large and small plants. The simple correlation coefficient between $\mathrm{DF2RD} \equiv (\mathrm{RDL} - \mathrm{RDS})/\mathrm{RDA}$ and RDA is -0.53 for 24 industries,[19] where RDS is R&D intensity for firms with 1 to 999 employees, RDL with no less than 1,000 employees, and RDA for the entire industry. In industries with intensive R&D the difference of R&D intensity was relatively small. This implies that the variance of R&D intensity among industries is larger in small plants (the coefficients of variation of RDL and RDS are 0.69 and 1.08, respectively). Therefore, if we assume that R&D functions to absorb current technology, the effect of R&D in determining LTF is stronger in the small plants than in large ones.

Plant-level specialization indexes run in the same direction in determining interindustry differences in efficiency as that shown in table 10.6, which imputes the association mainly to the negative and significant association between SPE4 and LTFL. If diversification is greater in large plants, these results conflict with those in chapter 2, which shows a positive and significant association between SPE4 and LTF. The coefficient of SPE4 showed a sensitivity to the method employed. In a simultaneous equations analysis, the presence of R&D and MULTI can affect the sign of the coefficient of SPE4 because of their close relation to diversification. However, even if a simultaneous equations analysis is applied to the two industry sectors, the signs of the SPE4 coefficients do not change; these coefficients are 0.2839 (1.34) for small plants and −0.4341 (1.98) for large plants, where asymptotic t-ratios appear in parentheses. The coefficient for small plants is positive as in chapter 2, but it is insignificant; the coefficient for large plants is negative.

This result should caution us about interpreting the positive association between LTF and SPE4 as an indicator of excess diversification, because it is hard to explain the negative association between SPE4 and LTFL by that hypothesis. One alternative explanation of the negative association between DF1 and SPE4, which is implied by the asymmetric effect of SPE4 on LTFL and LTFS, is provided by Marris (1964) and Yoshida et al. (1981). They hypothesized that the relation between profitability and diversification is inverted U-shaped and that some level of diversification maximizes the profitability. In industries with low optimal diversification both small and large plants will refrain from diversification. In industries with high optimal level of diversification only larger firms will benefit from diversifying their products thanks to their R&D activity and opportunities associated with their large scales. Therefore the level of diversification is heterogeneous and increases with firm scale. This causes technical inefficiency. Efficiency should decrease with diversification among the whole industries. In small plants the same relation should stem from uneven chances to diversify optimally. In large plants insufficient levels of diversification can cause the observed positive relation between diversification and efficiency. That is, in some industries with low diversification, firms do not diversify because the optimal level is low, whereas in other industries they exhibit low diversification because investment cost is fixed, and so on. Hence by a kind of filtering effect the average level of efficiency is lower than in industries with high diversification. These relations are further investigated in the next section in the discussion of the effect of productivity differences.

An important factor in the U.S. study was firm-level diversification. It was not analyzed in the Japanese study because data are not available. Although RSIZ had a significantly positive but small effect on intraindustry differences in the United States, that result does not hold for divided industries in Japan.

Some other variables are examined for possible effects on discrepancies in efficiency. The first is PRGM, which had different effects on efficiency in the two industry sectors. Its influence can resemble that of R&D. While R&D can exert the two effects noted above, PRGM works as a proxy of innovative activities. Therefore, if R&D works to enhance efficiency as discussed, PRGM does the opposite. That is, PRGM represents a disturbance, and small plants lagging farther behind frontier technology will exhibit impaired efficiency.

GRWT is reported to reduce U.S. intraindustry differences in efficiency despite the expectation that the accelerated turnover of small plants in rapidly expanding industries would produce a positive association. This variable had no differential effect on efficiency in the two sectors in table 10.6, but it might nonetheless affect discrepancies because of inhibiting effects hidden in the core model.

DREG and TARSUB are forms of governmental intervention that can have an asymmetric influence on the two sectors depending on the focus of government policies (especially DREG). The difference in the coefficients of DREG in table 10.6 suggests that regulations impair large-plant efficiency. Last the asymmetrical effect of SUBC on small plants, as indicated in table 10.6, holds according to our hypothesis in chapter 2. As hypothesized, it has a direct influence on the subcontractor's efficiency but a derivative one on the contractor.

The effects of these variables are now examined, starting with the variables that were used in the U.S. study:

$$DF1 = 0.444 - 5.02R\&D - 2.60RSIZ - 0.484^{**}SPE4, \tag{3}$$
$$(1.18) \quad (0.488) \quad (2.45)$$

$\bar{R}^2 = 0.043, \quad N = 71.$

The coefficients of both R&D and RSIZ are consistent with previous results but not significant. A negative association with plant-level specialization expected from table 10.6 is confirmed in the significant coefficient SPE4. Even when other factors such as exports, advertisement, and growth rates are introduced, the coefficients of R&D and RSIZ remain insignificant.

The next two equations result when R&D and RSIZ are replaced by the remaining variables:

$$DF1 = 0.394 + 0741TARSUB - 0.092DREG - 0.475^{*}SPE4$$
$$(1.74) \quad (1..58) \quad (2.61)$$

$$- 0.275SUBC + 0.004GRWT,$$
$$(-1.81) \quad (1.88)$$

$\bar{R}^2 = 0.120, \quad N = 71;$

$$DF1 = 0.409 + 0.766TARSUB - 0.095DREG - 0.488^{*}SPE4$$
$$(1.78) \quad (1.61) \quad (2.64)$$

$$- 0.305SUBC + 0.004GRWT - 0.005PRGM$$
$$(1.85) \quad (1.92) \quad (0.49)$$

$\bar{R}^2 = 0.109, \quad N = 71.$

The coefficients of TARSUB and DREG take opposite signs: As TARSUB increases the discrepancy, DREG reduces it. The regression results in table 10.6 imply that DREG's negative coefficient reflects regulation's selective effect on large plants. Contrary to the selective effect of DREG TARSUB's positive effect suggests that tariff and subsidy protection makes the heterogeneity of efficiency to increase among small industries. DREG takes high values in petroleum and coal, food, chemical, and transport equipment industries (airplanes and steel vessels), and TARSUB is high in leather, textile, and food industries. Besides food industries, it is apparent that direct regulation is aimed at industries with relatively large plants, whereas protection favors industries with small plants. This pattern is consistent with DREG's stronger effect on efficiencies of large plants and TARSUB's stronger effect on efficiencies of small plants.[20]

SUBC's negative coefficient is consistent with the hypothesis that small firms are likely to be subcontractors and large firms the contractors. If the subcontractor and contractor are in the same four-digit industry, efficiency is increased by this relationship, and this is reflected in the subcontractor's performance.

GRWT has a positive effect on the discrepancies in efficiency; this is consistent with the hypothesis that growth-related disturbances push small units farther from equilibrium. This relationship was not found in the United States.

Despite their consistent signs the significance of the coefficients is low except for SPE4. DREG's coefficient is not significant even at 10 percent in a two-tailed test (as the other coefficients are). PRGM's low significance is consistent with the inference that R&D in Japan is related to absorbing international frontier technology.

When DF2 replaces DF1, there is very little change. We will examine in the next section the effectiveness of this regression equation when the predicted values are used in models to explain productivity and profitability.

10.5 Productivity and Efficiency

10.5.1 Discrepancy in Productivity between Large and Small Plants

It was noted previously that the dual structure of industries can be seen in the discrepancy in productivities between small and large plants. Two variables are employed to indicate this discrepancy: $DF1VAN \equiv VANL - VANS$, and $DF2VAN \equiv (VANL - VANS)/(VANL + VANS)$, where VANL is value added per worker for large plants, and VANS for small plants. The mean of DF1VAN for 232 industries is 143.3 and is significantly different from 0 ($t = 9.03$). However, $\rho(DF1VAN, VANL) = 0.599$, and $\rho(DF1VAN, VANS) = -0.001$. Considering that VANL and VANS are highly correlated, these statistics imply that DF1VAN could depend mainly upon the entire industry's value added per worker. The normalized index DF2VAN then would be more suitable for comparative analysis. The mean of DF2VAN is 0.1096, and it also is significantly different from 0 ($t = 11.77$). ρ(DF2VAN, VANL) = 0.336, and ρ(DF1VAN, VANS) = -0.223, so dual structure is reflected in the discrepancies.

Discrepancies in productivity are associated with discrepancies in capital–labor ratios. Two variables demonstrate this: DF2KN $\equiv$ (KNL $-$ KNS)/(KNL $+$ KNS), and DF2KL $\equiv$ (KLL $-$ KLS)/(KLL $+$ KLS), where KNL(KNS) is total tangible assets per worker for large(small) sectors of industries, and KLL(KLS) is total tangible assets per labor input measured by compensation for workers. The means of DF2KN and DF2KL are, respectively, 0.175 and 0.102, both significantly different from 0 (t-statistics are 14.91 and 10.52). K/N is 17.5 percent greater in the large sectors, and K/L is 10.2 percent greater. Moreover the means of KNL and KNS are significantly different ($t = 2.56$), as are the means of KLL and KLS ($t = 2.26$). The distributions of these difference variables are shown in table 10.7, which illustrates the prevalence of positive discrepancies. Note that 22 percent of the industries still show higher value added per worker in their small plants, 15 percent for K/N and 25 percent for K/L.

Table 10.7
Distribution of differences in selected variables between large and small plants of industries (numbers of cases)

Range	VA/N	K/N	K/L	PCD2
$-0.50--0.40$	0	0	0	2
$-0.40--0.30$	0	0	0	4
$-0.30--0.20$	0	0	1	13
$-0.20--0.10$	11	8	12	40
$-0.10--0.00$	41	27	45	91
0.00–0.10	73	54	75	127
0.10–0.20	54	47	43	45
0.20–0.30	30	41	35	19
0.30–0.40	15	25	10	4
0.40–0.50	6	21	9	1
0.50–0.60	1	4	1	0
0.60–0.70	1	4	1	0
0.70–0.80	0	1	0	0
0.80–0.90	0	0	0	0
0.90–0.00	0	0	0	0

Table 10.8
Average values of selected variables by two-digit industry group

Industry group	DF2VAN	DF2KN	PCD2
Food, beverages, and tobacco	0.10569	0.08062	0.03123
Textiles	0.01938	0.07407	0.00239
Textiles products	0.08292	0.11528	−0.01156
Wood and wood products	0.02992	0.05771	−0.01034
Furniture and fixtures	0.08637	0.11245	0.03566
Pulp and paper products	0.17172	0.37980	−0.02524
Printing and publishing	0.13076	0.11855	−0.00661
Chemical products	0.14275	0.16879	0.05640
Petroleum and coal products	−0.05569	−0.07045	0.01783
Rubber products	0.23676	0.31541	0.02087
Leather and leather products	0.03525	0.09092	0.01301
Earthen and related products	0.04602	0.03415	0.01794
Iron and steel materials and products	−0.05647	0.06320	−0.05040
Nonferrous metal materials and products	0.17828	0.21753	0.08360
Fabricated metal products	0.13247	0.21032	0.04635
Ordinary machinery	0.15022	0.29202	−0.03237
Electrical machinery	0.34004	0.45805	0.03178
Transport equipment	0.14439	0.31460	−0.13310
Precision equipment	0.25697	0.42344	−0.04866
Other	0.14386	0.18845	0.03131

Table 10.8 reports weighted averages of these variables for the two-digit industry groups. While in electrical machinery, precision equipment, and rubber products industries DF2VAN shows high values, in petroleum and coal and in iron and steel industries value added per worker is larger in the small sectors. This tendency is also seen in K/N. The correlations ρ(DF2VAN, DF2KN) and ρ(DF2VAN, DF2KL) are high: 0.672 and 0.523. The dual structure demonstrated by these discrepancies is typical for Japan.

10.5.2 Efficiency as a Determinant of Discrepancies in Productivity

We now turn to determine the effect of the discrepancy in technical efficiency on relative productivity in large and small plants. Because on average no efficiency difference exists, its effect is neutral even if there exists the expected positive association between differences of productivity and efficiency. Yet, as was seen in tables 10.4 and 10.7, there is much variation among industries even though the intersectoral differences are not large. Discrepancies in productivity also vary among sectors, so some part of productivity differences may be due to differences in efficiency. We will use a regression analysis to explain differences in productivity. The dependent variable is DF2VAN. $\overline{\text{DFLTF}}$, the predicted value from equation (3), and DF2KN or DF2KL are included in the independent variables. Much of the elevated value added per worker in large plants is due to the higher ratios of capital to labor.

One aspect of dual structure is a lower wage rate in SMEs, alleged to let them endure disadvantages in capital markets. It is very difficult to obtain a suitable measure of the discrepancy in the wage rate because one would need to control carefully for differences in the quality of labor employed, so no direct analysis is offered here.[21] However, PART (proportion of part-time workers) could indicate if there is greater opportunity for small plants to hire workers at lower wage rates. In view of this, the coefficient of this variable should be negative.

Some further explanation may be in order here because it is not clear whether part-time labor is used more intensely in SMEs than in large establishments. In 1978 ratio of part-time employees to full-time employees was 8.2 percent for establishments with 1 to 299 employees and 1.9 percent for those with 300 or more employees.[22] However, this is rather recent phenomenon. In 1960 the ratios were 6.3 percent and 8.4 percent, respectively. Part-time labor is cheaper for small establishments than large ones. The average hourly wage for part-time female workers was 14 percent higher in establishments with 1,000 or more workers than in those with less than 1,000 workers.[23] The discrepancy could be even greater if one takes into account the fact that in large establishments workers receive more supplemental compensation than in small ones.

If large and small plants have the same production frontiers, the output–labor ratio is a function of the capital–labor ratio. Other variables employed as determinants of productivity are those thought to affect profitability. As determinants of discrepancies of efficiency TARSUB and DREG, which represent governmental intervention, had opposite effects: TARSUB depressed the efficiency of small plants, and DREG the efficiency of large plants. These sources of inefficiency can affect productivity directly as well. The effect of efficiency on productivity is in the probability of inefficient plants not surviving. Tariff protection can work to undermine productivity in small units by easing competitive pressure. DREG's role would be similar, with the same negative effect on efficiency. Small plants can adapt to growth in demand or changes in technology asymmetrically. As GRWT increases DF1, it appears to diminish efficiency in small plant sector. Large increases in demand makes it possible for small plants with low productivity to survive. If increased demand is met mostly by new small entrants, they get temporary rents. Therefore the sign of GRWT cannot be predicted. R&D intensity has a stronger effect on efficiency in small sectors than in large sectors, although no significant effect on discrepancies in efficiency can be identified. R&D can give large firms the advantage if it creates barriers to entry.[24] PRGM, which measures productivity growth rate, works in a way similarly to R&D because attaining best current technology is harder for small plants. Therefore PRGM could be positively correlated with productivity differences.

KSHI is an index of the lumpiness of capital investment. A large initial investment can work as a filter[25] to enhance efficiency of surviving small firms. On the other hand, the increased profitability of an oligopolistic core due to KSHI's function as a barrier to entry can appear as a difference in productivity.

In chapter 2 PCMA (price-cost margin) was found to decrease with diversification. The assumption that large multiplant firms are more diversified yields two alternative hypothesis already mentioned: One considers that situation to involve excess diversification of the large plants, and although it can explain the positive association between SPE4 and LTF, it conflicts with the negative association between SPE4 and LTFL. The other infers from diversified large plants the suboptimal diversification of small plants, which can explain the positive association between SPE4 and LTF and is consistent with the negative association between SPE4 and LTFL. The first hypothesis implies a positive relationship between SPE4 and productivity differences because excess diversification reduces the productivity of the large plants. The second hypothesis implies a negative relationship. However, this effect should operate through efficiency differences and hence could be hidden in the analysis of differences in productivity. Note that these two hypotheses do not contradict each other because excess diversification in larger plants and suboptimal diversification in smaller plants can occur at the same time.

Other variables that are considered to influence large and small plants asymmetrically are ADV (advertising intensity), TCHMSAL (payments for imported technology/sales), and EXPT (exports/sales). All these activities incur considerable fixed costs that work to the advantage of large plants. Therefore the coefficients of these variables are expected to be positive.

The results of regression analyses are shown in table 10.9. Regardless of whether K/L or K/N is used as the capital–labor ratio, the discrepancy in

Table 10.9
Regression analyses determining discrepancies in productivity between small and large plants

DF2VAN = −0.439

+1.07**	$\overline{\text{DFLTF}}$	+0.455*	DF2KN	+0.201*	DREG
(2.22)		(4.41)		(3.21)	
−0.003	GRWT	−0.38	TARSUB	−3.04**	PART
(1.24)		(0.89)		(2.02)	
−0.007	KSHI	+0.52	SPE4	+1.03	ADV
(1.17)		(1.87)		(0.58)	
+0.24**	TCHMSAL	+2.69	R&D	−0.005	PRGM
(2.10)		(0.74)		(0.69)	
−0.031	EXPT				
(0.229)					

$\overline{R}^2 = 0.540$, $N = 71$

DF2VAN = −0.44

+1.30**	$\overline{\text{DFLTF}}$	+0.279**	DF2KL	+0.238*	DREG
(2.43)		(2.31)		(3.44)	
−0.003	GRWT	−0.64	TARSUB	−3.83**	PART
(1.22)		(1.38)		(2.32)	
−0.015**	KSHI	+0.54	SPE4	+2.22	ADV
(2.42)		(1.71)		(1.15)	
+0.36**	TCHMSAL	+5.16	R&D	−0.005	PRGM
(3.05)		(1.30)		(0.75)	
−0.11	EXPT				
(0.75)					

$\overline{R}^2 = 0.435$, $N = 71$

DF2VAN = −0.272

+1.68**	$\overline{\text{DFLTF}}$	+0.505*	DF2KN	+0.18*	DREG
(2.21)		(5.48)		(4.61)	
−0.002	GRWT	−3.17**	PART	−0.007	KSHI
(1.02)		(2.30)		(1.32)	
+0.324	SPE4	+0.18	TCHMSAL		
(1.53)		(1.94)			

$\overline{R}^2 = 0.562$, $N = 71$

DF2VAN = −0.432

+1.27**	$\overline{\text{DFLTF}}$	+0.32*	DF2KL	+0.27*	DREG
(2.61)		(2.74)		(4.44)	
−0.003	GRWT	−0.63	TARSUB	−4.23**	PART
(1.28)		(1.40)		(2.63)	
−0.015**	KSHI	+0.54	SPE4	+0.35*	TCHMSAL
(2.60)		(1.79)		(2.97)	
+4.78	R&D				
(1.24)					

$\overline{R}^2 = 0.444$, $N = 71$

Note: * = 1 percent level of significance; ** = 5 percent level of significance.

productivity depends on the discrepancy in efficiency, with coefficients that are significant at 5 percent in a two-tailed test. This implies that to some extent the dual structure could be due to differences in efficiency. DF2KL and DF2KN show the expected positive associations with productivity.

The effects of DREG, TARSUB, SPE4, and GRWT have been included through their influence on DFLTF. Nonetheless, they have direct effects on the productivity difference, although only the coefficient of DREG is significant. DREG depresses the efficiency of large plants, but it seems to contribute positively to their value added, which is consistent with the hypothesis that regulations create rents. TARSUB's effect on large and small plants is opposite to that of DREG's, although its coefficient is not significant. SPE4's coefficient is positive, supporting the hypothesis of overdiversification in the large plants, but it is significant at only the 10 percent level in a two-tailed test. As noted previously, suboptimal diversification levels of small plants are not precluded by this result. GRWT works in favor of productivity in small plants; this could be due to advantages from flexibility. However, its effect is not strongly significant. The coefficient of PART is negative and significant, which confirms the advantage of small plants in employing part-time labor for lower wages. Still, flexible use of part-time labor is available to large plants as well, so more detailed study of this result is necessary.

The coefficient of KSHI is negative in all four equations but not significant when the difference of K/N is used as a control variable. Its effect is not consistent with its function as an entry barrier. It could be affected by outliers, since in the petroleum and steel industries value added per worker is greater in small plants; both industries are considered typical examples of process industries which have high capital–labor ratios. However, our regression analysis does not include the petroleum industry, and when we exclude the remaining two steel industries from our data set, higher t-statistics result. The filtering effect of necessary fixed capital would increase homogeneity in the plants that survive screening. That is, large fixed capital investment does not allow much discrepancy in assets between large and small plants. The hypothesis is supported by the high correlation of $\rho(\text{DF2KN, KSHI}) = -0.608$.

Among other variables thought to work in favor of large plants, only TCHMSAL has the expected significant positive coefficient. R&D and PRGM do not suggest any definite effect of technology growth on productivity differences. This could reflect Japanese SME's intense efforts to absorb current technology, as suggested by Okimoto and Saxonhouse (1987).

10.6   Effects on Differences in the Price-Cost Margin

The effect of the price-cost margin difference on technical efficiency found in chapter 2 sheds indirect light on the role of small plants. The analysis implied that the high performance of large units is related to the low technical efficiency of the industry as a whole. We ruled out that the relatively high performance of large units was due to their high efficiency, but we could not test in chapter 2 the hypothesis that small units have low efficiency.

Now a direct analysis is possible of the relationship between the differences in price-cost margins and efficiency levels. Our simple strategy employs a set of determinants of differences in price-cost margins that includes discrepancies in the levels of efficiency along with other structural variables.

The dependent variables in this analysis are $PCD1 \equiv PCML - PCMS$ and $PCD2 \equiv (PCML - PCMS)/(PCML + PCMS)$, where PCML (PCMS) is price-cost margin of the large (small) plant sector. The means of these variables among 346 industries are 0.0057 for PCD1 and 0.0086 for PCD2. The t-statistics testing the hypothesis that the values are not different from 0 are 1.78 and 1.25, so the hypothesis cannot be rejected at 5 percent in two-tailed tests. The signs point to better performance in the larger establishments, but the distribution of PCD2 shown in table 10.7 indicates that only 57 percent of the values are positive. The data in table 10.8 aggregated to two-digit industries imply that differences among industries are narrower than those found in productivity. In chemical products and nonferrous industries large plants achieve superior performance, while in the transport equipment industry they do worse.

The set of exogenous variables to explain the difference includes $\overline{DFLTF}$, defined previously, and $DFKS \equiv (KSL - KSS)/(KSL + KSS)$, where KSL(KSS) is the ratio of total tangible assets to total shipments of large (small) plant sectors. The latter variable is used to control for differences in the ratio of turnover by plant scale among industries. The variables that are thought to influence productivity differences through profitability are also included as independent variables, for reasons parallel to those given above.

The results are shown in table 10.10. The coefficients of $\overline{\text{DFLTF}}$ are significantly different from 0 at 1 percent in two-tailed tests, which indicates a positive effect on performance of technical efficiency. Note again that this interindustry effect implies no overall tendency. The coefficient of DFKS is not significant in any equation, perhaps because the differences among industries are greater than those between industries' subdivisions.

Patterns of signs and significance levels of coefficients of other variables are almost the same as when determining productivity differences: positive and significant for DREG, negative and insignificant for TARSUB, GRWT, and PRGM, negative and significant for PART. The differences occur in TCHMSAL, which lost significance, and SPE4 and EXPT, which gained. KSHI, ADV, and R&D have no significant coefficients, and some of their signs are changed from the previous analysis.

As implied by employing the same variables to determine both profitability and productivity, the effect on productivity differences of discrepancies in efficiency may be through differences in the price-cost margin. To examine this hypothesis, the regression analysis with DF2VAN as the dependent variable is repeated with the estimate of the difference in price-cost margins ($\overline{\text{PCD2}}$) included as an independent variable. The estimate comes from the fourth equation in table 10.10; by using the estimated values, we retain the recursive structure of simultaneous equations while avoiding possible bias from correlated disturbances.

DF2KN(DF2KL) are also employed as explanatory variables to control for differences in the capital–labor ratio. So is PART because its effect is assumed to operate through the use of cheaper inputs rather than profitability. This allows operation at a different part of the production frontier. To examine whether the DFLTF's effect on DF2VAN is through PCD2, $\overline{\text{DFLTF}}$ is also included.

Table 10.11 presents the results. As expected, the coefficient of $\overline{\text{PCD2}}$ is significantly positive, which confirms the effects of structural variables and the efficiency discrepancy on differences in productivity. On the other hand, the coefficient of $\overline{\text{DFLTF}}$ turns to be negative and insignificant. This relation supports the hypothesis that the effect of efficiency on productivity is through the price-cost margin.

The value of $\bar{R}^2$ when productivity is determined only by $\overline{\text{PCD2}}$ and DF2KN falls little below the value when productivity is determined by the

Table 10.10
Regression analyses determining discrepancies in the price-cost margin between small and large plants by difference in efficiency and structural variables

PCD1 = −0.214

+0.65*	$\overline{\text{DFLTF}}$	+0.455	DFKS	+0.065**	DREG
(3.48)		(0.73)		(2.62)	
−0.002	GRWT	−0.01	TARSUB	−1.21**	PART
(1.76)		(0.08)		(2.09)	
+0.001	KSHI	+0.26**	SPE4	−0.49	ADV
(0.69)		(2.38)		(0.73)	
+0.06	TCHMSAL	+0.14	R&D	−0.004	PRGM
(1.51)		(0.10)		(1.61)	
+0.13*	EXPT				
(2.66)					

$\bar{R}^2 = 0.241, N = 71$

PCD2 = −0.465

+1.47*	$\overline{\text{DFLTF}}$	+0.033	DFKS	+0.14**	DREG
(3.46)		(0.57)		(2.55)	
−0.004	GRWT	−0.16	TARSUB	−2.79**	PART
(1.85)		(0.45)		(2.12)	
+0.003	KSHI	+0.58**	SPE4	−1.38	ADV
(0.65)		(2.38)		(0.91)	
+0.12	TCHMSAL	−0.63	R&D	−0.012**	PRGM
(1.29)		(0.20)		(2.05)	
+0.28**	EXPT				
(2.49)					

$\bar{R}^2 = 0.206, N = 71$

PCD1 = −0.224

+0.65*	$\overline{\text{DFLTF}}$	+0.055*	DREG	−0.002**	GRWT
(5.04)		(3.66)		(2.22)	
−1.11**	PART	+0.26*	SPE4	+0.073**	TCHMSAL
(2.11)		(3.41)		(2.10)	
−0.004	SPE4	+0.11**	TCHMSAL		
(1.66)		(2.63)			

$\bar{R}^2 = 0.280, N = 71$

PCD2 = −0.456

+1.35*	$\overline{\text{DFLTF}}$	+0.12*	DREG	−0.003	GRWT
(4.58)		(3.29)		(1.94)	
−2.56**	PART	+0.55**	SPE4	−1.68	ADV
(2.12)		(3.16)		(1.18)	
+0.112	TCHMSAL	−0.01**	PRGM	+0.25**	EXPT
(1.55)		(1.99)		(2.45)	

$\bar{R}^2 = 0.244, N = 71$

Note: * = 1 percent level of significance; ** = 5 percent level of significance.

Table 10.11
Regression analyses determining discrepancies in the price-cost margin between smaller and larger plants by difference in profitability

DF2VAN = −0.021			
−0.287	$\overline{\text{DFLTF}}$	+0.892* $\overline{\text{PCD2}}$	+0.592* DF2KN
(1.40)		(3.50)	(8.51)
+1.04	PART		
(0.95)			
$\overline{R}^2 = 0.506$, $N = 71$			
DF2VAN = −0.018			
−0.178	$\overline{\text{DFLTF}}$	+0.795** $\overline{\text{PCD2}}$	+0.559* DF2KL
(0.71)		(2.54)	(5.23)
+0.33	PART		
(0.25)			
$\overline{R}^2 = 0.268$, $N = 71$			
DF2VAN = 0.008			
+0.703*	$\overline{\text{PCD2}}$	+0.567* DF2KN	
(3.21)		(8.39)	
$\overline{R}^2 = 0.504$, $N = 71$			
DF2VAN = 0.055			
+0.682**	$\overline{\text{PCD2}}$	+0.545* DF2KL	
(2.56)		(5.28)	
$\overline{R}^2 = 0.284$, $N = 71$			

Note: * = 1 percent level of significance; ** = 5 percent level of significance.

exogenous structural variables and DF2KN, showing that only a little information is lost by aggregating the effects. On the other hand, there is a relatively large difference between the values of $\overline{R}^2$ in regression equations with DF2KL. Considerable information is lost by that aggregation, so it remains possible that some structural variables influence productivity directly. However, PART failed to show its expected effect on productivity differences.

10.7 Summary

In this chapter the dual structure in Japanese manufacturing industries was investigated from the standpoint of technical efficiency. We analyzed the variation among industries of variables representing intraindustry differences between large and small establishments. We applied regression analyses to three sets of discrepancies: differences in technical efficiency, differences in price-cost margin, and differences in productivity (measured by value added per worker). To facilitate the comparison of technical efficiency we introduced a "modified" COLS method that extends the ordinary COLS estimator to cases subject to type I and type II failure with at least the same precision.

We found within the industries a significant difference only in mean productivity. There was no evidence that large plants have a significant advantage in technical efficiency or in their price-cost margin. Therefore the difference in productivity observed in almost all industries could not have been caused by superior technical efficiency in the large plants.

Nevertheless, technical efficiency possesses a direct connection with the price-cost margin productivity.[26] This relationship is established by the classical iterative least-squares method. For this reason we cannot rule out that in each industry low productivity in the small plants could be due to poor efficiency.

About half of the variance of discrepancies in productivity is explained by differences in the capital–labor ratio, and in the components of the price-cost margin caused by efficiency discrepancies and other structural factors. Among the structural variables governmental intervention proved to have robust effects. By using a dummy for regulation, we found that government intervention could depress efficiency, especially that of large plants. Still, government intervention can exert a strong positive effect on productivity and price-cost margins. Intensive use of imported technology proved to have a positive effect on productivity. It is not clear, however, if large plants benefited from technology imports because of the advantage of scale or if the variable represented an aspect of the production frontier that both sectors face. The discrepancy in productivity could also be related to some difference in technology, or it could be characteristic of factor markets. More detailed studies of the differences in the observed production frontier are necessary. That is the next step of this program of research.

Notes

1. The same tendency is seen in the distribution system. See Yoshino (1971).

2. See Takizawa (1980), fig. 1.

3. *Census of Manufactures*, 1978; the smallest-size group was not included because company statistics were not available in the census. *Report on the Census of Production*, 1986; this ratio is the comparison between firms with 24 to 499 employees and firms with not less than 500 employees. *Statistiches Jahrbuch für die Bundesrepublik Deutschland*, 1970; this ratio is the

comparison between firms with 10 to 499 employees and firms with not less than 500 employees.

4. Yokokura (1984, 450) reported that effective rates of interest paid on debt, which is defined as (interest paid + discount − interest earned)/(loans + debentures − deposits), are 12.1 percent for firms with more than 300 employees and 12.4 percent for firms with less than 300 employees in 1981. This shows a discrepancy between large and small enterprises, but its magnitude is far smaller than reported by Caves and Uekusa (1976), who concluded that a difference of more than 50 percent exists between the effective costs (although with a definition of capital cost a little different from Yokokura's). They stated that this large difference seems not to be explainable by risk premiums.

5. Koike (1987, 325). He also stated that "Japan's wage differentials by size of firm are not unusual and are comparable to those of EC countries when we examine the data by worker skill classifications."

6. For example, see Ikeo (1986) and comments on that paper.

7. For this point and reviews of previous studies, see CB, pp. 116–118.

8. As OSW, p. 70, indicates, the probability of type 1 failure approaches 1/2 when $\sigma_u^2 \to 0$.

9. For a Monte Carlo analysis of these problems see subsection 2.2.2 in chapter 2.

10. OSW, p. 70.

11. Another possible way is to set restrictions on the OLS estimation of the stochastic production function. However, unlike restrictions on regression coefficients, restrictions on the moments of residuals are prohibitively hard to treat.

12. OSW, p. 80.

13. See Johnston (1972), sec. 13.1.

14. See chapter 2, table 2.9.

15. If included, however, this variable retains its sign and significance and seems to have no influence on the coefficients of other variables.

16. Including PCMD in the core model leaves the signs and significance of all these coefficients unchanged.

17. However, note that there is no statistical evidence that firms in Japan direct R&D effort more intensely toward applied and development research than do firms in the United States. Although the definitions of basic, applied, and development research may differ between the two countries, the ratio of basic research to total R&D expenditure is higher in Japan than in the United States. See Suzuki and Miyagawa (1986, 137–138) or Wakasugi (1986, 54–55).

18. *Kagaku gijutsu chōsa houkoku*, 1978.

19. The classification of industries is based on a special two-digit classification prepared for *Kagaku gijutsu chōsa houkoku*.

20. While DREG's differential effect is implied in table 10.6, TARSUB's differential effect is not clear in the table. This is due to the method employed to investigate exogenous variables by adding them one by one to the core model, which may not be suitable for DREG and TARSUB. When both are included in the core model, the coefficients of TARSUB are −0.3130 for small plants and −0.0614 for large plants. The difference is consistent with a positive association between TARSUB and DF1.

25. One of the studies to address this point is Ono (1973).

26. *Establishment Census, Japan*, 1978.

27. *Survey on Employment of Tertiary Industry*, 1978.

28. According to *Report on the Survey of Research and Development*, 1977, the ratio of R&D expenditure to sales differs little between large and small firms engaging in R&D activities:

1.2 percent for firms with less than 1,000 employees, 1.6 percent for firms with not less than 1,000 employees. However, the proportions of companies engaging in R&D activity differ remarkably: 71.3 percent and 9.6 percent, respectively.

29. CB, p. 127.

30. CB, p. 1.

References

Caves, R. E., and M. Uekusa. 1976. *Industrial Organization in Japan.* Washington: Brookings Institution.

Caves, R. E., and D. R. Barton. 1990. *Efficiency in U.S. Manufacturing Industries.* Cambridge: MIT Press.

Johnston, J. 1972. *Econometric Methods.* 2d ed. New York: McGraw-Hill.

Ikeo, K. 1986. Kinyū Seido no Micro Bunseki (A microeconomic analysis of financial systems). In K. Kaizuka and E. Ono, eds., *Nihon no Kinyū Sisutemu* (The Financial System in Japan). Tokyo: Tokyo University Press.

Kagaku Gijutsu Chō. 1977. *Kagaku Gijutsu Chōsa Houkoku* (Report on the Survey of Research and Development).

Koike, K. 1987. Human resource development. In K. Yamamura and Y. Yasuba, eds. *The Political Economy of Japan: The Domestic Transformation,* vol. 1. Stanford: Stanford University Press.

Kusuda, Y., Y. Hisashi, and N. Masato. 1979. Wagakuni ChūShō Kigyō ni okeru Kigyō idō no Bunseki (An analysis of mobility by firm scale in Japanese small- and medium-scale manufactures). *Keizai Bunseki* 76 (August): 1–45.

Marris, R. 1964. *The Economic Theory of "Managerial" Capitalism.* New York: Free Press.

Okimoto, D. J., and G. R. Saxonhouse. 1987. Technology and the future of economy. In K. Yamamura and Y. Yasuba (eds.) *The Political Economy of Japan: The Domestic Transformation,* vol. 1. Stanford: Stanford University Press.

Olson, J. A., P. Schmidt, and D. M. Waldman. 1980. Monte Carlo Study of Estimators of Stochastic Frontier Production Functions. *Journal of Econometrics* 13 (May): 67–82.

Ono, A. 1973. *Sengo Nihon no Chingin Kettei* (An Analysis of Wage Determination in Postwar Japan). Tokyo: Tōyō Keizai Shinpōsha.

Shinohara M. 1961. *Nihon Keizei no Seichō to Junkan* (Growth and the Business Cycle in Japanese Economics). Tokyo: Sōbunsha.

Sōrifu Tōkeikyoku. 1978. *Jigyōsho Tōkei Chōsa Houkoku* (Establishment Census of Japan).

Sōrifu Tōkeikyoku. 1977. *Syūgyō Kouzou Kihon Chōsa Houkoku* (Survey on Employment in Tertiary Industries).

Statistisches Jahrbuch für die Bundesrepublik Deutschland. 1970. Stuttgart: W. Kohlhammer.

Suzuki, K., and T. Miyagawa. 1986. *Nohon no Kigyō Tōshi to Kenkyū Kaihatsu Senryaku* (Investments and R&D Strategies of Japanese Firms). Tokyo: Tōyōkeizai Shinpōsha.

Takizawa, K. 1980. ChūShō Kigyō (Small and medium-size businesses). *Keizaigaku Daijiten.* Tokyo: Tōyōkeizai Shinpōsha.

Yokokura, H. 1984. ChūShō Kigyō (Small and medium-size businesses). In R. Komiya et al., eds., *Nihon no Sangyōseisaku.* Tokyo: Tokyo University Press.

Yosihara, H., A. Sakuma, H. Itami, and T. Kagono. 1981. *Nihon Kigyo no Takakuku Senryaku* (Diversification Strategies of Japanese Firms). Tokyo: Nihonkeizai Shinbunsha.

Yoshino, M. Y. 1971. *The Japanese Marketing System: Adaptation and Innovation.* Cambridge: MIT Press.

Wakasugi, R. 1986. *Gijutsu Kakushin to Kenkyū Kaihatsu no Keizai Bunseki* (An Economic Analysis of Innovation and R&D Activities). Tokyo: Toyōkeizai Shinpōsha.

11 Technical Efficiency in Japanese and U.S. Manufacturing Industries

Akio Torii and Richard E. Caves

11.1 Introduction

Building on extensive analyses of the technical efficiency of Japanese and U.S. manufacturing industries and the factors explaining differences among industries,[1] this chapter compares industrial efficiency in the two countries. That comparison can be either casual or ambitious. At a minimum we can simply compare and contrast the findings of the two national investigations about interindustry differences. For a richer approach we can match industries in the two countries' standard industrial classifications and determine statistically what factors affect the relative efficiency of the matched industries. A further step involves drawing conclusions about comparative frontier productivity levels in the matched industries, measured by inferring relative production frontiers attainable in the two countries' branches of an industry from their relative average productivity and the two industries' levels of technical efficiency. In this chapter we pursue the second and third of these steps of comparative analysis.

From evidence on the industrial countries' historical levels of net output per head, the United States apparently led the industrial world in industrial productivity for at least a quarter century after World War II, and probably for an even longer time before the war. Although U.S. productivity certainly has not stopped increasing, other industrial countries, notably Japan, have been catching up and match U.S. productivity levels in at least some industries (see chapter 12). The U.S. lead evidently rested not just on the country's strength as a fecund source of innovations and productivity improvement but also, if less demonstrably, on relatively competitive markets and efficient organization of enterprise and factory. The long period of relatively undisturbed industrial development since the 1940s has seen the gradual loss of the U.S. productivity (frontier) advantage through diffusion, imitation, and many other processes. But it is not clear whether an advantage in technical efficiency has also been lost; indeed we lack hard evidence on whether such an advantage has existed.

This situation poses many important questions for our analysis; indeed it is easy to overdramatize them. Can we determine which country's manufacturing sector is the more technically efficient? How similar are the forces determining technical efficiency in the two countries? Are differences between their estimated levels of efficiency significantly related to differences in the underlying structures and environments of the two countries industries? Are factors giving rise to technical-efficiency differences intrinsic and structural, or are they subject to choices made by public policy? Are they stable, or are they likely to change in the course of economic evolution? Our attempt to investigate these critical issues bumps into limitations intrinsic to the methodology of frontier production functions as well as other constraints. Nonetheless, we persevere to see what constraints curb our ability to draw conclusions, and what research investments might serve to relax those constraints.

11.2 Background and Hypotheses about Comparative Efficiency

11.2.1 Comparative Summary of National Findings

The hypotheses we use to study the comparative efficiency of U.S. and Japanese industries necessarily flow from the hypotheses developed and tested about efficiency levels in each country separately. Therefore we summarize briefly the determinants of industries efficiency in each nation and use them to set priorities for the comparative analysis. The hypotheses tested and confirmed by each study fall into four groups. The first two address questions of competition and business organization that matter for welfare, the second two aspects of inefficiency that lack simple normative implications.

Competition

In both countries efficiency decreases with concentration in highly concentrated industries, but both also yield an internal optimal level of concentration below which efficiency decreases with competition. The optimal level of concentration seems lower in the United States.[2] The implication that efficiency is depressed in the most competitive industries is discussed below. Import competition promotes efficiency in the more concentrated U.S. industries. It is not a significant influence in Japan, although there is some evidence that tariffs reduce efficiency. The difference in the effects of international competition is consistent with the export orientation of many of Japan's more concentrated industries and the increasing exposure of their U.S. counterparts to import competition.

Business Organization

Both studies found that business organization influences efficiency, but the specific results differ considerably. In the United States enterprise diversification, especially the control of an industry's plants by enterprises based in other industries, reduces efficiency. In Japan, diversification "inbound" to an industry if anything increases its efficiency. The contrast accords with the much greater incidence of enterprise diversification and diversifying mergers in the United States.[3] Whether this contrast persists for matched industries is an important question. In Japan, but not in the United States, diversification at the plant level significantly reduces efficiency, as does the extent of multiplant operation by the larger enterprises.

The Japanese study developed theoretically the implications of costs to managers of attaining efficiency, getting empirical results that seem to suggest diseconomies of scale in the managerial cost of attaining (or restoring) efficiency (lumpy replacement costs could also account for this). The U.S. inquiry, setting up the test differently, got results leaning in the opposite direction. Both studies, however, obtained evidence consistent with the hypothesis that inefficiencies (or negative profits) among an industry's smaller firms and plants contribute strongly to the degree of inefficiency for the industry as a whole. This pattern could well result (as the U.S. study suggested) from new entrepreneurs' uncertainty about their ability levels. In Japan the pattern may be related to the traditional dualistic structures of industries and the factor-market pricing patterns that sustained them, although this dualism clearly seems to be disappearing (Patrick and Rohlen 1987).

The operation of labor-management relations differs greatly between Japan and the United States in ways consistent with more impairment of efficiency in the United States. Although the effect of labor relations on efficiency was not tested for Japan, the degree of unionization was found to reduce efficiency in U.S. industries in which large-size plants are prevalent.

The subcontracting relation in Japan is thought to enhance efficiency by improving the division of labor and concentrating incentives, without offsetting losses through contractual failure and bargaining costs (Patrick and Rohlen 1987). Its influence on efficiency in Japan was found to be positive although not statistically significant. In the U.S. counterparts of those Japanese industries with heavy subcontracting, relationships between suppliers and customers are diverse and exhibit contractual elements. We therefore want to know whether the incidence of subcontracting significantly influences differences in efficiency levels.

In Japan efficiency decreases with the importance of nonproduction workers in the industry's work force, consistent with the diverse activities of nonproduction workers and the diverse ways in which their activities can be organized in relation to manufacturing establishments. Although this relation did not appear for the United States, other aspects of the U.S. results point to the same conclusion.

Dynamic Disturbances

Both studies found that technical inefficiency as measured increases with the incidence of dynamic disturbances. U.S. efficiency decreases with the dispersion of vintages of machinery (although not structures); this relation could not be tested directly in Japan, but efficiency was found to decrease with the plant's capital-replacement costs. Efficiency decreases with some types of dynamic disturbances, but not the same types in both countries. U.S. efficiency decreases with the importance of research and development activities, apparently because of the uneven distribution of the rents that they generate. Japanese efficiency decreases with the industry's growth rate (and perhaps its rate of productivity growth). Some evidence was found that Japanese efficiency decreases with the variance of the industry's rate of growth (not tested for the United States).

We expected Japanese industries, less buffered from the 1973 energy shock than their U.S. counterparts, to show inefficiency due to energy-saving technologies that remained incompletely adopted in 1977. Efficiency nonetheless perversely appears to be positively related to energy-intensity in both Japan and the United States.[4] We will check whether the analysis of matched industries can explain this anomaly.

Sources of Static Heterogeneity

Both studies found that efficiency decreases with certain natural sources of heterogeneity, such as product differentiation. In each country efficiency decreases with an industry's advertising intensity, apparently due to the uneven distribution of rents stemming from first-mover advantages. The U.S. study did not find any effect due to goods' structural heterogeneity. A negative effect of export intensity was found for the United States, expected because exporting activity is unevenly distributed among companies and plants. It exerted no robust effect in Japan, however.

The countries' different economic geographies account for their differing sources of static heterogeneity. The large geographic size and uneven population density of the United States suggest that industries serving local (regional) markets exhibit heterogeneous productivity levels and hence greater apparent inefficiency. This was confirmed. For related reasons industries heavily reliant on raw materials were expected to show less uniform efficiency levels, a hypothesis that also found some support in the United States. The following analysis provides another opportunity to check these findings.

11.2.2 Hypotheses about Matched Industries

This summary of results generates its own list of hypotheses to test on matched U.S.–Japan industries. They take two basic forms. Some hypotheses are not on their faces country specific, so we expect the same mechanism to connect the efficiency level to the exogenous variable in each country. Differential efficiency should depend on differential levels of the exogenous variable. That is, suppose that the hypothesis relates some efficiency measure EFF to an exogenous variable X_i in a way that is not country specific. Then we expect to estimate $EFF_J = a_J X_{iJ}$ and $EFF_U = a_U X_{iU}$, with $a_J = a_U$. If in addition we estimate $EFF_U - EFF_J = a_D(X_{iU} - X_{iJ})$, we expect $a_D = a_U = a_J$. The coefficients will not be equal if the mechanism is not the same in the two countries. Equality could also fail if the distributions of X_{iU} and X_{iJ} differ markedly (e.g., suppose that one of them exhibits no variance), the amount of random disturbance differs, or for various other reasons.

Besides these inference about coefficients of differentials in regressors, the estimation of a_D can also have tactical uses. We may have priors about differences in the strength of some mechanism in the two countries that can be tested directly. X_i may be measured less well in one country than the other, and the estimation of a_D provides some basis for assessing the suspected measure.

The other source of hypotheses testable on matched industries is some institution or mechanism thought to operate in one country but not the other.[5] Examples cited above include subcontracting in Japan and enterprise diversification in the United States. Suppose that the assumption of specificity to one country were false, for example, that subcontracting in

Japan has an equally effective counterpart in long-term contracts with suppliers in the United States in those industries where subcontracting is widely used. Then the incidence of subcontracting would have no influence on differential efficiency, whereas it would favorably affect Japan's relative efficiency if the United States possessed no comparably effective institution. The ability to test hypotheses of this sort is an important advantage of our matched-industries design over simply stacking the Japanese and U.S. industry samples without matching.[6]

Table 11.1 summarizes the hypotheses that we hope to test and the exogenous variables available for testing them. It also contains a sign prediction based on economic theory and the results of the separate studies of technical efficiency; this prediction is intended only as a rough guide because it loses the shadings of theoretical and empirical confidence contained in the preceding discussion. Efficiency differences are expressed in the form of United States *minus* Japan levels, as are all of the exogenous variables appearing in the first section of the table. Thus, if an exogenous variable is expected to increase technical efficiency in each (either) country, its difference should increase the difference in technical efficiency. The final two sections of the table contain variables that pertain only to one country (or are available only for one)—first the United States, then Japan. A variable expected to increase efficiency in the U.S. industry but not in the Japanese counterpart is assigned a positive sign; a variable expected to increase efficiency in Japan but not the United States should exert a negative effect on the U.S.–Japan efficiency difference.

Definitions of the variables are general and do not report other than essential differences between countries in their construction. Exact definitions and sources stated in Caves and Barton (1990) and chapter 2 of this volume will not be repeated here.

11.3 Sample of Matched Industries and Efficiency Differences

To test the hypotheses established in the last section, we had to match industries in the United States and Japanese standard industrial classifications and determine the adequacy of the sample of industries for which technical efficiency differences can be calculated. These steps are reported in this section, along with an evaluation of the efficiency measures for matched industries.

Table 11.1
Hypotheses about differences in technical efficiency, matched United States and Japanese manufacturing industries, with notation and sign predictions

Symbol	Definition	Expected sign
U.S.–Japan differences		
ADVDFUJ	Ratio of total sales-promotion outlays to total industry sales	−
C4MDFUJ	Share of industry shipments accounted for by largest four firms, adjusted for import competition	?
EXPTDFUJ	Ratio of industry exports to industry shipments	−
INDDFUJ	Number of prosecutions for collusion-related offenses under competition-policy laws (Sherman Act Section 1 indictments for U.S., Fair Trade Commission decrees for Japan)	−
MULDFUJ	Measure of extent of multiplant operation by leading firms in the industry	?
PRTDFUJ	Estimated fraction of employees who work part-time (in Japan, compensation of part-time workers divided by employee compensation)	+
PRWDFUJ	Ratio of production workers to total employees	+
RDSDFUJ	Research and development outlays divided by industry sales	−
ROTGDFUJ	Rate of growth of real output	−
RSZDFUJ	Median plant size (shipments) divided by total industry shipments	?
SKLDFUJ	Standard deviation of plants' capital–labor ratios, obtained in estimating frontier production functions	−
SPEDFUJ	Establishment specialization ratio (shipments by establishments of products classified to other industries divided by total shipments)	+
UNIDFUJ	Fraction of production workers who are union members	−
Variables pertaining to United States only		
DIV	Sum of complements of enterprise coverage and specialization ratios ("inbound" plus "outbound" diversification)	−
IOSECT	Sum of input coefficients for agricultural, fisheries, forestry, and mining sectors (from input–output table)	−
RADSHIP	Radius within which 80 percent of industry shipments traveled to customers within United States	−
VINTM	Measure of the dispersion of vintages of the industry's machinery stock (sum of percentage less than 5 and more than 20 years old, 1976)	−
Variables available for Japan only		
SUBC	Payments for subcontracted work divided by total material cost	−
ENER	Cost of purchased energy divided by total materials cost (available for both countries but assumed inherent in industry technology, hence measured for only one)	+
PCMD	Difference between price-cost margin of largest plants accounting for 50 percent of industry shipments divided by price-cost margin in remaining (small) plants	+

Table 11.1 (continued)

Symbol	Definition	Expected sign
DREG	Dummy indicating intensity of public regulation (2 if both price and entry regulated [entry by permission or license]; 1 if both price and entry regulated [entry by registration]; zero otherwise)	+
GRWTVC	Variance of growth of industry shipments, 1969–78	+
SUBTVA	Current receipts of public subsidies divided by total industry value added	+
TARF	Receipts of customs duties divided by total value of imports classified to the industry	+
TCHMSAL	Total payments made under new and continuing contracts for technology imports	+
TCHXSAL	Total revenues received under new and continuing contracts for technology exports	−

11.3.1 Matching of Industries and Number of Measures Available

The Japanese and U.S. standard industrial classifications both provide rather fine breakdowns of manufacturing industries at their four-digit levels—the levels at which the technical efficiency estimates were developed. Although at one time industries could be matched quite fully between the two classification systems, even by matching aggressively, we could identify only 205 industries whose products were deemed to overlap sufficiently to warrant their inclusion in the analysis. We estimated roughly the proportion of shipments matched for each industry retained in the analysis as follows:

Percent of shipments matched	Number of industries
100%	71
90–100	37
80–90	20
70–80	18
60–70	29
50–60	30

The number of industries available for comparative analysis is further reduced by the loss of those for which technical efficiency proved impossible to estimate. These include both industries for which no estimates were attempted (because too few plants supplied data to the census) and

Table 11.2
Distribution of matched industries and available measures of technical efficiency among
major industrial sectors

Sector	LTE		LTF		SKEW		Number matched
	Japan	United States	Japan	United States	Japan	United States	
20 Foods and beverages	5	10	2	8	16	23	23
21 Tobacco	0	1	0	1	0	1	2
22 Textiles	4	5	3	5	7	8	9
23 Apparel	2	6	2	4	5	10	11
24 Wood products	1	4	1	4	5	9	9
25 Furniture	0	2	0	2	1	3	3
26 Paper products	1	1	1	1	2	5	5
27 Printing, publishing	1	2	1	2	4	4	4
28 Chemicals	7	11	5	11	15	18	18
29 Petroleum	1	3	1	2	2	4	4
30 Rubber and plastics	0	1	0	1	1	1	2
31 Leather, footwear	1	3	1	3	4	5	5
32 Stone, clay, glass	7	4	5	3	12	17	18
33 Metals	3	6	1	5	10	14	16
34 Metal fabrication	5	8	5	8	10	15	15
35 Machinery	12	8	8	7	18	20	20
36 Electrical equipment	9	7	6	7	15	15	16
37 Transport equipment	0	3	0	3	4	8	8
38 Instruments	4	6	4	5	5	6	6
39 Miscellaneous	4	6	3	6	10	11	11
Total	67	97	49	88	146	197	205

industries for which type I or type II failures occurred in the estimation of
technical efficiency. Skewness of course is not affected by estimation failures, so many more observations are available on skewness (SKEW) than
on the standard or extended Lee-Tyler efficiency measures (LTE, LTF).

Table 11.2 shows for each efficiency measure by major (two-digit) industries the number of industries matched and the number of industries in
each country for which each measure could be secured. The industries not
represented in the table were distributed fairly evenly among two-digit
sectors. SKEW is computed for all but eight U.S. industries and was
computed for three-fourths of the Japanese industries. Accordingly, the
number of industries for which SKEW is available for both countries is
quite large: 144. Because of type I and type II failures, the standard (LTE)
and adjusted (LTF) measures of technical efficiency were available for
substantially fewer industries (roughly half as many as SKEW), and the

number for Japan was smaller than for the United States (especially LTF). However, the industries subject to estimation failures in the two countries were rather independent of each other, so the number of industries with paired observations on LTE and LTF was quite small, 42 and 27, respectively.

Since our objective is to compare technical efficiency in matched industries, the small size of the matched sample is problematic. The sample is reasonably random for the two countries' manufacturing sectors, which is desirable, but the number for LTF, in particular, is too small to supply enough degrees of freedom. Although SKEW provides three times as many observations as LTE, it is unclear what interpretation to place on the variance among positive values of SKEW. We could assume that increasing positive values of SKEW indicate a decreasing probability that an industry harbors substantial technical inefficiency, that is, that random errors are positively skewed in the sample and no appreciable component in the residuals is due to technical inefficiency. Instead, we could suppose that positive skewness results where only a few plants are efficient and the large majority are inefficient, as Harris (1988) has pointed out. We will nonetheless employ comparative values of SKEW in our analysis of comparative technical efficiency. As a dependent variable SKEW will fail to confirm a hypothesis about comparative efficiency if the hypothesis is false or if the assumption about SKEW is incorrect; confirmation of the hypothesis would validate SKEW as a measure of efficiency.[7]

To check the results of this reduced industry sample, we reestimated the core phase 2 models for Japan and the United States using only the industries for which observations on LTE are available in both countries. A sample of 30 industries (22 degrees of freedom) is available for the United States and a sample of 22 industries (13 degrees of freedom) for Japan. The Japanese model holds up quite well: All signs are preserved, although *t*-ratios are greatly reduced. The U.S. equation does badly, however, with more than half of the signs changing. The chances for analyzing comparative efficiency (LTE) are not very good.

11.3.2 Comparative Levels of Efficiency in Matched Industries

The first question we consider is which country's industries on average show more inefficiency. In our view, frontier production functions, applied to real world data, are not well positioned to answer that question. First, they yield several different measures of efficiency whose mean values differ

Table 11.3
Differences in mean technical efficiency, United States and Japan

	United States	Difference	Japan	Significance of difference
Average technical efficiency				
LTE	0.671		0.705	$t = 2.34$
	(0.088)		(0.096)	
LTF	0.624		0.655	$t = 1.61$
	(0.106)		(0.106)	
Skewness (SKEW)	−0.768		−0.681	$t = 0.93$
	(0.902)		(0.990)	
U.S.–Japan difference				
LTE		−0.0248		$t = 0.22$
		(0.1144)		
LTF		−0.00205		$t = 0.01$
		(0.1666)		
SKEW		−0.1029		$t = 0.08$
		(1.289)		

substantially. Second, many small differences exist in the coverage and putative accuracy of the two countries' underlying census data and in the tactical choices made in formulating and estimating frontier production functions. Although we are not aware of any that should systematically and substantially bias the estimated differences in average efficiency, we cannot dismiss the possibility. Therefore we will assume that average technical efficiency differs only if the data yield gross differences.

The top half of table 11.3 concerns the mean values of the technical-efficiency measures for the matched industries summarized in table 11.2. As table 11.2 shows, the total number of industries represented differs, and the two sets overlap only partially for each efficiency measure. It appears that estimated efficiency is higher for Japan than for the United States in each measure. The standard test for differences between the means indicates that the difference is statistically significant for LTE but not for LTF or SKEW. The standard deviations of the two countries' efficiency measures are very similar. That fact suggests the absence of an overriding difference in either the structural factors determining efficiency or the pervasiveness of market (and other) forces tending to promote it. A stricter test of intercountry differences is performed in the last half of table 11.2, where we report the means and standard deviations of the differences between efficiency measures for the matched industries. The standard deviations are very large, and hence the mean differences are not remotely significant. Although the signs of all the differences between means and mean differences in table 11.3 point to higher technical efficiency in Japan than the United States, this cannot be considered a statistically significant conclusion.

We can also compare average efficiency using skewness if we assume that positive skewness indicates probable efficiency. Negative skewness indicating technical inefficiency was present in about 80 percent of U.S. manufacturing industries, a slightly larger proportion than in Japan (74 percent). Although the difference in type I errors suggests less inefficiency in Japan, we hesitate to embrace this line of reasoning. In fact U.S. industries had proportionally fewer type I errors than industries in *any* other country for which frontier production functions have been estimated on a broad sample of industries, including Great Britain, Australia, and Chile. Therefore that the United States at the bottom of the industrial efficiency rankings is not a convincing conclusion.

11.3.3   Correlations between Efficiency Measures

The contrast between the top and bottom halves of table 11.3 suggests that the correlations between efficiency measures for matched Japanese and U.S. industries must be quite low, for example,

LTEJ, LTEU   0.218

LTFJ, LTFU -0.286

SKEWJ, SKEWU   0.062

The positive correlation for LTE is not statistically significant ($t = 1.42$), and the negative correlation for LTF in fact comes closer to statistical significance ($t = 1.55$). The correlation for SKEW is not significant ($t = 0.75$).

The measures of technical efficiency in matched industries could of course be uncorrelated for two reasons. Each might be responding to its own determinants that are specific to the country/industry cell; if values of these determinants differ, the efficiency measures for matched industries need not be correlated. Alternatively, the underlying determinants could be industry specific but not country specific and highly correlated between the two countries, but the processes by which they determine technical efficiency could differ substantially, giving rise to uncorrelated efficiency measures in matched industries. These two reasons are not mutually exclusive.

Given the low correlation between U.S. and Japanese efficiency measures, is there any chance that the differences in the three efficiency measures are likely to be related to the same exogenous factors? We took the difference between each U.S. efficiency measure and its Japanese counterpart (for industries in which both exist) and calculated the correlations between the differences for the three efficiency measures (denoted LTEDFUJ, LTFDFUJ, and SKWDFUJ for the standard and extended Lee-Tyler measures of average efficiency and for skewness, respectively). The correlations are

LTEDFUJ, LTFDFUJ   0.759 $t = 5.70$

LTEDFUJ, SKWDFUJ   0.752 $t = 7.03$

LTFDFUJ, SKWDFUJ   0.603 $t = 3.70$

Each is highly significant. The correlations between these pairs of differences are substantially higher than the correlations for the individual efficiency measures between the two countries which we reported above. They support the hypothesis that the differences are real properties of the pairs of matched industries and not sensitive to properties of the method of measuring efficiency.

11.4   Determinants of Differences in Technical Efficiency

11.4.1. Cross-Sectional Regression Analysis

The findings of section 11.3 are cautiously promising for testing hypotheses about efficiency differences in matched industries. Positive factors are the high correlations between the various pairs of efficiency differences; negative factors are the few observations (skewness excepted) and the low correlations between U.S. and Japanese industries' efficiency measures.

Because LTFDFUJ has so few observations and is highly correlated with LTEDFUJ, we decided to concentrate on LTEDFUJ and SKWDFUJ as dependent variables. We applied the same style of analysis as for LTE in the two countries separately. With so many hypotheses, multicollinear regressors, and missing observations on the exogenous variables, we did not simply confront each dependent variable with all of the exogenous variables at once. We began with a group of regressors that theory and evidence from the national studies suggested would be important explanatory factors. After confirming this conjecture and checking for robustness, we added other variables individually, then in groups, to assess the stability of the model and the incremental gains in explanatory power. It is important to acknowledge this procedure and its implication that threshold levels of t-statistics should be raised somewhat to compensate for the unavoidable element of "fishing."

We focus first on LTEDFUJ because of its superior theoretical standing as a measure of efficiency. Equation 4.1 in table 11.4 shows the core variables that explain the differential efficiency. LTEDFUJ decreases with the relative distance of each country's concentration ratio from the level that maximizes efficiency (C4ADFUJ) and with the relative prevalence of trade-union organization (UNIDFUJ). It increases with the utilization of part-time employees (PRTDFUJ), the relative rate of growth of output (ROTGDFUJ), and the importance of technology imports to the Japanese industry (TCHMSAL). All but the last variable represent differential versions of hypotheses that were strongly supported in at least one of the national studies of the interindustry determinant of efficiency. Differential R&D spending (RDSDFUJ) did not prove robustly significant, despite the strong negative effect of the R&D/sales ratio on measured efficiency in the United States. However, RDSDFUJ is significantly correlated with Japanese technology imports, 0.24, suggesting that TCHMSAL may play the same role of proxying the uneven distribution of innovation rents in Japan that R&D/sales does for the United States.

Most factors outside this core proved not to be statistically significant, but the exceptions warrant notice. In equation 4.2 the raw materials intensity of the U.S. industry's inputs (IOSECT) exerts a negative influence on relative efficiency that is weak but stable to specification changes. It supports the conjecture that heterogeneous (local?) raw materials inputs matter more for the United States than Japan. Equation 4.3, however, shows that an important factor depressing on U.S. efficiency, enterprise diversification (UDIV), does not affect differential efficiency. We also checked for a number of influences specific to Japan, especially those coming from public policy. Equation 4.4 adds three variables. The Japanese tariff (TARF) has a highly significant positive effect on differential efficiency, presumably through a negative effect on Japanese efficiency.[8]

Table 11.4
Basic determinants of difference between expected technical efficiency, United States and Japan (LTEDFUJ)

Equation	Constant	C4ADFUJ	UNIDFUJ	ROTGDFUJ	PRTDFUJ	TCHMSAL	$\bar{R}^2$/degrees of freedom
4.1	−0.100	−0.004† (3.36)	−0.002* (2.56)	+0.004** (2.34)	+0.382** (1.84)	+0.227** (1.95)	0.290 / 30
4.2	−0.074	−0.004† (3.42)	−0.002* (2.94)	+0.005* (3.09)	+0.368** (1.86)	+0.178−0.355IOSECT (1.54) (1.67)	0.345 / 28
4.3	−0.076	−0.004† (2.93)	−0.002* (2.68)	+0.004** (2.54)	+0.661* (3.04)	+1.252**−0.043UDIV (2.12) (0.55)	0.366 / 24
4.4	−0.205	−0.004† (3.07)	−0.001* (2.77)	+0.004* (2.94)	+0.480* (2.78)	+0.364*+0.019DREG (3.49) (0.45)	
			−21.14*SUBTVA + 2.324*TARF − 0.344**TCHXSAL (3.36) (4.34) (1.76)				0.542 / 26
4.5	−0.227	−0.004† (3.70)	−0.002* (3.00)	+0.004* (3.18)	+0.436* (2.50)	+0.318**+2.089*TARSUB (3.15) (3.94)	0.486 / 28

Note: Levels of significance: when one-tailed, * = 1 percent, ** = 5 percent; when two-tailed, † = 1 percent, ‡ = 5 percent.

We also expected that Japan's rate of industrial subsidy (SUBTVA) would indicate the preservation of inefficient units, depress Japanese efficiency, and raise differential efficiency. However, its influence in equation 4.4 is significantly negative. The explanation is easy to find in the underlying zero-order correlation coefficients: The same industries are assisted by both tariffs and subsidies, so the correlation of TARF and SUBTVA is 0.53. Also one industry (U.S. SIC 2052, cookies and crackers) is an extreme outlier due to peculiarities of Japanese policy (Shōda 1981). It is reasonable to suppose that the effects of tariffs and subsidies on efficiency in the affected industries are similar. If we assume this and add TARF + SUBTVA = TARSUB and drop industry 2052, we obtain equation 4.5. TARSUB takes a significant positive coefficient, suggesting a negative effect of these policies on efficiency in Japan. If C4MDFUJ replaces C4ADFUJ (not shown), its significant positive coefficient indicates that relative efficiency rises with relative imports-adjusted seller concentration. These two variables are discussed below.

The determinants of differential skewness, SKWDFUJ, are reported in table 11.5. Equation 5.1 shows the same core of regressors as equation 4.1. The sign of C4ADFUJ is reversed, while the other signs agree with the preceding discussion and results. Only PRTDFUJ and TCHMSAL are significant in one-tail tests, the latter at 10 percent. In general, then, LTEDFUJ and SKWDFUJ do not lead to the same conclusions about differential efficiency. What we did discover about SKWDFUJ is that certain variables not significant for LTEDFUJ become so for SKWDFUJ. In equation 5.2 these are differential rates of R&D spending (RDSDFUJ), differential exporting rates (EXPTDFUJ), U.S. enterprise diversification (UDIV), and the distance shipped by U.S. producers (RADSHIP). The relative incidence of competition-policy violations (INDDFUJ) is weakly significant with the appropriate sign, but the variable representing relative departures from the internal optimum concentration ratio (C4ADFUJ) is not significant. In the similar equation 5.3 the expected positive coefficient of Japan's technology imports (TCHMSAL) is weakly significant, even though differential R&D spending is controlled.[9]

A simple way to evaluate the divergent results for LTEDFUJ and SKWDFUJ is to check the zero-order correlations between differential efficiency and key exogenous variables. We included other differential-efficiency measures not used in the regression analysis—those for LTF,

Table 11.5
Basic determinants of difference between skewness, United States and Japan (SKWDFUJ)

Equation	Model	$\bar{R}^2$/degrees of freedom
5.1	$-0.500 + 0.012$C4ADFUJ $- 0.002$UNIDFUJ	
	(1.45) (0.54)	
	$+ 0.0005$ROTGDFUJ $+ 2.952$**PRTDFUJ	
	(0.04) (1.72)	
	$+ 1.166$TCHMSAL	0.023
	(1.47)	115
5.2	$0.288 - 0.392$**RDSDFUJ $- 0.261$**INDDFUJ	
	(2.30) (1.85)	
	$- 0.042$*EXPTDFUJ $+ 0.014$C4ADFUJ	
	(2.69) (1.20)	
	$- 0.007$UNIDFUJ $+ 0.002$*RADSHIP $- 2.269$*UDIV	0.279
	(1.09) (3.52) (2.69)	66
5.3	$0.047 - 0.422$*RDSDFUJ $- 0.288$**INDDFUJ	
	(2.74) (2.09)	
	$- 0.040$*EXPTDFUJ $- 0.008$UNIDFUJ	
	(2.61) (1.30)	
	$+ 0.001$*RADSHIP $- 1.751$**TCHMSAL	0.296
	(3.32) (1.74)	66

Note: Levels of significance: when one-tailed, * = 1 percent, ** = 5 percent; when two-tailed, † = 1 percent, ‡ = 5 percent.

average technical inefficiency ATI, and lambda λ. The positive effect of C4MDFUJ on LTEDFUJ is evident in the correlation coefficient for that and indeed all the other measures except SKWDFUJ. In parallel, C4ADFUJ is negatively correlated with the efficiency differentials except SKWDFUJ and positively correlated with the inefficiency differentials. That pattern continues through a series of other variables, suggesting this rough generalization: Where a hypothesis is supported for one but not the other of SKWDFUJ and LTEDFUJ, the expected result agrees with the zero-order correlations of the other efficiency measures not used in the regression analysis.[10]

These results are undeniably scant, and the lack of consistency between LTEDFUJ and SKWDFUJ impels caution in drawing conclusions. What can be said is that each dependent variable yields substantial confirmation of results from the interindustry studies undertaken in the two countries separately. Allowing for all the problems of restricted sample sizes, differences in the measurement of variables, and the like, we feel that the results offer moderate support for the hypothesis that the same general types of mechanisms generate technical efficiency in both countries. The high correlations of the U.S.–Japan differences in the various efficiency measures, together with the modest number of confirming regression results (and the absence of serious inconsistencies), seem to support that position.

11.4.2 Correlations among National Variables for Matched Industries

The preceding analysis leaves open a number of questions about the exogenous variables for the matched industries. Differential efficiency could be unrelated statistically to a difference between exogenous variables for various reasons: because the relation fails to hold in both countries in the reduced sample; because the partial relation holds in at least one but is obscured by random noise, cross-correlations, or different-shaped functions; because the national exogenous variables are highly correlated with each other, so their difference is a random variable. This list is not complete, but it indicates some of the problems.

We extended the analysis in two ways. First, we reestimated models of the determinants of LTEDFUJ with the country-difference regressors separated by country. The coefficients for the two components reveal the intercountry differences both in magnitude and in their significance levels.

Second, for each exogenous variable that we could measure for both countries, we calculated a correlation matrix that includes the variable for each country and its difference, as well as LTEDFUJ, SKWDFUJ, and their national components. We computed these correlations over the maximum number of observations available and then for only the observations available for LTEDFUJ. We discovered an interesting piece of information: that the cross-national correlation between, say, LTEJ and an exogenous variable measured for the United States sometimes exceeds the correlation of LTEJ with the variable measured for Japan. What follows is a selective summary of findings from these extensions. Table 11.6 reports the regression results; each model is based on equation 4.1, with only the national components of selected difference variables reported (other coefficients proved quite stable and are not shown).

Concentration of Producers and Competition Policy

Concentration enters the national cross-sectional models as a quadratic, which is why we used the C4ADFUJ form in table 11.4. We also investigated the linear difference between imports-adjusted national concentra-

Table 11.6
Determinants of expected technical efficiency (LTEDFUJ): different coefficients for U.S. and Japanese components of differences

Equation	Coefficients of components of U.S.-Japan differences		$\bar{R}^2$/degrees of freedom
	United States	Japan	
6.1	$-0.004^{\ddagger}$C4AU	$+0.004^{\ddagger}$C4AJ	0.265
	(2.34)	(2.46)	29
6.2	0.0008C4MU	-0.0025C4MJ	0.096
	(0.58)	(1.80)	29
6.3	0.051INDU	$+0.024$INDJ	0.360
	(1.36)	(1.69)	29
6.4	-0.002^{*}UNIU	$+0.001$UNIJ	0.320
	(3.01)	(1.31)	29
6.5	0.374**PARTU	-0.863PARTJ	0.268
	(1.77)	(0.65)	29
6.6	-0.480ADVU	-3.903^{**}ADVJ	0.430
	(0.61)	(2.01)	24
6.7	-0.0004ROUTGU	-0.004^{**}ROUTGJ	0.274
	(0.01)	(2.33)	29

Note: Each equation also included a constant term and the variables C4ADFUJ, UNIDFUJ, ROTGDFUJ, TCHMSAL, and PRTDFUJ except when the components of one of these differences were entered separately. Levels of statistical significance: when one-tailed, * = 1 percent, ** = 5 percent; when two-tailed, ‡ = 5 percent.

tion ratios: C4MDFUJ. Equation 6.1 shows the relationship to C4A to be almost identical in magnitude and significance in the two countries. When C4MDFUJ (and not C4ADFUJ) is entered as a determinant of LTEDFUJ, it takes a positive coefficient that is significant in some specifications. Equation 6.2 shows that the result depends on the Japanese component.

The underlying correlations shed light on these findings. As other studies have found, concentration is highly correlated between the matched industries: 0.399. Because mean concentration in each country (especially Japan) is less than the level estimated to maximize efficiency,[11] the national efficiency measures (both LTE and SKEW) are positively correlated with national concentration, but the relation is stronger for Japan. This pattern translates into positive but not significant correlations between LTEDFUJ and C4MDFUJ (0.129) and between SKWDFUJ and C4MDFUJ (0.053).[12]

The national optimal concentration levels diverge enough that C4AU and C4AJ are uncorrelated. Consistent with equation 6.1, the negative correlations between efficiency and an industry's difference from optimal concentration are more evident for Japan than for the United States; they lead to a negative but insignificant correlation between LTEDFUJ and C4ADFUJ: -0.190. It is important to the regression result that LTEJ be substantially correlated with the divergence from the optimum of U.S. concentration (C4AU): -0.191.

INDDFUJ, the difference in competition-policy actions, is expected to depress efficiency, and its coefficient takes that sign but is not significant ($t = -1.16$). In equation 6.3, however, the U.S. term as well as that of the Japanese takes a positive coefficient. The expected result is obtained with SKWDFUJ, however.[13] The unclear pattern with LTE reflects the high correlation between INDJ and INDU (0.428), which supports the casual impression that producers' inclinations to engage in collusion depend on market-structure characteristics that are largely independent of the national economic environment. As equation 6.3 suggests, the negative correlation between LTEDFUJ and INDDFUJ (-0.088) stems mostly from the negative correlation between LTEJ and INDJ (-0.158).[14]

Union Membership

In equation 6.4 the negative effect of union organization on LTEDFUJ is seen in both the United States and Japan, although the U.S. relation is stronger; the same holds when SKWDFUJ is the dependent variable.[15] This pattern directly corresponds to the underlying correlations for SKEW. In the sample used for the regression analysis of LTEDFUJ, however, the negative relation is surprisingly stronger for Japan (LTEJ and UNIJ, -0.340) than for the United States (LTEU and UNIU, -0.178). Union membership is significantly correlated between countries (0.320), once again limiting the information value of the difference between them.

Business Organization

Because of its strong tendency to depress efficiency in the United States, enterprise diversification is a phenomenon of considerable interest. Unfortunately, it could not be measured in parallel fashion for Japan. We did determine that its negative correlation with LTEU is substantial in the sample used to estimate LTEDFUJ (-0.254), but LTEJ is uncorrelated with U.S. diversification in that sample (-0.006). Either enterprise diversification in Japan does not affect efficiency, or (what is less likely) it is uncorrelated with diversification in the United States.

The extent of multiplant operation of the leading companies is highly correlated in the two countries (0.411) and thus may not be very sensitive to the greater spatial dispersion of the U.S. economy. LTE is negatively correlated with multiplant operation in each country (LTEU and MULTIU, -0.178; LTEJ and MULTIJ, -0.152). Because each country's efficiency level is also correlated with the other's multiplant operation, the hypothesis draws little support in the correlation of the differentials or in the regression analysis. We have no statistical leverage against it.

LTEDFUJ is related neither to SPEDFUJ, the difference in plant-level diversification, nor to its national components separately, but SKWDFUJ increases with differential specialization, mostly by the United States.[16] Plant-level specialization in the two countries is uncorrelated: 0.068. Efficiency increases with specialization more from correlations in the United States than Japan, although it was significant for Japan but not the U.S. national analysis.

As equation 6.5 shows, the significant effect of part-time employment on LTEDFUJ comes through the United States. Part-time employment in the two countries is uncorrelated, suggesting important differences in national ways of organizing work (different methods of measurement might also be responsible). Both efficiency measures LTE and SKEW are strongly correlated with part-time work for the United States but not for Japan.

Research and Development and Advertising Outlays

We saw that research and development functions as a disturbance, reducing apparent efficiency for the United States but not Japan. The difference in R&D spending rates reduces SKWDFUJ but not LTEDFUJ. LTEDFUJ is unrelated to either national variable, while SKWDFUJ shows the expected significant negative relation to RDSU but none to RDSJ. An important constraint on testing R&D's differential effect is the very high correlation between RDSU and RDSJ, 0.612. LTE in each country shows a weak negative correlation with that country's research intensity, but LTEDFUJ and RDSDFUJ are uncorrelated. SKWDFUJ and RDSDFUJ are correlated (-0.143), but that relation actually depends on a positive correlation between SKEWJ and RDSU: 0.169. Could that reflect the state of diffusion of U.S. technology to Japan as of 1977?

LTEDFUJ's nonsignificant negative relation to the difference in advertising/sales ratios (ADVDFUJ) actually becomes a negative relation to both ADVU and ADVJ in equation 6.6, the latter significant. ADVU and

ADVJ are even more highly correlated in the two countries (0.647) than
are RDSU and RDSJ. The differentials LTDFUJ and ADVDFUJ are
accordingly uncorrelated: −0.020. The negative association between advertising intensity and efficiency seems to operate strictly in the United
States (LTEU and ADVU, −0.278; LTEJ and ADVJ, 0.147).[17]

We can group with the dynamic disturbances from research and advertising the industry's real rate of growth. The positive effect of differential
growth on efficiency (table 11.4) turns out to operate entirely in Japan
(equation 6.7). This result is perverse, however, in relation to the cross-
sectional analysis of LTEJ reported in chapter 2, so it is probably an
artifact of the reduced sample.

Export Intensity

Exporting activity is typically spread quite unevenly among an industry's
companies and plants. It thus can appear to increase technical inefficiency,
as we concluded for SKWDFUJ but not for LTEDFUJ. When the model
of SKWDFUJ is reestimated with the national export ratios entered separately, the coefficients are the same for the two countries though that
for Japan is more significant.[18] The export intensities of the matched
industries are surprisingly highly correlated: 0.370. For both efficiency
measures the negative correlation is stronger in the United States than in
the Japan. That pattern diverges from the regression results, but it is
consistent with the Japanese industries' greater export orientation.

11.5   Technical Efficiency and Average Productivity

11.5.1   Context and Objectives of the Investigation

The relative technical efficiency of U.S. and Japanese industries concerns
the question of their overall levels of relative productivity. Given appropriately measured variables, for any industry in each country we can write its
frontier level of efficiency as its average efficiency divided by its rate of
technical efficiency. With industries matched between the two countries,
relative technical efficiency is the product of relative average efficiency and
(inverted) relative technical efficiency. Such constructed measures of relative frontier efficiency might be useful in studies of international comparative advantage and of technology diffusion as well as in the assessment of
various public policy issues.

Our objective here is more limited: to investigate the association between relative output (value added) in the two countries and its putative determinants, the quantities of inputs and estimated relative efficiency. The exercise can be regarded either as locating a missing variable in the analysis of production or as validating our measures of technical efficiency. We also test some hypotheses about the relative positions of the two nations' efficiency frontiers.

Most previous research on productivity in the United States and Japan has taken a highly aggregated approach. Chavas and Cox (1990), for example, found that productivity in both countries' manufacturing sectors was seriously reduced by the 1973 energy price shock, but both were apparently back on track by 1977, the year of our study. More relevant here is the disaggregated analysis of Jorgenson, Kuroda, and Nishimizu (1987), who employed a sophisticated procedure to analyze productivity growth rates in 30 matched sectors. They found that by the 1970s Japan's advantage in labor-productivity growth depended on heavier rates of capital expenditure, and during 1973–79 Japan enjoyed no substantial corresponding advantage in the growth of total factor productivity. They classified sectors as to the year in which the productivity gap closed between the two countries or (alternatively) remained open in 1979. In the raw materials processing and intermediate goods industries (except for lumber and wood products, precision instruments, and other miscellaneous manufacturing) all gaps had closed by 1979, although more remained open in light consumer goods industries and investment goods industries. These results suggest that a simple cross-sectional analysis of relative productivity in 1977 should not be vitiated by the observation of relative productivity in many out-of-equilibrium situations.

11.5.2 Analyzing Relative Productivity

Although the technical efficiency measures were obtained through the estimation of production functions for each industry and country, for a variety of reasons that approach cannot be extended to the analysis of relative productivity in matched industries. Instead, we rely on simple approaches that seek to make sensible use of weak data on outputs and inputs aggregated to the industry level. Two such approaches were explored.

Common Production Function, Flexible Scale

One approach (method 1) was developed by Davies and Caves (1987, ch. 2) and applied to matched British and U.S. industries; it is also applied to Australian and U.S. industries in this volume (chapter 6). It assumes in the first instance that all industries in both countries utilize the same Cobb-Douglas production function, although one not constrained to constant returns to scale. It yields the relationship:

$$VPW_i = EFF_i \cdot CAP_i^\alpha \cdot TYP_i^{\alpha+\beta-1},$$

where VPW_i is the logarithm of value added per employee in the U.S. industry divided by value added per employee in its Japanese counterpart, CAP_i is the logarithm of total assets per employee in the U.S. industry divided by assets per employee in its Japanese counterpart, TYP_i is the logarithm of typical (median) plant size in the U.S. industry divided by typical plant size in its Japanese counterpart, and EFF_i is relative efficiency, obviously related to the national measures of technical efficiency.

We can derive this relation with explicit attention to technical efficiency. Define VA as value added, N as labor input, and AS as value of capital input. The technical efficiency model implies the following relationship for industry i's jth plant:

$$\left(\frac{VA}{N}\right)_{ij} = f_i\left(\left(\frac{AS}{N}\right)_{ij} N_{ij}\right)\exp(-u_{ij})\exp(v_{ij}),$$

where f is a production function. By averaging this equation for plants in each industry, we get

$$\left(\overline{\frac{VA}{N}}\right)_i = \iint f_i\left(\left(\frac{AS}{N}\right)_{ij} N_{ij}\right) dg_i^1\left(\frac{AS}{N}\right) g_i^2(N_i)\, d\left(\frac{AS}{N}\right) dN$$

$$\cdot \int \exp(-u_{ij})g^3(u)\, du \cdot \int \exp(v_{ij})g^4(v)\, dv$$

$$= \iint f_i\left(\left(\frac{AS}{N}\right)_{ij} N_{ij}\right) g_i^1\left(\frac{AS}{N}\right) g_i^2(N_i)\, d\left(\frac{AS}{N}\right) dN \cdot \text{LTE}_i$$

as $\int \exp(-u_{ij})g^3(u)\, du = \text{LTE}_i$, and $\int \exp(v_{ij})g^4(v)\, dv = 1$. Here the g^i are distribution functions for the variables, and appropriate interdependences between variables and the same technology in every plant in the same industry are assumed. Next we assume that $f_i = a_0(AS/N)^{\alpha_i}N^{\alpha_i+\beta_i-1}$. Then

$$\overline{\log\left(\frac{\overline{VA}}{N}\right)_i} = a_i^0 + a_i^1 \overline{\log\left(\frac{\overline{AS}}{N}\right)_i} + a_i^2 \overline{\log(N_i)} + \log(\text{LTE}_i).$$

We approximate averages of logarithms by logarithms of averages. In most distributions this approximation does not diverge more than a few percent. Therefore

$$\log\left(\frac{\overline{VA}}{N}\right)_i = a_i^0 + a_i^1 \log\left(\frac{\overline{AS}}{N}\right) + a_i^2 \log(\overline{N}) + \log(\text{LTE}_i).$$

Subtracting this equation for the United States from that for Japan, we get:

$$\log(\text{VPW}_i) = \log\left(\frac{\text{LTE}_i^U}{\text{LTE}_i^J}\right) + a_{iU}^1 \log(CAP_i)a_{iU}^2 + \log(TYP_i)$$
$$+ \Delta a_i^0 + \Delta a_i^1 \log(JCAP_i) + \Delta a_i^2 \log(JTYP_i).$$

Here $\Delta a_i^k = a_{iU}^k - a_{ij}^k$ $(k = 0, 1, 2)$ and U and J indicate countries as before.[19] The difference in average productivity is divided into three parts. The first term represents the difference in technical efficiency, the next two differences due to input composition and plant scales, and the last three differences in frontier technologies. Although the assumption that every industry uses the same technology is very strong, the model provides an attractive framework both for the relationship of technical efficiency to average productivity and for testing hypotheses about differences in efficiency frontiers.[20]

This model can be estimated from readily available data, including as a regressor either LTEU/LTEJ or a function relating SKEWU to SKEWJ by means of a transformation of SKEW that brings it into the (0, 1) range comparable to LTE:

$$\text{LSKW} = \log\left(\frac{\text{ASKEW}_{iU}}{\text{ASKEW}_{iJ}}\right),$$

where $\text{ASKEW}_{ij} = 1/[1 + \exp(-\text{SKEW}_{ij})]$. We expect the regression coefficient of relative technical efficiency to be $+1$; the positive coefficients of the CAP and TYP terms should supply reasonable estimates of the production-function coefficients. A problem in applying this method (and also the next) is how to treat relative product prices in the U.S. and Japanese counterpart industries. No adjustment would be needed if both sell at the same world price (adjusted for exchange rate). We discuss alternatives below.

Industry-Specific Production Function, Constant Returns

An alternative way to approach the analysis of relative average efficiency (method 2) avoids the restrictive assumption that all industries share the same production function. It requires only that the coefficients of each industry's production function be the same in both countries, but it does need the assumption of constant returns to scale. It also requires the assumption that producers in each country optimize their capital-labor proportions in light of the economy's parametric ratio of wages to capital rentals. With these two assumptions made, an estimating equation can be derived that makes VPW_i depend only on technical efficiency in each country and the ratio of value added per worker to the capital–labor ratio in one country. In fact the estimation indicated by this latter procedure produced coefficients that matched a priori restrictions rather poorly, although its qualitative conclusions closely resemble those of method 1. Therefore we do not report the details of method 2.

11.5.3 Statistical Results

Controlling Relative Prices

Implementing either method 1 or method 2 requires some procedure for dealing with interindustry differences in relative output prices. Previous applications to Canada and Australia have assumed that their domestic market prices are set equal to the world prices of goods plus tariffs and international shipping costs. This assumption is not implausible for nations with strongly import-competing manufacturing sectors; it worked reasonably well for Canada although not for Australia (see chapter 6). Davies and Caves (1987) sought to improve on this by using quantity and price data reported in the British and American censuses of production to obtain rough measures of actual relative prices. We attempted that same procedure, which seemed much more plausible for both the United States and Japan.

It did not prove easy to implement, and we could obtain credible estimates of relative prices for only 56 of the 144 matched industries for which SKWDFUJ is available. Many sources of inaccuracy intrude, such as qualitative differences in the two countries' products. Also U.S. data are reported with more disaggregation than Japanese data, allowing distortions to enter in the aggregation process. The industries lost included those with no unit-price statistics (69), different methods of measuring quantities

(7), suppressed data (4), and no overlap in the commodities on which data were reported (8). The relative-price term entering into the regression models is designated RPR, and it takes the value of zero for industries whose relative-price values could not be calculated.

Statistical Results

Application of both methods established two preliminary conclusions:

1.   Each model's fit is much better for industries exposed to significant international trade than for sheltered industries. This difference must rest on the fact that nontraded goods industries cater strongly to national tastes, making their goods noncomparable in attributes and frustrating our efforts to measure relative prices. Extensively traded goods, even when differentiated, must be more strictly comparable between countries. We defined the variable TRADE as the sum of the ratios of exports to shipments and imports to total supply for both the U.S. industry and its Japanese counterpart; it is used below to select subsamples of the more trade-exposed industries.

2.   The results are unfortunately sensitive to the way we measure labor input in the two countries. One procedure is to relate value added and the capital stock to the total number of employees, production and nonproduction, and to include in method 1's model the term PRW, defined as the logarithm of the ratio of production workers/employees in the U.S. industry to its counterpart in Japan. (A parallel procedure is used for method 2.) The other procedure simply ignores the nonproduction-worker input and measures labor input as production workers. Although the former procedure seems analytically preferable, it generally does not fit the data as well. Results will be reported on both bases.

The basic results from method 1 are shown in table 11.7, in which the first section reports the model fitted to all observations and subsequent ones truncate the sample by values of TRADE; extreme outlying observations on RPR are also dropped. Equations designated E use total employment to measure labor input, and those designated P production workers only. The neoclassical core of the model is significant and correctly signed for all observations. It remains generally well behaved as the threshold for TRADE is increased. When TRADE < 0.05, only the measure of relative plant size (TYP) is significant, whereas it becomes insignificant in the

Table 11.7
Effect of international-trade exposure on determinants of relative average productivity

Equation	LSKW	CAP	TYP	RPR	PRW	Constant	$\bar{R}^2$/degrees of freedom
All observations							
7.1E	−0.005	0.072**	0.064*	0.244*	−0.443*	0.441	0.164
	(0.20)	(1.67)	(2.89)	(2.83)	(2.68)		133
7.1P	−0.007	0.096**	0.090*	0.143	—	0.263	0.145
	(0.25)	(2.28)	(4.11)	(1.64)			133
TRADE < 0.05, 0.5 < RPR < 2.0							
7.2E	−0.040	0.027	0.116*	0.060	−0.733**	0.567	0.352
	(1.00)	(0.36)	(2.99)	(0.21)	(2.09)		37
7.2P	−0.051	0.087	0.128*	−0.167	—	0.312	0.235
	(1.09)	(1.01)	(3.09)	(0.52)			38
Trade > 0.1, 0.5 < RPR < 2.0							
7.3E	0.051	0.098	0.031	0.478**	−0.140	0.386	0.109
	(1.24)	(1.75)	(1.05)	(2.39)	(0.66)		69
7.3P	0.055	0.112**	0.058**	0.169	—	0.294	0.136
	(1.55)	(2.38)	(2.23)	(0.92)			69
Trade > 0.2, 0.5 < RPR < 2.0							
7.4E	0.060	0.083	0.020	0.503**	−0.113	0.430	0.123
	(1.31)	(1.28)	(0.57)	(2.38)	(0.35)		52
7.4P	0.063**	0.083**	0.049**	0.157	—	0.374	0.128
	(1.81)	(1.69)	(1.71)	(0.90)			52

Note: In E equations value added and capital assets are normalized by total employment, and relative production-worker proportion of total employment (PRW) is included as a regressor. In P equations value added and capital assets are normalized by production workers, so PRW is omitted. Levels of statistical significance (one-tailed): * = 1 percent ** = 5 percent.

traded goods subsamples. This pattern conforms to one's expectation that producers participating in a world market should realize scale economies fully, whereas in domestic markets national producers are more likely to choose outputs that do not exhaust scale economies. The terms $JCAP$ and $JTYP$ from the theoretical model never proved statistically significant and were dropped from the models of table 11.7; their deletion has no substantial effect on any conclusions reported below.

The relative efficiency measure LSKW is not significant or even properly signed for the full sample or for nontraded goods. It rises to (generally) 10 percent significance once TRADE > 0.1, doing better in the equations based on production-worker input. It retains that level of significance as TRADE is increased to 0.5, even as the subsample's size shrinks and other regressors lose their significance. This pattern supports the conjecture that

Table 11.8
Estimated differences in frontier efficiency between U.S. and Japanese two-digit sectors

Sector	Intercept shift	t-statistic
20 Food products	0.646	5.82
22 Textiles	0.160	1.31
24 Wood products	0.248	1.88
28 Chemicals and allied products	0.225	2.06
29 Petroleum products	−0.045	−0.26
30 Rubber and plastic products	−0.015	−0.08
32 Building materials	0.060	0.63
33 Primary metals	−0.202	−1.64
34 Fabricated metal products	−0.030	−0.19
35 Nonelectrical machinery	−0.187	−1.89
36 Electrical equipment	−0.306	−2.77
37 Transportation equipment	−0.256	−1.34
38 Instruments	−0.236	−1.96
39 Miscellaneous manufacturing	−0.163	−1.54

Note: Each shift coefficient is taken from an equation with LVATPW as dependent variable, with LSKW, CAP, TYP, RPR, $JCAP$, and $JTYP$ included as regressors. The industry sample includes those for which the tradable goods index exceeds 15 percent.

the outputs and activities of traded goods industries are substantially more comparable internationally. As with method 2, the coefficient of LSKW is much lower than the theoretical expectation.

The results of table 11.7 have their disappointing aspects, but they seem to warrant an effort to identify sources of difference in the U.S. and Japanese production frontiers. Before testing substantive hypotheses, we examine table 11.8, which reports intercept shifts for two-digit sectors in the U.S. standard industrial classification that contributed sufficient industries to the sample. The coefficients are taken from models that include $JCAP$ and $JTYP$, with the sample truncated at TRADE > 0.15 (values of 0.1 and 0.2 yield about the same results). Not surprisingly, the United States holds a significant advantage in food, wood products, and chemicals, Japan in metals and the durables and machinery industries.

In table 11.9 we proceed to test a series of hypotheses about relative frontier positions:

1. Subcontracting arrangements in Japan raise the efficient frontier without offsetting losses due to agency problems. In the first line of table 11.9 payments to subcontractors as a fraction of total materials costs are seen to lower U.S. relative to Japanese productivity; the coefficient is highly significant and robust to specification changes.

Table 11.9
Tests of hypotheses about relative production frontiers

	All industries		TRADE > 0.10	
Hypothesis	Employees	Production workers	Employees	Production workers
Subcontracting	−0.924*	−0.888*	−1.723*	−1.567*
	(3.40)	(3.21)	(3.87)	(4.21)
Relative R&D	−0.001	0.024	−0.015	0.015
	(0.03)	(0.80)	(0.37)	(0.44)
Japan technology acquisition	−0.077	−0.043	−0.169	−0.062
	(0.39)	(0.22)	(0.69)	(0.30)
Factory coordination	−0.043	−0.003	−0.085**	−0.029
	(1.11)	(0.08)	(2.18)	(0.82)
U.S. capital vintage	−0.010**	−0.005	−0.012**	−0.008**
	(2.29)	(1.13)	(2.54)	(1.93)

Note: Each regression coefficient is taken from a model that also includes the variables LASKWRAT, CAP, TYP, RPR, JCAP, and JTYP (also PRW when total employees serve as the labor-input measure); t-statistics appear in parentheses. Levels of statistical significance (one-tailed): * = 1 percent; ** = 5 percent.

2. The frontiers' positions depend on relative stocks of R&D knowledge (proxied by flows, RDSDFUJ). This hypothesis finds no support.

3. Japan's position is improved by technology acquisition efforts measured by the sum of R&D spending and of payments for technology imports, expressed as a fraction of shipments. This hypothesis also finds no support.

4. Japanese personal and cultural qualities raise Japan's relative frontier in industries whose technologies require coordination of the activities of large numbers of skilled workers (as suggested by the results for SIC 35–38 in table 11.8). The variable used is employees per plant in the United States in large plants accounting for one-half of industry shipments. The significance of its correctly signed coefficient is highly sensitive to the model's specification, so the test is indecisive.

5. Because of vintage effects U.S. industries with substantial amounts of old capital are constrained to operate on a lower frontier. The measure that we used is the sum of the percentages of plant and of equipment that were more than 20 years old in 1976. Its effect is negative and generally significant.

11.6   Conclusions

Because the chapter's specific findings are rather numerous, we characterize them generally rather than summarizing them in detail. This effort to relate technical and frontier efficiency in two countries is constrained by a number of limitations of the methodology of frontier production functions and the data available. Statistical results accordingly are weak or indecisive on many points. Nonetheless, it seems clear that the transnational comparative analysis is worthwhile. It fortifies a number of findings about the determinants of technical efficiency in the United States and Japan. Many of these amount to statistical confirmation of commonplace observations. Nonetheless, commonplace observations are not necessarily right, so the contribution to knowledge would not seem trivial.

The research embraced an attempt to explore the relationship among average productivity, technical efficiency, and the relative positions of U.S. and Japanese production frontiers. This can be done only in a simple way, but it seems fairly successful at that level. The statistical results support the basic approach and also allow tests of hypotheses about relative frontier efficiency, supporting Japan's advantage with the subcontracting system and in factory efficiency in the large-scale assembly-type industry and documenting the drag of elderly capital vintages in the United States. No results were obtained for research and development, consistent with the hypothesis that by 1977 each country's research activities had settled at their privately optimal levels.

Notes

We gratefully acknowledge the assistance of Denkitsūshin Fukyū Zaidan for enabling Torii's period of residence at Harvard University and the Division of Research, Harvard Business School, for supporting Caves's research.

1. Chapter 2 of this volume on Japan; Caves and Barton (1990) on the United States.

2. Different concentration measures were used (Herfindahl for Japan, four-firm for the United States), so only a rough comparison is possible.

3. Our efficiency measures pertain to the year 1977, before a wave of leveraged buyouts and reconcentration by diversified enterprises presumably alleviated the U.S. situation. The contrast between the two countries is consistent with Aoki's (1987) analysis of Japanese enterprise and the institutions of corporate control.

4. The sign of the significant coefficient reverses in Japan when two-stage least squares is employed. Also in the United States indirect effects of energy-saving investments were seen in the negative relation of efficiency to plants' dispersions of capital–labor ratios within industries.

5. The expectations of equal effects in both countries and an effect in only one are limiting cases convenient for exposition.

6. For hypotheses that are neither country specific nor confined to a narrow subset of manufacturing industries, the advantages of matching are less compelling. They consist of avoiding "false positive" conclusions that could arise when one country's sample lacks industries that strongly embody a particular effect, and of reducing biases due to regressors included in the analysis being correlated with omitted variables that are associated with particular industries.

7. For the United States Caves and Barton (1990, ch. 4) concluded that industries with positive skewness have various traits consistent with absence of significant technical ineffi-ciency but also that they present noisier data and/or their production functions were esti-mated less well. They also found (table 6.6) that the conclusions about the interindustry determinants of technical efficiency are fairly similar between skewness and average technical efficiency. For Australia (chapter 6), hypotheses about technical efficiency were tested with notably more success on skewness than on average technical inefficiency, although the qualitative findings were quite similar. The difference in degrees of freedom, substantially favoring skewness, seems an important source of the result.

8. It would be natural to test this hypothesis in a comparative form, but the limited number of matched industries for which U.S. data can be obtained discouraged that step.

9. It seems reasonable that research intensity and the importance of technology inflows should both have substantially influenced measured efficiency in Japan in 1977. By that year Japan's great increase in research had reached a level of rough parity with other industrial countries (Okimoto and Saxonhouse 1987; Owen 1988). Payments for imported technology were still growing at 6 percent annually, although they had slowed from a 21 percent growth rate in the 1960s (Uekusa 1987, p. 490).

10. We note the exceptions. RADSHIP's association is confined to SKWDFUJ. Signs for TCHMSAL conflict among the various efficiency differentials.

11. The values estimated to maximize efficiency were 40.5 and 47.9 percent for the United States and Japan, respectively, using the four-firm concentration ratio divided by one plus imports' share of total supply.

12. Significance tests will not be quoted for individual correlation coefficients. Degrees of freedom vary from case to case. Roughly speaking, when LTEDFUJ is involved, the thresh-old for 5 percent significance is about 0.29; when SKWDFUJ is involved, the threshold is about 0.18; for other variables it generally falls between these two values.

13. When equation 5.2 is reestimated with the national competition–policy terms taking different slopes, both coefficients are positive.

14. In the U.S. study (Caves and Barton 1990) IND's influence occurred through an interac-tion with levels of producer concentration. Uekusa (1987) argued that a substantial reduction in distortions due to collusion has taken place in Japan, but it was only beginning around 1977.

15. The result is consistent with Koike's (1987) argument that the contrast between U.S. and Japanese union organization and activity has been overdrawn.

16. With SKWDFUJ as the dependent variable, the t-statistic on SPEDFUJ's coefficient is 1.69. For the national components the coefficients (t-statistics) are 0.050 (2.01) and -0.021 (-0.120).

17. Similarly Caves and Uekusa (1976) found that sales-promotion barriers to entry seem less entrenched in Japan.

18. The coefficients (t-statistics) are -0.042 (-1.49) for the United States and 0.041 (2.53) for Japan.

19. In order to estimate this equation we assume $\alpha_{iU}^1 = \alpha_U^1$, $\alpha_{iU}^2 = \alpha_U^2$, $\Delta\alpha_i^0 = \Delta\alpha^0$, $\Delta\alpha_i^1 = \Delta\alpha^1$, $\Delta\alpha_i^2 = \Delta\alpha^2$.

20. The estimating equation differs only slightly from the one obtained by Davies and Caves (1987, 20) in which the last two terms pertain to the numerator (not the denominator) country and allow intercountry differences in parameters of the production function.

References

Aoki, M. The Japanese firm in transition. In Yamamura and Yasuba (1987), pp. 263–288.

Caves, R. E., and D. R. Barton. 1990. *Efficiency in U.S. Manufacturing Industries*. Cambridge: MIT Press.

Caves, R. E., and M. Uekusa. 1976. *Industrial Organization in Japan* Washington: Brookings Institution.

Chavas, J.-P., and T. L. Cox. 1990. A non-parametric analysis of productivity: The case of U.S. and Japanese manufacturing. *American Economic Review* 80: 450–464.

Harris, C. M. 1988. *Technical Efficiency in Australian Manufacturing Industries*. Occasional Paper No 4. Canberra: Bureau of Industry Economics.

Jorgenson, D. W., M. Kuroda, and M. Nishimizu. 1987. Japan–U.S. industry-level productivity comparisons, 1960–1979. *Journal of the Japanese and International Economies* 1: 1–30.

Koike, K. 1987. Human resource development and labor-management relations. In Yamamura and Yasuba (1987), pp. 289–330.

Okimoto, D. I., and G. R. Saxonhouse. Technology and the future of the economy. In Yamamura and Yasuba (1987), pp. 385–419.

Owen, R. F. 1988. The evolution of Japan's relative technological competitiveness since the 1960's: A cross-sectional, time-series analysis. Working Paper No. WP-88.009. Faculty of Economics, Limburg University.

Patrick, H. T., and T. P. Rohlen. 1987. Small-scale family enterprises. In Yamamura and Yasuba (1987), pp. 331–384.

Shōda, Y. 1981. Syokuryōhin sangyō no sangyō-chosei (Regulation in the food industry). In S. Sekiguchi, ed., *Nihon no Sangyō-Chōsei* (*Regulation in Japan*). Tokyo: Nihon-Keizai Sinbunsha.

Yamamura, K., and Y. Yasuba, eds. 1987. *The Political Economy of Japan, The Domestic Transformation*, vol. 1. Stanford: Stanford University Press.

12 Productivity Growth and Technical Efficiency in OECD Industrial Activities

Fabienne Fecher and Sergio Perelman

12.1 Introduction

Two major challenges in economics are the measurement of productivity growth and the research of explanations of its variability across countries, industrial sectors, and over time. In this chapter we attack both issues. First, we apply the frontier analysis approach in order to estimate productivity growth and technical efficiency in an international, intersectoral and intertemporal framework. That is, we analyze the efficiency not of the firm in its national industry, but the national sector relative to the world industry. Second, we test well-known hypotheses pertaining to the relationship between these performance indicators and a selected set of variables.

Aggregate production data recently made available for several OECD countries and all industrial sectors enable us to estimate total-factor productivity growth (TFP) over the period 1971 to 1986 using an alternative approach to the traditional index number techniques. This approach allows us to distinguish the contribution of technological progress and efficiency changes to TFP.

The starting point of this approach, first proposed by Nishimizu and Page (1982), is the estimation of a parametric production frontier allowing for the measurement of technological progress. Technical efficiency is then calculated, for each production unit, as the distance between the frontier and the observed output. Total factor productivity growth measure is finally obtained by summing up estimated temporal changes in efficiency and technological progress.

Productivity improvement in economic activities is thus regarded as the consequence of two rather different factors. On the one hand, the adoption of technical innovations in processes and in products, pushing the frontier of potential production upward, is measured by technological progress. On the other hand, efficiency change reflects the capacity of firms to improve production with given inputs and available technology.

Clearly productivity and technical efficiency are not neatly separable either in theory or in practice. The distinction that is adopted in the literature is therefore somewhat artificial, but it can offer an important added dimension to test different factors that are supposed to be at the root of these two indicators of performance. Needless to say, no one has yet come up with a full explanation of productivity and efficiency both in levels and in growth rates. However, some determinants are commonly recognized. Classical trade theory invokes the macroeconomic "climatic" factors as the main determinants of the Ricardian factors that explain comparative advantage. In this study technical efficiency reflects these Ricardian factors and is explained not only by the climatic factors but also by a set of microeconomic determinants. Available data on competitive conditions, innovation, and production structures for most OECD countries and sectors utilized in our analysis allow us to test these conjectures in a large-scale, cross-sectional, and intertemporal context.

This chapter is organized as follows. In section 12.2 we present some methodological considerations concerning the estimation of a parametric stochastic production frontier and the measurement of productivity and efficiency. Section 12.3 is devoted to the presentation of OECD data used in the analysis. In section 12.4 we present the main results on TFP measurement and its decomposition.[1] In section 12.5 we describe some of the best known hypotheses about determinants of technical efficiency levels and productivity growth rates. In section 12.6 we test the explanatory power of these determinants. A final section contains the conclusions.

12.2   Frontier Analysis and TFP

The most important difference between frontier analysis and traditional index number approach to TFP lies in one assumption: the existence of an unobservable function, the production frontier, corresponding to the set of maximum attainable output levels for a given combination of inputs. We represent this so-called best-practice function $g[\cdot]$, as follows:

$$y^F(t) = g[x(t), t],\tag{1}$$

where $y^F(t)$ is the potential output level on the frontier at time t, and $x(t)$ is a vector of inputs. It is assumed that function $g[\cdot]$ satisfies the usual regularity conditions and that there exists an appropriate aggregate index of output.

Thus any observed output $y(t)$ using $x(t)$ for inputs can be expressed as

$$y(t) = y^F(t)e^{u(t)} = g[x(t), t]e^{u(t)},\tag{2}$$

where $u(t) \leq 0$ is the rate of technical efficiency $[0 < e^{u(t)} = y(t)/y^F(t) \leq 1]$ corresponding to observed output $y(t)$.

The derivative of the logarithms of equation (2) with respect to time is then given by equation (3):

$$\frac{\dot{y}(t)}{y(t)} = g_x \frac{\dot{x}(t)}{x(t)} + g_t + \dot{u}(t), \tag{3}$$

where g_x and g_t denote respectively the output elasticities of $g[x(t), t]$ with respect to $x(t)$ and t and dotted variables indicate time derivatives.

As indicated by equation (3), output changes can be broken down in three main components. The first one corresponds to input changes weighted by output elasticities, the second, g_t, is the rate of technological progress of the best practice frontier and, the last one, $\dot{u}(t)$, represents the technical efficiency change during period t.

Following Nishimizu and Page (1982), we define the rate of total-factor productivity change, TFP, as the variation in output not explained by input changes. That is, for production unit i,

$$\text{TFP}_i(t) = g_t + \dot{u}_i(t), \tag{4}$$

the sum of technological progress, measured at the frontier level, and the change in efficiency observed at the individual level.

To estimate this indicator of productivity growth, the starting point is the estimation of the unobservable production frontier indicated by equation (1). Among the methods proposed to infer this frontier on the basis of observable data, parametric methods are appropriate for the estimation of functional forms. Alternative stochastic and deterministic approaches can be used for this purpose.[2] To estimate a cross-national and intertemporal frontier function, as is desired here, we adopt the stochastic approach proposed by Aigner, Lovell, and Schmidt (1977) and Meeusen and van den Broeck (1977).

For this purpose let us write again equation (2) in the form:

$$y(t) = g[x(t), t]e^{\varepsilon(t)}, \tag{2}$$

where $\varepsilon(t) = u(t) + v(t)$ is a composed error term combining technical efficiency, $u(t)$, assumed to be half-normal distributed with standard error σ_u, and a random term, $v(t)$, assumed to have the usual proprieties, that is, normal distribution, null mean and standard error σ_v. Once an analytical form is given to this frontier, it can be estimated by maximum likelihood techniques. We thereby obtain unbiased and efficient estimators for all the parameters in the model, including σ_v and σ_u. Nevertheless, given the stochastic nature of the frontier estimated in this way, only a conditional measure of technical efficiency can be estimated. This measure, indicated here by $E[u(t)] = E[u(t)|\varepsilon(t)]$, was proposed by Jondrow et al. (1982) and can be obtained easily from estimated residuals and variance components.

Turning now to the specification of function $g[\cdot]$, we adopt here a linear (Cobb-Douglas) approximation of the form:

$$\log y_{ri}(t) = \sum_{s=1}^{S} \left[\alpha_s + \sum_{k=1}^{K} \beta_{k,s} \log x_{k,ri}(t) + \gamma_s t \right] Z_r + v_{ri}(t) + u_{ri}(t), \qquad (5)$$

$r = 1, \dots, S, i = 1, \dots, I,$ and $t = 1, \dots, T,$

where r and s indicate the industrial sector and Z_r is a sectoral dummy variable ($Z_r = 1$ for $r = s$, and 0 otherwise). Furthermore i and k indicate, respectively, the country and the production factors. Two remarks are in order. First, as can be noted, function (5) is assumed to represent an overall frontier corresponding to all sectors, countries, and periods (years) in the sample. Nevertheless, each sector will be distinguished by proper output elasticities ($\beta_{k,s}$), technological progress (γ_s) and intercepts (α_s), allowing for different sectoral production technologies.[3] Second, technological progress is assumed to be neutral. This means that second-order terms, allowing for accelerated or embodied technological progress, were neglected. Several tests were done on the data with more elaborate translog functions, but they did not give satisfactory results, as is often the case with aggregate international data on production. Other details on the specification of this function and on the definition of variables are presented in the next section.

12.3   Variable Definitions and Data

The data used in this study, covering the major industrial branches of 13 OECD countries, were recently made available from the OECD International Sectoral Data Base (ISDB) whose detailed description is given in Meyer-zu-Schlochtern (1988). The main characteristic of this data base is that it contains the basic information on output, labor, and capital needed for the estimation of a production frontier.

Output is defined as value added (GDP) net of indirect taxes, at constant prices and in U.S. dollars corresponding to 1980 purchasing power parities. Note that like capital formation this variable is obtained on a national accounts basis and corresponds to sectoral aggregates in accordance with the International Standard Industrial Classification (ISIC). Labor is defined as total employment, self-employed included, and is measured by the number of individuals. Capital is estimated by means of a perpetual inventory method. The source for the estimation of the capital stock is data on gross fixed capital formation, assumed to have service lives and scrapping rates specific to each sector and country.[4]

Table 12.1 presents the average annual growth rates of these variables over the period 1971 to 1986.[5] Note that among the sectors in the ISDB,[6] we selected all the manufacturing sectors as well as among the services sectors those that seem most similar technologically to manufacturing. Data on manufacturing sectors for Australia and United Kingdom are missing due to lack of information on indirect taxes in GDP. The growth rates presented in table 12.1 reveal some interesting facts:

1. In almost all sectors and countries, employment falls, especially in textiles and basic metal products. Only two (nonmanufacturing) sectors display positive growth rates in employment: electricity, gas, and water; transport, storage, and communications. Canada is the only country that consistently exhibits increases in employment for all the selected industrial activities.

2. The growth in capital shows a very different pattern. Overall, sectors and countries experience positive rates of capital accumulation over the period analyzed. The average growth rates generally exceed 2 percent, with the only exception of textiles. Furthermore Canada and Japan show the highest average rates of accumulation in the sample.

3. The pattern of growth in value added is less clear. On the one hand, some sectors such as chemicals and machinery and equipment show high positive rates over the period as do services sectors such as electricity and transportation. On the other hand, the textiles and construction sectors experience near-zero growth rates.

Returning to the specification of the production frontier (5), we note that the choice of value added to measure output implies the assumption of separability between intermediate goods and capital and labor inputs.

Table 12.1
Average annual growth rates of value added, labor, and capital by country and sector,
1971–86

		Countries				
Sectors		Australia	Belgium	Canada	Germany	Denmark
Manufacturing sectors						
Wood, cork,	Value added	—	—	4.2	0.01	2.4
and furniture	Labor	—	—	3.0	−1.8	−1.0
	Capital	—	—	4.4	2.3	2.5
Chemicals	Value added	—	9.6	6.1	3.2	5.7
	Labor	—	0.03	3.3	−0.3	0.9
	Capital	—	4.7	5.9	2.3	3.1
Food, drink,	Value added	—	2.0	1.8	1.6	3.8
and tobacco	Labor	—	−1.5	1.3	−1.2	−0.7
	Capital	—	2.8	4.0	1.5	3.3
Machinery	Value added	—	4.1	5.3	2.5	3.4
and equipment	Labor	—	−1.3	1.9	−0.6	0.7
	Capital	—	5.0	4.4	4.1	4.0
Basic metal	Value added	—	2.2	2.0	0.6	3.2
products	Labor	—	−2.9	1.0	−2.2	−2.1
	Capital	—	1.9	4.0	1.4	3.9
Nonmetallic	Value added	—	0.7	2.8	0.4	−0.5
mineral	Labor	—	−4.6	1.3	−2.3	−2.4
products	Capital	—	2.1	4.3	1.5	2.3
Paper and	Value added	—	1.7	2.7	1.2	0.9
printing	Labor	—	−2.2	2.4	−2.3	−0.9
	Capital	—	3.7	3.7	2.7	3.2
Textiles	Value added	—	−0.5	3.2	−1.4	1.9
	Labor	—	−4.9	0.2	−4.8	−3.1
	Capital	—	1.1	2.8	−0.5	2.0
All manufac-	Value added	—	2.8	3.5	1.0	2.6
turing	Labor	—	−2.5	1.8	−1.9	−1.1
	Capital	—	3.0	4.2	1.9	3.0
Services sectors						
Construction	Value added	1.7	−0.4	3.5	0.0	−2.5
	Labor	0.3	−2.6	1.6	−1.6	−1.8
	Capital	5.6	1.5	5.3	0.9	2.3
Electricity,	Value added	5.5	3.9	5.9	3.5	5.6
gas, and water	Labor	2.3	−2.5	2.3	0.9	1.1
	Capital	3.3	3.4	5.4	3.9	3.5
Transport,	Value added	6.5	1.9	5.2	3.5	0.8
storage, and	Labor	1.5	0.5	1.5	0.2	0.7
communica-	Capital	4.0	5.7	4.6	3.8	3.4
tions						
All services	Value added	4.6	1.8	4.8	2.3	1.4
	Labor	1.4	−1.5	1.8	−0.2	0.04
	Capital	4.3	3.5	5.1	2.9	3.1

Table 12.1 (continued)

Countries

France	Britain	Italy	Japan	Netherlands	Norway	Sweden	United States	All
—	—	3.4	—	—	1.6	−0.4	2.9	2.0
—	—	−0.3	—	—	−0.8	−2.3	0.6	−0.4
—	—	4.0	—	—	4.6	3.5	2.9	3.5
3.3	—	4.4	7.6	6.3	3.4	2.4	3.5	5.0
−1.5	—	−0.5	−0.8	−0.8	−0.6	0.2	0.6	0.2
0.5	—	1.9	4.6	4.2	3.7	3.3	3.2	3.5
2.8	—	3.0	−2.6	3.9	0.8	−0.2	2.7	1.8
0.8	—	−0.3	2.4	−2.0	−0.2	−1.1	−0.7	−0.4
2.7	—	1.6	6.5	5.0	3.9	2.8	2.5	3.2
1.2	—	2.5	10.6	2.4	2.5	2.5	4.9	3.8
−1.8	—	−0.3	0.7	−2.1	0.3	−0.1	0.6	−0.1
6.3	—	4.5	7.8	1.8	4.5	3.3	4.6	4.4
1.0	—	2.7	4.1	1.9	2.9	1.6	−1.0	1.9
−3.3	—	−0.8	−2.5	−1.8	−1.4	−2.2	−2.9	−1.8
0.9	—	2.9	4.0	2.8	3.5	2.1	2.2	2.7
−1.4	—	2.0	−0.05	2.5	0.5	−1.4	1.7	0.8
−3.5	—	−1.1	−0.7	−3.0	−0.3	−3.5	−0.4	−1.8
1.1	—	2.9	5.4	3.6	3.6	3.1	2.0	2.9
2.5	—	3.1	4.7	1.6	1.4	1.9	2.7	2.1
−0.5	—	−0.2	−0.4	−1.3	−0.5	0.1	1.2	−0.4
1.5	—	0.6	6.2	4.2	4.7	2.9	3.4	3.4
−2.1	—	1.8	0.5	−3.9	−2.5	−3.4	1.9	−0.3
−3.8	—	−1.0	−3.2	−9.0	−5.4	−6.2	−1.8	−3.9
−0.9	—	0.8	2.2	−1.3	2.9	2.4	1.5	1.3
1.0	—	2.9	3.5	2.1	1.3	0.4	2.4	2.1
−1.9	—	−0.6	−0.6	−2.9	−1.1	−1.9	−0.3	−1.1
1.8	—	2.4	5.3	2.9	3.9	2.9	2.8	3.1
−2.0	−0.6	−0.2	0.4	−1.7	3.5	0.7	0.2	0.3
−2.5	−0.3	−1.5	1.0	−2.9	1.1	−1.9	2.6	−0.6
1.7	1.8	1.5	7.6	4.9	6.1	3.0	1.8	3.4
1.8	1.5	1.3	6.1	—	2.9	6.5	3.6	4.1
0.6	−1.7	0.7	1.2	—	1.8	1.3	1.7	0.8
4.4	1.4	4.0	6.8	—	4.4	3.1	3.1	3.8
2.6	2.4	3.6	2.6	2.3	3.5	4.0	3.1	3.3
0.8	−0.6	1.5	0.4	0.2	0.4	1.0	1.0	0.7
4.2	1.9	5.5	5.7	4.1	1.9	3.4	2.4	3.8
0.8	1.1	1.6	3.0	0.3	3.3	3.8	2.3	2.5
−0.3	−0.9	0.2	0.8	−1.3	1.1	0.2	1.8	0.3
3.4	1.7	3.6	6.7	4.5	4.2	3.1	2.4	3.7

Another assumption that we adopt for the estimation of function (5), constant returns to scale, is commonly made in productivity analysis. Alternative estimation carried under unrestricted functions indicates slight increasing returns to scale for several sectors, but with performance indicators not different from those presented here.

To illustrate the relative importance of bias in traditional productivity measurement with respect to TFP measured as indicated in section 12.2, we will present in the next section the results corresponding to a Tornqvist index of the form (Christensen and Jorgenson 1970):

$$\text{IND}(t) = \log\left[\frac{y(t)}{y(t-1)}\right] - \sum_{k=1}^{K}\left[\frac{w_k(t) + w_k(t-1)}{2}\right]\log\left[\frac{x_k(t)}{x_k(t-1)}\right], \quad (6)$$

where $w_k(t)$ indicates the share of input k in total cost. Input share for labor is defined as labor compensation in total value added and capital share is operating surplus in GDP, two variables included in the ISDB data set.

12.4   Productivity and Efficiency Indicators

To apply the approach presented in section 12.2 to the measurement of productivity growth, the first step is the estimation of the stochastic production frontier represented by equation (5). In table 12.2 we present the ML estimators corresponding to each industrial sector and other parameters allowing for the estimation of the variance components of the error term ε.[7] We obtain $\sigma_v^2 = 0.076$, $\sigma_u^2 = 0.027$, and thus $\sigma_\varepsilon^2 = 0.103$. The random component and the efficiency term hence represent respectively 75 percent and 25 percent of total variance, so the majority of changes in output levels not explained by structural production relations or by changes in input factors must be interpreted as random. Assuming that these random components are the consequences of measurement errors and of various factors out of the control of firms, such as changes in demand or in relative prices, efficiency indicators will be largely free of biases induced by these factors.

Elasticities of production illustrate the basic characteristics of sectoral production structures. We observe that textiles and construction are the most labor-intensive sectors while the basic metal sector appears as the most capitalistic.

Table 12.2
Estimated parameters of stochastic production frontier

| Sectors | Intercept (α_s) | Production elasticities | | Technological progress (γ_s) |
		Labor $(\beta_{1,s})$	Capital[a] $(\beta_{2,s})$	
Wood, cork, and furniture	−3.48 (9.9)	0.867 (7.7)	0.133	0.012 (1.3)
Chemicals	−2.49 (15.3)	0.524 (8.6)	0.476	0.023 (4.9)
Food, drink, and tobacco	−2.36 (7.1)	0.555 (4.9)	0.445	0.011 (1.3)
Machinery and equipment	−3.02 (6.9)	0.754 (5.6)	0.246	0.021 (2.5)
Basic metal products	−2.02 (8.2)	0.362 (3.9)	0.638	0.004 (0.5)
Nonmetallic mineral products	−3.16 (11.6)	0.799 (8.1)	0.201	0.008 (1.0)
Paper and printing	−2.95 (10.8)	0.738 (7.4)	0.262	0.011 (1.4)
Textiles	−4.13 (8.3)	0.932 (6.9)	0.068	0.028 (2.7)
Construction	−3.51 (10.2)	0.945 (9.1)	0.055	0.004 (0.5)
Electricity, gas, and water	−2.66 (11.3)	0.783 (7.2)	0.217	0.021 (2.9)
Transport, storage, and communications	−3.28 (12.0)	0.806 (7.6)	0.194	0.016 (1.9)

$n = 1853$
Log-likelihood = 197.1
$\sigma_v/\sigma_u = 1.677$ (8.9)
$\sigma_\varepsilon = (\sigma_v^2 + \sigma_u^2)^{1/2} = 0.321$ (28.1)

Note: t-test statistics appear in parentheses.
a. Estimated under the assumption of constant returns to scale.

Technological progress is estimated, sector by sector, as the derivative of production with respect to time. From equation (5) technological progress is equivalent to the γ_s coefficient. These estimated values are reproduced in the last column of table 12.2. Some sectors are more dynamic than others in the adoption of technological progress. Chemicals, textiles, machinery and equipment, and electricity, gas, and water exhibit annual rates higher than 2 percent over the period. Three sectors, basic metals, nonmetallic mineral products, and construction, have rates lower than 1 percent per year, followed by three other traditional industrial sectors (wood, food and paper) that just reach the annual rate of 1 percent. Note that we assume here that general knowledge disseminates immediately and costlessly throughout the OECD countries, which have approximately the same level of development. The assumption seems warranted because basic information spreads through technical journals, professional organizations, and interpersonal commercial contacts and as literature, scientists, and business managers move freely across international borders.

Table 12.3
Estimated levels of technical efficiency

		Countries				
Sectors	Periods	Australia	Belgium	Canada	Germany	Denmark
Manufacturing sectors						
Wood, cork,	1971–79	—	—	0.86	0.81	0.53
and furniture	1980–86	—	—	0.81	0.75	0.61
Chemicals	1971–79	—	0.67	0.90	0.90	0.70
	1980–86	—	0.88	0.71	0.87	0.74
Food, drink,	1971–79	—	0.86	0.88	0.70	0.66
and tobacco	1980–86	—	0.87	0.80	0.76	0.74
Machinery and	1971–79	—	0.81	0.89	0.84	0/66
equipment	1980–86	—	0.85	0.85	0.83	0.62
Basic metal	1971–79	—	0.80	0.87	0.72	0.46
products	1980–86	—	0.86	0.72	0.74	0.54
Nonmetallic	1971–79	—	0.75	0.85	0.80	0.67
mineral products	1980–86	—	0.85	0.68	0.82	0.66
Paper and	1971–79	—	0.79	0.88	0.76	0.76
printing	1980–86	—	0.83	0.82	0.81	0.73
Textiles	1971–79	—	0.77	0.87	0.81	0.68
	1980–86	—	0.84	0.85	0.80	0.76
Services sectors						
Construction	1971–79	0.82	0.83	0.87	0.78	0.74
	1980–86	0.87	0.86	0.92	0.80	0.66
Electricity, gas,	1971–79	0.42	0.82	0.77	0.70	0.46
and water	1980–86	0.41	0.89	0.74	0.64	0.53
Transport,	1971–79	0.75	0.90	0.75	0.80	0.76
storage, and	1980–86	0.84	0.86	0.80	0.85	0.68
communications						

The second step in the estimation of TFP growth by the approach described in section 12.2 consists in the estimation of technical efficiency for each observation in the sample. As indicated there, given the stochastic nature of the frontier estimated, only a conditional measure of efficiency can be obtained. In table 12.3 we reproduce the conditional mean levels of technical efficiency reached by each sector in each country during the 1971–1979 and 1980–1986 periods. This table gives an insight into the relative position and evolution of technical efficiency in OECD industrial sectors. These results confirm the leading position of the U.S. sectors, whose efficiency levels dominate those of the other countries in six sectors during the 1970s. In the 1980s we note a relative loss of efficiency with only four dominating activities. In some cases, as apparently for Danish sectors,

Table 12.3 (continued)

Countries							
France	Britain	Italy	Japan	Netherlands	Norway	Sweden	United States
—	—	0.82	—	—	0.83	0.87	0.86
—	—	0.87	—	—	0.80	0.86	0.87
0.66	—	0.76	0.91	0.38	0.82	0.80	0.90
0.70	—	0.81	0.91	0.41	0.77	0.73	0.86
0.91	—	0.92	0.83	0.69	0.58	0.82	0.86
0.91	—	0.93	0.65	0.74	0.31	0.75	0.88
0.87	—	0.84	0.57	0.57	0.83	0.76	0.92
0.84	—	0.83	0.81	0.62	0.78	0.73	0.91
0.89	—	0.53	0.91	0.87	0.91	0.49	0.87
0.90	—	0.55	0.93	0.87	0.90	0.55	0.71
0.79	—	0.84	0.68	0.86	0.85	0.83	0.90
0.80	—	0.88	0.67	0.89	0.80	0.81	0.89
0.75	—	0.88	0.74	0.81	0.72	0.72	0.91
0.75	—	0.92	0.82	0.83	0.68	0.71	0.89
0.85	—	0.89	0.40	0.83	0.83	0.86	0.84
0.84	—	0.88	0.53	0.87	0.83	0.79	0.86
0.78	0.71	0.81	0.70	0.88	0.70	0.82	0.91
0.79	0.66	0.82	0.61	0.86	0.77	0.87	0.85
0.87	0.62	0.95	0.89	—	0.86	0.82	0.87
0.82	0.55	0.93	0.89	—	0.80	0.85	0.84
0.79	0.70	0.79	0.83	0.90	0.74	0.70	0.91
0.77	0.72	0.78	0.83	0.90	0.78	0.72	0.90

poor estimated efficiency levels must be attributed to the omitted scale factor.

The last step is to sum up changes in efficiency and technological progress. These indicators are presented in table 12.4 with those obtained by the application of the index number approach, defined in equation (6) as IND. Note that mean annual growth rates are estimated for most countries and sectors over the period (1971–1986) except for France (1977–1984) and Japan (1974–1985). Three main results can be derived from table 12.4:

1. The two alternative measures of productivity, TFP and IND, are highly correlated $[\rho_{(TFP,IND)} = 0.83]$ but with significant differences in several

Table 12.4
Average annual rates of growth in technical efficiency and total-factor productivity, 1971–86

		Countries				
Sectors		Australia	Belgium	Canada	Germany	Denmark
Manufacturing sectors						
Wood, cork,	Efficiency	—	—	−0.02	0.1	2.5
and furniture	TFP	—	—	1.2	1.3	3.7
	IND	—	—	0.1	0.5	2.4
Chemicals	Efficiency	—	3.8	−0.3	−0.1	1.4
	TFP	—	6.2	2.0	2.3	3.7
	IND	—	7.3	1.2	2.3	3.5
Food, drink,	Efficiency	—	0.2	−0.7	0.5	1.6
and tobacco	TFP	—	1.3	0.3	1.6	2.6
	IND	—	1.1	−0.6	1.6	3.0
Machinery and	Efficiency	—	1.1	0.1	−0.1	−0.3
equipment	TFP	—	3.2	2.2	2.0	1.8
	IND	—	4.4	2.2	2.0	2.0
Basic metal	Efficiency	—	0.8	−0.3	0.1	3.6
products	TFP	—	1.2	0.1	0.5	4.0
	IND	—	4.1	0.2	1.8	3.3
Nonmetallic	Efficiency	—	2.3	0.2	0.7	0.05
mineral	TFP	—	3.2	1.1	1.6	0.9
products	IND	—	3.6	−0.3	1.3	0.4
Paper and	Efficiency	—	0.8	−0.4	0.8	−0.4
printing	TFP	—	1.9	0.7	1.9	0.7
	IND	—	3.0	−0.7	2.0	0.9
Textiles	Efficiency	—	0.8	0.03	0.2	2.2
	TFP	—	3.6	2.9	3.0	5.0
	IND	—	3.0	2.2	2.2	3.7
All manufactur-	Efficiency	—	1.4	−0.2	0.3	1.3
ing	TFP	—	2.9	1.3	1.8	2.8
	IND	—	3.8	0.6	1.7	2.4
Services sectors						
Construction	Efficiency	0.3	0.8	0.3	0.8	−1.3
	TFP	0.7	1.2	0.7	1.2	−0.9
	IND	−0.8	0.5	1.1	0.8	−2.2
Electricity, gas,	Efficiency	1.9	1.7	0.6	−0.3	2.8
and water	TFP	4.1	3.9	2.8	1.8	4.9
	IND	2.6	2.7	1.1	0.7	2.4
Transport,	Efficiency	1.9	−0.3	1.0	0.5	−1.6
storage, and	TFP	3.5	1.3	2.6	2.1	−0.04
communications	IND	3.9	−0.2	2.6	1.9	−1.2
All services	Efficiency	1.4	0.7	0.6	0.4	0.01
	TFP	2.8	2.1	2.0	1.7	1.4
	IND	1.9	1.0	1.6	1.1	−0.4

Table 12.4 (continued)

Countries

France	Britain	Italy	Japan	Nether-lands	Norway	Sweden	United States	All	Technolog-ical progress
—	—	1.0	—	—	0.3	−0.03	− 0.3	0.6	
—	—	2.2	—	—	1.5	1.1	1.5	1.8	1.2
—	—	1.0	—	—	0.5	−0.1	1.4	0.8	
1.4	—	0.9	0.8	6.6	−0.3	−1.3	−0.3	1.0	
3.7	—	3.2	3.2	8.9	2.1	1.0	2.1	3.4	2.3
—	—	4.0	4.3	—	2.2	1.5	1.7	3.1	
0.01	—	0.3	−6.6	1.8	−5.4	−1.2	0.4	−0.8	
1.1	—	1.3	−5.5	2.8	−4.4	−0.2	1.5	0.3	1.1
0.8	—	2.1	−7.4	3.0	−0.8	−0.4	2.5	0.6	
−0.5	—	−0.2	5.1	2.0	−0.5	−0.2	0.2	0.5	
1.6	—	1.9	7.2	4.1	1.6	1.9	2.3	2.6	2.1
0.9	—	1.4	6.6	—	1.3	2.0	3.1	2.6	
0.3	—	1.2	0.2	0.1	0.1	1.5	−1.2	0.6	
0.7	—	1.5	0.6	0.5	0.5	1.9	−0.8	1.0	0.4
2.7	—	2.3	1.6	—	2.3	3.8	−0.4	2.2	
0.2	—	0.7	−1.1	1.7	−0.5	−0.04	0.2	0.4	
1.1	—	1.5	−0.2	2.5	0.4	0.8	1.0	1.3	0.8
0.7	—	1.4	−1.9	2.6	−0.8	−0.1	1.4	0.8	
1.0	—	0.4	1.7	0.2	−0.5	−0.1	−0.1	0.2	
2.1	—	1.5	2.8	1.3	0.6	1.0	1.0	1.3	1.1
2.7	—	2.6	1.3	1.2	0.6	1.3	1.0	1.4	
−0.6	—	−0.1	1.3	0.9	−0.1	−0.3	0.3	0.4	
2.2	—	2.7	4.1	3.8	2.7	2.5	3.1	3.3	2.8
0.6	—	1.9	1.6	3.9	1.2	1.4	3.0	2.3	
0.3	—	0.5	0.2	1.9	−0.8	−0.2	−0.04	0.4	
1.8	—	2.0	1.7	3.4	0.6	1.3	1.4	1.9	1.5
1.4	—	2.1	0.9	2.7	0.8	1.2	1.7	1.7	
−0.1	−0.6	0.5	−1.4	0.2	1.7	1.0	−0.7	0.2	
0.3	−0.2	0.9	−1.1	0.5	2.0	1.4	−0.3	0.5	0.4
−0.3	−1.1	0.0	−3.6	−0.9	1.3	1.1	−2.3	−0.4	
−0.9	0.6	−0.2	0.4	—	−1.0	1.3	−0.3	0.6	
1.2	2.8	1.9	2.5	—	1.1	3.5	1.9	2.8	2.1
−1.1	1.4	−1.9	0.6	—	−0.4	3.9	1.2	1.2	
−0.3	0.8	−0.2	−0.2	−0.1	1.0	0.8	0.02	0.3	
1.3	2.4	1.4	1.4	1.5	2.6	2.5	1.6	1.9	1.6
1.0	2.1	1.1	1.2	0.5	2.4	2.0	1.4	1.5	
−0.4	0.3	0.03	−0.4	0.04	0.5	1.1	−0.3	0.4	
0.9	1.7	1.4	0.9	1.0	1.9	2.4	1.1	1.7	1.4
−0.1	0.8	−0.3	−0.6	−0.2	1.1	2.3	0.1	0.7	

cases. Nishimizu and Page (1982) showed that these differences arise basically from the way in which each approach chooses to estimate elasticities of production with respect to capital and labor. Remember that in the framework of frontier analysis these elasticities correspond to the estimated best-practice production function, while under the index number approach they are inferred from input shares in value added. Moreover note that our estimates of IND are quite similar to those obtained by Englander and Mittelstädt (1988), who estimated total factor productivity from the same data but with a simpler methodology.[8]

2. The part of growth in TFP due to changes in technical efficiency varies greatly among sectors and countries. Nevertheless, we observe that leading countries such as the United States and Germany realize very weak gains in efficiency, probably because of the high levels of efficiency reached in the past. On the other hand, small countries such as Denmark and Belgium display high rates of efficiency growth in several sectors.

3. Changes in technical efficiency account on average for a relatively small part of TFP growth. This is the case for almost all sectors studied, except for those characterized by low technological progress. Given that technological progress is positive in all industrial sectors analyzed, negative TFP

Table 12.5
Annual average rates of TFP by sector and period

Sectors	Unweighted means 1971–73	1974–75	1976–79	1980–82	1983–86	All
Manufacturing sectors						
Wood, cork, and furniture	4.0	−1.4	2.2	−0.2	2.9	1.8
Chemicals	6.0	−1.8	5.0	0.8	4.7	3.4
Food, drink, and tobacco	2.2	2.6	1.7	−1.0	−3.2	0.3
Machinery and equipment	3.4	0.8	3.1	2.0	3.1	2.6
Basic metal products	0.1	−2.9	2.3	−1.9	5.2	1.0
Nonmetallic products	3.5	−1.8	1.9	−1.0	2.7	1.3
Paper and printing	2.2	−1.6	2.6	0.2	1.7	1.3
Textiles	4.3	2.6	3.0	3.6	2.8	3.3
All manufacturing	3.2	−0.4	2.8	0.3	2.5	1.9
Services sectors						
Construction	1.4	0.01	0.5	0.3	0.4	0.5
Electricity, gas, and water	5.6	1.3	3.3	0.2	3.1	2.8
Transport, storage, and communications	2.6	0.6	2.6	0.7	2.2	1.9
All services	3.1	0.6	2.1	0.4	1.9	1.7

values in table 12.4 correspond to cases where the estimated loss in efficiency more than offsets technological improvement.

In table 12.5 TFP growth is broken down by time period. We distinguish five periods in order to expose the crisis years of 1974–75 and 1980–82. Two sets of average TFP rates are also calculated, the first unweighted and the second weighted by GDP values. As expected, overall sectors experience productivity slowdown or decline in 1974–75 and 1980–82 periods. The only exception is textiles and to some extent machinery and equipment (in 1980–82). Only two sectors exhibit decreasing rates of productivity in the latter period, food and construction (see weighted data). As noted before, these sectors together with basic metals display the lowest rates of productivity over the entire period. Nevertheless, the basic metal sector reaches a rate of 3 percent in the last three years covered by the data. It seems that the important reorganizations of metallurgy conducted in almost all countries began to bear fruit.

When the data are organized by country, with few exceptions all countries experienced on average a slowdown in productivity growth during both crisis periods. One of the well-known exceptions is Japan, which displayed the highest average TFP growth rate (near to 5 percent) during the second oil crisis but the lowest rate (− 6.6 percent) during the first shock.

Table 12.5 (continued)

| Sectors | Weighted means | | | | | |
	1971–73	1974–75	1976–79	1980–82	1983–86	All
Manufacturing sectors						
Wood, cork, and furniture	3.4	−0.01	1.9	−0.3	2.2	1.6
Chemicals	3.6	0.4	3.4	1.3	3.1	2.6
Food, drink, and tobacco	2.1	0.9	1.4	0.7	−1.4	0.5
Machinery and equipment	2.6	−0.4	4.0	2.4	3.7	3.0
Basic metal products	1.1	−2.7	1.2	−2.0	2.7	0.3
Nonmetallic products	2.7	−2.4	2.1	−0.4	2.0	1.1
Paper and printing	2.1	−1.0	2.1	0.6	1.3	1.3
Textiles	3.4	2.3	2.9	3.9	2.8	3.1
All manufacturing	2.6	−0.3	3.0	1.4	2.7	2.2
Services sectors						
Construction	0.6	0.3	0.2	−0.6	−0.2	0.0
Electricity, gas, and water	4.4	1.5	1.9	0.7	2.7	2.1
Transport, storage, and communications	2.5	0.9	2.1	1.0	2.0	1.8
All services	1.9	0.7	1.2	0.3	1.3	1.1

12.5 Determinants of Efficiency and Productivity

The indicators of technical performance just presented can vary between industrial sectors, countries and over time for a variety of reasons. In this section, we review some of the best known determinants of technical performance as measured by technical efficiency levels and total factor productivity growth rates. For identifying these explanatory factors, we borrow heavily from Caves and Barton (1990). However, we first need to consider whether these factors, derived either from mere conjectures or from solid theoretical analyses, bear the same implications for our aggregate sectoral OECD data as for their data on establishments within sectors.

The main difference between the two approaches lies in the construction of the production frontiers. On the one hand, from micro data we can estimate an industrial sector's frontier exclusively from available information at the national level. This means that the measure of technical efficiency derived in this way is conditional to the efficiency realized within that country, and the possibility of international differences is neglected. On the other hand, when we build technical frontiers with international data on sectoral aggregates within countries, the results are more general because they cover a large number of production experiences. However, these results could be misleading because they consider the sum of all micro units in a sector as a unique production unit and assume away differences among firms within each national industry. Except for these methodological differences, we think that most of the hypotheses about efficiency and productivity proposed by Caves and Barton (1990) can be used here, because we are dealing with essentially identical issues. Nevertheless, data availability prevents us from testing as many hypotheses as Caves and Barton.

We now turn to these alleged determinants of efficiency and productivity. They are classified into three groups. The first group includes competitive conditions such as concentration and trade exposure as well as tariff and nontariff barriers. The second group captures innovation arising from both R&D efforts and the catching-up process. The third group includes production characteristics such as the capital–labor ratio, the capital replacement rate, and the rate of output growth.

12.5.1 Competitive Conditions

Concentration

Caves and Barton (1990) suggested that when production is concentrated in the hands of a few large producers inefficiency can appear through three mechanisms: (1) the absence of strong competition among sellers permits inefficient production units to survive, (2) imperfect competition generates its own forms of inefficiency when partial collusive bargains in oligopoly induce rent-seeking forms of nonprice competition, and (3) the fewer the market's participants, the fewer independent experimenters seek better ways to carry out the sector's activities. All these mechanisms are consistent with efficiency levels decreasing with the concentration of producers. Concerning productivity growth, concentration could lead to greater R&D intensity, which in turn would increase it (Scherer 1986, ch. 8).[9] But all these relations seem better checked empirically than settled on a priori grounds. We use a sectoral four-firm seller concentration ratio:[10]

CONC = percentage of employment accounted for the four largest firms, 1978.

It is measured by Yamawaki, Sleuwaegen, and Weiss (1989) from data on the firm size distribution by employment size class for five EC countries (Germany, France, Italy, The Netherlands, and Belgium) instead of by sales (due to data limitation). This concentration ratio, available for 1978 at the three-digit level of the NACE classification, has been aggregated at the two-digit level of the ISIC classification using the production value as a weight.

International Trade

The extent of competition may be also measured by the openness of the market to imports. In theory the more open is the market to foreign competition, the smaller the opportunity for inefficiency and weak productivity gains. However, a high import ratio could actually indicate that the industrial sector is inefficient and not that foreign competition drives out the inefficiencies. Thus we expect a positive link between imports and productivity and a dubious relation with efficiency level. International competition also varies with the sector's ability to export. The greater the ability of a sector to export, the greater its international competitiveness and hence the higher its level of efficiency and its productivity growth rate. The following variables are defined and used to indicate the international trade conditions of an industrial sector:

MS = sectoral imports divided by production plus imports,

XS = sectoral exports divided by production,

ΔMS = MS annual growth rate,

ΔXS = XS annual growth rate.

The annual data on imports, exports, and production come from the Compatible Trade and Production Data Base (COMTAP) developed by the OECD. They are classified according to the ISIC nomenclature and available from 1961. All data are expressed in current values converted to U.S. dollars using current exchange rates.

Tariff and Nontariff Barriers

Protection by tariffs is thought to reduce the competitive pressure from foreign competition. Thus we conjecture that both technical efficiency and productivity should be worsened by tariff barriers. However, a tariff is not the only source of restriction on imports competition because nontariff barriers can also shelter domestic suppliers. Here we investigate the effects of both tariff and nontariff barriers, although the power of these tests is limited by the availability of detailed sectoral statistics. We employ the following national measure of tariff barriers:

TARIFF = national customs and import duties divided by the values of imports, 1980.

The data come from two OECD sources, respectively, the *Revenue Statistics of OECD Member Countries*, 1965–85 (1986), and the *National Accounts* (1989).

Noguès et al. (1986) calculated various indexes of effective protection by nontariff barriers in industrial countries for selected manufacturing sectors. To construct these variables, they disaggregated total imports by product and by country of origin. Then they summed up the values of those imports subject to nontariff barriers and divided them by total imports. Quantitative barriers include prohibitions, quotas, and discretionary import authorizations. Other barriers are classified into three groups: voluntary export restraints, tariff quotas, and monitoring measures (surveillance on price and volume and antidumping duties). We choose the following variables:

NTAR1 = national quantitative import restriction in manufacturing, 1983,

NTAR2 = all national nontariff barriers to imports in manufacturing, 1983.

12.5.2   Innovation

R&D Activities

From an empirical point of view, it is generally accepted that a main factor in productivity growth is the R&D activities (Griliches 1979). This concept refers to the amount of technology created within a sector or its "own technology base" as opposed to its use of "imitated technology." An innovation, when first introduced, shifts upward the sector's best-practice frontier and increases its rate of technological progress. However, at the same time it imputes inefficiency to the countries that are not able to manage this change. Thus we expect the inefficiency level and the growth in productivity to increase with R&D. The variable that we use is

R&D = Sectoral research and development spending as a percentage of value added.[11]

Historical statistics on research and experimental development activities in OECD member countries are collected every two years through international surveys and stored in the OECD Science and Technology Databank.[12] These data on sectoral R&D expenditures, which have been available since 1967, are expressed in dollars at the fixed-price levels and purchasing power parities of 1980.

R&D Spillover

A major distinctive feature of R&D activities is that sectors undertaking projects cannot completely appropriate all the benefits they generate. They are unable to exclude others from free-riding. This is called the *spillover effect of R&D* (Griliches 1979; Mohnen 1989). It should affect efficiency and productivity in the same way as R&D. Among the possible measures of spillover, we choose to build an international intrasectoral one. We construct this variable for a given sector by simply summing up the

R&D expenditures in that sector of the five most R&D intensive countries (United States, Japan, Germany, France, and United Kingdom).[13] It is given by

SPILL = R&D spillover gained by a sector as a percentage of its value
        added.[14]

The Netherlands are excluded from this analysis because of missing or incomplete data.

Catching-up Process

Another crucial source of growth in productivity is the use of knowledge gained through imitation. All countries indeed have some ability to imitate technology as well as the economic, social and institutional structures of the leader country. Our approach assumes, as is customary in the literature on diffusion, that the diffusion of internationally available knowledge follows a logistic curve. This mechanical process means in the framework of our analysis that the countries which start from a low level of efficiency are the ones that can increase their productivity growth rates the most. A number of empirical studies of this process have been carried out (Abramovitz 1986; Dollar and Wolff 1988; Dowrick and Nguyen 1989). We use lagged technical efficiency levels as proxies for the catching-up process:

CAUP = lagged level of technical efficiency.

12.5.3   Production Structures

Capital Formation

An industrial sector's efficiency level and productivity growth rate are also affected by capital formation. Because much new technology is embodied in new vintages of capital, an increase in capital formation can speed the rate of introduction of new technology and therefore increase the rate of technological progress. As in the R&D case, this process can cause some countries to appear inefficient at least in the short term. Indeed the effect of any change in capital stocks depends on the past investments in relatively fixed equipment, on the manager's ability in controlling the new inputs mix, but also on institutional difficulties in adopting too many changes too fast. But part of the new capital investment since the mid-1960s has been made in order to comply with safety regulations and pollution rules and should not improve productivity. Thus we expect overall a mitigated effect on efficiency and productivity. We seek to control for this with

$\Delta(K/L)$ = annual growth rate of capital–labor ratio,

I/K = ratio of gross investment to capital stock.

Data on capital stock, gross investment, and total employment come from the OECD International Sectoral Data Base.

Growth in Output

A rapid growth in output reflects significant increases in demand, which in turn put pressure on the capacity utilization as capacity becomes insufficient to meet demand. In this case there will be room for all in the market including the inefficient. On the other hand, the growth in demand can raise productivity and efficiency in ways not yet controlled. Growth in production develops ability and fosters experimentation to identify, combine, and exploit production factors (learning by doing), promote economies of scale, allow for a finer division of labor, and so on. In these circumstances output growth may increase efficiency, and it should always affect productivity change positively. However, this last relation must be tested carefully. Indeed, as Caves and Barton (1990) explain, the relation can be spurious for two reasons: (1) "productivity growth lowers the product's relative price and increases the quantity bought;" (2) "change in output is one component of the measurement of productivity changes." We use the following variable:

ΔGDP = annual growth rate of gross domestic product measured for the individual sector.

Value-added data are also available from the ISDB.

12.6. Main Findings

In this section we test the significance of these factors in explaining technical efficiency levels and productivity growth rates. To clarify the presentation, we divide the results in two sections dealing, respectively, with total factor productivity growth and technical efficiency levels. The method used is the correlation technique. Correlation rather than regres-

Table 12.6
Analysis of variance of technical efficiency and TFP

Variable	Between effects		Within effects	Total variance
International				
	Country	Country · sector	Country · sector · time	
Efficiency	4.27 (22.5)	10.97 (58.0)	3.68 (19.5)	18.92 (100.0)
TFP	0.08 (1.2)	0.32 (5.2)	5.77 (93.6)	6.17 (100.0)
Intertemporal				
	Time	Time · country	Time · country · sector	
Efficiency	0.13 (0.7)	5.32 (28.1)	13.47 (71.2)	18.92 (100.0)
TFP	0.52 (8.4)	1.11 (18.0)	4.54 (73.5)	6.17 (100.0)
Intersectoral				
	Sector	Sector · time	Sector · time · country	
Efficiency	0.45 (2.4)	0.58 (3.0)	17.89 (94.6)	18.92 (100.0)
TFP	0.13 (2.2)	1.16 (18.6)	4.88 (79.2)	6.17 (100.0)

Note: Values in parentheses indicate percentages of total variances.

sion analysis is chosen for two reasons: ambiguous causation (e.g., efficiency and trade exposure) and missing data on some important exogenous variables. Most of the tests are implemented on pooled international sectoral time-series data for the 8 manufacturing sectors in 11 OECD countries over the period 1971 to 1986. However a more detailed analysis by sector, country and period is presented. Tables 12.7 and 12.8 summarize the results.

But before proceeding with these tests, we first analyze the variance composition of the two main variables under study: technical efficiency levels and total-factor productivity changes. In table 12.6 we report the between and within effects corresponding to the three dimensions of these variables: international, intersectoral, and intertemporal. The first column of table 12.6 shows that the international effect represents 22.5 percent of the total variance of technical efficiency but only 1.2 percent of the variance of TFP growth. The intertemporal dimension explains only 0.7 percent of the variance of technical efficiency but 8.4 percent of TFP variable's total variance. Intersectoral effects represent only 2 percent of the total variance of either. The second column of table 12.6 shows that combined international and intersectoral dimensions explain 80.5 percent (22.5 + 58.0 percent) of total technical efficiency variance but only 6.4 percent (1.2 + 5.2 percent) of TFP's variance. On the other hand, the crossed effects "time · country" and "time · sector" explain, respectively, 26.4 percent

(8.4 + 18.0 percent) and 20.8 percent (2.2 + 18.6 percent) of the total variance of TFP growth. Summing up this evidence, we draw two conclusions. First, most of the variance of technical efficiency comes from international and intersectoral differences. This indicates that structural factors such as competitive conditions ought to explain efficiency levels. Second, the variance of TFP growth stems mainly from intertemporal differences. This indicates that dynamic factors such as innovation should better explain TFP growth.

12.6.1 Total Factor Productivity Change

Consider first the group of variables pertaining to competitive conditions. In table 12.7 the variables ΔMS and ΔXS have highly significant correlation coefficients with the expected positive signs. These results hold both at the sectoral and national levels as well as over time. Only one sector—textiles—and two countries—Denmark and France—present no significant association. For Italy and the United States only exposure to imports increases TFP, while for Japan only competition in exports matters. A second indicator of competitive conditions is the concentration ratio, which has a negative and significant effect on TFP $[\rho_{(TFP,CONC)} = -0.392^{**}]$. However the small number of observations ($N = 29$) inhibits drawing any strong conclusions and makes irrelevant any more detailed analysis. Hence this result is not presented in table 12.7. The tariff and nontariff barriers are not significantly related to TFP. Note that the correlation values $[\rho_{(TFP,TARIFF)} = -0.250; \rho_{(TFP,NTAR1)} = 0.077,$ and $\rho_{(TFP,NTAR2)} = 0.156]$ are based on data available only for 1983 and at the national level.

We turn now to the analysis of innovative factors presented in table 12.7. The correlation for all observations shows that TFP increases with the importance of spending on research and development. In the disaggregated analysis few significant relations appear although when significant the correlation coefficients take positive signs. These occur for the chemicals, basic metal, and textiles sectors as well as in Belgium and France. Note that as expected the significant relationship disappears during the two oil crisis periods (1974–75 and 1980–82). R&D spillover (SPILL) also spurs TFP. The correlations closely resemble those for R&D except for the negative significant coefficient in food and the lack of significant relation in chemicals. Again TFP does not gain from foreign R&D during the crisis periods. The catching-up hypothesis is supported by the

Table 12.7
Correlation of TFP and sector characteristics, by sector, country, and period

	Competitive conditions		Innovation			Productive structures		
	ΔMS	ΔXS	R&D	SPILL	CAUP	I/K	Δ(K/L)	ΔGDP
All observations	0.195***	0.171***	0.106***	0.109***	−0.187***	−0.081***	−0.011	0.739***
Sectors								
Wood, cork, and furniture	0.347***	0.254***	0.000	0.179*	−0.314***	0.001	−0.199**	0.759***
Chemicals	0.155**	0.179**	0.162***	0.064	−0.340***	−0.090	0.042	0.807***
Food, drink, and tobacco	0.310***	0.226***	−0.069	−0.241***	0.202***	−0.101	0.101	0.858***
Machinery and equipment	0.231***	0.264***	0.109	−0.054	−0.283***	0.140*	−0.131*	0.732***
Basic metal products	0.194***	0.129	0.159**	0.184**	−0.251***	−0.223***	−0.134*	0.781***
Nonmetallic mineral products	0.339***	0.216***	0.060	−0.015	−0.243***	−0.135*	−0.012	0.787***
Paper and printing	0.140*	0.211***	0.006	−0.052	−0.180*	−0.076	0.101	0.864***
Textiles	−0.023	0.120	0.142*	0.034	−0.247***	−0.003	0.158**	0.567***
Countries								
Belgium	0.332***	0.335***	0.320***	0.321***	−0.486***	0.026	−0.118	0.855***
Canada	0.304***	0.229***	0.086	0.170*	−0.405***	−0.216***	0.007	0.819***
Germany	0.368***	0.253***	0.052	0.048	−0.039	0.030	−0.174**	0.783***
Denmark	−0.004	0.025	0.141	0.153	−0.354***	−0.193**	−0.038	0.845***
France	−0.022	−0.026	0.342***	0.321**	−0.370***	−0.237*	−0.218	0.750***
Italy	0.551***	0.119	0.117	0.115	−0.126	0.084	0.151*	0.800***
Japan	0.022	0.261**	0.066	0.148	−0.171	0.064	0.257**	0.668***
Netherlands	0.296***	0.315***	—	—	−0.328***	−0.065	−0.033	0.829***
Norway	0.227***	0.197**	0.117	0.082	0.261***	−0.117	0.001	0.724***
Sweden	0.255***	0.286***	0.054	0.043	−0.143*	−0.198**	−0.026	0.707***
United States	0.279***	0.060	0.050	0.014	−0.132	0.088	−0.468**	0.738***
Periods								
1971–73	0.162**	0.143**	0.128*	0.043	−0.277***	−0.152**	0.020	0.722***
1974–75	0.270***	0.173**	−0.093	−0.018	−0.046	−0.035	0.024	0.751***
1976–79	0.206***	0.116**	0.173***	0.153***	−0.322***	−0.065	0.063	0.697***
1980–82	0.140**	0.183***	0.050	0.013	−0.056	0.007	−0.155***	0.792***
1983–86	0.042	0.210***	0.160***	0.230***	−0.102*	−0.196***	0.153***	0.730***

Note: The significance of the coefficients, P [$H_0 = 0$], is indicated as follows: *** = $P < 1$ percent, ** = 5 percent > P > 1 percent, and * = 10 percent > P > 5 percent.

results. Indeed CAUP is found to be significantly correlated with TFP in most disaggregated categories. Two exceptions are the food sector and Norway, where CAUP exhibits a positive significant relationship. Other expected exceptions concern the three leading countries—the United States, Japan, and Germany—which along with Italy fail to support the catching-up conjecture. Moreover the two crisis periods seem to impede this process. Note that over time R&D, SPILL, and CAUP appear complementarily significant during the same periods. Catching-up and R&D spillover may be furthered by a sector's own R&D efforts. Cohen and Levinthal (1989) argued that R&D enhances the ability to assimilate and exploit existing knowledge.

Tests of the two sets of factors concerning productive structures are reported in the last three columns of table 12.7. Capital intensity shows an ambiguous effect on TFP. If I/K has a weak negative correlation with TFP, $\Delta(K/L)$ shows no significant relation overall. The detailed analysis does not clarify the relation between capital formation and TFP because both positive and negative effects appear. However, some interesting results deserve emphasis. First, the variable I/K exhibits very high negative and significant coefficients in the basic metal sector, in Canada, Denmark, and Sweden, and in the two extreme periods. This could indicate that for these special cases new investments embodiment effect influences positively TFP only with a long lag not controlled by the tests. Second, the capital–labor ratio growth rate reveals some interesting features: opposite significant associations, with the wood and textiles sectors, respectively, negative and positive; strong negative significant relations for Germany and the United States and at the same time a positive significant association for Japan; and a remarkable switch from a negative to a positive association over the two last periods. As expected, TFP increases with the growth rate in output. Verdoorn's law (Bairam 1987) is confirmed. However, the magnitude and the similarity of the coefficients call for a cautious interpretation.

12.6.2 Technical Efficiency Levels

Correlations of the same groups of variables with technical efficiency levels are presented in table 12.8. A caveat affects their interpretation. As indicated in section 12.2, we measure technical efficiency from the distance between the observed output–input combination and the frontier. If we were dealing with microeconomic data in a steady-state framework, ineffi-

Table 12.8
Correlation of efficiency and sector characteristics, by sector, country, and period

	Competitive conditions		Innovation		Productive structures	
	MS	XS	R&D	SPILL	I/K	ΔGDP
All observations	-0.147***	-0.163***	-0.113***	-0.310***	0.095***	0.141***
Sectors						
Wood, cork, and furniture	-0.808***	-0.370***	0.107	-0.686***	0.287***	0.144
Chemicals	-0.287***	-0.559***	-0.132	-0.435***	0.163**	0.140*
Food, drink, and tobacco	0.220***	-0.124	-0.137*	-0.807***	-0.166**	0.231***
Machinery and equipment	-0.240***	-0.344***	0.075	-0.177**	0.303***	0.138*
Basic metal products	-0.392***	0.055	-0.406***	-0.479***	0.142*	0.151*
Nonmetallic mineral products	0.092	0.038	-0.169**	-0.164**	0.033	0.252**
Paper and printing	-0.053	-0.247***	-0.205***	-0.553***	0.009	0.249***
Textiles	0.198***	0.124	-0.585***	0.010	-0.118	0.051
Countries						
Belgium	0.251***	0.177*	-0.484***	-0.423***	-0.440***	-0.030
Canada	0.139	0.032	-0.268***	-0.191**	0.294***	0.437***
Germany	0.075	0.414***	0.595***	0.548***	0.377***	0.269***
Denmark	-0.395***	-0.337***	-0.185**	-0.484***	-0.249***	0.248***
France	0.195	0.336***	-0.692***	-0.688***	0.250**	-0.003
Italy	-0.117	0.102	-0.329***	-0.451***	0.126	0.080
Japan	-0.052	-0.002	0.485***	0.448***	0.306***	0.282***
Netherlands	0.206**	-0.255***	—	—	-0.095	-0.098
Norway	0.460***	0.392***	0.278***	0.122	-0.023	0.196**
Sweden	-0.102	-0.532***	-0.717***	-0.254***	0.314***	-0.032
United States	-0.434***	0.263***	0.008	-0.191**	0.440***	0.358***
Periods						
1971–73	-0.262***	-0.316***	-0.137*	-0.223***	-0.090	0.143**
1974–75	-0.211***	-0.262***	-0.151*	-0.389***	-0.001	0.152*
1976–79	-0.206***	-0.224***	-0.128**	-0.405***	0.172***	0.101*
1980–82	-0.084	-0.121**	-0.092	-0.305***	0.205***	0.219***
1983–86	-0.013	0.016	-0.079	-0.231***	0.133**	0.120**

Note: The significance of the coefficients, P [$H_0 = 0$], is indicated as follows: *** = P < 1 percent, ** = 5 percent > P > 1 percent, and * = 10 percent > P > 5 percent.

ciency optimally measured could be attributed only to management slack. However, in our dynamic aggregate setting where the production frontier shifts up over time, an additional source of efficiency arises in the lag of adjustment to these new technological conditions. This lag explains why factors such as R&D that push the frontier upward can involve an apparent loss in efficiency.

Let us now comment on table 12.8, beginning with the hypotheses about competitive conditions. Among the competitive conditions noted in table 12.8, higher import levels (MS) appear to be associated with high levels of inefficiency. As explained previously, a high import ratio could actually indicate that the industrial sector is inefficient and not that foreign competition drives out inefficient domestic producers. However, in two sectors largely nontraded—food and textiles—and three small countries— Belgium, the Netherlands, and Norway—imports competition improves significantly efficiency. Higher export levels (XS) also coincide surprisingly with higher inefficiency. The detailed picture of these relationships is less clear: In some countries—Germany, France, Norway and the United States—exports competition increases efficiency. Note that international competition does not exert any significant effect on efficiency levels in some cases (nonmetallic sector, Canada, Italy, and Japan, as well as in the last period). The concentration ratio as well as tariff and nontariff barriers have no significant relation with efficiency [$\rho_{(eff, CONC)} = -0.154$; $\rho_{(eff, TARIFF)} = 0.286$; $\rho_{(eff, NTAR1)} = 0.255$; $\rho_{(eff, NTAR2)} = 0.516$]. As indicated before, this absence of correlation may be due to incomplete data for these variables.

The second group of potential determinants relating to innovation is reported in table 12.8. The correlations show that technical efficiency decreases with the importance of a sector's R&D spillover, that is, when other countries' R&D is higher. In most of the sectors and countries the R&D spillover, shifting the frontier up, creates an apparent inefficiency for the production units not able to manage this change. Germany and Japan, two highly R&D-intensive countries, improve their efficiency. The sector's spending on research and development exerts the same influence over time. Germany, Japan, and Norway remain the exceptions. Over time this phenomenon plays a role until 1979 and then disappears.

Finally, we test the link between efficiency and production structure in table 12.8. I/K has weak positive significant association with efficiency, which supports the hypothesis that technology embodied in new capital can improve this measure of performance. Nevertheless, in the food sector, as for Belgium and Denmark, capital intensity is negatively correlated with efficiency. ΔGDP has also a positive influence on efficiency levels. All the significant coefficients have the expected positive signs. The three leading countries—Germany, Japan and the United States—are among those that strongly display this effect.

12.7 Conclusions

The main objectives of this chapter were twofold. First, we measured the productivity gains and technical efficiency levels attained by each industrial sector in a panel of OECD countries by means of a parametric production frontier. Second, we tested the relation of these two indicators of performance to a set of variables corresponding to three aspects of industrial activities: competitive conditions, innovation, and productive structures.

The results indicate that, on the one hand, total-factor productivity growth is on average more a consequence of technological progress, measured as the shift of the best-practice production function, than the result of technical efficiency improvements estimated as the individual temporal changes in the position relative to the frontier. On the other hand, they confirm that competition is a main determinant of technical efficiency, while innovation, especially R&D spillover, is a main determinant of productivity growth. Furthermore the detailed results allow us to identify the specific characteristics of industrial sectors and countries as well as the prevailing relations over time.

Nevertheless, the results presented here call for more research. For instance, production technologies and technical change were modeled on the basis of rather restrictive assumptions such as constant returns to scale and neutral technological progress. We expect that more disaggregated data, including all information on intermediate inputs such as energy, will allow us to relax some of these assumptions. We also hope that more complete information on structural variables such as levels of regulation and concentration indicators will be available in the near future.

Notes

The authors are research assistants in the Department of Economics, University of Liège, B.4000 Liège, Belgium. We thank Richard Caves, Pierre Pestieau, and Hideki Yamawaki for their comments and suggestions.

1. In these four sections we follow closely Fecher and Perelman (1989).

2. For a survey of alternative frontier approaches, see Lovell and Schmidt (1988).

3. Estimating all sectoral production functions as an unique frontier is a way to avoid identification problems. As is known (Aigner, Lovell, and Schmidt 1977), positive skewness of composed residuals in function (5) precludes the estimation of technical efficiency. This type of error was encountered when we tried to estimate a separate frontier for each sector but vanished when we worked with the whole panel of data.

4. See Meyer-zu-Schlochtern (1988) for more specific assumptions.

5. The countries studied are Australia, Belgium, Canada, Germany, Denmark, France, the United Kingdom, Italy, Japan, the Netherlands, Norway, Sweden, and the United States.

6. It is worth noting that the ISDB sectors are undesirably broad and constrained to that breadth by the OECD data.

7. ML estimation is performed by the LIMDEP software developed by Greene (1989). Note that the hypothesis of negative skewness of residuals was accepted on the basis of a previous OLS estimation.

8. In Englander and Mittelstädt (1988) total-factor productivity change is estimated as in (6), but the weights w_k, are assumed constant over time.

9. This relation between R&D and productivity growth is discussed in subsection 12.5.2.

10. In many studies effects of competing imported goods are incorporated in the adjustment of concentration ratios. Here we treat imports separately.

11. Note that R&D expenditures are generally expected to affect production performance only with a lag. To take into account this fact, we define the R&D ratio as follows: $R\&D_t = \sum_{i=1}^{l} \theta_i R\&D_{t-i}/GDP_t$. We opt for a simple bell-shaped lag structure over a period of four years with $\theta_i = (0.2, 0.3, 0.3, 0.2)$.

12. In implementing such a framework of analysis, we had to deal with the problem of missing R&D data. We decided to replace missing values by interpolated ones.

13. For these five countries the own R&D is excluded from the R&D spillover.

14. For the reason presented in note 11, we define the spillover ratio as follows:

$$SPILL_t = \sum_{i=1}^{l} \frac{\theta_i SPILL_{t-i}}{GDP_t}.$$

References

Abramovitz, M. 1986. Catching-up, forging ahead and falling behind. *Journal of Economic History* 46: 385–406.

Aigner, D. J., C. A. K. Lovell, and P. J. Schmidt. 1977. Formulation and estimation of stochastic frontier production function models. *Journal of Econometrics* 6: 21–37.

Bairam, E. I. 1987. The Verdoorn law, returns to scale and industrial growth: A review of the literature. *Australian Economic Papers* 26: 20–42.

Caves, R. E., and D. R. Barton. 1990. *Efficiency in U.S. Manufacturing Industries.* Cambridge: MIT Press.

Christensen, L. R., and D. W. Jorgenson. 1970. The measurement of US real capital input, 1929–1967. *Review of Income and Wealth* 15: 293–320.

Cohen, W. M., and D. A. Levinthal. 1989. Innovation and learning: The two faces of R&D. *The Economic Journal* 99: 569–596.

Dollar, D., and E. N. Wolff. 1988. Convergence of labor productivity among industrial countries, 1963–1982. *Review of Economics and Statistics* 70: 549–558.

Dowrick, S., and D. T. Nguyen. 1989. OECD comparative economic growth 1950–1985: Catching-up and convergence. *American Economic Review* 79: 1010–1030.

Englander, A. S., and A. Mittelstädt. 1988. Total factor productivity: Macroeconomic and structural aspects of the slowdown. *OECD Economic Studies* 10: 7–56.

Fecher, F., and S. Perelman. 1989. Productivity growth, technological progress and R&D in OECD industrial activities. In G. Krause-Junk, ed., *Public Finance and Steady Economic Growth, Proceedings of the 45th Congress of the International Institute of Public Finance*. The Hague: Fondation Journal Public Finance.

Greene, W. 1989. *Econometric Analysis*. New York: Macmillan.

Griliches, Z. 1979. Issues in assessing the contribution of research and development to productivity growth. *Bell Journal of Economics* 10: 92–116.

Jondrow, J., C. A. K. Lovell, I. S. Materov, and P. Schmidt. 1982. On the estimation of technical inefficiency in the stochastic frontier production function model. *Journal of Econometrics* 19: 233–238.

Meeusen, W. and J. van den Broeck. 1977. Efficiency estimation from Cobb-Douglas production functions with composed error. *International Economic Review* 18: 435–444.

Meyer-zu-Schlochtern, F. J. M. 1988. An international sectoral data base for thirteen OECD countries. Working Paper No. 57. Department of Economics and Statistics, OECD.

Mohnen, P. 1989. New technologies and inter-industry spillovers. Paper prepared for the OECD International Seminar on Science, Technology, and Economic Growth, Paris.

Nishimizu, M., and J. M. Page. 1982. Total factor productivity growth, technological progress and technical efficiency change: Dimensions of productivity change in Yugoslavia, 1967–1978. *Economic Journal* 92: 920–936.

Noguès, J. J., A. Olechowski, and L. A. Winters. 1986. The extent of nontariff barriers to imports of industrial countries. World Bank Staff Working Paper No. 789. Washington.

OECD. 1986. *Revenue Statistics of OECD Member Countries, 1965–85*. Paris.

OECD. 1989. *National Accounts, 1975–87. Detailed Tables*. Paris.

Scherer, F. M. 1986. *Innovation and Growth: Schumpeterian Perspectives*. Cambridge: MIT Press.

Yamawaki, H., L. Sleuwaegen, and L. W. Weiss. 1989. Industry competition and the formation of the European common market. In L. W. Weiss, ed., *Concentration and Price*. Cambridge: MIT Press.

Index